GENDER, LAW
& JUSTICE

GENDER, LAW & JUSTICE

A CUSTOM TEXTBOOK FROM
FERNWOOD PUBLISHING

Edited by
Gillian Balfour, Carolyn Brooks, Wendy Chan,
Elizabeth Comack, Ellen Faulkner, Gayle MacDonald,
Kiran Mirchandani, Bernard Schissel and A.J. Withers

Compiled for Emily van der Meulen
Department of Criminology, Ryerson University

FERNWOOD PUBLISHING
HALIFAX & WINNIPEG

Editing: Mark Ambrose Harris
Cover design: John van der Woude
Printed and bound in Canada

Published by Fernwood Publishing
32 Oceanvista Lane, Black Point, Nova Scotia, B0J 1B0
and 748 Broadway Avenue, Winnipeg, Manitoba, R3G 0X3

www.fernwoodpublishing.ca

Fernwood Publishing Company Limited gratefully acknowledges the financial support of the Government of Canada through the Canada Book Fund, the Manitoba Department of Culture, Heritage and Tourism under the Manitoba Publishers Marketing Assistance Program and the Province of Manitoba, through the Book Publishing Tax Credit, for our publishing program. We are pleased to work in partnership with the Province of Nova Scotia to develop and promote our creative industries for the benefit of all Nova Scotians. We acknowledge the support of the Canada Council for the Arts, which last year invested $153 million to bring the arts to Canadians throughout the country.

Library and Archives Canada Cataloguing in Publication

Gender, law & justice : a custom textbook from Fernwood / compiled by Emily van der Meulen.

Includes bibliographical references.
ISBN 978-1-55266-891-7 (paperback)

1. Sociological jurisprudence--Canada. 2. Sex and law--Canada.
3. Women--Social conditions--Canada. 4. Women--Legal status, laws, etc.--Canada. I. Van der Meulen, Emily, 1977-, compiler

KE4399.G46 2016   342.7108'78   C2016-904296-0
KF4483.C57G46 2016

CONTENTS

MARRIAGE AND THE FAMILY / 67

VIOLENCE / 115

RACISM AND COLONIALISM / 137

LABOUR / 305

DRUGS / 349

ABOUT THE BOOKS

Gillian Balfour and Elizabeth Comack (eds.), 2014, *Criminalizing Women: Gender and (In)Justice in Neo-liberal Times,* 2nd edition. Fernwood Publishing.

Carolyn Brooks and Bernard Schissel (eds.), 2015, *Marginality and Condemnation: An Introduction to Criminology,* 3rd edition. Fernwood Publishing.

Elizabeth Comack (ed.), 2014, *Locating Law: Race, Class, Gender and Sexuality Connections,* 3rd edition. Fernwood Publishing.

Ellen Faulkner and Gayle MacDonald (eds.), 2009, *Victim No More: Women's Resistance to Law, Culture and Power.* Fernwood Publishing.

Kiran Mirchandani and Wendy Chan, 2007, *Criminalizing Race, Criminalizing Poverty: Welfare Fraud Enforcement in Canada.* Fernwood Publishing.

A.J. Withers, 2012, *Disability Politics and Theory.* Fernwood Publishing.

ABOUT THE AUTHORS

Gillian Balfour is an associate professor in the Department of Sociology at Trent University. Her publications include two editions of *Criminalizing Women* (co-edited with Elizabeth Comack, 2006, 2014) and *The Power to Criminalize: Violence, Inequality and the Law* (co-authored with Elizabeth Comack, 2004).

Suzanne Bouclin is an associate professor at the Faulty of Law, University of Ottawa. She holds a PhD in law from McGill in which she explores law through film theory and feminist methodologies. She also writes on the legal regulation of particular groups including street-involved people and marginalized workers.

Susan C. Boyd is a distinguished professor in the Faculty of Human and Social Development at the University of Victoria. Her publications include *More Harm Than Good: Drug Policy in Canada* (with Connie Carter and Donald MacPherson, 2016), *From Witches to Crack Moms: Women, Drug Law, and Policy, 2nd edition* (2015), *Killer Weed: Marijuana Grow-ops, Media and Justice* (with Connie Carter, 2014), *Raise Shit! Social Action Saving Lives* (with Bud Osborn and Donald MacPherson, 2009) and *With Child: Substance Use During Pregnancy, A Woman-Centred Approach* (with Lenora Marcellus, 2006).

Carolyn Brooks is an associate professor in the Department of Sociology at the University of Saskatchewan. She is co-editor of three editions of *Marginality and Condemnation: A Critical Introduction to Criminology* (with Bernard Schissel, 2002, 2008, 2015). Her research and publications focus on youth resilience, violence, visual and community based research methods.

Chris Bruckert is a professor in the Department of Criminology at the University of Ottawa. She has done extensive research on and activism for the sex work industry in Canada including being a member of Prostitutes of Ottawa-Gatineau Work, Educate and Resist (POWER).

Wendy Chan is a professor in the Department of Sociology and Anthropology at Simon Fraser University. She is the author of five books including *Racialization, Crime and Criminal Justice in Canada* (co-authored with Dorothy Chunn, 2014), *Criminalizing Race, Criminalizing Poverty* (co-authored with Kiran Mirchandani, 2007) and *Crimes of Colour* (co-edited with Kiran Mirchandani, 2001).

Dorothy E. Chunn is a professor emerita of sociology at Simon Fraser University. She has published much in feminism, law and social change, crime, madness and welfare including *The Legal Tender of Gender: Welfare, Law and the Regulation of Women's Poverty* (co-edited with Shelley Gavigan, 2010) and *Reaction and Resistance: Feminism, Law and Social Change* (co-edited with Susan C. Boyd and Hester Lessard, 2007).

Linda Coates is an associate professor in the Department of Psychology at Okanagan College. She does research and publishing on language and violence, particularly on representations of violence in the legal system, the media, the helping professions and social policy.

Elizabeth Comack is a professor in the Department of Sociology at the University of Manitoba. Her recent publications include *Criminalizing Women, 2nd edition* (co-edited with Gillian Balfour, 2014), *Locating Law: Race/Class/Gender Connections, 3rd edition* (2014), *"Indians Wear Red" Colonialism, Resistance and Aboriginal Street Gangs* (co-authored with Larry Morrissette, Lawrence Deane and Jim Silver, 2013), *Racialized Policing: Aboriginal People's Encounters with The Police* (2012), *Out There/In Here: Masculinity, Violence and Prisoning* (2008) and *The Power to Criminalize: Violence, Inequality and the Law* (co-authored with Gillian Balfour, 2004).

Ellen Faulkner is an instructor with the Department of Criminology, Vancouver Island University. Her most recent publications include "Sexualities and Difference: The Criminalization of Lesbian, Gay, Bisexual, Transgendered, and Queer (LGBTQ) People in Canada" in Barbara Perry (ed.), *Diversity, Crime and Justice in Canada* 2nd edition (2016) and "Homophobic Sexist Violence in Canada: Trends in the Experiences of Lesbian and Bisexual Women in Canada" in Brenda Cranney and Sheila Molloy (eds.), *Canadian Woman Studies*, 3rd edition (2015).

Nahanni Fontaine was elected as a NDP MLA to the Manitoba Legislature in April 2016. Prior to that she was the Special Advisor on Aboriginal Women's Issues Cabinet Committee of the Manitoba government.

Monica Freitas took Walls to Bridges (W2B, formerly Inside-Out) courses while incarcerated at Grand Valley Institution for Women. She firmly believes in the W2B mission and vision, and looks forward to using her experiences and education to advocate and educate society about the "injustice" of the justice system.

Shelley A. M. Gavigan is a professor of law at Osgoode Hall Law School, York University. Her recent publications include *The Politics of Abortion* (with Jane Jenson and Janine Brodie, 2002), *The Legal Tender of Gender: Welfare, Law and the Regulation of Women's Poverty* (co-edited with Dorothy Chunn, 2010) and *Hunger, Horses and Government Men: Criminal Law on the Aboriginal Plains* (2012).

Nyki Kish is a member of the Walls and Bridges Collective at Grand Valley Institution, where she is serving a life sentence. She is a writer, activist and musician.

Gayle MacDonald is associate vice-president of research and professor of sociology/ women's studies at Mount Saint Vincent University. Her publications include *Victim No More: Women's Resistance to Law, Culture and Power* (co-edited with Ellen Faulkner, 2009), *Sex Workers of the Maritimes Talk Back* (co-authored with Leslie Ann Jeffrey, 2006), *Feminism, Law, Inclusion: Intersectionality in Action* (co-edited with Rachel Osborne and Charles Smith, 2005) and *Social Context and Social Location in the Sociology of Law* (2002).

Bonnie McAuley took Walls to Bridges (formerly Inside-Out) courses and was a member of the Walls to Bridges Collective while serving a twenty-five-year sentence at Grand Valley Institution for Women.

Kiran Mirchandani is a professor in leadership, higher and adult education at Ontario Institute for Studies in Education. Her recent publications include *Phone Clones: Authenticity Work in the Transnational Service Economy* (2012), *The Future of Lifelong Learning and Work: Critical Perspectives* (co-edited with David Livingstone and Peter Sawchuk, 2008), and *Criminalizing Race, Criminalizing Poverty: Welfare Fraud Enforcement in Canada* (co-authored with Wendy Chan, 2007).

Debra Mollen is an associate professor in the Department of Psychology and Philosophy at Texas Woman's University. Her recent publications include "The Pedagogical Strategies of Implementing Story from a Feminist Perspective," in *Telling Stories: The Art and Science of Storytelling as an Instructional Strategy* (with Jennifer Mootz, 2015), "Spiritual Maturity as a Moderator of the Relationship between Christian Fundamentalist and Shame" in the *Journal of Psychology and Theology* (with Kathryn Keller and Lisa Rosen, 2015) and "Reproductive Rights and Informed Consent: Toward a More Inclusive Discourse" in *Analysis of Social Issues and Public Policy* (2014).

Patricia Monture was a citizen of the Mohawk Nation, Grand River Territory. Sadly, she passed away in November 2010, at the age of 52. She was a professor in the Department of Sociology and the University of Saskatchewan. Her publications include two books *Thunder in My Soul: A Mohawk Woman Speaks* (1995) and *Journeying Forward: Dreaming First Nations Independence* (1999).

Janet E. Mosher is an associate professor at Osgoode Hall Law School, York University. She is co-editor of *Constructing Crime: Contemporary Processes of Criminalization* (with Joan Brockman, 2010) and *Disorderly People: Law and the Politics of Exclusion in Ontario* (with Joe Hermer, 2002). She is the co-author of several reports including "Take the Story, Take the Needs, and DO Something: Grassroots Women's Priorities for Community-Based Participatory Research and Action on Homelessness" (with Emily Paradis, 2012).

Colette Parent was a professor (retired) in the Department of Criminology at the University of Ottawa. She has worked on the issues of sex work, criminalization of women, violence against women and feminist theories in criminology.

Penny Ridley conducted part of the research for her chapter for her undergraduate honours thesis in psychology at the University of Victoria under the supervision of Linda Coates.

A.J. Withers works with the Ontario Coalition Against Poverty and is a PhD student in social work at York University. A.J.'s publications include *The Healing Power of Domination: Interlocking Oppression and the Origins of Social Work* (co-authored with Chris Chapman, forthcoming), *Disability Politics and Theory* (2012) and stillmyrevolution.org.

FEMINISM AND THEORY

Chapter 1

RACE, CLASS, GENDER AND THE LAW
An Introduction

Elizabeth Comack

From: *Locating Law: Race, Class, Gender, Sexuality Connections*, 3rd edition, pp. 1–8 (slightly revised and reprinted with permission).

One of the primary concerns within the sociology of law has been to understand the "law-society relation." Underlying this concern is the belief that law has a distinctly social basis; it both shapes — and is shaped by — the society in which it operates. A main objective of the sociology of law is to explore this law-society relation or, as the title of this book implies, to locate law. More specifically, we propose that to understand the law-society relation, we need to place law within the nexus of race, class and gender relations in society.

As individuals, our interactions and experiences are very much governed by our social positioning in society, and that social location is contoured and conditioned by three key elements: our race, our class and our gender. But these three elements do more than specify "difference" between individuals; they are used to divide, separate and categorize. In short, race, class and gender constitute the primary bases on which inequality is produced and maintained — though they are not the only bases: sexual orientation and disability are at least two significant others.

Historically, inequalities of race, class and gender have been an imbedded feature of Canadian society. It is a sad fact that our history is tainted by the systemic processes of colonization and forced dependency of the Indigenous people of this territory. This history includes not only the appropriation of their land, but also the transfer of their populations to geographical areas more often than not devoid of the natural resources needed to sustain traditional or any other useful economic practices. It includes the forced removal of their children to residential schools, where physical and sexual abuse became an all-too-common practice in the drive to "assimilate" them to the ways of the supposedly "civilized" white settler society. This historical legacy is one that mainstream Canadian society is only beginning to fully comprehend in terms of its long-lasting effects on the lives of Aboriginal people and on their communities. As Geoffrey York (1990: xiii) notes, "Most Canadians are better acquainted with the history of native people in the eighteenth and nineteenth centuries than they are with the unsavoury realities of recent years." Consider the following.

- During the 1960s, in what became known as the "Sixties Scoop," child welfare agencies removed Aboriginal children from their families, communities and cultures, placing them in non-Aboriginal families. These interventions carried on through the 1970s and 1980s. Between 1971 and 1981 alone, the agencies shipped over 3,400 Aboriginal children off to adoptive parents in other communities and sometimes in other countries (Hamilton and Sinclair 1991: 520). This pattern of family disruption continues to the present day. Of the roughly 30,000 children aged fourteen and under in Canada who were in foster care in 2011, nearly half (48 percent) were Aboriginal children. In 2011, 14,255 (3.6 percent) of Aboriginal children were in foster care, compared with 0.3 percent of non-Aboriginal children (Statistics Canada 2013a).

- Aboriginal people — First Nations, Métis and Inuit — constitute one of the poorest groups in Canadian society. Almost 1.2 million people reported Aboriginal identity in the 2006 Census, representing 3.8 percent of the total Canadian population (Statistics Canada 2008). In 2005, 18.7 percent of Aboriginal families and 42.8 percent of unattached individuals who identified as Aboriginal experienced low income, compared to 8.4 percent of families and 28 percent of unattached individuals who were non-Aboriginal (Collin and Jensen 2009).

- While levels of educational attainment for Aboriginal Canadians have improved in recent years, they are still considerably lower than non-Aboriginal Canadians. Only 68 percent of Aboriginal young adults aged twenty-five to thirty-four have completed their high school certificate, compared to 90 percent of non-Aboriginal Canadians of the same age group. The figure is even lower — 49 percent — for Aboriginal young adults living on-reserve (Vital Signs Canada 2009).

- Substandard and overcrowded housing is a pressing issue in many First Nations communities. In 2006, 28 percent of First Nations people were living in a home in need of major repairs, compared with just 7 percent of the non-Aboriginal population. First Nations people were five times more likely than non-Aboriginal people to live in crowded homes (Statistics Canada 2008).

- Potable water, adequate sanitation, and waste disposal services are re-sources that many Canadians take for granted. Yet in November 2010, 117 First Nations communities were under drinking water advisories (Campaign 2000 2011).

- Aboriginal people living in urban centres also encounter impoverished conditions. In 2006, 54 percent of Aboriginal people lived in an urban centre; 291,035 Aboriginal people — or 25 percent of the total Aboriginal population — lived in nine of the nation's thirty-three census metropoli-tan areas (CMAS). Some 57 percent of First Nations children and 42 per-cent of Métis children living in CMAS were members of low-income fami-lies. Among non-Aboriginal children, the low-income rate in CMAS was 21 percent (Collin and Jensen 2009).

- Impoverished living conditions undermine the health of a community. Aboriginal people have shorter life expectancies and a higher risk of suf-fering from infectious diseases such as tuberculosis and chronic illnesses such as diabetes. The projected life expectancy for First Nations people is seventy-eight years for women and seventy-three years for men, compared to eighty-three and seventy-nine for non-Aboriginals in Canada (Campaign 2000 2012).

- Impoverished conditions can also generate a sense of hopelessness and despair. While the suicide rates vary widely in First Nations communi-ties, the youth suicide rate in these communities is still between three and seven times greater than in Canada overall (Campaign 2000 2011).

The experiences of other racialized groups who historically made Canada their home have been similarly marked by inequities and dispossession. At various points the treatment of the Chinese, Japanese, East Indians, Jews and other groups has been characterized by both overt and subtle forms of discrimination. Signs of discrimination continue to the present day.

- Canada is increasingly becoming a racially diverse nation. In the 1980s, racialized groups (not including Aboriginal people) accounted for less than 5 percent of the Canadian population. In 2011, nearly 6,264,800 people identified themselves as a member of the visible minority population. They represented 19.1 percent of Canada's total population, compared with 16.2 percent in the 2006 Census. Statistics Canada estimates that racialized Canadians will make up 32 percent of the population by 2031 (Block and Galabuzi 2011: 6; Statistics Canada 2013b).

- Racialized Canadians experience inequality in the labour market. They earn only 81.4 cents for every dollar paid to non-racialized Canadians, and the work they are able to attain is much more likely to be insecure and temporary. For example, racialized Canadians are overrepresented in a range of business services ranging from call centres to security services that tend to be low-paid and with few or no benefits (Block and Galabuzi 2011: 11, 10).

- Racialized Canadians and their families are more likely to experience poverty. There were 1.1 million racialized persons living in poverty in Canada in 2006. Although this group made up only 4 percent of the population, they represented 32 percent of all persons living in poverty (National Council of Welfare 2012: 2). Poverty rates for racialized families are three times higher than for non-racialized families. In 2005, 19.8 percent of racialized families lived in poverty compared to 6.4 percent of non-racialized families (Block and Galabuzi 2011: 15).

- Educational attainment does not ensure economic well-being for racialized individuals. According to 2006 Census data, 32 percent of racialized persons aged twenty-five to sixty-two living in poverty had a university certificate or degree, compared with 13 percent of non-racialized persons in the same age category who were living in poverty (National Council of Welfare 2012: 9).

- Newcomers are especially vulnerable to poverty. Persons from racialized groups make up 54 percent of all immigrants in Canada; however, they make up 71 percent of all immigrants living in poverty (National Council of Welfare 2012: 5).

- Racialized groups in Canada experience discrimination not just in the labour market and workplace but also in education, housing and social services (Reitz and Banerjee 2007; Henry et al. 2006; Dion 2001; Bolaria and Li 1988).

As a group, women have also encountered inequalities in the labour market and elsewhere. Women's wages, for instance, have historically been only a portion of the wages earned by male workers and, despite advances in recent years, continue to lag behind men's. Historically, women were denied basic rights of citizenship — like the right to vote, to own property once married, and to hold public office. While most Canadian women won the right to vote in federal elections in 1918, Aboriginal women (and their male counterparts) could not vote until 1960 (and provincially in Quebec until 1969). The desperate economic situation of many Canadian women has resulted in what is referred to as the "feminization of poverty."

- Women are the majority of the poor in Canada. In 2007, 9.4 percent of Canadian women (over 1.5 million) were living on a low income (Collin and Jensen 2009).
- Single-parent families are especially vulnerable to poverty. Lone-parent families account for 16 percent of all families in Canada; the vast majority (80 percent) of lone-parent families are headed by women. Over one-half (52.1 percent) of lone mothers with children under six live in poverty (Collin and Jensen 2009; Campaign 2000 2012).
- In Canada it is not enough to have a job to stay out of poverty. Many poor people do work full-time or part-time. In 2007, for example, working-poor families accounted for 31 percent of all low-income families (Collin and Jensen 2009). Women, particularly immigrant and visible-minority women, make up 60 percent of minimum-wage workers. Statistics Canada figures show that a full-time minimum wage earner living in a large city falls $6,000 below the poverty line (UFCW Canada 2013; Statistics Canada 2009).
- Women continue to be paid less than men. They make about 71 percent of what men earn for full-year, full-time work. Education does not eliminate the wage gap: women with university degrees employed full-year, full-time earn 30 percent less than equally educated men. Women earn less than men even if they work in the same sectors or in the same jobs. There are no occupations in which women's average earnings exceed men's, not even female-dominated areas such as clerical work and teaching (Williams 2010; CRIAW 2005).
- Women bear most of the responsibility for caring for young children and the elderly. Statistics Canada (2011a) reports that regardless of a child's age, women spend more time on their care than men do; women with children up to the age of four spend six hours thirty-three minutes per day caring for them, while the corresponding duration for men is three hours seven minutes. Women also comprise the majority of the more than two million Canadians who provide care to elders. Many of these caregivers are still in the paid workforce and find themselves curtailing their paid work by working fewer hours or retiring earlier than planned in order to at-

tend to unpaid caregiving. The value to the Canadian economy of women's (unpaid) caregiving work is estimated to be in the range of $25 billion to $31 billion annually (Zimmerman 2013).

- Women are still missing in the corporate boardrooms of the nation. They hold just 12 percent (690 of 5,746) of corporate officer positions in Canada. Nearly half (244) of Canada's top 560 companies have no women on their boards (Catalyst 2011).

While Canadians prefer to think of their country as a "land of opportunity," where class inequalities do not prevail, the statistics belie that perception. Class inequalities have not only always existed in Canada, these inequities have actually been increasing in the past two decades in tandem with capitalist globalization, corporate restructuring and downsizing, and the dismantling of the Canadian welfare state and its social programs.

- According to Campaign 2000's 2012 Report Card on Child Poverty in Canada, 979,000, or 14.5 percent, of Canadian children live in poverty.
- The first Canadian food bank opened in Edmonton, Alberta, in 1982. By 2008, the country had over 700 food banks (Food Banks Canada 2008). According to Hunger Count 2012, an annual survey of food banks and emergency food programs carried out by the Canadian Association of Food Banks, during one month in 2012, 882,188 Canadians used a food bank — a population equal to the province of New Brunswick, the city of Ottawa, or the city of Edmonton. Some 38 percent of food bank clients are children and youth (Food Banks Canada 2012).
- Divide the Canadian population into income quintiles, five groups, each 20 percent of the population. In 2007, the average after-tax income of families in the highest income quintile was 5.4 times that of families in the lowest income quintile; those in the highest quintile earned 47.1 percent of the total income in Canada while those in the lowest income quintile earned only 4.2 percent. Spending on basic necessities (food, shelter and clothing) accounted for 52 percent of total spending by households in the lowest income quintile and for only 28 percent of total spending by households in the highest income quintile (Collin and Jensen 2009: 6).
- There were 24.6 million tax filers in Canada in 2007. The richest 1 percent made more than $169,000 and had an average income from all sources of $404,000. The richest 0.1 percent made more than $621,000 and had an average income of $1.49 million. The richest 0.01 percent made more than $1.85 million and had an average income of $3.83 million. The richest 1 percent has seen its share of total income double, the richest 0.1 percent

has seen its share almost triple, and the richest 0.01 percent has seen its share more than quintuple since the late 1970s (Yalnizyan 2010).

- While there are some 1.3 million corporations in Canada, sixty Canadian-based firms account for 60 percent of all corporate profit. In 1950, the average profit of a firm within the top sixty was 234 times larger than an average firm in the corporate universe. By 2007, that number had risen to 14,278 — a sixty-fold increase in six decades (Brennan 2012).

- Canada's CEO Elite 100 — the 100 highest paid CEOs of companies listed in the TSX Index — had an average annual compensation of $8.38 million in 2010, representing a 27 percent increase over the $6.6 million average the previous year. In contrast, Canadians working full-time, full-year earned $44,366 in 2010, which means that Canada's CEO Elite 100 make 189 times more than Canadians earning the average wage. This wage gap has been growing: in 1998, the highest paid 100 Canadian CEOs earned 105 times more than the average wage (Mackenzie 2012).

- The wealthiest Canadian is publisher David Thomson. In 2012, his net worth was estimated at $20.10 billion. Following Thomson are Galen Weston (Loblaws) at $8.20 billion, Arthur, James and John Irving (oil) at $8.07 billion, Edward Rogers (communications) at $6.41 billion, James Pattison (industrialist) at $6.14 billion, and Jeffrey Skoll (eBay) at $4.55 billion (Canadian Business n.d.).

The recognition of these inequalities along race, class and gender lines raises important social and political questions, not the least of which concerns the role of law. What role has law historically played in generating today's inequalities? Is law part of the problem or part of the solution in alleviating inequities based on race, class and gender? Can we use law as a mechanism or strategy to achieve substantive social change?

References

Block, Sheila, and Grace-Edward Galabuzi. 2011. *Canada's Colour Coded Labour Market: The Gap for Racialized Workers.* Ottawa and Toronto: Canadian Centre for Policy Alternatives and The Wellsley Institute.

Bolaria, B. Singh, and Peter S. Li (eds.). 1988. *Racial Oppression in Canada* (2nd edition). Toronto: Garamond Press.

Brennan, Jordan. 2012. *A Shrinking Universe: How Concentrated Corporate Power Is Shaping Income Inequality in Canada.* Ottawa: Canadian Centre for Policy Alternatives.

Campaign 2000. 2011. *2011 Report Card on Child and Family Poverty in Canada: Revisiting Family Security in Insecure Times.* Toronto: Family Service Toronto. <campaign2000. ca/reportCards/national/2011EnglishRreportCard.pdf>.

____. 2012. *2012 Report Card on Child and Family Poverty: Needed: A Federal Action Plan to Eradicate Child and Family Poverty in Canada*. Toronto: Family Service Toronto. <campaign2000.ca/reportCards/national/C2000ReportCardNov2012.pdf>.

Catalyst. 2011. "Catalyst Census Finds Few Women Corporate Officers." <catalyst.org/media/catalyst-census-finds-few-women-corporate-officers>.

Collin, Chantal, and Hilary Jensen. 2009. *A Statistical Profile of Poverty in Canada*. Ottawa: Library of Parliament. <parl.gc.ca/content/lop/researchpublications/prb0917-e.pdf>.

CRIAW (Canadian Research Institute for the Advancement of Women). 2005. CRIAW *Fact Sheet: Women and Poverty* (3rd edition). <criaw-icref.ca/indexFrame_e.htm>.

Dion, Kenneth. 2001. "Immigrants' Perceptions of Housing Discrimination in Toronto: The Housing New Canadians Project." *Journal of Social Issues* 57, 3.

Food Banks Canada. 2012. *Hunger Count 2012: A Comprehensive Report on Hunger and Food Bank Use in Canada, and Recommendations for Change*. <foodbankscanada.ca/getmedia/3b946e67-fbe2-490e-90dc-4a313dfb97e5/HungerCount2012.pdf.aspx?ext=.pdf>.

Hamilton, Alvin C., and Murray Sinclair (commissioners), 1991. *Report of the Aboriginal Justice Inquiry of Manitoba: The Justice System and Aboriginal People*, Volume 1. Winnipeg: Queen's Printer.

Henry, Frances, Carol Tator, Winston Mattis, and Tim Rees. 2006. *The Colour of Democracy: Racism in Canadian Society* (3rd edition). Toronto: Harcourt Brace and Company.

Mackenzie, Hugh. 2012. *Canada's CEO Elite 100: The 0.01%*. Ottawa: Canadian Centre for Policy Alternatives.

National Council of Welfare. 2012. *Poverty Profile: Special Edition*. Ottawa: National Council of Welfare Reports (January). <publications.gc.ca/collections/collection_2012/cnb-ncw/HS51-2-2012S-eng.pdf>.

Reitz, Jeffrey, and Rupa Banerjee. 2007. "Racial Inequality, Social Cohesion and Policy Issues in Canada." In Keith Banting, Thomas J. Courchene and F. Leslie Seidle (eds.), *Belonging? Diversity, Recognition and Shared Citizenship in Canada*. Montreal: Institute for Research on Public Policy.

Statistics Canada. 2008. *Aboriginal Peoples in Canada in 2006: Inuit, Métis and First Nations, 2006 Census*. <12.statcan.ca/census-recensement/2006/as-sa/97-558/pdf/97-558-XIE2006001.pdf>.

____. 2009. "Perspectives on Labour and Income: Minimum Wage." Catalogue no. 75-001-X. <statcan.gc.ca/pub/75-001-x/topics-sujets/pdf/topics-sujets/minimumwage-salaireminimum-2008-eng.pdf>.

____. 2011a. "Cases in Adult Criminal Court, by Province and Territory, 2009/2010." <statcan.gc.ca/tables-tableaux/sum-som/l01/cst01/legal19a-eng.htm>.

____. 2013b. "2011 National Household Survey: Aboriginal Peoples in Canada: First Nations People, Métis and Inuit." *The Daily* (May 8). <statcan.gc.ca/daily-quotidien/130508/dq130508a-eng.htm>.

UFCW Canada. 2013. "By the Numbers: Minimum Wage in Canada by Province for 2011." <ufcw.ca/index.php?option=com_content&view=article&id=2359%3Aby-the-numbers-cpi&Itemid=306&lang=en>.

Vital Signs Canada. 2009. *Learning: Aboriginal High School Completion Rates*. <vitalsignscanada.ca/en/research-54-learning-aboriginal-high-school-completion>.

Williams, Cara. 2010. "Economic Well-being." *Women in Canada: A Gender-Based Statistical Report*. Ottawa: Statistics Canada.

Yalnizyan, Armine. 2010. *The Rise of Canada's Richest 1%*. Ottawa: Canadian Centre for Policy Alternatives.

York, Geoffrey. 1990. *The Dispossessed: Life and Death in Native Canada*. London: Vintage Books.

Zimmerman, Lillian. 2013. "The Caregiving Crunch." Herizons Magazine (Winter).

Chapter 2

THE FEMINIST ENGAGEMENT WITH CRIMINOLOGY

Elizabeth Comack

From: *Criminalizing Women: Gender and (In)Justice in Neo-liberal Times*, 2nd edition, pp. 12–46 (reprinted with permission).

The feminist engagement with criminology began almost fifty years ago, when pioneers in the discipline such as Marie-Andrée Bertrand (1967) and Frances Heidensohn (1968) first called attention to criminology's amnesia when it came to women. Heidensohn (1968: 171), for instance, described the analysis of women and crime as "lonely uncharted seas" and suggested that what was needed was a "crash programme of research which telescopes decades of comparable studies of males." Since that time, feminist work in this area has developed at a fast pace, to the point where it has become increasingly difficult to keep abreast of the research and publications on women and crime.

There is little doubt about the validity of Heidensohn's claim that women traditionally have been neglected in criminology. Like other academic disciplines, criminology has been a decidedly male-centred enterprise. Despite the use of generic terms — such as "criminals," "defendants" or "delinquents" — criminology has historically been about what men do, so much so that women have been invisible in mainstream criminological theory and research. This is not to say, however, that women have been completely ignored. From criminology's inception, there have been some (rather dubious) efforts to make sense of women and girls who come under the purview of the criminal justice system. Variously referred to as monsters, misfits and manipulators, women — and especially women who engaged in criminal activity — were relegated by early criminologists to the status of "Other."

Historically, feminist engagement with criminology emerged out of the various ways in which women as an object of knowledge production were understood (or ignored) by the criminological discipline over time. Feminists have not only challenged these understandings but also promoted alternative claims about women and their involvement in crime. This kind of intellectual history is wide-ranging. Much has happened over the past five decades — both within academia and the wider society — that has played a role in instigating and contouring the kinds of work that feminists have undertaken in this area. Like all knowledge production, therefore, the rendering of an intellectual history in this chapter will at best be partial.

THE INVISIBLE WOMEN OF MAINSTREAM CRIMINOLOGY

To a certain extent the male-centredness of criminology makes sense when you examine the official statistics on crime. In 2011, women comprised only 21 percent of adults charged with Criminal Code offences in Canada, while men made up the lion's share — 79 percent — of those charged (Brennan 2012: 20). In Australia, females made up 25 percent of individuals charged in three states (Victoria, Queensland and South Australia) in 2009–10 (Australian Institute of Criminology 2011: 69). A similar percentage exists for the United States, where females made up 25 percent of those arrested in 2010 (Snyder 2012: 2). Yet, even though this sex/crime ratio has long been recognized in the discipline, most mainstream criminologists have never really stopped to question it. Instead, they proceeded to develop theories of crime causation that took men — or, more accurately, poor inner-city Black men — as their subject, even when the theorist was intent on framing a general theory of crime ostensibly applicable to the whole population.

This invisibility of women can be easily demonstrated by examining some of the mainstream theories that make up the criminological canon. Robert Merton's (1938) anomie theory, for example, was offered as a general theory explaining crime in relation to the strain that results from the disjunction between culture goals (like monetary success) and institutionalized means (education, jobs). While Merton's theory reflected sensitivity to class inequalities, the same could not be said with regard to an awareness of gender inequalities. If lower-class individuals were more likely to engage in crime because of a lack of access to the institutionalized means for achieving monetary success, it follows, then, that women — who as a group experience a similar lack of access — should also be found to commit their share of crime as a consequence of this strain. But the statistics tell us that this is not the case.

Like anomie theory, Edwin Sutherland's (1949) differential association theory was presented as a general theory of crime. Sutherland focused on the processes by which individuals learn definitions of the legal code as either favourable or unfavourable, and posited the existence of a "cultural heterogeneity" in society with regard to social assessments that were pro- and anti-criminal. Yet, this "general" theory only applied to half the population. Sutherland suggested that while men were individualistic and competitive, women were more altruistic and compliant. So, while cultural heterogeneity could account for men's involvement in crime, it did not seem to apply to women, leading Sutherland to surmise that women were an exception or anomaly in his theory because they displayed a "cultural homogeneity."

Travis Hirschi's (1969) control theory was also characterized by a neglect of the female. While other criminologists focused their attention on explaining deviance, Hirschi turned the tables and set out to explain conformity. Since women appear to be more conformist than men (given, for example, their underrepresentation in crime statistics), it would have made sense for Hirschi to treat women as central to his analysis. Nevertheless, despite having collected data on females, he simply set these data aside and — like his colleagues — concentrated on males.

With the advent of labelling and conflict theories in the 1960s and 1970s, the potential for a more gender-inclusive approach to crime increased. Nonetheless, while Howard Becker's (1963) labelling theory raised the question of "Whose side are we on?" and advocated an approach to deviance that gave voice to those who were subjected to the labelling process, it was never fully realized in the case of women. Similarly, Ian Taylor, Paul Walton and Jock Young's *The New Criminology* (1973), which offered up a devastating critique of traditional criminological theories, failed to give even a mention to women.

WOMEN AS OTHER:
MONSTERS, MISFITS AND MANIPULATORS

Women were not completely ignored in criminological thought. A small body of work, dating back to the nineteenth century, attempted to account for women's involvement in crime. What could be classified as the early approaches to explaining women's crime began in 1895 with Cesare Lombroso and William Ferrero's *The Female Offender*, followed by W.I. Thomas's *The Unadjusted Girl* in 1923, Sheldon Glueck and Eleanor Glueck's *Five Hundred Delinquent Women* in 1934, and Otto Pollak's *The Criminality of Women* in 1950. While differences exist between these approaches, they all share in common the view of women as "other" than men, and women who engage in criminal activity as even more so. For these theorists, it is women's "inherent nature" that accounts for both the nature and extent of their criminality. In particular, women are cast as sexual beings, and women's sexuality is at the root of their involvement in crime.

Lombroso and Ferrero based their theorizing on an examination of the physical characteristics of a group of 119 "criminal" women, which they compared with a control group of 14 "non-criminal" women. In applying the concepts of atavism (the idea that some individuals were born criminals) and social Darwinism (the idea that those who get ahead in society are the most fit to survive), they suggested that women as a group possessed limited intelligence. Women were also less sensitive to pain than men, full of revenge and jealousy, and naturally passive and conservative. These traits had a physiological basis. For instance, Lombroso and Ferrero (1895: 109) assert that women's passivity was demonstrated by the "immobility of the ovule compared to the zoosperm." Atavistically, women offenders were considered to display fewer signs of degeneration than men. The reason, according to Lombroso and Ferrero, was that women (and non-white males) had not advanced as far along the evolutionary continuum as (white) males, and so could not degenerate as far. Given that women were relatively "primitive," the criminals among them would not be highly visible. However, those women who were criminal were cast as excessively vile and cruel in their crimes. They ostensibly combined the qualities of the criminal male with the worst characteristics of the female: cunning, spite and deceitfulness. Lacking "maternal instinct" and "ladylike qualities," criminal women were deemed to be "monsters":

> The born female criminal is, so to speak, doubly exceptional as a woman and as a criminal. For criminals are an exception among civilized people, and women are an exception among criminals ... As a double exception, the criminal woman is consequently a *monster*. Her normal sister is kept in the paths of virtue by many causes, such as maternity, piety, weakness, and when these counter influences fail, and a woman commits a crime, we may conclude that her wickedness must have been so enormous before it could triumph over so many obstacles. (Lombroso and Ferrero 1895: 151–52; emphasis added)

Like Lombroso and Ferrero, W.I. Thomas (1923–1967) framed his theorizing about women on presumed "natural" or biological differences between men and women. Thomas suggested that human behaviour is based on four wishes: desires for adventure, security, response and recognition. These wishes corresponded to features in the nervous system that were expressed as biological instincts of anger, fear, love and the will to gain status and power. However, Thomas asserted that men's and women's instincts differed both in quantity and quality. Since women had more varieties of love in their nervous systems, their desire for response was greater than men's. According to Thomas, it was the need to feel loved that accounted for women's criminality, and especially for their involvement in prostitution.

Sheldon Glueck and Eleanor Glueck (1934) continued in this same tradition with their book *Five Hundred Delinquent Women*. The Gluecks described the women in their study as a "sorry lot. Burdened with feeblemindedness, psychopathic personality, and marked emotional instability, a large proportion of them found it difficult to survive by legitimate means" (Glueck and Glueck 1934: 299). The view of criminal women as Other is clearly evident: "This swarm of defective, diseased, antisocial misfits ... comprises the human material which a reformatory and a parole system are required by society to transform into wholesome, decent, law-abiding citizens! Is it not a miracle that a proportion of them were actually rehabilitated?" (Glueck and Glueck 1934: 303).

Two decades later, Otto Pollak attempted to account for what he described as the masked nature of women's crime. Skeptical of the official data on sex differences in crime, Pollak (1950) suggested that women's crime was vastly undercounted. He put forward the view that female criminality was more likely to be hidden and undetected. According to Pollak, women were more often the instigators than the perpetrators of crime. Like Eve in the Garden of Eden, they manipulated men into committing offences. Women, he claimed, were also inherently deceptive and vengeful. They engaged in prostitution and blackmailed their lovers. As domestics they stole from their employers, and as homemakers they carried out horrendous acts on their families (like poisoning the sick and abusing children). According to Pollak, woman's devious nature was rooted in her physiology. While a man must achieve erection in order to perform the sex act (and hence will not be able to conceal orgasm), a woman can fake orgasm (Pollak 1950: 10). This ability to conceal orgasm supposedly gave women practice at deception.

Pollak also argued that the vengefulness, irritability and depression that women encountered as a result of their generative phases caused female crime. For example, menstruation drove women to acts of revenge by reminding them of their inferior status (and their ultimate failure to become men). The concealed nature of their crimes, the vulnerability of their victims, and their chivalrous treatment by men who cannot bear to prosecute or punish them combined to mask women's offences. When these factors are taken into account, according to Pollak, women's crimes are equal in severity and number to those of men.

For these early criminologists, then, the women involved in crime were monsters, misfits or manipulators. While we can look back on these constructions of women with some amusement, it bears noting that these kinds of knowledge claims about women and the reasons for their involvement in crime have not disappeared. Throughout the 1960s, researchers continued to rely on the assumptions and premises of the earlier approaches. John Cowie, Valerie Cowie and Eliot

Slater (1968), for example, in the tradition of Lombroso and Ferrero, looked for "constitutional predisposing factors" to explain female delinquency. In a similarly disparaging manner, the same authors (1968: 167) characterized delinquent girls as "oversized, lumpish, uncouth and graceless." Gisela Konopka (1966), in extending Thomas' analysis, equated sexual delinquency in girls with a desperate need for love. Following on the footsteps of Otto Pollak, a more contemporary version of these theories links hormonal changes associated with women's menstrual cycles to their involvement in crime.

Premenstrual syndrome (PMS) has been described as a condition of "irritability, indescribable tension" and a "desire to find relief by foolish and ill-considered actions," something that is thought to occur during the week or two prior to the onset of menstruation (Frank, cited in Osborne 1989: 168). With no biomedical tests for determining its existence, PMS is the only "disease" not dependent on a specific type of symptom for its diagnosis. Nevertheless, PMS has been argued to be a cause of violent behaviour in women who suffer from it. Premenstrual syndrome gained popularity as an explanation for women's criminality in the 1980s, when it was introduced in two British court cases as a mitigating factor in homicide (Luckhaus 1985). Research linking PMS to women's criminality has been criticized for its methodological deficiencies (Morris 1987; Kendall 1991, 1992). As an explanation for women's involvement in crime, however, PMS clearly locates the source of the problem in women's "unruly" bodies. Because of their "nature," women are supposedly prone to madness once a month.

ENTER FEMINISM...

In its initial stages, feminist criminology took the form of a critique of the existing approaches to explaining crime. Writers such as Dorie Klein (1973), Carol Smart (1976, 1977), Eileen Leonard (1982), Allison Morris (1987) and Ngaire Naffine (1987) took issue with the sexism of criminological theories — socially undesirable characteristics were attributed to women and assumed to be intrinsic characteristics of their sex.

With regard to the early approaches to explaining crime (offered by Lombroso and Ferrero, Thomas, the Gluecks, and Pollak), Heidensohn (1985: 122) noted how they lent an aura of intellectual respectability to many old folk tales about women and their behaviours. Their constructions of the "female offender" reflected the widely held assumptions about "women's nature," including the good girl/bad girl duality and a double standard that viewed sexual promiscuity as a sign of amorality in women but normality in men. Relying on common sense, anecdotal evidence and circular reasoning — that is, "things are as they are because they are natural, and they are natural because that is the way things are" (Smart 1976: 36) — the early theorists failed to call into question the structural features of their society and the gendered roles of men and women. For these early criminologists, sex (a biological difference) and gender (a cultural prescription) were equated as one and the same, with the "ladylike" qualities of the middle-class and upper-class white woman used as the measuring rod for what is inherently female. Feminist criminologists castigated these early theories for being not only sexist, but also racist and classist.

Mainstream theories of crime (such an anomie, differential association, social control, labelling, and conflict theories) came under a similar scrutiny. The invisibility of women and the failure to adequately explain or account for women's involvement in crime led feminist criminologists to label such theories as not just mainstream but "malestream." As Loraine Gelsthorpe and Allison Morris asserted,

> theories are weak if they do not apply to half of the potential criminal population; women, after all, experience the same deprivations, family structures and so on that men do. Theories of crime should be able to take account of *both* men's and women's behaviour and to highlight those factors which operate differently on men and women. Whether or not a particular theory helps us to understand women's crime is of *fundamental*, not marginal, importance for criminology. (Gelsthorpe and Morris 1988: 103; emphasis added)

Kathleen Daly and Meda Chesney-Lind (1988) refer to one issue raised by the feminist critique of the mainstream theories as the "generalizability problem": can theories generated to explain males' involvement in crime be modified to apply to women? Several feminist criminologists responded to this problem by attempting to make the mainstream theories of crime "fit" women.

Eileen Leonard (1982), for example, in a reformulation of Merton's strain theory, suggested that females are socialized to aspire to different culture goals than are males, in particular relational goals concerning marriage and having children. Following this line of reasoning, women's low rate of criminal involvement compared to men could be explained by the relatively easy manner in which females can realize their goals. Nevertheless, as Allison Morris (1987) notes, such a formulation relies on an idealized and romanticized version of women's lives. Not only does it display an insensitivity to the strains and frustrations associated with women's familial role (raising children and maintaining a household), it fails to acknowledge the very real and pressing economic concerns that women confront in the process (making ends meet and paying the bills).

Such efforts to revise mainstream theories of crime to include women have been referred to as the "add women and stir" approach (Chesney-Lind 1988a). Part of the difficulty with this project is that women are presented merely as afterthoughts, not as integral to the arguments being developed (Gelsthorpe and Morris 1988). Naffine (1997: 32) captures a more significant problem with this effort: "The point of these exercises has been to adapt to the female case, theories of crime which purported to be gender-neutral but were in fact always highly gender specific. Not surprisingly, the results have been varied and generally inconclusive."

A second issue raised by the feminist critique of mainstream criminology is one that Daly and Chesney-Lind (1988: 119) refer to as the "gender-ratio problem." Why are women less likely than men to be involved in crime? What explains the sex difference in rates of arrest and in the variable types of criminal activity between men and women? Attention to the gender-ratio problem sparked a multitude of studies in the 1970s and 1980s on the criminal justice system's processing of men and women (see, for example, Scutt 1979; Kruttschnitt 1980–81, 1982; Steffensmeier and Kramer 1982; Zingraff and Thomson 1984; Daly 1987, 1989). Much of this research was guided by Pollak's assertion of chivalry on the part of criminal justice officials. Are women treated more leniently than men? As in the generalizability problem, the results were mixed. For instance, research that supported this chivalry hypothesis indicated that when it does exist, chivalry benefits some women more than others — in particular, the few white, middle-class or upper-class women who come into conflict with the law. It also appears to apply only to those female suspects who behave according to a stereotypical female script, that is, "crying, pleading for release for the sake of their children, claiming men have led them astray" (Rafter and Natalizia 1981: 92). In this regard, Nicole Rafter and Elena Natalizia argue that chivalrous behaviour should be seen as a means of preserving women's subordinate position in society, not as a benign effort to treat women with some special kindness. Naffine (1997: 36), however, points to a larger problem with this research. By turning on the question of whether women were treated in the same way as men, or differently, the chivalry thesis (and its rebuttal) took men to be the norm: "Men were thus granted the status of universal subjects, the population of people with whom the rest of the world (women) were compared" (Naffine 1997: 36).

At the same time, in the 1970s and 1980s, another thesis was attracting considerable criminological attention. The "women's liberation thesis" posited that women's involvement in crime would come to resemble men's more closely as differences between men and women were diminished by women's greater participation and equality in society. As reflected in the work of Rita Simon (1975) and Freda Adler (1975), the thesis suggested that changes in women's gender roles would be reflected in their rates of criminal involvement. Simon argued that the increased employment opportunities that resulted from the women's movement would also bring an increase in opportunities to commit crime (such as embezzlement from employers). Adler linked the apparent increase of women in crime statistics to the influence of the women's movement and suggested that a "new female criminal" was emerging: women were becoming more violent and aggressive, just like their male counterparts.

The women's liberation thesis "captured the imagination of the media and practitioners" (Morris and Gelsthorpe 1981: 53, cited in Gavigan 1993: 221). While law enforcement officials were quick to affirm its tenets, charging that the women's movement was responsible for triggering a massive crime wave, the media had a heyday with its claims, featuring headlines such as "Lib takes the lid off the gun moll" (*Toronto Star* 15 May 1975, cited in Gavigan 1993: 222). Nevertheless, representations of emancipated women running amok in the streets and workplaces did not hold up under closer scrutiny (see, for example, Chesney-Lind 1978; Weiss 1976; Steffensmeier 1980; Naffine 1987). Smart (1976), for one, noted that the women's liberation thesis was premised on a "statistical illusion" in that the supposed increases in women's crime were being reported as percentages. Given the small base number of women charged with criminal offences, it did not take much of a change to show a large percentage increase. Holly Johnson and Karen Rodgers (1993: 104) provided an example of this problem using Canadian data. Between 1970 and 1991, charges against women for homicide increased by 45 percent, but that figure reflected a real increase of only fifteen women charged. As well, while the women's movement was primarily geared toward privileged white women, poor women and women of colour were most likely to appear in police and prison data. These women were not inclined to think of themselves as "liberated" and — far from considering themselves as feminists — were quite conventional in their ideas and beliefs about women's role in society. For many feminist criminologists, the main difficulty with the women's liberation thesis — similar to the chivalry thesis — was that it posed a question that took males to be the norm: were women becoming more liberated and thus more like men, even in their involvement in crime? In Naffine's (1997: 32) judgment, the thesis that women's liberation causes crime by women has been "perhaps the most time-consuming and fruitless exercise" in criminology.

Another effort to attend to the gender-ratio problem was put forward by John Hagan and his colleagues (Hagan, Simpson, and Gillis 1979, 1987; Hagan, Gillis, and Simpson 1985), who combined elements of feminist theory with Hirschi's control theory to fashion a power-control theory of sex and delinquency. Focusing attention on the gender roles and differential socialization of males and females, power-control theory was designed to explain the sex differences in delinquency by drawing linkages between the variations in parental control and the delinquent behaviour of boys and girls. More specifically, Hagan and his colleagues suggested that parental control and adolescents' subsequent attitudes toward risk-taking behaviour are influenced by family class relations. They distinguished two ideal types of family: the patriarchal family, in which the husband is employed in an authority position in the workforce and the wife is not employed outside the home; and the egalitarian family, in which both husband and wife are employed in authority positions outside the home. Hagan and his colleagues suggested that in the former a traditional gender division exists, whereby fathers and especially mothers are expected to control their daughters more than their sons. Given the presence of a "cult of domesticity," girls will be socialized to focus their futures on domestic labour and consumption activities, while boys will be prepared for their participation in production activities. In the egalitarian family, parents will redistribute their control efforts such that girls are subject to controls that are more like the ones imposed on boys. "In other words, in egalitarian families, as mothers gain power relative to husbands, daughters gain freedom relative to sons" (Hagan, Simpson, and Gillis 1987: 792). As such, the authors predicted that these differ-ent family forms will produce differing levels of delinquency in girls: "Patriarchal families will be characterized by large gender differences in common delinquent behaviours, while egalitarian families will be characterized by smaller gender dif-ferences in delinquency" (Hagan, Simpson, and Gillis 1987: 793).

While Hagan and his colleagues endeavoured to place delinquency by girls in a broader structural context (by attending to the labour force participation of parents), they made an important assumption: if a woman is working for wages, there will be "equality" within the household. Their formulation does not pay enough attention to the nature of women's paid work and to other variables that might be in operation (such as how power and control may be exercised between males and females within the household). As well, Chesney-Lind regards power-control theory as a variation on the women's liberation thesis because it links the emergence of the egalitarian family with increasing delinquency among girls. In effect, "mother's liberation causes daughter's crime" (Chesney-Lind 1989: 20, cited in Boritch 1997: 71).

FEMINIST EMPIRICISM:
COUNTERING BAD SCIENCE

In their engagement with criminology during the 1970s and 1980s, feminists tended to work within the confines of positivist social science. In other words, they subscribed to the belief that the methods of the natural sciences (measure-ment and prediction) could be applied to the study of social life. Their critiques of mainstream work in the discipline amounted to the claim that what was being produced was "bad science." In her elaboration of different feminist epistemologies, philosopher Sandra Harding (1990) named this approach "feminist empiricism." Feminist empiricists in criminology held that bringing women into the mix and attending more rigorously to the methodological norms of scientific inquiry could rectify women's omission from the criminological canon. Feminist empiricism is very much reflected in the attempts to reformulate the mainstream theories of crime to include women. It is also reflected in the empirical research conducted to test the chivalry hypothesis and women's liberation thesis.

Yet, given the difficulties encountered in the efforts to respond to the generalizability and gender-ratio problems — in particular, the tendency to take men as the standard or measuring rod — many feminist criminologists saw the need to "bracket" these issues for the time being in order to understand better the social worlds of women and girls (Daly and Chesney-Lind 1988: 121). Maureen Cain (1990) took this suggestion further. She noted that while feminist criminologists needed to understand women's experiences, existing criminological theory offered no tools for doing this. Therefore, feminists needed to transgress the traditional boundaries of criminology, to start from outside the confines of criminological discourse. In carrying out this project, feminist criminologists drew inspiration from the violence against women movement.

TRANSGRESSING CRIMINOLOGY: THE ISSUE OF MALE VIOLENCE AGAINST WOMEN

At the same time as feminists were fashioning their critiques of criminology, the women's movement in Canada and other Western countries was breaking the silence around the issue of male violence against women. This violence was understood as a manifestation of patriarchy — the systemic and individual power that men exercise over women (Brownmiller 1975; Kelly 1988).

As a political movement united around improving the condition and quality of women's lives, feminism in the 1970s took as one of its key issues the provision of support to women who had been victimized by violence. One of the first books ever published on the subject of domestic violence was Erin Pizzey's (1974) *Scream Quietly or the Neighbours Will Hear You*. Pizzey is also credited for opening, in England in 1971, one of the first refuges for battered women and their children. Rape crisis centres and shelters for abused women also began to appear in Canada in the 1970s. With their establishment came the recognition that male violence against women was a widespread and pervasive phenomenon.

In the early 1980s, the Canadian Advisory Council on the Status of Women (CACSW) estimated that one in every five Canadian women will be sexually assaulted at some point in her life, and one in every seventeen will be a victim of forced sexual intercourse. In 1981, CACSW released a report, *Wife Battering in Canada: The Vicious Circle*. Linda MacLeod, author of the report, noted, "Women are kicked, punched, beaten, burned, threatened, knifed and shot, not by strangers who break into their houses or who accost them on dark streets, but by husbands and lovers they've spent many years with — years with good times as well as bad" (MacLeod 1980: 6). She estimated that, every year, one in ten Canadian women who is married or in a relationship with a live-in partner is battered.

More recently, in 1993, Statistics Canada released the findings of the Violence Against Women (VAW) Survey. The first national survey of its kind anywhere in the world, the VAW Survey included responses from 12,300 women (see Johnson 1996). Using definitions of physical and sexual assault consistent with the Canadian Criminal Code, the survey found that one-half (51 percent) of Canadian women had experienced at least one incident of physical or sexual violence since the age of sixteen. The survey also confirmed the results of other research in finding that women face the greatest risk of violence from men they know. "Almost half (45%) of all women experienced violence by men known to them (dates, boyfriends, marital partners, friends, family, neighbours, etc.), while 23% of women experienced violence by a stranger (17% reported violence by both strangers and known men)" (Statistics Canada 1993: 2). The VAW Survey also found that 29 percent of ever-married women had been assaulted by a spouse.

A pivotal moment in the violence against women movement occurred on December 6, 1989, when a man entered a classroom at the École Polytechnique in Montreal, separated the men from the women students, proclaimed, "You're all a bunch of feminists," and proceeded to gun them down. He killed fourteen women and wounded thirteen others that day. The gunman's suicide letter explicitly identified his action as politically motivated: he blamed "feminists" for the major disappointments in his life. Police also found a hit list containing the names of prominent women. The "Montreal Massacre" served in a most profound way to reinforce what women's groups across the country had been arguing for two decades: that violence against women is a serious social problem that takes many forms, including sexual harassment in the workplace, date rape, violent sexual assaults and wife abuse.

The violence against women movement had a number of implications for the work of feminist criminologists. First, the movement allowed feminists to break away from the confines of mainstream criminology, which had been complicit in the social silencing around male violence against women. Official statistics suggested that crimes like rape were relatively infrequent in their occurrence. Victim surveys — which asked respondents whether they had been victimized by crime — indicated that the group most at risk of victimization was young males, not women. Most mainstream criminologists took these data sources at face value. They seldom questioned whether (and why) acts like rape might be underreported, undercharged or underprosecuted, or the extent to which victim surveys had been constructed in ways that excluded the behaviours that women feared most. When criminologists did turn their attention to crimes like rape, the focus was on the small group of men who had been convicted and incarcerated for the offence, and these men were typically understood as an abnormal and pathological group. Much of traditional criminology also tended to mirror widely held cultural myths and misconceptions about male violence against women (such as women "ask for it" by their dress or their behaviour; see Morris 1987; Busby 2014). In his "classic" study of forcible rape, for example, Menachem Amir (1967, 1971) introduced "victim precipitation." This concept states that some women are "rape prone" (because of their "bad" reputation) and others invite rape by their "negligent and reckless" behaviour (by going to bars or hitchhiking) or their failure to react strongly enough to sexual overtures. Amir's work blamed the victim for the violence she encounters. In these terms, the issue of male violence against women pointed to significant knowledge gaps in mainstream criminology and encouraged a host of studies by feminist criminologists intent on rectifying this omission (see Dobash and Dobash 1979; Klein 1982; Stanko 1985; Gunn and Minch 1988).

Second, the violence against women movement brought to the fore the issue of engaging with the state to address the issue — especially in light of law's role historically in condoning the violence, for example, by granting husbands the right to consortium (which legally obligated wives to provide sexual services to their husbands such that there was no such thing as, let alone a crime of, rape in marriage) and the right to chastise their wives (which meant that husbands had the authority to use force in order to ensure that wives fulfilled their marital obligations) (Dobash and Dobash 1979; Edwards 1985; Backhouse 2002). While some feminist criminologists joined with other women's advocates and academics in lobbying the state to reform laws relating to sexual assault and domestic violence, others engaged in critical treatises on the wisdom of engaging the criminal justice system to promote feminist concerns (see Snider 1985, 1991, 1994; Smart 1989; Lös 1990; Faith and Currie 1993; Comack 1993; Martin and Mosher 1995).

Finally, in pointing to the widespread and pervasive nature of male violence against women, the movement raised the issue of the impact that violence has on women who come into conflict with the law. Several quantitative studies in the 1990s began to expose the extent of abuse experienced by women caught up in the criminal justice system. In interviewing women serving federal sentences, Margaret Shaw and her colleagues (1991) found that 68 percent had been physically abused as children or as adults, and 53 percent were sexually abused at some point in their lives. Among Aboriginal women, the figures were considerably higher: 90 percent said that they had been physically abused, and 61 percent reported sexual abuse (Shaw et al. 1991: vii, 31). Another study of women in a provincial jail (Comack 1993) found that 78 percent of the women admitted over a six-year period reported histories of physical and sexual abuse. To address this issue of the relation between victimization and criminalization, several feminist criminologists adopted the position known as "standpoint feminism" (Harding 1990).

STANDPOINT FEMINISM:
WOMEN IN TROUBLE

Influenced by Cain's call to transgress the boundaries of criminology and discover more about the lives of the women who were coming into conflict with the law, standpoint feminists began to dig deeper into the lives of women who came into conflict with the law. As Naffine (1997: 46) notes, while standpoint feminism assumed a number of forms — ranging from the assertion that women are the "experts" of their own lives to the proposal that an adequate social science must be capable of grasping the forms of oppression that women experience — the overall intention was "to place women as knowers at the centre of inquiry in order to produce better understandings of women and the world." Central to much of this research were links between women's victimization and their criminal involvement.

In the United States, Mary Gilfus (1992) conducted life history interviews with twenty incarcerated women to understand their entry into street crime. Most of these women had grown up with violence; thirteen of them reported childhood sexual abuse, and fifteen had experienced "severe childhood abuse" (Gilfus 1992: 70). Among the women Gilfus interviewed were eight African Americans. While there were no race-based differences in reported abuse, the African American women were more likely than their white counterparts to grow up in economically marginalized families. Violence, loss and neglect were prevalent themes in their narratives about their childhoods. Violence was also a common feature of their relationships with men: sixteen of the twenty women had lived with violent men. Repeated victimization experiences, drug addiction, involvement in the sex trade, relationships with men involved in street crime, and the demands of mothering: these themes marked the women's transitions from childhood to adulthood.

Beth Richie's (1996) study focused on African American battered women in prison. Richie (1996: 4) developed a theory of "gender entrapment" to explain the "contradictions and complications of the lives of the African American battered women who commit crimes." According to her, gender entrapment involves understanding the connections between violence against women in their intimate relationships, culturally constructed gender-identity development, and women's participation in illegal activities. In these terms, battered Black women were "trapped" in criminal activity in the same way that they were trapped in abusive relationships.

Working in Canada, Ellen Adelberg and Claudia Currie (1987a, 1993) reported on the lives of seven women convicted of indictable offences and sentenced to federal terms of imprisonment. Regularly occurring themes in these women's lives included "poverty, child and wife battering, sexual assault, and women's conditioning to accept positions of submissiveness and dependency upon men," which led Adelberg and Currie to conclude: "The problems suffered by women offenders are similar to the problems suffered by many women in our society, only perhaps more acutely" (Adelberg and Currie 1987b: 68, 98).

My own work, *Women in Trouble* (Comack 1996), was built around the stories of twenty-four incarcerated women. The women's stories revealed complex connections between a woman's law violations and her history of abuse. Sometimes the connections are direct, as in the case of women sent to prison for resisting their abusers. Janice, for instance, was serving a sentence for manslaughter. She talked about how the offence occurred:

> I was at a party, and this guy, older guy, came, came on to me. He tried telling me, "Why don't you go to bed with me. I'm getting some money, you know." And I said, "No." And then he started hitting me. And then he raped me. And then [pause] I lost it. Like, I just, I went, I got very angry and I snapped. And I started hitting him. I threw a coffee table on top of his head and then I stabbed him. (Cited in Comack 1996: 96)

Sometimes a woman's law violations are located in the context of her struggle to cope with the abuse and its effects. Merideth, for example, had a long history of abuse, beginning with her father sexually assaulting her as a young child, and extending to several violent relationships with the men in her life. She was imprisoned for bouncing cheques — she said she was writing the cheques to purchase "*new things to keep her mind off the abuse.*"

> I've never had any kind of conflict with the law. [long pause] When I started dealing with all these different things, then I started having problems. And then I took it out in the form of fraud. (Cited in Comack 1996: 86)

Sometimes the connections are even more entangled, as in the case of women who end up on the street, where abuse and law violation become enmeshed in their ongoing, everyday struggle to survive. Another incarcerated woman, Brenda, described her life on the street:

> Street life is a, it's a power game, you know? Street life? You have to show you're tough. You have to beat up this broad or you have to shank this person, or, you know, you're always carrying guns, you always have blow on you, you always have drugs on you, and you're always working the streets with the pimps and the bikers, you know? That, that alone, you know, it has so much

fucking abuse, it has more abuse than what you were brought up with! ... I
find living on the street I went through more abuse than I did at home. (Cited
in Comack 1996: 105–6)

This kind of work subsequently became known as "pathways research" — a
term that has been applied to a variety of different studies, all of them sharing the
effort to better understand the lives of women and girls and the particular features
that helped lead to their criminal activity (see, for example, Chesney-Lind and
Rodriguez 1983; Miller 1986; Arnold 1995; Heimer 1995; and Chesney-Lind
and Shelden 1998; DeHart 2008). In considering this research, Kathleen Daly
(1992, 1998) suggests that there is a feminist composite or "leading scenario" of
women's lawbreaking:

> Whether they were pushed out or ran away from abusive homes, or
> became part of a deviant milieu, young women began to engage in petty
> hustles or prostitution. Life on the streets leads to drug use and addiction,
> which in turn leads to more frequent lawbreaking to support their drug
> habit. Meanwhile, young women drop out of school because of pregnancy,
> boredom or disinterest in school, or both. Their paid employment record
> is negligible because they lack interest to work in low-paid or unskilled
> jobs. Having a child may facilitate entry into adult women's networks
> and allow a woman to support herself in part by state aid. A woman may
> continue lawbreaking as a result of relationships with men who may also
> be involved in crime. Women are on a revolving criminal justice door,
> moving between incarceration and time on the streets. (Daly 1998: 136)

Daly maintains that although this leading scenario draws attention to the
gendered contexts that bring girls to the streets, and to the gendered conditions
of their survival once they get there, questions continue to linger. In particular,
"What lies in the 'black box' between one's experiences of victimization as a child
and criminal activities as an adult? Is there something more than economic survival which propels or maintains women in a criminalized status?" (Daly 1998:
136–37). Drawing on pre-sentence investigation reports dealing with the cases of
forty women convicted in a New Haven felony court between 1981 and 1986, Daly
maps out five different categories: street women, harmed and harming women, battered women, drug-connected women, and a final category that she labels "other
women." Arguing for a more multidimensional approach to why women get caught
up in crime, she proposes three other routes — in addition to the leading scenario
of the street woman — that lead women to felony court: 1) abuse or neglect suffered as a child, an "out of control" or violent nature; 2) being (or having been) in
a relationship with a violent man; and 3) being around boyfriends, mates or family

members who use or sell drugs, or wanting more money for a more economically secure and conventional life (Daly 1998: 148).

Overall, these efforts to draw out the connections between women's victimization experiences and their lawbreaking activities had the benefit of locating law violations by women in a broader social context characterized by inequalities of class, race and gender.

INTERSECTIONALITY

While gender was the starting point for analyzing criminalized women's lives, it soon became apparent to feminist criminologists that they needed to somehow capture the multiple, fluid and complex nature of women's identities and their social relations. Much of the impetus for this recognition came from the critiques offered by women of colour and Indigenous women of the tendency for white feminists to theorize "Woman" as a unitary and homogeneous group. As Marcia Rice (1989: 57) noted, while feminist criminologists had succeeded in challenging stereotypical representations of female offenders, Black women and women from developing countries were "noticeably absent in this discourse," and when attempts were made to incorporate Black women's experiences into feminist writings, there were few attempts "to develop perspectives which take into account race, gender and class simultaneously." As Mohawk scholar Patricia Monture-Angus (1995: 177–78) tells us, "It is very difficult for me to separate what happens to me because of my gender and what happens to me because of my race and culture. My world is not experienced in a linear and compartmentalized way. I experience the world simultaneously as Mohawk and as woman … To artificially separate my gender from my race and culture forces me to deny the way I experience the world."

In response to this critique, feminist criminologists embraced "intersectionality," a concept first highlighted by Kimberlé Crenshaw (1989) to theorize the multiple and complex social relations and the diversity of subject positions involved. Crenshaw argues that the experience of oppression is not singular or fixed but derives from the relationship between interlocking systems of power. With regard to the oppression of Black women, Crenshaw explains, "Because the intersectional experience is greater than the sum of racism and sexism, any analysis that does not take intersectionality into account cannot sufficiently address the particular manner in which Black women are subordinated" (1989: 140). Adopting the notion of intersectionality, therefore, means that rather than viewing class, race and gender as additives (that is, race + class + gender), we need to think about these concepts — and the relations and identities they represent — as simultaneous forces (that is, race x class x gender) (Brewer 1997).

In contrast to the women's liberation thesis, which argued that women's

involvement in crime was a consequence of their "emancipation," feminist criminologists adopted an intersectionality approach to connect women's involvement
in crime to poverty. In recent decades, poverty has increasingly taken on a "female
face" — especially in terms of the number of single-parent families headed by
women (Gavigan 1999; Little 2003; Chunn and Gavigan here). As more and more
women are confronted with the task of making ends meet under dire circumstances,
the link between poverty and women's lawbreaking has become more obvious.
But so too has the move by the state to criminalize those who must rely on social
assistance to get by. Using an intersectionality approach, Kiran Mirchandani and
Wendy Chan (2007) document the move in British Columbia and Ontario to
criminalize welfare recipients through the pursuit of "fraudulent" claimants. In
the process, they argue that this "criminalization of poverty" is also racialized and
gendered in that women of colour have borne the brunt of this attack.

A focus on the intersections of gender, race and class also helped to explain some
forms of prostitution or sex trade work (Brock 1998; Phoenix 1999). According to
Holly Johnson and Karen Rodgers (1993: 101), women's involvement in prostitution is a reflection of their subordinate social and economic position in society:

> Prostitution thrives in a society which values women more for their
> sexuality than for their skilled labour, and which puts women in a class of
> commodity to be bought and sold. Research has shown one of the major
> causes of prostitution to be the economic plight of women, particularly
> young, poorly educated women who have limited *legitimate* employment
> records.

Maya Seshia's (2005) research on street sexual exploitation in Winnipeg revealed
that poverty and homelessness, colonialism and the legacy of residential schools,
and gender discrimination and generational sexual exploitation all combined to
lead cisgender and transgender women to become involved in the sex trade.

In learning more about the lives of women and the "miles of problems" (Comack
1996: 134) that brought them into conflict with the law — problems with drugs
and alcohol use, histories of violence and abuse, lack of education and job skills,
and struggles to provide and care for their children — feminist criminologists
took pains to distance their work from formulations that located the source of
women's problems in individual pathologies or personality disturbances. Instead,
the intersecting structural inequalities in society — of gender, race and class — that
contour and constrain the lives of women provided the backdrop for understanding women's involvement in crime. As British criminologist Pat Carlen (1988: 14)
noted, "Women set about making their lives within conditions that have certainly
not been of their own choosing."

BLURRED BOUNDARIES:
CHALLENGING THE VICTIM/OFFENDER DUALISM

Efforts to draw connections between law violations and women's histories of abuse led to a blurring of the boundaries between "offender" and "victim" and raised questions about the legal logic of individual culpability and law's strict adherence to the victim/offender dualism in the processing of cases (for not only women, but also poor, racialized men). Blurring the boundaries between offender and victim also had a decided influence on advocacy work conducted on behalf of imprisoned women. For instance, *Creating Choices*, the 1990 report of the Canadian Task Force on Federally Sentenced Women, proposed a new prison regime for women that would incorporate feminist principles and attend to women's needs (see TFFSW 1990; Shaw 1993; Hannah-Moffat and Shaw 2000; Hayman 2006). The near-complete absence of counselling services and other resources designed to assist women in overcoming victimization experiences (see Kendall 1993) figured prominently in the Task Force's recommendations.

As Laureen Snider (2003: 364, and 2014: ch 10) notes, feminist criminologists at that time succeeded in reconstituting the female prisoner as the "woman in trouble." Less violent and less dangerous than her male counterpart, she needed help, not punishment. When women did engage in violence, it was understood as a self-defensive reaction typically committed in a domestic context (Browne 1987; Jones 1994; Dobash and Dobash 1992; Johnson and Rodgers 1993). Heidensohn (1994) considers this feminist work to be a positive contribution. In comparing her research in the 1960s and 1990s, she argues that the later female prisoners were better equipped to share their standpoints. In the past, not only did women "not easily find voices, there were only limited discourses in which they could express themselves and few places where such expressions could be made" (Heidensohn 1994: 31). According to Heidensohn, feminist research provided these women "with a particular language, a way of expressing themselves" (1994: 32).

Nevertheless, while the concept of blurred boundaries and the construct of the woman in trouble were important feminist contributions to criminology, they were to later have particular ramifications for the ability of feminist criminologists to counter competing knowledge claims — ones founded on representations of women not as victims but as violent and dangerous.

POSTMODERN FEMINISM:
CRIMINALIZED WOMEN

In addition to feminist empiricism and standpoint feminism, a third position has informed the work of feminist criminologists over the last decade or so. "Postmodern feminism" emerged largely as a critique of the other two positions. In particular, postmodern feminists reject the claims to "truth" proposed by scientific objectivity. "Reality," they say, is not self-evident, something that can simply be revealed through the application of the scientific method. While the postmodern critique of empiricism does not negate the possibility of doing empirical research — that is, of engaging with women, interviewing them, documenting their oral histories (Smart 1990: 78–79) — postmodernists are skeptical of attempts to challenge male-centred approaches by counterposing them with a more accurate or correct version of women's lives. Given the differences within female perspectives and identities, they question whether such diversity can be formulated or expressed in a single account or standpoint of women.

Feminist empiricism and standpoint feminism are still very much firmly grounded on a modernist terrain. Postmodern feminism, however, "starts in a different place and proceeds in other directions" (Smart 1995: 45). While modernist approaches are characterized by the search for truth, the certainty of progress, and the effort to frame grand narratives about the social world, postmodernism draws attention to the importance of "discourse" — "historically specific systems of meaning which form the identities of subjects and objects" (Howarth 2000: 9). Discourses are contingent and historical constructions. As David Howarth describes it, their construction involves "the exercise of power and a consequent structuring of the relations between different social agents" (2000: 9). Through the method of deconstruction — which involves taking apart discourses to show how they achieve their effects — postmodernists endeavour to reveal how certain discourses (and their corresponding discursive practices or ways of acting) come to dominate in society at particular points in history.

Adopting a postmodern epistemology has led feminist criminologists to interrogate the language used to understand women's involvement in crime. Carol Smart (1989, 1995), Danielle Laberge (1991) and Karlene Faith (1993), among others, point out that crime categories (such as "crimes against the person," "crimes against property" or "public order offences") are legal constructions that represent one way of ordering or making sense of social life. In these terms, the offences for which women are deemed to be criminal are the end result of a lengthy process of detection, apprehension, accusation, judgment and conviction; they constitute the official version of women's actions and behaviours. As well, crime categories are premised on a dualism between the criminal and the law-abiding, which reinforces the view of women involved in crime as Other and thereby misses their similarities with non-criminal women. In this respect, women who come into conflict with the law are in very many ways no different from the rest of us. They are mothers, daughters, sisters, girlfriends and wives, and they share many of the experiences of women collectively in society. Given that crime is the outcome of interactions between individuals and the criminal justice system, Laberge (1991) proposed that we think not in terms of criminal women but of criminalized women.

Throughout the 1990s, in addition to the increasing influence of a postmodern epistemology, feminist criminologists also began to draw heavily on the ideas of the French poststructuralist theorist Michel Foucault. Much of Foucault's (1977, 1979) writing was concerned with the relation between power and knowledge. Rejecting the notion that power was a "thing" or commodity that can be owned, Foucault concentrated on the mechanisms of power that came with the development of what he called the "disciplinary society," characterized by the growth of new knowledges or discourses (such as criminology, psychiatry and psychology) that led to new modes of surveillance of the population. For Foucault, knowledge is not objective but political; the production of knowledge has to do with power. A reciprocal relation exists between the two: power is productive of knowledge, and knowledge is productive of power. In his later work, Foucault (1978) replaced his notion of power/knowledge with the concept of "governmentality" to address the specific "mentality" of governance — the links between forms of power and domination and the ways in which individuals conduct themselves.

Australian criminologist Kerry Carrington (1993) employed Foucault's notion of power/knowledge to explore how certain girls come to be officially defined as delinquents. Critical of feminist work depicting male power over women as direct, monolithic, coercive and repressive, Carrington emphasized the fragmented, fluid and dispersed nature of disciplinary power. In a similar fashion, British criminologist Anne Worrall (1990) adopted a Foucauldian approach to explore the conditions under which legal agents (judicial, welfare and medical) claim to possess knowledge about the "offending woman" and the processes whereby such claims are translated into practices that classify, define and so domesticate her behaviour. Taking a critical view of feminist studies of women's punishment because of their failure (among other things) to take gender seriously as an explanatory variable, Adrian Howe (1994) argued for the need to consider the gendered characteristics — for both women and men — of disciplinary procedures in advancing the project of a postmodern penal politics.

Feminist postmodernism has had a decided impact on the trajectory of feminist criminology. Not interested so much in the task of explaining *why* women come into conflict with the law, those who work in this area raise important *how* questions, such as how women and girls are constituted or defined by professional discourses, and how particular techniques of governance (in a number of different sites) work to contain, control or exclude those who are marginalized in society. The postmodern attention to discourse has also opened the way to a questioning of the kinds of language used by criminologists and criminal justice officials. Under the tutelage of postmodernists, terms such as offenders, inmates, clients and correctional institutions — although still widely disseminated — are no longer uncontested.

Nevertheless, at the same time as feminist criminologists were being influenced by the epistemological and theoretical shifts occurring within academia during the 1990s, shifts in the socio-political context and a series of notable events relating to the issue of women and crime were having a significant impact on the work of feminist criminologists. More specifically, as the century drew to a close, neo-liberal and neo-conservative political rationalities had begun to take hold and were readily put to work in the construction of women and girls as violent, dangerous — and downright "nasty."

THE SHIFTING SOCIO-POLITICAL CONTEXT: NEO-LIBERALISM AND NEO-CONSERVATISM

In the initial phases, the efforts of the women's movement to address women's inequality in society were fed by a sense of optimism. Given the expressed commitment by the Canadian state to the ideals of social citizenship (what came to be called the Keynesian welfare state) — that all citizens had a right to a basic standard of living, with the state accepting responsibility for the provision of social welfare for its citizenry — the prospects of realizing substantive change on issues like violence against women and women's treatment by the criminal justice system seemed bright. This change was made all the more possible with the entrenchment of the *Canadian Charter of Rights and Freedoms* in 1982, and especially the invoking of section 15 (the equality section) in 1985, which prohibited discrimination on the basis of sex. In a climate that appeared to be favourable to hearing women's issues, feminists and women's advocates organized and lobbied throughout the 1980s to bring about a number of changes (including reforms to rape legislation and the provision of resources for women in abusive relationships) and launched human rights and Charter challenges to address the unfair treatment of imprisoned women. With regard to women in prison, many observers took the government's acceptance of the *Creating Choices* report in 1990 as a sign that a sea change was underway, that substantive reform was possible.

Yet, the 1980s also saw a distinct shift in the socio-political terrain. Under the sway of globalization, the state's expressed commitment to social welfare was being eroded. In its place, neo-liberalism became the new wisdom of governing. "Neo-liberalism" is a political rationality founded on the values of individualism, freedom of choice, market dominance and minimal state involvement in the economy. Under neo-liberalism, the ideals of social citizenship are replaced by the market-based, self-reliance, and privatizing ideals of the new order. As political scientist Janine Brodie (1995: 57) explains it:

> The rights and securities guaranteed to all citizens of the Keynesian welfare state are no longer rights, universal, or secure. The new ideal of the common good rests on market-oriented values such as self-reliance, efficiency, and competition. The new good citizen is one that recognizes the limits and liabilities of state provision and embraces her or his obligation to work longer and harder in order to become more self-reliant.

In this era of restructuring, government talk of the need for deficit reduction translated into cutbacks to social programs (McQuaig 1993), and gains that the women's movement had realized in the previous decade were now under serious attack (Brodie 1995; Bashevkin 1998; Rebick 2005).

In the criminal justice arena, these economic and political developments ushered in an extraordinary expansion in the scope and scale of penalization. Rising crime rates and a growing economic recession in the 1980s gave way to a crime-control strategy that rejected rehabilitation and correction as the goals of the criminal justice system and replaced them with a concern for "risk management": the policing and minimization of risk that offenders pose to the wider community. Under this neo-liberal responsibilization model of crime control (Hannah-Moffat 2002), criminals are to be made responsible for the choices they make: "Rather than clients in need of support, they are seen as risks that must be managed" (Garland 2001: 175).

But neo-liberalism was not the only ideology to inform criminal justice practices. Subjecting the economy to market forces and cutting back on social welfare meant that increasing numbers of people were left to fend for themselves, without the benefit of a social safety net. As well, the precariousness of middle-income families engendered a social anxiety that easily translated into fear of crime — especially of those groups and individuals left less fortunate by virtue of the economic transformations. Calls for more law and order became louder. In tandem with neo-liberalism, therefore, a "neo-conservative rationality," premised on a concern for tradition, order, hierarchy and authority, fostered crime-control policies aimed at "getting tough" on crime. Zero-tolerance for domestic violence, "supermax" prisons, parole-release restrictions, community notification laws and boot camps for young offenders increasingly became the order of the day (Comack and Balfour 2004: 42–43).

This broader neo-liberal and neo-conservative socio-political context proved to be significant in framing how a number of events that occurred in the 1990s came to be understood. These events — and the ways in which they were being framed in the public discourse — were instrumental in assertions about women and girls that had much in common with constructions that had prevailed in earlier times.

VIOLENT WOMEN AND NASTY GIRLS

One decisive event was the Karla Homolka case. In July 1993, Karla Homolka was sentenced to twelve years in prison for her part in the deaths of two teenaged girls, Kristen French and Leslie Mahaffy. Homolka's sentence was part of a plea bargain reached with the Crown in exchange for her testimony against her husband, Paul Bernardo. The Crown had entered into this plea bargain prior to the discovery of six homemade videotapes that documented the sexual abuse and torture of the pair's victims — including Homolka's younger sister, Tammy. Bernardo was subsequently convicted of first-degree murder, kidnapping, aggravated sexual assault, forcible confinement and offering an indignity to a dead body. He was sentenced to life imprisonment in September 1995 (McGillivray 1998: 257).

During Bernardo's trial the real challenge came in trying to explain the role of Homolka, the prosecution's key witness. As Helen Boritch (1997: 2) notes, "Among the various professionals who commented on the case, there was a general agreement that, as far as serial murderers go, there was little that was unusual or mysterious about Bernardo. We have grown used to hearing about male serial murderers." Homolka, however, was the central enigma of the drama that unfolded, transforming the trial into an international, high-profile media event.

The legal documents and media accounts of the case offered two primary readings of Homolka. The first reading constructed her as a battered wife, one of Bernardo's many victims (he had also been exposed as "the Scarborough rapist"). A girlish 17-year-old when she first met the 23-year-old Bernardo, Homolka had entered into a relationship that progressed to a fairy-tale wedding (complete with horse-drawn carriage) and ended with a severe battering (complete with darkened and bruised raccoon eyes). According to this first reading, Homolka was under the control of her husband, having no agency of her own. Like other women who find themselves in abusive relationships, she was cast as a victim and diagnosed as suffering from the Battered Woman Syndrome, a psychological condition of "learned helplessness" that ostensibly prevents abused women from leaving the relationship (see Walker 1979, 1987). The representation of Homolka as a battered wife and "compliant victim" of her sexually sadistic husband (Hazelwood, Warren, and Dietz 1993) was meant to bolster her credibility as a prosecution witness and validate her plea bargain.

This first reading was met with strong resistance in the media and public discourse, leading to the second reading. Journalist Patricia Pearson (1995), for one, vigorously countered the picture of "Homolka as victim" and instead demonized her as a "competitive narcissist" willing to offer up innocent victims (including her own sister) to appease the sexual desires of her sociopathic husband. In a similar fashion, other writers offered diagnoses such as "malignant narcissism": "This personality cannot tolerate humiliation. It is capable of destroying others in the service of meeting its ego needs" (Skrapec, cited in Wood 2001: 60).

Despite their divergent viewpoints, both of these readings relied on the discourse of the "psy-professions" (psychology, psychotherapy and psychiatry) to make sense of Homolka. Feminist criminologists offered competing knowledge claims, for instance, by pointing out that women are seldom charged with the offence of murder and, when they do kill, women are most likely to kill their male partners — or that while Homolka's middle-class background and lifestyle set her apart from the vast majority of women charged with criminal offences, her efforts to conform to the standard feminine script (dyed blond hair, fairy-tale wedding) put her in company with a host of other women. But these claims were seldom heard. Instead, the cry that "Women are violent, too!" grew louder, even to the point of arguing that women's violence was quantitatively and qualitatively equal to that of men's.

In a widely publicized book, *When She Was Bad: Violent Women and the Myth of Innocence*, Pearson (1997; see also Dutton 1994; Laframboise 1996) argued not only that "women are violent, too," but also that their violence can be just as nasty as men's. Following on the footsteps of the 1950s criminologist Otto Pollak, Pearson (1997: 20–21) suggested that women's violence was more masked and underhanded than men's: women kill their babies, arrange for their husbands' murders, beat up on their lovers, and commit serial murders in hospitals and boarding houses. Nevertheless, argued Pearson (1997: 61), when their crimes are discovered, women are more likely to receive lenient treatment from a chivalrous criminal justice system. In a fashion that hearkened back to other early criminologists, Pearson (1997: 210) also stated: "Female prisoners are not peace activists or nuns who were kidnapped off the street and stuck in jail. They are miscreants, intemperate, willful and rough."

Pearson drew support for her position from studies that utilize the Conflict Tactics Scale (CTS) to measure abuse in intimate relationships. Most criminologists who use this scale have found equivalent rates of violence by women and men (Straus 1979; Straus and Gelles 1986; Straus, Gelles, and Steinmetz 1980; Steinmetz 1981; Brinkerhoff and Lupri 1988; Kennedy and Dutton 1989). Despite the scale's popularity, however, it has been subject to extensive critiques (DeKeseredy and MacLean 1998; DeKeseredy and Hinch 1991; Dobash et al. 1992; Johnson 1996). Nevertheless, Pearson argued that such critiques amounted to unwarranted attacks by feminists and their supporters, who were invested in a gender dichotomy of men as evil/women as good. In this regard, unlike earlier conservative-minded criminologists, Pearson asserted that women were no different than men. While feminists were intent on gendering violence by drawing its connections to patriarchy, Pearson (1997: 232) was adamant that violence be de-gendered: violence was simply a "human, rather than gendered, phenomena."

Framing the issue in neo-liberal terms, violence was a conscious choice, a means of solving problems or releasing frustration by a "responsible actor imposing her will upon the world" (Pearson 1997: 23).

While the Homolka case generated extensive media attention on the issue of women's violence, the spectre of the "nasty girl" was added into the mix with the killing of 14-year-old Reena Virk by a group of mostly teenaged girls in November 1997. Early on, in 1998, six girls were convicted of assault for their part in Virk's death. In 1999, Warren Glowaski was convicted of second-degree murder. In April 2005, after three trials, Kelly Ellard was convicted of second-degree murder.

According to the court documents, Virk was confronted by a group of girls under a bridge in Victoria, B.C., and accused of stealing one of their boyfriends. When she tried to leave she was punched and kicked, and one of the girls stubbed out a cigarette on her forehead. Glowaski testified at his trial that he and Ellard had followed Virk across the bridge and confronted her a second time. The pair kicked and stomped her until she was unconscious and then dragged her body to the water's edge, where she subsequently drowned. While Ellard admitted to being an active participant in the initial attack on Virk, she denied any involvement in the second attack. Asked in court whether the thought of seeing Reena left crumpled in the mud made her upset, Ellard replied, "*Obviously — I am not a monster*" (Armstrong 2004: A7).

Ellard's statement notwithstanding, events like the beating and murder of Reena Virk generated a series of media exposés on the "problem" of girl violence. As one CBC documentary, *Nasty Girls* (airing on March 5, 1997), put it: "In the late 1990s almost everything your mother taught you about polite society has disappeared from popular culture, and nowhere is this more apparent than in what is happening to our teenage girls. Welcome to the age of the nasty girls!" (cited in Barron 2000: 81). Girls, so we were told, were not "sugar and spice" after all — but "often violent and ruthless monsters" (McGovern 1998: 24).

These depictions of women and girls as violent, dangerous and downright nasty were also playing out in relation to what was then the only federal prison for women in Canada — the P4W.

LOMBROSO REVISITED?
FRAMING THE P4W INCIDENT

In February 1995, CBC-TV's *Fifth Estate* aired a video of an all-male Institutional Emergency Response Team (IERT) entering the solitary confinement unit at the Prison for Women (P4W) in Kingston, Ontario, and proceeding to extract women from their cells, one by one. The video showed the women's clothing being removed (in some cases the men forcibly cut it off) and the women being shackled and taken to the shower room, where they were subjected to body cavity searches. The program reported that after the segregation cells were completely emptied (including beds and mattresses), the women were placed back in the cells with only security blankets for clothing.

Some of the women were kept in segregation for up to eight months afterward. They were given no hygiene products, no daily exercise, no writing materials and no contact with family. Their blankets were not cleaned for at least a month. As part of the program, reporter Ann Rauhala also interviewed several of the women, who recounted their feelings of violation and degradation and drew similarities to their past experiences of being raped and sexually victimized.

When the report of Justice Louise Arbour (1996) into the events of April 1994 was released two years later, the CBC's news program *The National* re-televised segments of the program, including the IERT video. Emails posted on *The National's* discussion site in response to the segments revealed pieces of the public discourse that prevailed around women prisoners:

> While I can see how some of the pictures shown could be disturbing to some viewers, I am more disturbed at your handling of the story … These women were not ordinary citizens … They are in a correctional facility because they are CONVICTED FELONS, not Sunday School Teachers.
>
> Myself, I would see nothing wrong with a guard beating these inmates every once in a while! After all they lost their rights when they committed their crimes in the first place.
>
> Don't give me the bleeding heart crap. This is what has screwed up society. These women created their own situation — let them deal with the fallout.
>
> The women involved in this incident were the creators of their own misfortune — both in the short term and the long term … In recent years, it seems that the courts and government have become too lenient with the likes of these women, and men for that matter. The special interest groups and the "politically correct" that are constantly fighting for the rights of prisoners only undermine the rights of law-abiding citizens.

Clearly, the neo-conservative calls to "get tough on crime" — especially in relation to women — were finding supporters in the public at large. Much like the early criminological constructions of women involved in crime, these CBC viewers rejected the depiction of the women as victims and instead saw them as Other, roundly deserving of the brutal treatment they received.

Such law and order populism was no doubt instrumental in bolstering a neo-liberal realignment by the Correctional Service of Canada when it came to implementing the *Creating Choices* recommendations (TFFSW 1990). *Creating Choices* had been silent around the issue of women's violence. According to Shaw (2000: 62), "Overall, the report portrayed women as victims of violence and abuse, more likely to injure themselves than others as a result of those experiences." The April 1994 event, however, was held out as evidence to the contrary. The CSC maintained that calling the male IERT to the women's prison had become necessary to contain "unruly women" after a fight had broken out between six of the prisoners and their guards. In 1996, in a move that marked an about-turn from the Task Force's women-centred approach and the attendant focus on addressing women's needs, CSC adopted a new scheme for managing women prisoners, the Offender Intake Assessment Scheme, designed for male prisoners. Now, women's needs — including the need to recover from experiences of victimization — were to be redefined (in neo-liberal terms) as risk factors in predicting a woman's likelihood of reoffending. That same year the CSC announced that all women classified as maximum security would not be allowed at the new regional centres (including the Aboriginal healing lodge) that had been constructed on the basis of the *Creating Choices* recommendations. Instead, the women were to be housed in maximum-security facilities located inside men's prisons. As well, CSC implemented a new mental health policy for women thought to be experiencing psychological and behavioural problems. In contrast to its initial endorsement of the *Creating Choices* report, therefore, the government was clearly moving in a different direction.

FEMINIST CRIMINOLOGISTS RESPOND TO THE BACKLASH

The apparent ease with which the neo-conservative and neo-liberal readings of events like the Homolka case, the Virk killing and the P4W incident took hold in the public discourse was emblematic of the dramatic shifts in the socio-political context that were occurring in the 1990s. For the most part, these readings can be interpreted as part of a powerful backlash against feminist knowledge claims, especially the efforts by feminist criminologists to blur the boundaries between offender and victim. In what Snider (2004: 240) refers to as the "smaller meaner gaze of neo-liberalism," the sightlines were closely fixed. "'Victims' were those who suffered from crime, not those who committed it — and the higher their social class, the more traditional their sexual habits and lifestyles, and the lighter their color, the more legitimate their victim status became" (Snider 2004: 240). Feminist criminologists would respond to this backlash on a number of fronts.

Committed to the view of criminalized women as victims in need of help rather than punishment, feminist criminologists were initially caught off guard by the Homolka case. To be sure, the woman in trouble envisioned by feminist criminologists was not a privileged young woman who engaged in sadistic sex crimes. But repeating the refrain "Homolka is an anomaly, Homolka is an anomaly" did little to prevent her from becoming the public icon for women caught up in the criminal justice system — women who are likely to be racialized, poor and convicted of property crimes rather than of violent sex offences (see Comack 2014).

With Pearson's assertions about women and violence continuing to hold sway in the popular press, feminist criminologists countered by offering up pointed critiques of her work. In her review of *When She Was Bad*, for instance, Meda Chesney-Lind (1999) took Pearson to task for her routine conflation of aggression and violence. "This is either very sloppy or very smart, since anyone familiar with the literature on aggression ... knows that when one includes verbal and indirect forms of aggression (like gossip), the gender difference largely disappears" (Chesney-Lind 1999: 114). Similar to those who claim merit in the women's liberation thesis, Pearson also based her argument on percentage increases in women's arrests for violence, "without any mention of the relatively small and stable proportion of violent crime accounted for by women or the fact that small base numbers make huge increases easy to achieve" (Chesney-Lind 1999: 115). Pearson's misuse of research findings, which Chesney-Lind saw as rampant throughout the book, included citing a study that found women's prison infractions to be higher than men's to support her claim that women in prison are "miscreants, intemperate, willful and rough" (Pearson 1997: 210). What Pearson neglected to mention was that these women were being charged with extremely trivial forms of misconduct, such as having "excessive artwork" on the walls of their cells (that is, too many family photos on display). Chesney-Lind concluded her review by acknowledging that feminist criminologists must theorize women's aggression and women's violence, but that "we need a nuanced, sophisticated, and data driven treatment — and most importantly — one that begins by placing women's aggression and violence in its social context of patriarchy" (1999: 118).

Jennifer Kilty and Sylvie Frigon (2006) offer such a nuanced account in their analysis of the Homolka case. Reinterpreting the two readings of Homolka — battered wife versus competitive narcissist — as depictions of her as either "in danger" or "dangerous," they argue that these constructions are interrelated rather than mutually exclusive. While emphasizing that the abuse Homolka endured at the hands of Bernardo does not excuse her criminality, they maintain that it did constrain her choices. As such, she was *both* a "woman in danger" *and* a "dangerous woman." Kilty and Frigon (2006: 58) argue, therefore, "Rather than constructing these two concepts as dialectically opposed one must understand them as being interdependent, or more accurately, as along a continuum."

Other feminist criminologists intent on understanding the interconnections between women's experiences of violence and their own use of violence have adopted this shift away from dualistic (victim/offender) thinking and toward the use of a continuum metaphor. Introduced by Karlene Faith (1993) in her book *Unruly Women*, the "victimization-criminalization continuum" is used to signify the myriad of ways in which women's experiences of victimization — including not only violence but also social and economic marginalization — constrain or narrow their social supports and available options and leave them susceptible to criminalization. The continuum, therefore, draws on insights from intersectionality theory to showcase how systemic factors (relating to patriarchy, poverty and colonialism) contribute to women's vulnerability to victimization, thereby restricting their agency or capacity to make choices. Unlike the more linear imagery of the pathways approach, Elspeth Kaiser-Derrick (2012: 63) suggests that the continuum can be envisioned as a web, "with many incursions and redirections from external forces (broad, structural issues like poverty and discrimination, as well as events within women's lives often stemming from those structural issues such as relationship dissolution or the removal of children by the state)."

Gillian Balfour (2008) adopts the victimization-criminalization continuum to explore the relationship between the inordinate amounts of violence experienced by Aboriginal women and the increase in their coercive punishment by the criminal justice system. Balfour argues that — despite the introduction in 1996 of sentencing reforms to encourage alternatives to incarceration (specifically, the provision for conditional sentences to be served in the community and the addition of section 718.2[e] to the Criminal Code, which encourages judges to consider alternatives to imprisonment for Aboriginal people) — women's narratives of violence and social isolation have been excluded in the practice of Canadian sentencing law, leading to spiralling rates of imprisonment for Aboriginal women. Kaiser-Derrick (2012) also utilizes the victimization-criminalization continuum to inform her analysis of cases involving Aboriginal women in light of the *Gladue* (1999) and *Ipeelee* (2012) decisions of the Supreme Court of Canada relating to how judges are to undertake a sentencing analysis when Aboriginal defendants come before the court. Focusing on cases for which conditional sentences are or were previously an available sanction, Kaiser-Derrick found that judges translate discourses about victimization and criminalization into a judicial approach that frames sentences for Aboriginal women as "healing oriented"; in essence, Aboriginal women's victimization experiences are interpreted by the courts as precipitating a need for treatment in prison (see also Williams 2009).

Feminist criminologists also responded to the backlash against feminist knowledge claims by undertaking research to evaluate the claim that women are "men's equals" in violence. To explore qualitative differences in men's and women's violence, for example, Vanessa Chopyk, Linda Wood and I drew a random sample of 1,002 cases from police incident reports involving men and women charged with violent crime in the city of Winnipeg over a five-year period at the beginning of the 1990s. While studies that utilize the Conflict Tactics Scale have concluded that a sexual symmetry exists in intimate violence (men are as likely as women to be victims of abuse, and women are as likely as men to be perpetrators of both minor and serious acts of violence), we found a different picture in the police incident reports (Comack, Chopyk, and Wood 2000, 2002). First, the violence tactics used by men and women differed in their seriousness. Men were more likely to use their physical strength or force against their female partners, while women were more likely to resort to throwing objects (such as TV remote controls) during the course of a violent event. Second, female partners of men accused of violence used violence themselves in only 23 percent of the cases, while male partners of women accused of violence used violence in 65 percent of the cases. This suggests that the violence that occurs between intimate partners is not "mutual combat." Third, almost one-half (48 percent) of the women accused — as opposed to only 7 percent of the men accused — in partner events were injured during the course of the event. Finally, in incidents involving partners, it was the accused woman who called the police in 35 percent of the cases involving a female accused (compared with only 7 percent in those involving a male accused). Interpreting calls to the police as "help-seeking behaviour" on the part of someone in trouble suggests that in more than one-third of the cases involving a woman accused, she was the one who perceived the need for help. Nevertheless, the woman ended up being charged with a criminal offence.

These findings are supported by data from the General Social Survey conducted by Statistics Canada, which show the scope and severity of spousal violence to be more severe for women than for men. Female victims of spousal violence were more than twice as likely to be injured as were male victims (42 percent versus 18 percent). Women were almost seven times more likely to fear for their lives (33 percent versus 5 percent), and almost three times as likely to be the targets of more than ten violent episodes (20 percent versus 7 percent) (Mahony 2011: 10). In countering the arguments made by writers like Pearson, then, the feminist agenda placed the issue of women's violence and aggression in a prominent position (see also Renzetti 1998, 1999; Marleau 1999; Chan 2001; Mann 2003; Morrisey 2003; Comack and Balfour 2004).

In the wake of the moral panic generated by media reports of a violent crime wave by girls (Schissel 1997, 2001), feminists also set out to counter the claim that girls were becoming "gun-toting robbers" (Pate 1999: 42; see also Artz 1998; Barron 2000; Chesney-Lind 2001; Bell 2002; Burman, Batchelor, and Brown 2003; Alder and Worrall 2003). In her analysis of official statistics on youth crime, Heather Schramm (1998) warned that any arguments about a dramatic increase in the rate of girls' offending should be interpreted with caution. The theme here was similar to the critique of the women's liberation thesis: because only a small number of girls are charged with violent offences, changes in the rates of girls' violent crime inflate drastically when expressed as a percentage. Marge Reitsma-Street (1999) pointed out that the majority of the increase in the rate of girls' violent crime could be accounted for by an increase in the charges of common or level-one assault (for example, for pushing, slapping and threatening). Anthony Doob and Jane Sprott (1998: 185) concluded that the rising rate of girls (and youths in general) being charged with violent crimes did not indicate an increase in the nastiness of girls; rather, the change "relates more to the response of adult criminal justice officials to crime than it does to the behaviour of young offenders."

As well, feminist criminologists drew on postmodern insights to counter the legal and media representations of the Virk killing. Specifically, by framing the murder in terms of the "empty concept" of "girl violence" (Kadi, cited in Batacharya 2004: 77), dominant approaches rarely addressed the issues of "racism, sexism, pressures of assimilation, and the social construction of Reena Virk as an outcast," and "when they were addressed, it was always in the language of appearance" (Jiwani 2002: 441). In Yasmin Jiwani's view, the erasure of race/racism in judicial decision-making and in the media coverage of the case was "symbolic of the denial of racism as a systemic phenomenon in Canada" (2002: 42; see also Batacharya 2004; Jiwani 2006).

Feminist criminologists also engaged in extensive critiques of the use of male-centred risk scales for managing women prisoners (Stanko 1997; Hannah-Moffat and Shaw 2001; Chan and Rigakos 2002). They provided critical commentaries on the apparent transformation of the original feminist vision of *Creating Choices* to fit neo-liberal and neo-conservative correctional agendas (Hannah-Moffat and Shaw 2000), and they reflected on the lessons to be learned from efforts to refashion prison regimes (Hannah-Moffat 2002; Hayman 2006). Countering the tendency of the legal establishment and media to revert to individualized and pathologized renderings of women prisoners — an approach placing the spotlight on the personal failings of these women while keeping the political and economic factors that drive prison expansion in the shadows — some feminist criminologists began the work of connecting "the individual and personal with macroeconomic and geopolitical analyses" in the context of the global expansion of women's imprisonment (Sudbury 2005b: xvi).

THE POWER AND THE CHALLENGE

From invisibility and the Othering of women to the emergence of feminist criminology in the 1970s and the particular pathways that feminist criminologists have followed as they put women at the centre of their knowledge production: over the past fifty years we have slowly moved from Heidensohn's "lonely uncharted seas" to reach the point where it has become increasingly difficult to keep abreast of the research and writing on women and crime. In their own ways, the different epistemological positions of feminist empiricism, standpoint feminism, and postmodern feminism have enabled an incredible growth in knowledge about women and crime. Because of this work, we now know so much more about the lives of criminalized women — who they are, the social contexts in which they move, and the processes by which they are regulated and controlled — far more than we would have thought possible some five short decades ago. Still, feminist criminology has not developed in a vacuum. In the past fifty years feminist criminologists have drawn energy and insights from work in other arenas — particularly the violence against women movement — as well as responding to events and developments occurring within the ever-changing socio-political climate.

As Snider (2003, 2014) notes, it is one thing for feminists to produce particular discourses about women and crime, and it is quite another to have those discourses heard.

> Knowledge claims and expertise always work to the advantage of some and the detriment of others, strengthening some parties and interests while weakening others. Those with power to set institutional agendas, with superior economic, political, social and moral capital, are therefore able to reinforce and promote certain sets of knowledges while ignoring, ridiculing or attacking others. (Snider 2003: 355)

But the feminist engagement with criminology is by no means complete. As the chapters in this book demonstrate, it is very much a vibrant, continuing process. And in these neo-liberal times, meeting the challenge of containing — and especially countering — dominant understandings about women and crime is all the more necessary.

References

Adelberg, E., and C. Currie (eds.). 1987b. "In Their Own Words: Seven Women's Stories." In E. Adelberg and C. Currie (eds.), *Too Few to Count: Canadian Women in Conflict with the Law*. Vancouver: Press Gang.

____. 1987a. *Too Few to Count: Canadian Women in Conflict with the Law*. Vancouver: Press Gang.

____. 1993. *In Conflict with the Law: Women and the Canadian Justice System*. Vancouver: Press Gang.

Adler, F. 1975. *Sisters in Crime*. New York: McGraw-Hill.

Alder, C., and A. Worrall. 2003. *Girls' Violence: Myths and Realities*. Albany: State University of New York Press.

Amir, M. 1967. "Victim Precipitated Forcible Rape." *Journal of Criminal Law and Criminology*

58, 4.

____. 1971. *The Patterns of Forcible Rape*. Chicago: University of Chicago Press.

Arbour, The Honourable Justice Louise (Commissioner). 1996. *Commission of Inquiry into Certain Events at the Prison for Women in Kingston*. Ottawa: Solicitor General.

Armstrong, J. 2004. "'I Am Not a Monster,' Ellard Says." *Globe and Mail*, July 8: A7.

Arnold, R. 1995. "The Processes of Victimization and Criminalization of Black Women." In B.R. Price and N. Sokoloff (eds.), *The Criminal Justice System and Women*. New York: McGraw Hill.

Artz, S. 1998. *Sex, Power, and the Violent School Girl*. Toronto: Trifolium Books.

Australian Institute of Criminology. 2011. *Australian Crime: Facts & Figures: 2011*. <aic.gov. au/publications/current%20series/facts/1-20/2011/4_offender.html>.

Backhouse, C. 2002. "A Measure of Women's Credibility: The Doctrine of Corroboration in Sexual Assault Trials in Early Twentieth Century Canada and Australia." *York Occasional Working Papers in Law and Society*. Paper #1.

Balfour, G. 2008. "Falling Between the Cracks of Retributive and Restorative Justice: The Victimization and Punishment of Aboriginal Women." *Feminist Criminology* 3.

Barron, C. 2000. *Giving Youth a Voice: A Basis for Rethinking Adolescent Violence*. Halifax: Fernwood Publishing.

Bashevkin, S. 1998. *Women on the Defensive: Living Through Conservative Times*. Toronto: University of Toronto Press.

____. 2002. *Welfare Hot Buttons: Women, Work, and Social Policy Reform*. Toronto: University of Toronto Press.

Batacharya, S. 2004. "Racism, 'Girl Violence,' and the Murder of Reena Virk." In C. Alder and A. Worrall (eds.), *Girls' Violence: Myths and Realities*. Albany: State University of New York Press.

Becker, H. 1963. *The Outsiders*. New York: Free Press.

Bell, S. 2002. "Girls in Trouble." In B. Schissel and C. Brooks (eds.), *Marginality and Condemnation: An Introduction to Critical Criminology*. Halifax: Fernwood Publishing.

Bertrand, M-A. 1967. "The Myth of Sexual Equality Before the Law." Fifth Research Conference on Delinquency and Criminality. Montreal, Centre de Psychologies et de Pédagogie.

____. 1969. "Self-Image and Delinquency: A Contribution to the Study of Female Criminality." *Acta Criminologica* 2.

____. 1999. "Incarceration as a Gendering Strategy." *Canadian Journal of Law and Society* 14, 1.

Boritch, H. 1997. *Fallen Women: Female Crime and Criminal Justice in Canada*. Toronto: Nelson.

Brennan, S. 2011. "Canadian's Perceptions of Personal Safety and Crime, 2009." *Juristat* (December). <statcan.gc.ca/pub/85-002-x/2011001/article/11577-eng.pdf>.

____. 2012. "Police-Reported Crime Statistics in Canada, 2011." *Juristat* (July 24).

Brewer, Rose M. 1997. "Theorizing Race, Class, and Gender: The New Scholarship of Black Feminist Intellectuals and Black Women's Labour." In R. Hennessy and C. Ingraham (eds.), *Materialist Feminism*. London: Routledge.

Brinkerhoff, M., and E. Lupri. 1988. "Interspousal Violence." *Canadian Journal of Sociology* 13, 4.

Brock, D. 1998. *Making Work, Making Trouble: Prostitution as a Social Problem.* Toronto: University of Toronto Press.

Brodie, J. 1995. *Politics on the Margins: Restructuring and the Canadian Women's Movement.* Halifax: Fernwood Publishing.

Browne, A. 1987. *When Battered Women Kill.* New York: Free Press.

Brownmiller, S. 1975. *Against Our Will: Men, Women and Rape.* New York: Simon and Schuster.

Burman, M., S. Batchelor, and J. Brown. 2003. "Girls and the Meaning of Violence." In E. Stanko (ed.), *The Meanings of Violence.* London: Routledge.

Busby, K. 2014. "'Sex Was in the Air': Pernicious Myths and Other Problems with Sexual Violence Prosecutions." In E. Comack (ed.), *Locating Law: Race/Class/Gender/Sexuality Connections* (third edition). Halifax and Winnipeg: Fernwood Publishing.

Cain, M. 1990. "Towards Transgression: New Directions in Feminist Criminology." *International Journal of the Sociology of Law* 18.

Carlen, P. 1988. *Women, Crime and Poverty.* Milton Keynes: Open University Press.

Carrington, K. 1993. *Offending Girls: Sex, Youth and Justice.* Sydney: Allen and Unwin.

Chan, W. 2001. *Women, Murder and Justice.* London: Palgrave.

Chesney-Lind, M. 1978. "Chivalry Re-Examined." In L. Bowker (ed.), *Women, Crime and the Criminal Justice System.* Lexington, MA: Lexington Books.

____. 1999. "Review of 'When She Was Bad: Violent Women and the Myth of Innocence.'" *Women and Criminal Justice.*

____. 2001. "Are Girls Getting More Violent? Exploring Juvenile Robbery Trends." *Journal of Contemporary Criminal Justice* 17, 2.

____. 2004. "Feminism and Critical Criminology: Towards a Feminist Praxis." Division on Critical Criminology — American Society of Criminology. <critcrim.org/critpapers/chesney-lind1.htm>.

Chesney-Lind, M., and N. Rodriguez. 1983. "Women Under Lock and Key." *The Prison Journal* 63.

Chesney-Lind, M., and R. Shelden. 1998. *Girls, Delinquency and Juvenile Justice.* California: Wadsworth.

Comack, E. 1993. *Women Offenders' Experiences with Physical and Sexual Abuse: A Preliminary Report.* Winnipeg: Criminology Research Centre, University of Manitoba.

____. 1996. *Women in Trouble.* Halifax: Fernwood Publishing.

____. 2014. "Making Connections: Introduction to Part II." In G. Balfour and E. Comack (eds.), *Criminalizing Women: Gender and (In)Justice in Neo-liberal Times,* 2nd edition. Halifax and Winnipeg: Fernwood Publishing.

Comack, E., and G. Balfour. 2004. *The Power to Criminalize: Violence, Inequality and the Law.* Halifax: Fernwood Publishing.

Comack, E., V. Chopyk, and L. Wood. 2002. "Aren't Women Violent Too? The Gendered Nature of Violence." In B. Schissel and C. Brooks (eds.), *Marginality and Condemnation: An Introduction to Critical Criminology.* Halifax: Fernwood Publishing.

Cowie, J., V. Cowie, and E. Slater. 1968. *Delinquency in Girls.* London: Heinemann.

Crenshaw, K. 1989. "Demarginalizing the Intersection of Race and Sex: A Black Feminist Critique of Antidiscrimination Doctrine, Feminist Theory and Antiracist Politics." *The University of Chicago Legal Forum* 140.

Daly, K. 1987. "Discrimination in the Criminal Courts: Family, Gender, and the Problem of Equal Treatment." *Social Forces* 66, 1.

____. 1989. "Rethinking Judicial Paternalism: Gender, Work-Family Relations, and Sentencing." *Gender and Society* 3, 1.

____. 1992. "Women's Pathways to Felony Court: Feminist Theories of Lawbreaking and Problems of Representation." *Southern California Review of Law and Women's Studies* 2.

____. 1998. "Women's Pathways to Felony Court: Feminist Theories of Lawbreaking and Problems of Representation." In K. Daly and L. Maher (eds.), *Criminology at the Crossroads: Feminist Readings in Crime and Justice.* New York: Oxford.

Daly, K., and M. Chesney-Lind. 1988. "Feminism and Criminology." *Justice Quarterly* 5, 4.

DeHart, D. 2006. "Pathways to Prison: Impact of Victimization in the Lives of Incarcerated Women." *Violence Against Women* 14, 12.

DeKeseredy, W., and R. Hinch. 1991. *Woman Abuse: Sociological Perspectives.* Toronto: Thompson.

DeKeseredy, W., and B. MacLean. 1998. "'But Women Do It Too': The Contexts and Nature of Female-to-Male Violence in Canadian Heterosexual Dating Relationships." In K. Bonnycastle and G. Rigakos (eds.), *Unsettling Truths: Battered Women, Policy, Politics, and Contemporary Research in Canada.* Vancouver: Collective Press.

Dobash, R.E., and R. Dobash. 1979. *Violence Against Wives: A Case Against the Patriarchy.* New York: Free Press.

____. 1992. *Women, Violence and Social Change.* London: Routledge.

Dobash, R., R.E. Dobash, M. Wilson, and M. Daly. 1992. "The Myth of Sexual Symmetry in Marital Violence." *Social Problems* 39, 1 (February).

Doob, A., and J. Sprott. 1998. "Is the 'Quality' of Youth Violence Becoming More Serious?" *Canadian Journal of Criminology* 40, 2.

Dutton, D. 1994. "Patriarchy and Wife Assault: The Ecological Fallacy." *Violence and Victims* 9.

Edwards, S. 1985. "Gender Justice? Defending Defendants and Mitigating Sentence." In S. Edwards (ed.), *Gender, Sex and the Law.* London: Croom Helm.

Faith, K. 1993. *Unruly Women: The Politics of Confinement and Resistance.* Vancouver: Press Gang Publishers.

____. 1995. "Aboriginal Women's Healing Lodge: Challenge to Penal Correctionalism?" *Journal of Human Justice* 6, 2.

Faith, K., and D. Currie. 1993. *Seeking Shelter: A State of Battered Women.* Vancouver: Collective Press.

Foucault, M. 1977. *Discipline and Punish: The Birth of the Prison.* New York: Vintage.

____. 1978 [1991]. "Governmentality." In G. Burchell, C. Gordon, and P. Miller (eds.), *The Foucault Effect: Studies in Governmentality.* Chicago: University of Chicago Press.

____. 1979. *History of Sexuality: An Introduction* (Vol. 1). London: Penguin.

Garland, D. 2001. *The Culture of Control: Crime and Social Order in Contemporary Society.* Chicago: University of Chicago Press.

Gavigan, S.A.M. 1993. "Women's Crime: New Perspectives and Old Theories." In E. Adelberg and C. Currie (eds.), *In Conflict with the Law: Women and the Canadian Justice System.* Vancouver: Press Gang Publishers.

____. 1999. "Poverty Law, Theory and Practice: The Place of Class and Gender in Access to Justice." In E. Comack (ed.), *Locating Law: Race/Class/Gender Connections*. Halifax: Fernwood Publishing.

Gelsthorpe, L. and A. Morris. 1988. "Feminism and Criminology in Britain." *British Journal of Criminology* 23.

Gilfus, M. 1992. "From Victims to Survivors to Offenders: Women's Routes of Entry and Immersion into Street Crime." *Women and Criminal Justice* 4, 1.

Glueck, S., and E. Glueck. 1934. *Five Hundred Delinquent Women*. New York: Alfred A. Knopf.

Gunn, R., and C. Minch. 1988. *Sexual Assault: The Dilemma of Disclosure, The Question of Conviction*. Winnipeg: University of Manitoba Press.

Hagan, J., A.R. Gillis, and J. Simpson. 1985. "The Class Structure of Gender and Delinquency: Toward a Power-Control Theory of Common Delinquent Behavior." *American Journal of Sociology* 90.

Hagan, J., J. Simpson, and A.R. Gillis. 1979. "The Sexual Stratification of Social Control: A Gender-Based Perspective on Crime and Delinquency." *British Journal of Sociology* 30.

____. 1987. "Class in the Household: A Power-Control Theory of Gender and Delinquency." *American Journal of Sociology* 92, 4 (January).

Hannah-Moffat, K. 2002. "Creating Choices: Reflecting on Choices." In P. Carlen (ed.), *Women and Punishment: The Struggle for Justice*. Cullompton: Willan Publishing.

Hannah-Moffat, K., and M. Shaw (eds.). 2000. *An Ideal Prison? Critical Essays on Women's Imprisonment in Canada*. Halifax: Fernwood Publishing.

Hannah-Moffat, K., and M. Shaw. 2001. *Taking Risks: Incorporating Gender and Culture into the Assessment and Classification of Federally Sentenced Women in Canada*. Ottawa: Status of Women Canada.

Harding, S. 1990. "Feminism, Science, and the Anti-Enlightenment Critiques." In L. Nicholson (ed.), *Feminism/Postmodernism*. London: Routledge.

Hayman, S. 2006. *Imprisoning Our Sisters: The New Federal Women's Prisons in Canada*. Montreal and Kingston: McGill-Queen's University Press.

Hazelwood, R., J. Warren, and P. Dietz. 1993. "Compliant Victims of the Sexual Sadist." *Australian Family Physician* 22, 4 (April).

Heidensohn, F. 1968. "The Deviance of Women: A Critique and an Enquiry." *British Journal of Sociology* 19, 2.

____. 1985. *Women and Crime*. London: Macmillan.

____. 1994. "From Being to Knowing: Some Issues in the Study of Gender in Contemporary Society." *Women and Criminal Justice* 6, 1.

Heimer, K. 1995. "Gender, Race and Pathways to Delinquency." In J. Hagan and R. Peterson (eds.), *Crime and Inequality*. Stanford: Stanford University Press.

Hirschi, T. 1969. *Causes of Delinquency*. Berkeley: University of California Press.

Howarth, D. 2000. *Discourse*. Buckingham: Open University Press.

Howe, A. 1994. *Punish and Critique: Towards a Feminist Analysis of Penality*. London: Routledge.

Jiwani, Y. 2002. "Erasing Race: The Story of Reena Virk." In K. McKenna and J. Larkin (eds.), *Violence Against Women: New Canadian Perspectives*. Toronto: Inanna Publications.

____. 2006. *Discourses of Denial: Mediations of Race, Gender, and Violence*. Vancouver: UBC Press.

Johnson, H. 1996. *Dangerous Domains*. Toronto: Nelson.

Johnson, H., and K. Rodgers. 1993. "A Statistical Overview of Women and Crime in Canada." In E. Adelberg and C. Currie (eds.), *In Conflict with the Law: Women and the Canadian Justice System*. Vancouver: Press Gang Publishers.

Jones, A. 1994. *Next Time She'll Be Dead: Battering and How to Stop It*. Boston: Beacon Press.

Kaiser-Derrick, E. 2012. "Listening to What the Criminal Justice System Hears and the Stories it Tells: Judicial Sentencing Discourses about the Victimization and Criminalization of Aboriginal Women." Master of Laws thesis, University of British Columbia.

Kilty, J.M., and S. Frigon. 2006. "From a Woman in Danger to a Dangerous Woman, the Case of Karla Homolka: Chronicling the Shifts." *Women and Criminal Justice* 17, 4.

Kelly, L. 1988. *Surviving Sexual Violence*. Minneapolis: University of Minnesota Press.

Kendall, K. 1991. "The Politics of Premenstrual Syndrome: Implications for Feminist Justice." *Journal of Human Justice* 2, 2 (Spring).

____. 1992. "Dangerous Bodies." In D. Farrington and S. Walklate (eds.), *Offenders and Victims: Theory and Policy*. London: British Society of Criminology.

____. 1993. *Program Evaluation of Therapeutic Services at the Prison for Women*. Ottawa: Correctional Service Canada.

Kennedy, L., and D. Dutton. 1989. "The Incidence of Wife Assault in Alberta." *Canadian Journal of Behavioural Science* 21.

Kilty, J.M., and S. Frigon. 2006. "From a Woman in Danger to a Dangerous Woman, the Case of Karla Homolka: Chronicling the Shifts." *Women and Criminal Justice* 17, 4.

Klein, D. 1982. 1973. "The Etiology of Female Crime: A Review of the Literature." *Issues in Criminology* 8, 3.

Konopka, G. 1966. *The Adolescent Girl in Conflict*. Englewood Cliffs: Prentice Hall.

Kruttschnitt, C. 1980–81. "Social Status and Sentences of Female Offenders." *Law and Society Review* 15, 2.

____. 1982. "Women, Crime and Dependency." *Criminology* 19, 4.

Laberge, D. 1991. "Women's Criminality, Criminal Women, Criminalized Women? Questions in and for a Feminist Perspective." *Journal of Human Justice* 2, 2.

Laframboise, D. 1996. *The Princess at the Window*. Toronto: Penguin.

Leonard, E.D. 1982. *Women, Crime and Society: A Critique of Theoretical Criminology*. New York: Longman.

Little, M. 2003. "The Leaner, Meaner Welfare Machine: The Ontario Conservative Government's Ideological and Material Attack on Single Mothers." In D. Brock, (ed.), *Making Normal: Social Regulation in Canada*. Scarborough: Nelson Thompson Learning.

Lombroso, C., and E. Ferrero. 1885 [1985]. *The Female Offender*. New York: Appleton.

Lös, M. 1990. "Feminism and Rape Law Reform." In L. Gelsthorpe and A. Morris (eds.), *Feminist Perspectives in Criminology*. Milton Keynes: Open University Press.

Luckhaus, L. 1985. "A Plea for PMT in the Criminal Law." In S. Edwards (ed.), *Gender, Sex and the Law*. Kent: Croom Helm.

MacLeod, L. 1980. *Wife Battering in Canada: The Vicious Circle*. Ottawa: CACSW.

Mahony, T. 2011. *Women in Canada: A Gender-Based Statistical Report Women and the Criminal Justice System*. Ottawa: Statistics Canada. <statcan.gc.ca/pub/89-503-x/2010001/article/11416-eng.pdf>.

Mann, R. 2003. "Violence Against Women or Family Violence? The 'Problem' of Female Perpetration in Domestic Violence." In L. Samuelson and W. Antony (eds.), *Power and Resistance: Critical Thinking About Canadian Social Issues* (third edition). Halifax: Fernwood Publishing.

Marleau, J. 1999. "Demanding to Be Heard: Women's Use of Violence." *Humanity and Society* 23, 4.

Martin, D., and J. Mosher. 1995. "Unkept Promises: Experiences of Immigrant Women with the Neo-Criminalization of Wife Abuse." *Canadian Journal of Women and the Law* 8.

McGillivray, A. 1998. "'A Moral Vacuity in Her Which Is Difficult if Not Impossible to Explain': Law, Psychiatry and the Remaking of Karla Homolka." *International Journal of the Legal Profession* 5, 2/3.

McGovern, C. 1998. "Sugar and Spice and Cold as Ice: Teenage Girls Are Closing the Gender Gap in Violent Crime with Astonishing Speed." *Alberta Report* 25.

McQuaig, L. 1993. *The Wealthy Banker's Wife: The Assault on Equality in Canada*. Toronto: Penguin.

Merton, R. 1938. "Social Structure and Anomie." *American Sociological Review* 3 (October).

Miller, E. 1986. *Street Woman*. Philadelphia: Temple University Press.

Mirchandani, K., and W. Chan. 2007. *Criminalizing Race, Criminalizing Poverty*. Halifax: Fernwood Publishing.

Monture-Angus, P. 1995. *Thunder in My Soul: A Mohawk Woman Speaks*. Halifax: Fernwood Publishing.

Morris, A. 1987. *Women, Crime and Criminal Justice*. London: Blackwell.

Morrisey, B. 2003. *When Women Kill: Questions of Agency and Subjectivity*. London: Routledge.

Naffine, N. 1987. *Female Crime: The Construction of Women in Criminology*. Sydney: Allen and Unwin.

____. 1997. *Feminism and Criminology*. Sydney: Allen and Unwin.

Osborne, J. 1989. "Perspectives on Premenstrual Syndrome: Women, Law and Medicine." *Canadian Journal of Family Law* 8.

Pate, K. 1999. "Young Women and Violent Offences." *Canadian Women's Studies* 19.

Pearson, P. 1995. "Behind Every Successful Psychopath." *Saturday Night* 110 (October).

____. 1997. *When She Was Bad: Women's Violence and the Myth of Innocence*. Toronto: Random House.

Phoenix, J. 1999. *Making Sense of Prostitution*. London: Palgrave.

____. 2002. "Youth Prostitution Police Reform: New Discourse, Same Old Story." In P. Carlen (ed.), *Women and Punishment: The Struggle for Social Justice*. Portland: Willan Publishing.

Pizzey, E. 1974. *Scream Quietly or the Neighbours Will Hear You*. London: Penguin.

Pollak, O. 1950. *The Criminality of Women*. Philadelphia: University of Philadelphia Press.

Rafter, N.H., and E.M. Natalazia. 1981. "Marxist Feminism: Implications for Criminal Justice." *Crime and Delinquency* 27.

Rebick, J. 2005. *Ten Thousand Roses: The Making of a Feminist Revolution*. Toronto: Penguin.

Reitsma-Street, M. 1999. "Justice for Canadian Girls: A 1990s Update." *Canadian Journal of Criminology* 41, 3.

Renzetti, C. 1998. "Violence and Abuse in Lesbian Relationships: Theoretical and Empirical

Issues." In R. Bergen (ed.), *Issues in Intimate Violence.* Thousand Oaks: Sage.

____. 1999. "The Challenge to Feminism Posed by Women's Use of Violence in Intimate Relationships." In S. Lamb (ed.), *New Versions of Victims: Feminists Struggle with the Concept.* New York: New York University Press.

Rice, M. 1989. "Challenging Orthodoxies in Feminist Theory: A Black Feminist Critique." In L. Gelsthorpe and A. Morris (eds.), *Feminist Perspectives in Criminology.* Milton Keynes: Open University Press.

Richie, B. 1996. *Compelled to Crime: The Gender Entrapment of Battered Black Women.* New York: Routledge.

Schissel, B. 1997. *Blaming Children: Youth Crime, Moral Panics and the Politics of Hate.* Halifax: Fernwood Publishing.

____. 2001. "Youth Crime, Moral Panics and the News: The Conspiracy Against the Marginalized in Canada." In R. Smandych (ed.), *Youth Crime: History, Legislation, and Reform.* Toronto: Harcourt Canada.

Schramm, H. 1998. *Young Women Who Use Violence — Myths and Facts.* Calgary: Elizabeth Fry Society of Alberta.

Scutt, J. 1979. "The Myth of the 'Chivalry Factor' in Female Crime." *Australian Journal of Social Issues* 14, 1.

Seshia, Maya. 2005. *The Unheard Speak Out.* Winnipeg: Canadian Centre for Policy Alternatives–Manitoba.

Shaw, M. 2000. "Women, Violence, and Disorder in Prisons." In K. Hannah-Moffat and M. Shaw (eds.), *An Ideal Prison? Critical Essays on Women's Imprisonment in Canada.* Halifax: Fernwood Publishing.

Shaw, M., K. Rodgers, J. Blanchette, T. Hattem, L.S. Thomas, and L.Tamarack. 1991. *Survey of Federally Sentenced Women: Report of the Task Force on Federally Sentenced Women.* User Report 1991–4. Ottawa: Corrections Branch, Ministry of Solicitor General of Canada.

Simon, R. 1975. *Women and Crime.* Lexington: D.C. Heath.

Smart, C. 1976. *Women, Crime and Criminology: A Feminist Critique.* London: Routledge and Kegan Paul.

____. 1977. "Criminological Theory: Its Ideology and Implications Concerning Women." *British Journal of Sociology* 28, 1.

____. 1989. *Feminism and the Power of the Law: Essays in Feminism.* London: Routledge

____. 1990. "Feminist Approaches to Criminology or Postmodern Woman Meets Atavistic Man." In L. Gelsthorpe and A. Morris (eds.), *Feminist Perspectives in Criminology.* Milton Keynes: Open University Press.

____. 1995. *Law, Crime and Sexuality.* London: Sage.

Snider, L. 1985. "Legal Reform and Social Control: The Dangers of Abolishing Rape." *International Journal of the Sociology of Law* 13, 4.

____. 1991. "The Potential of the Criminal Justice System to Promote Feminist Concerns." In E. Comack and S. Brickey (eds.), *The Social Bias of Law: Critical Readings in the Sociology of Law* (second edition). Halifax: Fernwood Publishing.

____. 1994. "Feminism, Punishment and the Potential of Empowerment." *Canadian Journal of Law and Society* 9, 1.

____. 2003. "Constituting the Punishable Woman: Atavistic Man Incarcerates Postmodern Woman." *British Journal of Criminology* 43, 2.

____. 2004. "Female Punishment: From Patriarchy to Backlash?" In C. Sumner (ed.), *The Blackwell Companion to Criminology*. Oxford: Blackwell.

____. 2006. "Relocating Law: Making Corporate Crime Disappear." In E. Comack (ed.), *Locating Law: Race/Class/Gender/Sexuality Connections* (2nd edition). Halifax: Fernwood Publishing.

____. 2014. "Making Change in Neo-liberal Times." In G. Balfour and E. Comack (eds.), *Criminalizing Women: Gender and (In)Justice in Neo-liberal Times, 2nd edition*. Halifax and Winnipeg: Fernwood Publishing.

Snyder, H. 2012. *Arrest in the United States, 1990–2010*. Washington: Bureau of Justice Statistics. <bjs.gov/content/pub/pdf/aus9010.pdf>.

Stanko, E. 1985. *Intimate Intrusions: Women's Experience of Male Violence*. London: Routledge and Kegan Paul.

____. 1997. "Conceptualizing Women's Risk: Assessment as a Technology of the Soul." *Theoretical Criminology* 1, 4.

Statistics Canada. 1993. "The Violence Against Women Survey." *The Daily*, 18 November.

Steffensmeier, D., and J. Kramer. 1982. "Sex-Based Differences in the Sentencing of Adult Criminal Defendants." *Sociology and Social Research* 663.

Steinmetz, S. 1981. "A Cross-cultural Comparison of Marital Abuse." *Journal of Sociology and Social Welfare* 8.

Straus, M. 1979. "Measuring Intrafamily Conflict and Violence: The Conflict Tactics (CT) Scales." *Journal of Marriage and the Family* 41, 1.

Straus, M., and R. Gelles. 1986. "Societal Changes and Change in Family Violence from 1975 to 1985 as Revealed by Two National Surveys." *Journal of Marriage and the Family* 48.

Straus, M., R. Gelles, and S. Steinmetz. 1980. *Behind Closed Doors: Violence in the American Family*. New York: Doubleday.

Sudbury, J. (ed.). 2005a. *Global Lockdown: Race, Gender, and the Prison-Industrial Complex*. London: Routledge.

____. 2005b. "Introduction: Feminist Critiques, Transnational Landscapes, Abolitionist Visions." In J. Sudbury (ed.), *Global Lockdown: Race, Gender, and the Prison-Industrial Complex*. New York: Routledge.

Sutherland, E. 1949. *Principles of Criminology* (fourth edition). Philadelphia: J.B. Lippincott.

Taylor, I., P. Walton, and J. Young. 1973. *The New Criminology*. London: Routledge and Kegan Paul.

TFFSW (Task Force on Federally Sentenced Women). 1990. *Creating Choices: The Report of the Task Force on Federally Sentenced Women*. Ottawa: Correctional Service of Canada.

Thomas, W.I. 1923 [1967]. *The Unadjusted Girl*. New York: Harper and Row.

Walker, L. 1979. *The Battered Woman*. New York: Harper and Row.

____. 1987. *Terrifying Love: Why Battered Women Kill and How Society Responds*. New York: Harper Collins.

Weiss, J. 1976. "Liberation and Crime: The Invention of the New Female Criminal." *Crime and Social Justice* 6.

Williams, T. 2009. "Intersectionality Analysis in the Sentencing of Aboriginal Women in Canada: What Difference Does It Make?" In E. Grabham, D. Cooper, J. Krishnadas, and D. Herman (eds.), *Intersectionality and Beyond: Law, Power and the Politics of Location*. New York: Routledge-Cavendish.

Wood, T. 2001. "The Case Against Karla." *Elm Street Magazine*, April.

Worrall, A. 1990. *Offending Women: Female Lawbreakers and the Criminal Justice System.* New York: Rutledge and Keagan Paul.

____. 2002. "Rendering Women Punishable: The Making of a Penal Crisis." In P. Carlen (ed.), *Women and Punishment: The Struggle for Justice.* Cullompton: Willan Publishing.

Zingraff, M., and R. Thomson. 1984. "Differential Sentencing of Women and Men in the U.S.A." *International Journal of the Sociology of Law* 12.

Cases Cited

R. v. Gladue, [1999] 1 SCR 699

R. v. Ipeelee, [2012] SCC 13

Chapter 3

AGENCY AND RESISTANCE
Debates in Feminist Theory and Praxis

Ellen Faulkner and Gayle MacDonald

From: *Victim No More: Women's Resistance to Law, Culture and Power*, pp. 9–17 (slightly revised and reprinted with permission).

Feminism's third wave is built on both the politics of second-wave feminism and the backlash that responded to it within a postmodern, neo-liberal world, where culture rather than politics is taken to be the key area of resistance (Miller 2008: 28). Feminist activism began in North America as a collective movement. The "personal is political" became its rallying cry, its mantra for a revolution for how to think/act about and to understand the differences between the sexes. Many achievements came as a result of this foment: pay equity, daycares, sexual assault centres, and transition houses for battered women and their children. No longer could legislators, policymakers or pundits ignore the plight of women. No longer would jokes about women's roles be easily delivered in Parliament. Indeed, the Democratic race for leadership in the U.S. showed for the first time how a white woman or a Black man could actually become president of the United States, something some of us thought we would not live to see.

But what does all of this mean to the women's movement? Backlash in the press, such as resistance to Mary Koss' research on date rape on university campuses and to Take Back the Night marches and No-Means-No date rape campaigns (Stringer 2001; Roiphe 1993; Wolf 1993; Kamen 1993; Koss and Harvey 1991; Gilbert 1991,

1992, 1993; Koss and Oros1982; Koss 1988), spells out a feminism that, for the most part, is no longer the "in" social movement. It's considered passé (Gillespie 1994). Moreover, negative publicity has been used to bolster claims for financial cutbacks to feminist organizations. In 2006, the Conservative government "cut funding to the Status of Women Canada secretariat and to the Court Challenges program that funded citizens and groups fighting laws they believe violated the Charter of Rights and Freedoms" (Mallick 2006). Then the Tories "killed all funding for women's groups that do advocacy, lobbying, or research" (Mallick 2006). This signalled that a diversified political challenge is necessary to combat neo-liberal policies. Environmental movements (largely spearheaded by women) have become more compelling to youth as they look forward to a resource-ravaged planet and all of its incumbent difficulties. Books on disasters of all types environmental (Jacobs 2004; Rees 2004; Smith 2004; Aptekar1994) and capitalism gone amok (Klein 2007, 2001) comingle in people's consciousness with self-help books on everything from Tantric sex to Buddhist mediation.

We argue, however, that there are movements still afoot (Boyd 2004), collective, individual and cultural, and many of them involve women. We argue that collective action on class, race and gender has changed emphasis, reoriented into issues of identity politics (Mathen 2004; Spivak 2008, 1988; Spivak, Chakravorty and Harasym 1990), of cultural challenge and of legal resistance (MacKinnon 2008). This resistance is largely due to a reaction to the circumstances, labelling and experience of the female "victim."

In this anthology, we trouble the concept of victim. We do so to enable the reader to see the work of women in resistance. We hope to offer the beginnings of a framework of resistance, one that explores the moments *beyond* victimization, how women do not stay crushed and broken, but move on, build and grow. We note the types of resistance as we find them, in settings of collective or individual political organizing, legal reforms and cultural norms and labels that criminalize. We find these examples in arenas of political resistance, identity formation and as tools of survival.

ACTIVISM REVISITED

In the eighties feminists focused on anti-pornography, anti-prostitution, anti-censorship and pro-workers' rights, initiatives that presumed the workability of the "woman as victim" model. This model attempted to empower women by suggesting that the sexual assault victim, the sex trade worker, the woman victimized by pornographers or sweatshops and the woman sexualized in her trade union could be a survivor rather than a victim. This was a necessary political step and one we do not hesitate to support. Further, the movement has transitioned from a collective politic to individual resistance, and some individual resistance tactics have morphed back into a collective politic. We see this as a necessary political step in the next frontier of women's rights, the international stage. This transitioning was, in part, a direct response to issues imperative to the movement, identity politics arising from postcolonialist resistance, for example, and transnational feminisms both fusing and fracturing simultaneously. Rather than an aberration, or a seemingly erratic pattern, such political patterns are not only effective but highly "on the ground" responsive to issues that women face every day across the globe. Not unlike the resistance to global capitalism, the tendency to "umbrella" women's resistance (Lewis 2005) at the international level has fractured some movements, fused others. But the women's movement lives on, largely reactive to the label of "victim" and seeking changes on both individual and structural levels.

Early feminisms, for all their achievements, stayed in a victim framework. Women were rendered passive, yet again, not by patriarchal ideology, but by reductionist explanations of the place of women: battered, assaulted and harassed. But to *name* these issues, as critical as that is for the healing of women so victimized, is but part of the political battle. Woman-as-victim is not an emancipatory cry that encourages all women to join efforts in combating patriarchy. It is, at its core, highly analogous to the right-wing, conservative agendas that would keep women politically passive, smiling stewards of male futures, still adhering to "men's way" in the boardroom and the bedroom. It is not what our mothers and sisters intended at all.

The early movement was narrow. It had to be. A wide net, a grand focus, could not have achieved what our foremothers needed — whether that was the vote, shelter from harm, pasteurized milk, pay equity or extended maternity leave. This strategy had its victories but it also had its problems. For example, feminism as it used to be rarely included women of colour (Moraga and Anzaldúa 2003; Bhopal 2002; Allen 1992; Ware 1992; Omolade 1989; Spelman 1988; Giddings 1985; Lorde 1984; Avakian 1981; hooks 1981; Smith 1979; Hood 1978; Joseph and Lewis 1981) or fully explained differences of sexuality (Atkinson 1974; Myron and Bunch 1975; Rich 1980; Cornwell 1983). Some women were still marginalized, particularly so when it came to discussions of women and the law. Discussions of child custody in North America, for example, did not include what was happening in Europe, and discussions of violence, even on a structural level concerning sexual assault, could not explain fully the systematic rape that war has produced in the past few decades.

Alternatively, those who choose not to conceptualize women as victims argue that women's work in the sex trade industry, pornography and the underground economy is empowering for women. Turning victim language on its head, sex trade workers who fight for union rights suggest that archaic notions of consensus building and transformation are just that — archaic, so that the models of sex discrimination feminism represents often do not work for all women. True resistance, therefore, can be found through examining the *specificity* of women's conditions, the legal, social and cultural structures that disempower women, and the transformative power of negating the label of victim. Resistance then becomes a way of life, a survivor response or a political action. *Resistance is manifest either individually or collectively, at the local level or at the level of the state, as a first response or a last resort.*

What is unique in this collection is the rapport between this scholarship and resistance, relative to women's relationships to law, politics and culture (Chunn, Boyd, Lessard 2007; Boyd 2007; Boyd, Young, Brodsky and Day 2007; Boyd and Rhoades 2006). Through narrative, theory, fieldwork, case studies and/or legal policy, this anthology documents resistance in particular ways. Women in these chapters resist dominant practices in the social world in favour of more fluid, resistant and life-giving strategies to enable change in their own lives. By exposing language, experience and legal policy to this type of analysis, we can more fully understand the nature of the resistant experience for what it is, a subversion of normative practice.

In thinking about the ways in which women resist, we can turn to North American women's political awakenings, involvement with the battered women's movement, the sexual assault crisis centre movement and women's studies courses as examples. Participation in annual Take Back the Night marches, No-Means-No date rape campaigns and women's collectives entailed mobilizing, lobbying and fundraising, all of which contributed to social justice and social change for women. These actions for social change liberated many; yet, the promise of liberation had its contradictions. Research on racism in the women's movement, for example, has been resisted in women's studies programs (Moraga and Anzaldúa 2003; Bhopal 2002; Allen 1992; Ware 1992; Spelman 1988; Giddings 1985; Lorde 1984; Avakian 1981; hooks 1981; Smith 1979). But what of the resistance strategies employed by women cross-culturally? Are the strategies of resistance available to North American women viable alternatives to, say, women in Europe?

THEORY AND PRAXIS

The forms of resistance we observe in this anthology are wide-ranging. Activism is a highly visible form of resistance, and known to most. There are others. For example, legal responses to women's social problems are not necessarily recognized as resistance. Law reform and legal challenges are considered institutional responses, which do not fall into the same category as political protests. But as this volume attests, international actions, such as the response to war crimes in Bosnia (Gödl 2007) and analysis of the United Nation's mobility clauses and the implications for child custody (Bromwich 2009) can indeed be categorized as resistance, and resistance of the most critical kind.

Resistance is rarely documented as a powerful political strategy, especially when women are its primary agents. As an institution and as praxis, law rarely has room for agency, and even less so for the agency of women. Women are most often depicted in particularized ways by law, most significantly, as victims, usually as sexualized victims. As Mary Eberts (n.d.) has often indicated, law deals only with the sexual aspects of women's lives: pregnancy, motherhood, sexual assault. Less visible in legal cases are the more common places of women's victimization: of work, of pension and of increased tax burden (Johnson 2002). One salient reason for this is that law acts as a social mirror (Bell 1994), reflecting back to us how we socially organize the world in gendered terms. In other words, if we organize the world in ways that only emphasize women's sexuality, we render invisible those areas of women's lives in which other types of victimization occur. There is no room in this scenario, for example, for women who are victims of war, of harassment at work or of international child abduction. The means by which women from diverse backgrounds are able to resist depends on context, location, support and the ability to strategize in order to survive with dignity and determination. In this volume, we present women who all have the ability to resist, despite differences of class, race, gender identity, and ethnicity and nationality.

Law does not usually recognize resistance *as* resistance (Jeffrey and MacDonald 2006). Collective political action, individual actions or legal challenges by social groups are considered suspect. Claims to knowledge and power are often considered anormative, or simply ignored (Foucault 1976, 1977). Despite such examples, there have been considerable concerns among feminists about relying on legal structures to further women's interests (Smart 2002, 1995; Smart and Brophy 1985). These concerns stem in part from the patriarchal legacy in law, reflected in the dominance of men in virtually all aspects of law making and law enforcement, including the judiciary, the legal profession and Parliament. At the same time, some feminists favour using legal institutions as part of a broader effort to change society. There has been ongoing interest not only in studying the impact of particular laws and measures on women, but in taking a more introspective look at how women are treated within the legal profession and the courts (Hagan and Kay 1995; Brockman 2001).

First- and second-wave feminists resisted oppression and domination, and, through consciousness raising, political action and transformation, fought to have women recognized within law. Marxists and radical feminists questioned participating in the legal system because it was created and sustained by a "dominant sex class" (Smart 2002; Smart and Brophy 1985). Poststructuralists and postmodernists deconstructed damaging labels applied to women who do not fit neatly into dichotomous legalistic categories and have questioned the workability of the legal institution itself. The transformation of social, political and legal institutions might signal to women that they have won the battle, but lost the war. Liberal humanist values seem to prevail within formal social institutions, leaving out diverse voices and experiences. The "legal woman," like the "rational man," reconceptualized by feminist theory, remains white, middle-class, propertied, married, heterosexual and educated. Those who do not fit within the dominant conceptual framework often become othered and excluded. This is the case for women who experience sexual assault (Coates and Ridley 2009), abuse (Rosenberg 2009), sexual harassment (Profitt 2009) or even addiction (Toner 2009).

To summarize, much consciousness raising in the women's movement for social change (for example, Betty Friedan's *The Feminine Mystique*, Simone de Beauvoir's *The Second Sex*, Germaine Greer's *The Female Eunuch*, Del Martin and Phyllis Lyon's *Battered Wives*, Ti-Grace Atkinson's *Amazon Odyssey*, Mary Daly's *Gyn/Ecology*) drew upon stories women told of how they resisted male domination. These political analyses allowed women to document experience and make connections with other women so that the personal became the political, in the process breaking down barriers between women and providing alternative methods of resistance and survival. However, fractures in the women's movement challenged these political alliances, threatening to disconnect women from each other over issues of identity, location, class and race. Feminist theory became weakened as it attempted to be too many things to too many diverse groups. Further, it became evident that feminist theory may "need" victims perhaps a little too much.

What we mean by this is that victim precipitation models that fail to investigate context, specificity and intersectionality have ended up labelling and reimposing social control mechanisms (Elias 1993). What is problematic about this direction is not the presence of victims but the absence of chronology; the treatment of victimization as fixed, rather than fluid, as a state of being, rather than a "journey of life" process. Simply put, victims do not stay victims. They heal, regroup, move on (Profitt 2000). Those who do not move on, who stay traumatized by the experience, are a minority. An example that flies directly in the face of the construction of victim is included in recent work (Jeffrey and MacDonald 2006) on sex workers. Radical theory encourages us to transform our thinking about women and men who work in the sex trade, educating us about the workers' agency to organize, unionize and enjoy the work that they do, a far cry from the victimization model consistently used by feminists (LeMonchek 1997; Jeffrey and MacDonald 2006).

Agency, for feminist theorists, has been "embodied" in the subject of dissent and enacted, at times, through political protest (Parkins 2000; Stern 2000). It may be that second- and third-wave feminisms have more in common than they believe. Resistance can include both an understanding of the institutional and personal oppressions women experience while at the same time providing options for self-determination, through individual identity, or political and/or collective social movements.

NEW SOCIAL MOVEMENTS

Those who criticize the apolitical nature of (some) new social movements tend to see modern society as predominantly capitalist. Although they may have transcended traditional Marxist positions on the role of "old social movements," they remain wedded to a conception of capitalism as a systemic form of domination that must ultimately be challenged in political terms. (Buechler 1995: 453)

Despite the contention that there has been a "fall" from collective to individual resistance, there is no consensus that this fall from grace ever took place. Historian Charles Tilly documents a long history of social movement in the West as a result of large-scale social changes and political conditions, so that "social movements still select tactics from essentially the same repertoire of contention that became established in the nineteenth century" (cited in Staggenborg 2008: 4). According to Tilly, "social movements are one form of contentious politics," which included "special-purpose associations or coalitions and engaged in strategies such as demonstrations, petition drives, public statements, and meetings — various tactics that make up the modern social movement repertoire" (cited in Staggenborg 2008: 5). "Based on this contentious politics approach, Sidney Tarrow (1998: 4) provides a succinct definition of social movements as 'collective challenges, based on common purposes and social solidarities, in sustained interaction with elites, opponents, and authorities'" (Staggenborg 2008: 5). Suzanne Staggenborg argues that it is necessary to consider the historical context of the multiplicity of modern social movement themes and forms of agitation. She concludes that modern social movements are extensions of, rather than apolitical and ahistorical forms of, contentious politics.

Given the historical lineage of social movements and their common characteristics over time, the argument that an economic class base is required to drive collective action requires reassessment. Rather than reject economic issues, new social movements extend the focus on class to include claims for recognition of environmental issues, globalization, feminism, gay and lesbian issues, and Aboriginal protest (Larana, Johnston and Gusfield 1994; Mooers and Sears 1997; Kauffman 1990; Staggenborg 2008; Buechler 1995; Marcus 1982; Kaplan 1979; Ramos 2008).

However, Steven M. Buechler (1995: 450) thinks that there is little consensus on anything to do with new social movement theories in relation to older left-leaning forms of political activism. New social movements may be part of a cycle of move-ments — drawing from the cycle of protest in the sixties and seventies influenced by the New Left and feminism. Buechler argues that unfortunate dichotomies are created when theorists try to define what is political versus what is cultural. Buechler agrees with McAdam (1994) that "all movements are cultural in some way" (Buechler 1995: 451). All movements play a representational or symbolic func-tion. Buechler writes: "all movements take explicit or implicit political stances ... [and] are complex and cannot be explained using inflexible binaries" (1995: 451).

A number of characteristics of new social movement theories validate the cul-tural theoretical perspective. First, such theories "represent a major form of social activism whose social base is sometimes best defined in something other than class terms, whether that be gender, ethnicity, race, sexuality, or age" (Buechler 1995: 456). Second, these theories "may be best characterized not in terms of a social base rooted in conventional statuses, but rather in terms of values and goods with which participants agree" (Buechler 1995: 456). Third, despite the criticism of a lack of class base, "there does appear to be an elective affinity between a middle-class location and new social movements" (Buechler 1995: 456). Finally, Buechler concludes that there is no one new social movement theory but multiple theories and he proposes a typology, an "ideal typical sensitizing construct," a heuristic tool. Buechler divides new social movement theories into political and cultural versions, which are not mutually exclusive but rather have related characteristics that overlap (1995: 457).

NEW SOCIAL MOVEMENTS AND FEMINISM

According to Suzanne Staggenborg (2008: 23, Table 2.1.) new social movement theories originate in large-scale social and political changes and the mobilization of everyday networks and organizational structures motivated by new types of grievances. An important feature of new social movements is their international collective identity, known as the global justice movement, which utilizes sub-merged networks and new types of structures, constituents and ideologies. The key outcomes are new types of values, identities and organizations using diverse cultural innovations.

Staggenborg explains how resistance to neo-liberal policies is a key factor in the development of the global justice movement (2008: 127). This movement and its allies (feminists, environmentalists, labour activists, students, community activists, churches, Aboriginal peoples) grew out of resistance to neo-liberal economic poli-cies. The actors include the concerned citizens who organized coalitions against the Canada–U.S. Free Trade Agreement, both nationally and transnationally, those who opposed the Meech Lake Accord (Hampton 2008) and people working in environmental struggles. Coalition building increased with the formation of the Council for Canadians, which shifted the focus from Canada to the international concerns of safe water, for example. All such coalitions were concerned with extending social justice. Staggenborg thinks that submerged networks are critical to the success of the global women's movement, as well as many other initiatives, such as cultural and political activities "connecting issues of sexism with interlocking oppressions of race, class, and sexuality in cultural and political projects" (2008: 85).

Staggenborg calls third-wave feminism the global women's movement because it focuses on international issues, including violence against women and reproductive rights (2008: 81–87). The global women's movement includes transnational women's networks formed via the U.N. and NGOs, a focus on economic issues that connect the personal with the political, a critique of policies associated with neo-liberalism and resulting economic strategies and an analysis of how "women's unpaid labour is required to compensate for cutbacks in government services and how these economic policies affected the everyday lives of poor women" (Staggenborg 2008: 82–83). Staggenborg defines the global justice movement as a transnational movement that "began linking various socio-economic and political problems to neo-liberal policies" (2008: 127). Activists created a master frame "that diagnosed specific problems as consequences of neo-liberalism and its practice by international financial institutions" (Ayres 2004, 2005, cited in Staggenborg 2008: 127). Examples of strategies include the use of the Internet to raise awareness and make global linkages, raising public awareness of the poverty-enhancing effects of neo-liberal policies, and political acts using new cultural forms. Tactics such as parallel summits, blockades, teach-ins, street theatre, rallies, protests and marches provide non-violent ways in which to challenge World Trade Organisation reform and support the dismantling of capitalism. Demonstrations challenge the exploitation of sweatshop workers and promote a global living wage, ethical trading and anti-corporate activity (Klein 2001). The result is a diverse anti-sweatshop global movement forging alliances with unions, environmentalists, students, feminists and community activists to lobby against lack of workplace standards and exploitation of women in developing countries (Staggenborg 2008: 135). Staggenborg sees a difference between second-wave feminists, who initiated the idea of the personal being political, and international feminists, who expand "on this insight to connect macro-level economic policies to women's everyday lives" (Antrobus 2004, cited in Staggenborg 2008: 34).

The global justice movement has been successful for a number of reasons, not least of which has been the creation of international linkages that raise awareness of the exploitation of workers and the environment by international trade and monetary practices. In doing so, the global justice movement has utilized a number of political strategies and cultural forms to challenge the negative impacts of global capitalism.

Women use numerous strategies of resistance when confronted with the obstacles of patriarchal practices. Their stories, studies, and practices speak volumes to the courage, persistence and patience of women's resistance to being labelled "victim." Women resist institutional structures, social norms, and legal codes in order to change the circumstances of their lives. We found their practices and their stories surprising, sometimes shocking and always inspiring. It is our sincere hope that you will to.

References

Allen, Paula Gunn. 1992. "Who Is Your Mother? Red Roots of White Racism." *The Sacred Hoop: Recovering the Feminine in American Indian Traditions*. Boston: Beacon.

Antrobus, Peggy. 2004. *The Global Women's Movement: Origins, Issues and Strategies*. London: Zed Books.

Aptekar, L. 1994. *Environmental Disasters in Global Perspective*. Toronto: G.K. Hall; New York: MacMillan.

Atkinson, Ti-Grace. 1974. *Amazon Odyssey*. New York: Links Books.

Avakian, Arlene Voski. 1981. "Women's Studies and Racism." *New England Journal of Black Studies* 31–36.

Ayres, Jeffrey M. 2004. "Framing Collective Action Against Neoliberalism: The Case of the 'Anti-Globalization' Movement." *Journal of World-Systems Research* 10, 1: 11–34.

____. 2005. "From 'Anti-Globalization' to the Global Justice Movement: Framing Collective Action against Neoliberalism." In B. Podobnik and T. Reifer (eds.), Transforming Globalization. Leiden, Netherlands: Brill.

Bell, Shannon. 1994. *Reading, Writing and Rewriting the Prostitute Body*. Indianapolis: Indiana University Press.

Bhopal, Kalwant. 2002. "Teaching Women's Studies: The Effects of 'Race' and Gender." *Journal of Further and Higher Education* 26, 2: 6–16.

Boyd, S.C. 2004. *From Witches to Crack Moms: Women, Drug Law, and Policy*. Durham, NC: Carolina Academic Press.

Boyd, Susan, and Helen Rhoades. 2006. Law and Families: The International Library of Essays on Law and Society. Aldershot: Ashgate.

Boyd, Susan, Margot Young, Gwen Brodsky, and Shelagh Day (eds.). 2007. *Poverty: Rights, Social Citizenship and Governance*. Vancouver: University of British Columbia Press.

Brockman, Joan. 2001. *Gender in the Legal Profession: Fitting or Breaking the Mould*. Vancouver: University of British Columbia Press.

Bromwich, Rebecca Jaremko. 2009. "Flight: Women Abuse and Children's Habitual Resistance in The Hague Convention on International Child Abduction." In E. Faulkner and G. MacDonald (eds.), *Victim No More: Women's Resistance to Law, Culture and Power*. Halifax and Winnipeg: Fernwood Publishing.

Buechler, S.M. 1995. "New Social Movement Theories." *The Sociological Quarterly* 36, 3: 441–64.

Chunn, Dorothy E., Susan B. Boyd and Hester Lessard (eds.). 2007. *Reaction and Resistance: Feminism, Law and Social Change*. Vancouver: University of British Columbia Press.

Coates, L., and P. Ridley. 2009. "Representing Victims of Sexualized Assault." In E. Faulkner and G. MacDonald (eds.), *Victim No More: Women's Resistance to Law, Culture and Power*. Halifax and Winnipeg: Fernwood Publishing.

Cornwell, A. 1983. *Black Lesbian in White America*. Tallahassee, FL: Naiad Press.

Eberts, Mary. n.d. *Sexual Assault and the Common Law: A New Perspective*. Toronto: Tory, Tory, DesLauriers and Binnington.

Elias, Robert. 1993. *Victims Still: The Political Manipulation of Crime Victims*. London, New Delhi, Newbury Park: Sage Publications.

Foucault, Michel. 1976. *Histoire de la sexualité*. Paris: Gallimard.

____. 1977. *Discipline and Punish: The Birth of the Prison*. New York: Pantheon Books.

Giddings, Paula. 1985. *When and Where I Enter: A History of Black Women's Movement*. New York: Bantam.

Gilbert, Neil. 1991. "The Phantom Epidemic of Sexual Assault." *The Public Interest* 103: 54–65.

____. 1992. "Realities and Mythologies of Rape." *Society* (May-June): 4–10.

____. 1993. "Examining the Facts: Advocacy Research Overstates the Incidence of Date and Acquaintance Rape." In Richard Gelles and Donileen Loseke (eds.), *Current Controversies in Family Violence*. Newbury Park, California: Sage Publications.

Gillespie, Marcia. 1994. "The Posse Rides Again." Editorial. *Ms. Magazine* May/June.

Gödl, Doris. 2007. "Challenging the Past: Serbian and Croatian Aggressor/Victim Narratives." In Tadeusz Krauze (ed.), *International Journal of Sociology*. New York: M.E. Sharpe.

Hagan, John, and F. Kay. 1995. *Gender in Practice: A Study of Lawyer's Lives*. New York: Oxford University Press.

Hampton, A.S.C. 2008. "I Don't Think Canadians Are Going to Sit Still and Let it Happen": The New Brunswick Ad Hoc Committee on the Constitution and Citizens' Response to the Meech Lake Accord. Master's thesis, University of New Brunswick. (January).

Hood, E.F. 1978. "Black Women, White Women: Separate Paths to Liberation." *Black Scholar* 9, 7: 45–56.

hooks, bell. 1981. *Ain't I a Woman? Black Women and Feminism*. South End Press.

Jacobs, Jane. 2004. *Dark Age Ahead*. Vintage Press.

Jeffrey, Leslie Ann, and Gayle MacDonald. 2006. *Sex Workers in the Maritimes Talk Back*. Vancouver: University of British Columbia Press.

Johnson, Rebecca. 2002. *Taxing Choices: The Intersection of Class, Gender, Parenthood and the Law*. Vancouver: UBC Press.

Joseph, G., and J. Lewis. 1981. *Common Differences: Conflicts in Black and White Feminist Perspectives*. New York: Anchor Press.

Kamen, Paul. December 1993. "Erasing Rape: Media Hype an Attack on Sexual-Assault Research." FAIR: Fairness and Accuracy in Reporting. Available at <http://www.fair.org/index.php?page=1218> accessed October 2008.

Kaplan, S.J. 1979. "Literary Criticism." *Signs* 4, 3: 514–27.

Kauffman, L.A. 1990. "The Anti-Politics of Identity." *Socialist Review* 20, 1.

Klein, N. 2001. *No Logo: Taking Aim at the Band Bullies*. U.K.: Harper Collins.

____. 2007. *The Shock Doctrine: The Rise of Disaster Capitalism*. Toronto: Alfred A. Knopf Canada.

Koss, Mary. 1988. "Hidden Rape: Sexual Aggression and Victimization in a National Sample of Students in Higher Education," In A. Wolbert Burgess, (ed.), *Rape and Sexual Assault* Vol. 2. New York: Garland Publishing.

Koss, M., and C. Oros. 1982. "Sexual Experiences Survey: A Research Instrument Investigating Sexual Aggression and Victimization." *Journal of Consulting and Clinical Psychology* 50, 3.

Koss, Mary P., and Mary R. Harvey. 1991. *The Rape Victim. Clinical and Community Interventions*. Second edition. Newbury Park, CA: Sage Publications.

Larana, E., H. Johnston, J.R. Gusfield (eds.). 1994. *New Social Movements: From Ideology to Identity*. Temple University Press.

LeMoncheck, L. 1997. *Loose Women, Lecherous Men: A Feminist Philosophy of Sex*. Oxford University Press.

Lewis, Stephen. 2005. *Race Against Time: Searching for Hope in AIDS Ravaged Africa*. Toronto: Anansi Press.

Lorde, Audre. 1984. *Sister Outsider: Essays and Speeches*. Berkeley, CA: Crossing Press.

MacKinnon, Catharine A. 2008. *Are Women Human? And Other International Dialogues*. Cambridge, MA: Harvard University Press.

Mallick, H. 2006. "Pay attention, feminists." *CBC News Online*. Analysis and Views. October 6. Available at <http://www.cbc.ca/news/viewpoint/vp_mallick/20061006.html> accessed June 4, 2008.

Marcus, J. Spring 1982. "Storming the Toolshed." *Feminist Theory* 7, 3: 622–40.

Mathen, C. 2004. "Transgendered Persons and Feminist Strategy." *Canadian Journal of Women and the Law* 16, 2: 291–316.

McAdam, Doug. 1994. "Culture and Social Movements." In E. Larana, H. Johnston, and J.R. Gusfield (eds.), *New Social Movements: From Ideology to Identity*. Philadelphia: Temple University Press.

Miller, Michelle. 2008. *Branding Miss G: Third Wave Feminists and the Media*. Toronto: Sumach Press.

Mooers, C., and A. Sears. 1997. *Organizing Dissent: Contemporary Social Movements in Theory*. Toronto: Garamond Press.

Moraga, Cherrie L., and Gloria E. Anzaldúa (eds.). 2003. *This Bridge Called My Back – Writings by Radical Women of Color*. Third edition. Third Woman Press.

Myron, N., and C. Bunch (eds.). 1975. *Lesbianism and the Women's Movement*. Baltimore, MD: Diana Press.

Omolade, Barbara. 1985. "Black Women and Feminism." In Hester Eisenstein and Alice Jardine (eds.), *The Future of Difference*. New Brunswick, N.J.: Rutgers University Press.

Parkins, W. 2000. "Protesting Like a Girl: Embodiment, Dissent and Feminist Agency." *Feminist Theory* 1, 1.

Profitt, Norma Jean. 2000. *Women Survivors, Psychological Trauma, and the Politics of Resistance*. New York, London, Oxford: Haworth Press.

____. 2009. "'Not a Tough Enough Skin?': Resisting Paternalist Relations in Academe." In E. Faulkner and G. MacDonald (eds.), *Victim No More: Women's Resistance to Law, Culture and Power*. Halifax and Winnipeg: Fernwood Publishing.

Ramos, H. 2008. "Aboriginal Protest." In S. Staggenborg (ed.), *Social Movements.* Don Mills, ON: Oxford University Press.

Rees, M. 2004. *Our Final Hour: A Scientist's Warning: How Terror, Error, and Environmental Disaster Threaten Humankind's Future in This Century — On Earth and Beyond.* New York: Basic Books.

Rich, Adrienne. 1980. "Compulsory Heterosexuality and Lesbian Existence." *Signs: Journal of Women in Culture and Society* 5, 4: 631–90.

Roiphe, Katie. 1993. *The Morning After: Sex, Fear, and Feminism.* London: Hamish Hamilton.

Smith, Barbara. 1979. "Racism and Women's Studies." *Frontiers: A Journal of Women's Studies* 5, 1: 48–49.

Rosenberg, Karen. 2009. "Playing Games With the Law: Legal Advocacy and Resistance." In E. Faulkner and G. MacDonald (eds.), *Victim No More: Women's Resistance to Law, Culture and Power.* Halifax and Winnipeg: Fernwood Publishing.

Smart, Carol. 2002. *Feminism and the Power of Law.* London & New York: Routledge.

Smart, C., and J. Brophy. 1985. "Locating Law: A Discussion of the Place of Law in Feminist Politics." In J. Brophy and C. Smart (eds.), *Women In Law: Explorations in Law, Family and Sexuality.* London, Boston, Melbourne, and Henley: Routledge & Kegan Paul.

Smith, Barbara. 1979. "Racism and Women's Studies." *Frontiers: A Journal of Women's Studies* 5, 1: 48–49.

Smith, K. 2004. *Environmental Hazards: Assessing Risk and Reducing Disaster.* Fourth edition. New York: Routledge.

Spelman, Elizabeth. 1988. *Inessential Woman. Problems of Exclusion in Feminist Thought.* Boston: Beacon Press.

Spivak, G.C. 1988. *In Other Worlds: Essays in Cultural Politics.* New York: Routledge.

_____. 2008. *Other Asias.* MA, USA; Oxford, UK; Victoria, Australia: Blackwell.

Spivak, Gayatri Chakravorty, and Sarah Harasym. 1990. *The Post-Colonial Critic: Interviews, Strategies, Dialogues.* New York; London: Routledge.

Staggenborg, S. 2008. *Social Movements.* Don Mills, ON: Oxford University Press.

Stern, D. 2000. "The Return of the Subject? Power, Reflexivity and Agency." *Philosophy & Social Criticism* 26, 5.

Stringer, Rebecca. 2001. "Blaming Me, Blaming You: Victim Identity in Recent Feminism." *Outskirts: Feminism Along the Edge* 8. University of Australia. Available at <http://www.chloe.uwa.edu.au/outskirts/archive/volume8/stringer> accessed October 2008.

Tarrow, S. 1998. *Power in Movement: Social Movements and Contentious Politics.* Second edition. Cambridge: Cambridge University Press.

Toner, Jean. 2009. "Resistance and Recovery: Three Women's Testimony on Addiction and Collective Sites of Recovery." In E. Faulkner and G. MacDonald (eds.), *Victim No More: Women's Resistance to Law, Culture and Power.* Halifax and Winnipeg: Fernwood Publishing.

Ware, V. 1992. *Beyond the Pale: White Women, Racism and History.* London: Verso.

Wolf, Naomi. 1993. Fire With Fire: The New Female Power and How it Will Change the 21st Century. London: Chatto & Windus.

MARRIAGE AND THE FAMILY

Chapter 4

FEMINISM, LAW AND "THE FAMILY"
Assessing the Reform Legacy

Dorothy E. Chunn

From: *Locating Law: Race, Class, Gender, Sexuality Connections*, 3rd edition, pp. 232–256 (slightly revised by and reprinted with permission).

Even a cursory retrospective reveals that institutions such as state, law and family are not always and everywhere the same, either in a given society or in societies with similar histories. Rather, they are formed and reformed at particular transformative moments within the constraints of specific kinds of social organization (Garland 1985). Canada has undergone three major transformative moments since 1840: the consolidation of a white settler society and development of industrial capitalism and a laissez-faire state; corporate capitalism and a welfare state; and transnational capitalism and a neo-liberal form of state (Brodie 1995; Christie 2000; Chunn 1992; Moscovitch and Albert 1987; Siltanen 2002; Ursel 1992).

These changes in capitalist organization and social relations have been accompanied by analogous transformations in patriarchal relations exemplified by the authoritarian, welfare and egalitarian models of family, respectively (Eichler 1997). Despite differences between them, all three models are variations on the nuclear family form, which historically has been premised on heterosexual marriage, the sexual division of labour and the public/private split (Barrett and McIntosh 1982), and that recently has expanded to include same-sex civil marriage.[1] Common-law couples have also obtained varying degrees of recognition in law and policy since the 1980s (Holland 2000). Thus the nuclear family form has been, and continues to be, dominant in Canadian law and social policy related to the "private" sphere (Boyd 1997a; Chunn, Boyd, and Lessard 2007; Cossman and Fudge 2002; Eichler 1997; Luxton 2011).

Analyses of socio-legal reforms that have contributed to transformations of state, law and family in capitalist societies reveal that reform is an inherently contradictory phenomenon (Chunn 1992; Donzelot 1980; Garland 1985). Because they are always the outcome of political struggle and negotiation, reforms invariably generate both positive and negative effects, which, in turn, are mediated by gender, race, class, sexual orientation, disability and so on. On one hand, then, law and social policy help reproduce and perpetuate the status quo (and inequalities) by supporting particular forms of social and family organization. On the other hand, law and public policy are not simply unitary instruments of oppression that are the monopoly of white, bourgeois, heterosexual men (Boyd 1997a; Brophy and Smart 1985; Gavigan 1993, 1999).

Like their counterparts in other Western market societies (Dale and Foster 1986; Gordon 1990), feminists and the organized women's movements in Canada have played a major role in campaigns for legal and policy reforms and have therefore contributed to important transformations (Adamson, Briskin, and McPhail 1988; Bacchi 1983; Christie 2000; Landsberg 2012; McCormack 1991; Ross 1995). These campaigns have been very much informed by particular feminist explanations of why and how women are subordinated and the best means of bringing about change — explanations that incorporate distinct conceptions of the state, law and family. During the late nineteenth and early twentieth centuries, first-wave maternal feminism (Bacchi 1983; Christie 2000; Roberts 1979) was the dominant feminist influence on the family-related legislation and policies that helped to create the Canadian welfare state and to entrench a welfare model of family in law and social policy (Andrew 1984; McCormack 1991; Ursel 1992). Similarly, since the 1960s, second-wave liberal feminism has strongly influenced socio-legal reforms that are based on an egalitarian model of family and have contributed to the deconstruction of the welfare state in Canada (Boyd 1997a; Brodie 1995; Chunn, Boyd, and Lessard 2007; Cossman and Fudge 2002; Eichler 1997).

This chapter assesses the role played by feminists in both the historical construction and the contemporary reordering of the Canadian welfare state through their successful advocacy of legislation and policies governing the "private" sphere of the family.[2] As we shall see, the socio-legal reforms promoted by both first-wave maternal feminists and second-wave liberal feminists had contradictory and differential effects, suggesting that in the end, women's oppression can only be eradicated through systemic change — change that challenges patriarchal ideologies and discourses and transforms the nuclear family form that sustains them. While this is indeed a daunting project when undertaken in a neo-liberal climate, there are strategies that Canadian feminists could adopt to obtain legislation and policies that will challenge the nuclear family form at its ideological and structural roots and revitalize the movement to achieve substantive equality (equal outcomes) for all women.

FIRST-WAVE REFORMS:
MATERNAL FEMINISM

In Canada and elsewhere, the catalyst for the emergence of an organized women's movement during the nineteenth and early twentieth centuries was the legal invisibility of women, particularly married women. Much legislation and policy governing families in laissez-faire states were derived from an authoritarian model of the nuclear family, which gave husbands and fathers total legal control over their wives and children. Under the so-called "unity doctrine," a husband and wife became one person, and that person was the husband; a married woman thus became a mere extension of her patriarch-husband, with the same status as "an infant or institutionalized incompetent" (Kieran 1986: 41). Forcing poor and/or First Nations women to marry thus became a priority for authorities in the Canadian laissez-faire state (Backhouse 1991; Carter 2008). While single women had more rights than their married sisters, a major impetus for the rise of first-wave feminism was a desire to challenge and end the legal subordination of women, especially white, middle-class women.

In Canada, maternal feminism was the first-wave feminist perspective that most influenced family related law and policy. It was premised on the assumption that men and women are different but complementary in nature and that, therefore, they excel in "separate but equal" spheres of activity. Following from this assumption, the "masculine" traits of providing and protecting predispose men to enter the public sphere of production (business, politics, the professions), while the "feminine" qualities of nurturing and caregiving make women uniquely suited to the private realm of reproduction (the family). In their political work, then, maternal feminists embraced conceptions of state, law and family and advocated reforms compatible with the assumption that women and men have sex-specific traits, capabilities and needs.

The latter belief translated into an uncritical acceptance of the traditional nuclear family form. For maternal feminists, the "normal" family was a nuclear unit, based on a heterosexual marriage relationship, in which each member had a specific role. Husbands/fathers protected and provided for their dependants; wives and mothers nurtured and cared for other family members; children existed in a "natural" state of dependency on their parents. A "natural," sexual division of labour between the spouses mirrored the public/private split in society more generally (Chunn 1990; Gavigan 1988).

Along with adherence to the nuclear family form, most maternal feminists initially accepted the nineteenth-century liberal notion of the state as a neutral arbiter of the common good. Only after some experience with the laissez-faire state did they begin to articulate the reformist view that safeguarding the common good might require state intervention on behalf of disadvantaged groups — such as women and children — to ensure that they received protection and support. In the words of first-wave feminist Nellie McClung (1976: 322), "More and more the idea is growing upon us that certain services are best rendered by the state, and not left to depend on the caprice, inclination, or inability of the individual."

For maternal feminists, law became the pivotal instrument of social engineering through which an interventionist state could address women's devalued status relative to men. They believed women were subordinate to men mainly because their central roles as wives and mothers within the family were not legally recognized. Thus, solving the problem did not require a revolution; rather, it involved merely the abolition of the unity doctrine and the implementation of legislation and policies that would give women legal rights in the private sphere of reproduction. To that end, maternal feminists supported women's suffrage — not to move women into the public world of business and politics, but because the right to vote would give women the political power to influence the men who made family related law and policy.

Although first-wave maternal feminists did not challenge the sexual division of labour, they did "politicize the personal" through their efforts to acquire legal standing for women in their "proper sphere" of the family. They were especially concerned about reinforcing women in their motherhood role and keeping mother-headed families together in the midst of apparent "social disorganization" generated by the rapid industrialization and urbanization of Canada between 1880 and 1940 (Roberts 1979; Ursel 1992). From the 1880s onward, maternal feminists fought for legislation and policies that gave mothers and wives some rights when a marriage failed or when a male breadwinner was otherwise absent. In general, maternal feminists contributed to reforms that collectively shaped the welfare-state structures that regulated the private sphere of family or reproduction. In the process they helped to revamp the two-tiered, class-based system of family law that the English had transplanted to Canada. On the first level, which related primarily to the propertied classes, the reform of divorce, custody and property law benefited those middle-class and upper-class women who could afford legal counsel. On the second level, the reform of family welfare laws related to guardianship, maintenance and support assisted some economically marginal women (Chunn 1992; Snell 1991).[3]

A historical review of specific family related legal and policy reforms advocated by maternal feminists in Canada illustrates these patterns. With regard to custody and guardianship law, for instance, Canadian courts often upheld the absolute right of fathers to legal control of their children under English common and statutory law throughout the nineteenth century (Backhouse 1991; Boyd 2003; Kieran 1986). By the turn of the twentieth century, however, feminists and other reformers had obtained legislation in a number of provinces that, to some degree, recognized the importance of women's motherhood role (Boyd 2003). In addition, an 1897 court decision in British Columbia laid the foundation for what became known as the "tender years" doctrine, by authorizing judges to award custody of children under the age of seven to non-adulterous mothers who were deemed "fit" parents (Backhouse 1991: 204). This principle — that "all other things being equal, a young child should be with its natural mother" — came to dominate custody and guardianship decisions in the twentieth century and ended the presumption of automatic "paternal" right to children of a marriage.

By 1900, married women had also acquired new property rights. Under the unity doctrine, a wife was legally obligated to give all property acquired before or during marriage to her husband, including land, furniture, money and even the clothes on her back. However, three successive reform waves during the nineteenth century led to the enactment of married women's property laws, which introduced separate property regimes in some provinces, beginning with Ontario in 1884. The concept of separate property meant that both wives and husbands had the right to acquire, administer and dispose of any personal property whether it was obtained before or during marriage; and if the relationship failed, each partner kept what was hers or his (Backhouse 1992; Chambers 1997).

As with custody and guardianship, the authoritarian model of family that underpinned the unity doctrine allowed men to divorce or abandon their wives and children, leave them without any means of support, and still retain legal control over them (Kieran 1986: 49). From the 1880s onward, however, rapid industrialization and urbanization brought disproportionate numbers of women and children to growing cities in advance of their male breadwinners, and many of these mother-led families ended up destitute because their husbands/fathers never arrived. When female and child poverty became increasingly visible in urban centres, feminists and other reformers sought legislation that compelled men to support their dependants. Starting in 1888 with the Ontario Deserted Wives' Maintenance Act, most provinces enacted legislation that introduced a legal obligation on husbands and fathers to support their dependants after marital separation or face sanctions, including jail. After World War I, many provinces passed similar laws imposing a financial obligation on the putative father in cases of unmarried parenthood (Chambers 2007; Chunn 1992; Ursel 1992).

The post-World War I era also saw provincial states assume the financial role of employer through the payment of mothers' pensions/allowances in cases in which the male protector/breadwinner was absent from the family through death or mental or physical incapacity or when a male deserter could not be found. Although "a broad spectrum of articulate, middle-class Canadians" had promoted such an income-support policy since the turn of the twentieth century, only the increase in mother-led families during the war, which fuelled a perception that the (nuclear) family was in crisis, provided a sufficient catalyst for implementing this reform (Strong-Boag 1979: 25). "Deserving" women were awarded allowances to help them fulfil their "natural" domestic role by enabling them to engage in part-time rather than full-time outside employment or to earn wages without leaving home. Recipients of pensions/allowances were analogous to state employees and were expected to supplement their government salaries with other earnings (Strong-Boag 1979: 27; see also Christie 2000; Gavigan and Chunn 2007; Little 1998).

Contradictory and Differential Effects of First-wave Reforms

Like all reforms, the family-related legislation and policies promoted by first-wave feminists had both intended and unintended consequences in practice. On the positive side, women benefited from the reforms in a number of ways.

First, they received explicit legal recognition of the unpaid nurturing and caregiving work that women perform in their role as mothers (and, to a lesser degree, as wives) and a concrete acknowledgement that the "private" sphere of reproduction was important and should be taken into account when a marriage ended through separation, divorce or mutual agreement. Specifically, the tender years doctrine assisted some women in their attempts to gain custody or guardianship of their children. Similarly, desertion legislation and enforcement mechanisms, such as family courts, gave women without financial means the legal assistance to obtain spousal and child support (Chunn 1992).

Second, reforms such as the provincial mothers' pensions/allowances policies represented some recognition of state responsibility to oversee the well-being of the disadvantaged and, if necessary, to contribute materially to their subsistence rather than leaving the burden to families and charities in the private sector or to local governments. During the interwar period, increasing numbers of women received allowances/pensions from the state. In British Columbia, for example, the number of mothers or foster mothers receiving allowances more than doubled between 1919–1920 (636), when pensions were introduced, and 1938–1939 (1,751), while the amount expended by the province between 1927–1928 and

1938–1939 increased from $612,645 to $790,101 notwithstanding the 1930s Depression (Strong-Boag 1979: 26, 28–30; Christie 2000).

Finally, although statistics are incomplete, feminist-supported laws and policies to shore up the nuclear family arguably left many poor white women and children without male breadwinners at least marginally better off than they might otherwise have been. For instance, the early family courts in Ontario collected substantial sums for women and children, as did the government official who handled unmarried mothers' cases (Chunn 1992). Clearly, separate property regimes also saved some women from the destitution that previously befell many wives when a marriage ended (Backhouse 1992; Kieran 1986).

In retrospect, however, the negative effects of first-wave-inspired reforms are obvious. Taking the nuclear family as a given, maternal feminists promoted reforms that sanctified rather than challenged that model, thereby helping to entrench in law and policy a definition of family as one based on heterosexual marriage, a sexual division of labour and the public/private split. Privileging "the family" and women's role in it reinforced their subordination to, and dependency upon, men in several ways.

Historically, heterosexual marriage has been premised on a sexual double standard: women, but not men, must be chaste before and monogamous during marriage. The family-related legislation and policies obtained by maternal feminists and other reformers all incorporated and therefore reinforced this double standard. Whether women applied for custody, maintenance or mothers' allowances, they were routinely scrutinized for sexual purity and moral fitness. Women who breached the "norms" of good motherhood were routinely denied custody of their children (Boyd 2003). "Uncondoned adultery" by a wife automatically barred her from obtaining spousal maintenance after marital breakdown and was a ground for the rescinding of existing support orders (Chunn 1992). Likewise, moral laxity disqualified women as "deserving" recipients of mothers' allowances or of other public financial assistance. Moreover, under the "man in the house" rule, a woman who resided with a man became ineligible for state benefits because authorities assumed that he must be supporting her, yet the same rule did not apply to men (Little 1998; Strong-Boag 1979). Thus, women who adhered to the sexual double standard were rewarded; the morally "undeserving" were punished through the loss of their children, denial of financial assistance, and even criminal prosecution (Chambers 2007; Gavigan 1993; Martin 1992).

Similarly, the failure of maternal feminists to attack the sexual division of labour meant that legal and policy reforms gave married women more power within the family — not so much in their own right as women, but because of their role in social reproduction, particularly as mothers (Brophy and Smart 1985; Chunn 1992). Thus, women's unpaid, intrafamilial motherwork, wifework and housework (Rosenberg 1990: 58–61) were assumed, and the economic dependency of women within marriage remained intact, ultimately to be underlined by cases such as *Murdoch v. Murdoch* (1973, 1975), which revealed a basic weakness of separate property regimes.

The Murdochs were Alberta ranchers who separated in 1968 after twenty-five years of marriage. During that time, Irene Murdoch had done not only domestic work but also enough ranch work that her husband did not need to hire a ranch hand. When she sued for half-interest in their property, cattle and other assets, the Supreme Court of Canada decided that Irene Murdoch was entitled to alimony but had no claim to the property, because she had not made "a direct financial contribution" to the ranch. The unpaid work she had done for twenty-five years was "the work done by any ranch wife." In short, Mr. Murdoch held the title to "his" property, and Irene Murdoch could not claim a share of it under the existing separate property regime in Alberta (Kieran 1986: 142).

Maternal feminists also espoused legislation and policies that reinforced the idea of "separate spheres" and, hence, the public/private distinction so central to the liberal state. Since "the family" fell on the private side of the divide, they strongly advocated the use of state power to enforce familial responsibility for the costs of social reproduction (Fudge 1989) by holding men legally accountable for maintaining their dependants even after marital separation or divorce. Thus, a woman would be maintained in her "natural" role as caregiver and housekeeper when a male breadwinner was no longer part of the family unit. The problem with privatized responsibility was that, despite the considerable sums of money collected on behalf of women and children by state agencies such as family courts, the majority of men defaulted on or were chronically in arrears with their support payments (Chunn 1992). Moreover, even when the state assumed some direct financial responsibility for social reproduction through such policies as mothers' allowances, the emphasis remained on individual family units and case-by-case assessment of eligibility (Gavigan and Chunn 2007; Little 1998).

Finally, the differential effects of the legislation and policies supported by first-wave feminists must be underscored. Maternal feminists focused solely on differences *between* women and men and, hence, on sex/gender comparisons, and they did not examine differences *among* women and *among* men generated by race, ethnicity, class, sexual orientation and disability. As a consequence, the family-related reforms they promoted were premised on assumptions that reflected primarily the experiences of white, middle-class, heterosexual women (and men). Not surprisingly, then, it was precisely such women, and to a lesser extent their counterparts in the "respectable" working classes, who were best able to adhere to the "norms" governing the traditional nuclear family and who benefited most from law reforms related to custody, property and support. The reforms did help some white women among the working and dependent poor, especially single mothers, but the price of assistance from the paternalistic state was increased surveillance and scrutiny of family life (Chunn 1992; Little 1998). Lesbians, racialized women, Aboriginal women and disabled women remained invisible in the pertinent statutes and public policies. Moreover, most First Nations women living on-reserve did not live in nuclear family units and were governed entirely by the federal Indian Act. Therefore, provincial legislation and policies related to marriage, matrimonial property, maintenance and other family matters were irrelevant to their lives (Turpel 1991). Likewise, First Nations women have been embroiled more often in guardianship battles with the state than with the fathers of their children (Monture 1989; Monture-Angus 1995).

Notwithstanding the negative and differential impact of the reforms they advocated, first-wave maternal feminists played a major role in transforming a family law system that accorded married women virtually no rights into one in which women had rights based on their status as wives and mothers. Together with other reformers, they helped to undermine the authoritarian model of family that still underpinned much legislation and policy in the laissez-faire state and to entrench the welfare model of family that underpinned legislation and policy in the emerging interventionist state. The resulting system of family-related law and policy remained intact until the 1960s and 1970s, when another generation of feminist reformers came of age under very different social, economic and political circumstances.

SECOND-WAVE REFORMS:
LIBERAL FEMINISM

Second-wave feminism was one of many organized, equality-seeking movements that emerged in Canada and other liberal democracies during the 1960s — a period of welfare-state consolidation, prosperity and rising expectations among traditionally marginalized groups. Unlike some other groups, however, women were not a minority of the population and most had acquired basic civil and legal rights. The impetus for second-wave feminism was the realization that gaining legal visibility had not ended women's subordination to men. On the contrary, existing law and policy had codified the dependency of women on men. Thus, if women were to be free, it was necessary to repeal inherently paternalistic legislation and policies based on a welfare model of family and state. It was also necessary to implement socio-legal reforms premised on an egalitarian model of family and the principles of gender neutrality and formal equality in both the public and private spheres (Adamson, Briskin, and McPhail 1988).

Liberal feminism was the second-wave feminist perspective that most influenced family-related law and policy. Like maternal feminists, liberals focused on sex/gender comparisons, but they assumed "sameness," not "difference." Following this assumption, women have the same capabilities as men, yet few develop their full potential because they are socialized to adopt the "feminine" role of caregivers and housekeepers and, if they do enter the public realm, most do not have the same freedom to pursue opportunities as men. For liberal feminists, then, the key to women's liberation was for women to become more like men through resocialization and participation in the world of men. Thus, liberal feminists embraced somewhat different conceptions of state, law and family than did their maternal feminist predecessors, and they advocated reforms compatible with the assumption that there are no sex-specific traits, capabilities and needs (Boyd and Sheehy 1986; Chunn and Lacombe 2000).

Nonetheless, liberal feminists continued to embrace the maternal feminist view of the traditional nuclear family as the "norm" and assumed that most women would marry and bear children. Unlike first-wave feminists, however, they made a direct link between "liberation" and women's economic independence. Therefore, while they did not overtly critique the nuclear family form, liberal feminists implicitly challenged the idea of separate spheres and the sexual division of labour by arguing for the movement of married women en masse out of the home into paid employment. Once women were economically viable, equality with men would follow (Boyd and Sheehy 1986; Chunn and Lacombe 2000).

In contrast to maternal feminists, second-wave liberal feminists viewed the paternalistic welfare state as a cause of women's continued subordination, and they embraced a more classical liberal conception of the state as a mediator or umpire, particularly in the public sphere. Liberal feminists assumed that once women gained the same access and opportunity to compete in the public sphere as men, the state would not treat their interests any differently from those of men. Like their first-wave precursors, however, liberal feminists believed that discrimination against women could be removed through a process of incremental reform without any fundamental restructuring of social institutions (Boyd and Sheehy 1986; Chunn and Lacombe 2000).

Consequently, second-wave feminists retained the maternal feminist emphasis on law as a major vehicle for achieving and guaranteeing women's equality. In Canada, the *Report of the Royal Commission on the Status of Women* (Canada 1970) established the second-wave reform agenda for the next two decades. A quintessentially liberal-feminist document, the report emphasized the implementation of gender neutrality and formal equality in law and policy, and based on these principles it set out numerous recommendations for reform that would collectively make women's equality with men a reality. Overall, liberal feminists helped bring about an overhaul of the family related law and social policy that maternal feminists had fought for and, thus, contributed to a restructuring of the Canadian welfare state (Andrew and Rodgers 1997).

Whereas maternal feminists fought to enhance the position of women within the family, their second-wave successors wanted legislation and policies that would allow flexibility and interchangeability of roles for women and men in both the private and public spheres. Beginning with the implementation of the first federal Divorce Act in 1968, Canada's family law system was extensively reformed and now incorporates an egalitarian as opposed to a welfare model of (nuclear) family (Eichler 1997). Legislation and policies are based on principles of gender neutrality and formal equality, and there are no rights to custody, property and financial support based on sex/gender (Mossman and MacLean 1986, 1997).

Current family law and policy related to parenting, for example, rest on the assumptions that women are no more predisposed than men are to care for children and that fathers and mothers are equally capable of parenting. Therefore, when a marriage ends, custody of children should be based on the determination of what best serves their interests. The gender neutral "best interests of the child" principle thus displaced the tender years doctrine, which gave preference to fit mothers of young children in custody and access decisions (Boyd 2003).

Parental-leave policies also incorporate the notion of equal parenting. A 1990 amendment to the Unemployment Insurance Act (now the Employment Insurance Act) allowed either parent to take ten weeks of partially paid leave following the birth or adoption of a child. The rationale for parental leave is the reduction of work-family conflict and the potential for changing the sexual division of labour both at home and in the workplace (Iyer 1997). Amendments to the EI Act in 2001 extended parental leave "significantly"; mothers and/or fathers can now take up to thirty-five weeks of partially paid leave to care for their young children (Madsen 2002: 12). The national maternity and parental leave benefit program also withstood a constitutionality challenge in 2005 when the Supreme Court of Canada handed down a unanimous judgment that the benefit was "indeed properly administered federally" (Calder 2006).

Today the principles of gender neutrality and formal equality also govern federal and provincial marital property laws. Following the Supreme Court of Canada's 1973 decision in *Murdoch*, women's groups joined with other reformers to rectify the weaknesses in legislation based on the concept of separate property regimes. Now the division of marital property is based on the principle of equalization incorporated in a deferred community property regime. As a general rule, separate property rights exist so long as a marriage is intact, but if the relationship ends, all marital property is to be shared equitably, albeit not necessarily equally, between the spouses (Steel 1985). Moreover, the concept of property has been expanded greatly to include "virtually anything of which one could conceive," including such assets as pensions and academic degrees (Morton 1988: 260).

With regard to financial support, contemporary family law is based on the

principle of spousal self-sufficiency and equal parental responsibility for maintaining children. Gone are the sex-specific clauses in the divorce, desertion and
other family-related legislation promoted by first-wave feminists, clauses that
imposed a legal obligation on men to maintain wives and children and required
women to be non-adulterous to qualify for support. The legislation now applies to
both marriages and common-law unions. The courts assume that in most cases of
marital breakdown each spouse can attain economic independence and contribute
financially to the upkeep of their children. Therefore, spousal support is viewed as
unnecessary or as short-term assistance awarded for the sole purpose of allowing
a dependent partner to become self-sufficient. As stated in *Maw v. Maw* (1985):
"Absent an agreement to maintain, only where self-sufficiency is not possible can
there be a lifetime obligation to support."

Since the 1960s, however, the increasing number of people, primarily women
and children, who are impoverished following a marital breakdown has generated
court decisions and public policies aimed at ensuring the payment of spousal
and child support that is awarded. The historical pattern of default on support
orders did not disappear when new provincial family relations laws were enacted
during the 1970s and 1980s, and several provinces (including British Columbia,
Manitoba and Ontario) created maintenance-enforcement programs to reduce the
astronomical rate of non-compliance. Such programs are state-ordered collections
on behalf of persons who are not receiving spousal or child support; for example,
an individual who consistently fails to make payments without good reason may
have his or her wages garnisheed.

Some aspects of family welfare law have also undergone a gender-neutral transformation. For example, the "man in the house" rule has become the "spouse in the
house" rule in the social assistance legislation of every province (Cossman 2002;
Gavigan 1999; Martin 1992; Mossman and MacLean 1997).

Contradictory and Differential Effects of Second-wave Reforms

The overhaul of family-related legislation and policies achieved, in part, by second-
wave feminists has generated effects no less contradictory and differential than
those produced by socio-legal reforms enacted through the efforts of first-wave
feminists (Andrew and Rodgers 1997; Busby, Fainstein, and Penner 1990; Chunn,
Boyd, and Lessard 2007). On the positive side, family and welfare law based on the
principles of gender neutrality and formal legal equality ended the blatant sexual
discrimination and enforced dependency embedded in the old desertion statutes
and mothers' allowances legislation. As noted above, for example, the new legislation did not contain adultery clauses, and thus women were no longer held legally
accountable to a sexual double standard.

The introduction of parental leave also reinforces the feminist critique of the sexual division of labour. By creating the option for fathers to assume childcare responsibilities in the private sphere, the policy helps to undercut the pervasive belief that women "by their nature" are predisposed towards, and better at, "motherwork" than men (Rosenberg 1990). Similarly, the policy has the potential to improve women's position in the public sphere because they can remain attached to the paid labour force on leave while they stay home to care for a child, rather than leaving the ranks of the employed altogether as was the case historically (Iyer 1997).

Another positive result of second-wave family law reforms was the increased recognition of women's economic contribution to marriage through the implementation of deferred community property regimes for the spousal division of family assets upon marital breakdown. Redefining property to include social benefits such as pensions and intangible assets such as academic degrees has benefited many women: those who, like Irene Murdoch, had never been part of the paid workforce when divorce ended a long-time marriage; and women who periodically left the labour force and/or worked part-time to accommodate child-care responsibilities during a marriage (Keet 1990; Steel 1985).

Finally, the family-related socio-legal reforms promoted by second-wave feminists have recognized, to some degree, different types of cohabitation; specifically, that many heterosexual and same-sex common-law relationships resemble legal marriages (Holland 2000). For instance, the Supreme Court of Canada judgment in *M. v. H.* left the door open to include same-sex as well as heterosexual common-law unions in all family law provisions related to support (Gavigan 1999). This case involved the claim of a lesbian for spousal support from her financially better-off former partner. In 1999, the SCC upheld an earlier Ontario Court of Appeal decision, which accepted M.'s argument that the Ontario Family Law Act discriminated on the basis of sexual orientation because it did not apply to same-sex partners, one of whom was dependent upon the other when the relationship ended.

With regard to property, historically, family property law applied only to married, heterosexual couples. However, common-law couples were sometimes able to use constructive trust doctrine when dividing property at the end of a relationship. In the 1986 case of *Anderson v. Luoma*, for example, the British Columbia Supreme Court applied the principle of unjust enrichment to the facts of the case and imposed the remedy of constructive trust. The two women had lived together for ten years, but title to houses and property that they shared "tended to be in the name of the substantively better off Luoma" (Gavigan 1995: 110). Nonetheless, the BCSC required Luoma to "share the property she and Anderson had acquired and/or lived in together" (Gavigan 1995: 116). More recently, the provisions of family property law are being extended to common law couples. For example, under British Columbia's new Family Law Act, which came into force in March 2013, the rules governing property division now apply to unmarried spouses who have lived in a marriage-like relationship for at least two years as well as to married couples.

Although few regret the repeal of legislation and policies rooted in paternalism, feminists have been confronted with the unpleasant reality that implementing formal legal equality in family law and social welfare did not end women's structured dependency, and actually intensified it in some instances upon marital breakdown (Andrew and Rodgers 1997; Busby, Fainstein, and Penner 1990). But why and how does legislation based on an egalitarian model of family and principles of gender neutrality and formal equality continue to help reproduce and sustain women's inequality? Liberal feminists did not foresee that strict adherence to the principle of formal equality in the absence of substantive equality inevitably produces unequal outcomes; treating unalikes in the same way merely perpetuates differences. In short, like maternal feminists before them, liberal feminists ultimately failed to challenge the ideological and structural roots of the nuclear family form. This failure to interrogate prevailing assumptions about the normality of heterosexual marriage, the sexual division of labour and the public/private split was reflected in legal practice, where decision-making about custody, property and spousal/child support often has been detrimental for women.

For example, fathers' rights groups insist that they are seriously disadvantaged vis-à-vis mothers in the legal system, yet statistics and analyses of decision-making about custody and access suggest otherwise (Boyd 2003; Boyd and Young 2002; Menzies 2007; see also Collier and Sheldon 2006). Overall, child custody law based on gender neutrality and formal equality has given fathers more power to lay claim to their children than they had before the law was changed, and with no corresponding increase in their caregiving obligations. Since the 1970s, the percentage of cases in which mothers retain sole custody of children after a separation or divorce by agreement with the fathers has dropped, and, in contested cases, men have a good chance of "winning" either sole or joint custody (Bertoia and Drakich 1993; Bertoia 1998; Boyd 2003: 103–5). Indeed, the number of joint custody awards "rose significantly" during the 1990s, sometimes in the absence of parental agreement and/or evidence of parental ability to cooperate (Boyd 2003: 130). Likewise, since the late 1980s, judicial decisions in cases involving disputes over access of non-custodial fathers to their children often have favoured fathers over mothers (Bourque 1995; Boyd 2003; Taylor, Barnsley, and Goldsmith 1996).

These trends reflect the combined influence of ideologies about family, motherhood, fatherhood and equality on judicial interpretations of the very malleable "best interests of the child" principle (Boyd 2003; Drakich 1989). Taking the nuclear family based on heterosexual marriage as the norm, many judges assume that it is in the best interests of children to have ongoing contact with two opposite-sex, biological parents, and they conceptualize former spouses and their children as a "post-divorce family" (Boyd 1997b, 2003). In Canada and elsewhere, they are handing down judgments about custody and access based on assumptions that children must have a father in their lives and that contemporary men are actually equally involved in parenting their children (Boyd 2003; Drakich 1989). Such decisions not only privilege the traditional nuclear family, but also ignore other pertinent factors: some fathers are bad role models, others are abusive, and most fathers do not contribute equally to the care of their children prior to a separation or divorce (Bourque 1995; Boyd 1997b, 2003; Taylor, Barnsley, and Goldsmith 1996). Moreover, studies of fathers' rights advocates show that they do not necessarily want sole responsibility for children or an equal division of child care and responsibility. Instead, they want either greatly expanded access or equal status as legal parents, which really is a demand "to continue the practice of inequality in post-divorce parenting but now with a legal sanction" (Bertoia and Drakich 1993: 612).

It is too soon to know how judges will interpret the "best interests" principle in determining custody of children when same-sex spouses divorce. Historically, however, the judicial privileging of heterosexual marriage boded ill for a lesbian who left a heterosexual union and ended up in a custody dispute with her former husband. The outcomes in contested cases involving young children through the 1980s after the implementation of gender-neutral law reveal that, regardless of her parenting abilities, a lesbian mother almost always lost custody to the father unless she appeared to fit the norms of the "good" mother — white, middle-class and heterosexual (Arnup 1989; Boyd 2003). The B.C. Supreme Court decision in *Elliott v. Elliott* is one of the most explicit judicial statements on the need for mothers to be, or appear to be, heterosexual (Sage 1987). Mr. Elliott gained custody of his 7-year-old daughter, who had been living with her mother, because Ms. Elliott had established a live-in relationship with a lesbian partner. Clearly equating the "best interests" of the child with a heterosexual family environment, the court said: "Whatever one might accept or privately practise, I cannot conclude that indulging in homosexuality is something for the edification of young children" (Sage 1987: 1, 8). During the 1990s, judicial homophobia did not disappear, but the sanctioning of lesbian mothers became less overt. Judges no longer cited a live-in homosexual relationship as the sole ground for denying a mother custody. Rather, they began to consider the effects of a parent's "lifestyle" on children (Boyd 2003: 111–12).

Ideological assumptions about motherhood, fatherhood and the sexual division of labour also strongly influence judicial interpretations of the "best interests" principle. On one hand, the idea that women's primary work is the altruistic care and nurture of other family members means that judges often equate best interests with the stay-at-home mother. Therefore, a woman who engages in full-time or part-time paid employment in order to support her children — which is increasingly the case even for mothers with young children — may be viewed as abandoning them to pursue her own selfish interests. As a result she may lose custody to her husband, especially if he has a new homemaker-wife, a housekeeper or some other surrogate mother to look after the children (Boyd 1997b, 2003). On the other hand, the idea that men's primary work is to protect and materially provide for other family members means that fathers need only to demonstrate some interest in parenting or do some child care to be seen as "super dads," while the work that many women perform routinely is expected and therefore not specifically noteworthy.

Similar thinking influences judicial application of the "friendly parent" provision in the federal Divorce Act, which directs courts to operate on the principle that children should have as much contact with each parent as is in their "best interests." The onus clearly is on a custodial mother to facilitate contact between children and their father, even if he has been physically or sexually abusive. Otherwise the mother risks losing custody for being uncooperative and putting her own interests before those of the children (Boyd 2003; Rosnes 1997). In *LiSanti v. LiSanti* (1990), for example, the wife took her children to a women's shelter to escape the alleged abuse of her husband, who was then awarded interim custody of the children. According to the court, Mrs. LiSanti's "abrupt departure" was "a complete denial of the husband's custodial rights," and "the best interests of the children, were they ever first considered by her, would have militated against such a result" (*LiSanti v. LiSanti* 1990). Thus, although Canadian law contains no presumption in favour of joint legal custody, women are often forced to accept de facto or formal joint custody arrangements with fathers (Bourque 1995; Boyd 2003). Moreover, fathers' rights advocates increasingly use the discourse of "shared parenting" and "shared responsibility," making it even more difficult for mothers to contest fathers' applications for access or custody without seeming unreasonable (Boyd 2003).

The same ideologies of family, work and equality have governed judges' interpretations of the ostensibly gender-neutral principle of self-sufficiency in decisions about spousal and child support. Clearly, the courts have tended to assume that women and men are equally capable of being self-supporting after marital breakdown, and they have interpreted self-sufficiency not based on a previous standard of living but on earning any sort of living at all. Therefore, although marriage puts most women in a position of economic dependency (both in the family and in the market), the courts have not considered the substantive inequality in the postdivorce economic situations of most women relative to men, and they expect both spouses to achieve financial independence either immediately or in a very short time after the marriage ends. This condition naturalizes the sexual division of labour that "causes" women's economic dependency. Thus, until recently, women's unpaid domestic labour and the wage gap between women and men engaged in paid employment have been largely invisible in judicial decision-making about spousal and child support. Yet many older women have been full-time homeworkers, and many more women have had interruptions in their paid employment and/or have worked part-time in order to care for children during a marriage, with an obvious impact on their earning potential after a separation or divorce (Keet 1990; Morton 1993). In 2008, for example, even women with full-time, full-year paid employment made only 71.4 percent of the earnings of their male counterparts in Canada, and among all earners that year women made just under 64.4 percent as much as men (Cool 2010).

Not surprisingly, women are still much more likely than men to be plunged into poverty when a marriage ends, and since the 1950s, female poverty has increased significantly along with the divorce rate. In 1951, one in every twenty-four marriages ended in divorce; by 1990 the rate was one in every 2.4 marriages (Mossman and MacLean 1997: 119). Moreover, although the number of divorces levelled off during the 1990s and has shown recent declines, it was estimated in 2008 that 41 percent of marriages from that year will end in divorce before the thirtieth year of marriage, "an increase from 36 [percent] in 1998" (Kelly 2012: 2). Therefore, the issue of financial responsibility for an ex-spouse who does not attain self-sufficiency has become a pressing question.

Since the mid-1980s, the Supreme Court of Canada has adopted two different positions in cases in which the spouses themselves agreed to a set time limit on support payments, but one spouse subsequently has asked for continued support. The first involved the application of the so-called "causal connection test," which required the spouse requesting an extended period of support to demonstrate "that he or she has suffered a radical (and unforeseen) change in circumstances flowing from an economic pattern of dependency engendered by the marriage" (Bailey 1989). Because it is difficult to establish, a spouse seeking continued support has often been unable to demonstrate causal connection, and the courts have tended to treat the original spousal agreement as a binding contract with an emphasis on the principle of self-sufficiency and independence.

In contrast, the Supreme Court has adopted a more interventionist stance in some cases in which court-ordered spousal support has ended and the recipient spouse requesting a continuation would otherwise become a state dependant on social assistance. The 1992 Supreme Court decision in *Moge v. Moge* accepted the claim of the ex-wife that her former husband, who had not lived with her for many years, should continue to pay spousal support. For the first time a Canadian court was swayed by the argument that women's unpaid contributions to a marriage, such as domestic labour and childcare, typically were undervalued in spousal support awards and that this undervaluing is linked to greater female poverty as divorce and separation increase. Thus, "the responsibility for women's poverty should rest wherever possible with a man with whom they have had a recognized relationship" (Boyd 1996: 176–77).

Clearly, then, family law reforms promoted by liberal feminists and implemented since the 1960s have continued the historical emphasis on familial responsibility for the costs of reproduction (Fudge 1989). This individualized focus in law and policy has reinforced the public/private distinction and contributed to the impoverishment of women and children (Boyd 1997a). For example, the maintenance-enforcement programs established in some provinces have reduced the default rate on support payments, and the federal Child Support Guidelines adopted in 1997 have set out minimum levels of support; but neither policy can eliminate or even substantially ameliorate poverty, because both spousal and child support awards are generally so low (Eichler 1991; Robson 2004). Emphasizing individual responsibility for the "personal" also pre-empts the creation of new social programs. The use of tax exemptions and/or credits for childcare expenses incurred by parents perpetuates the idea that social reproduction is a private rather than a public concern (Eichler 1997). Moreover, social reproduction remains primarily women's work, because the financial rewards for the work of caring for children are so low that men have no incentive to change the sexual division of labour (Ferguson 1998; Iyer 1997).

The trend to reduce social responsibility for poverty is especially clear in the area of welfare law. Although the "spouse in the house" rule is gender-neutral, it is almost always applied to women receiving welfare benefits who live with men rather than the reverse (Cossman 2002; Carruthers 1995; Martin 1992). A mother on social assistance who lives with an abusive man is often afraid to leave him lest he report the live-in relationship to welfare authorities (Mosher et al. 2004). As well, the 1990s welfare reforms have left virtually no one "deserving" of state assistance. Even mothers of young children are expected to attain self-sufficiency and independence through welfare to work programs or, alternatively, to obtain support from non-state sources such as ex-spouses and other family members or through another spousal relationship (Mosher et al. 2004; see also Chunn and Gavigan 2004; Klein and Long 2003; Mosher's chapter here).

Finally, like their first-wave precursors, liberal feminists did not anticipate the differential impact of the family-related legislation and policies they promoted. Again, white, middle-class, and upper-class heterosexual women and, to a lesser extent, their counterparts in the more affluent sectors of the working class have benefited the most overall from the reordering of family law since the 1960s. Poor women and/or racialized women, Aboriginal women and women with disabilities have been disproportionately less able to use legislation and policies based on gender-neutrality and formal equality (Andrew and Rodgers 1997; Boyd 1997a).[4]

Class differences are important in relation to property, for instance. A deferred property regime is of little relevance to many couples who have no property to split when their relationship dissolves. Or, if common property exists, it is most often a house with a mortgage, so there is nothing to divide except mutual debt. Similarly, child and spousal support obligations imposed on the working poor may mean that two families are impoverished rather than one (Mossman and MacLean 1997).

Childcare policies generate the same disparities. During the 1980s, only slightly more than 50 percent of pregnant women in paid employment claimed maternity benefits under unemployment insurance, probably because the benefit was so low that only women and/or couples with a good income to begin with could afford to do so. The situation is even worse under the Employment Insurance Act because the benefit remains low (55 percent of insurable earnings), eligibility is based on hours and not weeks worked, and the weekly payment has been reduced over time with a maximum of weekly benefit rate in 2015 of only $524 (Iyer 1997: 187; Madsen 2002: 40–43; Service Canada 2014). Without an employer or personal savings top-up, the maternity and parental leave program is not an option for many women. Similarly, tax credits and exemptions for childcare are most helpful to more affluent professional women and couples who can afford to hire domestic workers or support a stay-at-home mother (Macklin 1992). None of these programs are especially accessible for single, low-income parents, most of whom are women and/or members of racial and ethnic minorities (Madsen 2002: 47). Moreover, the growing reliance of affluent families on poor, racialized women to provide childcare has created conflicts among feminists about the exploitation of some women by other, more privileged women (Arat-Koç 1990; Bakan and Stasiulis 1997).

Undeniably, second-wave feminist support for individualized solutions to the problem of women's subordination has helped some women. At the same time it is painfully apparent that a diversity of Canadian women face difficulties that simply were not part of the picture of women painted by the 1970 *Royal Commission on the Status of Women* (Andrew and Rodgers 1997; Bannerji 1993; George 1998; Herman 1994; Monture-Angus 1995; Razack 1998; Wendell 1996). The negative and differential effects of family related reforms promoted by second-wave feminists reflect, in part, some "fatal flaws" of the liberal-feminist approach.

First, liberal feminism does not problematize the state, law and family. Liberal conceptions of these institutions — the state as "umpire," law as the protector of equality rights, the family as nuclear and private — are taken as givens. They are viewed as homogeneous rather than differentiated and contradictory, timeless as opposed to historically and culturally bounded. Because of a singular focus on enabling women to act and be the same as men, liberal feminism also tends to conceptualize sex and gender in terms of a simple nature/nurture dichotomy. Since biology is not destiny, it is differential socialization of women and men on the basis of biological characteristics that has created sex inequality, which, in turn, is sustained through discriminatory law and policy.

This conceptualization of gender equates socialization with passivity (that is, the individual is acted upon), assumes that socialization is the same for all women and for all men, and ignores the contexts of socialization (Connell 2009). Thus, liberal feminists do not see the need to analyze the structural embeddedness of patriarchal relations in state, law and family; the different forms and content of patriarchal relations in different types of social organization; or how differences generated by race, ethnicity, class, sexual orientation and disability shape the social construction of gender. Consequently, they cannot explain the state's role in (re) producing gender relations and the privatization of the reproductive sphere or how patriarchal discourses and ideologies are reflected in and (re)produced through law.

Second, the liberal-feminist explanation of women's subordination is premised on a conceptualization of inequality as unequal opportunity and access to the world of men. From this perspective, the liberal, capitalist state is basically sound, and achieving equality for women is a matter of addition and subtraction: (re)socialize women to be more "masculine" and men more "feminine"; move (married) women into paid labour; and implement reforms to entrench and guarantee sex equality. Although it implicitly challenges the sexual division of labour, this approach to women's liberation rests on an acceptance of the public/private split and leaves it intact. Simply moving women into paid work does not lead to equality. Most women straddle the production/reproduction divide, and they confront structured inequality on both sides: low-paid clerical and service work and unpaid domestic work (the double day). This structured inequality cannot be rectified by piecemeal reform and (re)socialization. Women's oppression can only be eradicated through systemic change that will not only challenge patriarchal ideologies and discourses but also transform the nuclear family form that sustains them.

PROSPECTS FOR "REFORM" IN THE NEO-LIBERAL STATE

The problem for feminists is how to mount such a challenge in the climate of neo-liberalism. While liberal feminism helped to create the reform agenda for the second wave of the women's movement during the 1970s and 1980s, the nature of both the productive process and the state has undergone transformations. "Vampire capitalism" has replaced welfare capitalism through globalization — which entails the radically increased mobility of capital and the international organization of production and distribution — and through restructuring — which involves the reordering of national economic, social and political systems in keeping with the values of globalization and transnational capital (Cohen 1997: 30). In Canada, as elsewhere, this highly gendered development has brought about significant changes in social relations and women's structural position as well as a very different landscape for the feminist engagement with the state to address women's subordination. The "playing field" has been transformed, and even the limited redistributive gains made by second-wave feminists are now being attacked and eroded. Feminists find themselves engaged in "politics on the margins" as they try to defend what is left of the paternalistic welfare state that they critiqued so strongly in the past (Bezanson 2006; Bezanson and Luxton 2006; Braedley and Luxton 2010; Brodie 1995).

A central task for feminists is to challenge the neo-liberal idea that now pervades public culture — the idea of "the 'inevitability' of the market as the main regulator of social life" (Cohen 1997: 30; Cohen and Brodie 2007; Cohen and Pulkingham 2009; Siltanen 2002). In the context of 1960s liberal optimism and with the best of intentions, second-wave liberal feminists sought to achieve women's equality through the implementation of legislation and policies based on a non-interventionist state, gender-neutral law and an egalitarian model of the nuclear family. The neo-liberal twist on these conceptualizations of state, law and family — embodied in notions of the genderless international citizen and privatization — has rendered structured inequality and women/gender invisible (Cossman and Fudge 2002; Wiegers 2002). While an anti-feminist backlash has diluted and even erased the feminist impact on contemporary law and policy, many feminists continue to see law and the state as critical sites of struggle against the new world order (Brodie 1995; Chunn, Boyd, and Lessard 2007; Chunn and Gavigan 2004; Cohen and Brodie 2007; Cossman and Fudge 2002). Nonetheless, it is also clear that sociolegal reforms per se cannot end women's subordination; women cannot litigate their way to substantive equality. Therefore, feminists must think carefully about the unintended as well as intended consequences of the reforms they advocate and strategize about how they can inject potentially transgressive proposals for family related law and policy into the political and public cultures (Boyd 1997a; Cossman and Fudge 2002; Luxton 2011).

Specifically, feminists need to engage with state power at all levels, defend what remains of the welfare state, and advocate reforms that challenge and subvert the privileged status of the traditional nuclear family model in law and policy. While there is no blueprint for change, feminists could pursue a number of existing proposals for family related legislation and policies that would contribute to the implementation of a "social responsibility" model of family; one that focuses on "minimizing inequalities that are the result of being married or being a parent instead of on [formal] equality" (Eichler 1997: 130). In the area of custody and access, linking the "best interests of the child principle" to "a meaningful and progressive 'pro-family' social policy" could be a step in that direction. Placing caregiving/domestic work in the context of social responsibility for children would help to deprivatize the work of social reproduction, which historically has been taken for granted and rendered invisible (Boyd 2003: 224). It would also take the pressure off individual mothers who have been penalized historically if they do not meet the expectations of "good motherhood" encapsulated in the traditional nuclear model of family (Boyd 1997b: 272; Mosoff 1997).

Other reforms would also challenge the historical onus on the (private) family to assume the costs of reproduction (Cossman and Fudge 2002). For instance, the total elimination of the sexist and paternalistic elements in welfare law and its administration — particularly the "spouse in the house rule" — would improve the financial and legal position of sole-support mothers (Gavigan 1993, 1999). Another change that would benefit many women and children would be to end the policy of provincial governments whereby any income that a welfare recipient receives from sources such as child support payments and the child tax benefit is automatically deducted from social assistance payments (Wiegers 2002). An even more comprehensive reform would entail the implementation of a state-subsidized system of child support that would guarantee a minimum income, not only to lone-parent families but also to parents in low-income families regardless of marital status. This reform would address the issue of child poverty, which cannot be resolved through child and spousal support payments alone (Eichler 1997: 155–56; Wiegers 2002).

Legislation and programs recognizing the inextricable links between women's paid and unpaid work and explicitly challenging the sexual division of labour would also help establish social responsibility for reproduction in Canada. While policies such as pay and employment equity aimed at creating equality of opportunity for women (and other equity-seekers) may benefit those who have "good" jobs in the public sector or in large firms, they do nothing for the majority of people entering a deteriorating labour market — people who only have equal opportunity to find "bad" jobs. To address the inequalities that women confront in both the home and paid employment we need reforms to labour law and policy that recognize the gendered nature of work and the political will of the state "to regulate the labour market in a way that minimizes competition and exploitation at the bottom" (Fudge 1996: 261–63; see also Cohen and Pulkingham 2009). In addition, specific policies, such as a national daycare plan that is not implemented through contracting out to private, non-unionized agencies, would help to socialize the costs of reproduction and to address women's inequality (Friendly and Prentice 2009). Similarly, reforms to maternity and parental leave programs that raise the monetary benefits and increase the length of the leave period would make them accessible to those women (and men) who cannot afford to take leave under existing programs (Calder 2006; Iyer 1997; Madsen 2002).

Obtaining legislation and policies based on a social responsibility model of family would go some way towards the deconstruction of the neo-liberal agenda and the regressive conceptualizations of state, law and family that underpin it. Working alone and in alliances with other equality-seeking groups, feminists can mount powerful ideological and political resistance to the status quo. The market as social regulator is not inevitable. Substantive equality for all women and men can be achieved.

Notes

I am indebted to Elizabeth Comack for her excellent editing skills, good humour and forbearance.

1   The Civil Marriage Act (SC 2005 c.33) went into effect on July 20, 2005. The Act extended equal access to civil marriage to same-sex couples.

2   A comprehensive review of feminist impact on family related law and policy is beyond the scope of this chapter. Instead, I draw on selected examples to illuminate the intended and unintended effects of socio-legal reforms in this area over time.

3   In English Canada there is also a two-tiered system of family law based on jurisdiction. The federal government exercises jurisdiction over marriage and divorce. The provinces are responsible for the solemnization of marriage and the administration of justice. In Quebec, family law and policy are based on the Civil Code of Quebec (SQ 1991, c.64), which was inherited from France.

4   However, it is important to note that, like women, other historically disadvantaged groups in Canada have achieved formal equality since the 1960s. For instance, lesbians and gay men obtained legal recognition of their formal equality rights with respect to family and same-sex marriage in a decade. See Young and Boyd (2006) for a feminist analysis of the contradictory effects of those reforms.

References

Adamson, Nancy, Linda Briskin, and Margaret McPhail. 1988. *Feminist Organizing for Change: The Contemporary Women's Movement in Canada*. Toronto: Oxford University Press.

Andrew, Caroline. 1984. "Women and the Welfare State." *Canadian Journal of Political Science* 17.

Andrew, Caroline, and Sandra Rodgers (eds.). 1997. *Women and the Canadian State*. Montreal: McGill-Queen's University Press.

Arat-Koç, Sedef. 1990. "Importing Housewives: Non-Citizen Domestic Workers and the Crisis of the Domestic Sphere in Canada." In Meg Luxton, Harriet Rosenberg, and Sedef Arat-Koç (eds.), *Through the Kitchen Window: The Politics of Home and Family* (2nd ed.). Toronto: Garamond.

Arnup, Katherine. 1989. "'Mothers Just Like Others': Lesbians, Divorce and Child Custody in Canada." *Canadian Journal of Women and the Law* 3.

Bacchi, Carol Lee. 1983. *Liberation Deferred? The Ideas of the English-Canadian Suffragists, 1877–1918*. Toronto: University of Toronto Press.

Backhouse, Constance. 1991. *Petticoats and Prejudice: Women and Law in Nineteenth-Century*

Canada. Toronto: Osgoode Society.

____. 1992. "Married Women's Property Law in Nineteenth-Century Canada." In Bettina Bradbury (ed.), *Canadian Family History: Selected Readings.* Toronto: Copp Clark Pitman.

Bailey, Martha J. 1989. "Pelech, Caron, and Richardson." *Canadian Journal of Women and the Law* 3, 2 (December).

Bakan, Abigail and Daiva Stasiulis (eds.). 1997. *Not One of the Family: Foreign Domestic Workers in Canada.* Toronto: University of Toronto Press.

Bannerji, Himani (ed.). 1993. *Returning the Gaze: Essays on Racism, Feminism and Politics.* Toronto: Sister Vision Press.

Barrett, Michele, and Mary McIntosh. 1982. *The Anti-Social Family.* London: Verso and NLB.

Bertoia, Carl. 1998. "An Interpretive Analysis of the Mediation Rhetoric of Fathers' Rightists: Privatization Versus Personalization." *Mediation Quarterly* 16, 1.

Bertoia, Carl, and Janice Drakich. 1993. "The Fathers' Rights Movement: Contradictions in Rhetoric and Practice." *Journal of Family Issues* 14, 4.

Bezanson, Kate. 2006. *Gender, the State and Social Reproduction: Household Insecurity in Neo-Liberal Times.* Toronto, ON: University of Toronto Press.

Bezanson, Kate, and Meg Luxton (eds.). 2006. *Social Reproduction: Feminist Political Economy Challenges Neo-Liberalism.* Montreal: McGill-Queen's University Press.

Bourque, Dawn. 1995. "'Reconstructing' the Patriarchal Nuclear Family: Recent Developments in Child Custody and Access in Canada." *Canadian Journal of Law and Society* 10, 1.

Boyd, Susan B. 1996. "Can Law Challenge the Public/Private Divide? Women, Work, and Family." *Windsor Yearbook of Access to Justice* 15.

____. (ed.). 1997a. *Challenging the Public/Private Divide: Feminism, Law, and Public Policy.* Toronto: University of Toronto Press.

____. 1997b. "Looking Beyond Tyabji: Employed Mothers, Lifestyles, and Child Custody Law." In Susan B. Boyd (ed.), *Challenging the Public/Private Divide.* Toronto: University of Toronto Press.

____. 2003. *Child Custody, Law, and Women's Work.* Toronto: Oxford University Press.

Boyd, Susan B., and Elizabeth A. Sheehy. 1986. "Feminist Perspectives on Law." *Canadian Journal of Women and the Law* 2, 1.

Boyd, Susan B., and Claire Young. 2002. "Who Influences Family Law Reform? Discourses on Motherhood and Fatherhood in Legislative Reform Debates in Canada." *Studies in Law, Politics and Society* 26.

Braedley, Susan, and Meg Luxton (eds.). 2010. *Neoliberalism and Everyday Life.* Montreal: McGill-Queen's University Press.

Brodie, Janine. 1995. Politics on the Margins: Restructuring and the Canadian Women's Movement. Halifax: Fernwood Publishing

Brophy, Julia, and Carol Smart (eds.). 1985. *Women-in-Law.* London: Routledge and Kegan Paul.

Busby, Karen, Lisa Fainstein, and Holly Penner (eds.). 1990. *Equality Issues in Family Law.* Winnipeg: Legal Research Institute of the University of Manitoba.

Calder, Gillian. 2006. "A Pregnant Pause: Federalism, Equality and the Maternity and Parental Leave Debate in Canada." *Feminist Legal Studies* 14.

Canada. 1970. *Report of the Royal Commission on the Status of Women*. Ottawa: Queen's Printer.

Carruthers, E. 1995. "Prosecuting Women for Welfare Fraud in Ontario: Implications for Equality." *Journal of Law & Social Policy* 11.

Carter, Sarah. 2008. *The Importance of Being Monogamous: Marriage and Nation Building in Western Canada to 1915*. Edmonton: University of Alberta Press.

Chambers, Anne Lorene. 1997. *Married Women and Property Law in Victorian Ontario*. Toronto, ON: University of Toronto Press. Published for the Osgoode Society for Canadian Legal History.

Christie, Nancy. 2000. *Engendering the State: Family, Work, and Welfare in Canada*. Toronto: University of Toronto Press.

Chunn, Dorothy E. 1990. "Boys Will Be Men, Girls Will Be Mothers: The Regulation of Childhood in Vancouver and Toronto." *Sociological Studies in Childhood Development* 3.

____. 1992. *From Punishment to Doing Good: Family Courts and Socialized Justice in Ontario 1880–1940*. Toronto: University of Toronto Press.

Chunn, Dorothy E., Susan B. Boyd, and Hester Lessard (eds.). 2007. *Reaction and Resistance: Feminism, Law and Social Change*. Vancouver, BC: UBC Press.

Chunn, Dorothy E., and Shelley A.M. Gavigan. 2004. "Welfare Law, Welfare Fraud, and the Moral Regulation of the 'Never Deserving' Poor." *Social & Legal Studies* 13, 2 (June).

____ (eds.). 2012. *The Legal Tender of Gender: Welfare, Law, and the Regulation of Women's Poverty*. Oxford: Hart Publishing.

Chunn, Dorothy E., and Dany Lacombe. 2000. "Introduction." In Dorothy E. Chunn and Dany Lacombe (eds.), *Law as a Gendering Practice*. Toronto: Oxford University Press.

Cohen, Marjorie Griffen. 1997. "From the Welfare State to Vampire Capitalism." In Patricia Evans and Gerda Wekerle (eds.), *Women and the Canadian Welfare State*. Toronto: University of Toronto Press.

Cohen, Marjorie G., and Janine Brodie. 2007. *Remapping Gender in the New Global Order*. New York: Routledge.

Cohen, Marjorie G., and Jane Pulkingham (eds.). 2009. *Public Policy for Women: The State, Income Security, and Labour Market Issues*. Toronto, ON: University of Toronto Press.

Collier, Richard, and Sally Sheldon (eds.). 2006. *Fathers' Rights Activism and Law Reform in Comparative Perspective*. Oxford: Hart.

Connell, Raewyn. 2009. *Gender in World Perspective* (2d ed.). Cambridge: Polity Press.

Cool, Julie. 2010. *Wage Gap Between Women and Men*. Ottawa, ON: Library of Parliament Research Publications.

Cossman, Brenda. 2002. "Family Feuds: Neo-Liberal and Neo-Conservative Visions of the Reprivatization Project." In Brenda Cossman and Judy Fudge (eds.), *Privatization, Law, and the Challenge to Feminism*. Toronto: University of Toronto Press.

Cossman, Brenda, and Judy Fudge (eds.). 2002. *Privatization, Law, and the Challenge to Feminism*. Toronto: University of Toronto Press.

Dale, Jennifer, and Peggy Foster. 1986. *Feminists and State Welfare*. London: Routledge and Kegan Paul.

Donzelot, Jacques. 1980. *The Policing of Families*. New York: Pantheon.

Drakich, Janice. 1989. "In Search of the Better Parent: The Social Construction of Ideologies of Fatherhood." *Canadian Journal of Women and the Law* 3, 1.

Eichler, Margrit. 1991. "The Limits of Family Law Reform, or the Privatization of Female and Child Poverty." *Canadian Family Law Quarterly* 7.

____. 1997. *Family Shifts: Families, Policies, and Gender Equality*. Toronto: Oxford University Press.

Ferguson, Evelyn. 1998. "The Child-Care Debate: Facing Hopes and Shifting Sands." In Baines, Carol, Sheila Neysmith, Patricia Evans (eds.), *Women's Caring: Feminist Perspectives on Social Welfare* (2nd. edition). Toronto: Oxford University Press.

Friendly, Martha, and Susan Prentice. 2009. *About Canada: Childcare*. Halifax and Winnipeg: Fernwood Publishing.

Fudge, Judy. 1989. "The Privatization of the Costs of Reproduction." *Canadian Journal of Women and the Law* 3.

____. 1996. "Rungs on the Labour Law Ladder: Using Gender to Challenge Hierarchy." *Saskatchewan Law Review* 60.

Garland, David. 1985. *Punishment and Welfare*. Brookfield, VT: Gower.

Gavigan, Shelley A.M. 1988. "Law, Gender and Ideology." In Anne F. Bayefsky (ed.), *Legal Theory Meets Legal Practice*. Edmonton: Academic Printers and Publishing.

____. 1993. "Paradise Lost, Paradox Revisited: The Implications of Familial Ideology for Feminist, Lesbian, and Gay Engagement to Law." *Osgoode Hall Law Journal* 31, 3.

____. 1995. "A Parent(ly) Knot: Can Heather Have Two Mommies?" In Didi Herman and Carl F. Stychin (eds.), *Legal Inversions: Lesbians, Gay Men and the Politics of Law*. Philadelphia: Temple University Press.

____. 1999. "Legal Form, Family Forms, and Gender Norms: What Is a Spouse?" *Canadian Journal of Law & Society* 14.

Gavigan, Shelley A.M., and Dorothy E. Chunn. 2007. "From Mothers' Allowance to Mothers Need Not Apply: Canadian Welfare Law as Liberal and Neo-Liberal Reforms." *Osgoode Hall Law Journal* 45, 4.

George, Usha. 1998. "Caring and Women of Colour: Living the Intersecting Oppressions of Race, Class, and Gender." In Carol Baines, Patricia Evans, and Sheila Neysmith (eds.), *Women's Caring* (2nd edition). Toronto: Oxford University Press.

Gordon, Linda (ed.). 1990. *Women, the State and Welfare*. Madison, WI: University of Wisconsin Press.

Herman, Didi. 1994. *Rights of Passage: Struggles for Lesbian and Gay Legal Equality*. Toronto: University of Toronto Press.

Holland, Winnifred. 2000. "Intimate Relationships in the New Millenium: The Assimilation of Marriage and Cohabitation?" *Canadian Journal of Family Law* 17, 1.

Iyer, Nitya. 1997. "Some Mothers Are Better Than Others: A Re-examination of Maternity Benefits." In Susan. B. Boyd (ed.), *Challenging the Public/Private Divide*. Toronto: University of Toronto Press.

Keet, Jean. 1990. "The Law Reform Process, Matrimonial Property, and Farm Women: A Case Study of Saskatchewan, 1980–1986." *Canadian Journal of Women and the Law* 4, 1.

Kelly, Mary B. 2012. *Divorce Cases in Civil Court, 2010/2011*. Ottawa, ON: Statistics Canada.

Kieran, Sheila. 1986. *The Family Matters: Two Centuries of Family Law and Life in Ontario*. Toronto: Key Porter.

Klein, Seth and Andrea Long. 2003. *A Bad Time to Be Poor*. Vancouver: Canadian Centre for Policy Alternatives-BC.

Landsberg, Michele. 2012. *Writing the Revolution*. Ottawa, ON: Feminist History Society.

Little, Margaret. 1998. *No Car, No Radio, No Liquor Permit: The Moral Regulation of Single Mothers in Ontario, 1920-1997*. Toronto: Oxford University Press.

Luxton, Meg. 2011. *Changing Families, New Understandings*. Ottawa: Vanier Institute of the Family.

Macklin, Audrey. 1992. "*Symes v. M.N.R.*: Where Sex Meets Class." *Canadian Journal of Women and the Law* 5, 2.

Madsen, Lene. 2002. "Citizen, Worker, Mother: Canadian Women's Claims to Parental Leave and Childcare." *Canadian Journal of Family Law* 19.

Martin, Dianne L. 1992. "Passing the Buck: Prosecution of Welfare Fraud; Preservation of Stereotypes." *Windsor Yearbook of Access to Justice* 12.

McClung, Nellie. 1976. "What Will They Do with It?" In Ramsay Cook and Wendy Mitchinson (eds.), *The Proper Sphere*. Toronto: University of Toronto Press.

McCormack, Thelma. 1991. *Politics and the Hidden Injuries of Gender: Feminism and the Making of the Welfare State*. Ottawa: CRIAW/ICREF.

Menzies, Robert. 2007. "Virtual Backlash: Representations of Men's 'Rights' and Women's 'Wrongs' in Cyberspace." In Dorothy E. Chunn, Susan B. Boyd, and Hester Lessard (eds.), *Reaction and Resistance: Feminism, Law, and Social Change*. Vancouver: UBC Press.

Monture, Patricia. 1989. "A Vicious Circle: Child Welfare and the First Nations." *Canadian Journal of Women and the Law* 3, 1.

Monture-Angus, Patricia. 1995. *Thunder in My Soul: A Mohawk Woman Speaks*. Halifax: Fernwood Publishing.

Mosoff, Judith. 1997. "'A Jury Dressed in Medical White and Judicial Black': Mothers with Mental Health Histories in Child Welfare and Custody." In Susan B. Boyd (ed.), *Challenging the Public/Private Divide: Feminism, Law, and Public Policy*. Toronto: University of Toronto Press.

Morton, Mary E. 1988. "Dividing the Wealth, Sharing the Poverty: The (Re)formation of 'Family' in Law in Ontario." *Canadian Review of Sociology and Anthropology* 25, 2.

____. 1993. "The Cost of Sharing, the Price of Caring: Problems in the Determination of 'Equity' in Family Maintenance and Support." In Joan Brockman and Dorothy E. Chunn (eds.), *Investigating Gender Bias in Law: Socio-Legal Perspectives*. Toronto: Thompson Educational Publishing.

Moscovitch, Allan, and Jim Albert (eds.). 1987. *The 'Benevolent' State: The Growth of Welfare in Canada*. Toronto: Garamond Press.

Mosher, Janet, Patricia Evans, Margaret Little, Eileen Morrow, Jo-Anne Boulding, and Nancy VanderPlaats. 2004. *Walking on Eggshells: Abused Women's Experiences of Ontario's Welfare System*. Toronto. <dawn.thot.net/abuse.html>.

Mossman, Mary Jane, and Morag MacLean. 1986. "Family Law and Social Welfare: Toward a New Equality." *Canadian Journal of Family Law* 5.

____. 1997. "Family Law and Social Assistance Programs: Rethinking Equality." In Patricia M. Evans and Gerda R. Wekerle (eds.), *Women and the Canadian Welfare State*. Toronto: University of Toronto Press.

Razack, Sherene. 1998. *Looking White People in the Eye: Gender, Race, and Culture in Courtrooms and Classrooms*. Toronto: University of Toronto Press.

Roberts, Wayne. 1979. "'Rocking the Cradle for the World': The New Woman and Maternal

Feminism, Toronto, 1877–1914." In Linda Kealey (ed.), *A Not Unreasonable Claim*. Toronto: Women's Press.

Robson, Krista. 2004. "Unfair Guidelines: A Critical Analysis of the Federal Child Support Guidelines." *Journal of the Association for Research on Mothering* 6, 1.

Rosenberg, Harriet. 1990. "The Home Is the Workplace: Hazards, Stress and Pollutants in the Household." In M, Luxton, H. Rosenberg, and S. Arat-Koç (eds.), *Through the Kitchen Window*. Toronto: Garamond Press.

Rosnes, Melanie. 1997. "The Invisibility of Male Violence in Canadian Child Custody and Access Decision-Making." *Canadian Journal of Family Law* 14, 1.

Ross, Becki L. 1995. *The House That Jill Built: A Lesbian Nation in Formation*. Toronto: University of Toronto Press.

Sage, Barbara. 1987. "B.C. Lesbian Mother Denied Custody of Daughter." *The Lawyers' Weekly* 6, 38.

Service Canada. 2014. "Employment Insurance — Important Notice about Maximum Insurable Earnings for 2015." <servicecanada.gc.ca/eng/ei/information/maximum2015.shtml>.

Siltanen, Janet. 2002. "Paradise Paved? Reflections on the Fate of Social Citizenship in Canada." *Citizenship Studies* 6, 4.

Snell, James G. 1991. *In the Shadow of the Law: Divorce in Canada, 1900–1939*. Toronto: University of Toronto Press.

Strong-Boag, Veronica. 1979. "'Wages for Housework': Mothers' Allowances and the Beginnings of Social Security in Canada." *Journal of Canadian Studies* 14, 1.

Taylor, Georgina, Jan Barnsley, and Penny Goldsmith. 1996. *Women and Children Last: Custody Disputes and the Family Justice System*. Vancouver: Vancouver Custody and Access Support and Advocacy Association.

Turpel, Mary Ellen. 1991. "Home/Land." *Canadian Journal of Family Law* 10, 1.

Ursel, Jane. 1992. *Private Lives, Public Policy: 100 Years of State Intervention in the Family*. Toronto: Women's Press.

Wendell, Susan. 1996. *Rejected Body: Feminist Philosophical Reflections on Disability*. New York: Routledge.

Wiegers, Wanda. 2002. *The Framing of Poverty as "Child Poverty" and Its Implications for Women*. Ottawa: Status of Women Canada.

Cases Cited

LiSanti v. LiSanti, 1990, 24 RFL (3d) 178 (OPC)

Maw v. Maw, [1985] 44 RFL (2d) 364 (BCSC)

Murdoch v. Murdoch, (1973), 41 DLR (3d) 367 (SCC)

Murdoch v. Murdoch, [1975] 1 SCR 423

Chapter 5

IN DEFIANCE OF COMPULSORY MOTHERING

Voluntarily Childfree Women's Resistance

Debra Mollen

From: *Victim No More: Women's Resistance to Law, Culture and Power*, pp. 138–151 (reprinted with permission).

Feminists, as Carolyn Morell cogently argues, have had a capricious relationship with resistance. Perhaps this is because of what resistance commands. Resistance necessitates questioning, action and subversion. It demands a challenging of the status quo and requires effort and impetus. Resistance's antithesis — reception — connotes accession and does not demand such motility. Resistance might be especially pernicious when acted upon by members of disenfranchised groups because of the potential for harm.

This chapter focuses on the lives of nine voluntarily childfree women and how they have resisted the traditional role of women as mothers. Because of the significant social sanctioning of pronatalism, the degree of resistance women need to forge in the face of pressures to become mothers is often substantial. As "woman" and "mother" are still largely conceptualized synonymously, particularly in pronatalist countries, the act of resisting motherhood requires a kind of gender rebellion. In many cases, this rebellion begins in the earliest stages of gender identity development and traverses a lifetime. Legal implications in the face of mounting restrictions in access to contraception and abortion in the United States are also addressed.

IMAGES AND CONCEPTUALIZATIONS OF CHILDFREEDOM

Women who choose not to have children violate a gender norm so implicit in our culture that there is a dearth of suitable language to use in the discourse (Lisle 1999). "Childless" more often conjures images of those who cannot — not those who wish not to — have children. Stories of barren women like Rachel in the Bible are replete with shame and guilt, while several childfree characters in Greek mythology are seen as warriors marked by heroism and chastity. Freud equated normal female development with motherhood. He wrote, "Her new relation to her father may start by having as its content a wish to have a penis at her disposal, but it culminates in another wish — to have a baby from him as a gift" (Freud 1949: 77). William Inge, the 1950s-era U.S. playwright, created several leading characters who were childfree wives. They were seen as "lonely, disillusioned, narcissistic, unfulfilled, sexually frustrated (or inadequate), unhappily married, immature, and psychologically maladjusted" (Koprince 2000: 252). As Lisle (1999: 66) lamented, the profile of the childfree woman "has left us with a heritage that is both troubling and inspiring, one composed of expansive archetypes and constrictive stereotypes … in an idealized or demonized form, a saint or a devil but rarely as normal or fulfilled."

Politicians and religious leaders have extolled the virtues of parenthood. Frequently, political enthusiasm for parenting emerges on the heels of periods of great feminist activity and has racist, ethnocentric nuances that translate to backlash for women and ethnic minorities. In 1903, Theodore Roosevelt condemned white women for not procreating, fearful of the influx of immigrants (Griffin 1996). In a 1905 speech to the National Congress of Mothers, Roosevelt analogized women's obligation to have a minimum of six children to men's responsibilities to fight for the country. To abstain from childbirth was a selfish act (Lisle 1999). While such overt pronatalist directives might seem dated, nearly all United States presidential campaigns in the past twenty years have continued to depict the ubiquitous representation of adults who have children (Clausen 2002). The needs and concerns of adults without children continue to be disregarded (Burkett 2000; Clausen 2002).

More recently, a professor of biblical studies lamented about the freedom those who choose not to have children relish: "Such couples forget that true freedom is service to Christ, and that God knows better than we what makes for true happiness" (Van Leeuwen 2003: 24). In California, Reverend Sun Myung Moon unashamedly remarked to a group of two thousand people that all women should bear children and should a woman choose not to have a child, "I'm sorry to say, you're disqualified as a woman" (Lattin 2001: A28). In other words, a woman's very legitimacy may be called into question should she subvert and refuse to become a mother.

RESEARCH FINDINGS ON CHILDFREEDOM

There is substantial research support for the notion that childfree adults are perceived less favorably than their parenting peers. LaMastro (2001) studied 254 undergraduate students to determine perceptions of childfree people. Participants read short passages about married couples who had no, one, two or six children. They were queried regarding whether they believed the couple had freely chosen their family size and then asked to respond to a series of statements about reasons for the attributions they made. Results indicated that perceptions of childfree adults were more negative than for parents and, regardless of whether their childfreedom was assumed to be voluntary or involuntary, adults without children were perceived as less caring, sensitive and kind than parents.

Mueller and Yoder (1999) studied childfree women and found they were stigmatized as being unhappily married, selfish, too career-involved, not nurturing and irresponsible. Likewise, Park (2002) found that the childfree participants in her study were regarded as being self-centred, cold, materialistic and strange. Two feminist academics (Letherby and Williams 1999) who drew on their own life experiences as childfree women, provided accounts in which they felt challenged, intruded upon with unsolicited advice and comments, and seen as selfish and worthy of pity. Both women found themselves excluded from conversations with colleagues and friends, which tend to focus nearly exclusively on children.

MANAGING STIGMA

Riessman (2000) discussed the implications of stigma among women from South India. She conducted interviews with thirty-one married women without children to gain understanding about how they construct their lives, their reasons for not having children and the social support available to them considering their unconventional lifestyle. Nearly all the participants reported feeling marginalized by others, with those from the lowest socio-economic backgrounds experiencing the most intense reactions. Those from exceptionally impoverished homes reported feeling dismayed at being called *machi*, a word meaning a farm animal that cannot breed. Those from economically privileged backgrounds managed to avoid such harsh characterization but stated that they still experienced invasive questions about childbearing that many found insulting. Coping with stigma ranged from remaining silent to engaging in resistant thinking and strategic avoidance of people and settings where criticisms were likely to flourish.

Morell (1993) interviewed thirty-four intentionally childfree women between the ages of forty and seventy-eight. While there was considerable diversity among the women's individual autobiographies, the author noted the presence of subversive desires in all the interviews. The women all expressed the wish for something beyond what is normally deemed appropriate for their gender. They wanted self-expression, autonomy, education and economic independence. Challenging the stereotype that women who do not want children are upper-middle-class, Morell (1993) found that almost 75 percent of the women she interviewed came from poor or working-class backgrounds and expressed some desire for class mobility and for opportunities and experiences typically not available to them. She concluded by discussing the resistance needed to overcome traditional gender role expectations regarding motherhood.

Byrne (2000: 14) studied childfree single women living in Ireland to determine how they managed the stigma of their relationship status. She wrote: "Groups of people are stigmatized on the basis that they share social or personal characteristics which cause others to exclude them from normal social interaction. The characteristics are regarded as problematic in that they disrupt the basis of expected behavior" (Byrne 2000:14). Byrne found that the women were regularly asked about their single status, including their childfreedom. She found that the women were frequently discredited in conversations with women who were parents, who insisted that the women could not possibly understand what is involved in childcare. In her study, Byrne found that single women employ various strategies to manage stigma, including refuting the importance of the stigmatized social identity, refusing to adhere to the stereotyped representation of the stigma and becoming comfortable with the identity that they choose.

GENDER IDENTITY AND GENDER ROLE RESISTANCE

Gender identity refers "not only to an individual's sense of self as a man or woman but also to his or her global sense of masculinity or femininity" (O'Heron and Orlofsky 1990: 134). Choosing not to live within culturally prescribed notions of gender can have an enduring impact on how one is viewed in the world. Resisting traditional gender conceptualizations is often cause for societal rejection and alienation, and can demand resilience and a measured defiance.

Relatedly, Abrams (2003) studied two groups of adolescent girls from distinctive communities in the San Francisco Bay Area to determine what strategies they employed for empowerment and resisting gender-based stereotypes as they formulated their gender identities. The author found that many of the adolescent girls actively resisted gender stereotypes by adopting more masculine forms of behaviour. She wrote that some of the girls "looked toward attributes of the 'masculine' such as physical strength and economic control, to transform the 'feminine' into a more privileged and powerful position" (Abrams 2003: 69).

In her study of fourteen women who self-identified as having been tomboys in childhood, Carr (1998: 549) remarked that "agency can emerge through resistance to gender socialization or norms." She surmised that the role of volition developed as her participants refused to give in to socially mandated gender roles. Like West and Zimmerman (1987), Carr rejected the notion of either passive acceptance of gender roles or deterministic biological differences, and embraced instead the component of choice in forging identity. In her study of twenty-six adolescent girls from two neighbouring communities, Williams (2002) also found the notion of "trying on gender," of girls experimenting with various roles, including the role of resistance to traditional expectations for females. She found that "resistance is evident as they test boundaries and assert themselves into male-defined territories" (Williams 2002: 36). Mandel and Shakeshaft (2000: 87) studied middle school youth and found that a small portion of adolescent girls rejected traditional definitions of femininity and that they "were often perceived as unfeminine because they exhibited … confidence, self-assuredness, toughness … independence, and were not focused on their looks."

A STUDY OF VOLUNTARILY CHILDFREE WOMEN'S RESISTANCE

Participants and Procedure

Nine voluntarily childfree women, ranging in age from thirty-two to fifty-one, in a Midwest state elected to participate in the study. Five participants self-identified as heterosexual, and of these, four were married and one was single. Two participants identified as lesbian living with their partners, and two participants identified as bisexual living with their partners (one female and one male). Eight of the participants were white with the remaining one of mixed ethnicity (Caucasian, African American and Native American). The participants reported practicing a variety of religions, including Judaism, Christianity and Wicca. Participants' education included high school graduate (n=2), associate's degree (n=1), bachelor's degree (n=1), master's degree (n=2) and doctoral degree (n=3). Personal income ranged from a low of $18,000 to a high of $84,000 annually, with an average of $41,000. All participants were assigned a pseudonym to protect their anonymity.

The investigation examined the responses women received from others in light of their choice not to have children and how they reacted to these responses. Their narratives were collected by three methods: through a semi-structured interview process, semi-structured journal entries and a focus group. Multiple methods of collecting narratives yield richer data as well as increasing validity (Patton 2002).

Interviews took place at the researcher's home, the homes of the participants or the workplaces of participants, depending on the participants' preferences. Each interview lasted between sixty and ninety minutes, was audiotaped and was transcribed verbatim. Member checks were performed to ensure accuracy and increase validity of the study. Participants received a copy of their transcript and provided commentary and correction.

The focus group occurred after the initial period of analysis had been conducted, so that participants could support or refute emergent themes and categories as well as meet in a supportive environment with other childfree women. The group met in a room with one-way observation capability housed in a university training clinic.

Refusal of Gender Role Conformity in Childhood

The women in the study demonstrated a resistant and even rebellious approach to socially mandated gender roles. For most, this resistance and rebellion initially emerged in childhood and became even more salient as they grew into adulthood. Many of them voiced an early rejection of activities and play experiences, such as playing with dolls, that are largely gender-prescribed. Five of the nine participants were self-described tomboys. For some, this meant a preference for opposite-sex endeavours. For example, Kate remarked,

> I played with dolls for a while, but I grew frustrated with them, because they wouldn't move the way I wanted them to move, and I remember throwing them and just saying, "these are stupid; I don't want to play with them anymore." I was a tomboy and I ended up being more involved in playing basketball and climbing.

Likewise, Kelly had no interest in dolls:

> I didn't want dolls. It wasn't that I wasn't given them. I didn't want them. I just wasn't interested. I used to get guns and holsters for Christmas. I wanted books and I got a microscope and phonograph and that kind of stuff. I just didn't want dolls and especially baby stuff. I didn't want the whole thing.

Among those women who recollected their early play with dolls were several accounts of realizing they played with them differently than did their peers or sisters. Some, when they looked back at their involvement with dolls, saw early rejections of the maternal role. Clarissa stated,

> I grew up with "aren't you a good mommy to your dolls?" kind of thing. The first time I remember sort of rejecting the mothering role was when I had a stuffed Snoopy. I got him at about five and I used to carry him around by his neck in the crook of my elbow. So consequently after carrying him around everywhere … his neck was about two inches in diameter and he was floppy headed … I used to throw him in the air and swing him around by his ears. People used to say, "don't do that to Snoopy … that's not how you'd be a good mother." And I remember thinking, he's a dog, I'm not his mother.

The accounts about play described in these narratives reflect instances of early resistance to prescribed gender roles. Several of the women expressed preferences for non-stereotyped pursuits, such as books, playing outdoors and games and activities that were often more physically active and exploratory than playing with dolls traditionally allows. Of those who did play with dolls, their narratives indicated either frustration by the dolls' limitations in movement or utility, or they resonated with accounts of doll play that was decidedly not nurturing nor maternal, such as Kate's description of her dolls as "stupid."

Similarly, the women in the investigation engaged in gender role resistance as they refused to be limited by socially derived meanings of what it means to be girls and women. It was apparent from the participants' narratives that the construct of gender — particularly making meaning of one's gender — figured prominently for them. All of the women reflected deeply about the meaning of gender and about their sense of themselves as girls and women. Concurrently, they exhibited an early, sometimes pervasive, refusal to live within the confines of typical gender role socialization. It could well be that this refusal — understood primarily as gender role rebellion — lay the foundation for a lifetime of questioning of these roles, of a skepticism and a healthy resistance to established societal expectations.

Experiencing Stigma

All nine women reported the experience of being pitied, criticized or in other ways stigmatized for being childfree. Stigmatization is, in this case, understood broadly and along a continuum from relatively mild incidents of dismissal to more severe experiences of reprobation. This stigmatization took several forms, which I have classified under five categories. The women (1) were often discounted when it came to discussions focused on children; (2) were sometimes expected to compensate by working extra hours; (3) were considered weird or abnormal and subjected to shock and dismay; (4) experienced pity; (5) experienced discrimination or abuse because of their choice.

Three of the women reported being discredited for not being parents when it came to the discussion of childcare and childrearing. In her interview, Chloe recalled interactions with her friend who has a child:

> She says things like, "Oh, you wouldn't understand because you don't want to have a kid." Or, you know, she'll call to tell me that the baby got its first tooth and she's like, "Well, I'm sure you don't care since you don't want to have kids." It's like she's on this superior level now because she had a baby and I can't relate.

Likewise, Kelly reported being silenced by her sister when the conversation turned to her nephew. In her interview she said,

There have been occasions when I've made the mistake of saying something to her about, "Well, I don't understand why [her son] couldn't do that." Or, "Why don't you just have [him] do that?" over a variety of different kinds of things. And her reply is, "You just don't understand, you've never been a mother. You don't understand."

Being dismissed and discredited seemed to result in the women's feeling isolated and exempt from the world of parenting as well as from their friends and relatives.

Three of the women had experienced being expected or asked to work extra hours based on the rationale that they had more time because they were childfree. Jennifer voiced an awareness of an expectation that she work late. She said, *"People expect me, because I don't have children, to be the one out of the group that stays late, because I don't have somebody at home that I have to run to."* Chloe, who is employed at the university, recalled what happened when she worked in another setting:

One of the jobs I used to work at was an optometry office. There were four other girls that worked there and at one point or another in the five years that I worked there, they all had kids. So it was like, "Oh, Chloe, so-and-so isn't here because she's on maternity leave, so would you care to work late?" or "Do you care to come in on Saturday because we know you don't have kids."

Three of the women reported that their normality has been called into question as women who have chosen not to have children. In her journal, Kelly vividly portrayed her feeling that, *"Those of us who may not be so drawn [to motherhood] remain, at best, enigmas to most people, and at worse, mutants."* Chloe and Jennifer reported feeling that professionals, friends and relatives speculated about whether they were "normal." Chloe described a pervasive questioning of her normalcy in her interview and in her journal:

If you say you just don't want to [have children], it's like, "What's wrong with you? What did your mom do to you?" People expect you to have kids and if you don't, they either think you can't or you're weird. I told one of my girlfriends that I was in a research study about voluntarily childless women and she said maybe I'd find out what's wrong with me.

The experience of being considered weird or abnormal sometimes contributed to perceptions of being excluded or shunned for the decision to be childfree. Jennifer recalled such an experience. She remembered the conversation in which an acquaintance began, *"'Well, can you not have children?' I said, 'No, we're fine. We just chose not to.' She just felt that there was something wrong with us. She has avoided us at parties and stuff."*

Jennifer also recalled an experience when she was in counselling to help her process through and better understand her upbringing, specifically her experience of growing up with alcoholic parents. In her interview, Jennifer described her frustration with one therapist who seemed compelled to link her upbringing with her decision not to have children:

> [The topic of remaining childfree began with] a general questioning about my own marital status, and, "Well, do you have any children?" kind of in that normal way, and when I said no, she said, "Well, are you going to have children?" and I said, "No," just rather confidently. Then the therapist asked me, you know, about the decision and then really tried to connect it back to adult children of alcoholics. I just felt like she overdid it. It happened rather immediately. I discovered that she really felt like most people wanted to have children and thought it was abnormal that someone didn't.

So, the reactions to participants as being abnormal for remaining childfree came not only from the general public but also from supposedly informed professionals. This questioning of normality was often followed by expressions of shock or disbelief, construed as a subset as described in the following section.

Six of the women in the study reported experiences in which others expressed shock and disbelief after learning of their voluntary childfreedom. Oftentimes the participants' experience of shock and disbelief seemed to be inextricably related to the questioning of their normality. Chloe recalled a conversation she had had with her husband's cousin, whom she had met only three times:

> I answered the phone and the first thing he said to me was, "Are you pregnant yet?" And I said, "No." "Why not?" I said, "Don't want to be." He goes, "Ah! What kind of answer is that?" (because he has two kids of his own).

The taken-for-granted assumption that any normal person would want to have children was articulated in various ways to these voluntarily childfree women. Naomi reported a similar reaction from her brother's wife:

> My sister-in-law that just had the baby, she was really shocked. We were sitting there talking about kids and I said, "I don't want any." She said, "Never?" She said, "It just shocks me, you know. Look at her with [my nieces and nephews]. She would be a good mother. It would be different if she hated kids but she doesn't hate kids." She was trying to say that's why she finds it hard for me not to want to be a mother. I said, "It's just not for me." She's had a change of heart now since she's had the second kid.

Clarissa reported that people are shocked and oftentimes confused about her decision not to have children. In her interview, she said,

> There are a couple who think, "Yeah, this is a fairly nice person" [then] they
> get around to asking if I have kids and I say no, they reach for a reason to
> try to make it consistent with "This seems like a nice, pleasant person." They
> can't fathom why someone who appears to be whatever, witty, fill in the blank,
> wouldn't have kids. People are just flabbergasted by that when they meet me.
> It's almost as if they're trying to re-categorize me as something other than
> [what I am, as] cold, unfeeling — I'm none of those things.

Lucy summarized the theme of others' shock and disbelief succinctly when she said, "People still do not know how to react to someone who chooses any sort of alternative way of life no matter what that alternative lifestyle choice may be. They are always suspicious of someone different from the norm."

Six of the women experienced pity as a common response from people who learned of their childfreedom, even when they were clearly informed about the volition in regards to their childfree status. Expressions of pity described by participants ranged from outright shame and disappointment to more subtle expressions of sorrow and encouragement to reconsider their decision. Chloe said, "People initially think, 'Oh, how awful for you that you don't want to have a child.'" During her interview, Kate recalled the reluctance of others to freely accept her decision and their subsequent encouragement that she re-think her choice:

> And my neighbour actually — who had the two kids — used to come over
> and say, "Why don't you… why aren't you a mom?" I said, "I don't want
> to be a mom." She was another one who said, "Oh, you'd be great at it." I've
> had neighbours and coworkers who have said things like that. It's been more
> questioning: "You'd have been a good mom. Why aren't you a mom?"

Both Jennifer and Naomi reported responses from others who assumed they were childfree only because they had not yet met the right man. Jennifer remembered reactions she received when she had been single and an active member of her church. She said, "It was more just kind of like, 'Oh well, when you meet the right person.' It was all just very patronizing." Likewise, Naomi's sister-in-law, who had initially expressed shock at learning of Naomi's decision not to have children, attributed her choice to not having yet met a suitable partner. Naomi said, "She said, 'I can understand now because you're not married and haven't met the right guy.'" The clear assumption was that Naomi would change her mind once she met the "right guy."

Three women recalled experiences of discrimination — two participants observed or heard of such incidents and the other directly experienced one — in response to being childfree. One woman experienced abuse. Clarissa, who currently works as a university professor, recalled what she observed when she worked for a Fortune 500 company. Her account reflected the dual suspicions against women who are both single and childfree. Furthermore, the coalescing of a single, childfree woman with increasing age suggests a multifaceted discrimination against women who do not conform to societal standards:

> If you were unmarried and a staff accountant, young, in your twenties, that's cool. But toward the end of your twenties, you better start looking for somebody [to marry]. If you got promoted through the ranks 'til you were in your mid-thirties and you made manager, that's where the speculation really started to grow. God forbid you be single, thirty-five, and childless. The idea that sacrificing a child and a relationship for a career — there was a sense of distrust. It was almost like if you would do that, I can't trust you. For the women it was as if in order to be viewed as a trustworthy coworker, you better not make it look like your career is the most important thing in your life because people will believe that you will steamroll over them to get what you want.

Lucy, who herself wanted a tubal ligation but did not actively seek the procedure due to the expense, wrote in her journal about the discrimination involved in women seeking permanent sterilization:

> Doctors are apparently reluctant to perform the surgery on young women for fear that she will change her mind. If the woman is married, [some doctors] will actually refuse [to perform the procedure] if the husband does not give his permission! I know a woman this happened to. She had to travel to another state to get her procedure.

Jennifer described what happened when she and her husband asked their physician to perform a vasectomy. She found the practice of refusing to grant a simple medical procedure blatantly discriminatory. In her interview she said,

> Well, one doctor, the physician we had been going to, just said, "No, it's not my policy ... I won't do it until a man is at least thirty-eight and has either had children or there's some real specific reason that they don't want to have children." So then we found somebody else and he was just kind of like, "I don't really feel very comfortable about this and I'd really like you to think about it more." And I just said, "Forget it," and we went to another guy and he was fine with it.

These examples can be construed as the subtle and usually unexamined ways that organizations and people with power — namely the corporate world and physicians — exert their influence over individuals and couples who do not have, nor want, children. In both cases, the discrimination is tied to the woman-as-mother (and person-as-parent) phenomenon, with those refusing to adhere to societal mandates the target of unfair treatment. Limiting the options of women who do not want children and who do not act, in Clarissa's words, "feminine enough" is understood as an example of discrimination.

One woman in the study reported having been abused in her first marriage in relation to the issue of children. Lucy discussed how her husband had been cajoling her to reconsider her decision not to have children. During her interview she recalled what happened between her husband and her:

> We were in the course of foreplay, were getting ready to have intercourse. We had been involved together for three years, had been married for about a year and [my husband] was big time, "I want children, I want children," very much pushing on the subject. We're getting ready to have intercourse and I'm like, "Excuse me, haven't we forgotten something here?" We used condoms as birth control and you really don't think after you're in a relationship with someone for three years you need to discuss every time whether or not you are going to use a condom. He was on top of me and just said, "No, I'm tired of waiting. I want a baby and I want a baby now."

In Lucy's story, her husband's demand for a child is interpreted as a desire to manipulate and control her. Such domination over women around the issue of reproduction symbolizes the greater societal patriarchy in which women's choices are routinely restricted, their personal power oftentimes usurped by men.

All nine women reported experiencing some degree of stigmatization due to their childfreedom. These experiences ranged from subtle but persistent questions from family members, coworkers and strangers to more blatant expressions of shock, dismay, pity and sympathy. In some cases, women reported having their sanity questioned, were discriminated against or observed such discrimination, or experienced sexual assault in an intimate relationship around the issue of children.

Saying No, Resisting the Mandate, and Getting Angry

In seven of the women's narratives, there were discernible examples of anger and frustration in response to societal and familial pressures to conform to proscribed gender roles. Some of the women struggled in their ability to say no and get angry, traditionally domains not largely acceptable for women. Some gave sarcastic responses to questions about their decision not to have children. Eventually most claimed to have developed an assertive voice to answer their doubters. This sense of assertiveness was incorporated into their sense of identity. Lois stated emphatically in her interview,

My responses have run the gamut. I did go through a period of time where I decided I was so sick of these questions [about my childfreedom] that I was going to answer every one of them sarcastically, and so I did. It was just to let them know it was a totally inappropriate question as far as I was concerned.

One of Chloe's tactics was to lie and tell those who asked her that she was unable — not unwilling — to have children. She noticed that people had contempt and scorn when she said she did not want to have children but that *"they feel sorry for you when you say you can't."* Coming to some resolve, Chloe continued, *"I'm not ashamed of it and I'm not embarrassed of it. I'm just to the point now where if you don't like what I have to say or the way I am, just don't be around me."* Clarissa has taken a similar no-nonsense response. In her interview, she said,

For those times I have said to women who have children, "I don't want them," I get a very defensive, "Well, what do you have against kids?" There's a real defensiveness that enters into that. I don't have anything against other people's kids. I don't want them.

Kate, too, arrived at some degree of peace in her quest to say no: *"I had to do a lot of therapy to realize that I can say no, or that I could do what I want to do, and not [only] make other people happy in life."* Jennifer recalled her experience of saying no to her therapist, who thought it was abnormal not to want children:

So I ended up asking her more about her views on having children and then after I discovered that she really felt like most people wanted to have children and thought it was abnormal that someone didn't, I said well we can't continue this relationship because I think it is normal.

Three of the women experienced a good deal of anger over being told what to do, being unfairly treated or being emotionally and/or physically coerced. They sometimes took calculated steps toward achieving some resolution and seemed empowered by their anger as it compelled them to make change. In response to the physician who had refused the couple's request for a vasectomy, Jennifer said,

I was just shocked. I wrote a long letter to him and said, "I find this appalling and you cannot refuse people who want a medical procedure that seems safe," and I really had a fit with him. I also told everybody that I knew that this guy picks and chooses what kind of medical procedures he wants to practise, and that's not fair. I was really angered by the whole thing because I was just like, "How dare you impose your values on us!"

Lucy, whose husband had attacked her and had refused to use birth control in an effort to get her pregnant, physically defended herself in response to the assault:

> *And I finally managed to get him off of me by kicking and screaming. I was trying to move all my weight toward his side of the bed where he had a gun hanging in a holster on the bedpost. But he finally got off and got out and I said, "Look, that was a terrorist tactic. The time to discuss these things is at the dinner table and not when someone is pinned underneath you with her legs spread." That was the one that really kind of nailed it for me.*

Naomi reported having an instinct to fight back when she sensed she was being manipulated, controlled or constrained. She talked about how she felt about some of the men she has dated:

> *It seems the ones that I tend to date that are my age, they tell me what to do, boss me around. The one that I did date, we dated for probably ten years and we just fought constantly for the same reasons: do this, don't do this. I dated one guy for six or seven months. He asked me to quit one of my jobs because he could never see me. But like I said, I'm not going to be told what to do.*

The Emerging Resilience: Feeling Strong in the Face of Stigma

In recent years, scholars have proposed definitions of resilience and studied the conditions under which it is most likely to flourish. Masten (2001: 228) defined resilience as "good outcomes in spite of serious threats to adaptation or development." In a study that discovered favorable coping skills among some women who had had abortions, resilience was encapsulated as the notion that "a person with a ... positive view of him- or herself, a sense of control over his or her own life, and an optimistic outlook on the future — all resources that should contribute to more positive appraisals of ... stressful life events" (Major, Richards, Cooper, Cozzarelli and Zubek, 1998: 737). Todd and Worell (2000: 119) studied resilience among low-income employed African American women and likened resilience to "a positive sense of well-being ... the manifestation of competence or effective functioning [in] the presence of serious stress or adversity."

The women in the study wrestled in their quest to have a positive sense of who they were in a culture that has often stigmatized and chastised them for their choice to remain childfree. Four of them implicitly questioned their normalcy and yielded to the notion that, having made an unorthodox choice, they are different. At times the notion of "different" seemed to be equated with abnormal or deviant. Chloe said, *"When I got into my twenties and everyone was saying, 'You've got to get married and have a kid,' I was like, 'Is there something wrong with me?'"* Similarly, Naomi stated, *"It's like I'm the different one."* In the focus group, Lois stated that she sees herself as different as well: *"I've just always been a little different than my friends and way different than society. It's just been across the board in my life."* Kelly recalled questioning her sense of normalcy as well:

> I used to wonder what is wrong with me because there are plenty of women that say, "Oh, a baby!" You know, a woman is walking with a baby and says, "Do you want to hold it?" No, I really don't.

In spite of those who questioned their normalcy, all nine women in the study expressed some sense of feeling strong, capable and empowered. This sense of resilience arose in the interviews, journals and focus group. During her interview, Nicole said,

> What I expect of myself is I try to build up and grow as a human being. I see myself as a woman who has chosen to live a certain way, who's also a very strong woman but is also real sensitive and caring and who likes herself. Kind of has a temper on occasion but that's okay.

Jennifer voiced a sense of pride regarding her decision. In her interview, she said, *"In some ways, I feel more like an empowered woman because I've resisted the social pressure to do this [have children]. So it makes me proud to be a woman and have made this choice."* Naomi saw herself as very capable and self-sufficient:

> I have the tendency to be very strong, very independent, very own-willed. I never settled and I think a lot of girls settled. I'm more independent than most women I know. I don't care a lot what other people think. I learned how to take care of myself.

Both Kate and Lois, who identified as lesbians, spoke about how being comfortable with their sexual orientation aided in their comfort with their decision not to have children. They had had ample experience with navigating a culture that has often stigmatized their lifestyle, and they had developed resilience in the face of the stigma that proved useful in other areas of their lives. In her interview, Lois said,

> My coming out as a lesbian was a huge, huge factor for me in my comfort level about not having children. I immersed myself in the lesbian culture ... I was one of those people who got to know it and help shape it. Through all those years that I was in a place where I would have really been questioning whether this is a good thing or not and having angst over it and stuff, I was in the midst of this incredibly lively culture that was giving birth to itself. We were all about being amazing, powerful, unique, creative women.

MOUNTING THREATS AGAINST CHOICE

Although abortion was made legal in the United States in 1973, prompt steps were taken to challenge and dismantle this law almost the moment it passed (Baird-Windle and Bader 2001). In the past fifteen years alone, tremendous strides have been accomplished by anti-choice politicians and private groups who collectively have increased the number of states with mandatory waiting periods, enacted restrictive teen parental notification and consent laws, restricted abortion for poor women and enforced mandatory counselling, which often includes lectures on and photos of fetal development (Benshoof 2002; Hontz 1998; Makin-Byrd 2002; Page 2006). When abortion restrictions are imposed, the choice about whether to become mothers is endangered. Women who do not want to become mothers but whose access to safe abortion is compromised must seek illegal abortions, thereby putting their health in jeopardy, or may face compulsory motherhood when abortion is not available as an option. Indeed, as legal restrictions continue to mount against abortion rights, women who self-abort may themselves be criminally prosecuted (Page 2006). Women in Portugal (Cancio 2005), Peru, Chile, the Dominican Republic, El Salvador and in nearly every African country face even harsher conditions for controlling and directing their own reproductive destinies (Senanayake and Newman 2002).

The right to choose whether or not to become a mother, once heralded and championed in the United States and elsewhere, has become, in many instances, both plausibly and legally prohibited. Those who have made the unorthodox choice to refuse the societal, religious, familial and national pressures to mother now face greater restrictions, moral condemnation and legal castigation which threaten the right to choose.

CONCLUSION

Being resolute in the face of stigmatization, particularly for women and people of colour, commands a sense of resilience and rebellion, a willingness to question societal mandates and to live with authenticity and purpose. Laws and policies that threaten, restrict or eliminate access to abortion signify that those women who wish not to have children quite literally live outside the law. Childfree women living in pronatalist societies can and do live outside the bounds of acceptability for their gender, and they do so with conviction.

References

Abrams, Laura S. 2003. "Contextual Variations in Young Women's Gender Identity Negotiations." *Psychology of Women Quarterly* 27: 64–74.

Baird-Windle, Patricia, and Eleanor J. Bader. 2001. *Targets of Hatred: Anti-abortion Terrorism.* New York: Palgrave.

Benshoof, Janet. 2002. "The Dismantling of Choice." *NCJW Journal* 25: 12.

Burkett, Elinor. 2000. *The Baby Boon: How Family-Friendly American Cheats the Childless.* New York: Free Press.

Byrne, Anne. 2000. "Singular Identities: Managing Stigma, Resisting Voices." *Women's Studies Review* 7: 13–24.

Cancio, Fernanda. 2005. "When Abortion Is a Crime: The Reality that Rhetoric Ignores." *Conscience* 25, 28.

Carr, C. Lynn. 1998. "Tomboy Resistance and Conformity: Agency in Social Psychological Gender Theory." *Gender and Society* 12: 528–53.

Clausen, Christopher. 2002. "Childfree in Toyland." *American Scholar* 71: 111–21.

Freud, Sigmund. 1949. *An Outline of Psychoanalysis.* New York: W.W. Norton.

Griffin, Katherine. 1996. "Childless by Choice: Can I Live a Rich, Balanced Life without Joining the Parenthood Procession?" *Health* 10: 98–104.

Hontz, J. 1998. "25 Years Later: The impact of Roe v. Wade." *Human Rights: Journal of the Section of Individual Rights and Responsibilities* 25: 8–11.

Koprince, Susan. 2000. "Childless Women in the Plays of William Inge." *Midwest Quarterly* 3, 251–64.

LaMastro, Valerie. 2001. "Childless by Choice? Attributions and Attitudes Concerning Family Size." *Social Behavior and Personality* 29: 231–44.

Lattin, Don. 2001. "In Oakland, Moon Stresses Family; Speech of Unification Church Criticizes Childless Women." *San Francisco Chronicle* March 13.

Letherby, Gayle, and Catherine Williams. 1999. "Non-Motherhood: Ambivalent Autobiographies." *Feminist Studies* 25: 719–29.

Lisle, Laurie. 1999. *Without Child: Challenging the Stigma of Childlessness.* New York: Routledge.

Major, Brenda, Caroline Richards, M. Lynne Cooper, Catherine Cozzarelli, and Josephine Zubek. 1998. "Personal Resilience, Cognitive Appraisals, and Coping: An Integrative Model of Adjustment to Abortion." *Journal of Personality and Social Psychology* 74: 735–52.

Makin-Byrd, Kerry. 2002. "The Doctor and the Woman: Comparing British and American Abortion Law." *Off Our Backs* March-April: 37–41.

Mandel, Laurie, and Charol Shakeshaft. 2000. "Heterosexism in Middle Schools." In N. Lesko (ed.), *Masculinities at School.* Thousand Oaks, CA: Sage.

Masten, Ann S. 2001. "Ordinary Magic: Resilience Processes in Development." *American Psychologist* 56: 227–38.

Morell, Carolyn. 1993. "Intentionally Childless Women: Another View of Women's Development." *Affilia: Journal of Women and Social Work* 8: 300–17.

Mueller, Karla, and Janice Yoder. 1999. "Stigmatization of Non-Normative Family Size Status." *Sex Roles* 41: 901–19.

O'Heron, Connie A., and Jacob L. Orlofsky. 1990. "Stereotypic and Nonstereotypic Sex Role Trait and Behavior Orientations, Gender Identity, and Psychological Adjustment." *Journal of Personality and Social Psychology* 58: 134–43.

Page, Cristina. 2006. *How the Pro-Choice Movement Saved America: Freedom, Politics, and the War on Sex.* New York: Basic Books.

Park, Kristin. 2002. "Stigma Management Among the Voluntarily Childless." *Sociological*

Perspectives 45: 21–45.

Patton, Michael Quinn. 2002. *Qualitative Research and Evaluation Methods.* Third edition. London: Sage.

Riessman, Catherine Kohler. 2000. "Stigma and Everyday Resistance Practices: Childless Women in South India." *Gender and Society* 14: 111–36.

Senanayake, Pramilla, and Karen Newman. 2002. "The Politics of Abortion in the Modern Age." *Conscience* 23, 12.

Todd, J.L., and Judith Worell. 2000. "Resilience in Low-Income, Employed, African American Women." *Psychology of Women Quarterly* 24: 119–28.

Van Leeuwen, Raymond C. 2003. "Is it all Right for a Married Couple to Choose to Remain Childless?" *Today's Christian Woman* 25, 24.

West, Candace, and Don H. Zimmerman. 1987. "Doing Gender." *Gender and Society* 1: 125-51.

Williams, L. Susan. 2002. "Trying on Gender, Gender Regimes, and the Process of Becoming Women." *Gender and Society* 16: 29–52.

VIOLENCE

Chapter 6

REPRESENTING VICTIMS OF SEXUALIZED ASSAULT

Linda Coates and Penny Ridley

From: *Victim No More: Women's Resistance to Law, Culture and Power*, pp. 109–124 (reprinted with permission).

How victims are represented has broad socio-political implications, including repercussions for therapeutic intervention. In this chapter we first argue for reclaiming the term "victim" to indicate that a wrong was done against another person and that it must be righted. Then we explain how accounts that conceal or ignore victim resistance, conceal violence and obfuscate perpetrator responsibility make it possible to blame and pathologize victims. We show how victims are represented in therapy articles, having analyzed 257 representations from twenty-nine published therapy articles for whether they presented the victim as passively affected by the violence (effects-based representations) or as actively responding or resisting the violence (response-based representations). Victims were overwhelmingly represented as "affected," that is, as passive, damaged and deficient. Finally, we present a detailed analysis of a case study excerpt to show how the account accomplishes a representation of the victim as an affected being and some problems with such an account. We argue that the acknowledgement of victims as active agents who resist the violence perpetrated against them is necessary to accurately understand violence and perpetrator responsibility and to stop victim blaming.

A central premise of this current study is that language is not a neutral medium for the transmission of information about reality but socially constitutes and transforms reality into versions or accounts. Language is central to virtually every response or intervention into violence. Professional therapists do not "objectively" identify or diagnose the problem to be worked on so much as they transform accounts of violence into suitable objects to which to respond (Davis 1986; Wade 2000). The identified problem becomes the focus of legal or psychotherapeutic action. Thus, the language used in therapy sessions not only illustrates current socio-historic trends and understandings about victims of violence, it also formulates them. It is through analyzing the language or discourse that we see social practices such as therapy in action.

A quick perusal of dictionaries, victimology journal articles and the Canadian Criminal Code reveals substantial similarities among definitions of "victim" of violence. These definitions typically require a person to have experienced "harm," "suffering" or "injury"; for example, a "person or thing injured or destroyed" (*Oxford Dictionary of Current English* 1993); "the first ingredient for victim status is the presence of harm, suffering or injury" (Burt 1983: 262); "a victim is any individual ... harmed or damaged" (Birkbeck 1983: 270) or "a person to whom harm was done or who suffered physical or emotional losses as a result of the offence" (Canadian Criminal Code 1985: 485).

Calling someone a "victim" seems to be an unproblematic expression of common sense. A person who committed an act of violence necessarily harmed or violated another living being — often in a manner that inflicted immense physical and emotional pain. In this light, labelling someone as a victim could be seen as an act of solidarity against such injustices. Miers (1983) articulates this position very clearly in his article on criminal injury compensation:

> The process of defining someone as a victim involves an expression of values about his suffering and our reactions to it. To call someone a victim is to attach a social label to him; it is to acknowledge that his suffering is undeserved and is a proper occasion for extending sympathy for mobilizing the institutional and other arrangements that have been made to alleviate his kind of suffering. (Miers 1983: 209)

Yet, within this very article, it becomes clear that rather than a gesture of solidarity, being ascribed the status of victim is more often an act of marginalization. For example, not all victims of violence are entitled to this "mobilization" of aid. Criminal injuries compensation policies specifically exclude those victims who can be judged as belonging to particular social categories. Among those who are or have been excluded are women who had been assaulted by their husbands or boyfriends, children who had been assaulted by their parents and people who had been judged on the "basis of character" or "way of life" to have "precipitated" or "deserved" the violence inflicted against them. Such negative attributions about victims appear to be common; for example, victims are frequently criticized for having "a victim mentality" (meaning that the person's interpretations of someone's actions as hostile were incorrect) or being "a *real* victim" (meaning that the person is inappropriately dwelling on the many difficulties facing them). We see in these statements totalizing negative representations; it is as if having been subjected to violence now fully constitutes the victimized person's identity. It is as if being victimized results in a deficient person. Moreover, victim-blaming theories that posit that persons precipitate their own victimization have been central in the development of victimology (cf. van Dijk 1999). Clearly, being ascribed the status of victim is not uniformly positive.

Some people have attempted to eliminate the negative characteristics or blame by denying their status as victim. For example, a poster from the 1985 International Women's Peace Conference featured a picture of a woman with the large caption, "No victim I." Women who have been raped or assaulted in other sexualized ways who deny their victimization can also be understood as resisting or avoiding negative social responses and exerting as much control as possible in their circumstances. By denying that she suffered sexualized violence, a woman can avoid others treating her as exaggerating the situation, lying, having caused the rape, wanting to be raped, being mentally disordered or doomed to experience long-term psychological symptoms. At the broader social level, many women use the term "survivor" instead of "victim." However, such name changes are unlikely to be widely successful in preventing the ascription of negative characteristics to victimized persons unless the underlying logic of and our role in creating such representations have been critiqued and understood. Some name changes may even be used to support negative stereotypes about persons who have been victimized. For example, a Crown prosecutor said that she opposed the use of the term "survivor" because she felt that those who used it were exaggerating the degree of danger and harm they suffered, as well as their inability to stop the violence. "You survive a plane crash," the prosecutor said, "not spousal assault." The fact that men inflict extreme violence on and even murder their spouses was ignored by this person, who is supposed to be a victim advocate and may someday become a judge.

In this chapter, we have chosen to use the term victim because we want to reclaim its meaning of indicating that a person was harmed, that violence is wrong and that victims must be supported rather than undermined. By itself, this reclaiming of the term victim is insufficient: victim-blaming attributions rely upon misrepresentations that ignore or conceal victim resistance, conceal violence and obfuscate perpetrator responsibility (the four operations of discourse). These misrepresentations tend to formulate the victim and perpetrator as affected beings but with different consequences: victims are blamed whereas perpetrators are excused. Below, we use the Interactional and Discursive View of Violence and Resistance to critique current understandings of violence and pose alternative representations (Coates and Wade 2004, 2007; Coates, Todd and Wade 2003; West and Coates 2004). Some of the main tenets of this framework are that violence is a unilateral and interpersonal act that is best understood in context; violence is deliberate; victims resist violence; and representations of violence are critical for violence research and intervention. Our position is that misrepresentations of victim resistance, violence and perpetrator responsibility lead to and support victim blaming.

VICTIM RESISTANCE

Most psychological theories about violence and explanations of victim behaviour are effects-based (Wade 2000). The underlying assumption in these theories, including socialization theories, learned helplessness theories and cycle of violence theories, is that the victim is an affected being. She is cast as passively accepting violence which then triggers or exposes psychological deficiencies or disorders. Such theories seem plausible as long as they are *not* examined from a language and social interaction perspective. When such a perspective is used to examine the behaviours of both victims and offenders in context and in sufficient detail, it becomes apparent that victim resistance is ubiquitous. In fact, we argue that whenever individuals are badly treated, they resist (Brown 1991; Burstow 1992; Hydén 1999; Kelly 1988; Reynolds 2001; Wade 1995b, 1997, 2000; Zemsky 1991). Wade (2000: 95) suggested that resistance takes many forms:

> Virtually any mental or behavioural act through which an individual attempts to expose, withstand, repel, stop, prevent, abstain from, strive against, impede, refuse to comply with, or oppose any form of violence or oppression, from disrespect to overt abuse, or the conditions that make such acts possible, may be understood as a form of resistance. Further, any attempt to preserve or reassert one's dignity, to imagine or establish a life based on respect and equality on behalf of one's self or others, including any effort to redress the harm caused by violence or other forms of oppression, represents a de facto form of resistance.

This statement regarding the scope of resistance is not definitive. Resistance is identified less by its physical form than it is by the meaning and situational logic of the actions from the victim's point of view.

Perhaps the most striking evidence of the ubiquity and significance of victims' resistance may be perpetrators' elaborate efforts to conceal and suppress it (Scott 1990). If victims were passive, perpetrators would not attack them when they were alone or isolated. Instead, perpetrators know that victims will resist and so they anticipate that resistance and take steps to overpower or conceal it. For example, rarely does a teenaged boy grab a girl's breasts or genitals in front of teachers, her six-foot father or police officers. Instead, anticipating that she will resist by calling out for help, he waits until she is alone or in the presence of people who are unlikely to help her, for example, his friends. When he grabs at the girl, if she knocks his hands away, he might grab her wrists and pin her arms so that she cannot move them. If the girl then attempts to free herself by jerking her body back, he takes action to prevent her from escaping. For example, he might drag her down to the ground so she cannot run away. If someone could be in hearing distance, and she is crying out, he might push her face into the ground so that her cries will be muffled. Perpetrators also know that victims will oppose their actions after the assault has ended; therefore, they actively discredit victims, present their actions as mutual, carefully project positive public images and engage in a wide range of other concealing behaviours.

Victims must consider the very real possibility that the perpetrator will inflict further violence, ranging from relatively mild censure and loss of privileges to extreme brutality, to any open acts of resistance. Consequently, open attempts by the victim to stop the violence, prevent the violence or re-assert her dignity are the least common form of resistance (Burstow 1992; Kelly 1988; Scott 1990). Instead, where power inequities exist, resistance at the interpersonal level tends to be covert — that is, concealed or disguised. Victims, for example, may go limp during an attack in an attempt to minimize the severity of the violence exerted against them. Victims may seem to be passive but will in fact be engaging in prudent resistance. For example, in the movie *The Color Purple*, while publicly appearing to be deferential to her abusive husband, the main character spits covertly in his glass before giving him a drink. In extreme circumstances, the only possibility for the realization of resistance may be in the privacy afforded by the mind (Wade 2000). For example, victims have described mentally removing themselves while being raped to prevent the perpetrator from "getting into their minds," mentally saying snappy comebacks to insults, or imagining a life without violence.

We argue that recognition of resistance, that is, that victims are acting upon the world rather than only being acted upon, is vital to an accurate understanding of the victim, the perpetrator and violence itself.

CONCEALING VIOLENCE

Research has shown that the severity, incidence and magnitude of violence against women is routinely concealed and minimized (Brownmiller 1975; Burt 1991; Clark and Lewis 1976; Coates 1997; Coates and Wade 2004, 2007; Ehrlich 2001; Ehrlich

1998; Estrich 1987; Gunn and Linden 1997). Sometimes, representations reduce or conceal the magnitude of the force used in the assault. For example, saying that "he pushed her and she fell to the ground" implies far less force than "he knocked her to the ground." The severity of the assault is often reduced by misrepresenting the acts as outside of the realm of violence; for example, rather than saying "he raped her," violence is frequently concealed by using terms that conveyed that the assault was bothersome (e.g., "molest"), an act of affection (e.g., "fondle"), playful (e.g., "it was a game") or sexual (e.g., "he had sex with her"). In fact, Lamb (1991: 250) found that academic articles on violence so effectively removed acts from the realm of violence that they "rarely projected an image of a man harming a woman."

A pervasive technique of concealing violence is to mutualize it, that is, to cast the victim as freely engaging in actions with the perpetrator (Coates and Wade 2004, 2007). For example, to describe a man grabbing a woman, holding her head still, forcing his mouth on hers and slobbering on her mouth as "they kissed" or even "he kissed her" is to mutualize it. Mutualizing descriptions misrepresent the nature of the social interaction by concealing the nature of the act and the agency of the perpetrator and the victim. Mutualizing descriptions place the acts within the domain of non-violence (e.g., sex, recreation), where the perpetrator and victim are co-agents, co-actors or co-participants. Perpetrators are not portrayed as acting upon and against the will and well-being of the victim but instead as acting with her. She becomes a partner in the joint activity. Even though the victim is cast as a participant in mutualizing descriptions, she is still assumed to be an affected being. Particularly in cases of sexualized assault, the victim is typically assumed to be passively participating. Her actions that do not fit the misrepresentation as mutual are routinely left out of the accounts or reformulated (Davis 1986). In this way, the inconsistency between the representation of the act as mutual and her actual actions are concealed. For example, accounts that describe assaults as "they were kissing" rarely include descriptions of how the victim was trying to turn her head away, crying to convey harm and protest, stiffening her body so that he had trouble pulling her close or holding her mouth rigidly closed to prevent him from sticking his tongue in her mouth. Describing an assault where a boy grabbed a girl's genitals and breasts as "they were engaged in horseplay" does not include a clear description of how the girl slapped his hands away, tried to run away or called out for help. In these accounts, how the perpetrator anticipated and overcame the victim's resistance may never come up for consideration. For example, the fact that the teenaged boy grabbed the girl's wrists after she slapped him, dragged her down to prevent her from running away and pushed her face into the ground so that her cries would be muffled are not only missing in mutualizing accounts, they are pre-emptively rendered out of place. Accounts that mutualize violence do not fully represent the extent of violence against the victim, and do reproduce or support assumptions about the passive, affected victim (effects-based representations). Two separate studies found the use of these representations to be associated with perpetrators receiving lower sentences (Coates et al. 2005; West and Coates 2004).

OBFUSCATING PERPETRATOR RESPONSIBILITY

Researchers have found that responsibility for violence against women is routinely obscured in newspapers, men's magazines, academic journals, the judicial system and therapy programs, even when women are murdered (Berns 2001). Linguistic techniques such as passive voice ("she was hit by John"), avoidance of agency ("she was raped") and nominalization (e.g., "wife battery") have been identified as obfuscating perpetrator responsibility (Bohner 2001; Coates, Bavelas and Gibson 1994; Henley, Miller and Beazley 1995; Lamb 1991; Lamb and Keon 1995; Penelope 1990; Trew 1979).

One way in which perpetrator responsibility is obscured is by representing their acts as non-deliberate. Often this is done by representing the perpetrator as being acted upon by an overwhelming force that is outside of his control (Coates 1997; Coates and Wade 2004, 2007; Marolla and Scully 1979; Morgan and O'Neill 2001; O'Neill and Morgan 2001; Sykes and Matza 1957). Common explanations that cast the cause of the assault as emotion (e.g., "he lost his temper," "he failed to control his emotions"), sexual drive ("I couldn't stop myself") or many other psychological phenomena ("I just lost it") all formulate the violence as non-deliberate by externalizing the postulated cause of the violence. The postulated cause is presented as if it were outside of the perpetrator's control. Similarly, explanations that represent perpetrators' actions as being mechanistically triggered by the victim, for example, "she pushed his buttons" or "she lead me on," also deny the deliberateness of the perpetrator's actions. When perpetrators' actions are presented as deliberate, their actions are concealed as arising from non-violent motivations or intentions (e.g., sexual drive, stress or emotion) and used to mitigate attributions of responsibility. For example, in Coates' research a number of men charged with raping their wives defended their actions as deliberate attempts to save or "jump-start" their marriages.

However, when examined in context, it is clear that perpetrators of diverse forms of personalized violence (e.g., sexualized violence, wife-assault, physical assault and workplace harassment) employ a number of strategies before (e.g., isolation of the victim, ingratiating behaviour, lies), during (e.g., physical violence, threats, interrogation, humiliation) and after assaults (e.g., concealing or denying the violence, minimizing the victim's injuries, blaming the victim, refusing to accept responsibility) to suppress or overpower victim resistance. When these actions are taken into account, it becomes very difficult to view these acts as non-deliberate.

The fact that perpetrators frequently seek to deny the deliberateness of their actions and present themselves as affected beings seems to stem from an intention to mitigate responsibility legally, socially and interpersonally. But perpetrators are not the only ones who obfuscate their responsibility. Similar representations are common in public, legal and psychological discourse (Coates 1997; Coates and Wade 2004; Morgan and O'Neill 2001; O'Neill and Morgan 2001). In the legal system, the use of excusing attributions is systematically related to the perpetrator receiving a more lenient sentence, particularly when the act was described as non-violent and non-volitional (Coates 1997). In fact, the language used by judges to describe the perpetrator and his violent actions were better predictors of sentence than legal factors (e.g., severity of violence, duration of attack or alcohol or drug use). Moreover, court mandated counselling was consistently for the reformulated, non-violent cause, such as anger management, not the violence. Even when men receive counselling for violence, their violence is frequently excused in the therapy sessions as non-deliberate (Morgan and O'Neill 2001; O'Neill and Morgan 2001).

VICTIM BLAMING

Our focus here is not the nature of victims' resistance, the concealment of violence or the obfuscation of perpetrator responsibility, but how the failure to acknowledge victim resistance, expose violence and clarify perpetrator responsibility makes it possible to blame and pathologize victims. In other words, these discursive operations make it possible to turn labelling someone a victim from an act of solidarity to an act of marginalization, even contempt. One can easily find examples of such victim blaming in diverse forms of socio-political and interpersonal violence, from European imperialism to sexualized assault. Strikingly, when victim resistance is mentioned, it is frequently characterized as deficiency or disorder. For example, slaves who resisted their imprisonment and mistreatment by escaping were diagnosed as having the mental disorder drapetomania, a condition that could be managed by beating the recaptured slaves (Gould 1996). Women who refuse to be content with their husbands' abusive behaviour are recast as clinically depressed or having a deficiency in character (Anderson 1999). Children who refuse to call the perpetrators "Dad" are reformulated as having attention deficit disorder or an attitude problem.

When violent behaviour has been uncovered, but the full extent of the violence and the perpetrator's responsibility for that violence is not clarified, consideration of the victim's resistance is typically displaced. In so doing, the question of how the perpetrator attempted to suppress that resistance cannot come up for consideration, and the deliberate and unilateral nature of violence remains concealed. Moreover, the displacement or concealment of victim resistance leaves victims open to being blamed for the violence perpetrated against them. If an act was not violent but mutual, then the perpetrator was not at fault; instead, the victim is making a false claim, is a woman scorned or has disordered thoughts.

Because resistance is so frequently overlooked, particularly in its more indirect and disguised forms, victims are generally represented in professional psychological discourse as passive recipients of abuse, that is, with effects-based representations. Victims are represented as socially conditioned individuals who seek out, submit to and participate in the violence that is forced upon them. The presumption that victims are passive then becomes the foundation for causal attributions that locate the source of victims' behaviour in their psychology alone. For example, people ask, "What is it about the victim that would lead her to be accept the violence that she endures?" "Why does she stay with him?" "Why does she pick guys like that?" "How could she let that happen?" and "Why didn't she tell somebody?" Such questions shift the focus away from the perpetrator's social behaviour of violence to a postulated, individualized problem with the victim. The mind of the victim becomes the focus of theories and interventions (Mardorossian 2002; Todd and Wade 2003). The victim is viewed as mentally deficient or disordered. The mental deficiencies or disorders are typically viewed as arising from or triggered by the victim's endurance of current or past violation.

The assumption of victim passivity can be used as a pretext to discredit victims and call into question the veracity of their testimony regarding the nature of the acts at issue. For example, the legal defence of presumed consent or mistaken belief rested on the notion that a lack of open and persistent resistance is equivalent to consent. The apparent lack of resistance also lends credence to the suggestion that the offender was not fully responsible for the assault because the victim did not clearly signal her refusal (Coates 2004; Ehrlich 1998). However, once the nature and situational logic of the victim's resistance is elucidated, it becomes very difficult to take seriously the suggestion that the victim accepted the violence, wanted it to occur or was responsible for it. Thus, our view is that victim blaming will occur as long as victim resistance is not adequately recognized as a basic premise, the nature of violent behaviour is not adequately understood, the full extent of the violence not adequately exposed and the extent of offenders' responsibility not adequately clarified. In short, it is likely to continue as long as we use effects-based theories of violence.

While we have articulated the above position from research and clinical experience, a study had not been conducted to systematically investigate the representation of victims of sexualized violence in clinical literature. In order to address this gap, we analyzed published case studies for whether they represented the victims as passive, that is, within an effects-based framework, or resisting, that is, within a response-based framework (Wade 1995b, 1997, 2000; Todd and Wade 2003; Todd 2002a; Todd 2002b). We sought (a) to gather information about the relative frequency with which therapists represent victims using effects-based or response-based interpretative repertoire, and (b) to critique representations of victims of sexualized violence.

METHOD

Articles for analysis were located through a search of PsycLIT for published case studies that contained the words "sexual assault" or "sexual abuse." The data had been previously gathered for a study on descriptions of sexual assault in which the first author had been involved. Articles that were included for analysis in the present study all met the following criteria: they (a) contained the phrases "sexual assault" or "sexual abuse, (b) described a case study (c) and contained descriptions of victims of sexualized assault. A total of twenty-nine professional case study journal articles were analyzed.

Five articles (17 percent) were randomly selected from the sample for the purpose of developing the system of analysis. This procedure was used to ensure that any patterns or findings from the study would not be unique to the cases used to develop the system of analysis (see Coates 1997). The system of analysis that was developed required the data to be analyzed in three stages: location of relevant sections of the articles for analysis, identification of time frame and analysis of function.

First, analysts identified all representations that referred to or described the mental or physical actions of sexualized violence victims for further analysis. General descriptions of victims or sexualized assault (e.g., "long-term effects of child sexual abuse include ..." or "this approach recognizes that sexual abuse during childhood has implications for one's sense of self..."), and descriptions that did not characterize the behaviour of the victim (e.g., "the sexual abuse began to take place before the victim's eighth birthday, not long after the family transferred from a country town to a coastal city") were eliminated from analysis. Descriptions that characterized sexualized violence as mutual (e.g., "she described her childhood sexual abuse experiences by her uncle which ranged from fondling to intercourse") were also excluded from analysis because they were investigated in other studies (Coates, 2000a, 2000b, 2000c; Coates, Bavelas and Gibson, 1994; Bavelas and Coates 2001; West and Coates 2004; Tatlock and Coates 2003).

Through this process, all representations located for analysis characterized the victim's mental or physical actions. The process of locating descriptions for analysis was highly reliable with independent analysts, one of whom was blind (i.e., did not know) to the position taken by the authors, agreeing 98 percent of the time. Reliability was assessed across 26 percent of the articles.

Second, analysts recorded whether representations described the victim or her actions during or after the assault. Representations that described the perpetration of violence and the victimized person's immediate responses to that violence were recorded as "during." Representations that focused on the victimized person after the assault (e.g., hours, days, weeks, or years later) were recorded as "after."

Third, the descriptions located in the first stage of analysis were re-examined to determine how they formulated the victim or her actions within the context of the case study (i.e., effects-based or response-based). Analysts answered a series of questions on a decision tree to aid them in deciding upon the function of the representations. Response-based representations were those that formulated (a) the victim as proficient or agentive (i.e., acting upon the world) or (b) her mental or physical actions as resisting, opposing or countering violence *in any way*. Effects-based representations were those that *clearly* formulated (a) the victim as deficient, passive or a mere object (i.e., acted upon) or (b) her actions as symptoms, abnormal or triggered by the violence.

The system of analysis developed from the subset of the data was then applied to the entire database. Inter-analyst reliability was assessed for 12 percent of the data. Overall reliability of the analysis of function for independent analysts, one of whom was blind to the position taken by the authors, was very high (97 percent agreement).

RESULTS AND DISCUSSION

Two-hundred and fifty-seven representations were located for analysis. The majority of representations (90 percent) were effects-based. These descriptions interpreted the victimized person or her actions as passive, ineffectual, damaged or deficient and in doing so cast her as dysfunctional. Thus, even though we would expect therapists to use representations that indicate their solidarity with the victim, they used representations that marginalized victims. For example, one therapist stated: "B. learned the victim role well … B did not know any alternative but to live as a victim." This representation casts the victim as having been passively conditioned to play a part in the violence (see Coates et al. 2005 and West and Coates 2004 for a discussion of some of the problems with representing victims of violence as participants). Her actions are merely mechanistic behaviours evoked by her past experiences. The victim's actions are so problematically controlled by her past conditioning that she passively accepts being victimized: "[B] was a non-survivor, as shown by her helplessness to end the abuse." Moreover, this totalizing negative characterization of the victim as a "non-survivor" is explicitly connected to her "helplessness" in stopping the violence inflicted upon her. In doing so, the therapist shifts responsibility for the violence from the perpetrator to the victim. The word "helplessness" bolsters the construction of the victim as passive. The term connects to the theory of learned helplessness or the idea that chronic abuse results in passive acceptance. In this way, the possibility that the victim resisted, opposed or countered the violence does not come up for consideration. Likewise, the conditions that supported the perpetrator's violence against the victim, such as inequalities in physical and social power, are not used to interpret the victim's actions, including her inability to stop the perpetrator from being violent. Instead, the victim herself is held responsible for the violence, and her deficient, psychological make-up becomes the object of intervention.

While there was a plethora of representations that cast the victim as passively affected, there was a paucity of representations that cast the victim as actively responding. Only 10 percent of the representations cast the victim as proficient, functional and mentally healthy in some way. One therapist, for example, wrote: "P. over-scheduled herself, she linked this with her history: as a child, her over-commitment was a legitimate escape from the physical danger of being at home." Here the author represents the client as actively responding to the violence committed against her. She kept herself very busy, which minimized her time at home — the place where she was most vulnerable to attack. In this way, the therapist constructed the client as volitional and strategic. However, the use of the terms "over-scheduled" and "over-commitment" reveal that the therapist interpreted the client's chosen strategy to be problematic. The therapist then construes "over-scheduling" to be the therapeutic problem to be addressed in the therapy. Once again, the therapeutic problem is removed from the social context within which it is occurring — that is, the experience of being violated — and placed in the mind of the victim. If the therapist had fully appreciated the client's behaviours as acts of resistance, the client would have been formulated as appropriately scheduling and committing her time. The therapist's reliance on an effects-based theory of violence results in the problem ultimately being with the victim's mind; she is cast as mechanistically repeating a maladaptive pattern of behaviour.

The majority of representations (73 percent) described victims' mental and behavioural actions in the aftermath of sexualized violence. Ninety-four percent of these representations were effects-based. In order to test the hypothesis that a therapist would more easily recognize a victim's active resistance to the perpetrator's violent actions when the resistance co-occurred with the violent actions, we further examined the representations of the victim or her actions during the actual assault. Of these representations, a significant majority (78 percent) still represented the victim's mental and behavioural actions as affected, that is, as passively acquiescing to the attack. Thus, even in a situation where it was reasonable to expect victim resistance (and even overt physical resistance), there was a dearth of response-based representations that conveyed accurate understandings and formulations of violence.

Therapists did not often switch between the two interpretative repertoires.

Authors tended to consistently formulate the clients and their actions as affected throughout the entire article. However, authors of effects-based representations sometimes formulated victims as somewhat actively responding by adopting a "coping" mechanism. Nevertheless, rather than viewing the victim as truly agentive (i.e., acting upon the world by resisting or opposing the violence), she was still formulated as an object without true agency. Her actions were merely mechanistically triggered by the violence and cast as maladaptive, dysfunctional or insufficient. For example, one therapist stated that: "powerful and overwhelming emotions were encased in a wall of protection deep inside ... [this] had been a functional and effective coping mechanism." Here, the therapist casts the victim as actively responding to the violence inflicted upon her by building a "protection wall" to cope with the violence. However, the "protection wall" was now judged to be dysfunctional, indicated here by the therapist's use of the past tense ("the wall had been functional"). Having evaluated the victim's response as dysfunctional, the problem was then placed inside the victim's mind, and she became the focus of the therapeutic intervention.

CASE STUDY EXCERPT

The following analysis of a case study excerpt is used to more fully illustrate the local accomplishment of effects-based representations as well as their consequence.

> The incest trauma had resulted in a narcissistic injury and a regression to archaic modes of defence. M. seemed to lack effective internalized systems for the promotion and maintenance of self-esteem and a stable self-representation. She coped by experiencing her own emotions and other aspects of herself as outside the self-representation.

In this short passage, the therapist's representation relies heavily on imputed unobservables (internalized systems, self-esteem, stable self-representation) that work together to discursively create the client as (a) damaged by the assaults and (b) possessing an internal (mental) deficiency. In order to support this interpretation, the author first creates a linear-mechanical, cause-effect relationship between the client's victimization and her behaviour. The trauma "resulted" in injury and regression and so currently determines the client's behaviours. Her actions are further rendered as negative by the author's characterization of "narcissistic injury" and "regression." Notice too that the injury is not physical or emotional pain, which arguably could be seen as a consequence of assault (the decision to show this pain or not, however, would not be an effect of the assault but a choice by an actively responding victim), but "narcissistic injury." The focus has become the inner workings of the client's mind rather than the interpersonal violence. In less than a sentence, the authors have established the victim as mentally damaged.

From a background of damage, it is then possible for the therapist (and readers) to accept that any implied actions by the victim (which are suggested by the phrase "modes of defence") are not deliberate and resourceful strategies but are flawed or dysfunctional repercussions of the damage caused by the assault. The therapist bolsters the position that the victim is deficient by the use of the word "archaic," which concisely characterizes the client's mental or behavioural actions as immature, outdated or obsolete modes of defence. In merely one full sentence, the victim has been constructed as damaged and her current behaviours as dysfunctional, that is, as a manifestation of the sexualized violence. The therapist has reformulated the client from having a situated external problem (i.e., her father committed acts of the sexualized violence against her) to having an internalized cause of the problems (i.e., "narcissistic injury" and "regression" resulting from the violence). The therapist then formulates a diagnosis based upon these imputed and internalized problems. The assault is reduced to a mere precipitating or triggering factor of the real internalized cause. The focus of the therapy becomes the aftermath of the violence. The importance of the sexualized violence has been identified in terms of its postulated effects on the victim. In contrast, the importance of the victim's subjective experience of sexualized violence and her responses to this violence have been precluded from consideration.

Next, the author draws upon these discursive constructions to further develop long-term victim deficiencies. The therapist asserts that the victim lacks the "effective internalized systems" that are necessary for the "promotion and maintenance of self-esteem" and "stable self-representation." The manifest implication of this sentence is that the victim chronically lacks self-esteem and stable self-representations.

The third sentence describes how the victim "coped" with the consequences of her deficits (i.e., missing internal systems) by "experiencing her own emotions and other aspects of herself as outside the self-representation." This sentence clearly illustrates the difference between coping and responding. The violence has caused the victim to be deficient and these deficiencies now cause her to have an abnormal self-representation with which she must cope. Her coping behaviour is a passive consequence of the effects of the violence and is not a strategy of resistance employed by the victim.

In this short excerpt, the problem that M. originally came into therapy with (i.e., the incest) was reformulated by the therapist into six internalized problems: two internal forms of damage (i.e., narcissistic injury and regression) and four internal deficiencies (lacking internal systems, poor self-esteem, unstable self-representation and difficulties experiencing herself). The original problem had temporal limits — the client had been victimized by her father at a particular time and place, whereas the reformulated problem has no such physical or temporal limits. The client's deficiencies are represented in such a way that they could conceivably be a lifelong condition.

GENERAL DISCUSSION

Victims typically seek therapy because they are experiencing "problems in living." In representing victims and their actions, one also formulates the reason for these problems. There was a plethora of effects-based representations of victims and their behaviours in this data. In the case studies analyzed, the therapists systematically represented the victim's physical, emotional or mental actions as symptoms or evidence of the damage, dysfunction or pathology created or activated by the perpetrator's violence. She was a victim: passive, damaged, deficient, unskilled, dysfunctional and even pathological. It was as if she was an object that was animated by the perpetrator when he committed violence against her and now needed to be re-animated by the therapist. The victim's status as object-to-be-activated was maintained throughout the articles analyzed.

In the effects-based representations, the ultimate cause of the victim's experience of difficulty was cast as personal deficiency and the problem was located in the mind of the victim. As illustrated in the case study excerpt, victims' experiences of violence and subjugation were relegated to the past, and therefore made less relevant to understanding the client's current problems in living. These representations discursively created a passive victim whose current actions were mere manifestations or mere effects of the violent force. The question, then, was why victims were still manifesting symptoms of this force when the sexualized violence had occurred in the past. The answer: she was psychologically damaged or had a pre-existing psychological deficiency that was triggered by the violence. She, or more precisely her mind, became the problem to be addressed. She was the ultimate reason she was experiencing problems in living — not any past or current violation or subjugation. In this way, therapists reformulated a social problem (violence) into an individualized one. The problem of violence became a problem in the victim's mind.

Also, effects-based representations separated the victim's actions from the social context within which they occurred. For example, when a victim gagged while telling the therapist about being orally raped, her actions were problematized as "puzzling fits" rather than clear communicative displays of what it was like to endure this sexualized violence. Imagine the smells, the taste, the feel of a man forcing his penis into your mouth and ejaculating. Imagine trying to breathe through this rape. Can there be a better way of communicating what it was like to be orally raped than gagging? Only by examining the victim's actions within context can we make sense of these actions. However, discursively constructing the victim and her actions as affected co-occurred with the therapist decontextualizing the victim's past and current actions.

Importantly, not a single article analyzed consistently represented victims of violence in a way that would be in line with the Interactional and Discursive View of Violence and Resistance. A few therapists formulated victims of violence as proficient, skilled and volitional at some time or in some manner. But victims of violence were never represented as uniformly volitional, proficient or mentally healthy. Instead, the few response-based representations were drowned in a sea of pathologizing, effects-based discourse. Therapists used the experience of having endured sexualized violence to fully constitute the victim's identity and her actions. Thus, rather than an act of solidarity, ascribing someone the status of victim within the therapy case studies was an act of marginalization. Victims were weak, deficient "others" who needed to be fixed by the presumably strong, proficient therapists.

The widespread use of effects-based representations may, in part, be accounted for by its apparent focus on the harm inflicted by the perpetrator. In other words, therapists, academics and others may have adopted the practice of representing victims in effects-based terminology because it appears to evince the severity of the perpetrator's actions. However, these representations replaced a careful consideration of the perpetrator's violence and the victim's suffering with the construction of a passive victim who was psychologically damaged and deficient. In this way, victims and their behaviours, and not the violence itself, became problematized. The victim's postulated damage and deficiencies became the problem to be addressed in therapy sessions. In doing so, the widespread commission of violence against women escaped being identified as sufficiently problematic. If the victim were active and not passive, or proficient instead of deficient, she would have stopped the violence, or not have been or continue to be affected by the violence. If she was not "maladaptive," "helpless," "anxious" or "predisposed" then there would not be a problem. Thus, the victim was not supported. Instead, these descriptions worked to simultaneously conceal violence, obfuscate the victim's resistance, blame and pathologize the victim and reduce the perpetrator's responsibility (see Coates and Wade 2004).

It is interesting to note that violent men who drop their wives off at therapy and instruct the therapists to "fix the bitch" are relying upon the therapists to utilize effects-based representations to support their violence (Wade 1997). They are counting on therapists to view the victims and not their violence as the problem warranting social intervention.

But what if we formulate the victim's actions not as passive effects but as considered responses that resist, oppose or counter violence? Then these actions, such as gagging when describing being orally raped, are not symptoms of pathology or deficiencies but evidence of health and proficiency (see Wade 2000; Weaver et al. 2005). Then, it is possible to view the victim's actions, which often seem extreme when examined in isolation, as continuing because she is demonstrating or communicating her refusal to be content with mistreatment. The problem for intervention would then remain the violence, and the therapist's role would become one of support and social activism.

If this position, as espoused in the Interactional and Discursive View of Violence and Resistance, has merit, then attempting to rid the client of actions of resistance that have been deemed to be problematic is analogous to treating starvation by eradicating hunger (Wade 2000). But hunger is not the problem; it is a healthy response to lack of food. In contrast, we can treat starvation by recognizing that a person's hunger is a sign of needing food and then provide her with food. We can approach her as an active, proficient, skilful and healthy person who has been violated and so could benefit from our support, not fixing. We could engage victims in discussions and write reports about victims of violence in such a way that violence is exposed, perpetrator responsibility clarified, victim resistance honoured and blaming or pathologizing of victims is contested.

It is important to state that we are not arguing that all therapists intentionally use these terms to conceal violence and blame victims. Effects-based representations are so common that they appear to be objective descriptions until carefully critiqued. It is not necessary to take an ideological position that embraces discrimination against women to produce and reproduce social injustice. Simply representing victims within the ubiquitous effects-based interpretative repertoire tends to support such injustice. Nor are we assuming that all therapists use these terms naively. Use of terms that ignore or reformulate victim resistance, conceal violence, excuse perpetrators and blame victims is frequently intentional, as is evidenced in the discourse of perpetrators and proponents of victim precipitation theories. The representations we use to describe victims and their actions have important implications for the promotion of social justice. We argue that accurate accounts of violence and victim resistance must be a focus of social intervention.

In this chapter, we report that representations of violence in therapy are overwhelmingly effects-based. Victims are represented as passive, damaged and deficient. We argue that recognizing victim resistance as it is accomplished in situ can be used to contest victim blaming. When the details of the victim's responses to and resistance against violence are acknowledged, it becomes difficult if not impossible to view the violence as mutual, the perpetrators actions as non-deliberate or the victim as wanting or putting up with violence. It becomes clear that psychological diagnoses about the mind of the victim are unnecessary; her actions do not need fixing. The social problem of violence needs to be addressed.

In our attempt to reclaim the term violence, we are taking the position that we cannot theoretically or practically simply "get past" victimization. We live in a social world where people will continue to commit violence against others, particularly those with less power or privilege. If we deny victimization, we will collude with the perpetrator in suppressing resistance and concealing violence. If victimization is not recognized, victims' responses will seem extreme and pathological. Victims will continue to be blamed, and the focus of intervention will continue to be the mind of the victim. We propose that we must elucidate victim resistance, expose violence and clarify perpetrator responsibility. In this way, we can support victims by contesting victim blaming attributions and recognizing the injustice committed against them. We can use the term victim to indicate solidarity, to recognize injustice and to commit to righting that injustice.

References

Anderson, I. 1999. "Characterological and Behavioral Blame in Conversations about Female and Male Rape." *Journal of Language and Social Psychology* 18: 377–94.

Bavelas, J.B., and L. Coates. 2001. "Is it Sex or Assault? Erotic vs. Violent Language in Sexual Assault Trial Judgments." *Journal of Social Distress and Homelessness* 10, 29–40.

Berns, N. 2001. "Degendering the Problem and Gendering the Blame: Political Discourse on Women and Violence." *Gender and Society* 15: 262–81.

Birkbeck, C. 1983. "'Victimology Is what Victimologists Do' but What Should They Do?" *Victimology* 8: 270–75.

Bohner, Gerd. 2001. "Writing about Rape: Use of the Passive Voice and other Distancing Text Features as an Expression of Perceived Responsibility of the Victim." *British Journal of Social Psychology* 40: 515–29.

Brown, L.M. 1991. "Telling a Girl's Life: Self-Authorization as a Form Of Resistance." In A.G. Rogers, C. Gilligan, and D.L. Tolman (eds.), *Reframing Resistance: Women, Girls, and Psychotherapy.* New York: Haworth Press.

Brownmiller, S. 1975. *Against Our Will: Men, Women and Rape.* New York: Bantam.

Burstow, B. 1992. *Radical Feminist Therapy.* Newbury Park: Sage.

Burt, M.R. 1983. "A Conceptual Framework for Victimological Research." *Victimology* 8: 261–69.

____. 1991. "Rape Myths and Acquaintance Rape." In A. Parrot and L. Bechhofer (eds.), *Acquaintance Rape: The Hidden Crime.* New York: Wiley.

Canadian Criminal Code, R.S.C. 1985, c. C-46.

Clark, L.M.G., and D. Lewis. 1976. *Rape: The Price of Coercive Sexuality.* Toronto: Women's Press.

Coates, Linda. 1997. "Causal Attributions in Sexual Assault Trial Judgements." *Journal of Language and Social Psychology* 16: 278–96.

____. 2000a. "Language and Violence: A Discourse Model of Violence." Duncan, BC: Women's Resistance Group.

____. 2000b. "The Treatment of Consent in Sexual Assault Cases." International Conference on Language and Social Psychology (ICLASP). Cardiff, Wales: UK.

____. 2000c. "Twice a Volunteer: Mutualizing Violence." Duncan, BC: Women's Resistance Group.

Coates, Linda, J.B. Bavelas, and J. Gibson. 1994. "Anomalous Language in sexual Assault Trial Judgements." *Discourse and Society* 5: 191–205.

Coates, Linda, Nathan Hoyt, Melissa Tatlock, and Krista West. 2005. "Mutualizing Violence: Concealment and Blame in Canadian Sexualized Violence Trial Judgments." University of Lethbridge.

Coates, Linda, Nick Todd, and Allan Wade. 2003. "Shifting Terms: An Interactional and Discursive View of Violence and Resistance." *Canadian Review of Social Policy* 52: 116–22.

Coates, Linda, and Allan Wade. 2004. "Telling It Like It Isn't: Obscuring Perpetrator Responsibility for Violence." *Discourse and Society* 15: 499–526.

____. 2007. "Language and Violence: An Analysis of the Four Discursive Operations." *Journal of Family Violence* 22, 7 (October): 511–522.

Davis, K. 1986. "The Process of Problem (Re)Formulation in Psychotherapy." *Sociology of Health and Illness* 8: 44–74.

Ehrlich, Susan. 1998. "The Discursive Reconstruction of Sexual Consent." *Discourse and Society* 9: 149–71.

____. 2001. *Representing Rape: Language and Sexual Consent.* London and New York: Routledge.

Estrich, Susan. 1987. *Real Rape: How the Legal System Victimizes Women Who Say No.* Cambridge, MA: Harvard University Press.

Gould, Stephan. 1996. *The Mismeasure of Man.* New York: W.W. Norton.

Gunn, Rita, and Rick Linden. 1997. "The Impact of Law Reform on the Processing of Sexual Assault Cases." *Canadian Review of Sociology & Anthropology* 34: 155–75.

Henley, N.M., M. Miller, and J. Beazley. 1995. "Syntax, Semantics, and Sexual Violence: Agency and the Passive Voice." *Journal of Language and Social Psychology* 14: 60–84.

Hydén, M. 1995. "Verbal Aggression as a Prehistory of Woman Battering." *Journal of Family Violence* 10: 55–71.

Kelly, L. 1988. *Surviving Sexual Violence.* Minneapolis: University of Minnesota Press.

Lamb, S. 1991. "Acts Without Agents: An Analysis of Linguistic Avoidance in Journal Articles on Men who Batter Women." *American Journal of Orthopsychiatry* 61: 250–57.

Lamb, S., and S. Keon. 1995. "Blaming the Perpetrator: Language that Distorts Reality in Newspaper Articles on Men Battering Women." *Psychology of Women Quarterly* 19: 209–20.

Mardorossian, Carine M. 2002. "Toward a New Feminist Theory of Rape." *Signs* 27: 743–75.

Marolla, J.A., and D.H. Scully. 1979. "Rape and Psychiatric Vocabularies of Motive." In E.S. Gomberg and V. Franks (eds.), *Gender and Disordered Behavior: Sex Differences in Psychopathology.* New York: Brunner/Mazel.

Miers, David R. 1983. "Compensation and Conceptions of Victims of Crime." *Victimology* 18, 1–2: 204–12.

Morgan, M., and D. O'Neill. 2001. "Pragmatic Post-Structuralism (II): An Outcomes Evaluation of a Stopping Violence Programme." *Journal of Community & Applied Social Psychology* 11: 277–89.

O'Neill, D., and M. Morgan. 2001. "Pragmatic Post-Structuralism: (I): Participant Observation and Discourse in Evaluating Violence Intervention." *Journal of Community & Applied Social Psychology* 11: 263–75.

Penelope, J. 1990. *Speaking Freely*. New York: Pergamon.

Reynolds, V. 2001. "Wearing Threads of Belonging: The Cultural Witnessing Group." *Journal of Child and Youth Care* 15: 89–106.

Scott, J.C. 1990. *Domination and the Arts of Resistance: Hidden Transcripts*. New Haven, CT: Yale University Press.

Sykes, Gresham M., and D. Matza. 1957. "Techniques of Neutralization: Theory of Delinquency." *American Sociological Review* 22: 664–70.

Tatlock, Melissa, and Linda Coates. 2003. "Disguising Violence: Violence in Children's Films." Manuscript in progress. St. Thomas University.

Todd, N. 2002a. "An Eye for an I: Response-based Work with Perpetrators of Abuse." Unpublished manuscript.

____. 2002b. "An Introduction to Response-based Counseling with Victims of Interpersonal Violence." Calgary, AB: Calgary Women's Emergency Shelter.

Todd, Nick, and Allan Wade. 2003. "Coming to Terms with Violence and Resistance: From a Language of Effects to a Language of Responses." In Tom Strong and Dave Pare (eds.), *Furthering Talk: Advances in the Discursive Therapies*. New York: Kluwer Academic Plenum.

Trew, Tony. 1979. "Theory and Ideology at Work." In R. Fowler, G. Kress, and T. Trew (eds.), *Language and Control*. London: Routledge and Kegan Paul.

van Dijk, J. 1999. "Criminal Victimization and Victim Empowerment in an International Perspective." In J. van Dijk, R. van Kaam, and J. Wemmers (eds.), *Caring for Crime Victims: Selected Proceedings of the 9th International Symposium on Victimology*. NY: Criminal Justice Press.

Wade, A. 1995b. "Resistance Knowledges: Therapy with Aboriginal Persons Who Have Experienced Violence." In P.H. Stephenson, S.J. Elliott, L.T. Foster and J.A. Harris (eds.), *Persistent Spirit: Towards Understanding Aboriginal Health in British Columbia*. Victoria, BC: Department of Geography: University of Victoria.

____. 1997. Small Acts of Living: Everyday Resistance to Violence and Other Forms of Oppression. *Contemporary Family Therapy* 19, 1: 23–39.

____. 2000. "Resistance to Interpersonal Violence: Implications for the Practice of Therapy." *Psychology*. Victoria, BC: University of Victoria.

Weaver, Jill, Nick Todd, Cindy Ogden, and Laura Craik. 2005. *Resistance to Violence and Abuse in Intimate Relationships: A Response Based Perspective*. Calgary: Calgary Women's Emergency Shelter.

West, Krista, and Linda Coates. 2004. "Representation and Responsibility: An Analysis of Sexual Assault Trial Judgments." Saint Thomas University, Fredericton, NB.

Zemsky, B. 1991. "Coming Out Against All Odds: Resistance in the Life of a Young Lesbian." In C. Gilligan, A.G. Rogers and D.L. Tolman (eds.), *Reframing Resistance: Women, Girls, and Psychotherapy*. New York: Haworth Press.

RACISM AND COLONIALISM

Chapter 7

CRIMINALIZING RACE

Wendy Chan

From: *Marginality and Condemnation: A Critical Introduction to Criminology*, 3rd edition, pp. 247–267 (reprinted with permission).

Recent efforts to monitor racial bias in the "carding" practices of the Toronto police force highlight the troubled history that racialized communities have with criminal justice institutions (Rankin and Winsa 2013). Carding or street checks is a police practice that involves stopping, questioning and documenting people in mostly non-criminal encounters. A study by the *Toronto Star* paper found that Black people in Toronto were more likely than white people to be carded in 2013, even though the overall number of people carded had dropped from previous years (Rankin and Winsa 2013). Critics contend that this is evidence of systemic discrimination. In response, the Toronto police force claims they are working hard to eliminate racial bias from police practices.

The above example highlights how the issue of race and criminal justice in Canada is a complex one, shaped to a large extent by historical policies and practices. In the present day, the issue of race and criminal justice simmers in the background, punctuated at times by well-publicized events such as the mistreatment of undocumented migrants to Canada or the tensions between Aboriginal communities and the state. Unlike the United States, Canada has not seen the same level of antagonism between racialized communities and the criminal justice system. However, this is not to say that the issue of racism and criminal justice in Canada is unproblematic. Perceptions and allegations of discriminatory treatment of racialized groups have been and continues to be commonplace, with problems of racial profiling, over-incarceration and inadequate responses to victimization, to name a few, receiving ongoing attention by policy-makers and critical scholars.

This chapter unpacks the complex relationship between race and criminal justice in Canada. My starting point is the recognition that race and racism in Canada are still very relevant. Contrary to claims that we now live in a post-racial society, there remains unresolved tensions between racialized minorities and the state. Within the criminal justice system, racialized Canadians, particularly Black and Aboriginal Canadians, continue to experience higher levels of criminalization and incarceration. Stereotypes about who is more likely to commit crimes or engage in deviant behavior (e.g., "driving while Black," "shopping while Black," "flying while brown") remain strong reference points in shaping public perceptions about crime, dangerousness, fear and safety. Mainstream media have reinforced specific messages about race and criminality, making it easier to justify the punitive treatment of racialized minorities. Furthermore, there is a deep reluctance to acknowledge that these problems are structurally rooted, rather than the work of a "few bad apples" in the justice system. The legacy of colonization and racial discrimination in Canada has shaped contemporary processes of criminal justice, with racial injustices reflecting the differential power relations between white and non-white groups over time. Thus, the unequal treatment of racialized minorities in the criminal justice system is not accidental. It is the result of both conscious and unconscious practices, individual choice, institutional dynamics and systemic practices. As Omi and Winant (1994) observe, the state is inherently racial in that it does not stand above racial conflicts, but is thoroughly immersed in racial contests. Racial injustices in the criminal justice system are a reflection of the wider society. Therefore, recognizing how racial discrimination is structurally embedded in the justice system is the first step towards eradicating the harms and injustices that stand in the way of social and political equality for racialized minorities in Canada.

This chapter is organized around three key sections. In the first section, I examine contemporary debates on race and crime in Canada and the different intellectual approaches that have shaped the research in this area. For example, the positivist tradition, which uses the concept of race as a socio-demographic variable to describe victims and offenders in empirical research, has played a significant role in developing ideas about crime and criminals. I examine the limitations of this approach as well as the problems of conducting research on race and crime in Canada when there is limited access to statistical data on the racial and/or ethnic background of victims and offenders. I explore the problems associated with conceptualizing race as a fixed identity, and I situate the impact of these problems in the context of the criminal justice system. For example, the tendency to view some racial groups as more prone to criminal behaviour than others is one consequence to emerge from "race thinking." Critical approaches to race and crime emerged as a counter to the positivist tradition. I highlight the key issues critical criminologists have focused on in striving for racial equality and anti-racist practices in the criminal justice system. This section ends with a brief discussion of why many critical scholars have turned to the concept of racialization to frame discussions about racism and criminal justice in Canada.

Section two critically examines racialized constructions of crime in Canada. Drawing on a range of different examples, I demonstrate how the practice, discourse and policies of criminal justice have been shaped by racial stereotypes and myths or misperceptions about racialized groups. As many critical criminologists have pointed out, definitions of crime and criminal behaviour focus on street crimes or property crimes rather than corporate or white-collar crimes. Typically, racialized minorities are overrepresented in so-called street crimes. This creates the perception that danger or threat is strongly associated with racialized individuals and groups. Increased police attention and harsher sentences are then justified in the name of crime control.

The final section of this chapter explores the other side of this dynamic — the ways in which processes of criminalization target racialized individuals and groups. While some scholars have highlighted how crime is racialized in Canada, other scholars add that racialized groups are also more likely to have their acts and behaviours labelled as deviant and/or criminal. As such, they are at greater risk of being policed, investigated and prosecuted. Practices of racial profiling, over-policing and increased detention have resulted in the disproportionate representation of Aboriginal people, racialized Canadians and non-citizens, migrants and refugees in the criminal justice system. The effects of criminalization on racialized people has been devastating — they are widely demonized as the cause of chaos and disorder, and they have been denied basic human rights. Paying attention to patterns of criminalization will expose how racism is embedded in criminal justice practices, how it influences decision making and reinforces stereotypes about racialized minorities.

Throughout this chapter, race is understood to be a socially constructed category where meanings are not fixed, but contested and transformed through political struggle. The concept of race has always been problematic, and many scholars use the term in inverted commas to highlight the complex, political and contested nature of is usage (Mason 2000). Some scholars have argued for the use of ethnicity instead. I believe that the term is still analytically relevant. When used as an analytical term rather than a descriptive one, it highlights the power relationships that have shaped contemporary social relations in Canada, even while still recognizing its problematic status.

Race also intersects with other social characteristics, such as gender, class and sexual orientation, to produce racialized positions. Where possible, I use an intersectional approach to raise awareness of the complexity in the lives of racialized minorities. For example, many Aboriginal women who have been battered choose not to call authorities for help because they do not want to further criminalize male Aboriginal members of their community. Their responses differ from many battered non-Aboriginal women due to the convergence of factors such as gender, race and social class. By taking a wider lens to the study of race and crime, I hope to capture the nuances of these convergences in influencing crime and victimization as well as criminal justice policy and practice.

THE CONSTRUCTION OF THE RACE-CRIME PROBLEM IN CANADA

Mainstream criminological research on race and crime conceptualizes race as a socio-demographic variable. Much of this research is positivist in orientation, with a focus on highlighting the crime patterns of different racial and ethnic groups and comparing them to other social groups to locate causative factors. One of the central claims of mainstream criminologists is that criminals are different from non-criminals and that it is these differences, "criminogenic properties," that compels them into crime. These differences can include having different biological or genetic features such as low IQ or testosterone levels, or they may be different social conditions such as poverty, education and age. Once these differences are identified, and an individual has gone through intervention, treatment and reform, that person can be steered away from deviant and criminal behavior. This body of scholarship typically relies on official statistics to provide victim and offender profiles or to establish the crime rates and incarceration rates of a particular racial group (Trevethan and Rastin 2004). In Canada, the most discussed racialized group in the criminal justice system is Aboriginal people (Wood and Griffiths 1996). This is likely attributed to their history of being overrepresented in the criminal justice system. Other racialized groups, such as Black Canadians and immigrants, have received sporadic attention from Canadian criminologists (Roberts and Doob 1997; Gordon and Nelson 1996).

There are many limitations to treating race as an independent variable in criminological research. While positivist criminology offers a detailed picture of who is involved in the criminal justice system, there are also fears that the research creates false pathologies that may be used to naturalize and reify racialized people as inherently criminal (Phillips and Bowling 2003). For example, official crime statistics have been heavily criticized for its overrepresentation of marginalized and vulnerable social groups. Furthermore, the racial categories found in official statistics are often adopted at face value, raising further questions about the role of these statistics in perpetuating racial inequalities. Seeing some racialized groups as more criminogenic than others not only reinforces negative racial stereotypes, but also leads to racialized groups being blamed for high levels of crime and delinquency. Methodologically, race scholars have pointed out how the classification of different racial groups is inconsistently defined (Mann 1993), and they question whether or not humankind can be divided according to skin colour. As geneticist James King (1981) explains, formulating a typology of races is an arbitrary exercise because there is no objective (biological) criteria for dividing humans in this way. Thus, attempts to develop a racial classification scheme cannot be easily divorced from the assumptions about human origins and group inferiority and superiority that inform these classification systems.

Efforts to move beyond crude and essentialist categorizations of racialized minorities have been taken up by critical criminologists who have adopted a different approach. Contrary to the positivist tradition, these criminologists regard race as the product of social interactions and argue that racial categories are not fixed and immutable, but fluid and subject to change. That is, race is a social idea where racial categories and meanings are constructed by the dominant group in society as one way to mark difference. Racial differences are used to justify discriminatory treatment and the differential allocation of rights and resources. Much of the work of critical criminologists centres on examining whether or not the treatment of offenders and victims by the criminal justice system is racially biased and highlighting differential trial outcomes and overrepresentation or underrepresentation in the prisons, for example. Comack's (2012) study of policing of Aboriginal communities is exemplary. She highlights how the relationship between Aboriginal people and the justice system is shaped by colonization, decades of mistreatment and inequality. As a result, Aboriginal people do not trust the police and are reluctant to cooperate with the justice system, while police officers have been accused of over-criminalizing Aboriginal people. For critical scholars, then, racial prejudice and discrimination are key factors in explaining the differential criminal justice treatment and outcomes of non-white offenders and victims. Tanovich (2008: 656) questions whether or not fundamental justice is possible for Aboriginal and racialized communities given the limited impact of reforms on racial injustice in Canada.

Whether consciously or unconsciously, criminological research has reproduced racial hierarchies, but it has also been the site of resistance. For example, although historically there were criminal anthropologists such as Lombroso arguing that criminals were evolutionary throwbacks and the "white races [were] the triumph of the human species" (cited in Miller 1996: 185), others such as Bonger were challenging the fascist movement and the superiority of Nordic peoples (Hawkins 1995: 23). Today, similar tensions within the study of race and crime persist, albeit in a more nuanced form. Positivist criminologists continue to analyze crime using official statistics and racial classification schemes, but they are cautious about claiming that racialized groups are more criminogenic as they recognize that unequal treatment affects the overrepresentation of racialized groups in the justice system. Critiques of biological determinism by critical criminologists also persist, with the added recognition that racial categories are unstable and that crime and definitions of crime are subject to change. Indeed, as they have pointed out, the socially constructed nature of both race and crime tells us more about systems of control and regulation and how the criminal justice system is used by the powerful to dominate and subordinate the powerless than it does about racial groups.

It is within this context of criminological scholarship that an ongoing debate has been taking place in Canada over whether or not the government should even be collecting data on race and crime. The Canadian government has never systematically collected race-based data in the criminal justice system, and as a result, it has been more difficult to provide a detailed portrait of the relationship between race and crime in Canada. While there is a wealth of information in the U.K. and the U.S. on this topic, there is much less research available in Canada. The only data that is routinely collected in this area are federal imprisonment rates for Aboriginal people. During the 1990s, Canadian criminologists were engaged in a lively debate over whether or not statistics on race and crime should be collected. Scholars such as Thomas Gabor (1994) argued that restricting access to this information is both "alarmist" and "paternalistic" and that the public should not be denied access to information about their security and safety (Gabor 1994: 154). Furthermore, race-based crime statistics can be used to challenge racial inequality by invalidating biological explanations of crime, by identifying areas of criminal justice practices that are in need of reform and by identifying problems that disproportionately impact minority communities (Wortley 1999). Scholars who support the continued ban on collecting raced-based crime statistics state that racism in the justice system can be studied without the need for race-based crime statistics (Johnston 1994). They express a number of concerns, such as fears that the police would not be able to collect reliable and accurate data, that the accuracy of race-based crime statistics would be hampered by the changing definitions of race and crime, that the public will misinterpret the data and that racism and discrimination against minority groups will increase as a result of this data (Johnston 1994; Roberts 1994). Instead of an all-or-nothing approach, Wortley (1999) suggests several compromises such as restricting who would have access to the data and the type of analysis that would be permitted with the data.

Successive governments in Canada have not indicated any interest in changing the status quo. What has changed since the 1990s is that many minority groups are now calling for the collection of race-based crime statistics in order to redress racial discrimination in the justice system (Owusu-Bempah and Millar 2010) because they recognize that the lack of race-based crime data is a double-edge sword: while not collecting data may prevent further racism and discrimination from taking place, the absence of race-based data also makes understanding racial discrimination and mistreatment by criminal justice officials much more difficult. More recently, Paul Millar and Akwasi Owusu-Bempah (2011) have made a spirited call for change, arguing that race-based crime data is necessary to conduct quantitative anti-racism research. They attempt to put more pressure on policy-makers to revisit the ban on data collection by claiming that criminal justice institutions in Canada are deliberately suppressing race-based crime data and that this is an attempt to avoid accountability and to "whitewash" the criminal justice system. Indeed, in this post-September 11 context, where racism has reached new heights in many minority communities due to fears around national security, previous concerns that race-based crime data would exacerbate or act as a justification for discriminatory behavior appear moot. Racial profiling, for example, is now routinely practiced by law enforcement agents, and many minority communities have suffered grave injustices (e.g., Arab and Muslim communities) without the ability to counter official claims and negative public perceptions due to the lack of data available.

Despite the absence of race-based crime statistics in Canada, criminologists have produced a small but rich body of qualitative scholarship examining topics such as racial profiling (Satzewich and Shaffir 2009), the criminal justice treatment of racialized Canadians (Anand 2000) and perceptions of crime and justice by minority communities (Oriola and Adeyanju 2011). Intellectual interest in this area of study remains strong, particularly by critical scholars carrying out research examining the treatment of racial minorities as an index of social control and how the criminal justice system is used to perpetuate racial inequality (Gordon 2006; Nelson 2011).

Yet critical researchers are increasingly wary of using the concepts "race" and "crime," with some scholars opting instead for terms like racialization and criminalization. As mentioned earlier, one significant consequence of this way of thinking has been the tendency to view entire communities as predisposed for criminal behavior by virtue of their racial identity. Furthermore, others suggest that race as an analytical concept in criminal justice is too limiting. Walsh and Yun (2011) argue that it would be more fruitful to consider race as both a biological reality *and* a social construction. Although there is no scientific basis to the category of race, the concept of race still exists and continues to be used in official and unofficial discourse. They state that "we cannot change the underlying reality, but we can certainly change our beliefs about the representation of that reality" (Walsh and Yun 2011: 1281).

An emphasis on racialization draws attention to the process in which racial understandings are formed and reformed in the creation of racialized positions, thus recognizing that social understandings and the implications and consequences of race change over time. For example, southern and eastern Europeans have been deracialized and assigned to the broad category of white. As Satzewich observes, "Many European groups that are now routinely thought of as white were far from being considered white as little as two or three generations ago ... Groups from the southern and eastern periphery of Europe were particularly prone to racialized othering" (2000: 277). Yet Omi and Winant (1994) are careful to point out that the creation and characterization of racial categories is a variable process that has played out differently for different groups. For example, Aboriginal people in Canada were subjected to harsh assimilation policies, and Asian and Black people were excluded from Canada; more recently, Arab and Muslim Canadians are labelled as terrorists. Different processes of racialization have resulted in a racial hierarchy that sees whites on top and minorities, particularly Aboriginal and African/Black Canadians, at the bottom (Omi and Winant 1994). In the context of criminal justice, decades of disproportionate representation of Aboriginal people in Canadian prisons is evidence that a certain type of "race thinking" makes this phenomenon possible. The state's capacity to wield such power over a certain segment of society demonstrates its ability to reproduce racial hierarchies and maintain racial hegemony. Thus, even if race has no essence, racism persists, and mapping out the complex manifestations of racism in the criminal justice system by highlighting the power differentials implicated in the practice of racism is a central feature of racialization.

Within Canadian society, racism is often either denied through claims that we live in a multicultural society and race no longer matters, or it is held to be an individual problem, rather than a structural or systemic issue. Where racial inequality occurs, it is often regarded as a problem "of the people who fail to take responsibility for their own lives" (Brown et al. 2005: vii) rather than an institutional problem. This view can be found across many social institutions in Canada, from police chiefs denying that racial profiling occurs (Satzewich and Shaffir 2009), to politicians labelling asylum seekers coming to Canada as illegitimate or illegal (Levine-Rasky 2012), to the mainstream media virtually ignoring the topic of racism altogether (Décoste 2013a). Yet, when you commit a crime, as Rachel Décoste (2013b) notes, your race matters. Compare the treatment of Rob Ford, ex-mayor of Toronto, or Mike Duffy, a Conservative senator, two public figures caught in crime-related scandals, to the treatment of racialized offenders, whom the previous minister of citizenship and immigration, Jason Kenny, would like to "deport without delay" from Canada (Décoste 2013b). In contrast, there has not been any discussion of a similarly punitive treatment for Rob Ford or Mike Duffy. For many race scholars in Canada, this double standard comes as no surprise. The multicultural discourse in Canada celebrates a tolerance of Aboriginal and racialized minorities while ignoring acts of colonial violence, genocide, residential schools and racist immigration

policies. Respect for racial differences are based on white decisions and their definition of what are *allowable* differences (O'Connell 2010: 540). While ethnic food
and cultural celebrations are welcomed, social and economic demands are not. As
Bannerji (1997: 35) states, "Multiculturalism is itself a vehicle for racialization. It
establishes Anglo-Canadian culture as the ethnic core culture while 'tolerating' and
hierarchically arranging others around it as 'multiculture.'" Dua, Razack and Warner
(2005) add that national mythologies operate to sustain Canada's vision of itself
as a white nation, even though many urban centres like Vancouver and Toronto
are increasingly moving towards a majority-minority population.

Problems of racial discrimination in Canada are more subtle today compared to
historical practices, but they have not disappeared. The everyday racism found in
body language or tone of voice is one that many racialized Canadians experience.
As one Ontario community organizer noted, "Racism is prevalent, persisting and
perpetually growing [in Canada]" (Douglas and Rosella 2013). In the criminal
justice system, racial discrimination takes on many forms — from not being able
to access services and programs, to harsher sentences and deaths in police custody.
The paucity of research in Canada has allowed culturally produced images of crime
and criminals, by mainstream media in particular, to reinforce racial stereotypes and
myths about crime and victimization. Like many Western states, criminal justice
in Canada is heavily racialized.

RACIALIZED CONSTRUCTIONS OF CRIME IN CANADA

In Ontario, allegations and counter-allegations of a race problem in the justice system led to a public inquiry into the issue of systemic racism in the criminal justice
system in the mid-1990s. The Commission's key findings were that Black males
in Ontario were significantly more likely to be stopped by the police, to receive
harsher treatment by judges, to be refused bail or release before trial and to be
given a prison sentence than whites or other racialized minorities (Commission
on Systemic Racism in the Ontario Criminal Justice System 1995). Other studies
show that close to one-quarter of those incarcerated in Canada are Aboriginal,
even though Aboriginal people make up only 4 percent of the population. Black
and Aboriginal inmates are dramatically overrepresented in Canada's maximum
security federal penitentiaries and segregation placements — they are also more
likely to have force used on them, to incur a disproportionate number of disciplinary charges, to be released later in their sentences and to have less access to day
or full parole (Correctional Investigator of Canada 2013).

Despite these findings, the problem of crime has been, and continues to be,
framed primarily as a problem of deviant, minority communities. Whether it is the
suggestion that these groups are "innately criminal" or that they possess deviant

cultural values, public anxieties about crime and chaos fuel the ongoing hostility about their presence and alleged criminal tendencies. Crime is racialized when individual behaviours are attached to the traits of a wider racial community or group such that "whole categories of phenotypically similar individuals are rendered pre-criminal and morally suspect" (Covington 1995: 547). In Canada, the pool of people that comprise the "dangerous classes" has been, and continues to be, drawn largely from racial and ethnic communities, thereby allowing for their over-policing and subsequent disproportionate representation in the criminal justice system (Roach 1996).

Monaghan documents how Aboriginal leaders at the end of the nineteenth century were subjected to a campaign of surveillance and labelled as "good" or "bad" characters, depending on their willingness to assimilate and promote the colonialist project of expansionism (2013: 499). Fears of Indigenous danger and backwardness led to Aboriginal activities being problematized as suspect and dangerous and to the construction of Aboriginal leaders as abnormal and deviant because they threatened the advancement of settler colonialism with their demands for rights and dignity (Monaghan 2013). Similarly, Mosher's (1996) historical study of Black offenders in Ontario at the turn of the twentieth century found that they were more likely to be imprisoned for public order offences such as prostitution or vagrancy and to receive harsher sentences than white offenders. D'Arcy's (2007) study shows that, in Toronto, the "Jamaican criminal" has become a taken-for-granted category of pathology who embodies a threat to public safety and from whom "we" need to be protected, a perception that has remained unchanged for decades (D'Arcy 2007).

Law and order campaigns targeting behaviours linked to racialized communities magnify the perception that crime is implicitly associated with these communities. The war on drugs in Canada is an example. Gordon (2006: 74) argues that it is typically working-class people and immigrants of colour who are the main targets in the "drug war" even though they are mostly small-time dealers and people in possession of cannabis. Furthermore, under the pretext of drug criminalization, the police have been able to intervene more broadly in these minority communities to maintain social order. Similarly, Silverstein's (2005) study of parole hearings found that the racial identity of inmates was a factor in the decision-making process for. Parole board members set out conditions using different standards depending on the inmate's racial background. Aboriginal inmates were required to have more community involvement in their rehabilitation compared to other inmates, while Hispanic and Asian inmates were required to demonstrate higher levels of shame for their crimes. These expectations, done in the name of protecting society, were often based on racial and ethnic stereotyping, and they raise many questions about fairness and due process in parole hearings (Silverstein 2005).

When crime rates rose during the 1990s in Canada, the government at the time implemented many tough-on-crime policies such as mandatory minimum sentences, longer maximum sentences, restricted access to parole and easier transfers for youths committing serious offences to adult courts. Public fear of crime and violence, and a perceived decline in public safety, created escalating anxiety amongst Canadians. These harsher policies and practices were not unusual, as the United States and the U.K. had enacted similar crime policies during this period. A number of high-profile cases also led the public to believe that the crime problem was caused by racialized offenders. For example, the 1994 Just Desserts case in Toronto, where Georgina Leimonis was shot and killed in the Just Desserts café by two men of Jamaican heritage, led to a moral panic where the public believed that there was a Jamaican crime wave in Toronto (D'Arcy 2007). Minority communities fought back against these claims, pointing out how only two years earlier, two police officers in the Toronto region were acquitted of killing Michael Wade Lawson, a 17-year-old Black youth, and Raymond Lawrence, a 22-year-old Jamaican immigrant. Nonetheless, the report by the Commission on Systemic Racism in the Ontario Criminal Justice System (1995) found that in the minds of criminal justice managers, planners and workers, crime is strongly associated with particular racialized groups. Thus, the explosion of "get tough" measures aimed at assuaging public fears about crime had an implicit racial subtext.

Several decades later, the march towards increased punitiveness continues, despite falling crime rates and overcrowded prisons. In the fall of 2013, Stephen Harper's Conservative Government passed crime legislation that included the controversial provision of mandatory minimum sentences. Many critics argue that a tough-on-crime agenda is no longer appropriate, while one United Nations group has criticized the legislation for being "excessively punitive" on youth and expressed concern about the fact that Aboriginal and Black children are already dramatically overrepresented in the criminal justice system (*Toronto Star* August 19, 2013; Canadian Press 2012). Critics add that successive studies have demonstrated that incarceration is ineffective and unsustainable and that draconian policies have had little influence on curbing undesirable behaviours (*Toronto Star* August 19, 2013).

Further criticism from Howard Sapers, the Correctional Investigator of Canada, highlights the depth of the problem. In his annual report, he notes that federal correctional centres are currently overcrowded, dangerous and violent, all factors that could potentially result in riots (Correctional Investigator of Canada 2013). Sapers observes that "the growth in the custody population appears to be policy, not crime driven" (Correctional Investigator of Canada 2013). In other words, the drive towards punitive criminal justice treatment is not undertaken due to problems with high crime rates. Rather, it is a symbolic gesture by politicians seeking to demonstrate their ability to govern, and this relies on using racialized minorities as scapegoats. These "reforms" find their support in public opinion rather than criminal justice experts and professionals, and these reforms give priority to the interests of victims and victims' families (Garland 2000).

It has been suggested by scholars that current crime policies are a symbol for other social anxieties such as high unemployment and increasing poverty (Wacquant 2001). The "Blackening" of the carceral system is part of a larger risk management project to surveil and neutralize populations that are superfluous to the global economy and deemed a threat to social stability (Wacquant 2001).

This phenomenon is not only racialized, but it is also deeply gendered. For example, in Canada, the number of Black inmates, the majority of whom are men, has increased 75 percent in the last ten years (Correctional Investigator of Canada 2013), highlighting how these individuals have become collateral damage in the current neo-liberal economic regime, where secure, full-time work is no longer the norm. While women are being funnelled into part-time, precarious employment, unemployed, racialized men are increasingly being managed by the penal system (Wacquant 2001). Government efforts to rehabilitate or retrain citizens have been displaced by strategies aimed at simply neutralizing and managing these populations. Thus, those who are unable to find a place for themselves in the labour market are penalized and criminalized, and this is more likely in racialized communities where there are higher levels of economic deprivation and poverty.

RACIAL PROFILING

The use of race as a proxy for dangerousness is best exemplified by the practice of racial profiling. Targeting individuals for law enforcement based on the colour of their skin demonstrates how race informs the contemporary understanding of who or what poses a risk to society. In Canada, the debate on racial profiling has mostly focused on whether or not police forces actual practice racial profiling. A series of articles on racial profiling in the *Toronto Star* in 2002 highlighted the use of racial profiling, such as stop and searches, by the Toronto police force, sparking an intense public debate. In a follow-up report, the African Canadian Community Coalition on Racial Profiling found that there is widespread evidence that racial profiling exists in the greater Toronto area, with Black people being the primary targets of police stop and searches (Brown 2004). There have been many subsequent reports confirming the use of racial profiling in other provinces.

Racial profiling in Canada is a controversial practice, and police forces have routinely denied that they racially profile, despite many complaints by racialized Canadians (Smith 2006). However, after September 11, racial profiling became more widely accepted as a necessary tool for combatting terrorism and maintaining national security. Bahdi (2003: 295) states that in the context of the war against terrorism, racial profiling debates focused on whether Canadian society can morally, legally or politically condone the practice. Arab and Muslim communities became key targets of law enforcement. Arabs and Muslims found themselves subjected to multiple layers of screening at Canada's borders, with pre-entry assessments, fingerprinting and interviews with security or border officials becoming a common routine for many who wished to travel. Stories of people being denied access onto a plane, removed from planes for praying, denied visas to other countries or questioned extensively about their Canadian identity played out in a context where public sympathy was in short supply and recourse to fair treatment was not a priority.

Several high-profile cases of Arab and Muslim people being mistreated demonstrates how different life is for them compared to other Canadians. Maher Arar, a dual Canadian and Syrian citizen, was detained at JFK airport in New York while en route home to Ottawa from a vacation. Arar was (falsely) accused by U.S. officials of being linked to al-Qaeda and was deported to Syria, where he was imprisoned for ten months, during which time he was beaten, tortured and forced to make a false confession (maherarar.net). A Commission of Inquiry into Arar's case found that he was cleared of all terrorism allegations. In a similar case, Abousfian Abdelrazik, a Black, Muslim Canadian citizen, was accused of being a supporter of al-Qaeda and a terrorist during a trip he took to Sudan to visit his sick mother in 2003 (Brown 2008). He was jailed and tortured for nine months but never charged. Abdelrazik was arrested again in November 2005 and released in July 2006 (Brown 2008). The Sudanese government formally exonerated Abdelrazik in 2005, finding that there was no evidence of any links to al-Qaeda or terrorism (Koring 2011).

The consequences, both intended and unintended, suffered by Maher Arar and Abousfian Abdelrazik, and the many other racialized minorities in Canada, suggests that their suffering is not inconsequential. The lives of these two men have been shattered by Canada's national security agenda, which allows the terrorist label to be applied to citizens as easily as it is applied to non-citizens. Bahdi (2003) argues that while some people may argue that the harms endured are justified as the price to pay for fighting terrorism, the consequences, when viewed from a community perspective of systematic exclusion and marginalization, are not insignificant. Acts of discrimination fuel the belief that members of Muslim and Arab communities are dangerous internal foreigners despite their citizenship status (Dhamoon and Abu-Laban 2009). As Bahdi (2003: 317) states, "Those who turn to racial profiling as an anecdote for uncertainty will find neither solutions nor comfort. Racial profiling will produce only illusions of security while heightening the disempowerment and sense of vulnerability of racialized groups in Canada."

The association in the minds of many people between crime and racialized groups stems from crime legislation and from the activities of law enforcement agencies. It is also reinforced by the disproportionate media coverage of racialized individuals involved in crime. Numerous studies have found that racialized minorities are underrepresented in positive roles and overrepresented in negative portrayals that link them to social disorder and criminal behavior (Larsen 2006). Furthermore, recurring images in the mainstream media of racialized people generally having undesirable, dangerous or inferior traits or behaviours reinforces biases about the guilt or innocence the defendant (Entman and Gross 2008). Thus, when news stories focus on violent crimes, racialized people are more likely to appear as the perpetrators rather than the victims (Entman and Gross 2008). When racialized people are criminally victimized, their experiences are either minimized or ignored altogether. For example, media coverage of the missing/murdered Aboriginal women in Canada highlights the value judgments made by media institutions in which white women are positively portrayed as legitimate, innocent and worthy victims — "the girl next door" — while Aboriginal women victims are largely ignored and rendered invisible (Jiwani and Young 2006). Amnesty International notes that this hierarchy of worthiness creates an underclass of victims that could increase the victimization of Aboriginal women since the message to the rest of society is that these women don't matter (Amnesty International 2009). Media stereotyping of racial groups exacerbates the mentality that Canadian society is composed of "us" and "them," making it much more difficult for racialized and marginalized groups and individuals to be heard and treated with dignity and respect.

Thinking about how crime is racialized allows us to interrogate the policies and practices in the criminal justice system that continue to subjugate racialized people by labelling and treating them as deviant and dangerous. Historically, the criminal justice system has been, and continues to be, a key institution used to control racialized populations. As the discussion in this section illustrates, racialized groups have been the targets of moral panics and continue to be stereotyped as the criminal other. As Angela Davis remarks, "The figure of the 'criminal' — the racialized figure of the criminal — has come to represent the most menacing enemy of 'American society'" (1998: 270). The legacy of institutional and systemic racism has brutalized many communities, leaving them socially excluded, economically impoverished and politically disenfranchised. The politicization of crime in Canada, evident in the most recent crime legislation by the Conservative Government, will do little to mend the problems of racial inequality in the justice system.

CRIMINALIZING RACIALIZED BODIES

Racialized communities are the target of law enforcement practices due in large part to how we define what is a crime and who are the criminals in our midst. However, these communities have also been constructed and identified by the state as problematic and in need of greater surveillance and control. The racialization of crime works in tandem with the criminalization of race, which refers to the ways that racialized groups and individuals are labelled and targeted by the state as undesirable, leading to their subsequent criminalization, illegalization, marginalization and exclusion. In this final section, I examine how different racial groups have been the objects of increased criminalization and how various state agencies have relied increasingly on criminal justice strategies to manage a broad range of social issues such as immigration and welfare services. As Simon (2007: 8) observes, we govern through crime when we see crime as "the problem through which we seek to know and act on the conduct of others." Crime provides the metaphors and narratives for those seeking to make claims on those who are being governed in a non-criminal context such as immigration, schools or the welfare system. Governments are then able to deploy the use of criminal law and its associated technologies and mentalities as crime becomes the dominant rationale for governance. Simon (2007) states that "governing through crime" is now the default response by many governments to social, political and economic problems, and this wider use of crime control strategies in non-criminal contexts has expanded the net of control and punishment in racialized communities.

Immigrants and Refugees as "Criminals"

Within the last decade, migrants and asylum seekers have increasingly become the objects of intense policing. As migration becomes synonymous with risk, many developed nations have securitized their borders as a strategy for managing contemporary anxieties and fears arising from the effects of globalization. A key strategy adopted by Canada and other Western states for preventing unwanted migrants and immigrants from entering their respective countries is to criminalize their activities. The increasing criminalization of immigration taking place across many Western nations is the result of immigration and criminal justice practices merging and unifying to fend off the "criminal alien" (Kanstroom 2005). Aas (2007) notes that the image of the "deviant immigrant" is not new and has been a recurring theme in social research. Foreigners were often depicted as possessing powerful criminal tendencies, and their appearance as a threat typically occurs in concert with global and national migratory movements (Aas 2007).

Current images of the "deviant immigrant" are a prominent feature in Canadian political and media discourse. For example, Jason Kenney, the previous minister for immigration, repeatedly referred to asylum seekers as "bogus" or "queue jumpers," suggesting that their need for state protection is not legitimate, particularly those who come from countries he claimed were "safe" (Levine-Rasky 2012). The mainstream media also routinely depicts refugees as the cause of chaos and disorder, suggesting that their troubled backgrounds and cultural differences make them unsuitable for Canada (Bradimore and Bauder 2011). The treatment of 492

Sri Lankan asylum seekers who came by cargo ship to the west coast of Canada in the summer of 2010 illustrates this process. They were portrayed and treated as deviant and criminal rather than given compassion and protection. All of the asylum seekers were detained for several months, including women and children, with most of them eventually being deported from Canada. The representation of the Sri Lankan asylum seekers as posing a very real threat, as being "different from us," underscores how poverty and racial difference, disguised as dangerousness, is mobilized to justify the violation of their human rights. The government's response in light of this event was to introduce legislation, the Protecting Canada's Immigration System Act, which would impose mandatory detention for those the government deems to be "irregular arrivals," by which they are primarily referring to large numbers of boat migrants. Not only would these migrants be automatically detained for up to one year, they would also have reduced access to health care and delayed access to permanent residency, family reunification and travel documents even if they were found to be "genuine" refugees (Alboim and Cohl 2012).

Immigrants who are not highly skilled and economically independent do not fit the government's image of immigrants who are worthy and desirable. Instead, these "undesirable" immigrants and migrants have been constructed as deviant for causing social problems or needing state protection. For example, the passage of a recent parliamentary bill (C-43 — Faster Removal of Foreign Criminals Act) seeking to expedite the process of removing "foreign criminals" has been criticized for suggesting that Canada is "overrun with foreign terrorists, escaped convicts, war criminals and the like" (*Huffington Post* 2012). Non-citizens who have been convicted of a crime and sentenced to six months imprisonment or more will be deported without access to the appeals process. Critics have described this bill as an American-style, "one strike and you're out" policy (Godfrey 2012). One major criticism of this policy is the removal of long-time permanent residents who have lived in Canada since childhood but never applied for citizenship. Lorne Waldman (2013) contends that this law has nothing to do with "foreign criminals" — it is about stripping appeal rights from permanent residents.

Immigration enforcement has been given higher priority over issues such as refugee protection or humanitarian cases. Within the Immigration and Refugee Protection Act is a long list of preventative and deterrent measures that have been added or bolstered to control non-citizens and police the external borders. Expanded visa regimes (travellers who come from countries that require a visa to enter Canada), increased fines and penalties for airlines transporting foreign nationals without proper documentation, increased use of immigration detention and greater denial of access to appeals demonstrates how "undesirable" immigrants have been rebranded as security and criminality risks. Their treatment by the state reinforces and reproduces the boundaries between citizen and non-citizen, between those who belong to the nation and those who do not, and, in the process, it offers us a very particular vision of national identity. Racial politics are deeply embedded in immigration policies, making it possible to routinely deny basic rights to racialized groups defined as outsiders.

As a result of growing suspicion and resentment towards immigrants and refugees, public support for all these harsh measures has been high. This is not a new phenomenon, as there have always been groups of immigrant and refugees that have been the targets of intolerance and hate. However, as more people migrate around the world due to wars, environmental disasters or economic turmoil, rather than providing support for migrants, Western governments have bolstered their exclusionary policies in order to demonstrate that they are in control of their borders. The current Canadian government has incorporated many criminal law practices into immigration proceedings without providing procedural protections to immigrants and refugees. Immigrants and refugees who arrive in Canada without proper documentation, who seek asylum or who arrive through irregular channels such as using the help of smugglers to escape have all been rebranded as criminals. One of the harshest criticisms levelled at the Canadian government is the use of prisons to detain immigrants, a practice that has been widely condemned by national and international organizations since many immigrants are detained for non-criminal offences and the mixing of non-criminals with criminals is seen as highly undesirable.

The criminalization of immigrants and refugees illustrates how the mythical figure of the "deviant immigrant" has come to embody the dangers, insecurities and perceived risks of a rapidly changing global environment (Melossi 2003). The connection between migration and crime has been reinforced by the construction and treatment of foreignness as a criminal threat, and it has paved the way for punitive and restrictive policies. Furthermore, when these policies and practices are based on the racially motivated stereotype of migrants as the cause of crime and disorder, it is much more difficult to challenge their legitimacy. As Bosworth (2011) observes, foreign offenders often have limited numbers of supporters, therefore governments seldom experience any qualms about disrupting social relationships or violating human rights.

Policing Non-white People

However, it is not just immigrants and refugees who are subjected to intrusive levels of surveillance and policing. Aboriginal communities have been particularly impacted by intensive policing practices and mistreatment. Black people in the Greater Toronto Area, for example, are grossly overrepresented in use of force statistics, especially in police shooting incidents (Wortley 2006). Not surprisingly, various studies conducted on minority views of the police have found that visible minorities have less confidence in the police (Cao 2011) and that Canadian-born minorities perceive the justice system to be more biased than people of colour born outside of Canada (Wortley and Owusu-Bempah 2009).

A number of high-profile incidents involving Aboriginal men point to the tense relationship between these communities and the criminal justice system. In 1998, Frank Paul was picked up by the police in Vancouver's downtown eastside for being drunk in a public place, placed in lockup, released, then taken into custody again where the sergeant in charge refused to accept him a second time. At the time of his second arrest, he could barely walk. Frank Paul was then left in an alleyway, where he was found dead of hypothermia a few hours later (Razack 2012: 909). Six Aboriginal men in Saskatchewan have also died as a result of mistreatment by the police. These men froze to death when they were given a "starlight tour" — the police picked up the intoxicated Aboriginal men, drove them to a remote area of town and then dropped them off, leaving them to find their way home (Comack 2012). In most cases of starlight tours, the men are only lightly dressed and not prepared for the cold weather. While Aboriginal leaders argued that the treatment of these men demonstrates the pervasive racism in the Saskatoon Police Service, the police force and its supporters denied any wrongdoing and claimed that the stories were myths (Comack 2012). Eventually, an inquiry was conducted into the death of one of the men, Neil Stonechild, with the conclusion that the police did not adequately investigate the case for fear that one of their own officers may have been involved his death (Cheema 2009: 91). A public inquiry was also held to investigate Paul's death, and although the report acknowledged how racism and colonialism contributed to Frank Paul's demise, in the end, no one was found criminally responsible for his death (Davies 2011). Finally, there is also the well-known case of Donald Marshall, a Mi'kmaq man from Halifax who was wrongly convicted of killing Sandy Seale in the 1970s. He spent eleven years in prison until he was finally released and an inquiry was held to investigate his wrongful conviction. The Commissioners for the Inquiry concluded that the criminal justice system had failed Donald Marshall (Hickman 1989). Not only did the courts accept perjured evidence, but also the Crown, the judge and even the defence lawyer for Marshall had made many errors in his case (Hickman 1989). It was only by coincidence that his innocence was finally established (Hickman 1989: 5).

While many of these well-known cases involved racialized men, racialized women's experiences of the criminal justice have not been significantly more positive. For example, their experiences of criminal victimization has often been minimized or dismissed by the justice system. It is not uncommon for police officers to view violence within racialized communities as normal or reasonable, and, therefore, when racialized women are victimized, they are often left with few options for seeking protection (Adelman et al. 2003). Furthermore, Aboriginal women's sexual victimization is often not believed in court trials and the harms they suffer are trivialized (Dylan, Regehr and Alaggia 2008). Racialized and indigenous women typically do not fit the role of the "ideal" or "authentic" victim of sexual assault because racial stereotypes depict them as more blameworthy and less deserving of protection (Randall 2010). Women in general are reluctant to report crimes of sexual assault or domestic violence, but racialized women, despite higher rates of victimization, are even less likely to seek legal redress through the justice system for fears of not being believed or being revictimized by the system (Regehr et al. 2008).

Race and Poverty

Poor people, particularly poor, racialized women, are typically portrayed as individuals with moral or psychological deficiencies (Fraser and Gordon 1994). Despite years of significant cutbacks in state support, the assumption held by many is that poor people deserve their life situations because they fail to rise up to the challenges of the labour market. Constructions of their poverty emphasize their pathological lifestyles, such as the belief that women of colour are hypersexed and promiscuous and that they have children to obtain more welfare money (Abramovitz 2006). Many people thus assume that poor people, especially poor, racialized individuals, are receiving state support illegitimately and believe that punitive action is needed to control this population. Municipalities across Canada have passed bylaws and legislation criminalizing the activities of poor people. Panhandling, squeegeeing, sleeping in public and loitering are activities that have been reconstituted as disorderly and result in criminal sanctions (Hermer and Mosher 2002). Welfare policies have also been recrafted with the presumption that recipients are "guilty until proven innocent," that their conduct needs to be carefully supervised and remedied by restrictive and coercive measures and that deterrence and stigma are necessary to modify behavior (Wacquant 2009: 79). This approach rejects racism and sexism, believing that anyone who really wants to work hard will succeed (Davis 2007). The convergence of penal and welfare practices illustrates how harsher treatment will be the default response to managing the problems of poverty.

MARGINALIZED AND CONDEMNED

The criminalization and marginalization of racialized communities has been made possible by depicting people of colour as less deserving of state protection or support and more likely to be in need of surveillance and control. For example, in 2005, concerns about gun violence by young Black men in Toronto led to explanations that the problem was one of family dysfunction, where many Black youths were growing up in households without a father figure (Lawson 2012). Media discourse at the time repeatedly highlighted how Black single mothers were failing to raise their children properly and how these Black youths were now becoming a dangerous class. Rarely was there acknowledgement of the structural barriers such as inadequate education or employment discrimination that shape and limit the possibilities of parenting in Black families. Even less talked about are the ways in which criminal justice practices, such as over-policing and racial profiling, destabilize Black families, which is seen most clearly in the high rates of incarceration for Black males and the high rates of Black, single-female parented families (Lawson 2012: 815–16) As a result, even as crime rates decline in the twenty-first century, the disproportionate representation of people of colour throughout Canada's justice system remains. Racialized patterns of crime and punishment are taking place in a context where public discourse about crime excludes and/or dismisses the problems of race and racism and, therefore, excludes any need to acknowledge or address issues of racial discrimination in the justice system. Yet, racism continues to shape the social and economic outcomes for many people, and while many social institutions may eschew racialized language in their policies, practices and discourse, the prevalence of racism's institutional entrenchment — most evident in the criminal justice system — is clear.

There is a deep reluctance in the justice system and, arguably, in Canadian society to address issues of racial discrimination and engage in meaningful discussions about the treatment of racialized Canadians. Even as criminal justice practices are now extending into other social institutions such as immigration and welfare services as a way to manage potential threats and security issues, and even though the co-optation of criminal justice policies and practices has a disproportionate effect on racialized communities, there is a "socially recurrent blindness to racism" present (Hesse 2011). Racism is no longer seen as a social problem, and discussions about race in the public sphere are taboo. As a result, practices of race privilege, racial discrimination and racial profiling are now denied public representation. There is a tendency to avoid any acknowledgement of racialization and state-racial arrangements, yet, under the threat of terror or crime, the state simultaneously enforces racial oppression through increased surveillance and policing. As the examples throughout this chapter highlight, there are many state policies and practices that disproportionately disadvantage racial groups but have been legitimated as necessary in order to protect Canadians. The discourse of risk and safety allows the state to police racialized people and communities, overriding equality laws. Thus, commitments to address racial inequalities and to uphold the values of equality, due process and justice dissolve.

References

Aas, F. 2007. *Globalization and Crime*. London: Sage Publications.

Abramovitz, M. 2006. "Welfare Reform in the United States: Gender, Race and Class Matter." *Critical Social Policy* 26, 2: 336–64.

Adelman, M., E. Erez and N. Shalhoub-Kevorkian. 2003. "Policing Violence Against Minority Women in Multicultural Societies: 'Community' and the Politics of Exclusion." *Police and Society* 7: 105–33.

Alboim, N., and K. Cohl. 2012. *Shaping the Future: Canada's Rapidly Changing Immigration Policies*. Toronto: Maytree Foundation.

Amnesty International. 2009. *No More Stolen Sisters*. London: Amnesty International Publications.

Anand, S. 2000. "The Sentencing of Aboriginal Offenders, Continued Confusion and Persisting Problems: A Comment on the Decision in R. v. Gladue." *Canadian Journal of Criminology* 42: 412–20.

Bahdi, R. 2003. "No Exit: Racial Profiling and Canada's War Against Terrorism." *Osgoode Hall Law Journal* 41, 2&3: 293–317.

Bannerji, H. 1997 "Geography Lessons: On Being an Inside/Outsider to the Canadian Nation." In L. Roman and L. Eyre (eds.), *Dangerous Territories: Struggles for Differences and Equality*. New York: Routledge.

Bosworth, M. 2011. "Deportation, Detention and Foreign-National Prisoners in England and Wales." *Citizenship Studies* 15, 5: 583–95.

Bradimore, A., and H. Bauder. 2011. *Mystery Ships and Risky Boat People: Tamil Refugee Migration in the Newsprint Media*. Metropolis BC, Working Paper Series 11-02.

Brown, J. 2008. "Ottawa Refuses to Help Canadian in Sudan: Lawyer." *Toronto Star*, April 28.

Brown, M. 2004. *In Their Own Voices: African Canadians in the Greater Toronto Area Share Their Experiences of Police Profiling*. Toronto: African Canadian Community Coalition on Racial Profiling.

Brown, M.K., M. Carnoy, E. Currie, T. Duster, D. Oppenheimer, M. Schultz and D. Wellman. 2005. *White-Washing Race: The Myth of a Color-Blind Society*. Berkeley: University of California Press.

Canadian Press. 2012. "Canada's Tough-on-Crime Agenda 'Excessively Punitive.'" *Canadian Press*, October 9.

Cao, L. 2011. "Visible Minorities and Confidence in the Police." *Canadian Journal of Criminology & Criminal Justice* 53, 1: 1–26.

Cheema, M. 2009. "Missing Subjects: Aboriginal Deaths in Custody, Data Problems, and Racialized Policing." *Appeal* 14: 84–100.

Comack, E. 2012. *Racialized Policing: Aboriginal People's Encounters with the Police*. Black Point, NS: Fernwood Publishing.

Commission on Systemic Racism in the Ontario Criminal Justice System. 1995. *Final Report*. Toronto: Queens Printer.

Correctional Investigator of Canada. 2013. *Annual Report of the Office of the Correctional Investigator 2012–2013*. Ottawa: The Correctional Investigator of Canada.

Covington, J. 1995. "Racial Classification in Criminology: The Reproduction of Racialized

Crime." *Sociological Forum* 10, 4: 547–68.

D'Arcy, S. 2007. "The 'Jamaican Criminal' in Toronto, 1994: A Critical Ontology." *Canadian Journal of Communications* 32: 241–259.

Davies, W.H. 2011. *Inquiry into the Death of Frank Paul. Final Report: Alone and Cold.* Victoria, BC: Ministry of the Attorney General, Criminal Justice Branch.

Davis, A. 1998. "Race and Criminalization: Black Americans and the Punishment Industry." In W. Lubiano (ed.), *The House That Race Built.* New York: Vintage Books.

Davis, D. 2007. "Narrating the Mute: Racializing and Racism in a Neoliberal Moment." *Souls* 9, 4: 346–60.

Décoste, R. 2013a. "Don't Ask, Don't Tell: Canada's Approach to Racism." *Huffington Post*, November 18.

____. 2013b. "When You Commit a Crime, Your Race Matters." *Huffington Post*, May 27.

Dhamoon, R., and Y. Abu-Laban. 2009. "Dangerous (Internal) Foreigners and Nation-Building: The Case of Canada." *International Political Science Review* 30, 2: 163–83.

Douglas, P., and L. Rosella. 2013. "Racism Is Prevalent, Persisting and Perpetually Growing, Experts Warn." *Mississauga.com*, November 25.

Dua, E., N. Razack and J. Warner. 2005. "Race, Racism, and Empire: Reflections on Canada." Social Justice 32, 4: 1–10.

Dylan, A., C. Regehr and R. Alaggia. 2008. "And Justice for All? Aboriginal Victims of Sexual Violence." *Violence Against Women* 14: 678–96.

Entman, R., and K. Gross. 2008. "Race to Judgment: Stereotyping Media and Criminal Defendants." *Law and Contemporary Problems* 71: 93–133.

Fraser, N., and L. Gordon. 1994. "A Genealogy of 'Dependency': Tracing a Keyword of the U.S. Welfare State." *Signs* 19, 2: 309–36.

Gabor, T. 1994. "The Suppression of Crime Statistics on Race and Ethnicity: The Price of Political Correctness." *Canadian Journal of Criminology* 36: 153–63.

Garland, D. 2000. "The Culture of High Crime Societies." *British Journal of Criminology* 40: 347–75.

Godfrey, T. 2012. "Proposed Deportation Law Under Fire." *Toronto Sun*, October 1.

Gordon, R., and J. Nelson. 1996. "Crime, Ethnicity and Immigration." In R. Silverman, J. Teevan and V. Sacco (eds.), *Crime in Canadian Society,* fifth edition. Toronto: Harcourt Brace.

Gordon, T. 2006. "Neoliberalism, Racism and the War on Drugs in Canada." *Social Justice* 33, 1: 59–78.

Hawkins, D. 1995. *Ethnicity, Race and Crime.* Albany: State University of New York Press.

Hermer, J., and J. Mosher. 2002. *Disorderly People: Law and the Politics of Exclusion in Ontario.* Halifax: Fernwood Publishing.

Hesse, B. 2011. "Self-Fulfilling Prophecy: The Postracial Horizon." *The South Atlantic Quarterly* 110, 1: 155–78.

Hickman, T.A. 1989. *Royal Commission on the Donald Marshall, Jr., Prosecution: Digest of Findings and Recommendations.* Halifax, N.S.

Huffington Post. 2012. "Canada: A Nation of Foreign Terrorists According to Bill C-43." October 23. At <http://www.huffingtonpost.ca/irwin-cotler/billc-43_b_2005209.html> accessed November 5, 2012.

Jiwani, Y., and M.L. Young. 2006. "Missing and Murdered Women: Reproducing

Marginality in News Discourse." *Canadian Journal of Communication* 31, 4: 895–917.

Johnston, J.P. 1994. "Academic Approaches to Race-Crime Statistics Do Not Justify Their Collection." *Canadian Journal of Criminology* 36: 166–74.

Kanstroom, D. 2005. "Immigration Law as Social Control." In C. Mele and T. Miller (eds.), *Civil Penalties, Social Consequences.* New York: Routledge.

King, J. 1981. *The Biology of Race.* Berkeley: University of California Press.

Koring, P. 2011. "Canadian Abousfian Abdelrazik Taken off United Nations Terror List." *Globe and Mail,* November 30. At <http://www.theglobeandmail.com/news/world/canadian-abousfian-abdelrazik-taken-off-united-nations-terror-list/article4179856/> accessed November 13, 2012.

Larsen, S. 2006. *Media & Minorities: The Politics of Race in News and Entertainment.* Lanham, MD: Rowman and Littlefield.

Lawson, E. 2012. "Single Mothers, Absentee Fathers, and Fun Violence in Toronto: A Contextual Interpretation." *Women's Studies* 41: 805–28.

Levine-Rasky, C. 2012. "Who Are You Calling Bogus? Saying No to Roma Refugees." *Canadian Dimension,* September 25. At <http://canadiandimension.com/articles/4959/> accessed November 11, 2012.

Mann, C. 1993. *Unequal Justice: A Question of Color.* Bloomington: Indiana University Press.

Mason, D. 2000. *Race and Ethnicity in Modern Britain.* Oxford: Oxford University Press.

Melossi, D. 2003. "'In a Peaceful Life': Migration and the Crime of Modernity in Europe/Italy." *Punishment and Society* 5, 4: 371–97.

Miller, J. 1996. *Search and Destroy: African-American Males in the Criminal Justice System.* Cambridge: Cambridge University Press.

Monaghan, J. 2013. "Settler Governmentality and Racializing Surveillance in Canada's North-West." *Canadian Journal of Sociology* 38, 4: 487–508.

Mosher, C. 1996. "Minorities and Misdemeanours: The Treatment of Black Public Order Offenders in Ontario's Criminal Justice System, 1892–1930." *Canadian Journal of Criminology* 38: 413–38.

Nelson, J. 2011. "'Partners or Thieves': Racialized Knowledge and the Regulation of Africville." *Journal of Canadian Studies* 45, 1: 121–42.

O'Connell, A. 2010. "An Exploration of Redneck Whiteness in Multicultural Canada." *Social Politics* 17, 4: 536–63.

Omi, M., and H. Winant. 1994. *Racial Formation in the United States From the 1960s to the 1990s.* Second edition. New York: Routledge.

Oriola, T., and C. Adeyanju. 2011. "Perceptions of the Canadian Criminal Justice System Among Nigerians: Evidence from a local Church in Winnipeg, Manitoba." *International Journal of Human Sciences* 8, 1: 635: 56.

Owusu-Bempah, A., and P. Millar. 2010. "Revisiting the Collection of Justice Statistics by Race in Canada." *Canadian Journal of Law and Society* 24, 1: 97–104.

____. 2011. "Whitewashing Criminal Justice in Canada: Preventing Research through Data Suppression." *Canadian Journal of Law and Society* 26, 3: 653–61.

Phillips, C., and B. Bowling. 2003. "Racism, Ethnicity and Criminology: Developing Minority Perspectives." *British Journal of Criminology* 43: 269–90.

Randall, M. 2010. "Sexual Assault Law, Credibility, and 'Ideal Victims': Consent,

Resistance, And Victim Blaming." *Canadian Journal of Women and the Law* 22: 397–433.

Rankin, J., and P. Winsa. 2013. "Toronto Police Propose Purging Carding Information from Database." *Toronto Star*, October 4.

Razack, S. 2012. "Memorializing Colonial Power: The Death of Frank Paul." *Law & Social Inquiry* 37, 4: 908–32.

Regehr, C., R. Alaggia, L. Lambert and M. Saini. 2008. "Victims of Sexual Violence in the Canadian Criminal Courts." *Victims & Offenders* 3, 1: 99–113.

Roach, K. 1996. "Systemic Racism and Criminal Justice Policy." *Windsor Yearbook of Access to Justice* 15: 236–49.

Roberts, J. 1994. "Crime and Race Statistics: Toward a Canadian Solution." *Canadian Journal of Criminology* 36: 175–85.

Roberts, J., and A. Doob. 1997. "Race, Ethnicity and Criminal Justice in Canada." *Crime and Justice* 21: 469–522.

Satzewich, V. 2000. "Whiteness Limited: Racialization and the Social Construction of 'Peripheral Europeans.'" *Social History* 66: 271–90.

Satzewich, V., and W. Shaffir. 2009. "Racism versus Professionalism: Claims and Counter-Claims about Racial Profiling." *Canadian Journal of Criminal and Criminal Justice* 51, 2: 199–226.

Silverstein, M. 2005. "What's Race Got to Do with Justice: Responsibilization Strategies at Parole Hearings." *British Journal of Criminology* 45: 340–54.

Simon, J. 2007. *Governing Through Crime.* New York: Oxford University Press.

Smith, C. 2006. "Racial Profiling in Canada, the United States, and the United Kingdom." In F. Henry and C. Tator (eds.), *Racial Profiling in Canada.* Toronto: University of Toronto Press.

Tanovich, D. 2008. "The Charter of Whiteness: Twenty-Five Years of Maintaining Racial Injustice in the Canadian Criminal Justice System." *Supreme Court Law Review* 40: 655–86.

Toronto Star. 2013. "Editorial: Harper Government's Tough-On-Crime Laws Are Outdated." August 19. At <http://www.thestar.com/opinion/editorials/2013/08/19/harper_governments_toughoncrime_laws_are_outdated_editorial.html>

Trevethan, S., and C. Rastin. 2004. *A Profile of Visible Minority Offenders in the Federal Canadian Correctional System.* Ottawa: Correctional Service of Canada.

Wacquant, L. 2001. "Deadly Symbiosis: When Ghetto and Prison Meet and Mesh." *Punishment and Society* 3, 1: 95–134.

____. 2009. *Punishing the Poor: The Neoliberal Government of Social Insecurity.* Durham: Duke University Press.

Waldman, L. 2013. "Faster Deportations Come at the Cost of Compassion and Fairness." *Globe and Mail*, May 14.

Walsh, A., and I. Yun. 2011. "Race and Criminology in the Age of Genomic Science." *Social Science Quarterly* 92, 5: 1279–96.

Wood, D., and C. Griffths. 1996. "Patterns of Aboriginal Crime." In R. Silverman, J. Teevan and V. Sacco (eds.), *Crime in Canadian Society,* fifth edition. Toronto: Harcourt Brace.

Wortley, S. 1999. "A Northern Taboo: Research on Race, Crime and Criminal Justice in Canada." *Canadian Journal of Criminology* 41: 261–74.

____. 2006. *Police Use of Force in Ontario: An Examination of Data from the Special Investigations Unit. Final Report.* Toronto, ON.

Wortley, S., and A. Owusu-Bempah. 2009. "Unequal Before the Law: Immigrant and Racial Minority Perceptions of the Canadian Criminal Justice System." *Journal of International Migration and Integration* 10, 4: 447–73.

Chapter 8

SURVIVING COLONIZATION
Anishinaabe Ikwe Street Gang Participation

Nahanni Fontaine

From: *Criminalizing Women: Gender and (In)Justice in Neo-liberal Times,* 2nd
edition, pp. 113–129 (reprinted with permission).

*If you have come here to help me you are wasting your time. But if you have
come because your liberation is connected to mine, then we can work together.*
— Lilla Watson, a Murri woman who has been active in the struggle of
Aboriginal peoples in Australia

In June 2003, several body parts were found along the shoreline of the Red River in
Winnipeg. They were quickly identified as belonging to Felicia Solomon Osborne, a
16-year-old girl from the Norway House Cree Nation. Few media sources bothered
to cover this story. Those that did stated that Felicia Solomon had gang ties and
had been working the streets.

The murder of Felicia Solomon raises questions about the lived experiences
of Aboriginal women — Anishinaabe Ikwe — and their participation in gangs.
Ultimately, however, the question becomes: what do we need to learn as a community about Aboriginal women and girls and the contemporary context in which
they find themselves? To address such a question, we need to hear from them.

At a gathering in the summer of 2003, several organizations — Southern
Chiefs' Organization (sco), Mother of Red Nations Women's Council of Manitoba

(MORN), and Ka Ni Kanichihk Inc. — resolved to reach out to Anishinaabe Ikwe in order to grasp and appreciate their standpoint with respect to gangs. It was agreed that the participants in the study ought to be interviewed in a culturally appropriate, safe manner. There was also a consensus that the study should be pursued and presented from within an Aboriginal framework because there is so little indigenously driven research or analysis on the issue. As both the Manitoba Aboriginal Justice Inquiry (Hamilton and Sinclair 1991) and the Royal Commission on Aboriginal Peoples (1996) recommended, all research and program development as it relates to Aboriginal peoples must be pursued by and for Aboriginal peoples so that it is more effective, responsive and culturally sensitive to the needs of the Aboriginal collective.

My purpose here is to report on some of the findings of this study. To be clear, this chapter is not about "Aboriginal street gangs." That is to say, I will not be discussing the creation, structure, hierarchy and activities of the "street gang" as an Aboriginal phenomenon. No. This chapter concerns Aboriginal women's and girls' particular experiences in relation to the gang. That being said, we require a broader context in which we can situate the participants of the study, one that deconstructs the traditional discourse offered to account for the phenomenon of the "street gang." Simply put, Aboriginal street gangs are not what the dominant white settler society socially constructs them — a malignant and deviant thorn in the side of a so-called upstanding, productive, middle-class, Christian civilization. Rather, Aboriginal street gangs are the result of the settler colonial context and experience in contemporary Canada.

SETTLER COLONIALISM AND THE COLONIAL EXPERIENCE

Colonialism, in the words of John McLeod (2000: 7), involved "a lucrative commercial operation, bringing wealth and riches to Western nations through the economic exploitation of others." In the Canadian context, colonialism involved the process by which Europeans erected a settler colonial society based on the seizure of the territories of the Indigenous population. While the appropriation of land was a key element of settler colonialism, this colonization process was unquestionably racialized. As Patrick Wolfe (2006: 388) explains, "Indigenous North Americans were not killed, driven away, romanticized, assimilated, fenced in, bred White, and otherwise eliminated as the original owners of the land but as Indians." European colonizers aimed to eradicate Indigenous societies — what Wolfe (2006: 403) refers to as "structural genocide" in that elimination was not a one-time occurrence but an organizing principle of settler colonial society. Settler colonization, as Wolfe points out, is "a structure rather than an event" and settler colonialism is "a specific social formation" (2006: 390, 401). As such, colonialism is not simply a historical artifact that has no bearing on contemporary events. The racialization of Aboriginal people — "the process through which groups come to be designated as different and on that basis subjected to differential and unequal treatment" (Block and Galabuzi 2011: 19) — has continued to the present day. As Sherene Razack (2007: 74) notes: "As it evolves, a white settler society continues to be structured by a racial hierarchy."

Edward Said's work on postcolonialism offers important insights into representations of the colonial experience. As McLeod (2000: 21) tells us, Said's interest was in "how the knowledge that the Western imperial powers formed about their colonies helped continually to justify their subjugation." Said observed that Western or Occidental powers spent considerable energies producing knowledge about the territories they dominated. But seldom did they endeavour to learn from and about the Indigenous inhabitants of those territories. Rather, their knowledge was founded on questionable assumptions about the "Orient" and its inhabitants that served to justify colonial domination. What Said called "Orientalism," then, "operates in the service of the West's hegemony over the East primarily by producing the East discursively as the West's inferior 'Other,' a manoeuvre which strengthens — indeed, even partially constructs — the West's self-image as a superior civilization" (cited in Moore-Gilbert 1997: 38–39). In these terms, criminal justice reports on the "Aboriginal street gang" can tell us something about how these gangs are represented in colonial discourse.

A report released by the Royal Canadian Mounted Police "D" Division, Manitoba, in 2004 stated:

> The last two decades have seen numerous street gangs rise within both urban and rural areas of Manitoba. Although there are not any strictly aboriginal street gangs, aboriginal membership in several gangs is quite dominant. Some of the major aboriginal-based street gangs in effect, per se, are the Manitoba Warriors, the Native Syndicate and the Indian Posse. Alliances and rivalries are sometimes formed between these gangs, other street gangs and even the Outlaw Motorcycle Gangs in order to control the drug trade, prostitution and other illegal activities.
>
> Recruitment of gang members is an on-going process that is done by most gangs in order to build the gang in both numbers and strength. Once focusing on the major urban centres, recruitment has now filtered into the aboriginal communities of Manitoba. A growing scenario consists of a member from the community being arrested and then later incarcerated. Upon incarceration, this person is then recruited into the gang. Some are compelled to join a gang within the correctional centre in order to ensure their protection for fear of being targeted by the gangs within the centre.

Others join to belong, because they know someone in the gang or are lured by the thought of quick money and the gang lifestyle. Upon their release, they return to their communities and begin gang activity there, including recruitment of new members. (McLeod 2004)

Similarly, the 2004 *Annual Report on Organized Crime in Canada* of Criminal Intelligence Service Canada asserted:

Aboriginal-based street gangs are generally involved in opportunistic, spontaneous and disorganized street-level criminal activities, primarily low-level trafficking of marijuana, cocaine and crack cocaine and, to a lesser extent, methamphetamine. The gangs are also involved in prostitution, break-and-enters, robberies, assaults, intimidation, vehicle theft and illicit drug debt collection. Although the gangs' capability to plan and commit sophisticated or large-scale criminal activities is low, their propensity for violence is high, posing a threat to public safety. (Criminal Intelligence Service Canada 2004)

These reports share in common an interpretation of the gang as a deviant subculture centred on criminal activity, a subculture that persists because of the attraction of the gang lifestyle to its members. What many, if not all, such reports fail to recognize is the historical and contemporary colonial context that precipitated the advent of Aboriginal street gangs. Gangs did not arise owing to the "gang lifestyle," as some commentators naively argue and try to convince the general public. Aboriginal gangs surfaced, developed and organized in response to the reality and experience of colonization and its perpetual legacy in our daily lives. Aboriginal gangs are the product of our colonized and oppressed space within Canada — a space fraught with inequity, racism, dislocation, marginalization, and cultural and spiritual alienation (Razack 2002). It is a space of physical and cultural genocide that continues to exist even at this very moment.

From first contact with Europeans, Indigenous peoples' cultures, political systems, economies, lands, and traditional social constructions and mores were systematically and methodically attacked. In this respect, there is nothing "postcolonial" about Aboriginal peoples' experience. They continue to endure dislocation, deculturalization, ecocide and forced assimilation. Indeed, the question often posed by outsiders is "why can't you people just leave that in the past?" Without a doubt, settler colonialism is alive and well in Canada, and remains an insidious force permeating every aspect of the lives of the original inhabitants and rightful owners of this land.

An important illustration of the lingering effects of colonialism is the altered power relations between the sexes within our Indigenous societies. Traditionally,

Anishinaabe Ikwe's roles and responsibilities encompassed every aspect of community life. As life-givers and primary caregivers, women were respected and had a significant role in the decision-making processes of the community. Social relations were of an equal nature and did not involve notions that one sex was superior to the other (Gunn Allen 1992; Anderson 2000). Unfortunately, as a result of the introduction of Christianity and forced Christian marriages, incorporation into a capitalist wage economy, residential schools and the introduction of alcohol, Aboriginal men's and women's roles changed significantly.

As Carol Devens (1992: 5) argues, "The friction between men and women is in fact the bitter fruit of colonization." This is not to imply that gendered roles and responsibilities would have remained static and unchanging, but that colonialism directed their development in ways that Indigenous peoples would not have chosen. As a consequence of colonial processes, Anishinaabe Ikwe are doubly victimized; they are disempowered and oppressed within both the Euro-Canadian mainstream and the Indigenous collective. Anishinaabe Ikwe have become what one prominent Winnipeg community member calls "collaterals of war." Leslie Spillett, the Executive Director of Ka Ni Kanichihk Inc., suggests, "In most wars women and children are collateral damage, and we can extend this concept in which 'gangs' constitute, within the Canadian colonial context, external/internal warfare whereby women and children are both victimized" (personal communication, October 20, 2005).

Surely, one contributing factor toward gang involvement for Anishinaabe Ikwe is the abject poverty faced by our communities. Elizabeth Comack and her colleagues (2013: 8) report on the astonishingly high poverty rates for Aboriginal peoples, particularly in inner-city Winnipeg:

> Aboriginal people are overrepresented among the ranks of Winnipeg's poor. In 2005 over four in ten (43 percent) Aboriginal people — compared to 16 percent of non-Aboriginal people — were living under the low-income-cut-off (LICO), Canada's unofficial but commonly used "poverty line." Almost six in ten (57 percent) Aboriginal children aged fourteen years and under in Winnipeg were living under the LICO, compared to 20 percent of non-Aboriginal children ... While 20 percent of Winnipeg's households were living in poverty in 2006, that figure was 40 percent for inner-city households. For Aboriginal households in the inner city, the figure was much higher — at 65 percent.

Anishinaabe Ikwe leaving poor socio-economic conditions in their home communities (First Nation reserves and Métis communities) often come to the city alone or with their families in search of equitable opportunities and a better standard of living, but instead find a dominant Euro-Canadian mainstream society that is culturally alien to and the antithesis of their own experiences. Most, if not all, Indigenous newcomers to the urban environment face myriad racist, alienating and patronizing realities firmly entrenched within mainstream social institutions (see, for example, Silver 2006).

A second contributing factor is the loss or interruption of Indigenous cultural identity. The Royal Commission on Aboriginal Peoples (1996) noted that a fundamental component in Aboriginal youth joining gangs is the loss or dislocation of traditional Aboriginal culture. John Berry (1994), who conducted interviews with Aboriginal peoples on the notion of cultural identity for the Royal Commission on Aboriginal Peoples, argued that "behavioural expression" among the Aboriginal population was the most "concrete feature" of their sense of identity. Looking at the use of an Aboriginal language and the "daily activities related to one's culture (e.g., language, social relations, dress, food, music, arts, and crafts)" as indicators of behavioural expression, Berry (1994) found:

> Of the total adult population (aged 15 years and over), 65.4% of North American Indians on Reserve (NAI), 23.1% of NAI off Reserve, and 17.5% of Métis were able to use their Aboriginal language; 74.6% of Inuit were able to do so. There is a similar results [sic] for children (aged 5 to 14 years), but with even lower levels: 44.3%, 9.0%, 4.9% and 67.0% respectively. For participation in traditional Aboriginal activities, the pattern is repeated. For adults, the participation rates were 65.2%, 44.8%, 39.8% and 74.1%; and for children, they were 57.5%, 39.5%, 28.7% and 70.2%.

Berry interpreted these data to mean that Aboriginal peoples, particularly children, had lost a considerable degree of cultural identity since the advent of colonization.

It is under these circumstances that Anishinaabe Ikwe, some as young as eleven, are recruited by gang members and often targeted for exploitation in the sex and drug trades. According to Karen Busby and her colleagues (2002: 94), of the girls and women working in the sex trade on the streets of Prairie Canada, a higher percentage were of Aboriginal descent (58 percent) than Caucasian (42 percent). However, within the province of Manitoba, particularly in Winnipeg, that figure is likely to be much higher. Some researchers estimate that 70 percent of the youth and 50 percent of adults involved in the sex trade in Winnipeg are Aboriginal (Seshia 2005).

LEARNING FROM ANISHINAABE IKWE

The collaborative, participatory project undertaken with Aboriginal women and girls was designed taking into consideration the expressed needs and concerns of the participants, that is to say, as the principal investigator, my main priority was to ensure that the participants felt safe and secure in sharing their narratives. I conducted a series of individual tape-recorded, life-history interviews (repeated over time) with nineteen Anishinaabe Ikwe at agreed-upon times and locations. More often than not, this involved picking up the participant and going out for breakfast or lunch. As part of the exchange, each of the participants got an honorarium and a tobacco tie as recognition of the spiritual connection that occurs when two people discuss ideas, experiences, beliefs and emotions.

The study participants ranged in age from thirteen to forty-four years and were from a variety of First Nation and Métis communities in Manitoba and Ontario. Geographically they came from both Northern and Southern regions. One woman was born in the United States but had left early on in her childhood to come back to Manitoba. The First Nations participants had lived both on- and off-reserve, reflecting the migratory reality of Indigenous communities. At the time of the interviews, six of the participants were housed at the Portage Correctional Centre (a women's jail) in Portage La Prairie, and four were living at a Winnipeg inner-city girls' group home. One woman was living in Northern Ontario, and the rest of the women lived in either central Winnipeg (downtown) or the notorious "North End," an area now both physically and socially constructed as poor, decrepit, violent, gang-infested and degenerated (see Silver 2010; Comack et al. 2013). Of the nineteen participants, all but two had parents who had attended state-regulated and mandated residential schools; seventeen of the participants had grandparents and extended family members who had attended residential schools. All of the participants reported that one or both of their parents had been involved in drugs and alcohol from early childhood. Most of the participants had experienced encounters with Child and Family Services; indeed, one 19-year-old participant had over 136 placements — all of them with non-Aboriginal families.

Their oral narratives[1] provided new insights into urban Aboriginal gender relations, power structures, and strategies for coping with cultural dislocation. Overall, the project provided an opportunity for Anishinaabe Ikwe involved in street gangs to shed light on their experience and to assert their contemporary identity to the broader community.

ANISHINAABE IKWE IN RELATION TO THE "STREET GANG"

More and more on a daily basis, in Winnipeg at least, we hear stories about Aboriginal women and girls with reference to the "increasing numbers" and "increasing violence" of female gang members or female gangs. Interestingly, however, only three of the participants in the study (the oldest ones) declared that there were Aboriginal female gang members or Aboriginal female gangs. These participants told me that at one time in Winnipeg (in the early 1980s), there was a semblance of a women's gang deriving from one of the first Aboriginal gangs in Manitoba, the Main Street Rattlers. According to Tamara, the Main Street Rattlers was born out of *"youth just hanging out, trying to survive."* Mary insisted that the formation of gangs in Winnipeg occurred as a result of youth hanging out at Rossbrook House, an inner-city neighbourhood centre for young people that, ironically, is described on its website as being established for the purpose of offering "a constant alternative to the destructive environment of the streets."[2] Tamara explained:

> From the Rattlers came the Overlords and then from the Overlords they split. They changed themselves to the Manitoba Warriors. And they started feuding, so they went and said, "Well, we are going to make our own little gang called the Indian Posse."

Lucy maintained that the gang was different back then:

> At that time, they seemed to have a code of ethics, kind of like, "do no harm" within the gang. They had a sisterhood and a brotherhood, it was a family. It was a fine line that was drawn in terms of the "do no harm" within the gang system. I remember a time when they thought it was honourable to fight with your hands, not with weapons. And that female gang members who were a part of the gang, a lot of them went into prostitution and they could not participate in the heavy use of drugs. It was frowned upon because of the "do no harm" philosophy. It was never worded that but just the way they had a reverence for each other in that way. If you got into heavier drugs, it was frowned upon from higher-ranking members in the gang.

Lucy was also of the view that relations between the sexes in these gangs were equal: "*But at that time it seemed like it was equal. Base power to both the male and female. Like, it was so closely relational. Like, you know, really cared for each other.*" By the early 1990s, she said, the core of the gang had "*quickly turned to something else.*" When I asked her why she thought this change had occurred, she replied:

> Because maybe not having the skill to be able to put forth their message. You

know, not having the resources. Not having the support of the community because of where they come from. Because in our own community they put value on the paper, on a degree. On some kind of status that puts us in a certain type of leadership. I started seeing pieces that were starting to go on because the crime started to become more intense and more violent, like break-ins and the robberies and what not. Of course, it was fuelled by addictions.

In opposition to these stories, most participants in the study maintained that there were now no female gang members or female gangs, only "old ladies," "bitches" and "hos," each with specific defined roles and responsibilities. Participants explained that Anishinaabe Ikwe had their connection to the gang only by virtue of their relationships with male gang members. While many participants had family relations with gang members (a father, brother, uncle, and/or cousin were in the gang), for the most part participants saw their connection to the gang as deriving from their relationship with a male gang member. This relation to male gang members defined and constructed particular aspects of women's and girls' experiences and spaces.

Old Ladies

Throughout the interviews, many participants referred to themselves as "so and so's old lady." Old ladies are the girlfriends of male gang members. That is to say, they are women or girls with whom male gang members have some semblance of a committed and loving relationship. Tamara explained that a women's position in the gang was to further their "old man's" place and space within the gang: "*It depends who your old man is too. What his role is within the gang.*" Many participants noted that some women had decision-making capacities in the gang as well, depending upon how they were perceived by male gang members. Tamara explained:

Her knowledge and her experience in the gang — they [male gang members] just analyze the situation with certain women. Like they think "Oh you are so fucking stupid, you don't know what the hell you are talking about" or "Hey, that's something to really think about." They categorize it like that.

Another participant, who happened to be the boss'[3] old lady, noted that once a woman is considered and known as an old lady, everyone knows, respects and ensures that place, particularly if her partner is incarcerated.

All those little men, they watch you. They follow you around or stop you for the old man ... even when he was in the Remand Centre. His little friends would come to my mom's and buzz me. I came down and he would be on the cell phone and ask why I am not answering the phone ... I went up North.

No one, nobody knew I went up North. Nobody. Just me and my mom. I don't know how they knew I went up North.

While Aboriginal gangs do not necessarily have written codes of ethics or behaviour, there are unspoken, expected, and prescribed protocols, rules and responsibilities that everyone — including old ladies — must adhere to. Primarily, old ladies were expected to be "good." Candace explained that to be good meant:

Don't drink or run around with guys or go to the bars. Just stay home, that's what they expect you to do. Why would you make your old lady stay at home and stay indoors? Don't go outside, talk, speak when spoken to, stuff like that.

Candace went on to explicitly note: "*Gang members and their old ladies aren't allowed to do drugs.*"

Old ladies were expected to "be solid" — which implies, in the instance of physical assault, that a woman would just take the beating. To be solid means that an old lady does not seek help from social-service agencies or the police, or that she does not try to leave her partner for a women's shelter. As Tamara explained:

If you get out of it, the other women just say, "Okay, well then you are not solid enough." They just kind of shun you ... for complaining. You don't mention it [abuse shelters] but if you mention something like that then your old man is going to get mad at you, "Why are you fucking talking that shit?"

Tamara also maintained that Anishinaabe Ikwe stay out of the physical assaults of other Anishinaabe Ikwe by their intimate partners as a way of "being solid" with the gang: "*You just stay out of it.*" Mary similarly argues that other old ladies had to stay out of each other's business:

We couldn't stop it because we had to take it like a woman. If your man beats you up, take it. That's your norm. That is normal. Like my ex, I got all my teeth knocked out from him and, you know, I got stabbed so many times. You just take it.

Candace shared one incident (of many) in which she was being physically assaulted. Her story showed that not only women, but also male gang members, do not report or intervene in domestic relationships.

He has beaten me up a couple of times around his friends. There is, like, twenty guys there. I was twenty-six and he must have been, like, thirty ... There would be, like, twenty of them when they went to drink and he beat me up right in front of them. He just got out of remand and he said I was dogging him — fooling around on him … They just watch. They stood back and watched. I can't believe it, a bunch of them could have stopped him, pulled him away from me 'cause he had me up against the wall off my feet. Like, he had his hands around my neck and he was just yelling at me.

The normalization of abuse and the pressures on the women to "be solid" mean that some old ladies will actually make up stories about being physically abused in order to fit in with the other old ladies. Cathy explained:

You have to just accept it. If it is not happening to you, then you are lucky and you just keep quiet about it. I heard one girl saying things that her old man had pushed her head into the mirror while she was putting makeup on but she didn't have any marks to show for it. We'd all be showing our marks, our bruises and she didn't have any marks so we didn't believe her. So when we're alone with our old man we ask him that we heard so and so was beating up on so and so and he'll confirm that it's not like that.

Nevertheless, many respondents emphasized that a kind of sisterhood cultivates among old ladies because they are going through the same struggles and joys and operate within the same gang context. As Candace explained it, "*We know each other and we know what we are going through and we all know what it is like.*" Cathy said:

It just seems like if you're with a man that's in a gang — like, all the women that are going out with these gang members — they are automatically friends, even if you don't like someone. You have to be polite to her when you go to their house. And your kids all hang out together too.

Even if an Anishinaabe Ikwe is no longer with a particular gang member, according to many participants she will always have that connection through her child or children. Tamara described this connection:

If you have a kid from a gang member you will always be involved in that gang even if it was twenty years ago, thirty years ago. You will always be connected, especially the kids, especially the kids. They are second generation. They are like blessed. They get blessed into the gang. It is like they don't have to do anything to be in a gang. It is automatically a gang member.

While an old lady's place in the gang is determined largely by her relation with a male gang member, Cathy maintained that old ladies had some semblance of decision-making capacities and other responsibilities within the gang. For instance, some old ladies were solicited for their advice by male gang members: "*When they were selling rock, they used to ask us, 'Should we go over here tonight?' or 'What area should we do?' or 'Whose place should we go to first?' That is what they would be doing, asking us.*" Cathy also explained that some old ladies were designated as "drivers," which involved chauffeuring male gang members to various locations for a variety of activities (picking up drugs, committing break-and-enters).

Bitches and Hos

Most, if not all, study participants argued that at the lower rung of the hierarchy of Anishinaabe Ikwe involved in street gangs were the "bitches" and "hos." These women and girls were not looked upon favourably and were always described in pejorative ways. Sabrina noted that gang members "*always have a girl [old lady] at home that they like and stay with. But at the same time they are fucking all these other girls. Man, bringing home shit.*" Sabrina went on to note that "bitches" and "hos" also get pregnant from gang members:

> But at the same time these girls run around, "like this is your baby" but mean-while, they are fucking all these other guys, so nobody really knows what is going on. A "bitch" are the girls that dress all skanky and they run around.

Lorna maintains that "*Bitches and hos are just the girlfriends that work the streets. They call them bitches and hos. They just feed them drugs.*" Candace referred to women and girls that work the streets as "*just money-makers.*" The possibility of attracting such negative labels, however, was an ever-present concern for many of the women. Sabrina, for instance, commented that even by simple association, a woman or girl could be considered a "bitch" or "ho":

> You hang out with a bunch of "hos" then you are going to look like a "ho." I try to stay away from all girls because they make you look bad. They bring you down. They want to go scamming shit.

In addition to highlighting the nature of women's and girls' participation in the gang, these narratives begin to reveal the pervasive nature of violence in the lives of Anishinaabe Ikwe. The subject of violence permeated the discussions with the women and girls, who spoke of intergenerational violence, residential school physical and sexual abuse, and intra-female violence. One predominant theme was that of violence between male gang members and women. Violence in interpersonal relationships was not just an experience encountered by the older women in the study. One participant, who was turning fourteen at the time of the interview, recounted how, when she was twelve, she was assaulted by a fourteen-year-old gang member:

> I used to hang out with other gang members. I went to this one house because there was this guy that I liked. He asked me if I wanted to come over. I stayed

there for a while. We usually got high, drank sometimes. This one day I said, "I want to go home." And all of a sudden, he turns out the lights. He had this white thing, it was hard. He started hitting me with it, yelling, "You're not fucking going anywhere." He was just hitting me and I was crying … When [her friend] went in [the room], he was like, "Get the fuck out of here!" and he starts hitting her. I tried running out of the room but he just grabbed me and slammed me against the wall. I was all bruised up and beaten up.

Of all the narratives I heard concerning interpersonal violence between male gang members and women, Candace's account of one particular incident (of the many more she was to encounter) had by far the most profound effect on me. Candace shared how, when she was around seventeen, she was pregnant with her first child and only a week away from her due date when she and her boyfriend got into an argument over another man at a party. The fight escalated to where her boyfriend "grabbed a knife out of nowhere."

And he stabbed me in the stomach. It hit the baby through the baby's back and it almost came out the stomach. So after that they rushed me, everybody left that party and they phoned the ambulance. The cops took him and they don't know where the weapon was. I was in the hospital. I don't remember being in the hospital but I was there. I had a cesarean, they took it out. It was stillborn. I was due the next week.

How can we begin to make sense of these narratives, in terms of what they tell us not only about the relations between women and men, but also about those between the women and girls involved in gang activity? Again we have to keep in mind that relations between Indigenous men and women pre-contact were of an equal, fluid nature, and that the processes of colonization have had a dramatic impact on relations between the sexes. As the Royal Commission on Aboriginal Peoples (1996) stated:

The stereotyping and devaluing of Aboriginal women, a combination of racism and sexism, are among the most damaging of attitudes that find expression in Canadian society. These attitudes are not held exclusively by non-Aboriginal people either … Members of powerless groups who are subjected to demeaning treatment tend to internalize negative attitudes toward their own groups. They then act on these attitudes in ways that confirm the original negative judgement.

Métis scholar Emma LaRocque (2002) also discusses this process of "internalization," whereby, as a result of colonization, Aboriginal peoples have come to judge themselves against the standards of the white society. According to LaRocque (2002: 149), part of this process entails "swallowing the standards, judgements, expectations, and portrayals of the dominant white world."

In these terms, the violence encountered by Anishinaabe Ikwe in their intimate relationships with men can be interpreted as a reflection of the patriarchal ideas about women (and how they should be treated) that prevail in the wider society. Jody Miller came to a similar conclusion in her research on girls' involvement in street gangs. Miller suggests that the girls strike a "patriarchal bargain" that allows them to reconcile the negative aspects of their gang affiliation with the perceived benefits. Miller points out that "the world around gang girls is not a particularly safe place, physically or psychically" (2001: 193). When young women in that social world are seen as such ready targets of violence and victimization, association with a street gang can offer at least some semblance of protection. Nevertheless, Miller found that

> many young women's means of resisting gender oppression within gangs tended to be an individualized response based on constructing gendered gang identities as separate from and 'better than' those of the girls around them in their social environments. It meant internalizing and accepting masculine constructs of gang values. (2001: 197)

To this extent, colonization has now taken on a new guise. While physical violence historically played a major role in ensuring colonial rule, violence is now taken up by our men and inflicted on our women within this new, internalized colonial regime. Given their disenfranchised and subordinate position both within the street gang and the wider society, it should not surprise us that Aboriginal women and girls would compete among themselves in an effort to negotiate their place and space. "Being solid," "taking it like a woman," and creating a distance from those women and girls who have less status therefore become important survival strategies.

SURVIVING COLONIALISM

Throughout each of the interviews, colonization and its impact on our Indigenous culture, traditions and existence permeated the discussions. While the study participants may not have named their lived experience using the language of colonialism, time and time again Anishinaabe Ikwe made references to "how it was before the 'White Man.'" It is within this colonial context that the role of the street gang as a source of support and resistance must be located.

Euro-Canadian dominant discourse would have us believe that the conditions in which Aboriginal peoples now find themselves derive primarily from the First

Nations' own lack of enterprise, poor work ethic ("lazy Indians"), and overall inadequate economic, political (corrupt), social (savage) and cultural (backwards) capacities. On the contrary, Aboriginal peoples' socio-economic, political, social and cultural conditions fundamentally derive from our collective experience of colonization. Christian missionary conversion mandates, state-regulated and executed residential school systems, the prohibition of voting, the forbidding of participation in traditional cultural and spiritual activities, and the entrenchment of the racist and sexist Indian Act are just a few of the many policies and strategies imposed upon the Indigenous collective. Each of these various activities has had — and continues to have — profound effects on generations of Aboriginal peoples in Canada.

In particular, think about the impact of the residential school system: Indigenous children as young as three were involuntarily taken away from parents, grandparents, and community and forced to live away for ten months at a time or, in some cases, years at a time. What happens to children, families, communities and nations when our children, who, as the "Circle of Law" teaches us, are the "Fire" and "Motivation" of the Indigenous collective, are taken away and "taught" (enforced, strictly regulated, brainwashed) that everything they knew, experienced and believed to be true about their world was "savage" and that they were "less than"? Children, families, communities and nations slowly die physically, socially, culturally and spiritually. The formation of Aboriginal street gangs primarily derives from this ancestral and generational colonial history and experience.

Given this context, many study participants not surprisingly relayed how their association with the gang provided them with a space in which they could be themselves and where they found solidarity and pride in being Indigenous. Tamara stated: "*What's the gang to me? Well, obviously, they have been around. They have been a support. They have been the backbone to me being alive and taking care of me.*" Cathy told me how the gang allowed her the freedom and strength to counter the dominant white society and claim her space as one of the original peoples of this land:

> *It is very powerful. Like, you know, they [white society] put you really down. I find they get ignorant and racist. Like, it is almost like you're dirt. And for me, I would just stand up and say, 'No, I'm not dirt.' You know, if they want to play the part, so can I. Reverse psychology because that is how dirty they get.*

Louisa asserted that the gang provided her with an environment in which she had a connection and understanding:

> *Strengths. I met a lot of friends. They took care of me and I always had money. It was someone I knew that was there for me and kind of helping me. When I was in that group home there were white, black people. It was okay but I was*

more happy being around my own people. And there were a couple of people from The Pas. It was nice to know somebody from The Pas. There was more understanding, like, I could understand too. I was like their little sister. That was cool.

In these terms, Aboriginal gangs do not develop solely because of a desire or need for money and power. Aboriginal gangs develop simply because our people are not afforded the same educational, employment, political and cultural opportunities as the rest of Canadian society. From the moment we take our first breath to the moment we take our last, we are under assault by virtue of the Indian Act. We start school only to learn that we were or are "savages" and are a burden on society. We do not see ourselves reflected positively in schools, work or government. It is only once we start to acknowledge and recognize this factor that we can begin to move to more worthwhile approaches in dealing with Aboriginal street gangs and, in particular, Aboriginal women's place and space.

The dominant discourse surrounding gangs mostly pertains to so-called "exiting" models premised on the notion that gang members just need to either formally (request to leave) or informally (hide out and eventually be forgotten) exit the gang. Unfortunately, this is far too simplistic a solution. Gangs provide members with a sense of family, both literally and symbolically (as in "you're my homie"). Many of the study participants noted the literal family connections that many gang members have. Freda maintained that even though gang members (and their old ladies) may be from different gangs, family connections override any prescribed gang norms or codes of behaviour. She said:

> *They are all connected through their families. Some will have a cousin that is a Warrior and his cousin will be an Indian Posse and then that one's sister or stepsister will be going out with a guy that is from Native Syndicate. If you are in the same room with all of them, it's a family gathering.*

That gang members end up being family members complicates whether or not it is ever truly possible to "leave the gang."

STREET GANGS: STRENGTH AND SURVIVAL

I have been only able to offer here a portion of the various narratives and themes shared by the study participants over the span of almost two years. Nevertheless, what I have endeavoured to show is that Aboriginal street gangs — and women's particular context within the gang — did and do not develop divorced from the settler colonial context in Canada. Contrary to what most may believe, colonialism is not something that occurred in the past. The colonial experiment in Canada has never ended — European settlers did not decolonize and go "back home." We are still under the rule of the colonizer, with all of its Western Euro-Canadian ethnocentric ideologies and institutions.

Conducting the interviews for this study was by far the most difficult research I have ever done, but I would not have traded one moment. I was so privileged to have time with these women. Far from the media portrayal of violent female equivalents of "thugs," these women represent the strength, perseverance and beauty of the Indigenous peoples in Canada. Remembering a time when our people, our nations and our cultures were thought to be "vanishing," I can see that these women counter that notion with their very struggle and, most importantly, survival. We were not supposed to be here. Indeed, that was the plan so methodically and strategically executed. But despite every imaginable assault, we are still here and, in some capacity or another, flourishing.

Notes

I would like to say "meegwetch" to Elizabeth Comack for all the support and help she provided throughout the process of writing this piece, particularly her wonderful editing. Truly, this paper would not have been completed had it not been for her time, energy and spirit.

1   I have not edited and/or grammatically altered the participants' narratives. Specifically, I wanted to ensure respect and appreciation for participants and what they had to say and did not feel I had the right or the authority to change anything that was so freely communicated and shared.

2   See <rossbrookhouse.ca/about/>.

3   A "boss" is a president of one of the gangs.

References

Anderson, K. 2000. A *Recognition of Being: Reconstructing Native Womanhood.* Toronto: Sumach Press.

Berry, J. 1994. "Aboriginal Cultural Identity." Report Prepared for the Royal Commission on Aboriginal Peoples. Ottawa: Department of Indian and Northern Affairs.

Block, S., and G.E. Galabuzi. 2011. *Canada's Colour Coded Labour Market: The Gap for Racialized Workers.* Ottawa and Toronto: Canadian Centre for Policy Alternatives and The Wellesley Institute.

Busby, K., P. Downe, K. Gorkoff, K. Nixon, L. Tutty, and J. Ursel. 2002. "Examination of Innovative Programming for Children and Youth Involved in Prostitution." In H. Berman and Y. Jiwani (eds.), *In The Best Interests of the Girl Child: Phase II Report.* Ottawa: Status of Women Canada.

Comack, E., L. Deane, L. Morrissette, and J. Silver. 2013. *"Indians Wear Red" Colonialism, Resistance, and Aboriginal Street Gangs.* Halifax and Winnipeg: Fernwood Publishing.

Criminal Intelligence Service Canada. 2004. "2004 Annual Report on Organized Crime in Canada." <cisc.gc.ca/annual_reports/documents/2004_annual_report.pdf>.

Devens, C. 1992. *Countering Colonization: Native American Women and Great Lake Missions, 1630–1900*. Berkeley: University of California Press.

Gunn Allen, P. 1992. *The Sacred Hoop: Recovering the Feminine in American Indian Traditions*. Boston: Beacon Press.

Hamilton, A.C., and C.M. Sinclair. 1991. *The Justice System and Aboriginal People: Report of the Aboriginal Justice Inquiry of Manitoba*. Vol. 1. Winnipeg: Queen's Printer.

LaRocque, E. 2002. "Violence in Aboriginal Communities." In K. McKenna and J. Larkin (eds.), *Violence Against Women: New Canadian Perspectives*. Toronto: Inanna.

McLeod, H. 2004. "A Glimpse at Aboriginal-Based Street Gangs." A Report for the Royal Canadian Mounted Police "D" Division, Winnipeg, Manitoba for the National Aboriginal Policing Forum held in Ottawa, ON. Hosted by Pacific Business and Law Institute, September 22 and 23.

McLeod, N. 2000. "Indigenous Studies: Negotiating the Space between Tribal Communities and Academia." *Expressions in Canadian Native Studies*. Saskatoon: University Extension Press.

Miller, J. 2001. *One of the Guys: Girls, Gangs, and Gender.* New York: Oxford University Press.

Moore-Gilbert, B. 1997. *Postcolonial Theory: Contexts, Practices, Politics*. London and New York: Verso.

Razack, S. 2002. *Race, Space and the Law: Unmapping a White Settler Society*. Toronto: Between the Lines.

____. 2007. "When Place Becomes Race." In T. Das Gupta, C.E. James, R. Maaka, G.-E. Galabuzi, and C. Andersen (eds.), *Race and Racialization: Essential Readings*. Toronto: Canadian Scholars' Press.

RCAP (Royal Commission on Aboriginal Peoples). 1996. *Report of the Royal Commission on Aboriginal Peoples*. Ottawa: Department of Indian and Northern Affairs. <collectionscanada.gc.ca/webarchives/20071115053257/http://www.ainc-inac.gc.ca/ch/rcap/sg/sgmm_e.html>.

Seshia, Maya. 2005. *The Unheard Speak Out*. Winnipeg: Canadian Centre for Policy Alternatives–Manitoba.

Silver, J. 2006. *In Their Own Voices: Building Aboriginal Communities*. Halifax and Winnipeg: Fernwood Publishing.

____. 2010. "Segregated City: A Century of Poverty in Winnipeg." In P. Thomas and C. (eds.), *Voices from the Prairies*. Regina: Canadian Plains Research Centre.

Wolfe, P. 2006. "Settler Colonialism and the Elimination of the Native." Journal of Genocide Research 8, 4.

Chapter 9

STANDING AGAINST CANADIAN LAW
Naming Omissions of Race, Culture and Gender

Patricia Monture

From: *Locating Law: Race, Class, Gender, Sexuality Connections,* 3rd edition, pp. 68–87 (reprinted with permission).

I have grown very impatient with Canadian law as a solution to problems that Aboriginal peoples, both as nations and as individuals, face in the Canadian mosaic. But to explain my conclusions and concerns about Canadian law and its impact on Aboriginal lives, I will need also to tell you how I situate myself against Canadian law as a Mohawk woman.

First of all, there is no single "Indian" reality. This is a formidable myth. It is a myth that has been accepted by all "mainstream"[1] disciplines that have an interest in studying "Indians." Professor Devon Mihesuah (Oklahoma Choctaw) articulates in her essay on American Indian women and history:

> There was and is no such thing as a monolithic, essential Indian woman. Nor has there ever been a unitary "worldview" among tribes, especially after contact and interaction with non-Indians, not even among members of the same group. Cultural ambiguity was and is common among Indians. Traditional Native women were as different from progressive tribeswomen as they were from white women, and often they still are. (Mihesuah 1998: 37–38)

This discussion is, therefore, only one comment on the ideas (or story) of one person, a Mohawk woman.

My impatience is also grounded in the fact that, as a Mohawk woman, I do not accept Canadian law as *the* single, viable and legitimate way of resolving disputes. My understanding is that Canadian law operates to perpetuate disputes. Consider how many Aboriginal claims — almost all the decisions recently heard by the Supreme Court of Canada — are resolved by the courts by sending them back to trial for a second time. This list includes cases heralded as great victories, such as *Sparrow* and *Delgamuukw*. Further, and more importantly, Canadian law from my standpoint is not the only option. I come from a peoples and a tradition that had rules and processes about dispute resolution that I experience as legitimate and viable. These rules and processes of dispute resolution are not simple, romantic visions of the past. They are present and viable in our communities today. I do not defer to the Canadian system any legitimacy solely because it is the only choice, because from my position it is not. Indigenous citizens of our nations have choices about dispute resolution traditions and mechanisms that are not necessarily available to Canadians.

As a Mohawk woman who came to study Canadian law, I am forever balancing the teaching, rules and principles of both systems. This balancing act probably leads me to different understandings about the structure and shape of Canadian law. This is not a visibility that operates solely because I come from a "different" culture. It becomes visible because of both my tradition and gender, realities that operate concurrently in interlocking ways. Sherene Razack (1998: 58) concurs with this observation and explains the serious consequence of the misunderstanding that culture and gender are separate realities:

> When women from non-dominant groups talk about culture, we are often heard to be articulating a false dichotomy between culture and gender; in articulating our difference, we inadvertently also confirm our relegation to the margins. Culture talk is clearly a double-edged sword. It packages difference as inferiority and obscures both gender-based and racial domination, yet cultural considerations are important for contextualizing oppressed groups' claims for justice, for improving their access to services, and for requiring dominant groups to examine the invisible cultural advantages you enjoy.

Understanding law from a place that is cultured and gendered offers advantages in my own understanding, but at the same time operates to the detriment of our position in the mainstream dialogue.

Part of the reason I feel advantaged is because I have a choice about legal systems. This has several consequences. I have never presumed that the Canadian legal system is the only system. Because I often "stand against" the principles on which Canadian law is founded, my position is critical. I do not take the principles of Canadian law for granted. Nor do I fail to see that the principles on which Canadian law is based are not absolutes. These principles were chosen. However, it is equally important to note that I will always defer to the standards of my first way to determine the value of participating in the Canadian legal system. At the same time I recognize that the choice I exercise is not always possible. This choice is a reflection of the privilege of my legal education. A person facing criminal charges or child welfare actions or defending Aboriginal lands does not exercise such a privilege (nor would I if I were in any of those circumstances). At the same time that I engage in legal method, I am constantly assessing that law against my Mohawk understanding of law. It is not that I expect courts to become suddenly Mohawk; I am just looking for a significant degree of respect built on an understanding that is at least bicultural and gendered.

This is contrary to how I see Canadian courts and non-Aboriginal academics using Aboriginal legal discourse. When quoted (which is entirely all too infrequently), my words, like the words of other Aboriginal scholars, are used as cultural evidence and not legal method.[2] This reminds me of a caution stated by Razack (1998: 61): "When racism and genocide are denied and cultural difference replaces it, the net effect for Aboriginal peoples is a denial of their right to exist as sovereign nations and viable communities."

When reading the Supreme Court of Canada's decision in Delgamuukw, I did not fail to notice that the eminent scholars the Court chose to quote were (significantly) all white men.[3] The failure to broaden the scope of their reading and reference (Matsudi 1988: 4–5) is most likely a reflection of the factums the lawyers presented to the courts. It is not that I think the Supreme Court of Canada should quote me. On a very personal level, I dread the day that this should ever occur.[4] It is, however, one of the notable but subtle ways in which Canadian law operates to exclude, omit, and deny difference. Or, if you prefer, it is how courts participate in perpetuating colonialism while ensuring that power — their power — continues to be vested in the status quo.

The oppression embedded in the legal process ranges from the subtle to the overt and obvious. Several cases in Canada have criminalized the actions of pregnant women — one of them an Aboriginal woman — who were abusing alcohol or drugs. The social realities, including the historic oppression of Aboriginal peoples, are not realities that courts readily consider in their decision-making process. In a detailed analysis of the *Big Pipe* case in the United States, where a Dakota woman found herself before the courts in just these circumstances, Elizabeth Cook-Lynn (Dakota) argues:

There is evidence that women, thought by the tribes to be the backbone of Native society and the bearers of sacred children and repositors of cultural values, are now thought to pose a significant threat to tribal survival. Indeed, the intrusive federal government now interprets the law on Indian reservations in ways which sanction *indicting* Indian women as though they alone are responsible for the fragmentation of the social fabric of Indian lives. As infants with fetal alcohol syndrome (FAS) and fetal alcohol effect (FAE) are born in increasing numbers, it is said that women's recalcitrant behavior (consuming alcohol and other drugs during pregnancy and nursing) needs to be legally criminalized by the federal system to make it a felony for a women to commit such acts. (Cook-Lynn 1996: 114–15)

These conditions — that the result of the tribal (that is, collective) oppression of Aboriginal peoples is now individualized within legal relations and that a greater burden is being placed on women for problems of social disorder and the resulting harms — also point to the inadequacy of an individualized system of law to resolve Aboriginal issues. The impact of the individualization of our legal relations moves Aboriginal nations further away from our traditions, which are kinship-based and collective. That women are the focus of these trends cannot escape our attention.

My impatience with law, with its theory and method, is grounded as well in the practical realization that long-term solutions are not available in Canadian law because of the very structure of that legal system. Granted, Aboriginal people are sometimes able to avail themselves of immediate solutions for the topical problems faced. Being represented by a counsel[5] who understands the history and being of an Aboriginal person may make a difference in a child welfare matter or the defence of a criminal charge. However, the consequence of being able to address immediate solutions is deceiving. It conceals that no significant change is occurring. I refuse to be satisfied with being better able to defend ourselves in small ways in particular circumstances as all that we can hope for.[6] This is one of the fundamental characteristics of oppression by assimilation. It appears as though change has occurred when it has not. This concern is even more pressing for women, especially for Aboriginal women who carry the weight of discrimination (race/culture) wound within discrimination (gender).

This impatience with Canadian law, conditioned on my understanding that it remains a problem for Aboriginal peoples and especially for Aboriginal women, is not a conclusion that is widely shared. It is essential, therefore, for me to state the reasons why I have reached this conclusion.[7] I spent a good five years of my life as a student of law and another five years as a law professor. Although now teaching in a sociology department, I am still reading cases and teaching about law. A preliminary examination of legal structure and theory clearly identifies that certain groups have not had an equal opportunity to participate in the process of defining social and state relations (including the law). Women, Aboriginal people and other so-called minorities have not shared in the power to define the relationships of the institutions of this country (including the university, the law courts, criminal justice institutions and social services).

CONSIDERING CHANGE:
ABORIGINAL PEOPLE AND THE
CANADIAN CRIMINAL JUSTICE SYSTEM

I am interested in a transformative change of the Canadian legal system; this is the kind of change that I consider significant. In Canada much has been made of the many initiatives taken "for" Aboriginal people in the justice system. There are court workers, hiring programs, Native liaison workers in prisons, Elder-assisted parole board hearings, sentencing circles and so on. All of these programs are mere "add-ons" to the mainstream justice system, and all of them operate on a shared presumption: if we can only teach Aboriginal people more about our system, then that system will work for them and they will accept it. Many of the programs and developments are packaged as cultural accommodations. This should be recognized for what it is: a misappropriation of culture. The programs are really based on the notion of Aboriginal inferiority, and if we Aboriginal people just become more knowledgeable about the Canadian system, the problem is solved. Culture has been used to obscure the structural racism in the Canadian criminal justice system. The failure of the system is placed squarely on the shoulders of Aboriginal people and not on the system, where it really belongs. This is not transformative change, because transformative change requires structural change in the system when it is required and necessary.

Not only are the reforms to the criminal justice system in Canada not transformative, but they have also not been fully successful. Because of my work in Canadian prisons (both men's and women's institutions), I do not question that the reforms have changed the incarceration experiences of Aboriginal people. This is an ameliorative and individual change in matters of criminal justice that is essential. However, real success would be demonstrated in decreased incarceration rates of Aboriginal people, which is not occurring. Aboriginal incarceration rates continue to increase, despite the new programs and accommodations. The collective experience of the justice system has not been transformed.

Much has been made of the establishment of sentencing circles in Canada. These circles, under the discretion of the judge, offer the Aboriginal accused the opportunity to be sentenced in a community process (Ross 1996: 192–98, 246–47).

But there is nothing intrinsically Aboriginal about these processes. We did not "sentence," and merely rearranging the furniture so we are sitting in a "circle" does not accomplish systemic or transformative change. Granted, a sentencing circle does borrow from Aboriginal traditions of dispute resolution as well as healing. Sentencing circles are accommodations of the mainstream process that may hold a better opportunity to provide a degree of comfort to community members, (Aboriginal) victims, and/or the Aboriginal accused. The sentencing circle may change the momentary experience of the Aboriginal person of criminal justice, but it does not really hold greater potential.

The concern that transformative progress is not being made is also visible in Canadian court decisions. In December 1997, when the Supreme Court of Canada released the decision in the Delgamuukw case, the central claim was the Aboriginal title of fifty-one hereditary chiefs of the Gitksan and Wet'suwet'en peoples. The decision was heralded as a great victory. I have difficulty with this conclusion, because the Supreme Court's decision was to return for retrial a case that had originally involved 374 days at trial and 141 days spent taking evidence out of court (Miller 1992: 3).[8] It is true that significant progress was made in the evidentiary rules, which had previously preferred the written document to oral history. These rules of evidence previously operated in Canadian law as a serious structural barrier to success in litigation brought by Aboriginal peoples. This diminishing of Aboriginal forms of history against non-Aboriginal written ways was a significant detriment in attempts to bring Aboriginal claims forward. The Court opined:

> Notwithstanding the challenges created by the use of oral histories as proof of historical facts, the laws of evidence must be *adapted* in order that this type of evidence can be *accommodated* and placed on an equal footing with the types of historical evidence that courts are familiar with which largely consists of historical documents. (*Delgamuukw v. British Columbia* 1998: 49–50, emphasis added)

Granted, the Court's benevolent respect for the consequences of the exclusion of oral history and the accommodation of the rules of evidence represents a great victory. However, when we examine the language of the judiciary, a different picture emerges. The Court has "adapted" its own rules of evidence to "accommodate" oral history — which is the same pattern of nominal change that I noted in my discussion of recent reforms to the criminal justice system. Here, the overall structure is not challenged, but just one unfortunate consequence of the evidentiary rules. If I believed that the only evidentiary rule that operated to the disadvantage of Aboriginal persons was this one, perhaps I would be more satisfied. The end result is that Aboriginal people walk away from this decision with lots more work to do.

Every place where evidentiary rules do not fit with our ways must be brought to the courts for review. This will be both time-consuming and money-consuming. Nonetheless, I recognize that the decision in *Delgamuukw* may make this change easier to accomplish. Regardless, it still leaves the burden on Aboriginal people to continually challenge the system forced on us. Transformative change would require that courts or legislatures take it upon themselves to complete an ameliorative review with the intent of removing all such barriers existing in Canadian law.

UNDERSTANDING OPPRESSION AND RESISTANCE

This analysis of the problems in the structure of Canadian law has thus far been primarily focused on race and culture. But it is essential that gender (both male and female) be wound into this story. By the time I reached law school, I understood that much of my identity was shaped on the recognition that I was oppressed. I was oppressed as an Indian.[9] I was oppressed as a woman. I was oppressed as an Indian woman. I do not experience these categories of "Indian" and "woman" as singular and unrelated. The experience of Indian and woman is layered. My choice to go to law school was premised on my desire to fight back against the oppression and violence that I had lived with as an Indian woman.[10] It was a journey of seeking solutions to both the immediate consequences and long-term impact of the criminal justice system on the lives of Aboriginal people I knew.

At one time I thought that ending my personal oppression only required the ability to fight back. Later I saw that the best place for me to fight oppression Canadian-style was in law. I wanted to be a criminal defence counsel. What I learned during my law-school years (and it is a lesson frequently reinforced in recent years) is that I am just too impatient for this kind of fighting back. Fighting back frequently only perpetuates the oppression, because all of your energy is directed at a "problem" you did not construct. When all of your energy is consumed in fighting back, transformative change remains elusive. This is one of the very real personal consequences of our inability to bring changes to the Canadian legal system that would make it truly inclusive.

Through the course of my legal education I began to learn that oppression is not of a unitary character. I experience it as both personal and collective (that is, directed at me not as an individual but as part of a people). I also experience oppression as layered. I now understand that the way I looked at the world back when I began to study law was naive or overly simple. Canadian law does not hold forth the hope or power to solve many of the issues that must be struggled with in our communities as the result of oppression at the hands of the Canadian state. Although the discussion here has focused on oppression — because oppression is what I feel as well as see in my daily life — it is essential to recognize that the oppression I have survived (and continue to struggle to survive on a daily basis) is the result of colonial beliefs and relationships. Colonialism is very easily understood. It is the belief in the superiority of certain ways, values and beliefs *over* the ways, values and beliefs of other peoples. Colonialism is the legacy that the so-called discovery of the Americas has left to the peoples who are indigenous to these territories. Colonialism is the theory of power, while oppression is the result of the lived experience of colonialism.

As a result of these colonial relationships, resistance became a key concept in understanding the relationship I held with law — and particularly with institutions of criminal justice — around and during the time of my law-school days. I know' that dictionary reading is not a sound academic pursuit or research methodology, but I thought it just might prove interesting (or an act of resistance/rebellion) and therefore a good place to start to understand resistance. Maybe I just wanted or needed the idea of resistance to be simple. I have lived resistance for a long time. For me a lot of complicated thoughts, ideas and feelings are conjured up by that word, because so much of my life experiences are about resisting. I have often understood my life in terms of resistance. A lot of what I do in the university is about resistance.

The *Concise Oxford Dictionary* provided me with four beautifully simple definitions of resistance:

1. refusing to comply;
2. hindrance;
3. impeding or stopping;
4. opposition. (Fowler and Fowler 1974: 1059)

These definitional standards of "refusing to comply," "hindrance," "impeding" or "opposition" are not the concepts that I want to build my life on. They are not the concepts I would choose, if I had choice. I know I deserve more than refusing, hindering or opposing. Mere resistance is not transformative. It often acts solely to reinforce colonial and oppressive relationships, not to destroy them. This is because resistance can be no more than a response to the power that someone else holds. Responding to that colonial power can actually operate to affirm and further entrench it.

Sometimes resistance is still a necessary part of the First Nations' bag of survival tricks. I am not disputing that. But resistance only gains mere survival, and often the survival gained is only individual. I cannot — and I suppose will not — believe that the Creator gave us the walk, gave us life, to have nothing more than mere resistance. In my mind, resistance is only the first step, and it is a small step in recovering who we are as original peoples. Resistance is only a first step away from being a victim.

I have a particular understanding of being victim and of being victimized. Like too many other Aboriginal people, I have been a victim. I was a victim of child sexual abuse, of a battering relationship, of rape. In the First Nations women's community, that does not make me exceptional. I can tell you the name of only one Aboriginal woman in this country who I know for sure has not survived incest, child sexual abuse, rape or battering. It is worse than that, because most of us do not survive just one single incident of abuse or violence. Our lives are about the experience of violence from birth to death, be it overt physical violence or psychological and emotional violence.

I also understand racism to be psychological and emotional violence (Monture 1993). Focusing solely on the physical aspects of violence both diminishes and disappears the full impact of violence in the lives of Aboriginal women. This is an important concept, and my hope is that it will be understood contextually. I offer this long quotation from the Task Force on Federally Sentenced Women — in which I participated — for just that purpose:[11]

> This survey report was prepared by two Aboriginal women (*Lana Fox and Fran Sugar*) who have been through the Canadian prison system. They gathered information for the study through interviews with 39 federally sentenced Aboriginal women in the community. The women spoke of violence, of racism, and of the meaning of being female, Aboriginal and imprisoned. They spoke of systematic violence throughout their lives by those they lived with, those they depended on and those they loved and trusted. Twenty-seven of the 39 women interviewed described experiences of childhood violence, rape, regular sexual abuse, the witnessing of a murder, watching their mothers repeatedly beaten, and beatings in juvenile detention centers at the hands of staff and other children.
>
> For many of the women, this childhood violence became an ongoing feature of life, and continued through adolescence into adulthood. Twenty-one had been raped or sexually assaulted either as children or as adults. Twenty-seven of the 39 had experienced violence during adolescence. However to these experiences were added the violence of tricks, rape and assaults on the streets. In addition, 34 of the 39 had been the victims of tricks who had beaten and/or raped them (12 of 39 had shared this experience and 9 had been violent toward tricks), some from police or prison guards. The violence experienced by these women is typically at the hands of men.
>
> The women also spoke of living with racism. Racism and oppression are the preconditions of the violence these women experience throughout their lives. (Correctional Service of Canada 1990: 63–64)

Both the forms of violence (physical, sexual, spiritual, emotional and verbal) and how violence is inflicted on Aboriginal women are multifaceted. Violence is not generally experienced as a single incident. The violence is cyclical. All too often, violence describes most of our lives. Even when we manage to create a safe environment in which to live our individual lives, the violence still surrounds us. Our friends, sisters, aunties and nieces still suffer. The violence becomes a fact of life and it is inescapable.

The methodology utilized by the Task Force on Federally Sentenced Women was an important component of the work that distinguished it from previous research on Aboriginal women. Culture was a significant concern of task force members involved in commissioning the research. As a result, the interviewers were not only Aboriginal women (of the same culture — Cree — as the majority of Aboriginal women who were serving federal sentences), but were also women who had previously served federal sentences. They, therefore, possessed a credibility among the population to be researched that most (academically trained) interviewers do not. Further, the research instrument was open-ended, which allowed the women interviewed to shape and tell their own stories. This was viewed as essential so as not to influence the research with non-Aboriginal and "straight"[12] views of incarcerated Aboriginal women. The interviewers were also central to the process of interpretation of the data, because they were able to contextualize the women's comments in their own experiences of incarceration. This methodology has been adopted in further research on Aboriginal women who have survived violence (McGillivray and Comaskey 1996).

Looking back, I now see how naive I was during the task force years. The task force embraced the philosophy of choices, which I was fully supportive of and thought was quite revolutionary at the time. But it did not work. While the words changed, the values and philosophy of "corrections" (that is, having the right to change a person because she committed a crime) were merely dumped into the new idea of "choices." Further, I now see that this choices philosophy is basically a middle-class concept.[13] Not all women incarcerated federally have equal access to the means required to exercise good choices. This is particularly true for Aboriginal women, who have the least access to socio-economic resources of any group of women in this country. In contrast, with the exception of its Chapter 2, the report was written by white women with at least middle-class access to services and middle-class experiences of the world. Although I do still think that the work of the task force held revolutionary potential, I would not agree to participate in future work in the same way.

The methodology I advocate involves the creation of a space (or spaces) for Aboriginal ways of knowing and understanding to occupy within more mainstream methodologies. Storytelling is a significant component of Aboriginal epistemologies (see Ladner 1996). How I understand Canadian law is influenced by my having been a victim. This methodology does not advocate "objective" knowledge (if, in fact, such a thing exists) but holds that personal experience, when contributed carefully to research agendas, adds both quality and authenticity.

I led part of my life as a victim. I used drugs and alcohol to hide from my feelings and from the memories of the individual acts of violence. In a way, for part of my life, I agreed to be victim. Then I learned how to resist — just a little — the violence that surrounded me. Eventually I moved beyond the victim place and learned how to be a survivor. Victims (as juxtaposed to survivors) often allow things to happen to them (and, therefore, research on Aboriginal women should not revictimize them). This is not an argument that alleges that victims are responsible for the violence done to them. They are not. Survivors, however, have begun to take care of themselves and have begun taking charge of their lives. Recovery — moving from victim to survivor — is a gradual process. Unfortunately, there are still moments when racism, sexism, and/or colonialism continue to have the power to turn me into a victim again and I am immobilized.

Some years back I got really tired of being a survivor. Just like I got tired of being a victim. I wondered for a long time, "Isn't there something more to life than victimization? Do I always have to be a survivor?" Just like I am now not satisfied with resistance as the most I can expect from life, with fighting back as the only mode of my existence, I was then not satisfied with being a survivor (Monture-Angus 1995: 53–70). Through reflection (and with the support of and many conversations with Elders and friends), I learned that we move beyond surviving to become warriors. This is the next "stage." I know this is not a linear process. Movement is not from one stage to the next with no going back. There is no graduation ceremony where the robes of victimization are shed for life. In my mind, I see it as a medicine wheel. The fourth stage is that of teacher. Teachers not only speak to the truth but they also offer ways in which we may change the reality we are living in.[14]

Many of the women I know in my life are warriors, as they are able to stand up and speak their truth. There are some men, fewer than the women (in my experience), who are "true" warriors. That statement is not meant to amaze or anger. It is the truth as I see it in my community. It is with a great hesitation that I even use this word, "warrior."[15] I have used it because I have not been able to find a better one in English. At the same time I realize that my language has no word for "warrior." In 1990, in the *Indian Times* published in the Mohawk territory of Akwesasne, the following was said (and I sadly do not know what the equivalent woman's word in the language is or if in fact there is a need for one): "We do not have a word for warrior [in the Mohawk language]. The men are called *Hodiskengehdah*. It means 'all the men who carry the bones, the burden of their ancestors, on their backs'" (Johansen 1993: 66).[16]

For me, warrior is both an image of responsibility and commitment. Warriors live to protect, yes, but, more importantly, to give honour to the people. Being a warrior means living your life for more than yourself. Warrior, in my mind, is not a man's word. It is not a fighting word. It is not a war word. Given what I have been told about many Indian languages, that you cannot use "he" or "she" in the same way that you do in the English language, I suspect that the word warrior is not gender-specific at all. Warrior is a "knowing your place in your community," "caring to speak your truth," "being able to share your gift," "being proud of who you are" word. Warrior, in the way I intend it, is not merely a resistance word. The way I have come to understand the warrior is as someone who is beyond resisting. Survivors resist. Resistance is one of many skills that a warrior might use. It is not their only way. Warriors also have vision. They dream for their people's future.

RESISTING THE INDIAN ACT

In offering the following discussion on the Indian Act, I hope to be able to provide an analysis that assists in our understanding of discrimination, oppression, colonialism and possible forms of resistance. As long as the Indian Act[17] remains in force, colonialism remains a vibrant force in Indian communities, and I recognize the need for strategies of resistance. The Indian Act can never define who I am as a Mohawk woman, nor can it ever define who my children are as Mohawk and Cree. There is no identity in the Indian Act, only oppression and colonialism.

It is important to look at what the Indian Act has done to our identities as "tribal" people. Bill C-31[18] is an excellent and recent example. I think the next time that somebody tells me that they are a "Bill C-31 Indian,"[19] I am going to scream. There is no such thing as a Bill C-31 Indian. Once a bill passes into law it is not a bill anymore (maybe this is just a little quirk I have as a result of my legal education). Everyone running around calling themselves Bill C-31 Indians is saying (technically and legally), "I am something that does not exist." If we have to be "Indians," then let's all just be "Indians." I would prefer if we could be Mohawk or Cree or Tlingit or Mi'kmaq or Saulteaux. That is who we really are. That is the truth. It is important to reclaim who we are at least in our thoughts.

I want to reject the ideology of reserves as something of "ours" and as something "Indian." Reserves were not dreamed up by Indians. Reserves were a step — a rather long step, in my opinion — down the colonial trail. What really troubles me about this is that we as Indian people respect that piece of postage stamp silliness. We need to ask ourselves (and then remember the answer): Where did that reserve come from? When the Creator, in her[20] infinite wisdom, put us down in our territories, did she say, "Okay. Here's your postage stamp, Trish. You get to go live at the Six Nations reserve"? The Creator did not do that. She gave us territories. I am now living in Cree territory, territory shared with the Métis people. An Elder back home told me more than a decade ago to stop thinking and talking in terms of reserves. Instead, he said, think about your territory.

Nowadays, the Indian Act also allows for another clever little distinction between Indians who live on this little square piece of land called a reserve and Indians who do not. You get certain "rights" or "benefits" if you live on the reserve, and only if you live on the reserve.[21] You can be tax-free. You can have health benefits. You are eligible for education benefits. Even Indians now also measure "Indian-ness" based on the on-reserve/off-reserve criteria created by the Indian Act. When we think in this way we are bought and paid for with those few trivial rights found in the legislation. If you live on 12th Street East in Saskatoon, forget it. You are not going to get any rights under the Indian Act because you do not live on the reserve. This is a problem that is not, at least initially, the fault of Indian people. One of the dangerous results of the federal government's Indian Act is how it divides (and that is a strategy of colonialism, because divided peoples are more easily controlled) our people from each other and the land.

It is even more disturbing to me that some Indians are going to see you as less Indian, as less authentic, if you reside off-reserve. This is incredibly narrow, legal, social and political thinking. It is one of the absolute seeds of oppression I must survive. We are mesmerized away from seeing our oppression in our efforts to ensure access to the nominal rights we have. In my mind, this means that the cost far outweighs the benefits under the Indian Act system. We spend untold amounts of energy (and money) fighting in political arenas and Canadian courts for a few "tax-free" and other assorted crumbs, rather than spending our energy shedding the shackles of our colonial oppression.[22]

Understanding the experience of women on the reserve exposes one way in which gender is important in this analysis. Many women have fled reserves because of the amount of gendered victimization they encountered there. In trying to escape the violence, part of their identity and access to that identity are torn away from them. Many of these women have not found better lives in the city (Hamilton and Sinclair 1991: 485; Dion Stout and Bruyere 1997).

Much literature has been written on the impact of the old section 12(1)(b) of the Indian Act, which stripped Indian women of their status upon marriage to a non-Indian.[23] But the majority of Indian women were never affected directly by this section of the Indian Act. By 1996, only about 104,000 persons had been added to the Indian register as a result of the 1985 amendments to the Indian Act (Ponting 1997: 68), and not all of these were women. The figures also include children (both male and female) of the women who had "married out"; those who had "voluntarily" enfranchised; families of enfranchised men; until 1951 those who had resided outside Canada for five years or more; and professionals and university graduates.

Perhaps my view is skewed because I was never victimized by the provisions of section 12(1)(b). However, in my experience, Indian women's lives have been more significantly hurt by overt violence, residential schools and child welfare agencies than they have by the restrictions of that section.

It is curious to consider where the preoccupation with former section 12(1)(b) comes from. One could postulate, for example, that it has come to the fore because it neatly parallels, albeit superficially, the agenda of the feminist movement. Women activists have long pointed to the unequal treatment of women in Canadian law. The *Lavell* and *Bedard* cases, which went to the highest court of the land, increased the visibility of this issue. Almost concurrently, national organizations of Native women were also forming. Many of these women were from urban areas, and section 12(1)(b) had a negative effect on their lives.[24] The issue of loss of women's status was, therefore, available to the mainstream women's movement in a way that did not force non-Aboriginal women to step out of their comfort zones and directly into Indian women's lives and communities.[25]

Understanding the consequences of the feminist intervention in Indian women's lives is even more enlightening. Not long ago I heard a CBC radio program in which two leaders of the women's movement were interviewed about the last few decades of change for women in Canada. One of the interviewer's questions focused on the relationship between Aboriginal women and "the movement." My pleasure at this question being on the interviewer's list quickly evaporated with the response. The women leaders bragged of the great success of the "coalition" in seeing the discriminatory provisions of the Indian Act removed and the women reinstated. The truth of the matter is that discrimination against women has not been removed from the Indian Act. This realization exposes the distance remaining between the women's movement and Indian women.[26]

There are several reasons why the women's boast does not reflect the concerns of Indian women. First of all, the reinstatement process does not put Indian men and Indian women in the same position. Men who married out (largely because their wives gained status) continue to be able to pass their status on to the children and at least their grandchildren. Indian women who are reinstated only pass a limited form of status onto their children (under section 6[2] of the Act), and nothing remains for their grandchildren. The discrimination is not removed from the Indian Act, as many assert. It has merely been embedded into the Act in such a way that it is less visible. Secondly, the women who were involuntarily disenfranchised because of their marriage to non-Indians do not receive any compensation for their loss of access to culture, ceremony and language during the years that they were prohibited from living on the reserve; nor was this ever considered, despite the serious harm that was often done to them as a result. The effect of the 1985 membership provisions has, in addition, the more general result of making membership more difficult to gain, which means that the size of the status Indian population will probably diminish into the future. I do not join in the celebration of the 1985 amendments. The cost of women's partial reinclusion has been too great.

There are further reasons why it is premature to suggest that gender discrimination has been removed from the Indian Act. There has yet to be completed a systematic gender review of the legislation and the effects of the operation of the legislation to determine if women are systematically excluded from other "benefits" in the Act. Certificates of possession, the system of property ownership on many reserves, are often only in the name of the male partner in a marriage. In the *Paul* and *Derrickson* cases, the Supreme Court of Canada disallowed the application of provincial matrimonial property law regimes on reserves.[27] Because the Indian Act is silent on the distribution of matrimonial property in cases of marriage breakdown, no matrimonial property regimes apply on reserves. This is a serious disadvantage to women. The 1985 amendments to the Indian Act only removed the most obvious and blatant discrimination against Indian women from the face of the legislation. It is inaccurate to translate this into an assertion that gender discrimination has been fully removed from the Act.

The Indian Act has not just done damage to those of us entitled to be registered under that statute. It is because the Indian Act excluded from registration certain people (such as the Métis) that some critics have argued that those excluded groups do not have any rights. They do not have the Indian Act and its colonized (twisted) form of thinking that a federal statute is the source of their rights. Rather, I think the Métis are "fortunate" because they do not have all that written colonization to hold them down. They, at least theoretically, have a clean "statutory slate." The Métis have neither treaty[28] nor the Indian Act to confine them. Their rights have not been as whittled away or tarnished by Canadian laws under the guise of granting rights or becoming civilized.[29] The separation of Aboriginal peoples by the kind of rights we possess is a strategy of divide and conquer, which is central in the process of colonization. The benefit from the strategy flows to the colonizer, because it is much too easy to control a people divided.[30] This is an ancient strategy of colonialism.

CLOSING THIS CIRCLE

In conclusion I want first to return to a discussion of methodology. When I finished law school I quite often described the feeling at graduation as the same feeling of relief combined with fear that I had after leaving an abusive man. It felt as though I had been just so battered for so long. Finishing law school is an accomplishment, yet I did not feel proud of myself. I just felt empty. This feeling forced me to begin considering why I felt the way I did. It was this process that began to reveal the ways in which law is fully oppressive to Aboriginal people.

This process of self-reflection is an obligation that I have as a First Nations person trying to live according to the teachings and ways of my people. But it is much more than a personal obligation. It is a fundamental concept essential to First Nations epistemology (see Ermine 1995: 101–12). It is a methodology.

The realization that law was the problem and not a solution of transformative quality was difficult for me to fully accept, because it made the three years I had struggled through law school seem without purpose. I did not want to believe it. Think about everything that First Nations people have survived in this country: the taking of our land, the taking of our children, residential schools, the criminal justice system, the outlawing of potlatches, sundances and other ceremonies, and the stripping of Indian women (and other Indian people) of their status. Everything we survived as individuals or as Indian peoples. How was all of this delivered? The answer is simple: through law. For almost every single one of the oppressions I have named, I can take you to the law library and I can show you where they wrote it down in the statutes and in the regulations. Sometimes the colonialism is expressed on the face of the statute books, and other times it is hidden in the power of bureaucrats who take their authority from those same books.

Still, so many people still believe that law is the answer. The reason why Canadian law just does not fully work for resolving Aboriginal claims — including those fundamentally concerning Aboriginal women — is quite simple. Canadian courts owe their origin to British notions of when a nation is sovereign. It is from Canadian sovereignty that Canadian courts owe their existence. Courts, therefore, cannot question the very source of their own existence without fully jeopardizing their own being. Courts cannot be forced to look at issues about the legitimacy (or, more appropriately, the lack thereof) of Canadian sovereignty as against the claims of Aboriginal sovereignties. The result is that Aboriginal claimants (women, men and nations) can never hope to litigate the issue that is at the very heart of our claims. This is what distinguishes much feminist litigation from Aboriginal "rights" litigation.

It is not just that the decisions of Canadian law are often the wrong decisions. It is more complex. I am interested in having a place, including a place in Canadian law, that feels right and fits right. This requires a place free from oppression. I cannot accomplish this through acts of (or a life of) mere resistance. The place I seek would not only allow me the space[31] and place to be a Mohawk woman, but also encourage me to be all that I am capable of being. It is a place that respects me for who I am as woman and for how I understand myself to be both a member of a nation as well as a confederacy. This is my dream.

Notes

The section of this chapter that deals with resistance was first published as "Resisting the Boundaries of Academic Thought: Aboriginal Women, Justice and Decolonization" in *Native Studies Review* 12(1) (1997).

1   I hesitate to use the word "mainstream," as by doing so I cooperate in the marginalization of my own people.

2   One example (with all due respect) I have come across is in the work of Kent McNeil (1998: 37).

3   There is one scholar whose work I am not familiar with and cannot determine gender from the name.

4   Being quoted is a fear because, as it now stands, it would locate my scholarship within what I experience as the rigid judicial framework, which is both conservative and gendered away from me.

5   It is more likely that an Aboriginal person will be able to put themselves in this position. However, there is no guarantee that an Aboriginal person has learned the necessary things in a Canadian law school to carry this awareness. Perhaps this is a failing of how we educate lawyers in Canadian law schools, or perhaps Aboriginal culture and tradition do not belong in a Canadian institution. (This is a complicated issue; perhaps a topic for another paper.) It is also possible that non-Aboriginal persons may be able to situate their ability to practice law in such a way that they embrace the "difference" of an Aboriginal client. I think Canadian universities (including law schools) have done a much better job of developing education programs that assist non-Aboriginal people in gaining access to significant amounts of Aboriginal culture, tradition and knowledge.

6   I mean no disrespect to the Aboriginal people who are able to sustain themselves in the daily practice of law. My point is simply to articulate one of the reasons, the structural reason, for why I do not have the patience for this kind of work.

7   I do not mean to suggest that I am the only "minority" scholar who has reached this conclusion. Please see, for example, the collection of papers edited by Adrien Katherine Wing (1997).

8   See *BC Studies: A Quarterly Journal of the Humanities and Social Sciences* 95 (Autumn 1992). The focus of this special issue, "A Theme Issue: Anthropology and History in the Courts," is the *Delgamuukw* decision at trial. Dara Culhane (1998) presents another excellent analysis of this case, Canadian law, and the discipline of anthropology.

9   Elsewhere I have explained: "I tell this story about naming because it is symbolic. Growing up 'Indian' in this country is very much about not having the power to define yourself or your own reality. It is being denied the right to say, 'I am!' — instead, always finding yourself saying, 'I am not!' In some places in the book, I have chosen to use the word Indian or First Nations, even recognizing that they can be viewed as excluding others. My experience is the experience of a person entitled to be registered under the Indian Act. Further, I have never been denied that right. These facts shape how I understand life, law and politics" (Monture-Angus 1995: 3).

10 Looking back, I understand both why "Flint Woman" (this is the Mohawk title of my first article, republished as the first chapter of my book *Thunder in My Soul*) emerged during

my last years at law school and why a few years after leaving law school I wanted to move beyond the image I had created. "Flint Woman" is the one who fights back. Now, more than a decade and a half after graduating from law school, I find that fighting back is no longer enough.

11   It is not my intention to appropriate the experiences of Aboriginal women who are federally sentenced. This was the first comprehensive study to collect and give voice to the stories of Aboriginal women and what they have survived. Further, I do not see a lot of difference between the lives of Aboriginal prisoners who are women and my life when the measure is what we survived growing up. Therefore, I do not judge their present circumstances or allow the experience to be an obstacle in creating friendships.

12   This term refers to individuals who have not been arrested and have never served terms of incarceration.

13   I am grateful to Stephanie Hayman of the Centre for Crime and Justice Studies, London, England, for bringing this concern to my attention.

14   I have a problem with a portion of the academic literature written by Aboriginal scholars (many of those who fit in this category, I would note, are men). Many of these scholars offer excellent critiques of colonialism, of where we have been, but offer little comment on where we should go.

15   I am not the first academic to borrow the imagery from our cultural experiences and contexts. Please see Gloria Valencia-Weber and Christine Zuni (1995).

16   Although Johansen is not a Mohawk or Aboriginal, the people of the community have supported his work. Douglas M. George (Kanentiio) states: "What was sorely lacking in previous books was a command of the facts *as the Mohawk people saw them*. Until Professor Johansen began his research, *no author had the trust and confidence of the Mohawk people necessary to write about the events that are as sensitive as they are terrifying*" (Johansen 1993: x; emphasis added). This criterion is far too infrequently considered in academia and the research generated on Aboriginal Peoples. It is indeed *on* the people — it is on our backs as it is without our consent, knowledge, and participation. Very few academics are even cognizant that their relationship with Aboriginal people and Aboriginal nations is something that must be considered. It is not as simple as returning the research to the community. This does nothing to displace the appropriation. Even well-intentioned researchers do not develop sustaining relationships, because the relationships are not in and of the community.

17   Whenever I discuss these particular sections of the Indian Act and its impositions on Indian women, I am reminded of a poem written by Lenore Keeshig-Tobias. Her poem, "(a found poem)," was borrowed (in part) from the Indian Act and creatively reconstructs former sections 11 and 12(1)(b). These two sections contained the gender discriminatory provision that disenfranchised women on "marriage out" (See Keeshig-Tobias 1983: 123–24).

18   Bill C-31 became law in 1985. It contains the provision allowing for the reinstatement of most individuals who were involuntarily disenfranchised by a variety of provisions in the Act (including the women who married out), and it creates the ability for bands to assume some level of control over their membership.

19   As this discussion focuses on the Indian Act, I adopt the language (Indian) of that Act in this section of the paper. The Indian Act applies only to those entitled to be registered

under section 6 of that Act.

20 Careful! This is no evidence that I have embraced feminist critiques of the English language (and it is a lesson in presumptions). I use the female pronoun because, as one Elder taught me, the word for Creator in our languages is neither male nor female. As so many people use the male pronoun when talking about the Creator, I have elected to always use the female in an effort to restore some balance into how we talk about the spiritual realm. Nia:wen Art Solomon.

21 When my family made the decision to move to my partner's reserve, I do not recall considering one of these "rights" or "benefits" as a reason to settle ourselves on the reserve. We moved to Thunderchild so our children would be raised with more family than just mom and dad. We wanted our children to have a chance to learn the language. We moved to the reserve to free the children from the racism in the city so that they would have a place to be free and to be who they are. We moved back to the reserve to be in a relationship with our community in an effort to step away from the pattern of colonialism embedded in our life. We moved back to the reserve to establish a stronger relationship with the land of my partner's territory.

22 I do not "blame" Indians for this, as the central experience of colonial oppression is the fight for daily survival. When you are busy trying to feed your children and just to make it to the next day, it is very difficult to see the "big picture" painted by our collective and individual oppression. This is one of the "privileges" I have in my life. I am no longer fighting for basic daily survival.

23 See, for example, Kathleen Jamieson (1978); Lilianne Krosenbrink-Gelissen (1991); and Native Women's Association of Canada (1986).

24 The most comprehensive analysis of the Native Women's Association of Canada and their part in the lobby to see section 12(1)(b) repealed does not consider these factors. See the work of Lilianne Krosenbrink-Gelissen (1991).

25 For example, the Canadian Advisory Council on the Status of Women funded a study produced by Kathleen Jamieson (an Indian woman) in 1978.

26 I am not asserting that the involvement of all feminists or women's rights activists and Aboriginal women is inappropriate. An excellent bridge-building discussion of the violence against all women is provided in Laureen Snider's (1998b) work. The work of Constance Backhouse (1991) also stands out in my mind as an example of feminist work involving Aboriginal women in an appropriate way.

27 For a fuller discussion, see Mary Ellen Turpel (1991: 17–40).

28 I mean no disrespect to the sacred nature of these alliances called treaties. However, a look at the situation of treaties in Canadian law makes it obvious why I hold such a view.

29 I do not believe that the individualized process for issuing script extinguished any "collective" land rights of the Métis. The script documents themselves are silent regarding extinguishment. In Canadian law, this is insufficient to create the extinguishment of land rights. With respect to our nation "lines," I will leave any further discussion for Métis citizens to write. To go further is to speak for the Métis (a distinct nation), and that is both unnecessary and improper.

30 This is not an argument in support of pan-Indianism. I have long believed that we must organize around nation status (and/or perhaps treaty territories).

31   I am not talking about a "safe space," which would presume that there is space outside
the safe space that is not safe. Conceding that much space is not an acceptable approach
for me.

References

Backhouse, Constance. 1991. *Petticoats and Prejudice: Women and Law in Nineteenth-Century Canada*. Toronto: Osgoode Society.

BC Studies: *The British Columbian Quarterly*. 1992. Special Issue on "Anthropology and History in the Courts." *BC Studies* 95.

Cook-Lynn, Elizabeth. 1996. *Why I Can't Read Wallace Stegner and Other Essays*. Madison: University of Wisconsin Press.

Correctional Service of Canada. 1990. *Creating Choices: Report of the Task Force on Federally Sentenced Women*. Ottawa: Solicitor General.

Culhane, Dara. 1998. *The Pleasure of the Crown: Anthropology, Law and First Nations*. Burnaby: Talonbooks.

Dion Stout, Madeleine and Catherine R. Bruyere. 1997. "Stopping Family Violence: Aboriginal Communities Enspirited." In J. Rick Ponting (ed.), *First Nations in Canada: Perspectives on Opportunity, Empowerment, and Self-Determination*. Toronto: McGraw-Hill Ryerson.

Ermine, Willie. 1995. "Aboriginal Epistemology." In Marie Battiste and Jean Barman (eds.), *First Nations Education in Canada: The Circle Unfolds*. Vancouver: University of British Columbia Press.

Fowler, H.W. and F.G. Fowler (eds.). 1974. *The Concise Oxford Dictionary*. Oxford: Clarendon Press.

Hamilton, Alvin C. and Murray Sinclair (commissioners). 1991. *Report of the Aboriginal Justice Inquiry of Manitoba: The Justice System and Aboriginal People*, Volume 1. Winnipeg: Queen's Printer.

Jamieson, Kathleen. 1978. *Indian Women and the Law in Canada: Citizens Minus*. Ottawa: Canadian Advisory Council on the Status of Women.

Johansen, Bruce E. 1993. *Life and Death in Mohawk Country*. Golden, Colorado: North American Press.

Keeshig-Tobias, Lenore. 1983. "(a found poem)." In Beth Brant (Degonwadonti) (ed.), *A Gathering of Spirit: Writing and Art by Native American Women*. Berkeley: Sinister Wisdom.

Krosenbrink-Gelissen, Lilianne E. 1991. *Sexual Equality as an Aboriginal Right: The Native Women's Association of Canada and the Constitutional Process on Aboriginal Matters*. Germany: Breitenbach Publishers.

Ladner, Kiera. 1996. "*Nit-acimonawinomaacimonakohci*: This is My Story About Stories." *Native Studies Review* 11, 2.

Matsudi, Mari. 1988. "Affirmative Action and Legal Knowledge: Planting Seeds in Plowed-Up Ground." *Harvard Women's Law Journal* 11.

McGillivray, Anne and Brenda Comaskey. 1996. *Intimate Violence, Aboriginal Women and Justice System Response: A Winnipeg Study*. Winnipeg: Manitoba Research Centre on Family Violence and Violence Against Women.

McNeil, Kent. 1998. "Defining Aboriginal Title in the 90s: Has the Supreme Court Finally Got It Right?" Unpublished lecture. Toronto: York University, March 25.

Mihesuah, Devon A. 1998. "Commonalty of Difference: American Indian Women and History." In Devon A. Mihesuah (ed.), *Natives and Academics: Researching and Writing about American Indians*. Lincoln and London: University of Nebraska Press.

Miller, Bruce (ed.). 1992. *B.C. Studies* 95 (Autumn).

Monture, Patricia. 1993. "I Know My Name: A First Nations Woman Speaks." In Geraldine Finn (ed.), *Limited Edition: Voices of Women, Voices of Feminism*. Halifax: Fernwood Publishing.

Monture-Angus, Patricia. 1995. *Thunder in My Soul: A Mohawk Woman Speaks*. Halifax: Fernwood Publishing.

Native Women's Association of Canada. 1986. *Guide to Bill C-32: An Explanation of the 1985 Amendments to the Indian Act*. Ottawa.

Ponting, J. Rick. 1997. *First Nations in Canada: Perspectives on Opportunity, Empowerment, and Self-Determination*. Toronto: McGraw-Hill Ryerson.

Razack, Sherene. 1998. *Looking White People in the Eye: Gender, Race, and Culture in Courtrooms and Classrooms*. Toronto: University of Toronto Press.

Ross, Rupert. 1996. *Returning to the Teachings: Exploring Aboriginal Justice*. Toronto: Penguin.

Turpel, Mary Ellen. 1991. "Home/Land." *Canadian Journal of Family Law* 10, 1.

Weber, Gloria Valencia and Christine Zuni. 1995. "Domestic Violence and Tribal Protection of Indigenous Women in the United States." *Women's Rights and Human Rights Law Journal* 69, 1–2.

Wing, Adrien Katherine. 1997. *Critical Race Feminism: A Reader*. New York: New York University Press.

Legal Cases

Delgamuukw v. British Columbia, [1998] 1 CNLR 21 (SCC)

REPRODUCTIVE JUSTICE

Chapter 10

CONSTRUCTING DIFFERENCE, CONTROLLING DEVIANCE
The Eugenic Model

A.J. Withers

From: *Disability Politics and Theory*, pp. 13–30 (reprinted with permission).

Eugenics is the belief that human evolution can be crafted by the encouraged breeding of people who are considered the most desirable — the "fit" — and the discouraged breeding of those who are considered the least desirable — the "unfit." Eugenics is inspired by evolutionary theory and operates under the assumption that humans can shape our own evolution in positive ways by engaging in selective breeding. The word itself is a creation of Sir Francis Galton, the father of eugenics, and is based on the Greek word *eugenes,* meaning well-born or good stock. While Galton's theories were first published in 1865, he did not coin the word eugenics until 1883 in *Inquiries into Human Faculty and Its Development.* The word Galton used prior to eugenics was "viriculture" (Galton 1907).

There are different ways of going about achieving eugenic goals and they are generally defined as either "negative" or "positive" eugenics. Negative eugenics focuses on the reduction of reproduction amongst those who are considered undesirable; positive eugenics focuses on increasing reproduction of those who are considered desirable. Further, eugenicists also differentiate between forms of eugenic programs. These programs can happen through insidious forms of control or coercion of reproduction, called passive eugenics, or through active eugenics

— the implementation of programs that force eugenics onto people (such as through sterilizations, prohibitions in marriages, segregation and murder).

In 1865, Galton formulated the theory of eugenics, and with it the first cohesive ideas about a class of disabled people, or the unfit, were born in modern Western society. Galton saw eugenics both as "the science of improving inherited stock, not only by judicious matings, but by all the influences which give more suitable strains a better chance" and as a way "to give the more suitable races … a better chance of prevailing speedily over the less suitable" (cited in Galton and Galton 1998: 99). Galton strongly believed that unfit people were reproducing at an alarming rate. He wanted to see "the undesirables be got rid of and the desirables multiplied" (cited in Black 2003: 16). Of course, Galton's views of fitness, or disability, were based on the social, cultural and economic views at the time.

The eugenic model conceptualized disability as being in the individual body and as inheritable. Simply, disabled people were unfit: unfit to live in society, unfit to exist. Eugenicists believed eugenics offered a "solution" to disability, a way to eradicate disability from society. This model envisioned disability as a threat to society and to those considered fit. Primarily, eugenics honed in on all of those individuals who were struggling in society (almost always as a result of existing social injustices), labelled them as disabled and targeted them for eradication. The eugenic model constructed disability with such rabid contempt that its proponents would, and did, do anything to get rid of the problem disabled people posed, including murder.

The early part of the twentieth century saw an explosion in support for eugenics. A boon to the cause occurred when Galton's cousin, Charles Darwin, publicly declared his support for eugenics (Wikler 1999). Eugenic organizations were established, including the American Breeders' Association's Eugenics Committee (1906) (Kimmelman 1983), the United Farm Women of Alberta (1916) (Nind 2000), the English Eugenics Education Society (1907) (Wikler 1999) and the Racial Hygiene Society (Germany, 1905) (Wikler 1999). A number of prominent people were involved in these organizations early on, including Alexander Graham Bell, Stanford professor Vernon Kellogg, U.S. Assistant Secretary of Agriculture Willet M. Hayes, Dutch geneticist Hugo de Vries (Kimmelman 1983), activist and soon-to-be Alberta MLA Irene Parlby, German biologist Alfred Ploetz (Black 2003) and, of course, Francis Galton (Kevles 1985). Eugenic movements also sprang up around the same time in Brazil, Norway and Russia, among many other places (Wikler 1999).

The eugenic movement had its peak in the 1930s and 1940s and declined after the defeat of the Nazis, who had implemented horrific mass eugenic policies. However, eugenics made up the foundation of the modern Western understanding of disability, and its influences can be found in other mainstream models of disability. Some of the eugenic attitudes about disabled people and their reproduction remain present today.

WHO IS "FIT" AND WHO ISN'T

The eugenic worldview was a binary one in which there were two classes of people: those considered "fit" and those considered "unfit." The unfit class created the foundation for what is considered disability today. Who is considered disabled today, along with women, racialized people, homosexuals, queers, poor and working-class people, were all considered disabled under eugenics (Davis 2002). All of these attributes were considered to be negative and perceived to be inheritable, thus they were all presumed to be physical conditions. The elimination of these conditions — the elimination of disability, eugenicists believed — would lead to a more productive and far less troubled society.

Feeble-mindedness had a number of different definitions. One of these definitions was being unable to finish third grade (Pfeiffer 1993). This definition failed to problematize the education system, the discrimination within it or any of the social factors that would prevent children from being able to attend or remain in school. Eugenicist Amos Butler (1921: 390) wrote, "Feeble-mindedness is one of the most potential [sic] destructive factors in our civilization. It produces more pauperism, more crime, more degeneracy, than any other one force." This ideology put the blame of social problems directly on those people who experienced the brunt of those problems. Therefore, eugenic ideas were highly popular amongst the upper (and growing middle) classes as eugenics explained away social problems by blaming the people who were the most negatively impacted by existing oppressions. The solution? Eliminate the people who cause the problems. With eugenics, there was no need for systemic change, only a change in who was a part of society.

Many of the eugenic solutions were adopted from Reverend Thomas Malthus. Malthus, a British author who wrote extensively about population, economics and politics in the late eighteenth and early nineteenth centuries, called for a widespread reduction in the global population. Malthus argued for the removal of poor laws and of the meagre poor-assistance systems of the time. He believed giving assistance to the poor would encourage them to have more children; thus, the population would increase, ultimately resulting in famine and war. Malthus (1888: 430) said, "We are bound in justice and honour formally to disclaim the *right* of the poor to support." Malthus held that the poor should be removed from society by encouraging death and disease:

> We should sedulously encourage the other forms of destruction, which we compel nature to use. Instead of recommending cleanliness to the poor, we should encourage contrary habits. In our towns we should make the

streets narrower, crowd more people into the houses, and court the return of the plague. In the country, we should build our villages near stagnant pools, and particularly encourage settlements in all marshy and unwholesome situations. But above all, we should reprobate specific remedies for ravaging diseases; and those benevolent, but much mistaken men, who have thought they were doing a service to mankind by projecting schemes for the total extrapolation of particular disorders. (1888: 412)

He went on to argue that increased mortality would reduce the population to a sustainable level that would not result in mass hunger.[1] From a eugenic perspective, it was not only acceptable to permit people to live in abject poverty, it was preferred. This would allow evolution to take its course and cull those considered unfit.

It was no coincidence that the eugenic movement developed shortly after the industrial revolution, as it provided the perfect explanation for massive disparities in wealth as well as the increasing poverty and suffering among the working-class. Eugenics provided those with power a justification for that power as well as a rationalization for the injustices and inequalities that industrial capitalism and colonialism brought forth in new and increasingly violent ways.

The unfit were largely classified as such because they were considered unproductive or underproductive within the capitalist economy. Leonard Darwin (1926: 366) argued that eugenic targets included "the immoral, the inefficient, the stupid, the unemployable, the weakly, etc." Many years later, eugenicist Frederick Osborn (1968: 105) would assert, "Achievement in building a home as well as success in other aspects of life constitutes a eugenic criterion." These statements illustrate the true motives of eugenic thought: to legitimize the oppression of groups of people by identifying them as defective, unfit and disabled, and to use that legitimacy to perpetuate oppression.

Eugenics formed a seemingly scientific way to establish an "other" and to legitimize "othering" — the process of establishing a group identity by stigmatizing and devaluing certain people. The individual and multiple identities of people who were labelled as "other" were replaced by one (negative) group identity or trait. Eugenics created the other as the unfit and targeted them for elimination.

Within eugenics, economic or political realities such as poverty are not caused by injustice but by genetically inherited traits. Social conditions and economic inequalities were considered individual heritable failings. Charles Davenport, one of the most prominent American eugenicists, argued that poor people were genetically unable to participate in competitive capitalist economies and support themselves. Davenport wrote:

[There are many people] who lack one or more traits that are necessary for them to take their part in forwarding the world's work under the conditions of competition afforded by the society in which they live. If they fail in their part they become private or public charges or a social menace. (1912a: 53)

This would make them unfit. Leonard Darwin, another well-known eugenics supporter and the son of Charles Darwin, also argued that social problems, such as poverty, were directly related to one's genetic or physical make-up:

Does not the housing difficulty in most cases merely indicate the impossibility of an economic rent being paid, an impossibility often due to an actual incapacity on the part of the tenant to do work equivalent in value to what is needed to supply a decent dwelling? (1926: 387)

From a eugenic perspective, one's ability to support oneself within the capitalist system was hereditary, and poverty and "pauperism" (begging or taking charity out of poverty) were biologically predetermined.

Racialized people received special notice from eugenicists. In the late nineteenth and early twentieth centuries, this category consisted of a number of ethnicities that are now considered white, including Irish people, Jewish people and Eastern European immigrants. This category of racialized people also consisted of groups who continue to be considered people of colour, Black people being the most vehemently targeted. These groups were entirely, or almost entirely, poor; therefore, they were seen as undesirable and unworthy. (Alternatively, they were seen as undesirable and unworthy so they were entirely, or almost entirely, poor). Galton established a ranking system for determining a person's fitness in which Black people were automatically ranked two grades lower than what he considered to be the least-fit white person (Province 1973). Edward East, in the 1919 text *Inbreeding and Outbreeding*, wrote that Black people were inferior to white people:

In reality the negro is inferior to the white. This is not hypothesis or supposition; it is a crude statement of actual fact. The negro has given the world no original contribution of high merit. By his own initiative in his original habitat, he has never risen ... In competition with the white race, he has failed to approach its standard. (1919: 253)

Racialized groups were often considered lazy as well. A 1931 genetics text reported that "in general, a Negro is not inclined to work hard" (cited in Beckwith 1993: 327).

At the First International Eugenics Congress (held in London in 1912) Davenport argued for the separation of racialized groups from white society because they "do not go well with our social organization" (1912b: 154). Davenport continued:

> For the Ethiopian has not undergone that selection that in Europe weeded out the traits that failed to recognize property rights, or that failed to give industry, ambition and sex control.[2] (1912b: 154)

Racist stereotypes and cultural differences, including understandings of property ownership, were all taken by eugenicists to be genetic faults or disabilities inherent to specific races or ethnic groups.

For eugenicists, racism and poverty were not social or economic problems; rather, they were natural and appropriate outcomes brought about by a host of inheritable defects. Capitalist colonial expansion, for which the appropriation of labour and land was essential, was justified by the believed natural inferiority of different groups. After all, Africans did not have the gene to respect property rights; therefore it wasn't really *their* land that was being stolen. This eugenic logic would have likely also extended to legitimize other colonial projects throughout the rest of the world.

The other groups that Davis (2002: 14) identifies as falling into "the rubric of feeble-mindedness and degeneration" were similarly categorized to legitimize social injustices. Homosexuals (and other gender transgressors[3]) were seen as deviant; however, there were competing eugenic arguments as to why. Some, like prominent eugenicist Havelock Ellis, thought they were genetically inferior and if they reproduced they would breed degenerate children (Ordover 2003). Others, like psychiatrist George Henry, believed that homosexuals who were from a sound genetic stock would not reproduce because of their homosexuality, posing a eugenic threat (Terry 1995).

Women were also eugenic targets; however, they were targeted differently depending on their social position. Rich and poor women were seen very differently in the late nineteenth and early twentieth centuries and were not categorized on any similar terms. Poor women were seen as a "different species" than rich women, according to Barbara Ehrenreich and Deirdre English in *Complaints and Disorders* (1976: 12). Poor women engaged in paid work and were frequently seen as carriers of disease. Because they were markedly different than rich women, it seems that much of the emphasis was put on their poverty. Under eugenic theory, however, they were paid special attention to because of the reproductive threat they posed: after all, they were the ones who brought even more poor children into the world.

Rich women (who were almost entirely, if not entirely, white) were pathologized in order to ensure the continuation and justification of sexism and patriarchy. Comments such as, "The man who does not know sick women does not know women," made by Dr. S. Weir Mitchell, reflected the sentiment of the time (cited in Ehrenreich and English 1976: 25). This pathologization of women, according to Ehrenreich and English (1976: 23), "seemed to take the malice out of sexual oppression: when you prevented a woman from doing anything active or interesting, you were only doing this for her own good."

Intellectually disabled people were also seen as unproductive, particularly in an increasingly industrial economy where work became more segmented and/or cognitively based (Harder and Scott 2005). While there was an integrated place for both physically and intellectually disabled people before the eugenic period, these people began to be viewed as "useless and unproductive" with the rise of industrial capitalism (Tait 1985–86: 451). This was the case, largely, because of disablist notions of productivity and the absence of accommodations for disabled workers, such as adjusting factory speeds, having a variety of training approaches, having a variety of time prompts and providing retraining as needed.

The groups that were targeted as eugenically unfit were targeted in ways that legitimized the status quo, propped up capitalism and justified the continued oppression of these groups out of biological necessity. All of these groups made up the original definition of disabled and were vilified and targeted as a result. "Feeble-minded" was not simply a politically incorrect turn of phrase — it was a label imposed on people to at once target certain groups and justify the systems that created them as separate in the first place.

REDUCING THE UNFIT:
IMMIGRATION

Eugenicists were determined to use any tool they could to reduce the populations of those they considered unfit. They had a number of successes in influencing governmental policies in Canada and the United States, particularly in keeping people they considered undesirable out of the country. In Canada, the 1886 Immigration Act prohibited "the landing in Canada of any immigrant or other passenger who is suffering from any loathsome, dangerous or infectious disease or malady" (cited in *Chee* 1905: headnote). An earlier version of the law called for the screening of "imbeciles, idiots and morons" (cited in Gillis 2001: A13).

The United States established similar policies of discrimination against disabled immigrants. In 1882, the federal government implemented a policy permitting the denial of entry to individuals who would potentially become a "public ward" (cited in Jaeger and Bowman 2005: 51). Medical exams for immigration purposes were initiated nine years later (Fairchild and Tynan 1994) because a key aim of immigration policy was to exclude disabled people (Longmore 2003). As of 1917, people could be barred for things like varicose veins, asthma, hernias, poor eyesight, flat feet and a gamut of other conditions; further, beginning in 1949, an individual could have their immigrant status in the United States revoked if a medical condition that was missed at the border was subsequently discovered (Jaeger and Bowman 2005).

These policies, coupled with clearly racist policies that established quotas for immigrants from certain countries, meant that most physically or intellectually disabled, racialized, and/or poor people would not be granted entry into either Canada or the United States.

STERILIZATION

While keeping disabled people out was effective, it did not address the many unfit people who were already within the country's borders. To do this, eugenicists focused their attention on limiting the reproduction of the unfit, specifically, through sterilization. Eugenics was not simply a way of understanding disability — it was a call to action, compelling its followers to urgently act to save the sanctity of the race. The United States enacted its first sterilization legislation in Indiana in 1907 (Kevles 1985). In all, about seventy thousand people were legally and forcibly sterilized between 1907 and 1970 (Black 2003). Of the thirty-three states with eugenic sterilization legislation, twenty-six had it in place by 1932 (Davis 1990).

The United States Supreme Court first addressed the issue of forced sterilization in the 1927 *Buck v. Bell* case. In this case, the court allowed the sterilization of a woman who had been labelled as feeble-minded. This was done despite arguments that the order would violate the woman's constitutional rights. Justice Holmes saw his decision as a benefit to society:

> It is better for all the world, if instead of waiting to execute degenerate offspring for crime, or to let them starve for their imbecility, society can prevent those who are manifestly unfit from continuing their kind. The principle that sustains compulsory vaccination is broad enough to cover cutting the Fallopian tubes … Three generations of imbeciles are enough. (1927: 207)

Thus the U.S. Supreme Court legally legitimized eugenics by finding that that the interests of the state, and those of the capitalist-driven economy, superseded individual rights. The eugenic model was upheld by the state and the eradication of disabled people became one of its goals.

In Canada, the Ontario government tried to impose forced sterilization legislation on people in 1912, but it did not pass (Kevles 2000). Alberta and British Columbia were more successful, each passing a Sexual Sterilization Act, in 1928 and 1933, respectively. Both provinces established eugenics boards to approve sterilizations of disabled or unfit people.[4] In Alberta, the Sexual Sterilization Act was enacted (according to George Hoadley, the bill's sponsor) to address the "need for the state to be protected from the menace which the propagation by the mentally diseased brings about" (Robertson 1996: n.p.). The Act called for sterilization in instances where there was a risk of "the transmission of any mental disability or deficiency to his progeny, or the risk of mental injury either to such person or his progeny" (*Muir v. Alberta* 1996). The legislation had a specific apparatus to determine who should be sterilized on the grounds of their perceived disability.

Alberta's Eugenics Board viewed itself as a social enforcer and used its power to eliminate undesirable members of society (even beyond what had been established in the legislation). The sterilization of individuals who did not meet the criteria set out in the law and the use of sterilization as punishment for difficult or deviant prison inmates are but a few of the abuses carried out through the Sexual Sterilization Act. Many disabled women had their uterus and/or ovaries removed in order to eliminate menstruation. These women, according to the Board, proved "difficult to handle and to keep clean during menstrual periods," or masturbated or showed "lesbian tendencies" (*Muir v. Alberta* 1996: para. 53). By approving the use of sterilization, the overzealous Eugenics Board was in reality deciding who was disabled and who should be permitted to reproduce. After 1930, the Board approved sterilizations in ten minutes or less (*Muir v. Alberta* 1996). In keeping with the logic of eugenics, sterilizations were often fuelled by sexist, racist and classist goals (Robertson 1996). Towards the end of the Albertan eugenic program, one-quarter of all sterilizations were performed on First Nations and Métis people even though they made up less than 3 percent of the population (Black 2003).

Because it was permanent, sterilization was the first choice for most eugenicists dealing with the genetic "threat" posed by the unfit. However, the growing birth control movement attracted eugenicists as well. There was an affinity between early feminists — most of whom were straight, white, middle- and upper-class — and eugenicists around the issues of birth control. Feminists saw eugenics as an opportunity to build support for their campaign for access to birth control information and instruments (or they saw birth control as an opportunity to promote eugenics). While birth control was not permanent, it had the potential to dramatically reduce the reproduction of eugenically targeted populations. Birth control could also become something that many women who were considered unfit would embrace, unlike sterilization.

FEMINIST COMPLICITY

With women as eugenic targets, first-wave feminists' adoption of the eugenic discourse presented not only the potential to win greater capacity to control their own reproduction, but also an opportunity to remove themselves out from under the eugenic umbrella. Early feminist campaigns endeavoured to overcome the fact that they had been labelled as disabled on account of their female "affliction" and to gain access to the same privileges as the rest of society. These campaigns worked to reinforce the oppression of all those groups that they left behind, including poor people, racialized people, homosexuals, queer and trans people and those who are still thought of as disabled today.

In fact, eugenics became front and centre in the discourse of the feminist campaign for birth control. One prominent feminist, Charlotte Perkins Gilman, said, "An active sense of social motherhood is desperately needed among women of today, if we are to put a stop to war, to cease producing defectives and to begin the conscious improvement of our stock" (cited in May 1995: 70). Victoria Woodhull (1893: 278) condemned the building of institutions and hospitals because "medical experts do all they can to keep alive the unfit brought together in these institutions, and destined, should they survive, to perpetuate a deteriorated race." Two of Canada's most famous suffragists, Nellie McClung and Emily Murphy, adamantly supported eugenics. These two women were integral in the campaign for Alberta's Sexual Sterilization Act (Devereaux 2005; Grekul 2008).

Margaret Sanger, likely the most famous of the early feminists, passionately campaigned for both birth control and eugenics. Initially, her focus was most strongly placed on women's right to limit their family size; however, she later began openly advocating for the implementation of sweeping eugenic policies. Sanger called for "a stern and rigid policy" in which the government would "give certain dysgenic groups in our population their choice of segregation or sterilization" (cited in Carlson 2010: 82). Sanger (1925: 5) also argued that "the Government of the United States deliberately encourages and even makes necessary by its laws the breeding — with a breakneck rapidity — of idiots, defectives, diseased, feeble-minded and criminal classes."

Eugenic ideas were not limited to a few first-wave feminists; rather, eugenics was a core component of first-wave feminism. The National Council of Women of Canada (1893) (Roberts 1979), National League of Women Voters (1920) (Lemons 1990), American Birth Control League (1921) (Ordover 2003), Birth Control Clinical Research Bureau (1923) (Engs 2000), Canadian Birth Control League (1924) (Prentice 1988), Planned Parenthood (1942) (Kline 2001)[5] and Birthright Inc. (1943) (Robitsche 1973) were early feminist groups; they were all founded by women, promoted some level of women's rights, had platforms founded on eugenic principles and worked diligently to have eugenic politics implemented.

By adopting eugenics, feminists effectively expanded their base of support and garnered support for the right to vote (as well as other rights) where they may not have had that support previously. For example, Robert Reid Rentoul, in the 1906 book *Race Culture or Race Suicide*, supported first-wave feminism because it was serving a eugenic purpose. Rentoul (1906: 47) said, "A great many of our social problems can only be dealt with if women will take up their proper position in public affairs, and give their time and attention to questions which men generally have little wish to tackle." A number of prominent men supported birth control as a feminist demand because these women successfully argued that birth control was an important eugenic tool that would assist in limiting the birth rate of those labelled as disabled.

Not only did the birth control campaign earn the burgeoning white, middle- and upper-class feminist movement an early win,[6] it also took these women out of what Davis (2002: 14) called "the rubric of feeble-mindedness" and into a new category of person. This person was the modern woman, a voter, for whom this era of feminism was built — the rich, white, straight woman, not yet equal, but on her way. As a part of this move towards the idea of the modern woman, these women worked to reinforce the notion that there was nothing wrong with (or disabled) about themselves by arguing that there was something seriously and dangerously wrong with the real disabled people: the poor, the racialized, the queer, the psychiatrized, the intellectually disabled and the physically disabled. As a result of the feminist movement, the eugenic model was recast. Privileged women were removed from the cage of disability in exchange for guarding the door.

By 1933, first-wave feminism was well established as a vehicle for eugenics. Birth control was increasingly widespread and eugenic sterilizations were taking place in large parts of North America and Europe. Additionally, forty-two American states had laws prohibiting interracial marriage; at least twenty-five of the state laws could result in a prison or hard labour sentence. In Pennsylvania, any free Blacks could be ordered back into servitude if they were convicted of violating the interracial marriage law (Newbeck 2004).

From a eugenic perspective, forced sterilization, birth control and anti-marriage laws for interracial couples appear to have been quite successful in reducing populations that were considered disabled. In the period from 1800 to 1820, there were ninety-three Black people for every one hundred white people in the United States. Between 1900 and 1920, there were forty-four Black people for every one hundred white people (Wilcox 1922). Additionally, in 1910, Black women's reproduction rates dropped to two-thirds of what they had been in 1880 (Roberts 1997). Some of the reduction in the proportion of Black population was caused by sterilization and restrictive, racist immigration legislation. Poverty, low life expectancy rates and other factors also worked to reduce Black populations.

NAZI EUGENICS

Canadian and American eugenic projects were well underway by the time Adolf Hitler was elected German Chancellor in 1933. Nazi Germany, under Hitler's leadership, adopted eugenic aims as state policy, initially copying many North American programs (Black 2003). Yet, this was not the first time Germany initiated eugenic policy. During World War I, the country starved tens of thousands of psychiatrized people to death — they were simply too low on the priority list to receive rations (Lifton 1986). Under Hitler, the systemic starvation of disabled people and other "useless eaters" became official state policy (Lifton1986) after a prolonged propaganda campaign to stigmatize these people as "life unworthy of life" (cited in Rees 2005: 177).

Hitler operated under the common eugenic belief that

> those who are physically and mentally unhealthy and unfit must not perpetuate their own suffering in the bodies of their children ... it is a crime and a disgrace to make this affliction all the worse by passing on disease and defects to innocent creatures out of mere egoism. (Hitler 1939: 243)

The Nazis passed the Law for the Prevention of Offspring with Hereditary Diseases on July 14, 1933 (Biesold 1999). While the precise number of people sterilized under the law will never be known, it is estimated that 200,000 to 375,000 people were sterilized on the grounds of hereditary disease (Lifton 1986; Biesold 1999).[7] Those targeted for sterilization were people with a number of what were considered to be hereditary diseases: psychiatric diagnoses, feeble-mindedness, blindness, Deafness, Huntington's disease, epilepsy, deformation and alcoholism (Lifton 1986). Beyond sterilization, disabled women in Nazi Germany were also subjected to forced abortions at any time during the pregnancy. The numbers of these torturous procedures are unknown; however, there are fifty-seven documented cases of Deaf women who were subjected to this horror (Biesold 1999).

Sterilization and forced abortion, however, weren't enough. Just before World War II started, Hitler decreed the expansion of "the authority of individual physicians, with the view to enable them, after the most critical examination in the realm of human knowledge, to administer to incurably sick persons a mercy death" (cited in Arad 1987: 9). This began the Nazi euthanasia programs. The word "euthanasia" is from the Greek meaning "good death" and is a clear misnomer in relation to the Nazi murders: doctors starved, gassed and drugged their patients to death.

Some doctors approached the executions with a morbid creativity. It was doctors who came up with the idea to make the gas chambers appear to be shower rooms so people would be willing to enter them (O'Neil 2001). Throughout the Holocaust, hundreds of thousands of disabled people who had previously been targeted by the Nazis for sterilization were actually killed (O'Neil 2001). While the numbers of people killed because of their medical diagnoses will never be known, an estimated 200,000 to 250,000 people were killed under the Nazi's T-4 program (Friedman 2004), including 85,000 to 105,000 inmates of mental institutions, 5,000 of them children (Lifton 1986).

Many disabled people who were targeted by the Nazis are largely excluded from these numbers as well. As Sandy O'Neil (2001: 69), author of the comprehensive *First They Killed the 'Crazies' and the 'Cripples'* writes, "Even taking low figures, demographically about 10 percent of any given population have some types of disabilities. This would mean 600,000 Jews with disabilities at a minimum."

To further complicate this position, in the context of Nazi society, being disabled and being Jewish could not be distinguished. At the time, to be Jewish was to be disabled. Hitler (1939: 243) wrote of Jews as having "the blood of an inferior stock." One's "Jewishness" was a part of the body, a blood disease that resulted in a number of physical and mental symptoms.

This argument is not an attempt to diminish the rabid anti-Semitism of Hitler and the Nazi Party; indeed, most Jews never would have been classified as eugenically unfit or disabled if not for anti-Semitism. Undeniably, six million Jews were killed because they were Jewish. In addition to being Jewish, however, they were also disabled under the eugenic model, which was grounds for killing someone. Within eugenic logic, it is impossible to parse apart disability from race, ethnicity, anti-sociality or sexual orientation — they are all categorized, albeit with different implications, as a form of unfit or deviant identity that lives in the body and in nature.

While the international community found the extermination of many groups abhorrent, this moral outrage was generally not extended to disabled people because of other countries' treatment of and attitudes toward disabled people. Germany would not pay out any compensation to those who were sterilized because the Nazis were considered to have legitimate genetic reasons (O'Neil 2001). Eugenic sterilizations continued in Canada, the United States, Sweden, Denmark, Finland and Switzerland after World War II (Spallone 1989).

NORTH AMERICAN EUGENICS AFTER WORLD WAR II

Following World War II, there was public recoil against eugenics. The graphic and horrifying images that came out of Germany from the Holocaust largely made eugenics distasteful. However, sterilization programs remained in practice. This may indicate a shift in the eugenic model's conceptualization of disability from marginality as disability to (so-called) legitimate genetic defect as disability, which would later bleed into the medical model.

Alberta's Sexual Sterilization Act was only repealed in 1972 after 2,822 people had been legally sterilized (*Muir v. Alberta* 1996). British Columbia's program was never implemented on the same scale as that of Alberta's. In B.C., there are 188 documented cases of people who were forcibly sterilized in the Essondale Provincial Mental Hospital before the law was repealed in 1973 (*E. (D.) v. R.* 2003).[8] Between 1940 and 1979 about 35,000 people were sterilized under eugenic legislation in the United States (Black 2003).[9]

These programs continued until the 1970s in many areas, but there were exceptions. In 1975, North Carolina enacted forced sterilization legislation, which was not repealed until 2003 (Silver 2003–2004). At least seven other states — Arkansas, Delaware, Georgia, Idaho, Mississippi, Vermont and Virginia — continued to have sterilization legislation after the turn of this century (Silver 2003–2004). While forced sterilization legislation was largely discontinued in the United States, eugenic sterilizations remained a regular occurrence. Most of these sterilizations were done to Black women, and many were performed without their knowledge.

Forced sterilizations continued in large numbers in the 1970s. Programs financed by the federal government resulted in the sterilization of 100,000 to 150,000 women a year in the early 1970s, and almost half of these women were Black (Black 2003). In 1972 alone, however, there were 200,000 sterilizations (Davis 1990). Many of these sterilizations occurred on the threat of withdrawal of social assistance (Roberts 1997).

America, over two decades after the Holocaust, was achieving sterilization rates of the same magnitude that Nazi Germany had accomplished (Roberts 1997). President Nixon reportedly believed that Black people, due to their genetic inferiority, would barely benefit from federal programming (Ehrlichman 1982). However, the government was willing to spend a massive amount on their forced sterilization. And, by the early 1970s, a quarter of First Nations women living on reservations in the United States had been sterilized (Ehrlichman 1982). The American government helped finance an even more successful eugenic sterilization program in Puerto Rico, which by 1968 saw the sterilization of one-third of all women there (Roberts 1997).[10] The targeting of the eugenically unfit continued, albeit more surreptitiously, after the fall of the Nazis.

Today in the United States, coerced sterilization remains commonplace. The lack, or inaccessibility, of state and federal funding for abortions means that many women cannot afford to get abortions even if they wanted one. Angela Davis (1990: 17) argues this policy has "effectively divested [poor women] of the right to legal abortions. Since surgical sterilizations ... remained free on demand, more and more poor women have been forced to opt for permanent infertility." While these sterilizations may not be legally forced, many women feel that they have no other options because of governmental policies.

The organization Project Prevention operates openly in the United States. Project Prevention pays women who are drug users or alcoholics $300 to get permanently sterilized. Project Prevention founder Barbara Harris (2009) says that "what separates this organization from many others is that we work to prevent a problem rather than spending the money we receive to treat one." An ad on Project Prevention's website shows a very young baby covered with a number of medical wires and tubes, including one on its nose, that take up about a quarter of the baby's face with the text: "Attention drug addicts and alcoholics, get birth control. Get $300. Make the call today: 888-30-CRACK."

The image on the advertisement makes it clear that it is these kinds of babies, disabled babies, which are purportedly being prevented through the project. The website also views the life of a disabled child solely as a financial drain or burden:

> The cost of hospitalization for a very low birth weight baby in need of intensive care can be as high as $150,000 or more. The annual medical cost of caring for cocaine-exposed babies nation wide has been estimated at 33 million for neonates, and as high as 1.4 billion during the babies' first year of life. (Project Prevention 1999: n.p.)

Focusing on the cost of medical care for these disabled children reduces lives to dollar amounts and harkens back to when eugenics was in its prime. The organization intones that the lives of disabled people are too expensive for our economy and our society and, therefore, should be prevented.

Project Prevention has paid about 3,850 people to keep from reproducing through long-term birth control (2,404 people) or sterilization (1,444 people). About half of the people who have been paid by Project Prevention not to have children are from racialized groups (Project Prevention 2011). The program has seen the sterilization or implementation of long-term birth control in drug addicts and alcoholics in every American state (Project Prevention 2011)

In Canada, a 1986 Supreme Court decision made sterilizations without consent for nontherapeutic purposes illegal. The case that set the precedent, *E. (Mrs.) v. Eve,* involved a twenty-four-year-old woman with an intellectual disability whose mother wished to have her sterilized. In this case, a lower court ruled that "the real and genuine object of the proposed sterilization was her protection. There was no overriding public interest against it" (*E. (Mrs.) v. Eve* 1986: para. 16). The Supreme Court overruled this decision, arguing that the intrusion on the person's civil liberties and permanent physical consequences cannot be overridden by any advantage from it. However, in the *Eve* decision, the Supreme Court left the door open to forced sterilization when it permitted nonconsensual sterilization for the "treatment of a serious malady" (*E. (Mrs.) v. Eve* 1986 para. 93). While the Supreme

Court set the burden high in respect to nonconsensual sterilization, there are no clear guidelines as to when or under what circumstances forced sterilization of disabled people would be justified.

There are myriad cases revealing that eugenics continues to operate through legal and medical frameworks today. Take, for example, the case of Martina Greywind, a pregnant woman charged with reckless endangerment in 1992 because she huffed paint during her pregnancy. After Greywind aborted her fetus, ensuring that a disabled baby would not be born as "a result" of her drug use, the charges against her were withdrawn (Roberts 1997). Every time a pregnancy is intervened upon to prevent disability, eugenics is operating. Every time someone is sterilized or administered birth control against their will or without their knowledge, eugenics is operating. Eugenics is insidious and pervasive and continues to be a threat to disabled people, especially racialized disabled people and/or disabled women.

Additionally, there are more simplistic forms of controlling the reproductive capacity of disabled women than sterilization. These include the nonconsensual, coerced or uninformed administration of birth control and eugenic pressures. Disabled women have been known to be administered Depo-Provera, a long-term birth control drug, without their consent (Canadian Women's Committee on Reproduction, Population and Development 1995). These practices are a form of passive eugenics that work to appropriate women's choice and reproductive capacity in order to eliminate disabled offspring.

Further, disabled women are pressured not to have children if those children could also become disabled. In 1968, eugenicist Frederick Osborn expressed this fact:

> Perhaps the most important function of the public is to create a climate of opinion that will put pressure on carriers of defect to reduce their reproduction, and on scientists in medicine and public health to put priority on all studies that might provide leads for effective action. (97)

This pressure has been applied to many different disabled women through genetic counselling and, at times, public outcry about their pregnancies.

One example of this was the public reaction when Bree Walker, a disabled anchorwoman, became pregnant. At a time when she should have been congratulated, she was faced with national public pressure to have an abortion. People were enraged and disgusted by the fact that someone would choose to have a child that had a fifty-fifty chance of inheriting the same disability. On a radio phone-in show, one listener said Walker "had no right to become pregnant and should have an abortion" (cited in Kallianes and Rubenfeld 1997: 210). Ms. Walker spoke out against the vocally disablist people pressuring her not to proceed with her pregnancy or vilifying her for getting pregnant. Walker says, "I was told by CBS management that this was a troublesome issue and that my choosing to speak out instead of just letting it go away presented a thorny issue for them" (cited in Cooper, n.d.a). Walker was condemned because of the eugenic values that are still held today, although they are rarely called that.

Eugenics continues to operate in the immigration system as well. While overtly racist quotas have been removed from Canadian and American immigration acts, their disablist intentions to exclude people who are "unfit" remain intact. In Canada, the Immigration and Refugee Protection Act (2001: s. 39 (1)(c)) states that one can be deemed inadmissible if their condition "might reasonably be expected to cause excessive demand on health or social services." In recent years, people have been excluded from entering Canada for conditions like arthritis (*Cohen v. Canada* 2006), cerebral palsy (*Kirec v. Canada* 2006), intellectual disabilities (*Sharma v. Canada* 2010) and for being quadriplegic (*Alibey v. Canada* 2004).

Immigration policies carry eugenic legacies, as do reproductive health programs in the United States. In 1968, Frederick Osborn (104) wrote, "Eugenic goals are most likely to be attained under a name other than eugenics." He went on to outline a number of eugenic achievements in postwar America, including the use of genetic counselling, which has dramatically increased since the 1960s. Eugenic organizations commonly changed their names, becoming "genetic" organizations,[11] and much of the racist, classist and disablist materials being taught in science classes before the war continued to be taught in the postwar era (see Winston et al. 2004; Paul 1985).

Frederick Osborn, Harry Laughlin of the Eugenics Record Office and a number of other prominent eugenicists founded the Pioneer Fund in 1937. According to the Pioneer Fund's website (n.d.b), the organization was founded "to advance the scientific study of heredity and human differences." The organization, which continues to operate to this day, distributes grants adding up to about $1 million a year (Miller 1994–1995) and has awarded money to a number of major colleges and universities (Pioneer Fund, n.d.b).[12] At the University of Waterloo, the Pioneer Fund has financed a current tenured professor, J. Philippe Rushton, who has done research trying to substantiate eugenic theories that Black people have higher sex drives and smaller brains than white people (Miller 1994–95). The Fund has also bankrolled current professor of educational psychology at the University of Delaware, Linda Gottfredson, who has put forward theories about the inferiority of Black people's intelligence (Miller 1994–95).

CONCLUSION

Eugenics has not disappeared; it is in our universities, in our courts, in our hospitals, at the border and on television. The eugenics model of disability lies at the foundations of how we think of disability today. Eugenics classified all people in one of two ways: fit or unfit. The entire category of unfit made up who was defined as disabled at the time. Disability, to a eugenicist, is an undesirable heritable flaw that threatens to destabilize society as a whole and should be eliminated. While eugenics often operates under other names and with less open aggression than it did in the past, it continues to function as an active consideration in a number of public policies, particularly within the medical system. As such, it is integral that we work to understand these histories, not just of the Nazi enemies who committed horrific atrocities, but of those atrocities done in our communities by our neighbours, our grandparents and even our heroes.

In understanding this past, we can recognize eugenics in our present and work to uproot it. Eugenic ideas about disability were and are formational ideas about what disability is and who is disabled.

Notes

1   Malthus did condemn aspects of society for being unjust. However, these views were largely overlooked by eugenicists.

2   Ethiopian was a term often used to describe all people of African descent.

3   While this is not the case today, at the time, homosexuals were considered to transgress the gender binary, with lesbians being considered masculine and gay men being considered feminine.

4   The British Columbian board was called the Board of Eugenics, whereas the Albertan board was called the Eugenics Board.

5   The American Birth Control League was actually renamed Planned Parenthood.

6   As a movement in North America, feminism addressed the issues and campaigned for the rights of upper-class and middle-class women. While there were poor and racialized women who fought for justice for women, they would not have been accepted or included in the first-wave feminist movement.

7   Lifton places the estimate between 200,000 and 350,000, while Biesold estimates 375,000.

8   Essondale Provincial Mental Hospital is now called Riverview Hospital. There may have been other sterilizations in other institutions or in the community, but these records are difficult to find or have been lost.

9   Seventy thousand sterilizations from 1900–1979 and 35,878 sterilizations from 1907–1940 (Black 2003).

10   Excluding girls and women who had gone through menopause.

11   See Withers 2012: chapter 3.

12   These include the University of California at Berkeley and Santa Barbara, University of Calgary, University of London, University of Illinois, University of Ulster, Johns

Hopkins University, University of Delaware, University of Western Ontario, University of Florence, University of Georgia, University of Texas and the University of Minnesota, Randolph-Macon Woman's College.

References

Alibey v. Canada (Minister of Citizenship and Immigration). 2004 FC 305.

Arad, Yitzhak. 1987. *Belzec, Sobibor, Treblinka: The Operation Reinhard Death Camps*. Bloomington: Indiana University Press [1999].

Beckwith, Jon. 1993. "A Historical View of Social Responsibility in Genetics." *Bioscience* 43, 5 (May).

Biesold, Horst. 1999. In William Sayers (trans.), *Crying Hands: Eugenics and Deaf People in Nazi Germany*. Washington D.C.: Gallaudet University Press.

Black, Edwin. 2003. *War Against The Weak: Eugenics and America's Campaign to Create a Master Race*. New York: Four Walls Eight Windows.

Buck v. Bell. 1927. 274 U.S. 200.

Butler, Amos W. 1921. "Some Families as Factors in Anti-Social Conditions." *Eugenics, Genetics and Family: 2nd International Congress of Eugenics, V.1*. New York: Garland Publishing [1984].

Canadian Women's Committee on Reproduction, Population and Development. 1995. "Canadian Policies and Practices in the Areas of Reproduction, Population and Development." *Canadian Women Studies* 15, 2/3 (Spring/Summer).

Carlson, Licia. 2010. *The Faces of Intellectual Disability: Philosophical Reflections*. Bloomington: Indiana University Press.

Cooper, Chet. n.d.a. "Bree Walker Interviewed by Chet Cooper." ABILITY *Magazine*. <abilitymagazine.com/walker_interview.html>.

Darwin, Leonard. 1926. *The Need for Eugenic Reform*. New York: Garland Publishing [1984].

Davenport, Charles B. 1912a. "The Family-History Book." *Eugenics Record Office Bulletin* 7 (September).

____. 1912b. "Marriage Laws and Customs." *Problems in Eugenics: 1st International Eugenics Congress Volume 1*. New York: Garland Publishing, 1984.

Davis, Angela. 1990. "Racism, Birth Control, and Reproductive Rights." In Marlene Gerber Fried (ed.), *From Abortion to Reproductive Freedom: Transforming a Movement*. Boston: South End Press 1990.

Davis, Lennard J. 2002. *Bending Over Backwards: Disability, Dismodernism, and Other Difficult Positions*. New York: New York University Press.

____. 1995. *Enforcing Normalcy: Disability, Deafness and the Body*. New York: Verso.

Devereaux, Cecily. 2005. *Growing a Race: Nellie L. McClung and the Fiction of Eugenic Feminism*. Montreal: McGill-Queen's University Press.

East, Edward, and Donald Jones. 1919. *Inbreeding and Outbreeding: Their Genetic and Sociological Significance*. Philadelphia: JB Lippincott.

Ehrenreich, Barbara, and Deirdre English. 1976. *Complaints and Disorders: The Sexual Politics of Sickness*. Westbury, NY: Feminist Press.

Ehrlichman, John. 1982. *Witness to Power: The Nixon Years*. New York: Simon and Schuster.

Engs, Ruth Clifford. 2000. *Clean Living Movements: American Cycles of Health Reform*.

Westport: Greenwood (2001).

Fairchild, A.L., and E.A. Tynan. 1994. "Policies of Containment: Immigration in the Era of AIDS." *American Journal of Public Health* 84, 12 (December).

Friedman, Saul S. 2004. *A History of the Holocaust*. Portland: Mitchell Vallentine.

Galton, David J., and Clare J. Galton. 1998. "Francis Galton: and Eugenics Today." *Journal of Medical Ethics* 24, 2.

Galton, Francis. 1907. *Inquiries into Human Faculty and its Development*. 2nd ed. London: J.M. Dent & Sons.

Gillis, Charlie. 2001. "Not Welcome: For Generations, Canada Has Restricted Immigration to the Healthy and Able, Preserving the Nation's Health Care Services from the World's Sick and Needy." *National Post*, March 30.

Grekul, Jana. 2008. "Sterilization in Alberta, 1928–1982: Gender Matters." *Canadian Review of Sociology* 45, 3 (August).

Harder, Henry G., and Liz R. Scott. 2005. *Comprehensive Disability Management*. Philadelphia: Elsevier Science.

Harris, Barbara. 2009. "End of Year Letter 2009: From Barbara Harris, Founder and Executive Director." Project Prevention. <projectprevention.org/whats-new/>.

Hitler, Adolf. 1939. *Mein Kampf.* New York: Hurst and Blackett.

Jaeger, Paul T., and Cynthia Ann Bowman. 2005. *Understanding Disability: Inclusion, Access, Diversity, and Civil Rights*. Westport, CT: Praeger Publishers.

Kallianes, Virginia, and Phyllis Rubenfeld. 1997. "Disabled Women and Reproductive Rights." *Disability and Society* 12, 2.

Kevles, Daniel J. 2000. "The Ghost of Galton: Eugenics Past, Present and Future." In Michael Alan Signer (ed.), *Humanity at the Limit: The Impact of the Holocaust Experience on Jews and Christians*. Bloomington: Indiana University Press.

____. 1985. *In the Name of Eugenics: Genetics and the Uses of Human Heredity*. Berkeley: University of California Press [1986].

Kimmelman, Barbara. 1983. "The American Breeders' Association: Genetics and Eugenics in an Agricultural Context, 1903–13." *Social Studies of Science* 13, 2 (May).

Kirec v. Canada (Minister of Citizenship & Immigration). 2006. FC 800.

Kline, Wendy. 2001. *Building A Better Race: Gender Sexuality, and Eugenics from the Turn of the Century to the Baby Boom*. Berkley: University of California Press.

Lemons, J. Stanley. 1990. *The Woman Citizen: Social Feminism in the 1920s*. Charlottesville: University Press of Virginia.

Lifton, Robert Jay. 1986. *The Nazi Doctors: Medical Killing and the Psychology of Genocide*. New York, Basic Books.

Longmore, Paul K. 2003. *Why I Burned My Book and Other Essays on Disability*. Philadelphia: Temple University Press.

Malthus, Thomas. 1888. *An Essay on the Principle of Population: Or, A View of Its Past and Present Effects on Human Happiness*. 9th ed. London: Reeves and Turner.

May, Elaine Tyler. 1995. *Barren in the Promised Land: Childless Americans and the Pursuit of Happiness*. Cambridge: Harvard University Press [1997].

Miller, Adam. 1994–1995. "The Pioneer Fund: Bankrolling the Professors of Hate." *The Journal of Blacks in Higher Education* 6 (Winter).

Newbeck, Phyl. 2004. *Virginia Hasn't Always Been for Lovers: Interracial Marriage Bans and the Case of Richard and Mildred Loving*. Carbondale: Southern Illinois University Press.

Nind, Naomi A. 2000. "Solving an Appalling Problem: Social Reformers and the Campaign for the Alberta Sexual Sterilization Act, 1928." *Alberta Law Review* 38, 2 (August).

Ordover, Nancy. 2003. *American Eugenics: Race, Queer Anatomy, and the Science of Nationalism*. Minneapolis: University of Minnesota Press.

Osborn, Frederick. 1968. *The Future of Human Heredity: An Introduction to Eugenics in Modern Society*. New York: Weybright & Talley.

O'Neil, Sandy. 2001. *First they Killed The 'Crazies' and the 'Cripples': The Ableist Persecution and Murders of People with Disabilities by Nazi Germany 1933–45, An Anthropological Perspective*. Ann Arbor, MI: UMI Dissertation Services.

Paul, Diane B. 1985. "Commentary: Textbook Treatments of the Genetics of Intelligence." *The Quarterly Review of Biology* 60, 3 (September).

Pfeiffer, David. 1993. "Overview of the Disability Movement: History, Legislative Record and Political Implications." *Policy Studies Journal* 21, 4.

Pioneer Fund. n.d.a. "About Us." <pioneerfund.org>.

Prentice, Alison L. 1988. *Canadian Women: A History*. San Diego: Harcourt Brace Jovanovich.

Project Prevention. 2011. "Statistics." At: <projectprevention.org/statistics>.

____. 1999. "Sad Reality." <projectprevention.org/the-sad-reality>.

Province, William B. 1973. "Geneticists and the Biology of Race Crossing." *Science* 182, 4114 (November).

Rees, Laurence. 2005. *Auschwitz: A New History*. New York: Public Affairs.

Rentoul, Robert Reid. 1906. *Race Culture or Race Suicide: A Plea for the Unborn*. New York: Garland Publishing [1984].

Roberts, Dorothy. 1997. *Killing the Black Body: Race, Reproduction, and the Meaning of Liberty*. New York: Pantheon Books.

Roberts, Wayne. 1979. "'Rocking the Cradle for the World': The New Woman and Maternal Feminism, Toronto, 1877–1914." *A Not Unreasonable Claim: Women and Reform in Canada, 1880s–1920s*. Toronto: Women's Educational Press.

Robertson, Gerald. 1996. "Appendix A." *Muir v. Alberta*, 132 D.L.R. (4th) 695 (AB. Crt. Q.B.), (Lexis 1056).

Robitsche, Jonas B. 1973. *Eugenic Sterilization*. Springfield: Charles C. Thomas.

Sanger, Margaret. 1925. "Introduction." In Margaret Sanger (ed.), *International Aspects of Birth Control, The Sixth International Neo-Malthusian and Birth Control Conference, Volume 1*. New York: American Birth Control League.

Sharma v. Canada (Citizenship and Immigration). 2010. FC 398.

Silver, Michael G. 2003–2004. "Eugenics and Compulsory Sterilization Laws: Providing Redress for the Victims of a Shameful Era in United States History Note." *George Washington Law Review* 72, 4 (April).

Spallone, Patricia. 1989. *Beyond Conception: The New Politics of Reproduction*. Massachusetts: Bergin and Garvey Publishers.

Tait, Janice J. 1985–86. "Reproductive Technology and the Rights of Disabled Persons." *Canadian Journal of Women and the Law* 1.

Terry, Jennifer. 1995. "Anxious Slippages Between 'Us' and 'Them.'" In Jennifer Terry and Jacqueline L. Urla (eds.), *Deviant Bodies: Critical Perspectives on Difference in Science and Poplar Culture (Race, Gender, and Science)*. Bloomington: Indiana University Press.

Wikler, Daniel. 1999. "Can We Learn From Eugenics?" *Journal of Medical Ethics* 25, 2.

Wilcox, W. F. 1922. "Birth Rate and Natural Increase of Whites and Negroes in the United States." In Raymond Pierpoint William (ed.), *Report of the Fifth International Neo-Malthusian and Birth Control Conference*. London: Heinemann.

Winston, Andrew, Bethany Butzer and Mark D. Ferris. 2004. "Constructing Difference: Heredity, Intelligence and Race in Textbooks, 1930–1970." In Andre S. Winston (ed.), *Defining Difference: Race & Racism in the History of Psychology*. Washington DC: American Psychological Association.

Woodhull, Victoria. 1893. "The Scientific Propagation of the Human Race; Or Humanitarian Aspects of Finance and Marriage." In Victoria C. Woodhull and Michael W. Perry, *Lady Eugenist: Feminist Eugenics in the Speeches and Writing of Victorial Woodhull*. Seattle: Inkling Books [2005].

Legal Cases

Chee, Re (1905), 11 B.C.R. 400. Quicklaw.

Cohen v. Canada (Minister of Citizenship & Immigration). (2006). 55 Imm. L.R. (3d) 21.

E. (D.) v. R., 2003 BCSC 1013.

E. (Mrs.) v. Eve, [1986] 2 S.C.R. 388.

Muir v. Alberta. 1996, 132 D.L.R. (4th) 695 (AB. Crt. Q.B.).

POVERTY

Chapter 11

THE CONSTRUCTION OF "WELFARE FRAUD" AND THE WIELDING OF THE STATE'S IRON FIST

Janet E. Mosher

From: *Locating Law: Race, Class, Gender, Sexuality Connections*, 3rd edition, pp. 198–224 (reprinted with permission).

In Ontario, as in many other social welfare states, dramatic reforms to social assistance (or welfare) programs were carried out in the 1980s and 1990s. Most profoundly, these reforms embodied a shift in the conceptual underpinning and moral foundation of state benefits for those in need — a move from the concept of entitlement based on need to a narrow contractualism that requires recipients to engage in work or work-readiness activities as a condition of benefits. This shift in conceptual underpinning — reflected most clearly in the adoption of "work-fare" — together with dramatic reductions in benefit levels, the reconstitution of single mothers as workers, and the construction of the menace of "welfare fraud" served to install waged work as a foundation of modern welfare regimes. While new discourses of "poverty reduction" and "social investment" have since entered the realm of social policy, they do not reflect a change in course but rather more fully entrench the centrality of waged work within welfare regimes. Through a mix of both carrots and sticks — the precise mix varying among jurisdictions — welfare has been reconstituted as the "pathway," the "springboard" or the "spur" to waged work.

The welfare reforms of the 1980s and 1990s were integral to the evolution of the "lean state," characterized by its focus on reduced labour time in production, the elimination of waste and the promotion of efficiency. It also depends on the maintenance of a flexible workforce able to rapidly contract or expand and shift tasks, and willing to work under any conditions (Sears 1999). In the lean state the employment at the bottom end of the labour market has become increasingly precarious: it consists of various forms of temporary and part-time work, high levels of uncertainty, few if any benefits, low wages, little control over labour processes, and not uncommonly, limited access to regulatory protections (Noack and Vosko 2011; Law Commission of Ontario 2012).

As Loïc Wacquant argues, the reorganization of the welfare state and the rise of precarious work go hand in hand with harsh, punitive state action: "The 'invisible hand' of the casualised labour market finds its institutional complement and counterpart in the 'iron fist' of the state which is being redeployed so as *to check the disorders generated by the diffusion of social insecurity*" (2001: 401–2). The iron fist of the state takes many forms in this redeployment: anti-panhandling ordinances; the policing of "disorder" and "incivilities"; police sweeps that remove homeless people from downtown cores; massive police presence and militaristic responses to social justice protests; the increased use of immigration detention; and the increased incarceration of poor people who have been forced by the unravelling of health and social services to survive on the margins of society. So while neo-liberalism is frequently associated with the withdrawal or "rolling back" of the state, this is true only in relation to particular functions. Rather, there has been a simultaneous "rolling out" of state regulation in the form of a stepped up law-and-order agenda (Peck and Tickell 2002).

Within Ontario's welfare system the iron fist of the state is manifest in the pounding blows of poverty delivered in the form of decreased benefit rates and in the penalties attached to the failure to adequately participate in work or work-related activities. But the iron fist of the state is most dramatically revealed by the state's approach to "welfare fraud."

At the time of introducing the major reforms in the mid-1990s, the Progressive Conservative (PC) government actively reinvigorated the long, historical association of criminality with the "undeserving poor" in its depiction of "welfare fraud" as a serious problem — indeed, one that was out of control and which required more and increasingly harsh measures to curb its proliferation. Mechanisms for the surveillance of welfare recipients were massively expanded and recipients policed in such a way to make them seem a threat to the public. This policing is infrequently carried out by the social control agents commonly associated with the criminal justice system; rather, it is undertaken by front-line welfare administrators, "eligibility review officers" and even the broader public.

The "crackdown" on "welfare fraud" served to construct welfare recipients as undeserving, as criminals intent on stealing the hard-earned dollars of taxpayers. In turn, this facilitated reductions in benefits, intense surveillance and disciplinary practices intended to reform flawed citizens. It also served to intensify the stigma attached to being in receipt of welfare benefits. Taken together, the welfare reforms facilitated the creation of a vulnerable class of low-wage workers.

The role law and its enforcement have played in facilitating the evolution of the lean state and maintaining a class of flexible low-wage workers becomes strikingly apparent through a comparison of the discourse and practices surrounding welfare fraud with those within the employment standards regime. The surveillance of employer compliance with legislated minimum standards of employment is extremely limited, and in that regime the criminal language of "fraud" or "theft" is seldom heard — notwithstanding the millions of dollars in outstanding wages owed to employees and the clear existence of employer practices that constitute criminal fraud. As it turns out, the iron fist of the state is deployed in the regulation of welfare recipients, the soft glove of the state in the regulation of employers.

The selective invocation of the language of criminal law and of the imagery of "the criminal" and the dramatically uneven enforcement practices — surveillance, policing and sanctions — tellingly reveal that the lean state strategically deployed the concept of welfare fraud to facilitate not only state retreat from social provision but the creation and maintenance of a class of vulnerable workers prepared to "accept" the limited, precarious work of the new economy.

FROM SOCIAL WELFARE TO NEO-LIBERALISM

Several of the social policies introduced in the post-World War II era removed certain matters entirely from the play of market forces, while others regulated the market to minimize and/or socialize risk. The provision of health care, for example, became the responsibility of the state. Social assistance, unemployment insurance, minimum standards of employment, minimum-wage legislation and a host of other measures acknowledged the vulnerability of each citizen to potential unemployment, ill health and disability, and material deprivation. The Keynesian welfare state explicitly attempted to mitigate, through social provision, the inequalities of wealth generated by a capitalist economic system (Broadbent 1999; Rittich 2007). Importantly, these policies reflected a view that there existed a *social* responsibility to provide protection against insecurity. Correspondingly, entitlement to such state support was widely regarded as a hallmark of citizenship.

Beginning in the 1970s and gaining momentum thereafter, a marked shift occurred in economic and social policy. The shift, heavily influenced by neo-liberalism, was pursued in the name of deficit reduction, global competition and family values. The federal government staged a marked retreat from the social policy arena, with its repeal of the Canada Assistance Plan Act (CAPA) and introduction of the Canada Health and Safety Transfer (CHST) in 1996 being particularly significant. While both programs provided mechanisms through which federal money could flow to the provinces and territories to support their welfare programs, they differed in two crucial respects. First, unlike CAPA, the CHST was a block fund for post-secondary education, health care and social services, with no stipulations attached as to how money is allocated between these areas. Second, receipt of federal money pursuant to CAPA depended upon the provincial and territorial governments respecting conditions articulated in the governing legislation. Among those conditions was a requirement that benefit levels be set in a manner that would "take into account" basic requirements (defined to include food, shelter, clothing, fuel, utilities, household supplies and personal requirement) of a person in need. CAPA had also stipulated, "no person shall be denied assistance because he refuses or has refused to take part in a work activity project." Neither of these conditions attached to the CHST and thus, provinces were free to condition the receipt of benefits upon mandatory participation in work or work-related activities and to set rates without any regard to basic requirements.

As social programs were being eliminated or substantially cut back, the market was given a freer rein. The creation of a "business-friendly" environment became an organizing mantra, and it led to reduced corporate taxes, the deregulation of business and the hollowing out of workers' entitlements. Increasingly, it was expected that citizens would meet their needs through the market, not through state provision. Within neo-liberal citizenship, state provision (but most particularly welfare) is regarded as the antithesis of citizenship; in other words, "social citizenship" within a neo-liberal paradigm is a conceptual oxymoron (McCluskey 2003: 789–90). The good, neo-liberal citizen is self-reliant and independent, providing for his needs through the market, and zealously guarding what he has earned through his market participation.[1] Wacquant (2001: 405) captures well the nature of the transformation:

> The Keynesian state that was the historic vehicle of *solidarity*, and whose mission was to counter the cycles and damaging effects of the market, to ensure the collective "well-fare" and to reduce inequalities, is succeeded by a Darwinian state that makes a fetish of *competition* and celebrates individual responsibility (whose counterpart is collective irresponsibility), and which withdraws into its kingly functions of "law and order," themselves hypertrophied.

WELFARE REFORM:
MAKING THE "UNDESERVING POOR" RESPONSIBLE

The welfare reforms introduced in Ontario by the PC government of Mike Harris were primarily enacted through the Social Assistance Reform Act, which itself contained two pieces of legislation: the Ontario Works Act, 1997 (OWA); and the Ontario Disability Support Program Act, 1997 (ODSPA). Since their enactment in 1997 only a few modest amendments have been made. Section 1 of the OWA articulates that its purpose is to establish a program that:

(a) recognizes individual responsibility and promotes self-reliance through employment;

(b) provides temporary financial assistance to those most in need while they satisfy obligations to become and stay employed;

(c) effectively serves people needing assistance; and

(d) is accountable to the taxpayers of Ontario.

This statement of purpose reflects a profound departure from the principle of entitlement to economic support that, while never fully realized in practice, nevertheless formed an articulated basis for both provincial and federal legislation. Indeed, only a decade earlier a government-commissioned report on social assistance in Ontario had identified a rights-based approach as a guiding principle of the social assistance regime, proclaiming, "All members of the community have a presumptive right to social assistance based on need" (Social Assistance Review Committee 1988: 10). But clearly, eroding Canadians' sense of entitlement to government support to meet basic needs was a move crucial to the neo-liberal project. In *Reducing Fraud and Waste in Income Security Programs in Canada*, a report prepared for the Fraser Institute, precisely this argument was advanced. Its authors maintained that reducing waste (seemingly state benefits that had not been earned or were not deserved) required removing the standard of need articulated in CAPA and replacing it "with a more general standard which makes explicit that the receipt of income security benefits in Canada is a privilege, not a right, and that appropriate behaviour and certain responsibilities are expected of recipients in return, both in terms of honesty and movement towards independence as rapidly as possible" (MacDonald, MacDonald, Blair 1995: 16–17). When introducing the legislation in the House, then Minister of Community and Social Services Janet Ecker stated, "Self-sufficiency [is] the overriding goal of social assistance" (*Hansard*, Nov. 25, 1997). This approach represented a dramatic reversal of the conceptualization of social assistance as a crucial safety net for people who would inevitably be temporarily or permanently cast off by a market economy.

Consistent with the view reflected in the legislative statement of purpose of the limited role of the state in meeting the needs of citizens, Ontario's PC introduced a 21.6 percent cut in benefit levels for Ontario Works, effective October 1995. The diminishment of rates to a level that placed recipients in conditions of abject poverty was justified by a particular political discourse: in an era emphasizing the goals of a "debt-free" government, individuals on social assistance were seen as getting a "free ride" and "something for nothing," and they ought, after all, to be self-sufficient. Welfare benefits were characterized as "generous," and it was widely asserted that welfare created a perverse incentive for many to opt for welfare over employment. Lowering rates, it was argued, would sharpen the spur of poverty and propel people into the labour market, where they would be prepared to accept virtually any work they could find. It would also help to ensure that those in precarious work stayed there. Since the 21.6 percent reduction, there have been occasional and modest increases, bringing the monthly rate for a single person to $599 in 2012. However, taking account of inflation, in real terms this is $225 less than what it was following the 21.6 percent cut (Stapleton 2012).

As Dean Herd, Andrew Mitchell, and Ernie Lightman (2005: 19) noted in relation to the reforms, "the ascendancy of workfarist policy-making in Ontario, as elsewhere, has coincided with — and is also reinforcing — fundamental shifts in the nature of work and in the organization of flexible labour markets." These shifts, which began in the mid-1970s, include the precipitous decline of the "standard employment relationship" — full-time, continuous, stable employment with good wages and benefits and opportunities for progression up a career ladder — and the growth of precarious work (temporary, casual, part-time, low-waged work with few or no benefits) (Noack and Vosko 2011). As Tom Zizys (2011) depicts, the labour market increasingly resembles an hourglass, with a decline of jobs in the middle and a growth at the bottom and top.

As section 1 of the OWA makes clear, recipients have an obligation to become and stay employed — to be self-reliant and responsible. Other provisions of the Act and the regulations put these obligations into operation in a variety of ways. Also critical is precisely who these provisions govern. Prior to the reforms, two statutes constituted social assistance in Ontario: the Family Benefits Act (FBA) and the General Welfare Assistance Act (GWAA). The FBA applied to single parents (overwhelmingly women) and those with disabilities that precluded their full labour-market participation. The GWAA applied to those who were able-bodied and, presumably, employable. Those on GWAA received lower benefit levels (the principle of less eligibility has long governed rates such that rates would always be below the lowest offered by paid employment) and were subject to a variety of work-related rules such as job searches. With the introduction of the OWA and the ODSPA, two significant changes occurred. First, single parents were recategorized with the able-bodied unemployed. In other words, they were reconfigured as workers, not parents, and were expected to be fully self-reliant. Second, it became substantially more difficult to qualify for the more generous ODSP benefits, both because of a new definition of disability and because of the impossibly difficult application process (Fraser, Wilkey, and Frenschkowski 2003). Previously understood to be part of the deserving poor, single parents and many persons with disabilities now found themselves among the undeserving poor. With their poverty assumed to be the result of individual character flaws, they were to be subjected to punitive work regimes to correct or diminish these flaws, which would presumably bring their conduct more in line with valued neo-liberal citizenship practices.

The obligation to be self-reliant, responsible and employed is enforced through statutory requirements to get a job and keep it and by the conditioning of the receipt of benefits upon participation in work readiness activities. Subject to few exceptions, adult beneficiaries are required to enter into "participation agreements" with the Ministry, spelling out the "employment assistance" activities that they will undertake in order to secure employment. Employment assistance activities include "community participation" or "employment measures," and among the latter are job searches, literacy testing, basic education and job-specific skills training, employment placement, supports to self-employment, screening for substance addiction, and participation in a program to complete high school or develop parenting skills. In addition, every adult beneficiary has an obligation to make reasonable efforts to accept and maintain employment "for which he or she is physically capable." If employed part-time, beneficiaries are to find full-time employment, and if employed and still eligible for assistance, obligated to find employment to increase their income.

Participation agreements are to be reviewed, in most cases, at least every three months to monitor ongoing eligibility, although particular events — refusing an offer of paid employment, for example — will trigger an immediate review. The Policy Directives identify four types of non-compliance: the refusal to accept employment or make reasonable efforts to maintain employment; the refusal to accept a referral for participation in an employment assistance activity; the refusal to accept an offer of a placement; and the failure to make reasonable efforts to meet participation requirements (Ontario, Ministry of Community and Social Services 2013). Until September 2010, the failure to comply with the participation agreement or make reasonable efforts as required resulted in the cancellation of benefits for a three-month period in the first instance, and six months for repeat infractions. The penalty periods are now one and three months for first and subsequent infractions, respectively (Ontario Regulation 310/10).

In introducing the legislation in 1995, then Premier Mike Harris heralded a new vision:

We're paying a significant number of people, over a million, by the way, of families, 300,000 to 400,000 to sit home and do nothing ... This [the PC government's approach] is breaking new ground. This is not easy. This is something that is a different philosophy. There is a philosophy, create a cycle of dependency, pay people more money to stay home and do nothing versus give people an opportunity, give them training, give them work experience, give them jobs. (*Hansard*, Sept. 28, 1995)

Harris's Minister of Community and Social Services chimed in, "People have got to learn again to take responsibility for themselves and their families and not to leave it to everyone else to do" (*Hansard*, Sept. 28, 1995).

Understood in this way, welfare represents a moral hazard, creating an enticing alternative to wage work and undermining the virtues of good citizenship. Those in receipt of welfare are represented as lacking the essential moral virtues of a work ethic, independence and self-reliance — as suffering fundamental and deeply harmful character flaws. This attribution of personal character flaws ignores the breadth and depth of the structural impediments to employment faced by most recipients, and it ignores the reality that most of them desire work but cannot secure or maintain it. Unemployment rates, workplaces that fail to accommodate those with disabilities, the lack of decent child care, and other structural barriers curiously disappear in the accounts that blame individuals for their poverty. Rather, the corrective, disciplinary measures ostensibly needed to inculcate virtue take centre stage: workfare and penalties for "failing" to participate; benefit reductions; the erosion of entitlement.

While there has been some acknowledgement of the lack of success in moving recipients off welfare and into employment (particularly over the medium and longer term), and of even less success in moving recipients out of poverty, the corrective measures currently under discussion continue to accept that the goal of welfare assistance is to move recipients into employment. New carrots (better employment supports, for example) and sharper sticks (time limited receipt of benefits) pattern these conversations (Lightman, Mitchell, and Herd 2010; Commission for the Review of Social Assistance 2012; Progressive Conservative Party 2011).

IMPLICATIONS FOR SINGLE MOTHERS

That the Ontario Works regime redefines most single mothers as workers reflects the rise of an ideology of the masculine worker-citizen (Korteweg 2003). Feminists have long argued that women have experienced a form of second-class citizenship because the caring labour performed overwhelmingly by women in the home has never been given the same material rewards (a wage, benefits, access to less stigmatizing forms of state support) or the same degree of respect and validation that paid employment has received (Evans and Wekerle 1997; Pateman 1989). And while advances had been made, especially in relation to women's entitlement to state benefits, the welfare reforms in Ontario greatly devalued women and their unpaid caring labour. In Ontario, single parents (overwhelmingly women) are exempted from workfare obligations only until their youngest child reaches school age (three or four years of age); in many jurisdictions the age is much younger (Smith et al. 2000). Unlike the messaging to white, middle-class mothers to stay at home and care for their young children, the caring labour of low-income mothers is almost completely devalued; indeed, the message is that they are not fit and worthy mothers at all (Pollack and Caragata 2010).

But in addition to the messaging to get a job, any job, and keep it, single women in receipt of Ontario Works assistance are frequently told, both explicitly and implicitly, to get a man, any man, and keep him. And a changed definition of "spouse" introduced by the PC government, even prior to the OWA and ODSPA, greatly expanded the circumstances in which a woman was presumed to have a man; that is, presumed to be living with a "spouse" and deemed to be receiving his support.

The so-called "man in the house" or "spouse in the house" rules have a lengthy history in Ontario, and certainly historically women's entitlement to benefits was strongly tied to judgments about their moral character and, in particular, their sexual chastity (Little 1998; Chunn and Gavigan 2004). Before 1987 a single recipient risked having her benefits terminated if a conclusion was made that she was not living as a single person, but rather living together with a man as husband and wife (the regime impacted almost exclusively upon women). In 1987, feminists and equality rights activists were successful in persuading the provincial government to introduce a definition of "spouse" for welfare purposes that largely tracked Ontario's Family Law Act. Importantly, this meant that couples could live together for three years before they would be deemed to be spouses for social assistance purposes and when, in fact, legal obligations of support would arise.

The PC government acted in October 1995 to again alter the definition of "spouse" for social assistance purposes, on this occasion changing it to more closely approximate its pre-1987 origins. This amended definition treated persons of the opposite sex presumptively as spouses if they shared a common residence. After this law was struck down as unconstitutional by the Ontario Court of Appeal in *Falkiner et al. v. Director, Income Maintenance Branch, Ministry of Community and Social Services and Attorney General of Ontario*, the government abandoned its appeal to the Supreme Court of Canada and in fall 2004 introduced a new definition. Apart from introducing a three-month "grace period," the new version largely tracked its predecessor, thus raising renewed questions about its constitutionality. A further amendment eliminated the prior distinction between spouses and same-sex partners to include both heterosexual and same-sex couples within the definition of spouse itself. In addition to those who declare themselves as spouses or have existing family law support obligations, at present spouses, for social assistance purposes, are any two persons who reside in the same dwelling (for at least three months), if "the extent of the social and familial aspects of the relationship between the two persons is consistent with cohabitation" and "the extent of the financial support provided by one person to the other or the degree of financial interdependence between the two persons is consistent with cohabitation" (Ontario Regulation 134/98 as amended). Sexual factors are not to be investigated or considered in determining spousal status. The definition continues to be vague and ambiguous, and frequently the facts relied upon to support a finding that one is "residing with" a "spouse" are extremely thin. If they are presumed to be supported by the men in their lives, women are cut off state benefits. Yet until they co-reside for three years, these men have no corresponding legal obligation to provide support. Women's well-being is left to the vagaries of men's good will (Mosher 2010).

The immediate impact of the definition introduced in 1995 was to cut more than 10,000 people off welfare — 89 percent of them women, and 76 percent single mothers — presuming that the men in their lives, who had no legal obligation to support them, would, in fact, do so (*Falkiner* 2002: para. 77; *Falkiner* 2000: para. 82). The impact has been to reinforce women's economic dependence upon men, and to deepen their vulnerability, to domestic violence in particular, by limiting their options to exit abusive relationships (Mosher et al. 2004; *Falkiner* 2002). On the one hand, then, the reforms presuppose the existence of nuclear families with entrenched gender roles that script men as the providers of material support, and women as the providers of domestic labour and sex. Men are assumed to be financially "responsible" and financially capable, and women are assumed to be economically dependent. On the other hand, if a woman has no man in her life upon whom the state can transfer responsibility for support, she is treated as a "worker" — and this is true whether she applies for welfare as a single person or together with a man as a "family," for should they qualify financially for benefits, both will be treated as workers and subject to the workfare regime.

WELFARE FRAUD AND PRESUMED CRIMINALITY: FRAUDS, CHEATS AND LIARS?

As noted, "welfare fraud" occupied a central position in the social assistance reforms of the mid-1990s. Indeed, the Ontario government expressly identified "fighting" welfare fraud as one of its three goals of welfare reform, and it successfully constructed welfare fraud as a social problem spinning out of control and requiring increasingly aggressive and punitive measures.

As Patrick Parnaby (2003) argues, claims-makers, in seeking to convince the public that a problem or condition is real and urgent, will attempt to ground the issue through the use of official statistics and/or through claims alleging its widespread nature. Certainly, those claiming the problem of welfare fraud used both of these methods. In constructing welfare fraud as a significant problem, rhetorical claims about its magnitude and harms abounded. In her affidavit in support of the government's position regarding the constitutionality of a lifetime ban on receipt of welfare benefits for those convicted of welfare fraud, the director of the Ontario Disability Support Program (ODSP), Debbie Moretta, detailed several initiatives undertaken by governments over the years to curb the problem. She concluded: "Despite initiatives to combat welfare fraud, it has remained a serious problem and was seen by the public to be insufficiently addressed by government. The zero tolerance policy is intended to deter welfare fraud, to ensure effective management of public funds and to restore public confidence in the welfare system" (Moretta 2003: para. 6). In other words, despite valiant attempts, the problem of welfare fraud had still to be contained, and harsher measures were required.

The invocation of explicitly criminal terms — "fraud," "cheats," "liars," "theft," "zero tolerance" and "crackdowns" — served to construct the problem as a criminal menace, and thus all the more serious and threatening. Welfare fraud "cheat sheets" were posted on the government's website, and accounts of complex frauds involving multiple fabricated identities appeared in local news media, all of it further contributing to the sense of serious criminality.

But the government's use of "official statistics" provides the most revealing window into the construction of the problem of welfare fraud. Capitalizing upon an enduring feature of the discussions — the lack of definitional clarity and precision as to just what constitutes "welfare fraud" — the "official statistics" widely circulated by the government included all of the errors that resulted in overpayments (but tellingly not underpayments) of welfare benefits. The government's *Welfare Fraud Control Report 2001–2002* exemplifies this collapsing of fraud and error (Ontario, Ministry of Community, Family and Children's Services 2003). The Report is permeated with the language of "fraud" — it makes reference to the Welfare Fraud Hotline, to the fraud-control database to track fraud investigations, to "anti-fraud measures [that] help catch welfare cheats and deter others from thinking about cheating," and to welfare fraud as a crime that the government is cracking down on through the introduction of a zero-tolerance policy (Ontario, Ministry of Community, Family and Children's Services 2003). The Report claims that "over $49 million was identified in social assistance payments that people were not entitled to receive and an estimated $12 million in avoided future costs" (Ontario, Ministry of Community, Family and Children's Services 2003). Given the general thrust of the report and its title, the message conveyed is that these dollars are directly attributable to welfare fraud.

But a close examination reveals a different picture. In 2001–2, of 38,452 fraud investigations only 393 resulted in convictions for welfare fraud (representing about 0.1 percent of the caseload); and there were 12,816 cases in which assistance was reduced or terminated as a result of eligibility reassessments. In more than 12,000 cases, then, "fraud" had not been established; no crime had been proven, and any dollars saved were not the result of "fraud" detection. While a modest number of these 12,000 cases may represent instances in which prosecution was not recommended even though a strong case existed, the vast majority were most likely instances in which an administrative rule had been broken, but without the requisite *mens rea* or intent necessary to constitute criminal fraud — in other words, they were problems that resulted from client misunderstanding, error or oversight. As noted in a more recent report of the Auditor General, overpayments occur for many reasons: changes in income, administrator error, changes in provincial policy and regulations, and on-going reliability issues with the provincial technology used to manage client files (Toronto 2008). But the Report, by collapsing all errors into fraud and through its use of terms such as "cheats," "cracking down on crime" and "zero tolerance," portrays a picture of criminal fraud as rampant and, correspondingly, of recipients as actual or potential criminals.

While the political rhetoric around welfare fraud has been tempered more recently in Ontario, it reappears during political campaigns and in response to particular media stories. During the 2011 provincial election, for example, the "Changebook" of the PC Party promised that "[the] worst repeat offenders of welfare fraud will face tough penalties, up to a lifetime ban" (Ontario PC Party 2011). Importantly, and as described in more detail below, surveillance practices have intensified over time.

COMPREHENDING THE COMPLEXITY OF THE WELFARE REGULATION SYSTEM

Governed by some eight hundred rules that determine eligibility, the welfare system has variously been described as "Kafkaesque" and "fiendishly difficult" to comprehend (*R. v. Maldonado* 1998). Many of the rules are counterintuitive, others incomprehensible, and it is extremely difficult to access accurate and timely information about the governing rules.

Commonly, recipients find themselves in situations in which they stand accused of "fraud" but have no idea that the rule they allegedly violated existed at all: that a loan or a cash advance is treated as income and has to be reported (and will be deducted dollar for dollar); that gifts may be treated as income and reportable; or that details about intimate relationships are expected to be disclosed (just what level of detail is far from clear). Given the number of rules and their complexity, recipients find it nearly impossible to live on welfare for any length of time without inadvertently breaking a rule; and in a regime in which virtually all rule violations are categorized as fraud — not only in the annual *Welfare Fraud Control Reports*, but often by those on the front lines in the administration of the system — "fraud" will of course be rampant, and virtually all recipients will be "fraudsters."

The approach taken in the *Welfare Fraud Control Reports* reflects the approach advocated in *Reducing Fraud and Waste in Income Security Programs*, the same report that argued for the elimination of an entitlement-based approach to income security. In the neo-liberal quest to reduce waste, a careful delineation between criminal and non-criminal conduct is argued to be irrelevant. The *Reducing Fraud and Waste* states:

> There is no clear-cut delineations [sic] of fraud and error in the sense that the dividing line, where error crosses into fraud, is based on the psychological construct of *intent*. And fraud is a legal term which applies when *intent* can be proven in a court of law. There are many cases investigated in which the investigator is sure that fraud occurred, however the strict rules of evidence may prevent the case being proven in court. This category could be referred to as "program abuse" … All of the categories of error and fraud overlap, and it is often a matter of convenience or legal requirements which determine how a particular case is labeled … "client error" is often the administrator's way of saying that intent to defraud could not be easily proven in court. (MacDonald, MacDonald, and Blair 1995: 7–8)

This analysis presupposes that client error is inevitably fraud. The rules of evidence just get in the way of proving it, or it is "inconvenient" to take the trouble to prove it. This view is, however, incompatible with what is known about how the system and recipients of benefits interface. The very complexity of the system and the difficulties of adequately communicating the rules make client error — and indeed significant system error — unavoidable. Moreover, the analysis simply disregards the importance of the construct that lies at the heart of criminal liability: the "guilty mind." If all rule breaches, irrespective of intent, are characterized as "fraud," every recipient who, through inadvertence, lack of knowledge/information, mental or cognitive disability, or misunderstanding breaches a rule is tainted with the moral brush of criminality. But in the effort to eliminate waste, characterizing that waste as the result of criminal fraud rather than recipient or administrative error helps to construct a more serious social problem — one that requires more aggressive, harsh and punitive responses.

LIVING UNDER A MICROSCOPE":
INVASIVE STRATEGIES FOR DETECTING
WELFARE "FRAUDSTERS"

To respond to this construction of welfare fraud as a serious problem, the government introduced a broad array of measures. In turn, the extent, breadth and severity of these measures serve to consistently reinforce the view of the severity of the "fraud" problem.

Eligibility Review Officers

Allegations of fraud or abuse are first reviewed by designated staff to determine if a more thorough review is required; if so, the file is referred for comprehensive investigation to an Eligibility Review Officer (ERO), who must prepare a written report for an ERO supervisor, including a recommendation regarding continuing eligibility and any overpayment, and whether to refer the matter to the police (Ontario, Ministry of Community and Social Services 2012). Province-wide more than 35,000 allegations were received in 2001–02; 52,000 in 2000–01. While more recent provincial data appear not to be available, for the City of Toronto more than 9,000 reviews were carried out in 2007 in response to allegations of fraud or abuse (identifying 700 overpayments and resulting in 15 criminal proceedings) (Toronto 2008).

The OWA and regulations grant significant powers to EROs to undertake their investigations of fraud allegations. They have the power to enter any place other than a dwelling if there exist reasonable grounds to believe that evidence relevant to eligibility may be found there; they also have the power to require the production of records. EROs have the right to obtain "information or material from a person who is the subject of an investigation ... or from any person who the officer has reason to believe can provide information or material relevant to the investigation" (Ontario Regulation 134/98, s.65). These powers are reinforced by subsection 79(3) of the Act, which makes it an offence to obstruct or knowingly give false information to a person engaged in an investigation.

In the course of their investigations, EROs will often seek information from landlords, neighbours, teachers and others who may know something of the circumstances of the recipient under investigation. Additionally, an investigation will often include a meeting with the person who is the subject of the investigation. While practices may have changed subsequently, research conducted in 2004 found that Charter cautions were not routinely provided during these meetings, even though the evidence gathered was regularly used against recipients in the event of subsequent criminal prosecutions (Mosher and Hermer 2005). Certainly one characterization of these meetings is that they are solely for the purpose of determining eligibility and are thus integrally connected to the enforcement of a regulatory regime. But a competing and compelling characterization is that they often take the form of de facto criminal investigations and, as such, require Charter warnings and limitations on the use of evidence so gathered. While the issue of when a regulatory investigation becomes a de facto criminal investigation has received significant attention in the context of income tax, it has received very little critical interrogation in the realm of welfare (*R. v. Jarvis* 2002). This omission is disconcerting, because it appears to be not uncommon for police and Crown attorneys to rely upon the investigations undertaken by EROs in their prosecution of persons accused of welfare fraud. Given the number of fraud investigations and given the statutory power of EROs to compel information, there is a strong concern that the Charter rights of recipients are being regularly violated.

A related concern is that recipients under investigation who are called in for a meeting with an ERO frequently do not fully understand the import of the interview or that the statements given may subsequently be used against them in a fraud prosecution. Moreover, fearing a possible criminal charge, and within a broad context in which fraud language is pervasive and recipients are constantly dehumanized, those accused (even inferentially) of fraud may agree all too readily to administrative sanctions such as terminations or overpayments (Mosher and Hermer 2005). Recipients are also understandably reluctant to complain about mistreatment during investigations. They are, after all, in a position of extreme vulnerability in their interactions with agents of the administrative regime, who can cut them off benefits, assess overpayments and refer matters to the police. Rocking the boat almost always promises to be more trouble than it is worth.

Surveillance Practices

Certainly a significant evolution in Ontario's welfare system has been the introduction of various technologies and practices to collect and verify personal information of recipients and beneficiaries with a view to "preventing and controlling" fraud. In the mid-1990s the province embarked upon a Business Transformation Project through an agreement with Anderson Consulting (now Accenture) to develop new technologies to manage and verify client information (Herd, Mitchell, and Lightman 2005). Since that time, a succession of reports by the provincial Auditor General notes modest improvements in these systems, but consistently calls for yet more steps to verify information, particularly with third parties. The Auditor General (2009 and 2011) has expressed particular concern that tips from the fraud hotline are being ignored or inadequately investigated and that the numbers of referrals to police are extremely low (reflecting approximately 1 percent of all tips across the three service municipalities audited). In response the Ministry reiterated that where sufficient evidence exists staff is directed to refer all cases of suspected welfare fraud to police, and promised to further improve fraud investigation practices "through the development of additional tools that support effective program management and oversight" (Provincial Auditor General 2009: 267). Then, in April of 2012, the Ministry introduced a new eligibility verification process with automated monthly validation of client financial information (City Auditor General 2012). Little trust is placed in the honesty and candour of recipients.

The amount of information required at the time of applying and during regular or risk-determined reviews is sweeping. So too is the scope of the consent to the collection and release of information that must be signed as a precondition to receipt of benefits. Documents required at the time of application include a SIN, health card, birth certificate and documentation to verify identify and legal status. Monthly bank statements, pay stubs, vehicle registration and evidence of shelter costs must be provided. Indeed any change in circumstance relevant to eligibility (not easily discerned given the complexity of the system) must be reported on a monthly basis. A detailed eligibility review is required every twelve months or more frequently depending upon "risk factors." These extensive and ongoing reporting requirements, together with a host of information-sharing agreements negotiated with a range of provincial and federal departments, permit the Ministry to gather, validate and share vast amounts of information about those in receipt of social assistance.

Recipients have described the experience of being on welfare as "living under a microscope" or "having one's life gone through with a fine-tooth comb," a time in which virtually everything they do is everyone's business (Mosher and Hermer 2005). The climate in their interactions with the system is permeated with suspicion and hostility. Constant fear is part of their everyday reality: fear of not being able to meet the basic needs of their children; fear of losing custody; fear of declining health; fear — especially for their children — of the impacts of social ostracism, stigmatization and discrimination; fear of breaching a rule; fear of someone calling the snitch line, which would lead to a hostile investigation. Front-line workers sometimes expressly cultivate this last fear. Recipients report being told by their workers that they know they must be up to something because it is just not possible to survive on their welfare cheques, and it will only be a matter of time before the workers figure out exactly what the recipients are up to. As Herd and Mitchell (2002: 8–9, 33) found in their research:

> The new system is more concerned with surveillance and deterrence, than it is with assisting people to find employment ... What is new is the intensity of surveillance and the technologies employed, the importation of private sector methods and standardised business practices ... Overall the mood of the focus groups was that the new system was inspiring a greater degree of suspicion and hostility ... more concerned with constant surveillance and treating "everybody like they're cheating the system."

In addition to EROs, the public too is charged with a responsibility — a civic duty — to engage in the project of surveilling and scrutinizing welfare recipients. Concerned citizens are actively encouraged to call a toll-free welfare fraud hotline, which can be done anonymously. Introducing the welfare fraud hotline on October 2, 1995, then Minister of Community and Social Services David Tsubouchi proclaimed in the House: "Welfare fraud is a problem that hurts the most vulnerable people in our society. Every cent that is paid to the wrong person through fraud is help taken from the needy" (cited in *Hansard*, Oct. 2, 1995). Noting that experience had shown hotlines to be an effective device to ensure that this misdirection does not happen, he projected savings of $25 million per year and invited the people of Ontario to call 1-800-394-STOP to help "stop fraud and to protect the system for people who really need help" (cited in *Hansard*, Oct. 2, 1995). The Ministry's website promises that calls will be taken "very seriously" and "every case will be investigated and, where appropriate, action will be taken" (Ontario, Ministry of Community and Social Services n.d.). While recent data appear not to be available, 6,527 people called the hotline in 2001–02, down from the 9,348 calls in 2000–01.

As the number of calls to the snitch line suggests (and in addition to calls to the snitch line, calls are also made directly to local Ontario Works or ODSP offices), recipients' lives are scrutinized intensely by non-state agents. Abusive boyfriends or spouses, landlords, local shop owners and neighbours have all taken up the government's invitation to participate in the surveillance project (Mosher and Hermer 2005). No doubt, class, gender and race stereotypes play into who calls to report what about whom. So, for example, class and race stereotypes of racialized women portray them as bad and potentially dangerous, as likely criminals. Dominant stereotypes caricature Aboriginal people as "living off the system" and being too lazy to get a job. Single mothers — especially those with children by more than one father — are seen as promiscuous, having children to increase welfare dollars, and likely to be hiding men in their homes. Under the gaze of surveillance by "concerned citizens" who harbour these stereotypes, virtually any racialized woman, any single mother or any Aboriginal person becomes someone who can be suspected of fraud and ought to be investigated. The sweep and impact of surveillance by non-state actors are therefore likely to have different impacts on particular groups of recipients: racialized peoples, women and, most pervasively, racialized women (Mirchandani and Chan 2005).

In addition, the snitch line is not uncommonly used for purposes completely extraneous to preventing or detecting fraud. Abusive men make false reports to further their power and control over women; landlords make false reports to facilitate the eviction of a tenant; and vindictive neighbours or other acquaintances make false or misleading reports simply out of spite (Mosher et al. 2004).

Harsh Penalties for Conviction: The Lifetime Ban and Incarceration

Perhaps the most punitive measures introduced in the new welfare fraud control regime were the penalties upon conviction: the government first introduced a three-month ban on receipt of welfare for a first conviction, with six months for subsequent convictions; and later a lifetime ban for a first conviction (for crimes committed after April 1, 2000). Thus, someone convicted of welfare fraud was automatically banned for life from receipt of social assistance. The constitutionality of the lifetime ban was under challenge when the Liberal government announced its repeal in December 2003, while at the same time introducing a revised Policy Directive making referral of cases by welfare administrators to the police mandatory in all cases in which there is sufficient evidence to suspect intent to commit fraud (*Broomer v. Ontario (A.G.)* 2002; Ontario, Ministry of Community and Social Services 2004). Although both the OWA and the ODSPA contain offence provisions that prohibit knowingly obtaining assistance to which one is not entitled, these provisions are never resorted to. Rather, it is the policy of the Ministry to deal with such matters as criminal, rather than provincial, offences.

Significantly, conviction for welfare fraud has long attracted disproportionately harsh punishments (Mosher and Hermer 2005; Martin 1992). With general deterrence as the articulated guiding principle, conviction for welfare fraud involving even small amounts of money (a few thousand dollars) presumptively gives rise to a sentence of incarceration. Welfare fraud is routinely characterized as a crime against every citizen of the community, as theft from those "genuinely in need," as a breach or abuse of public trust, as theft from the hard-working, generous, and charitably inclined taxpayer, and as the most despicable form of theft. This is true notwithstanding that the majority of cases involve situations of desperate need and extremely difficult personal circumstances and not the complex schemes of multiple identities that consume so much of the media's attention.

The Kimberly Rogers Case

The sentence given to Kimberly Rogers is indicative of this harsh approach to welfare fraud. Rogers pled guilty to the crime of fraud for having failed to disclose $13,468.31 in student loans that she had received over a three-year period while in receipt of Ontario Work benefits (*R. v. Rogers* 2001). In sentencing Kimberly Rogers, Mr. Justice Rodgers admonished her about the seriousness of the offence, concluding: "There is a jail term that is going to be involved, it just happens to be a jail term that will be served in your home, and not at the expense of the community. You have taken enough from the community." He proceeded to impose a conditional sentence of six months (a precondition for the imposition of a conditional sentence is a finding that the circumstances warrant incarceration), along with nineteen months' probation and a restitution order for the full amount. He declined to impose a community service order, concluding that because Rogers was pregnant she would soon be required to devote much time and attention to the care of her child. He added that he hoped she would raise her child "in a way that will instil the values that you appear to be missing, at least during this period of time."

So dehumanized was Kimberly Rogers in the eyes of the sentencing judge, that jail was too good for her; she did not deserve even that much. Rather, she was to fund her own incarceration. Just how she was to do that was not at all obvious; she had been in receipt of Ontario Workfare payments, but, as a consequence of the conviction, was subject to a three-month ban on eligibility. Under the terms of her conditional sentence she was permitted to leave her apartment for only three hours on Wednesday mornings — perhaps enough time to purchase the necessities of life when you have a decent income, but impossible for those who must scavenge for life's necessities.

About one month after her conviction and the revocation of her benefits, lawyers were able to successfully obtain an injunction, lifting the ban on the receipt of benefits, pending a constitutional challenge to the ban. In her decision granting the injunction, Madam Justice Epstein rejected the callous characterization of Rogers' circumstances advanced by the Ministry of the Attorney General in its argument that because she had managed to find ways of addressing her basic needs she had failed to demonstrate the "irreparable harm" necessary for the granting of an injunction. To the contrary, Justice Epstein concluded:

> Ms. Rogers has no reliable alternative source of income. She is at the brink of being homeless. She is at this moment unable to feed herself adequately. The medical evidence in the record is clear that as a pregnant woman in the last trimester of her pregnancy the applicant is exposed to serious and perhaps permanent health problems unless, at the very least, she has access to proper nutrition if not shelter. The irreparable harm is clear and obvious. (*Rogers v. Greater Sudbury (City) Administrator of Ontario Works* 2001: para. 13)

The judge went on to conclude:

> In the unique circumstances of this case, if the applicant is exposed to the full three month suspension of her benefits, a member of our community carrying an unborn child may well be homeless and deprived of basic sustenance. Such a situation would jeopardize the health of Ms. Rogers and the fetus thereby adversely affecting not only mother and child but also the public — its dignity, its human rights commitments and its health care resources. (*Rogers v. Greater Sudbury (City) Administrator of Ontario Works* 2001: para. 19)

Even with her benefits restored, after paying her rent Kimberly Rogers had extremely limited funds to support herself: a mere $18 per month by some accounts (see CAEFS 2013). Tragically, Kimberly Rogers died, eight months pregnant, in her apartment during a heat wave in August 2001. Although the coroner found the medical cause of her death to be a drug overdose, the recommendations of the coroner's jury — that the lifetime ban be revoked, that the state ensure those serving periods of house arrest be provided with adequate food, shelter and other necessities, that there be an evaluation of life circumstances and the consequences of conviction before prosecuting for welfare fraud, and that benefit rates be set in accordance with actual need — clearly suggest that the jury found existing welfare policies and practices to be at least partially to blame.

More recently, at least on occasion, courts have been prepared to grant a conditional discharge in circumstances where the accused presents as a reformed neo-liberal citizen. For example, in the case of R. v. Wilson, the accused failed to report the receipt of student loans and income from part-time employment, underreported child support and overreported the amount paid for rent (R. v. Wilson 2005). The amounts were significant: $20,000 in social assistance and $44,000 in rent subsidies. Ms. Wilson, at the time of sentencing, had obtained two bachelor degrees, was working full-time and was pursuing a master's degree. Although the Crown sought a conditional sentence of four to six months, Justice Lampkin ordered a conditional discharge. While agreeing with the Crown in the characterization of welfare fraud as a serious crime, Justice Lampkin reasoned that a conviction would result in the loss of her employment, the "community would lose her specialized training in child welfare," and she "would no longer be a contributing member of society" (2005: para.18).

EMPLOYMENT STANDARDS

Ontario's welfare regime, with its obsession regarding fraud, its wide net of suspicion and surveillance, and its harshly punitive approach to those who dare "take" more in order to survive, stands in stark contrast to state regulation of employer compliance with statutory minimum standards of employment. A comparison of the welfare and employment standards regimes reveals a very selective invocation of "criminal" discourses and practices at play. This selective, partial and strategic use of "criminal" law is very much aligned with the values and interests of neo-liberalism, deploying an iron fist against those already marginalized by poverty (and often by gender, race and disability) and extending a soft, placating glove to employers.

Ontario's Employment Standards Act, 2000 (ESA) creates several minimum statutory conditions of work, governing such matters as minimum wage, maximum hours of work, overtime compensation and vacation pay. Yet these minimum conditions, especially at the bottom end of the labour market where they matter most, are frequently disregarded. With distressing regularity employees are not compensated for overtime work, not paid their vacation pay or not paid at all for work done. The Ministry of Labour's mechanisms of enforcement are almost entirely reactive, dependent upon individual employees to come forward with complaints. In contrast to the welfare regime, with its intense surveillance and monitoring of compliance, the employment standards regime is characterized by an extremely limited monitoring of employer conduct.

As social assistance was being substantially reformed in the mid-1990s, so too was the regulation of employment. Emphasizing efficiency and flexibility, the Ontario government increased weekly maximum hours of work from forty-eight to sixty, changed the rules so that entitlement to overtime pay could, with employee consent, be calculated by averaging hours worked over four weeks, terminated an employee wage protection program, reduced the time in which workers could register formal complaints from two years to six months, and put a cap of $10,000 on monetary awards (Vosko, Tucker, Thomas, and Gellatly 2011). As Leah Vosko and her colleagues (2011: 11) argue, these changes undercut established principles of decent work, defined by the International Labour Organization as "jobs that provide income and employment security, equity, and human dignity." This includes the establishment of minimally acceptable conditions of work to protect workers against "employer exploitation due to unequal bargaining power" (Vosko et al. 2011: 2–3). While important reforms between 2004 and 2010 addressed to some degree the exploitative working conditions of live-in caregivers and workers employed by temporary help agencies, the 2010 Open for Business Act signalled yet further distancing from the principles of decent work.

Significantly, the Open for Business Act (OBA) amended the ESA to provide that a complaint would not be referred to an employment standards officer (ESO) for investigation unless the worker has taken certain steps to facilitate the investigation of the complaint (s.96.1). These steps may include the worker informing the employer that the worker believes the Act has been contravened and providing "such evidence and other information in writing as the Director considers appropriate" (s.96.1(3)). The Ministry's website counsels that "you generally must contact your employer or former employer." Notwithstanding the Ministry's claim that "most employers will want to do the right thing and they will often remedy the situation promptly and voluntarily, if they agree there is a valid claim" (Ontario, Ministry of Labour 2010), these new pre-conditions shifted the burden of investigation and enforcement onto those least able to bear it — employees in precarious work situations. While the Ministry's press announcement and other materials indicate that these requirements can be waived for "vulnerable employees," waivers are discretionary and create yet a further barrier.

The OBA also contains a new provision empowering Employment Standards Offices to pursue mediated settlements of complaints, raising concerns regarding the pressure on workers to settle for less than owed, indeed for amounts below the statutory minimums. There is also concern that the increased emphasis on private dispute settlement enables employers to avoid public denunciation and penalties. This is particularly so given that the effect of settlement is to deem the claim to have been withdrawn, to terminate the investigation and to halt other proceedings with the exception of a prosecution.

It is important to locate these recent changes in the broader context of enforcement practices. Vosko and her colleagues (2011: 4) describe three types of compliance: voluntary, reactive and proactive. Similarly, a report by the Law Commission of Ontario (2012) describes a mix of "soft" and "hard" law, the former consisting of voluntary compliance and self-regulation on the part of employers and the latter, orders to pay or comply and prosecutions. Within the employment standards system overall, considerable emphasis is placed on self-regulation, grounded in an assumption that "most employers will do the right thing" and will behave as "good corporate citizens" (Vosko et al. 2011: 15). Starting assumptions about deservedness and trustworthiness are notably different than those applied to welfare recipients.

Beyond self-regulation by employers, the system is primarily reactive, responding to individual complaints filed by workers and with an emphasis on negotiated settlements. An increase over a five-year period saw the number of claims rise from an average of 15,000 to 20,000 per year (Vosko et al. 2011: 31). A report by the Law Commission of Ontario (LCO) observed that the Ministry of Labour will act on third party and anonymous complaints; however, unlike the welfare fraud hotline, this mechanism "is not advertised and does not appear to be well known" (2012: 61). The LCO recommends the establishment of an advertised hotline, yet, mindful of concerns expressed by employers, recommends further that policy criteria be developed "to ensure that unfounded complaints do not trigger unwarranted inspections" (2012: 62). Again, the situation stands in marked contrast to the positioning of the welfare fraud hotline.

Notwithstanding that violations are found in a substantial percentage of complaints (for example, 70 percent in 2004 and 83 percent in 2012), the number of "expanded investigations," wherein individual complaints are used to launch broader investigations, has declined since the 1970s, when full audits were generally done to follow-up each individual case (Vosko et al. 2011: 17). More generally, there is relatively limited resort to proactive investigations, although the statutory tools and powers for proactive investigations or audits of employer practices and the expansive investigative powers of ESOs are similar to those of EROs. In the 1980s and 1990s, workplace inspections were almost nonexistent (Vosko et al. 2011:

27). In 2002–03, a total of 357 proactive investigations were undertaken (down significantly from 1,543 in 2000–01) (Ontario, Ministry of Labour 2003). The number has continued to fluctuate, dropping to near zero in 2004–05 (at which point the government announced that it was putting enforcement back on the agenda), raising to roughly 2,500 in 2005–06, dropping to about 1,100 in 2010–11 and up to 2,248 in 2011–12 (Vosko et al. 2011: 23).

For those individual employees who see the private complaint process through to its end, victory is often bittersweet. The record of the Ministry in enforcing orders to pay (a state order to pay the minimum required by law) made against employers can only be described as abysmal. In 2002–03, more than $16 million was outstanding in orders to pay alone, no doubt only a small fraction of the unpaid wages owing to employees in Ontario (Ontario, Ministry of Labour 2003). Vosko and her colleagues note that in 2009–10 wages assessed as owing through claims, proactive inspections and bankruptcies totalled more than $62 million, yet only roughly $18 million was collected. Significantly, $42.9 million owing was the result of bankruptcy or insolvency (Vosko et al. 2011: 22, 17).

Notwithstanding the availability under the ESA of prosecutions for violations of the Act and the prospect of substantial penalties upon conviction, prosecutions are extremely rare. In 2009–10, of the 20,762 claims investigated, finding employers owing $64.4 million to workers, only 86 fines and 298 tickets (usually for $360) were issued. The Ministry initiated only thirteen prosecutions of employers for breaches of the Act. The enforcement activity of proactive inspections appears to be most concerned with encouraging compliance rather than penalizing employers (Vosko et al. 2011: 24). As observed by the LCO, no guidelines or criteria exist to determine the use of sanctions and penalties, leading the commission to recommend that ESOs "be provided with specific policy direction and education to emphasize deterrence in selection of penalties and sanctions … in cases of repeat violations and wilful non-compliance" (2012: 65).

Unlike the welfare fraud context, the limited resort to prosecutions under the Provincial Offences Act is not a result of a policy to pursue criminal charges instead, because prosecutions for employer fraud under the Criminal Code are virtually unheard of. Tellingly though, a sizeable amount of employer conduct not only violates the ESA but satisfies the legal test for criminal fraud. For example, employers who hire with no intention of paying their employees are engaging in criminal fraud. Employers who hire when they know the business is about to go bankrupt (and consider the substantial percentage of monies owing that are the result of bankruptcy), or hire when existing employees have yet to be paid, may also be guilty of fraud (Slattery 2004). Yet not only are prosecutions under the Criminal Code for fraud exceedingly rare, there is no invocation of the language of fraud or criminality in official discourse. Employers — even those who hire intending not to pay their employees or who are repeat violators — are not labelled as criminals. There is no political or broad public outrage about the theft of the labour of vulnerable employees by unscrupulous employers; noticeably absent is the kind of moral anger expressed about welfare "fraudsters." And there has not been a massive ratcheting up of surveillance practices to "prevent and control" fraud and abuses, notwithstanding the millions of unpaid wages each year and the enormous number of workers harmed by these practices. To the contrary, resources and staffing for employment standards regulation in the 2009–10 budget put funding more than 10 percent below 1997 levels (Vosko et al. 2011: 30). The government did promise, but then retracted, additional monies for enforcement as part of its Poverty Reduction Plan. Ultimately, a Stop Wage Theft campaign mounted by workers — the only appearance of the language of criminality — was successful in its demand that the $6 million for enforcement proposed to be cut from the 2012 budget be restored.

Employers can flagrantly disregard the ESA with little possibility that they will be ordered to pay what is owing to their employees, with a fair measure of confidence that even if an order to pay is issued its enforcement can be avoided, with an abundance of confidence that they will not be prosecuted with an offence under the ESA, and with complete assurance that no criminal prosecution will ensue. They are trusted to "do the right thing." As Laureen Snider (2006b: 200) observes, "The ideological process that shapes the social distribution of blame has exonerated these kinds of harmful acts and, therefore, the actors responsible for them." At the same time, this ideological process has not exonerated — but rather inculpated and demonized — low-income people in receipt of social assistance. Employers and the waged work that they arguably generate are valorized within a neo-liberal paradigm; those without waged work, who turn to the state for support, are villainized.

EXACERBATING THE PROBLEMS OF THE MARGINALIZED

The hyper-surveillance within the welfare regime and attribution of criminality to those in receipt of welfare benefits work in tandem with the deregulated labour market in which minimum standards go unenforced and employer illegality goes largely unchecked. The constructed problem of welfare fraud, together with benefit reductions and workfare, has created a class of vulnerable workers prepared to "accept" the work available at the bottom end of the lean state — work that the state has allowed to become increasingly more precarious and exploitative. As Dean Herd and his colleagues (2005: 20) observe, "It is of the utmost significance that the context for increasingly harsh and restrictive welfare regimes is a labour market characterized by polarized job opportunity, with a particularly adverse effect on lower tiers of the labour market where social assistance recipients tend to compete."

But some do not even have the option of exploitative, marginal wage work. A good many people — persons with disabilities who do not qualify for OSDP benefits but whom the market will not accommodate, women with children who cannot find adequate care for their children while they work, women who resist the neo-liberal imperative of wage work to rear their children, and newcomers to Canada whom the market refuses to employ — will be intensely monitored, punished and dehumanized by the welfare system for their "failure" to be self-reliant. They will be personally blamed and subjected to efforts to reform them, to make them virtuous neo-liberal citizens. They will be compelled to make brutally agonizing choices: whether to report small amounts of money received from occasional under-the-table work that could be used to feed their children and would otherwise be deducted from their welfare cheques (they risk a possible fraud prosecution if welfare authorities later learn of this money); or whether to return to an abusive relationship in which basic material needs may be met, but where they are exposed to continuing physical and psychological harm. And many will come face to face with the other mechanisms that the state has deployed to punish poverty: restrictions on, and penalties for, street-level subsistence activities; incarceration for engaging in illegal activities undertaken to survive in the face of shrinking social support; and mounting hostility towards the poor — hostility that has been intensely fuelled by the construction of the problem of welfare fraud. They fall within what Wacquant describes as the "castaway categories," marginalized populations "ensnared in a *carceral-assistential net* that aims either to render them 'useful' by steering them onto the track of deskilled employment through moral retaining and material suasion, or to warehouse them out of reach" (Wacquant 2008: 18).

Notes

This chapter draws upon research undertaken for and funded by the Law Commission of Canada by the author and Professor Joe Hermer. Deep gratitude is owed to the Law Commission for its support of this work.
1   I use the male pronoun here because this is a view of the "self" commonly associated with men and frequently contrasted with a more relational "feminine" self.

References

Broadbent, Edward. 1999. "Citizenship Today: Is There a Crisis?" In Dave Broad and Wayne Antony (eds.), *Citizens or Consumers? Social Policy in a Market Society.* Halifax: Fernwood Publishing.

CAEFS (Canadian Association of Elizabeth Fry Societies). 2013. "Justice with Dignity: Remember Kimberley Rogers." < caefs.ca/wp-content/uploads/2013/04/rogers.pdf>.

Chunn, Dorothy E., and Shelley A.M. Gavigan. 2004. "Welfare Law, Welfare Fraud, and the Moral Regulation of the 'Never Deserving' Poor." *Social & Legal Studies* 13, 2 (June).

Commission for the Review of Social Assistance in Ontario. 2012. Brighter Prospects:

Transforming Social Assistance in Ontario. <mcss.gov.on.ca/documents/en/mcss/ social/publications/social_assistance_review_final_report.pdf>.

Evans, Patricia, and Gerda Wekerle. 1988. *Women's Work, Markets, and Economic Development in Nineteenth-Century Ontario.* Toronto: University of Toronto Press.

Fraser, John, Cynthia Wilkey, and JoAnne Frenschkowski. 2003. *Denial By Design... The Ontario Disability Support Program.* Toronto: Income Security Advocacy Centre.

Herd, Dean, and Andrew Mitchell. 2002. *Discouraged, Diverted and Disentitled: Ontario Works' New Service Delivery Model.* Toronto: Community Social Planning Council of Toronto and the Ontario Social Safety Network.

Herd, Dean, Andrew Mitchell and Ernie Lightman. 2005. "Rituals of Degradation: Administration as Policy in the Ontario Works Programme." Social Policy and Administration 39, 1: 65–79. <socialwork.utoronto.ca/Assets/Social%2BWork%2B Digital%2BAssets/SANE/Rituals%2Bof%2BDegradation.pdf>.

Korteweg, Anna C. 2003. "Welfare Reform and the Subject of the Working Mother: 'Get a Job, a Better Job, Then a Career.'" *Theory and Society* 32, 4.

Law Commission of Ontario. 2012. Vulnerable Workers and Precarious Work. <lco-cdo. org/vulnerable-workers-final-report.pdf>.

Lightman, Ernie, Andrew Mitchell and Dean Herd. 2010. "Cycling Off and On Welfare in Canada." Journal Social Policy 39, 4: 523–542.

Little, Margaret. 1998. *No Car, No Radio, No Liquor Permit: The Moral Regulation of Single Mothers in Ontario, 1920–1997.* Toronto: Oxford University Press.

MacDonald, C.A. (Tina), Duncan F. MacDonald, and Sheila Blair. 1995. *Reducing Fraud and Waste in Income Security Programs in Canada.* Edmonton: C.A. MacDonald & Associates.

Martin, Dianne L. 1992. "Passing the Buck: Prosecution of Welfare Fraud; Preservation of Stereotypes." *Windsor Yearbook of Access to Justice* 12.

McCluskey, Martha. 2003. "Efficiency and Social Citizenship: Challenging the Neoliberal Attack on the Welfare State." *Indiana Law Journal* 78.

Ministry of Labour. 2010. "New Legislation Modernizes Ontario's Employment Standards." News release. <labour.gov.on.ca/english/news/bulletin_ofba.php>.

Mirchandani, Kiran, and Wendy Chan. 2005. "The Racialized Impact of Welfare Fraud Control in British Columbia and Ontario." Canadian Race Relations Foundation. <crr.ca/divers-files/en/publications/reports/pubRacialized_Impact_Welfare.pdf >.

Moretta, Debbie. 2003. Affidavit Sworn August 29, 2003 in *Broomer v. Ontario (A.G.)* (June 5, 2002), Toronto 02-CV-229203CM3 (Ont. Sup. Ct.).

Mosher, Janet. 2010. "Intimate Intrusions – Welfare Regulation and Women's Personal Lives." In Mimi Ajzenstadt, Dorothy Chunn, and Shelley Gavigan (eds.), The Legal Tender of Gender. London: Hart, Onati Law & Society Series.

Mosher, Janet, Patricia Evans, Margaret Little, Eileen Morrow, Jo-Anne Boulding, and Nancy VanderPlaats. 2004. *Walking on Eggshells: Abused Women's Experiences of Ontario's Welfare System.* Toronto. <dawn.thot.net/abuse.html>.

Mosher, Janet, and Joe Hermer. 2005. *Welfare Fraud: The Constitution of Social Assistance as Crime.* Ottawa: Law Commission of Canada.

Noack, Andrea M., and Leah F. Vosko. 2011. "Precarious Jobs in Ontario: Mapping Dimensions of Labour Market Insecurity by Workers' Social Location and Context." <lco-cdo.org/vulnerable-workers-commissioned-papers-vosko-noack.pdf>.

Ontario. 1995 *Official Report of Debates (Hansard)*, 1st Sess., 36th Leg., October 2.

____. 1997. *Official Report of Debates (Hansard)*, 1st Sess., 36th Leg., November 25.

Ontario, Auditor General. 2009. "Ministry of Community and Social Services: Ontario Works Program." Chapter 3.11. <auditor.on.ca/en/reports_en/en09/311en09.pdf>.

____. 2011. "Ministry of Community and Social Services: Ontario Works Program." Chapter 4.11. <auditor.on.ca/en/reports_en/en11/411en11.pdf>.

Ontario, Ministry of Community, Family, and Children's Services. 2001. *Ontario Works: Controlling Fraud (Directive 45.0)*. Toronto: Ministry of Community, Family, and Children's Services.

____. 2003. *Welfare Fraud Control Report 2001–2002*. Toronto: Ministry of Community, Family and Children's Services.

Ontario, Ministry of Community and Social Services. 2004. *Ontario Works: Controlling Fraud (Directive 45.0)*. Toronto: Ministry of Community and Social Services.

____. 2012. Ontario Works, Controlling Fraud (Directive 9.7). Toronto: Ministry of Community and Social Services.

____. 2013. Ontario Works, Reviewing Eligibility (Directive 9.1). Toronto: Ministry of Community and Social Services.

Ontario PC Party 2011. "Changebook." <poltext.org/sites/poltext.org/files/plateformes/on2011pc_en_03042012_91448.pdf>.

Parnaby, Patrick. 2003. "Disaster Through Dirty Windshields: Law, Order and Toronto's Squeegee Kids." *Canadian Journal of Sociology* 28, 3.

Pateman, Carole. 1989. *The Disorder of Women: Democracy, Feminism, and Political Theory.* Stanford: Stanford University Press.

Peck, Jamie, and Adam Tickell. 2002. "Neoliberalizing Space." Antipode 34, 3: 380–404.

Pollack, Shoshana, and Lea Caragata. 2010. "Contestation and Accommodation: Constructions of Lone Mothers' Subjectively though Workfare Policy and Practice." Affilia: Journal of Women and Social Work 25, 3:264–277.

Rittich, Kerry. 2007. "Social Rights and Social Policy; Transformations on the International Landscape." In Aeyal M. Gross and Daphne Marak-Erez (eds.), Exploring Social Rights: Between Theory and Practice. Oxford: Hart Publishing.

Sears, Alan. 1999. "The 'Lean' State and Capitalist Restructuring: Towards a Theoretical Account." *Studies in Political Economy* 59, 91.

Slattery, Shannon. 2004. "The Criminal Law and the Employment Relationship: A New Perspective on Enforcing the Employment Standards Act." Paper on file with Janet Mosher.

Smith, Lauren, Paul Wise, Wendy Chavkin, Diana Romero, and Barry Zuckerman. 2000. "Implications of Welfare Reform for Child Health: Emerging Challenges for Clinical Practice and Policy." *Pediatrics* 106, 5.

Snider, L. 2006b. "Making Corporate Crime Disappear." In Elizabeth Comack (ed.), *Locating Law: Race, Class, Gender, Sexuality Connections,* 2nd edition. Halifax: Fernwood Publishing.

Social Assistance Review Committee. 1988. *Report of the Social Assistance Review Committee: Transitions.* Toronto: Queen's Printer, 1988.

Stapleton, John. 2012. "Of the 1%, for the 1%, to the 1%?" <openpolicyontario.com/of-the-1-for-the-1-to-the-1/>.

Toronto, Auditor General. 2012. "Toronto Employment and Social Services – Income Verification Procedures Can be Improved." <toronto.ca/audit/2012/TESS_Income_ Verification_Procedures_Oct_6_2012_Web.pdf>.

____. 2008. "Managing the Risk of Overpayments in the Administration of Overpayments of Social Assistance." <toronto.ca/audit/2008/managing_risk_social_assistance_ audit_report_may2008.pdf>.

Vosko, Leah F., Eric Tucker, Mark P. Thomas and Mary Gellatly. 2011. "New Approaches to Enforcement and Compliance with Labour Regulatory Standards: The Case of Ontario, Canada." <lco-cdo.org/vulnerable-workers-commissioned-papers-vosko-tucker-thomas-gellatly.pdf>.

Wacquant, Loïc. 2001. "The Penalisation of Poverty and the Rise of Neo-Liberalism." *European Journal on Criminal Policy and Research* 9.

____. 2005. "The Scholarly Myths of the New Law and Order Doxa." In Leo Panitch and Colin Leys (eds.), *The Socialist Register 2006: Telling the Truth.* New York: Monthly Review Press.

____. 2008. "Ordering Insecurity: Social Polarization and the Punitive Upsurge." Radical Philosophy Review 11(1): 1-19.

Zizys, Tom. 2011. "Working Better: Creating a High-Performing Labour Market in Ontario." Toronto: Metcalf Foundation. <metcalffoundation.com/stories/publications/ working-better-creating-a-high-performing-labour-market-in-ontario-2/>.0

Cases Cited

Broomer v. Ontario (A.G.) (2002), Toronto 02-CV-229203CM3 (Ont. Sup. Ct.) (June 5)

R. v. Jarvis, [2002] 3 SCR 757

R. v. Maldonado, [1998] OJ No. 3209 (Prov. Div.) (QL)

R. v. Rogers, [2001] OJ No. 5203 (Ct. of Jus.) (QL)

R. v. Wilson (2001), 49 Weekly Criminal Bulletin (2d) 492 (Manitoba Prov. Ct.)

R v. Wilson, 2005 ONCJ 21 (Can LII).

Rogers v. Greater Sudbury (City) Administrator of Ontario Works (2001), 57 OR (3d) 460

Legislation Cited

Ontario Works Act, 1997, O. Reg. 134/98

Ontario Works Act, 1997, O. Reg. 310/10

Open for Business Act, 2010 SO 2010, c.16.

Chapter 12

FROM WELFARE FRAUD TO WELFARE AS FRAUD
The Criminalization of Poverty

Dorothy E. Chunn and Shelley A.M. Gavigan

From: *Criminalizing Women: Gender and (In)Justice in Neo-liberal Times,* 2nd edition, pp. 197–218 (reprinted with permission).

In Canada and elsewhere, attacks on the policies and practices of the Keynesian welfare state since the late twentieth century have led to the dismantling and massive restructuring of social security programs for the poor. These sweeping welfare reforms, which intensified through the 1990s — aptly characterized by some as a war on the poor — have a disproportionate impact on poor women (see, for example, *Falkiner v. Ontario* 2002; Klein and Long 2003; Little 2001; McMullin, Davies, and Cassidy 2002; Mosher et al. 2004; Savarese and Morton 2005, Swan et al. 2008). As Lynne Segal (1999: 206–7) argues: "The continuing offensive against welfare provides, perhaps, the single most general threat to Western women's interests at present — at least for those many women who are not wealthy, and who still take the major responsibility for caring work in the home." Indeed, it is no exaggeration to say that welfare law is primarily (and ideologically) concerned with the lives and issues of poor women, especially lone-parent mothers.

Welfare "fraud" occupies a central place in this attack on the poor. "Fraudsters" have always been a state concern in most liberal democracies, but the preoccupation with welfare "cheats" in the late 1990s and early 2000s was unprecedented.

Although the preoccupation with welfare fraud is now less pronounced than it was a decade ago, the threat of it is still a weapon used against the poor. Moreover, it is only the most visible form of assault. In Ontario, for instance, the attack on welfare in the late 1990s also included deep cuts to the level of benefits (*Masse v. Ontario* 1996; see also Moscovitch 1997: 85), an expanded definition of "spouse" (*Falkiner v. Ontario* 2002), restructuring of the legislation from "welfare" to "work,"[1] mandatory drug testing, the introduction of a "quit/fire" regulation (which requires the cancellation or suspension of assistance to a recipient who resigns employment without just cause or is dismissed with cause),[2] the implementation of biometric finger-scanning (Little 2001: 26), anonymous snitch lines designed to encourage individuals to report suspected welfare abuse by their neighbours (see Morrison 1998; Morrison and Pearce 1995), and "zero-tolerance" in the form of permanent ineligibility imposed upon anyone convicted of welfare fraud (see *Rogers v. Sudbury* 2001: 5; *Broomer v. Ontario* 2002). In the past decade in Ontario, "welfare fraud" seems to have garnered less political and social attention than in the heyday of the attack on social assistance. However, the welfare system continues to operate within an ideological framework that shows welfare recipients as inherently "defrauding" the system.

This restructuring of welfare has shifted and been shifted by public discourse and social images (see Evans and Swift 2000; Golding and Middleton 1982; Misra, Moller, and Karides 2003; Mosher 2000; Mirchandani and Chan 2007). Few people, it seems, qualify as "deserving" poor anymore. Welfare fraud is welfare *as* fraud. Thus poverty, welfare and crime are linked.[3] Simply to be poor is to be culpable, or at least vulnerable to culpability.

Two Ontario women convicted of welfare fraud offer case studies of the culpable poor in the early period of neo-liberal welfare reform. In 1994 Donna Bond, a single mother of two teenage children, was charged with welfare fraud in the amount of $16,477.84 over a sixteen-month period — she had not disclosed a bank account in her annual update report.[4] At trial, Bond testified that she had saved, and deposited, all the money she had ever received from her part-time employment, baby bonus, child tax credits and income tax refunds (all of which she had disclosed in her annual reports to welfare). Initially she had planned to buy a car with this money, but then realized that her children would "require financial assistance to deal with [their serious health] problems in the years ahead" (*R. v. Bond* 1994: para.8). So she decided to set the money aside as a trust fund for them. Bond said she had "honestly believed that she did not have to report the savings because they were for the children" (*R. v. Bond* 1994: para.13).

The trial judge admitted to a dilemma:

> I was very impressed by the sincerity and achievement of the accused

and troubled by the paradox of criminalizing the actions of this woman who scrimped as a hedge against the future financial health needs of her children. If she had spent this money on drinking, or drugs, or in any other irresponsible way, there would be no basis for any criminal charge. A conviction seems to send the message it was wrong to be conscientious about the welfare of her children and foolish to be frugal. (R. v. Bond 1994: para. 14)

Convict he did, however. And he was neither the first nor the last "sympathetic" judge to enter a conviction for fraud against a welfare mother (see Martin 1992; Carruthers 1995). Arguably, this case is one in which reasonable doubt as to guilt ought to have existed. Had she not been convicted of welfare fraud, this normatively perfect mother might well have been a candidate for "Mother and Homemaker of the Year." Yet the trial judge found Bond culpable: "Her commendable frugality and her selfless motives for committing the offence [were only] matters for considera-tion on sentencing" (R. v. Bond 1994: para. 14).

Some seven years later, in the spring of 2001, Kimberly Rogers pleaded guilty to welfare fraud that involved receiving a student loan and welfare assistance at the same time (previously but no longer permitted by Ontario's legislation).[5] Because she was pregnant, and had no prior criminal record, the judge sentenced her to six months of house arrest. However, as a result of the Ontario government's zero-tolerance policy, which then stipulated three months, and later permanent, ineligibility of people convicted of welfare fraud, Rogers had no source of income (Keck 2002; MacKinnon and Lacey 2001: F1, F8). Seeking reinstatement of her benefits, she wrote in an affidavit to the court: "I ran out of food this weekend. I am unable to sleep and I cry all the time" (cited in Keck 2002). Through a court order, she did receive interim assistance pending the hearing of a challenge to the constitutionality of the new ineligibility rules (Rogers v. Sudbury 2001), but her rent ($450.00 per month) consumed the bulk of her monthly cheque ($468.00 per month). As a friend later observed, "No one can stretch $18.00 for a whole month" (MacKinnon and Lacey 2001: F8).

Isolated, in her eighth month of pregnancy, and confined to her tiny apartment, Kimberly Rogers died of a prescription drug overdose during a sweltering heat wave in August 2001. The circumstances of her death gave rise to a coroner's inquest in the fall of 2002. The coroner's jury made fourteen recommendations for changes in government policies and practices, including the repeal of the zero-tolerance lifetime ineligibility for social assistance as a result of welfare fraud (Ontario 2002; see also Eden 2003). Following their defeat of the ruling Conservatives in October 2003, the newly elected Ontario Liberal government did repeal the lifetime ban.[6] Although this was a welcome reform, Kimberly Rogers would still be liable to a welfare fraud conviction today and, if living under house arrest, she would still have only a pittance to live on after her rent was paid.

The *Bond* and *Rogers* cases raise many theoretical and empirical questions related to regulation, law and morality, and the relationship between them at particular historical moments. We draw on these cases to analyze the intensified criminalization of poverty signified by the shift from welfare fraud to welfare *as* fraud. We argue that the shift reflected a reformed mode of moral regulation in neo-liberal states. In contemporary society, neo-liberal ideologies and the conceptualization of welfare as fraud continue to harm the lives of the poor.

The concept of moral regulation was developed initially during the 1980s by Marxist-influenced theorists (see Corrigan and Sayer 1981, 1985; Hall 1980) who linked it to processes of state formation. Through the 1990s a number of Canadian scholars pointed to the importance of non-state forces and discourses in moral regulation, arguing that the state does not hold a monopoly on "social" and "moral" initiatives (Valverde and Weir 1988: 31–34; Strange and Loo 1997; Little 1998; Valverde 1991, 1998; see also Dean 1994, 1999; Hunt 1997, 1999b). In our view, however, the state never ceases to be a player, even when benched, ignored by some, or outmanoeuvred by others. Thus, it remains important to identify the links, forms and sites of state action and inaction.

We draw on a large body of socio-legal scholarship that has advanced this form of inquiry and analysis and illustrate our examination of shifting modes of moral regulation with reference to the historical treatment of poor women on welfare (see Little 1998; Gavigan and Chunn 2007).[7] We focus in particular on the always precarious position of such women within the overarching (apparently anachronistic) category of the "deserving poor" through the example of welfare legislation and policy.[8] The welfare law reform of the late 1990s and early 2000s and the continuing preoccupation with welfare fraud — the redefinition, restructuring, harassment, and disentitlement, coupled with the ever-present threat of criminal prosecution — suggest that the state and its coercive apparatus continue to play an important role that requires close analysis.

THE DOUBLE TAXONOMY OF MORAL REGULATION: COMPULSION AND SELF-REGULATION

Moral regulation has no agreed upon meaning, but most scholarship in the area begins with the collaborative work of Philip Corrigan and Derek Sayer. In *The Great Arch: English State Formation as Cultural Revolution*, they linked moral regulation to the "cultural" project of English state formation:

> Moral regulation: a project of normalizing, rendering natural, taking for granted, in a word "obvious," what are in fact ontological and

epistemological premises of a particular and historical form of social order. Moral regulation is coextensive with state formation, and state forms are always animated and legitimated by a particular moral ethos. (Corrigan and Sayer 1985: 4)

While Corrigan and Sayer placed the moral regulation project squarely within the realm of state actions and legal relations, other scholars theorizing regulation and control through the 1990s maintained that the state must be decentred (Valverde 1991), or its relationship with non-state agencies better appreciated (Valverde 1995), or erased as a significant player altogether (Valverde 1998). For Mariana Valverde, the heart of moral regulation or moral reform in a "moral capitalist setting ... is not so much to change behaviour as to generate certain ethical subjectivities that appear as inherently moral" (Valverde 1994: 216; see also Weir 1986). The focus is less on the material consequences of regulation or reform than it is on the discursive context.

Although sympathetic to this "decentring" emphasis, we want to argue for a renewed focus on social and state forces, and in particular on the contradictions and contributions of forms of law and state to gendered and anti-racist class struggles in the realm of moral regulation. Moral regulation must be situated expressly within the context of capitalist class relations and struggles — not least of which is capital's globalized attack on the "straw house" of the Keynesian welfare state. In developing our position, we draw on Stuart Hall's early work on law, state, and moral regulation; specifically, his analysis of the reformist sixties era of the "legislation of consent" in Britain, when laws relating to divorce, homosexuality, abortion and prostitution were liberalized (Hall 1980).

Hall's (1980: 2) organizing question is: "What was it about the shifts in the modality of moral regulation which enabled this legislation, plausibly, to be described as 'permissive'?" He notes that "the legislation of consent" contained "no single uncontradictory tendency" (Hall 1980: 7). By way of illustration, he looks at the influential Report of the Wolfenden Committee on prostitution and homosexuality and argues that it "identified and separated more sharply two areas of legal and moral practice — those of sin and crime, of immorality and illegality" (Hall 1980: 11). As a result, Wolfenden created "a firmer opposition between these two domains" and "clearly staked out a new relation between the *two modes of moral regulation — the modalities of legal compulsion and of self-regulation*" (Hall 1980: 11–12; emphasis added).

Wolfenden recommended decriminalization and "privatisation of selective aspects of sexual conduct" (Hall 1980: 13), notably off-street prostitution and homosexual relations between consenting adults in private, and increased regulation of visible sexual activities such as "street-walking" and "male importuning" that were "offences against [the] public sector" (Hall 1980: 10–11). Hall identifies the "double taxonomy" of the Wolfenden recommendations: toward stricter penalty and control, toward greater freedom and leniency (1980: 14). Here, then, was the core tendency of the permissive legislation of the 1960s: "*increased regulation* coupled with *selective privatisation* through contract or consent, both in a new disposition," a "more privatised and person-focused regulation, tacit rather than explicit, invisible rather than visible" (Hall 1980: 21; emphasis added). In short, a clearer distinction was made between "public" and "private," state and civil society (Hall 1980: 13).

In identifying the double taxonomy of control and penalty and freedom and leniency, or simultaneous deregulation and increased regulation, Hall reminds us of the complexity of the unity of the 1960s reforms. The state was pulled back and reinserted in different ways in the same pieces of legislation; its invisibility in one area was reinforced by its visibility in the other. Thus, "self-regulation" was inextricably related to increased "public" regulation. The lines between unacceptable public and permissible private conduct were more sharply drawn. In this way, two modalities of moral regulation, legal compulsion and self-regulation, one neither displacing nor transcending the other, coexisted in a complex unity.

Before applying this conceptualization of moral regulation to our exemplar of welfare fraud, we first examine welfare reform during the 1990s in order to consider the increased interest and legal shifts in the area of welfare fraud.

REFORMING WELFARE IN THE 1990s

Although concern about welfare fraud is not a new phenomenon, the unrelenting punitiveness of the crackdowns under neo-liberalism is. Anti-fraud campaigns during the 1970s and early 1980s (see Golding and Middleton 1982; Rachert 1990) led to the review and total restructuring of welfare policies in Canada and other Western countries through the 1990s (see Bashevkin 2002; Moscovitch 1997; Gustafson 2009). Here we focus primarily on Ontario reforms to illustrate the shift from welfare fraud to welfare *as* fraud.

A pivotal moment in the welfare history of Ontario occurred in 1988, when the Social Assistance Review Committee (SARC) released *Transitions*, a 600-page report with 274 recommendations on Ontario's social assistance system (Ontario 1988). The report devoted only seven pages to issues of "system integrity" and "welfare fraud" and yielded but two recommendations, which were motivated not out of any belief on the part of the Committee that fraud was rampant, but because they wanted to address and instil "public confidence" in the system (Ontario 1988: 384–86):

We have no evidence to suggest that fraud in the social assistance system is greater than it is in the tax system or the unemployment insurance system. Nevertheless, because public confidence in the social assistance system depends in large part on the belief that the funds are being well spent and that abuse is being kept to a minimum, we accept that some of the measures adopted to control social assistance fraud may need to be more extensive than they are in other systems. (Ontario 1988: 384)

Notably, however, the report identified adequacy of benefits as the "*single most important weapon in the fight against fraud in the system*" (Ontario 1988: 384).

Responding to the recommendations concerning "system integrity," Dianne Martin (1992) criticized the Committee for abandoning its own guiding principles, in particular its commitment to the creation of a welfare regime based on the dignity and autonomy of social assistance recipients. Martin (1992: 93) pointed out that the most reliable indicator (conviction rate) placed the incidence rate of welfare fraud in Ontario at less than 1 percent. She was particularly concerned about the disproportional criminalization and punitive treatment of women on welfare (Martin 1992: 91). The guiding sentencing principles stressed deterrence as "the paramount consideration" even where the case was "pitiful" (Martin 1992: 66; see also *R. v. Thurrott* 1971; Carruthers 1995). Deterrence continues to be "the paramount consideration" a judge should take into account when determining the appropriate sentence for welfare fraud (See *R. v. Collins* 2011; *R. v. Allan* 2008).

From an almost insignificant place in *Transitions*, the fight against welfare fraud emerged as a centrepiece of provincial welfare policy in Ontario during the 1990s, irrespective of governing political party (see Moscovitch 1997; Little 1998: 139–63; Morrison 1995). However, in the implementation of their election platform, "The Common Sense Revolution," the Conservatives under Premier Mike Harris introduced changes that were more neo-liberal than conservative (see Cossman 2002; Coulter 2009; Maki 2011: 50), including the most draconian welfare reforms of any Canadian province.[9] Taking their cue from the Klein administration in Alberta (see Denis 1995; Kline 1997), the Harris government made welfare — and in particular a vow to "crack down" on "fraud" — the core of its welfare policy (Ontario 2000a, 1999).

Almost immediately after its election in 1995, the Harris government implemented a 22 percent cut to welfare rates and redefined (that is, expanded) the definition of spouse in welfare law in order to disentitle a range of previously entitled recipients (see Gavigan 1999; Mosher 2000). All of Canada's welfare poor live on incomes that are thousands of dollars below the poverty line, but in post-1995 Ontario the welfare-rate cut widened the "poverty gap" even further (NCW 2005: 87, Figure 5.2; see also Little 2001; McMullin, Davies, and Cassidy 2002). Between 1995 and 2004, the household income of a single employable recipient of social assistance in Ontario fell from 48 to 34 percent of the federal government's low-income cut-off measure; the income of a single parent with one child dropped from 76 to 56 percent of the poverty line; and the income of a couple with two children on welfare fell from 67 to 50 percent of the poverty line (NCW 2005: 66, Table 5.1; see also Gavigan 1999: 212–13). Between 2004 and 2009, the household income of a single employable individual on social assistance in Ontario remained at 41 percent of the after-tax low-income cut-off. During this same time period, the income of a single parent with a child in Ontario rose from 69 to 77 percent of the low-income cut-off and the income of a couple with two children also rose from 59 to 65 percent of the low-income cut-off (NCW 2010: Table 13). Between 1990 and 2009, inflation increased by 45.9 percent. However, most welfare incomes in Canada did not increase at a similar rate. This left many people on welfare in Canada in worse positions than those who had received welfare decades earlier (NCW 2010: 8). Likewise, the impact of the expanded definition of spouse on single mothers was "devastating" (Little 2001: 27). In the eight months immediately following this reform, "more than 10,000 recipients were deemed ineligible under the new definition and cut off social assistance" (Little 2001: 26). Some 89 percent of those were women.

Further to these measures, the Harris government proudly announced its stance on welfare fraud: "The new zero tolerance policy is the first of its kind in Canada, and a key step in Ontario's welfare reforms."[10] Zero-tolerance meant permanent ineligibility for anyone convicted of welfare fraud, an exceptionally severe consequence given that the discourse and politics of welfare fraud have obscured the imprecision of what is considered to be fraud, and by whom. In Harris neo-liberal discourse, "fraud" came to encompass all forms of overpayments, whether resulting from administrative errors or not, including people in jail whose welfare should have been terminated upon incarceration, as well as formal fraud convictions. The government's own "Welfare Fraud Control Reports" tended to collapse categories, frequently failing to distinguish between benefit "reduction" and "termination," and the reasons therefore (see, for example, Ontario 2003). Yet, as the coroner who presided at the Kimberly Rogers inquest observed of the evidence that had been presented during the two months of hearings: "While overpayments are common, overpayments due to fraud are very uncommon" (Eden 2003). Indeed, research into abused women's experience of welfare within this discursive practice of welfare fraud (Mosher et al. 2004) as well as research into the nature and extent of welfare fraud (Mosher and Hermer 2005) reconfirms both the problem with definition and the sharp drop between "allegations" and actual convictions:

> The number of convictions [in Ontario] for 2001–02 (393 convictions) is roughly equivalent to 0.1 percent of the combined social assistance

caseload and one percent of the total number of allegations. Statistics from the Municipality of Toronto for 2001 provide a similar picture: *80 percent of 11,800 allegations made against recipients were found to be untrue, in 19 percent of the remaining allegations there was no intent to defraud,* 117 cases were referred to the Fraud Review unit, of these 116 were reviewed by a special review committee, 95 were referred on to the police and charges were laid or pending in 91 (less than one percent of the total allegations). (Mosher and Hermer 2005: 34; emphasis added)

One reason that 99 percent of the allegations of welfare fraud were unfounded may be that the "overwhelming majority of the $49 million [trumpeted in the Ontario Welfare Fraud Report for 2001–02 as going to undeserving recipients] can be attributed to errors, mistakes, oversights of one form or another, made by applicants and by administrators and not to fraud" (Mosher et al. 2004: 51).

The complexity of the rules and the reporting requirements facing welfare recipients have also become more difficult and intrusive in the time since the *Transitions* report was released (Morrison 1995: A12–A14; Mosher et al. 2004; Sossin 2004; Herd, Mitchell, and Lightman 2005), thereby increasing the likelihood that a recipient may unintentionally commit "fraud." As Lorne Sossin (2004) noted, the social assistance bureaucracy is so complex that it leads to a process of "bureaucratic disentitlement," whereby would-be recipients are denied benefits. For instance, the previous legislation permitted a welfare recipient to receive social assistance as well as an income-based student loan in order to attend college or university. However, as Kimberly Rogers learned, a change in the regulations ensured that a full-time student doing that runs the risk of a welfare fraud conviction (Keck 2002; MacKinnon and Lacey 2001; Ontario 2009).

Far from addressing a residual concern triggered by a few "cheats" (McKeever 1999: 261–70), policies of "enhanced verification," zero-tolerance, and permanent ineligibility illustrated a significant shift in the conceptualization of welfare. Along with ever more intrusive measures to ensure recipients' eligibility (Little 2001; Mosher 2014; Herd, Mitchell, and Lightman 2005), the Harris government created a snitch hotline to encourage the anonymous reporting of suspected fraud and abuse by neighbours. Rather than instilling public confidence in the social security system (Ontario 1988), these initiatives, which continue to the present day, encourage and maintain a lack of public confidence by conveying the impression that fraud was and is rampant, and that every person on welfare needs to be watched and reported on and tested.

The shift in the direction of increased surveillance and criminalization of welfare recipients — notably women on welfare — illustrates too that the coercive form of criminal law and the regulatory form of welfare law are inseparable. The Criminal

Code continues to be used to prosecute welfare recipients when fraud is suspected, and even "sincere, devoted mothers" like Donna Bond find themselves at risk of prosecution and conviction. Yet for all the heightened intensity and investigation of welfare fraud, the convictions boasted by the Ontario government in its own statistics have amounted to no more than 1.36 percent of the total number of welfare recipients in the province and less than 1 percent based on statistics from the National Council of Welfare (2005).[11]

WOMEN, WELFARE AND THE "NEVER DESERVING" POOR

Despite the contemporary shift in the prevailing mode of moral regulation, the welfare reforms of the 1990s did not mark a complete departure from past practices. On the contrary, Canadian welfare legislation and policy show important historical continuities (Abramovitz 1996; Little 1998; Mosher 2000). First, welfare policy has always been premised on the separation of the "deserving" from the "undeserving" poor. Second, the social support accorded to the deserving was, and continues to be, based on "the principle of less eligibility" — or the assumption that welfare recipients should not receive more money than the worst-paid worker in the labour force. Third, the "deserving" have always been at risk of falling into the ranks of the "undeserving." Single mothers on social assistance have been and are subjected to intrusive and "moral" surveillance of their homes, their cleanliness, their child-rearing abilities and their personal lives (Little 1998; see also Buchanan 1995: 33, 40; Mosher and Hermer 2005: 44; Mirchandani and Chan 2007: 52–53; Herd, Mitchell, and Lightman 2005). Fourth, there have long been criminal prosecutions for welfare fraud (Rachert 1990; Martin 1992: 52–97; Evans and Swift 2000).

What made the 1990s different from earlier times, then, was the ideological shift from welfare liberalism to neo-liberalism (see Stenson and Watt 1999; Clarke 2000). It was a shift that, however, still required a major state presence and resources. On one hand, the state was ideologically decentred but no less present (Denis 1995). The form of the state and its social policy shifted at the turn of the millennium; social programs designed to ameliorate or redistribute were eroded, laying bare a heightened state presence that continues to condemn and punish the poor. On the other hand, the effect of this ideological shift was a huge expansion in the category of "undeserving" poor. Virtually everyone is considered as "never deserving"; even those who do receive social assistance are viewed as temporary recipients who must demonstrate their willingness to work for welfare and who ultimately will be employed as a result of skills and experience gained through workfare and other government-subsidized programs.

Thus, lone-parent mothers who historically were more likely to be deemed "deserving" than were childless men and women are now no longer so "privileged"

(Buchanan 1995; Moscovitch 1997; Little 1998; Mortenson 1999; Mosher 2000; Swift and Birmingham 2000; Bashevkin 2002; Benshalom 2008; Crookshanks 2012), as even Canadian courts have begun to acknowledge that, as in *Falkiner v. Ontario* (2002: 504, para. 77), "the statistics unequivocally demonstrate that both women and single mothers are disproportionately adversely affected by the definition of spouse" in welfare law. As that case found, "Although women accounted for only 54% of those receiving social assistance and only 60% of single persons receiving social assistance, they accounted for nearly 90% whose benefits were terminated by the [new] definition of spouse" (p. 504, para. 77).

Similarly, Janet Mosher and her colleagues (2004: 56–59) found that welfare reforms have made women more vulnerable than ever to abusive men (see also NCW 2007; Brush 2011). Deep cuts to benefits increase women's dependence on material assistance from others to supplement their welfare cheques, and that assistance most often goes unreported. The expanded definition of spouse also makes it more likely that women will violate the "spouse in the house" rule. Abusive men take advantage of women's heightened vulnerability by reporting or threatening to report their current or past partners to welfare authorities, alleging fraud. As a result, women are trapped in abusive relationships. As one such woman said:

> *It was all to do with welfare. I just got into an abusive relationship that I could no longer get out of because now someone could accuse me of fraud.*
>
> *Um, it's like … if he gave me some money and we had an argument, he'd say something like, "I'm sure you didn't tell your worker that I gave you two hundred dollars the other day. You know, you could get in trouble for that."*
> (Cited in Mosher et al. 2004: 58)

Women face contradictory messages from "welfare-to-work" policies. Such policies simultaneously demand independence and self-sufficiency while at the same time requiring unquestioning obedience to welfare rules that preclude opportunities for long-term advancement (Crookshanks 2012; see also Gazso and Waldron 2009).

The contemporary expansion of the "undeserving poor" has required a massive redeployment but, arguably, not a reduction in the allocation of state resources to welfare. The downsizing of social assistance payments is accompanied by a concomitant increase in state-subsidized make-work and workfare programs that will ostensibly return participants to the labour force. There has also been a dramatic increase in the state-implemented technologies and programs aimed at ferreting out and punishing the "undeserving" poor (Mosher 2000; Swift and Birmingham 2000; Mosher et al. 2004; Savarese and Morton 2005; Gustafson 2009). For instance, the Harris Tories' lifetime ban following a conviction for welfare fraud ensured both a lifetime of (secondary) punishment (without parole) and unameliorated poverty.

The past and the present contexts in which welfare and welfare fraud are being framed, then, show important differences. We have witnessed a profound attack on the "social" — indeed, the erosion of social responsibility — and the "authoritarian" neo-liberal state is a key player in this attack. Despite the apparent transcendence of social relations and state forms (in favour of dispersed pluralities of power), moral regulation must be understood in relation to state and social policy.

MORAL REGULATION REVISITED

The increased emphasis on welfare and welfare fraud is tightly linked to the process of state reformation in liberal democracies. We concur with (moral regulation) scholars who argue that the success of the "new right" in Ontario and elsewhere cannot be reduced to economics and globalization. Rather, restructuring and the decline of the "social" must

> be understood in the context of a vast cultural offensive to transform society [in which] the ability to wield state power is essential ... Far from losing its sovereignty, the state reasserts its power over the lives of citizens ... It turns itself into the "authoritarian state," one of whose main characteristics is to usher in a new, more intense regime of moral regulation. (Denis 1995: 373; see also Hall 1988)

Again, as Hall (1980: 7) argued, the "legislation of consent" was shot through with contradictory tendencies, which made the "unity" of the various statutes involved "a necessarily complex one." Those contradictory tendencies are apparent in the welfare reform in Ontario and elsewhere during the 1980s and 1990s, a reform that restructured the relation between the two modes of moral regulation — self-regulation and compulsion. Specifically, the welfare reforms show a "double taxonomy" in the movement toward both expanded privatization and increased regulation. For one thing, they show the intensified individualization of poverty through the emphasis on personal responsibility, the imposition of self-reliance, and the relegation of former welfare recipients to the market (see also Cossman 2002; Benshalom 2008). The slight and grudging acknowledgement of social responsibility for the poor that marked the Keynesian state was rescinded. Now, as in the nineteenth century, poverty is a problem of individuals in civil society, and the solution to poverty is an individualized matter to be found principally in the labour market and/or marriage.[12]

This intensified individualization of poverty has major implications for lone-parent women. Historically, the "deserving" mother on welfare may have been "hapless" (Evans and Swift 2000) and "pitied, but not entitled" (Gordon 1994), but she was also a public servant of sorts so long as she was considered to be (morally) fit. The entry of both married and single women into the labour market altered the prevalent norm about the legitimacy of women's unemployment. After the welfare reforms of the 1990s, the necessity of the functions performed by mothers and housewives was no longer considered a reason for women to fail to attain economic self-sufficiency (Benshalom 2008). During the 1990s, Ontario and other governments began divesting themselves of public servants, including "welfare moms," and placed the emphasis on creating choices to work and become self-sufficient. Now work is strictly confined to the (private) market, and mother work no longer receives even the tacit recognition that it was accorded by Keynesian states. The promotion of individual responsibility and self-reliance and the equation of work with paid, private-sector employment are very clear in the statement of key principles underpinning Ontario's reformed welfare system: "Doing nothing on welfare is no longer an option ... Participation [in Ontario Works] is mandatory for all able-bodied people, including sole-support parents with school-aged children" (Ontario 2000b; see also Lalonde 1997).

Defining work as paid employment means that women who do unpaid work can no longer be dependent on the state, but they can work for welfare or be dependent on an individually responsible, self-reliant, employed spouse. The Harris government underscored this point by refining and expanding the "spouse in the house" rule on the ground that "no one deserves higher benefits just because they are not married."[13] In the decade or more after Mike Harris left power, the Liberal government refused to narrow the definition of spouse that was legislated by the previous government. Thus, while "welfare dependency" became a form of personality disorder signifying inadequacy, and was "diagnosed more frequently in females" (Fraser and Gordon 1994: 326), the "approved" alternative, or perhaps supplement, to the market for lone-parent women is marriage and the family (Murray 1990). As Segal points out: "This is why single mothers can be demonized if they *don't* work, even while married women with young children can be demonized if they *do*" (Segal 1999: 206). The "spouse in the house" rule also implicitly suggests that if a mother appears to be partnered with a male outside of legal marriage, she is not perceived as conforming with the moral code of the mother as caretaker (Gazso 2012).

Concomitant with the emphasis on an intensified individualization of poverty is the intensified state regulation and surveillance of dwindling numbers of public welfare recipients, now redefined as individuals who need "temporary financial assistance ... while they satisfy obligations to becoming and staying employed" (Ontario Works Act 1997, s. 1). Since welfare "is temporary, not permanent," according to the Ontario Works Act (s. 1), the state must ensure that public money is not being wasted on "fraudsters." The Ontario legislation invokes the neo-liberal language of self-reliance through employment, temporary financial assistance, efficient delivery and accountability to taxpayers.[14] While pouring extensive resources into the establishment of an elaborate and constantly expanding system of surveillance aimed at detecting and preventing fraud and misuse of the social assistance system, and concomitant with massive cuts to welfare rates, the government allocated considerable money for special staff with expanded powers to investigate welfare fraud: three hundred such investigators were hired in 1998–99 and the government later provided "additional funding for up to 100 more staff to do this work" (Ontario 2000b). Similarly, government resources were needed to create and maintain the Welfare Fraud Hotline and a province-wide Welfare Fraud Control Database, to implement biometric finger-scanning (Little 2001: 26) and to prosecute alleged "fraudsters." Clearly, the state will spend considerable public money to police welfare recipients — but not to provide for them.

If we move beyond what government authorities themselves say, it becomes evident that the moralization and criminalization of the poor in general and "welfare moms" in particular are far from seamless. Contradictions are evident both among those who apply welfare law and policy and among those who are the targets of moralization. Judicial decision-making, for instance, is not uniformly punitive in cases involving mothers charged with welfare fraud. Some criminal cases in which women were convicted of welfare fraud for "spouse in the house," and hence of not living as a single person, do illustrate the neo-liberal ideological shift from bad mothers to bad choices (see *R. v. Plemel* 1995; *R. v. Jantunen* 1994; *R. v. Slaght* 1995; and *R. v. Sim* 1980)

But not every woman charged with welfare fraud is convicted, or if convicted, sent to jail. Some judges go to lengths to ensure this. Donna Bond received a conditional discharge, fifty hours of community service, and six months' probation, all of which left her without a criminal record upon successful completion of the conditions.[15] In another Ontario case, Trainor J. refused to convict a battered woman for welfare fraud (*R. v. Lalonde* 1995; see also Carruthers 1995). Finally, the coroner's jury at the inquest into the house-arrest death of Kimberly Rogers made fourteen recommendations aimed at eliminating or softening the harsh welfare reforms that were implemented in Ontario during the 1990s.[16]

Recent case law suggests that some judges continue to be sympathetic to some individuals who are charged with welfare fraud. In *R. v. Wilson* (2005), Michelle Wilson received a conditional discharge and eighteen months' probation after she was charged with welfare fraud. Wilson had falsely reported that she was living with her parents and had also not disclosed the existence of student loans. Wilson was a single mother who had been able to obtain two Bachelor of Arts degrees and was working toward a Master's degree. Conditional discharges have been given to those who used welfare money to improve their current situation or if a conviction would undermine a person's current situation (*R. v. Ahmed* 2005; *R. v. Bjorn* 2004). Those who engage in blatantly fraudulent behaviour or who have used the welfare funds solely to augment their financial status usually face incarceration (*R. v. Collins* 2011; *R. v. McCloy* 2008; *R. v. Allan* 2008). In a similar trend in the United States, among persons charged with welfare fraud, those who succeed in becoming independent of state assistance are praised by judges and receive more lenient sentences (Kimmel 2007).

Accounts of "welfare mothers" also reveal diversity in practices among financial aid and front-line workers (Mortenson 1999). Some workers are empathetic and supportive; in *Lalonde*, for instance, welfare authorities had acquiesced to the man's presence in the home and only charged the woman after her partner "self-reported" his presence (*R. v. Lalonde* 1995). Others are punitive and controlling of their "clients" (Little 2001; Mosher et al. 2004; Powers 2005). Likewise, the poor, including "welfare mothers," are far from constituting a homogeneous category (Swift and Birmingham 2000; see also Gavigan 1999: 213–18). While welfare recipients arguably have a common class position, the ways in which they acquire that class position are diverse and mediated by other social relations of gender, race, sexual orientation and ability or disability that in turn influence how and the extent to which mothers on welfare, for instance, are active agents in shaping these relations.

In 2006 the overall poverty rate in Canada was 11 percent; for racialized persons the poverty rate was 22 percent (NCW 2006). With regard to labour-market participation, racialized Ontarians are far more likely to live in poverty, to face workplace barriers, and, when they have found employment, to earn less than the rest of Ontarians (Block 2010: 3). Furthermore, the disparate experiences of different racialized groups and poverty are missing in both academic literature and society at large (Gazso and Waldron 2009; Quadagno 2000). Indeed, the ways in which race and ethnicity influence a person's susceptibility to, and experience of, poverty call for examination — with a need also to question how factors such as race influence attitudes toward redistributive policies such as welfare. For example, research suggests that support for redistribution is lower when recipients are portrayed as Aboriginals (Harell, Soroka, and Ladner 2013).

Many women live in constant fear of scrutiny that may result in the loss of welfare assistance for not reporting income, having partners stay overnight, or being reported for child abuse and losing their children (Mortenson 1999: 122–23; Little 1998, 2001; *Falkiner v. Ontario* 2002: 515, paras. 103, 104). As a result, they engage in continual "self-censorship" of their activities (Little 1998: 180). Others resist or challenge welfare law and policy through the establishment of and participation in informal support networks of "welfare moms" and/or anti-poverty agencies and organizations (Buchanan 1995; Little 1998; Mortenson 1999). A significant component of neo-liberal welfare reform in Ontario was the overhauling of the social assistance administrative regime. Since the late 1990s, the social assistance administrative regime has been heavily, often intrusively, involved in the day-to-day lives of welfare recipients. The experience of welfare in Ontario is described by welfare recipients as dehumanizing, degrading and demoralizing (Herd, Mitchell, and Lightman 2005: 73).

Interview studies also reveal ideological contradictions among "welfare mothers." A few espouse the social Darwinism of neo-liberal law and policy. They see themselves as short-term, "deserving" welfare recipients who through workfare programs and/or their own hard work will become "contributing" members of society again (Mortenson 1999; see also Seccombe, James, and Walters 1998). Some also feel resentful of and more "deserving" than other mothers on welfare, who they believe are "faring better in the distribution of scarce resources, including jobs" (Swift and Birmingham 2000: 94–95). In contrast, others strongly reject the neo-liberal thrust of welfare legislation and policy, equating workfare programs and the rationales for them as government propaganda. One woman interviewed by Melanie Mortenson said she went to a workplace orientation and found that "it was unbelievably stupid." She added: "You have to be gung ho about making nothing and not getting any benefits or security, is basically what they're telling you in so many words ... It's a cheap labour strategy" (cited in Mortenson 1999: 66).

The regulation/deregulation contradiction in the area of welfare legislation and policy reforms aimed at the poor should also be viewed in the context of government actions related to the welfare of the affluent and the regulation of capital. Increased criminalization and punishment of welfare fraud have occurred simultaneously with the deregulation and "disappearance" of corporate crime (Snider 1999; see also Pearce and Tombs 1998: 567–75; Tombs 2002; Glasbeek 2002). Massive welfare cuts targeting poor people are implemented at the same time as huge corporate tax cuts, which, together with direct fiscal subsidies, arguably are forms of social welfare for the rich (see, for example, Young 2000; Abramovitz 2001; Klein and Long 2003). The deregulation and de facto decriminalization of corporate wrongdoing benefit a minority of (primarily) affluent white men, while the criminalization of poverty and the intensified prosecution of welfare fraud punish the poor disproportionately (see Beckett and Western 2001).

As Laureen Snider (2006: 205) points out, the disappearance of corporate crime does matter:

> Abandoning state sanctions has far-reaching symbolic and practical consequences. State laws are public statements that convey important public messages about the obligations of the employer classes ... The situation is paradoxical indeed: while crimes of the powerful were never

effectively sanctioned by state law, such laws are nonetheless essential to the operation of democratic societies.

The concomitant deregulation of corporate crime and increased punitiveness toward welfare fraud (and "street crime" more generally) suggest that in an authoritarian form of liberal-democratic state, government interventionism is redirected, not eliminated (Denis 1995: 368; see also Hall 1988). State withdrawal from Keynesian social programs and the economy occurs in tandem with government activism around issues such as youth crime and "terrorism" (Denis 1995: 369; see also Hermer and Mosher 2002). This shift in the focus of state interventionism has important implications for the regulation of the poor, and in particular, of lone-parent women.

"A BAD TIME TO BE POOR"

The reformed mode of moral regulation in Canada and elsewhere during the late twentieth century typified the reformed relationship between public and private under neo-liberalism. In Keynesian states a prevailing ideology of welfare liberalism provided a rationale for at least limited (public) state intervention to assist the "deserving" poor. In "authoritarian" neo-liberal states, a discursive shift to an emphasis on formal equality (sameness) has informed a new rationale for valorizing the (private) market as the only solution to poverty. As a result, to protect the public purse, anyone who asks for state assistance must be scrutinized carefully, and welfare can only be a stopgap measure prior to the recipients' entry into paid employment. Therefore, while non-state practices play a role in moral regulation, the state clearly continues to be a major player as well.

The ideological and discursive shifts from welfare liberalism to neo-liberalism have also had a drastic material impact. They have exacerbated the poverty of all welfare recipients, but particularly lone-parent women who historically were among the most "deserving." In some contemporary moral regulation scholarship, "poverty" is a discursive construct displacing the class analysis that characterized the Marxian-informed literature of the early 1980s (Corrigan and Sayer 1981, 1985; Hall 1980). Our analysis of the shift from welfare fraud to welfare *as* fraud supports those who continue to argue for the interconnectedness of the material, social and cultural and the need to look at the political and economic issues of redistribution as well as identity/self-formation (Fraser 1997; see also Roberts 1997; Segal 1999).

In the first decade of the twenty-first century, welfare law and policy shifted again, away from the excesses of the 1990s toward arguably more "humane" treatment of the poor. The moral regulation of the poor under neo-liberalism is not uniformly oppressive: courts sometimes refuse to convict, and some welfare workers are empathetic. In the decade following the neo-liberal welfare reforms, some governments even proclaimed a "kinder, gentler" approach to the poor. Following the election of the Ontario Liberals in 2003, for instance, Sandra Pupatello, the new minister of community and social services, said that the Harris Tories had treated people on welfare as "a typical punching bag," and she expressed the new government's commitment to a "series of reforms" so that "the system actually works for people."[17] The Liberal government subsequently eliminated the lifetime ban, increased welfare rates by 3 percent, and implemented several of the forty-nine recommendations contained in a government-commissioned report on ways of improving the province's welfare system (Matthews 2004).

After 2003, under a Liberal government, social assistance rates rose by 15 percent (Ontario 2013). However, these welcome changes did not substantially ameliorate the effects of the harsh welfare reforms of the late 1990s and early 2000s. The new Ontario government failed to heed calls for meaningful policy change to social assistance and obfuscated the severity and existence of gender and economic inequality (Coulter 2009).

Following the Liberal party's re-election in 2011, a commission was struck to investigate the social assistance system in Ontario. In 2012 the Commission for the Review of Social Assistance released its report, *Brighter Prospects: Transforming Social Assistance in Ontario*, recommending that the bureaucratic structure be simplified. Specifically, it recommended the elimination of half the rules and directives in the system (Ontario 2012: 17). The Commission also called for changes to the definition of spouse, stating that the spousal relationship definition should be altered to include two people who have lived together for at least one year (and not three months) (Ontario 2012: 22). By 2014, the Liberal government had failed to heed these two recommendations, which, if put into action, would enable women who need social assistance to navigate the system without unnecessary stress or indignity.

In the 2013 budget the Liberal government introduced a number of changes to social assistance, which it said were made to remove barriers and increase opportunities for workplace participation (Ontario 2013). Some of the changes would be beneficial for recipients of Ontario Works and the Ontario Disability Support Program (ODSP). Recipients would be able to keep the first $200 of employment earnings each month before their social assistance benefits were reduced (Ontario 2013). However, the 2013 Ontario budget changes were insufficient to address the severity of the problems that continue to plague welfare recipients (Income Security Advocacy Centre 2013).

Despite attempts to improve the state of the social assistance regime — and although the *Matthews Report* (Matthews 2004) incorporated the views of some low-income people and their advocates[18] — the Liberals did not follow up immediately with measures that would fundamentally alter the legacy of the Harris Tories.

While the Liberal government was much less focused on criminalizing welfare than was its predecessor in power, it did not make changes that would improve a welfare scheme that consistently fails those who need it. The new mode of moral regulation exemplified by the conceptualization of welfare *as* fraud remains in place. Early on, the Liberal government stated its commitment to "no tolerance" for welfare fraud (see Galloway 2004: A9).

Likewise, the Liberal government retained the conviction of successive governments that "employment provides an escape out of poverty," an especially problematic assertion "in the context of a labour market that is characterized by precarious, low-waged work" (Income Security Advocacy Centre 2005: 6). The "Great Recession" of 2008 further intensified pre-existing labour market problems with regard to employment prospects for welfare recipients. There have been less employment prospects for *all* Canadians. In times of declining economic growth, as there is less economic surplus to be distributed and lower levels of well-being, there is an increased risk that families at the lower end of the income distribution will fall into poverty (Quadagno 2000). The assertion that "employment provides an escape out of poverty" is also questionable given that additional factors such as gender or race can act as barriers to employment. For example, systemic discrimination in our society and institutions creates barriers of access, limited mobility and disproportionate concentrations of racialized labour in part-time and temporary employment (Pruegger, Cook, and Richter-Salomons 2009).

The overweening focus on paid employment militates against any significant increase in what the Liberal government has acknowledged are "unacceptably low" rates of assistance (Income Security Advocacy Centre 2005: 8). In 2013, Minister of Community and Social Services Ted McMeekin stated at a community consultation: "If it were up to me, I would raise social assistance rates by a lot more than $100. But it's not up to me" (Addison-Webster 2013). The benefits are so low that those on social assistance live below the poverty line "in a constant state of economic precariousness" (Income Security Advocacy Centre 2008). It is still "a bad time to be poor" (Klein and Long 2003), especially for the many lone-parent women and their children who have been relegated to the ranks of the "never deserving."

Notes

This chapter is a revised, edited version of Chunn and Gavigan 2004. We are indebted to and acknowledge with thanks Elizabeth Mullock (Osgoode JD 2013) for her excellent research assistance for the revisions. We also thank Elizabeth Comack, Gillian Balfour and Steve Bittle for their comments, and Laura Lunansky and Yui Funayama for research assistance on the earlier version of this chapter.

1   General Welfare Assistance Act, R.S.O. 1990, c. G.6, as rep. by Social Assistance Reform

Act, 1997, S.O. 1997, c. 25 enacting Ontario Works Act, 1997, S.O. 1997, c. 25, s. 1 [OWA] and Ontario Disability Support Program Act, 1997, S.O. c. 25, s. 2 [ODSPA]. The purpose of the Ontario Works legislation is to establish a program that, as expressed in s. 1:

(a) recognizes individual responsibility and promotes self-reliance through employment;

(b) provides temporary financial assistance to those most in need while they satisfy obligations to become and stay employed;

(c) effectively serves people needing assistance; and

(d) is accountable to the taxpayers of Ontario.

2   Ontario Works Act, 1997, O.Reg. 134/98, Reg. 33.

3   See Hermer and Mosher (2002) for commentary on Ontario's Safe Streets Act 1999, S.O. 1999, c. 8. This legislation renders illegal the street activity of "squeegee kids" and panhandlers.

4   Welfare recipients were then required to report annually on their circumstances, in order to ascertain continued eligibility for assistance. In Ontario financial eligibility is now "reverified" on at least an annual basis, and ongoing "verification" and reporting requirements have intensified. A recipient is obliged to self-report any change in circumstances immediately.

5   Ontario Works Act, 1997, O.Reg. 134/98, Reg. 9 (a) and (b), provide that no single person who is in full-time attendance at a post-secondary educational institution is eligible for assistance if the person is in receipt of a student loan or is ineligible for a student loan because of parental income.

6   The permanent ineligibility sections of the Regulations were repealed by O. Reg 456/03 made under the Ontario Works Act, 1997.

7   For a political economy approach to these issues, see Fudge and Cossman (2002).

8   The racist dimensions of welfare law should be emphasized. Historically, welfare legislation excluded (implicitly or explicitly) lone-parent, racialized and ethnic minority women. More recently, they have been disproportionately represented among the "undeserving" poor (see Roberts 1997; Chunn and Gavigan 2005).

9   See *Masse v. Ontario* (1996); *Rogers v. Sudbury* (2001); *Broomer v. Ontario* (2002).

10   Ontario Progressive Conservative government policy statement, Jan. 18, 2000, Ontario PC News and Headlines (mikeharrispc.com).

11   The statistics available from the Ontario Ministry of Community, Family and Children's Services reveal a steady decline in criminal convictions for welfare fraud: 1,123 in 1997–98; 747 in 1998–99; 547 in 1999–00; and 393 in 2001–02 (Ontario 1999, 2000a, 2000b, 2002, 2003: Table 1). With respect to the zero-tolerance lifetime ban, the Income Security Advocacy Centre reported that a total of 106 individuals became permanently ineligible to receive financial assistance due to welfare fraud offences committed between April 1, 2000 (when the ban took effect) and November 27, 2002 <www.incomesecurity.org>. See also Mirchandani and Chan (2007: 32), who note that there is a lack of reliable statistics both federally and provincially on the actual rates of welfare fraud.

12   This is illustrated clearly by the repeal of the General Welfare Act in Ontario, and the introduction in its place of Ontario Works legislation.

13 The Ontario Court of Appeal struck down this expanded definition of spouse for "its differential treatment of sole support mothers on the combined grounds of sex, marital status and receipt of social assistance, which discriminates against them contrary to s. 15 of the Charter" (*Falkiner v. Ontario* [2002]: 515 para. 105). Significantly, a person is deemed to be a spouse after three months' cohabitation; this is a much shorter time period of cohabitation (about two years and nine months shorter) than is required under Ontario's provincial family law legislation before spousal support obligations and entitlements are triggered.

14 See Ontario Works Act, 1997, s. 1 (a), (b), (c) and (d).

15 Sentencing took place on Sept. 19, 1994. *R. v. Bond* (1994) certificate of conviction (on file with the authors).

16 See "Verdict of Coroner's Jury into the Death of Kimberly Ann Rogers," released on Dec. 19, 2002. The coroner's inquest, which lasted two months, involved eight parties with standing, all represented by counsel, and forty-one witnesses. The jury heard that of the five thousand or so welfare recipients in Kimberly Rogers's home community of Sudbury, there were at most one or two convictions for welfare fraud annually. Evidence before the jury showed that "the Crown and the Courts were unaware that upon conviction the accused would be subject to a suspension of benefits." Recommendation 14 called for ongoing professional training of criminal justice personnel in this regard. The fourteen recommendations form part of a letter dated Jan. 17, 2003, sent by the presiding coroner, Dr. David S. Eden, to the chief coroner of Ontario (on file with the authors).

17 Ontario, Legislative Assembly, First Session, 38th Parliament, Official Debates (*Hansard*), no. 17A Wednesday Dec. 17, 2003, at 868.

18 Significantly, Aboriginal Peoples were not consulted about their social-service needs (Income Security Advocacy Centre 2005: 8).

References

Abramovitz, M. 1996. *Regulating the Lives of Women: Social Policy from Colonial Times to the Present* (second edition). Boston: South End Press.

____. 2001. "Everyone Is Still on Welfare: The Role of Distribution in Social Policy." *Social Work* 46, 4.

Addison-Webster, M. 2013. "Ted McMeekin Talks but Who Can Act on Social Assistance Rates?" *Toronto Star*, July 17. <thestar.com/opinion/commentary/2013/07/17/ted_mcmeekin_talks_but_who_can_act_on_social_assistance_rates.html>.

Bashevkin, S. 2002. *Welfare Hot Buttons: Women, Work, and Social Policy Reform.* Toronto: University of Toronto Press.

Beckett, K., and B. Western. 2001. "Governing Social Marginality: Welfare, Incarceration, and the Transformation of State Policy." *Punishment and Society* 3, 1.

Benshalom, I. 2008. "Regulating Work or Regulating Poverty: An Agenda of Inclusion or Exclusion in American Workplace Reform?" *Journal of Law and Equality* 6.

Block, S. 2010. *Ontario's Growing Gap: The Role of Race and Gender.* Ottawa: Canadian Center for Policy Alternatives.

Brush, L.D. 2011. *Poverty, Battered Women and Work in U.S. Public Policy.* New York: Oxford

University Press.

Buchanan, M. 1995. "The Unworthy Poor: Experiences of Single Mothers on Welfare in Chilliwack, British Columbia." M.A. thesis, Simon Fraser University, Burnaby.

Carruthers, E. 1995. "Prosecuting Women for Welfare Fraud in Ontario: Implications for Equality." *Journal of Law* and *Social Policy* 11.

Chunn, D.E., and S. Gavigan. 2005. "From Mother's Allowance to 'No Mothers Need Apply': Canadian Welfare Law as Liberal and Neo-Liberal Reforms." Presented at the Thirteenth Berkshire Conference on the History of Women (June). Claremont, CA.

Clarke, J. 2000. "Unfinished Business? Struggles over the Social in Social Welfare." In P. Gilroy, L. Grossberg, and A. McRobbie (eds.), *Without Guarantees: In Honour of Stuart Hall*. London: Verso.

Corrigan, P., and D. Sayer. 1981. "How the Law Rules: Variations on Some Themes in Karl Marx." In B. Fryer et al. (eds.), *Law, State, and Society*. London: Croom Helm.

_____. 1985. *The Great Arch: English State Formation as Cultural Revolution*. London: Basil Blackwell.

Cossman, B. 2002. "Family Feuds: Neo-Liberal and Neo-Conservative Visions of the Reprivatization Project." In B. Cossman and J. Fudge (eds.), *Privatization, Law, and the Challenge to Feminism*. Toronto: University of Toronto Press.

Coulter, K. 2009. "Women, Poverty Policy and the Production of Neoliberal Politics in Ontario Canada." *Journal of Women, Politics and Policy* 30.

Crookshanks, R. 2012. "Marginalization through a Custom of Deservingness: Sole-Support Mothers and Welfare Law in Canada." *Review of Current Law and Law Reform* 17.

Dean, M. 1994. "'A Social Structure of Many Souls': Moral Regulation, Government and Self-Formation." *Canadian Journal of Sociology* 19, 2.

_____. 1999. *Governmentality: Power and Rule in Modern Society*. London: Sage Publications.

Denis, C. 1995. "'Government Can Do Whatever It Wants': Moral Regulation in Ralph Klein's Alberta." *Canadian Review of Sociology and Anthropology* 32, 3.

Eden, Dr. D.S. 2003. Letter to Chief Coroner of Ontario re: Inquest into the Death of Kimberly Rogers. (Letter on file with D.E. Chunn and S.A.M. Gavigan).

Evans, P., and K. Swift. 2000. "Single Mothers and the Press: Rising Tides, Moral Panic, and Restructuring Discourses." In Sheila M. Neysmith (ed.), *Restructuring Caring Labour*. Toronto: Oxford University Press.

Fraser, N. 1997. *Justice Interruptus: Critical Reflections on the "Postsocialist" Condition*. New York: Routledge.

Fraser, N., and L. Gordon. 1994. "A Genealogy of Dependency: Tracing a Keyword of the U.S. Welfare State." *Signs* 19, 2.

Fudge, J., and B. Cossman. 2002. "Introduction: Privatization, Law and the Challenge to Feminism." In B. Cossman, and J. Fudge (eds.), *Privatization, Law and the Challenge to Feminism*. Toronto: University of Toronto Press.

Galloway, G. 2004. "Liberals Scrap Lifetime Ban for Those Who Cheat Welfare System." *Globe and Mail*, January 10.

Gavigan, S.A.M. 1999. "Poverty Law, Theory and Practice: The Place of Class and Gender in Access to Justice." In E. Comack (ed.), *Locating Law: Race/Class/Gender Connections*. Halifax: Fernwood Publishing.

_____. 2012. *Hunger, Horses, and Government Men: Criminal Law on the Aboriginal Plains.*

Vancouver: UBC Press.

Gavigan, S.A.M., and D.E. Chunn (eds.). 2007. "From Mothers' Allowance to Mothers Need Not Apply: Canadian Welfare Law as Liberal and Neo-Liberal Reforms." *Osgoode Hall Law Journal* 45.

____. 2010. *The Legal Tender of Gender: Law, Welfare, and the Legal Regulation of Women's Poverty.* Oxford: Hart Publishing.

Gazso, A. 2012. "Moral Codes of Mothering and the Introduction of Welfare-to-Work in Ontario." *Canadian Review of Sociology* 49.

Gazso, A., and I. Waldron. 2009. "Fleshing Out the Racial Undertones of Poverty for Canadian Women and Their Families: Re-envisioning a Critical Integrative Approach." *Atlantis* 34.

Glasbeek, H. 2002. *Wealth by Stealth: Corporate Crime, Corporate Law, and the Perversion of Democracy.* Toronto: Between the Lines.

Golding, P., and S. Middleton. 1982. *Images of Welfare: Press and Public Attitudes to Poverty.* Oxford: Martin Robertson.

Gordon, L. 1994. *Pitied But Not Entitled: Single Mothers and the History of Welfare.* Cambridge: Harvard University Press.

Gustafson, K. 2009. "The Criminalization of Poverty." *Journal of Criminal Law and Criminology* 99.

Hall, S. 1980. "Reformism and the Legislation of Consent." In National Deviancy Conference (ed.), *Permissiveness and Control: The Fate of the Sixties Legislation.* London: Macmillan.

____. 1988. "The Toad in the Garden: Thatcherism among the Theorists." In C. Nelson and L. Grossberg (eds.), *Marxism and the Interpretation of Culture.* Champaign: University of Illinois Press.

Harell, A., S. Soroka, and K. Ladner. 2013. "Public Opinion, Prejudice and the Racialization of Welfare in Canada." *Ethnic and Racial Studies.*

Herd, D., A. Mitchell, and E. Lightman. 2005. "Rituals of Degradation: Administration as Policy in the Ontario Works Programme." *Social Policy and Administration* 39.

Hunt, A. 1997. "Moral Regulation and Making-up the New Person: Putting Gramsci to Work." *Theoretical Criminology* 1, 3.

____. 1999a. "The Purity Wars: Making Sense of Moral Militancy." *Theoretical Criminology* l3, 4.

____. 1999b. *Governing Morals: A Social History of Moral Regulation.* Cambridge: Cambridge University Press.

____. 2002. "Regulating Heterosocial Space: Sexual Politics in the Early Twentieth Century." *Journal of Historical Sociology* 15, 1.

Income Security Advocacy Centre. 2005. *The Matthews Report: Moving Towards Real Income Security.* Toronto.

____. 2008. *Rethinking the Role of Social Assistance within a Poverty Reduction Strategy: A Submission to the Cabinet Committee for Poverty Reduction.* Toronto.

____. 2013. *Budget 2013 Analysis: Moving Forward on Social Assistance Reform.* Toronto.

Keck, J. 2002. "Remembering Kimberly Rogers." *Perception* 25.

Kimmel, E. 2007. "Welfare Law, Necessity and Moral Judgment." *Rutgers Journal of Law and Public Policy* 4.

Klein, S., and A. Long. 2003. *A Bad Time to Be Poor: An Analysis of British Columbia's New*

Welfare Policies. Vancouver: Canadian Centre for Policy Alternatives-B.C.

Kline, M. 1997. "Blue Meanies in Alberta: Tory Tactics and the Privatization of Child Welfare." In S.B. Boyd (ed.), *Challenging the Public Private Divide: Feminism, Law and Public Policy.* Toronto: University of Toronto Press.

Lalonde, L. 1997. "Tory Welfare Policies: A View from the Inside." In D. Ralph et al. (eds.), *Open for Business, Closed for People: Mike Harris's Ontario.* Halifax: Fernwood Publishing.

Little, M. 1998. *No Car, No Radio, No Liquor Permit: The Moral Regulation of Single Mothers in Ontario, 1920–1997.* Toronto: Oxford University Press.

____. 2001. "A Litmus Test for Democracy: The Impact of Ontario Welfare Changes on Single Mothers." *Studies in Political Economy* 66.

____. 2003. "The Leaner, Meaner Welfare Machine: The Ontario Conservative Government's Ideological and Material Attack on Single Mothers." In D. Brock, (ed.), *Making Normal: Social Regulation in Canada.* Scarborough: Nelson Thompson Learning.

____. 2005. *If I Had a Hammer: Retraining That Really Works.* British Columbia: UBC Press.

MacKinnon, M., and K. Lacey. 2001. "Bleak House." *Globe and Mail,* August 18.

Maki, K. 2011. "Neoliberal Deviants and Surveillance: Welfare Recipients under the Watchful Eye of Ontario Works." *Surveillance and Society* 9.

Martin, D. 1992. "Passing the Buck: Prosecution of Welfare Fraud; Preservation of Stereotypes." *Windsor Yearbook of Access to Justice* 12.

____. 2002. "Both Pitied and Scorned: Child Prostitution in an Era of Privatization." In B. Cossman and J. Fudge (eds.), *Privatization, Law and the Challenge to Feminism.* Toronto: University of Toronto Press.

Matthews, D. 2004. "Review of Employment Assistance Programs in Ontario Works and Ontario Disability Support Program." Report to The Honourable Sandra Pupatello, Minister of Community and Social Services. <mcss.gov.on.ca/documents/en/mcss/social/publications/EmploymentAssistanceProgram_Matthews_eng1.pdf>.

McKeever, G. 1999. "Detecting, Prosecuting, and Punishing Benefit Fraud: The Social Security Administration (Fraud) Act 1997." *Modern Law Review* 62, 2.

McMullin, J., L. Davies, and G. Cassidy. 2002 "Welfare Reform in Ontario: Tough Times in Mothers' Lives." *Canadian Public Policy* 28, 2.

Misra, J., S. Moller, and M. Karides. 2003. "Envisioning Dependency: Changing Media Depictions of Welfare in the 20th Century." *Social Problems* 50, 4.

Mirchandani, K., and W. Chan. 2007. *Criminalizing Race, Criminalizing Poverty.* Halifax: Fernwood Publishing.

Morrison, I. 1995. "Facts About the Administration of Social Assistance/UI that Criminal Lawyers Need to Know." In *Charged with Fraud on Social Assistance: What Criminal Lawyers Need to Know.* Department of Continuing Legal Education, Law Society of Upper Canada, March 25 [unpublished].

____. 1998. "Ontario Works: A Preliminary Assessment." *Journal of Law and Social Policy* 13.

Morrison, I., and G. Pearce. 1995. "Under the Axe: Social Assistance in Ontario in 1995." *Journal of Law and Social Policy* 11.

Mortenson, M. 1999. "B.C. Benefits Whom? Motherhood, Poverty, and Social Assistance Legislation in British Columbia." M.A. thesis, Simon Fraser University, Burnaby.

Moscovitch, A. 1997. "Social Assistance in the New Ontario." In D. Ralph, A. Régimbald, and N. St-Amand (eds.), *Mike Harris's Ontario: Open for Business, Closed to People.*

Halifax: Fernwood Publishing.

Mosher, J. 2000. "Managing the Disentitlement of Women: Glorified Markets, the Idealized Family, and the Undeserving Other." In S.M. Neysmith (ed.), *Restructuring Caring Labour*. Toronto: Oxford University Press.

____. 2006. "The Construction of 'Welfare Fraud' and the Wielding of the State's Iron Fist." In E. Comack (ed.), *Locating Law: Race/Class/Gender/Sexuality Connections* (second edition). Halifax: Fernwood Publishing.

____. 2014. "The Construction of 'Welfare Fraud' and the Wielding of the State's Iron Fist." In E. Comack (ed.), *Locating Law: Race/Class/Gender/Sexuality Connections* (third edition). Halifax and Winnipeg: Fernwood Publishing.

Mosher, J., P. Evans, M. Little, E. Morrow, J. Boulding, and N. Vanderplaats. 2004. *Walking on Eggshells; Abused Women's Experiences of Ontario's Welfare System: Final Report on the Research Findings on the Woman and Abuse Welfare Research Project*. Toronto: Osgoode Hall Law School. <yorku.ca/yorkweb/special/Welfare_Report_walking_on_eggshells_final_report.pdf>

Mosher, J., and J. Hermer. 2005. *Welfare Fraud: The Constitution of Social Assistance as Crime*. A Report Prepared for the Law Commission of Canada (July). Ottawa: Law Commission of Canada.

Murray, C., 1990. *The Emerging Underclass*. London: Institute of Economic Affairs.

NCW (National Council of Welfare). 2005. *Welfare Incomes 2004*. Ottawa: Minister of Public Works and Government Services Canada. (NCW Reports #123).

____. 2006. *Poverty Profile: Special Edition*. Ottawa: Minister of Public Works and Government Services Canada.

____. 2007. *First Nations, Métis and Inuit Children and Youth: Time to Act*. Ottawa: Minister of Public Works and Government Services Canada (NCW Reports # 127).

____. 2010. *Welfare Incomes 2009*. Ottawa: Minister of Public Works and Government Services Canada (NCW Reports #123).

Ontario. 1988. *Transitions: Report of the Social Assistance Review Committee* (SARC Report). Toronto: Queen's Printer.

____. 1999. *Welfare Fraud Control Report, 1997–98*. Ministry of Community and Social Services. Toronto: Queen's Printer.

____. 2000a. *Welfare Fraud Control Report, 1998–99*. Ministry of Community and Social Services. Toronto: Queen's Printer.

____. 2000b. *Making Welfare Work: Report to Taxpayers on Welfare Reform*. Ministry of Community and Social Services. Toronto: Queen's Printer.

____. 2002. Verdict of the Coroner's Jury into the Death of Kimberly Ann Rogers, held at Sudbury, Ontario. Office of the Chief Coroner.

____. 2003. *Welfare Fraud Control Report 2001–2002*, Table 1. Ministry of Community, Family and Children's Services. Toronto: Queen's Printer.

____. 2009. *Ontario Works Policy Directives*. Toronto: Queen's Printer.

____. 2012. *Brighter Prospects: Transforming Social Assistance in Ontario*. Commission for the Review of Social Assistance in Ontario. Toronto: Queen's Printer.

____. 2013. *News Release: Improving Social Assistance*. Toronto: Ministry of Community and Social Services.

Pearce, F., and S. Tombs. 1998. *Toxic Capitalism: Corporate Crime and the Chemical Industry*.

Aldershot: Ashgate and Dartmouth.

Powers, E. 2005. "The Unfreedom of Being Other: Canadian Lone Mothers' Experiences of Poverty and Life on the Cheque." *Sociology* 39.

Pruegger, V., D. Cook, and S. Richter-Salomons. 2009. *Inequality in Calgary: The Racialization of Poverty*. Calgary: City of Calgary Community and Neighbourhood Services—Social Research Unit.

Quadagno, J. 2000. "Another Face of Inequality: Racial and Ethnic Exclusion in the Welfare State." *Social Politics* 7.

Rachert, J. 1990. "Welfare Fraud and the State: British Columbia 1970–1977." M.A. thesis, Simon Fraser University, Burnaby.

Roberts, D. 1997. *Killing the Black Body: Race, Reproduction, and the Meaning of Liberty*. New York: Pantheon.

Savarese, J., and B. Morton. 2005. *Women and Social Assistance Policy in Saskatchewan and Manitoba*. Winnipeg: Prairie Women's Health Centre of Excellence.

Seccombe, K., D. James, and K. Walters. 1998. "'They Think You Ain't Much of Nothing': The Social Construction of the Welfare Mother." *Journal of Marriage and the Family* 60.

Segal, L. 1999. *Why Feminism? Gender, Psychology, Politics*. New York: Columbia University Press.

Sossin, L. 2004. "Boldly Going Where No Law Has Gone Before: Call Centres, Intake Scripts, Database Fields and Discretionary Justice in Social Assistance." *Osgoode Hall Law Journal* 42.

Snider, L. 1999. "Relocating Law: Making Corporate Crime Disappear." In Elizabeth Comack (ed.), *Locating Law: Race/Class/Gender Connections*. Halifax: Fernwood Publishing.

____. 2006. "Relocating Law: Making Corporate Crime Disappear." In E. Comack (ed.), *Locating Law: Race/Class/Gender/Sexuality Connections* (second edition). Halifax: Fernwood Publishing.

Strange, C., and T. Loo. 1997. *Making Good: Law and Moral Regulation in Canada*. Toronto: University of Toronto Press.

Stenson, K., and P. Watt. 1999. "Governmentality and 'the Death of the Social'? A Discourse Analysis of Local Government Texts in South-East England." *Urban Studies* 36, 1.

Swan, R., Linda L. Shaw, S. Cullity, J. Halpen, J. Humphrey, W. Limbert, and M. Roche. 2008. "The Untold Story of Welfare Fraud." *Journal of Sociology & Social Welfare* 35.

Swift, K., and M. Birmingham. 2000. "Location, Location, Location: Restructuring and the Everyday Lives of 'Welfare Moms.'" In S.M. Neysmith (ed.), *Restructuring Caring Labour*. Toronto: Oxford University Press.

Tombs, S. 2002. "Understanding Regulation?" *Social and Legal Studies* 11.

Valverde, M. 1998. *Diseases of the Will: Alcohol and the Dilemmas of Freedom*. Cambridge: Cambridge University Press.

____. 1995. "The Mixed Social Economy as a Canadian Tradition." *Studies in Political Economy* 47.

____. 1994. "Moral Capital." *Canadian Journal of Law and Society* 9.

____. 1991. *The Age of Light, Soap, and Water: Moral Reform in English Canada 1885–1925*. Toronto: McClelland and Stewart.

Valverde, M., and L. Weir. 1988. "The Struggles of the Immoral: Preliminary Remarks on

Moral Regulation." *Resources for Feminist Research* 17.

Weir, L. 1986. "Studies in the Medicalization of Sexual Danger: Sexual Rule, Sexual Politics, 1830–1930." Ph.D. dissertation, York University, Toronto.

Young, C. 2000. *Women, Tax and the Gendered Impact of Funding Social Programs Through the Tax System*. Ottawa: Status of Women Canada.

Cases Cited

Broomer v. Ontario (Attorney General), [2002] O.J. No 2196 (Ont. Sup Ct), online QL (OJ)

Falkiner v. Ontario (Ministry of Community and Social Services, Income Maintenance Branch), [2002] 59 OR *(3d)* 481, *[2002]* OJ No 1771 (Ont CA), online QL (OJ)

Masse v. Ontario (Ministry of Community and Social Services, Income Maintenance Branch), [1996] OJ No 363 (Ont Ct J (Gen Div)), online QL (OJ), leave to appeal denied, [1996] OJ No. 1526 (Ont CA), online (QL (OJ)

R. v. Ahmed, [2005] ABPC 38, [2005] AJ No 1112 (Alta Pro Ct), online QL

R. v. Allan, [2008] OJ No 2794 (Ont Supt Ct J), online QL (OJ)

R. v. Bond, [1994] OJ No 2185 (Ont Ct J (Gen Div)), online QL (OJ)

R. v. Bjorn, [2004] BCPC 127, [2004] BCJ No 1073 (BC Pro Ct) online QL

R. v. Collins, [2011] ONCA 182, [2011] 2 CNLR 256 (Ont CA), online QL (OJ)

R. v. Jantunen, [1994] OJ No 889 (Ont Ct (Gen Div)), online QL (OJ)

R. v. McCloy, [2008] ABPC 212, [2008] AJ No 1509 (Alta Pro Ct), online QL

R. v. Plemel, [1995] OJ No 4155 (Ont Ct (Gen Div)), online QL (OJ)

R. v. Sim, [1980] 63 CCC (2d) 376 (Ont Co Ct J (Cr Ct))

R. v. Slaght [1995] OJ No 4192 (Ont Ct (Gen Div)), online QL (OJ)

R. v. Thurrott, [1971] 5 CCC (2d) 129 (Ont CA)

R. v. Wilson, [2005] ONCJ 21, [2005] OJ No 382 (Ont Ct J), online QL (OJ)

Rogers v. Sudbury, [2001] 57 OR (3d) 460 (Ont Sup Ct)

Legislation Cited

General Welfare Assistance Act, RSO 1990, c G.6, as rep. by Social Assistance Reform Act, 1997, SO 1997, c 25 enacting Ontario Works Act, 1997, SO 1997, c 25, s.1 [OWA] and Ontario Disability Support Program Act, 1997, SO 1997 c. 25, s. 2 [ODSPA].

Chapter 13

DISCUSSIONS OF WELFARE FRAUD IN THE CANADIAN NEWS MEDIA

Kiran Mirchandani and Wendy Chan

From: *Criminalizing Race, Criminalizing Poverty: Welfare Fraud Enforcement in Canada*, pp. 22–44 (reprinted with permission).

Given the omnipresence of the media in our lives, their ability to educate, raise consciousness and influence attitudes is very powerful. The media maintain ritual order by acting as channels of connection between different parts of society (Carey 1989). This is particularly so in relation to public policy issues given that the public obtains information on policies primarily via the media (Falk 1994). The media are able to take an issue, intertwine it with ideological beliefs and portray ideas in ways that make them appear "natural" or commonsensical. Carey (1989) suggests that we need to understand the role the media play in representing shared beliefs through not only bringing people together and harmonizing differences but also through dividing people and reinforcing antagonism. As noted by Hackett (1991), the news media do not form a monolithic or closed system containing uniform representations. Rather, the press is a site of contestation.

Franklin outlines two perspectives on the role of the media in public policy debates:

> One view suggests that the press constitute ... a watchdog which is highly critical of government and its activities ... An alternative perception ... [is that the media] are merely conduits for the burgeoning flood

of handouts emanating from the expansive numbers of public relations experts, press officers and spin doctors employed by government, political parties and a range of special interest groups with policy agendas to promote. (Franklin 1999: 9)

Rather than a straightforward representation of facts, there is a complex interplay between media representations and the thoughts and actions of people in society. Tuchman (1978: 6) characterizes news as a "negotiated enterprise" that "transforms mere happenings into publicly discussable events." At the same time, not all interests or concerns are equally represented in the media. Hackett (1991: 52) notes that the mainstream news media are subordinate to society's power structure, systematically legitimizing a capitalist, patriarchal and militarist socio-political system.

As the analysis in this chapter reveals, the topic of welfare fraud is extensively debated in the Canadian news media, which is a site within which perspectives and approaches to fraud are contested. Depictions of welfare fraud neither simply reproduce hegemonic state representations, nor are they fully open to oppositional ideas. While oppositional voices exist, such as the *Toronto Star's* exposé on the inaccuracy of welfare figures (Landsberg 2000), much of the coverage in the mainstream Canadian press reproduces the assumption of the racial neutrality of fraud policies and remains largely silent on the lived experiences of recipients of colour. Indeed, much of the discussion of welfare fraud enforcement focuses on issues of poverty, financial costs and surveillance methods. Not only do these discussions pay little attention to the racialized nature of fraud enforcement policies, they often reify rather than challenge racial stereotypes. Few of the articles we analyze examine the impact of fraud enforcement policies on communities of colour and even fewer report on the experiences of people of colour on welfare.

The analysis in this chapter is based on a review of 607 articles in three Canadian newspapers (the *Toronto Star*, the *Globe and Mail*, and the *Vancouver Sun*). Only twenty articles contained any mention of racism. Four of these articles discussed the racism underlying the allegation that Toronto's Somali community comprised an organized fraud ring. In the remaining articles, racism was analyzed in relation to broader issues such as immigration, freedom of speech or employment rather than directly in reference to fraud policies. This is a conspicuous silence indeed! We argue that in the failure to make the link between welfare fraud enforcement and racism, the media reinforce the assumption that fraud policies have little racialized impact and that racism is disconnected to the conditions of poverty. This assumption of racial neutrality is also noted in the academic literature, which corroborates our view that extensive attention in the media coverage of social assistance is devoted to issues of poverty with little analysis of the links between poverty and racism.

MEDIA ANALYSES OF WELFARE AND POVERTY

Scholarly literature on how the media depict the welfare system, poverty and the poor highlight a number of important themes and issues. Although much of the literature is derived from studies done in the United States, the findings are nonetheless relevant in the Canadian context since media access in the twenty-first century is global in nature, and American and Canadian media enjoy a particularly interconnected relationship. Furthermore, the similarities in government and politics mean that Canada and the U.S. share a broadly similar approach to welfare although differences do exist. For example, although more dramatic in the U.S., both countries have cut back access to aid and welfare programs in the service of neo-liberal ideology. Both countries share the notion that encouraging hard work requires abolishing or reforming welfare programs to prevent "dependency" on the state. Promoting these ideas and setting the framework to portray poverty as contrary to the Canadian or American way of life has been made possible, in significant part, through the media.

Debates about the causes of poverty and how the state should assist the poor have always contained stereotypical images of welfare recipients. Contempt for the poor is the result of judging them according to how much they produce in the maintenance of capitalism; those considered "non-producing" are judged the harshest (Katz 1989). Media scholars note that the ongoing use of stereotypes in media discussions have resulted in an exaggerated, distorted and one-sided picture of poverty and welfare. Vicki Lens' research on welfare discourse in two major American daily newspapers found that the myths and values about welfare and the poor are communicated through language that emphasizes the "otherness" of welfare recipients, through a cataloguing of individual faults by the state in justifying its intervention in the regulation of individual behaviour and through negative portrayals of welfare recipients (2002: 141–42). Kanayama's (2003) examination of three national newsmagazines for over three decades in the U.S. found that the same stories were used over and over again to justify welfare reforms. These stories included ideas such as the belief that to be able-bodied and not working is a crime and that to digress from the moral standard of society is sinful (Kanayama 2003: 105). Within these stories, welfare recipients were given labels such as the "dependent underclass" and the "permanent underclass." However, it is the categories of "deserving" and "undeserving" poor, established in the eighteenth century, that continue to occupy a central role in how welfare recipients are represented (Kanayama 2003: 106). Other researchers have shown that the common stereotypes about welfare recipients contain little truth. Austin's examination of the frequency of criminal arrests amongst women welfare recipients in the U.S. found that, contrary to the conservative position, welfare reduces the financial pressure to break the law by providing a support network for at-risk individuals. Women receiving public assistance were less likely to return to risky activities like prostitution and the drug trade (Austin 2004: 99–100). Bullock, Wyche and Williams point out that omission in media stories can also perpetuate false assumptions about welfare recipients. They note that the media's failure to provide an appropriate context in their discussions about welfare reform and poverty leave audiences relying on stereotypes to fill in the gaps (2001: 241).

Along with the persistent use of stereotypes about welfare recipients, the selective use of language also reinforces a particular moral universe. Specific words or phrases can, as Lens (2002: 144) points out, encapsulate an entire ideology. The word "welfare" itself is one that "connotes to a great many people that the problem lies in the public dole which encourages laziness" (Edelman 1998: 135). Other terms like "dependency," "welfare fraud" or "welfare abuse" invoke images of individual failing and deviance rather than structural or systemic causes for the problems. The language used to categorize and describe poor people is also infused with a particular moral perspective. Terms such as "dependent poor," "non-deserving poor," "welfare migrants," "welfare queen" or the "dysfunctional poor" all serve to portray these people and their lives as "stupid, shameful, immoral, hopeless, abysmal, hated and/or hostile" (Kanayama 2003: 105). Many of these beliefs stem from conservative ideologies about self-sufficiency and individual responsibility. Researchers note how the language of conservatism, and the morality it implies, has dominated the public discourse on welfare, thus creating an ideology around welfare that has proven difficult to challenge. This ideology prevailed even during the Keynesian period (1950–1973), which was more liberal in terms of welfare relief. While the media may not have invented these terms, their use of them reinforces negative attitudes about welfare recipients and allows for their ongoing scapegoating as the cause of social problems and the enemy of the public (Kanayama 2003: 105).

Peter Dreier (2005) argues that the way the media define what constitutes a newsworthy story, how they allocate their resources and who they use as sources of information shape the type of story that ultimately gets told. For example, stories about urban problems in U.S. cities have for the most part been overwhelmingly negative and misleading, creating an image of social decay where crime, gangs, racial tensions, homelessness, AIDS and teen pregnancy persist unabated (Dreier 2005). Rarely do the media highlight solutions to these problems, conduct follow-up stories about an ongoing problem or controversy, show the efforts of poor and working-class families organizing to solve problems or highlight systemic policy solutions from other countries that show effective government policies at work (Dreier 2005: 198). Audiences are left with an apocalyptic vision of urban America without any knowledge that progressive urban policies do exist and are operating in pockets throughout the country. Dreier notes that this type of reporting "is a recipe for public distrust of government and suspicion of policies to improve economic social and environmental conditions" since audiences are not provided with the optimism of what is possible when ordinary people work effectively together (2005: 199). His analysis is instructive in demonstrating the detrimental impact the media can have in shaping our understanding of social issues like welfare and poverty.

As the research suggests, the media tend to focus on the so-called "non-deserving" poor while reinforcing negative stereotypes about most people who live under conditions of poverty. Not only are stereotypes and moralities deeply embedded in media discourse on welfare, but ideologies about gender and race have also been pivotal in shaping notions of entitlement to welfare. The gendered and racialized nature of media discourse on welfare has been a key theme and finding of many critical studies examining media coverage of this topic. Researchers point to the media's reliance on prejudiced views about gender and race to further demonize specific populations. Public animosity towards single mothers, particularly single Black or teenage mothers, has been heightened by media stories that create an image of welfare mothers as responsible for their own poverty and for the breakdown of the traditional nuclear family (Bullock, Wyche, and Williams 2001: 235). As media portrayals of single mothers move from hapless and objects of pity in the early 1980s to "bad" or troubling in the 1990s, single motherhood increasingly becomes regarded as a "choice" women make — thus to blame for their own misfortune (Evans and Swift 2000: 86). Rarely is women's poverty framed in structural terms, which acknowledges how the lack of access to affordable childcare and adequate wages contributes to their situation. Inaccurate portrayals by the media also create the impression that many welfare recipients are Black and that it is Black women who have the most children (Clawson and Trice 2000). As images of the urban poor come to dominate public depictions of poverty, it is primarily non-white neighbourhoods that are overrepresented in the media (Bullock, Wyche, and Williams 2001: 236), even though, for example, African Americans do not make up the majority of welfare recipients (Luther, Kennedy, and Combs-Orme 2005: 28). Research has also found that the poverty of Blacks was usually attributed to personal characteristics while the poverty of white welfare recipients was associated with situational causes (Luther, Kennedy, and Combs-Orme 2005: 29). Not surprisingly, some of the harshest criticisms made about welfare recipients are directed specifically at Black people in the U.S., and at Aboriginal people in Canada. The gendered and racial stereotyping that continues in the media has made it much easier for individuals as well as politicians to ignore the problems facing poor people and to dismiss or deny programs that may improve their situation.

MEDIA PORTRAYALS OF WELFARE:
FRAUD IN THREE CANADIAN PAPERS

Our study of how the print media depict the issue of welfare fraud is intended to help frame and add depth to our discussions with welfare recipients about their experiences with accessing social assistance. We do not aim to be comprehensive here as such a study is beyond the scope of this book and deserves full attention in its own right. However, it is still instructive to provide a preliminary examination of the way in which the media can influence our understanding of welfare fraud. We examined three Canadian broadsheet papers. The *Vancouver Sun* and the *Toronto Star* were selected as they are from the same region as the participants we spoke to in our interviews and thus offer an appropriate contextualization from which to understand our interview data. The *Globe and Mail* was selected as it is the only paper that offers a national focus within which to situate the discussion of welfare fraud. We chose articles using the keywords "welfare fraud" and studied those that focused directly on the issue. The final sample included 607 articles from all three papers over a thirteen-year period (1993–2006).

Although the data collection phase followed content analysis methods, our analysis of the articles was influenced by the procedures of critical discourse analysis, which constructs language as a social practice (Potter and Wetherell 1987). As Maneri and Wal (2005) summarize,

> critical discourse analysis focuses on the roles of ideology and power and their enactment and reproduction through discourse. It criticises the ways in which existing power inequalities and discrimination are maintained and reproduced through discourse. Discourse has not only pragmatic functions of persuasion and credibility enhancement but also socio-political functions of legitimisation and control.

Within this framework, rather than producing numerical summaries of trends in the data, we aimed to explore the ways in which the language of fraud was used in the articles. We "open coded" (Strauss and Corbin 1990) the articles, collapsed these codes into categories and organized the articles into five overlapping themes: the contextualization of welfare fraud and poverty, the extent and cost of welfare fraud, forms of fraud protection, racism and the enforcement of welfare fraud and the treatment of welfare recipients. We analyze each of these themes in turn and select a few representative articles for discussion. It comes as no surprise that the general public holds negative attitudes about the welfare system given that the overall tone of the media is predominately negative in their portrayal of welfare recipients and in their discussion of the welfare system.

The Contextualization of Welfare Fraud and Poverty

In their discussion of welfare fraud, the newspaper articles we examined frequently contextualize the issue around the broader problems of poverty and the welfare system. However, what is important here is how they frame the context and what type of information is made available to readers. The three papers examined use oppositional ideas like "deserving" and "undeserving" in reference to poor people; they tend to focus on the idea of poverty as a "cycle" which is tied in with the concept of "dependency" and blaming poor people for their situation. They take a more neutral stance when discussing cuts or freezes to welfare rates and the programs developed to encourage welfare recipients to return to work.

Although the terms "deserving" and "undeserving" are not used regularly in the articles, the attitudes that these categories convey are readily apparent. Many newspaper articles provide direct quotes that reinforce the myth that some people suffering from poverty are responsible for their own plight while the "real" victims of poverty need help and support. Politicians and criminal justice agents were regular sources for such claims:

> I think [welfare fraud] has become more socially unacceptable now. You're really stealing money from the poor. It bothers more people than any other type of fraud. (quote by Det. Sgt. Toye, "Computer battles welfare fraud," *Globe and Mail* February 22, 1994: A14)
>
> "Our new measures will help ensure that social assistance goes to people with genuine needs," Mr. Tsubouchi [Community and Social Services Minister] said, adding that it will protect the welfare system "by restoring the public's trust' in it." ("Ontario Tories crack whip on welfare: Latest measures include cheater hot line, home inspections and cuts to shelter allowances," *Globe and Mail* August 24, 1995: A7)
>
> "Welfare fraud hurts our most vulnerable Manitobans," Mitchelson [Social Services Minister] said, suggesting the money could be used by the really needy. ("Hotline targets welfare cheats in push to save $1.5 million," *Vancouver Sun* June 30, 1994: A6)
>
> "We must continue to take steps to ensure that welfare is there for those honest folks who are upgrading their education, improving their job skills or making the transition from welfare to work," Baird [Social Services Minister] said. ("17 people banned from collecting welfare," *Toronto Star* January 16, 2002: A3)

Edelman (1998: 132) argues that even though these categories are simplistic and inadequate, they nonetheless help us "to live with preexisting actions and beliefs and aids in interpreting news so as to perpetuate preexisting cognitive structures."

Furthermore, he claims that when these beliefs are subtly evoked through linguistic cues, the audience does not question the categories for being simplistic but rather embraces them as satisfying cognitive and emotional needs (Edelman 1998: 132). For some, the need to believe that poor people are to blame for their own poverty alleviates guilt, exonerates institutions from providing help and legitimizes the state's attempts to regulate the behaviour of the poor. Thus, it is not surprising to find that only a handful of articles discussed how welfare fraud, when compared to tax evasion by the rich, is lower in frequency and less costly. Many counterclaims disputing the charge that the problem of welfare fraud is burdening the welfare system were in the form of letters to the editor or as op-ed pieces:

> It is not the poor people and the unemployed who are defrauding the government, but the "corporate welfare bums," an apt phrase coined by the late NDP leader, David Lewis. The $3 billion to $4 billion in unpaid taxes from the multinational corporations in Ontario demand an immediate and independent investigation. However, Bob Rae and company do not seem to have the guts and integrity to go after these corporations, which never pay their fair share. During his election campaign and his first few months in office as premier, Rae piously announced that he was going to impose a 20 per cent tax on all the big corporations in Ontario. Another broken promise. And another betrayal of public trust. ("Another broken promise," letter to the editor, *Toronto Star* May 5, 1994: A22)
>
> Your paper displays an obvious double standard in covering fraud issues … Why are we subjected to huge headlines about speculation and allegations of welfare fraud by poor people, and blink-and-you-miss-it coverage of proven tax fraud involving middle-class people? ("Double standard pits middle class against poor," editorial by poverty advocate, *Vancouver Sun* January 13, 1994: B1)

Critics of the government have also pointed out how attempts to attack the poor in discussions about the problem of welfare fraud is made possible by claiming that the public doesn't understand the problems poor people face, by pointing out how the government has been using the welfare system as a scapegoat for budget deficits and by arguing that the management of the welfare system, not the recipients, is the problem:

> More important, fraud is a convenient opening for an attack on welfare itself. Welfare is an easy political target. It is easier to blame the poor for their poverty than to admit that it could happen to anyone. It's easier to attribute moral or character flaws to immigrants or visible minorities. We get mean-spirited when we are afraid and in the current economic climate

many people are afraid. ("Exploiting welfare fraud," editorial by poverty advocate, *Toronto Star* November 9, 1993: A19)

Canada's poor are caught in a war zone created by uncaring politicians, the president of the National Anti-Poverty Organization said Friday. "There is a virtual war, not against poverty but against people who are poor," Jean Swanson of Vancouver told a conference on poverty. Swanson accused politicians of viewing poor-bashing as an easy road to popularity. "Show me a politician who won't claim that zillions of dollars can be saved by cracking down on alleged but unproved welfare fraud," she said. ("Liberal welfare-fraud plan won't work, economist says," *Vancouver Sun* May 18, 1996: B3)

A careful look at the numbers suggests that as a class of people welfare recipients are actually far more honest than the public that so loves to abuse them ... Most of the problems with welfare seem to have less to do with the recipients than with the sloppy systems set up to administer the benefits. The total number of ripoff artists on the welfare rolls amounts to three per cent of the total caseload, just about the number that poverty action groups have been saying all along. ("Cheating, as well as charity, begins at home," *Vancouver Sun* March 24, 1995: A15)

Many of the articles we examined attempt to situate the problem of fraud within the broader context of welfare reforms, particularly cuts and freezes to welfare rates. Many of the comments point to the detrimental impact welfare reforms will have on poor people and why welfare fraud may increase as a result:

It's to their advantage. I'll tell you, once they start cutting rates and reducing the amount of money people get on welfare, you're going to increase welfare fraud and people working under the table, because people won't be able to survive with the lower rates. ("Metro hopes for OK on fingerprinting plan: Financial backing sought from province," comment by Toronto City councillor, Mr. Fortinos, *Globe and Mail* July 12, 1995: A1, A8)

Kwan predicted the new requirements for signing up for welfare and delays in getting a first cheque will drive desperate people to homelessness. And she said that many people, driven to desperation by reduced benefits and tight eligibility requirements, will get caught up in the new legislation's stiff penalties for welfare fraud. "People are going to be forced, in my view, to fraud the system," she said. ("Welfare reforms spark dissent: One Liberal backbencher says some provisions flawed; another fears for children," comment by Jenny Kwan, MLA. *Vancouver Sun* April 17, 2002: B1)

In this context, the elimination of the lifetime ban on receiving assistance when someone is convicted as fraud is widely celebrated as a significant victory:

> The McGuinty government accepted the jury's recommendation that it eliminate the ban on receiving social assistance when someone is convicted of welfare fraud. It deserves credit for taking that step. However, the jury also recommended that social assistance rates reflect the actual costs of housing and basic needs within each community. Instead, the government announced that rates would go up a mere 3 percent. (Smith and Chic 2004)

Yet, at the same time, the newspapers give contradictory messages that despite cutbacks, fraud is still fraud, and those who cannot abide by the new rules will be sought out:

> Just one day after social-assistance rates for one million people were slashed by 21.6 per cent, Community and Social Services Minister David Tsubouchi announced that a province-wide toll free line to catch welfare cheaters had begun operation. ("Ontario's welfare fraud 'hotline' in operation: Toll-free line centralizing those set up by municipalities called 'bumper-sticker' solution," *Globe and Mail* October 3, 1995: A10)
>
> While welfare fraud is difficult to measure, estimates have pegged it at about 3 per cent of the social-assistance caseload. With a welfare bill in Metro of about $1.2- billion last year, Mr. Fortinos estimates that at that rate of fraud the municipality stands to save $36-million a year after implementing positive ID. ("Metro hopes for OK on fingerprinting plan: Financial backing sought from province," *Globe and Mail* July 12, 1995: A1, A8)

Efforts to provide some background information on the issue of welfare fraud have a slightly positive impact on constructing a more sympathetic understanding of welfare recipients and poor people generally. However, newspapers also maintain their neo-liberal stance by reinforcing an "us" and "them" mentality through suggestions that even in difficult economic times, individual responsibility is paramount and structural barriers to employment are not at fault. Myths and stereotypes about welfare recipients bolster these views, providing convenient scapegoats that make the attempts to determine the extent and cost of welfare fraud somewhat superfluous, as the next section highlights.

Extent and Cost of Welfare Fraud

The lack of reliable statistics both provincially and federally on the actual rates of welfare fraud has resulted in debate over the validity of the reported figures. In both B.C. and Ontario, there has not been any attempt to consistently record rates of fraud. What many of the claims-makers agree on is that the problem of fraud is not significant, averaging around 3 percent per year:

> In British Columbia, where welfare investigators also review welfare files for fraud, a recent study conducted by Peat Marwick Thorne for the province's Ministry of Finance found that no more than 300 cases out of about 170,000 welfare recipients in B.C. — less than a quarter of 1 per cent — involved fraud charges in any one year since 1990. ("What are welfare boasts built on?" *Globe and Mail* March 30, 1994: A5)
>
> Between 1 per cent and 4 per cent of welfare recipients commit deliberate fraud, studies have consistently found. More people cheat on their income taxes and lie about their cross-border shopping than defraud the welfare system. ("Cheating less prevalent than gossip has it, studies indicate," *Globe and Mail* January 21, 1994: A8)
>
> What the provinces do have in common, however, is an inability to pinpoint exactly how much fraud exists in the welfare system. While a figure of 3 per cent of caseloads has gained wide currency, no one knows for sure the number of people who actually cheat. ("Crackdown on welfare cheats expected to save $50m," *Globe and Mail* March 30, 1994: A5)

The strategy of exposing the lack of data available and pointing to the weakness of the government's claims regarding the problem of fraud highlights how the media's relationship with the government is one of both friend and foe. Media criticism of the government, as Schudson (2002: 257) notes, is in itself newsworthy. Crucially, it also helps to re-assert their role as impartial, expert professionals in the mediation of the public sphere (Kaplan 2006: 182).

Despite the general acknowledgement that fraud rates are extremely low, cases of fraud receive widespread coverage, as did the conviction in the B.C. Provincial Court of a couple, Farideh Bavarsad and Ali Farshid Esmaeilnejad. The judge's remarks show the moral indignation against the recipients:

> By fraudulently claiming social assistance, the defendants were depriving others who genuinely needed the money and eroding the community's trust in the system ... You increase the cynicism of the people that think that welfare is just a bunch of fraudulent bums that do not deserve the money, and you ultimately reduce everyone's willingness to share and trust and be generous. (Matas 2005)

The lack of reliable statistics in conjunction with the sensationalist reporting of convictions has permitted governments to allege that fraud rates are high and that the problem requires immediate action, while critics charge that the figures have been exaggerated to perpetuate the myth of fraud:

> "The government is set to conduct a massive review of each of the 1.3 million cases currently on the welfare rolls in a bid to root out fraud and save taxpayers' money," said a government source familiar with the plan. ("Crackdown on welfare cheats expected to save $50m," *Globe and Mail* March 28, 1994: A5)
>
> The myth is rampant. Everyone seems to have a story about a neighbour's cousin who is cheating on welfare. But according to several studies done over the past decade, only a tiny minority of welfare recipients are defrauding the system. ("Cheating less prevalent than gossip has it, studies indicate," *Globe and Mail* January 21, 1994: A8)

A key point in these discussions that barely received any attention is the fact that many cases of welfare fraud involve administrative errors or misreadings of welfare statistics:

> At least one poverty activist disputed the fraud figures yesterday, saying many are not actually defrauding the system, but rather are people who've been rendered ineligible by the Harris government. "Every year the government puts out a report with vastly inflated fraud numbers," said Andrea Calver of the Ontario Coalition for Social Justice. ("Welfare fraud up, report says," *Toronto Star* November 23, 2000: A10)

The ambiguous nature of what constitutes fraud combined with the lack of reliable figures points to media that seem determined to help governments of the day punish poor people for their poverty. If the generally agreed figure of fraud is as low as 3 percent, the resources spent on pursuing fraudulent claims does not seem financially prudent. What then is the motivation for targeting and attacking poor people? As researchers Limbert and Bullock have noted, "By emphasizing declining welfare caseloads rather than the poverty-level wages earned by most former recipients, popular media ... has done little to challenge the legitimacy of the new regulations or the validity of policymakers claiming 'welfare reform' a success" (2005: 254).

Forms of Fraud Protection

A key theme in the articles we examined is the ways in which governments are taking action to prevent fraud in the welfare system. The newspapers discuss numerous techniques and approaches to reassure the public that the problem of welfare fraud is being taken seriously and that the measures employed will increase detection rates, resulting in allegedly significant savings to the public purse. However, not all interested parties agree that the forms of fraud protection in place are either adequate or effective. A strong debate is evident in the articles that raise doubts about some of the strategies proposed, since critics contend that "better" enforcement strategies often translate into punitive and criminalizing tendencies.

Several articles reveal a cynicism about the cost and efficiency of the new technological systems that were introduced as part of welfare reform in Ontario. This cynicism is countered by officials as noted in the following article:

> The system seems to have ended welfare fraud. Says Accenture Canada chairman David Seidel: "Before we built this [single province-wide] system, welfare in Ontario was on eight different systems that didn't talk to each other. People could apply for welfare in multiple jurisdictions and it would take a long time to catch up to them. There were people with gold Visa cards drawing welfare ... The system identified 42,000 ineligible cases, 25,000 overpayments and 8,000 underpayments." It eliminated $690 million in fraud and overpayments between 1996 and 2002. Accenture got its $180 million paycheck, which was contingent on such cost savings of at least $360 million. (Ticoll 2004)

The use of fingerprinting is one of the most discussed strategies in the articles. The governments in both provinces and their supporters argue that fingerprinting welfare recipients will have a dual purpose: to prevent double-dippers while also making it easier for recipients to cash their cheques:

> "Finger printing makes sure that if you're on the welfare system you can't get on again," said Donald Richmond, Metro's commissioner of community services. "So it's to prevent double-dipping at one end, but also to make it easier for people to get their cash at the other end." ("Fingerprint plan for welfare urged," *Globe and Mail* February 16, 1994: A1, A6)
>
> A new identification system is needed for welfare recipients, including high-tech identity cards and even mass fingerprinting, says Progressive Conservative Leader Mike Harris. "I'm personally not opposed to fingerprinting," Harris told reporters after detailing his welfare policies in a speech yesterday at the Ontario Association of Professional Social Workers. "If somebody wants benefits from the taxpayer, and assistance

from the taxpayers, it certainly makes sense." ("Fingerprinting way to cut welfare fraud, Harris says" *Toronto Star* October 28, 1994: A16)

Concerns regarding the use of fingerprinting include arguments that fingerprinting is too intrusive and will be difficult to enforce with individuals who have particular mental health problems. In addition, it has strong associations with the criminal justice system and many believe that welfare recipients will feel like they are being criminalized for being on welfare:

> "The whole finger printing issue doesn't address the real problem: The system tends to develop a dependency ... and fingerprinting isn't going to solve that," he [Mr. Szware] said. ("Computer battles welfare fraud," *Globe and Mail* February 22, 1994: A14)
>
> I hope I am not alone in my shock at the Orwellian paradox that Metro welfare recipients must give their fingerprints in order to receive the benefits of living in a caring society. The real criminals are the politicians who feed at the trough while thousands of Canadian children go hungry. Welfare fraud, indeed. What about political fraud? ("Following the money leads to purpose of finger scanning," letter to the editor, *Toronto Star* June 12, 1997: A28)
>
> Metro's plan to use fingerprint technology to reduce welfare fraud may be unnecessarily frightening for people with psychiatric illnesses who depend on welfare, advocates for the mentally disabled say. "Many of these people are already paranoid," said Scott Seiler, who heads a provincial committee that advises government on income issues affecting the disabled. "To ask these people to surrender their fingerprints to the welfare bureaucracy could put many of them over the edge," he said. "Many would simply refuse and drop off the system altogether." ("Special investigations unit set up to fight welfare fraud," *Toronto Star* May 9, 1996: A9)

Similarly, the hiring of more investigators and the development in some regions of a "fraud squad" have also received mixed reactions. While more investigators may catch more people attempting to defraud the system, like the issue of fingerprinting, critics find this approach excessive in relation to the seriousness of the problem:

> The Ontario government is cracking down on welfare fraud with a program it says is among the toughest in Canada. Community and Social Services Minister Tony Silipo announced yesterday that the government is hiring 270 inspectors to review almost 690,000 welfare cases — representing more than 1.3 million people — in an effort to eliminate fraud

and overpayment. ("What are welfare boasts built on?" *Globe and Mail* March 30, 1994: A5)

A new five-member special investigations unit based in the Lower Mainland is being struck to combat welfare fraud. Social Services Minister Joan Smallwood announced Thursday. As well, a senior Crown prosecutor will be assigned to work with the ministry to "expedite and ensure prosecution of those alleged to be defrauding the income assistance system," Smallwood told the legislature. ("Special investigations unit set up to fight welfare fraud," *Vancouver Sun* May 7, 1993: A3)

Three years ago, the Rae government set up expensive fraud squads in every welfare and family benefits office in Ontario. They have beat the bushes looking for fraud. They have found that there just isn't much there. They have, however, found substantial losses due to administrative error. If Metro wants to save money on welfare, the best way is to provide its case staff with adequate time and resources to reduce administrative overpayments. More care needs to be taken in keeping the books. It isn't politically sexy like fingerprinting. But unlike fingerprinting, it works. ("Welfare fingerprint plan won't save money," a lawyer specializing in social assistance law, *Toronto Star* May 9, 1997: A27)

Better record-keeping and information-sharing techniques combined with the establishment of a snitch line were also cited as possible strategies for improving detection. As noted in one article:

The city's so-called "snitch" hot line is such a success that Auditor-General Jeff Griffiths says he needs more staff to expose bureaucratic waste and even criminal behaviour. (Lewington 2003)

While there was less focus in the articles on fraud detection techniques, the ongoing attention paid to fraud protection suggests that discussing how to manage the problem of welfare fraud is a key theme. The effect of this is to remind readers that, despite claims otherwise, welfare fraud continues to be an important social issue that requires attention and solutions.

Enforcement and Racism

Public opposition to the growing costs of welfare has historically been linked in part to the claim that the growing number of immigrants in Canada is overburdening the welfare system. So entrenched is the belief that immigrants are a key source of problems that politicians confidently make statements like the following in public forums:

Refugees receiving fraudulent welfare cheques are costing Ontario taxpayers tens of millions of dollars, according to a secret federal report obtained by provincial Liberal Leader Lyn McLeod. ("Refugees accused of fraud: Ontario welfare 'pillage' reported," *Globe and Mail* October 28, 1993: A10)

Welfare is being doled out to 12,000 refugee claimants inside Canada who have been ordered deported or who are ducking criminal charges, an East York councillor claims ... "a quick cross-check of names between social service and enforcement agencies would weed out the ineligible claimants immediately, and enable clarification of status of many more," Papadakis said at a forum on crime he organized last night ... The get-tough theme was backed by federal Progressive Conservative candidate Ben Eng, a former Metro sergeant who quit the force in 1991 after sparking controversy by releasing statistics he compiled. His data suggested that refugees from Vietnam and mainland China commit a disproportionately high number of offences. ("Weed out ineligible refugee claimants crime forum told," *Toronto Star* April 29, 1993: A8)

Such claims end up labelling entire ethnic communities, and as is discussed in later chapters of this book, such racialization significantly structures the ways in which people of colour experience welfare. Such was the case when Lyn McLeod implied that the Somali community in Toronto was importing refugees to defraud the welfare system. Critics and members of the community challenged her claims, arguing that not only was she generalizing about the activities of a few to the many, but that her comments were racist in stereotyping all Somalis as criminal and that the impact of such comments from a high-profile politician would be difficult to reverse:

The angry Somali wanted Ms. McLeod to know that he worked 16 hours a day, seven days a week to support his family, that he was no welfare cheat and that he was enraged by her smear. He was doubly furious that she had not seen through the patently racist tone of a report that, based on the evidence of seven cases, found that "the Somali people are opportunists whose use of confusion and misrepresentation [is] unparalleled except by the Gypsies of Eastern and Western Europe" and that our "Western and primarily Christian-based way of life has little meaning or relevance to these people." ("Looking for hate in all the wrong places," *Globe and Mail* December 20, 1993: A10)

Thirteen local Somali organizations have united to fight the racism they say has dogged them since accusations of welfare fraud were made last month. They plan to form a coalition to try to kill the negative image of Somali refugees, which they say was created by federal documents referred to in the Ontario Legislature by Liberal Leader Lyn McLeod. About 400 attended the first meeting of the coalition yesterday. Many said they have been harassed by neighbours and strangers since the controversy erupted. ("Somalis in Ottawa ask McLeod for apology," *Toronto Star* November 7, 1993: A2)

Many critics of the government in both Ontario and B.C. argue that the enforcement of welfare fraud is inherently racist. Not only does it permit more suffering of an already vulnerable group, but marking out immigrants and refugees as key players in welfare fraud feeds into the ongoing racism that certain ethnic communities have been fighting against:

> Attacks on immigrants and refugees increasingly are taking the same form as attacks on the poor, the unemployed and those on social assistance. The more fear the media can create among the general public toward these vulnerable individuals, the easier it is for the government to push forward a conservative agenda. ("Marchi's consultations reek of farce Report revealed real, hidden agenda after process ended," *Toronto Star* October 3, 1994: A17)

As many race and poverty advocates have consistently argued, it is much easier to blame individuals and groups for causing these problems than it is to address and seek adequate solutions. Furthermore, by using penalties found in the criminal justice system, such as imprisonment, the message being sent is that anyone who commits welfare fraud is a criminal even though welfare policies and legislation are civil proceedings. Critics contend that the harsh penalties for welfare fraud are disproportionate to the seriousness of the problem:

> No one disputes the principle of punishing cheaters. But tough penalties already exist. Recipients convicted of fraud are barred from collecting benefits for three months after their first conviction and six months after subsequent ones. That's on top of the penalties-fines, restitution and even jail time-imposed by the courts ... "A lifetime ban is not proportional to the crime," said Shirley Hoy, the city's commissioner of community and neighbourhood services. Once again, it would appear, Queen's Park is making a big fuss about a small problem. ("Excessive crackdown," *Toronto Star* March 24, 2000: A1)

In light of the fact that many welfare recipients are prone to making mistakes on their applications due to language barriers and lack of access to translators as well as ignorance of the rules, it is difficult to understand the rationale for taking a tough stance on fraud unless the intent is to scapegoat poor and primarily racialized individuals:

> Peel Region gets many tips about people ripping off the welfare system. But social services director David Szware says most of the information comes from people who don't understand how welfare works. Seldom is abuse actually occurring, he says. ("Fraud tips on welfare usually groundless," *Toronto Star* February 24, 1994: B4)

Unfortunately, only a handful of articles presented a critical examination of the impact of welfare enforcement on communities of colour. As noted earlier, out of the 607 articles we analyzed, only 4 mentioned racism in relation to fraud protection. Discussions about immigrants tend to focus primarily on their immigrant status and descriptions of the fraudulent case being reported, thereby cementing the belief that people of colour are to blame for the problem of welfare fraud.

Treatment of Recipients

If the problem of welfare fraud is considered an important topic for the media, it is not necessarily the case that the treatment of welfare recipients is equally deserving of attention. Only a handful of articles discuss how welfare reforms treat recipients as criminals and deny or violate their rights, and almost all these articles refer only to the Kimberly Rogers case:

> Any government that would impose house arrest, probation and restitution, and then cut off a pregnant woman from collecting any money for even the most basic necessities, must seriously reconsider whether its policies are democratic, moral and just, Mr. Dewart said. "This is a case which cries out for an inquest." ("House arrest for welfare fraud ends in death," *Globe and Mail* August 15, 2001: A1, A6)
>
> Kimberly Rogers died in horrible, unjust circumstances. And unless the McGuinty government takes the advice of the jury that examined Rogers' death, others will die and continue to struggle in insecure and inhumane conditions. Rogers was convicted of fraud for violating the rules of social assistance. She made the mistake of collecting both social assistance and a student loan. For this "crime," Rogers was sentenced to six months house arrest. In the sweltering heat of the summer of 2001, confined to her Sudbury apartment and eight months pregnant, Rogers died. (Blackstock and Chic 2003)
>
> Privacy watchdogs fear a controversial agreement between the B.C

government and Ottawa to research job-training initiatives will constitute an unnecessary invasion of personal information. Under the agreement, which was reached last week without public fanfare, the provincial and federal governments agreed to share all personal information on welfare claims, employment insurance and job training programs. ("Privacy watchdogs criticize deal on information-sharing," *Vancouver Sun* January 13, 1998: A3)

One can see how welfare recipients will have difficulty challenging their treatment and the negative beliefs the public holds of them when papers publish comments such as the one made here by a local politician:

Welfare recipients should be automatically stripped of all privacy rights to ensure they don't bilk the public purse, a Thunder Bay politician says. "The right of the public to protect its money must outweigh the right of an individual to privacy," Alderman Evelyn Dodds told a legislative committee reviewing the Municipal Freedom of Information and Protection of Privacy Act. ("Welfare users should lose privacy rights, politician says," *Toronto Star* January 20, 1994: A15)

The lack of discussion in the media that humanizes welfare recipients and provides some insight into their situation only reinforces the myths and stereotypes. The three newspapers here have demonstrated that their coverage and reporting of welfare fraud will have little impact on providing an alternative understanding of the issue.

DISCUSSION

Falk (1994: 3) notes that conversations on public policy are enacted in the media in terms of the "simplification of stances and public positions, which are reported by the media as being adopted by interested groups, or 'stakeholders' as they are sometimes termed ... [This] sets the scene for a kind of public competition between the discourses — a case of duelling discourses." On one side are reports that argue that welfare recipients who can, should be working. Nothing is quite as disdainful as slothfulness, and we are told that society is divided between those who occupy the world of welfare and those who live outside of welfare. Therefore, to engage in fraudulent behaviour of the welfare system is nothing short of sinful. The morally loaded message of this story was told and retold countless times in the newspaper articles we reviewed. Welfare "cheats" do not deserve any sympathy, their behaviour is repugnant, and they deserve serious punishment. This perception of welfare recipients has shaped not only public attitudes towards poor people but successive attempts to reform the welfare system. On the other side are perspectives critical of state policies on welfare. This includes coverage on the inaccuracy of fraud control figures, the negative impact of the lifetime ban on the lives of those like Kimberly Rogers and the impact of the decline in social assistance rates on poverty. Common in these differing media discourses is an almost complete silence on the racialized impact of fraud protection measures and on the lived experiences of people of colour on welfare.

Our aim here is to demonstrate how three Canadian daily newspapers portray the issue of welfare fraud. Not surprisingly, our findings are consistent with previous studies, which argue that the media reinforce stereotypes about recipients, which includes both sexist and racist beliefs. Although some effort was made to provide counterclaims, the content of the articles are instructive for what they omit. Attempts to contextualize the problem of welfare fraud from the perspective of a welfare recipient were piecemeal at best. Readers are thus left with the impression that the media are in general agreement with the government over the need to rein in the problem of welfare fraud and find tough solutions to the problem. Sotirovic (2003: 133) argues that if people are not given the necessary information to generate alternative explanations, then "active processing may merely function to help individuals consolidate many similar stories they have already seen over time and reinforce rather than refute the effects of dominant media presentations on audience explanations."

Given that the dominant story of welfare fraud involves "undeserving" individuals taking money from those "in need," the so-called "undeserving" are rarely, if ever, seen as sympathetic characters. Moreover, racialized and gendered images of welfare recipients are deeply embedded in the media's definition of "undeserving." According to media images, it is only the elderly, children and people with disabilities that are the truly "needy." Increasing suspicion is cast on women as more and more middle-class women enter the labour market. The extensive reporting of particular cases, such as the one of D'Amour,[1] creates the impression that all women are defrauding the system, thus diluting the concerns raised by the Kimberly Rogers case of how women welfare recipients are treated. Racist stereotypes and prejudices in the media have intensified these suspicions. The belief that women of colour are having more babies in order to "live off" the state is one of myths created by media impressions. Furthermore, castigating entire ethnic communities as criminogenic not only increases public hostility but manipulates public fear of immigrants. By framing welfare fraud primarily in terms of racial stereotypes, any effort to build bridges across communities is undermined. That gender, intersecting with race, underpins the debate about welfare fraud highlights the extent to which media discourse on welfare contributes to the homogenizing tendencies present in society today. By channelling public fears and hostilities in misguided directions, stereotypical ideologies about sex and race remain intact, and punitive approaches against individuals and communities are justified on moral grounds. Dijk (1989) notes that the very framework for news gathering discriminates against groups that are less organized and that lack a "packaged" viewpoint and clearly identifiable spokesperson. He characterizes the lack of representation of the viewpoints of minority groups within the media as "discursive discrimination." As the analysis in later chapters of this book demonstrates, exploring the experiences of welfare recipients of colour allows for an understanding of the ways in which racialization is enacted and actively achieved through welfare enforcement policies.

Notes

1   D'Amour was convicted on welfare fraud because she did not claim employment income. The money collected from welfare was used to pay for her daughter's ballet lessons in Europe. Tracey Tyler, "Women's welfare fraud conviction upheld," *Toronto Star*, August 14, 2002.

References

Austin, A. 2004. "Public Assistance and the Pressure to Commit Crime: An Empirical Challenge to Conservative Criminology." *Journal of Poverty* 8, 1.

Blackstock, S., and J. Chic. 2003. "Scant Solace for the Poor." *Toronto Star*, December 19.

Bullock, H., K. Wyche and W. Williams. 2001. "Media Images of the Poor." *Journal of Social Issues* 57, 2.

Carey, J. 1989. *Communication as Culture: Essays on Media and Society.* New York: Routledge.

Clawson, R., and R. Trice. 2000. "Poverty As We Know It: Media Portrayals of the Poor." *Public Opinion Quarterly* 64.

Dreier, P. 2005. "How the Media Compound Urban Problems." *Journal of Urban Affairs* 27, 2.

Edelman, M. 1998. "Language, Myths and Rhetoric." *Society* 35, 2.

Evans, P., and K. Swift. 2000. "Single Mothers and the Press: Rising Tides, Moral Panic, and Restructuring Discourses." In S. Neysmith (ed.), *Restructuring Caring Labour*. Don Mills: Oxford University Press.

Falk, I. 1994. "The Making of Policy: Media Discourse of Conversations." *Discourse* 15, 2

Franklin, B. 1999. "Misleading Messages: The Media and Social Policy." In B. Franklin (ed.), *Social Policy, the Media and Misrepresentation.* London: Routledge.

Hackett, R. 1991. *News and Dissent: The Press and the Politics of Peace in Canada.* Norwood, NJ: Ablex Publishing.

Kanayama, T. 2003. "Magazine Coverage of Welfare Recipients 1969–1996: Media Rituals and American Society." *Journal of American and Canadian Studies* 21.

Kaplan, R. 2006. "The News About Institutionalism: Journalism's Ethic of Objectivity and Its Political origins." *Political Communication* 23: 173.

Katz, M. 1989. *The Undeserving Poor: From the War On Poverty to the War On Welfare.* New York: Pantheon.

Landsberg, M. 2000. "Ontario Tories Real Perpetrators of Welfare Fraud." *Toronto Star*, January 15.

Lens, V. 2002. "Public Voices and Public Policy: Changing the Societal Discourse on 'Welfare.'" *Journal of Sociology and Social Welfare* 29, 1.

Lewington, J. 2003. "'Snitch' Line Successful, Auditor-General Reports." *Globe and Mail*, September 11.

Limbert, W.M., and H.E. Bullock. 2005. "'Playing the Fool': U.S. Welfare Policy from a Critical Race Perspective." *Feminism and Psychology* 15, 3.

Luther, C., D. Kennedy, and T. Combs-Orme. 2005. "Intertwining of Poverty, Gender, and Race: A Critical Analysis of Welfare News Coverage from 1993–2000." *Race and Class* 12, 2.

Maneri M., and J. Wal. 2005. "The Criminalisation of Ethnic Groups: An Issue for Media Analysis." *Forum: Qualitative Social Research* 6, 3 (September). Online journal available at <http://www.qualitative-research.net/fqs-texte/3-05/05-3-9-e.htm> (accessed March 2007).

Matas, R. 2005. "Judge Blasts Pair Convicted of Eight-year Welfare Fraud." *Globe and Mail*, December 26.

Potter, J., and M. Wetherell. 1987. *Discourse and Social Psychology: Beyond Attitudes and Behaviour*. London: Sage.

Schudson, M. 2002. "The News Media as Political Institutions." *Annual Review of Political Science* 5: 249.

Smith, J., and J. Chic. 2004. "Government Fails Kimberly Rogers Again." *Toronto Star*, August 3.

Sotirovic, M. 2003. "How Individuals Explain Social Problems: The Influences of Media Use." *Journal of Communication* March.

Strauss, A., and J. Corbin. 1990. *Basics of Qualitative Research*. Newbury Park: Sage.

Ticoll, D. 2004. "Why a $180-million Computer Can't Deliver a Welfare Hike." *Globe and Mail*, July 15.

Tuchman, G. 1978. *Making News: An Analysis of the Construction of Reality*. London: Free Press.

Van Dijk, T.A. 1989. "Mediating Racism: The Role of the Media in the Representation of Racism." In R. Wodak (ed.), *Language, Power and Ideology: Studies in Political Discourse*. Amsterdam and Philadelphia: John Benjamins Publishing Company.

LABOUR

Chapter 14

THE INCALL SEX INDUSTRY
Gender, Class and
Racialized Labour in the Margins

Chris Bruckert and Colette Parent

From: *Criminalizing Women: Gender and (In)Justice in Neo-liberal Times*, 2nd edition, pp. 92–112 (reprinted with permission).

Prostitution has long (albeit inaccurately) been referred to as the world's oldest profession. It is striking, therefore, that the women employed in the sex industry have rarely been defined as workers — much less professionals — in either popular discourse or academic analysis. For the most part, until the 1960s, when symbolic interactionists shifted the focus (cf. Bryan 1965; Laner 1974; Velarde 1975; Heyl 1977, 1979), positivist accounts of prostitution dominated the debate (cf. Lombroso 1895 [1985]; Flexner 1920; Rolph 1955; Greenwald 1958; Glover 1969). In the 1970s new voices emerged. While radical feminists developed a gender-based analysis on the issue, sex workers in a number of countries — including Canada, the United States, England and the Netherlands — started to organize, to speak about their work, and to defend their interests in groups such as CORP, COYOTE, PROS, and the Red Thread. In opposition to the work of radical feminists, who perceived prostitution as victimization, the discourses that emerged from women within the industry emphasized the activity as work, thereby denouncing the legally defined classifications, moral subtext and conceptual baggage encapsulated in the term "prostitution."

The term "sex work," famously coined by Scarlet Harlot (Koyama 2002: 5), represents much more than a linguistic subtlety. It is a powerful concept that undermines normative assumptions as it compels reconsideration not only of the industry but also of the relegation of sexuality to the private realm. But this reframing continues to be challenged from a number of different quarters. In Canada counter-arguments were presented in submissions to the courts in the 2013 *Bedford* case, in which one current and two former sex workers challenged the constitutionality of Criminal Code sections 213(1)(c), 210, and 212(1)(j) that de facto criminalize sex work(ers) (see *Bedford v. Canada [Attorney General]* 2013). The Women's Coalition (2011) took a prohibitionist approach rooted in radical feminism when its members argued in their factum, "Prostitution is a global practice of sexual exploitation and male violence against women" (para. 3). By contrast, the Christian Legal Fellowship, REAL Women of Canada, and the Catholic Civil Rights League (2009) drew on the trope of the conservative right when they asserted, "Prostitution is immoral [and] it should be stigmatized" (para. 5) because it "violates the human dignity of both prostitutes and those who are witnesses to it" (para. 23).

Here we draw on qualitative research from two research projects to explore the implications, limits and potential for conceptualizing prostitution as sex work — specifically by integrating labour theory into criminology to examine the often overlooked but long-established commercial incall sex industry.[1] The term "incall sex work" emerged from the research and speaks to the subjective importance of specific labour structures. In contrast to outcall workers (such as escorts), incall workers provide sexual services to clients in establishments such as massage parlours, brothels and dungeons. While incall workers can be male or female and can also work as "independents" (by, for example, receiving clients in their own homes, hotel rooms or incall locations), our examination focuses on women who labour for third parties in an employment-like relationship.

A number of theoretical and political implications emerge when we think about women's work in the sex industry as classed, raced and gendered labour. The labour structure, labour process and experience of women workers in this sector are all key to this discussion, and so too are links to the work of working-class women labouring in other consumer services. Indeed, numerous points of convergence speak not only to the validity of framing sex work as "work," but also to the importance of rethinking women's labour in the new economy and destabilizing the private/public and sexuality/work dichotomies.

THEORIZING SEX WORK AS "WORK"

While feminist engagement with the question of prostitution dates back to the progressive era of the early twentieth century, it was in the 1970s, in the context of a broader rethinking of gender and patriarchy, that prostitution emerged as the symbol of the social, sexual and economic domination of women by men.[2] Within this framework developed by radical feminists, prostitutes — and by extension pornography performers and erotic dancers — emerged as victims. Their status as victims was seen to emanate from the capitalist and patriarchal social structures and the racism inscribed in discriminatory laws and their enforcement, from mistreatment and objectification by men (pimps and customers) who experience a sense of power over all women through the purchase of one representative member, and from the circumstances of their lives — based on the presumption that they were victims of childhood sexual abuse, incest and rape (cf. Millett 1971; Mignard 1976; James 1977; Barry 1979; Wilson 1983; Jeffreys 1985; O'Hara 1985; Wynter 1987).

This perspective continues to resonate in recent writing that asserts that sex work "itself is a form of sexualized male violence" (Day 2008: 28) existing "at the intersection of incest, rape, battery and torture" (Holsopple 1999: 49). Indeed, in this framing sex workers are not active agents but prostituted women (cf. Raphael and Myers 2010; Raphael, Reichert, and Powers 2010; Day 2008; Carter 2004; Lakeman, Lee, and Jay 2004; Farley 2003, 2004; Poulin 2004). These sex-work-as-violence feminists also continue to link prostitution to socio-economic structures, including gender stratifications, racialization and poverty that restrict options; colonization is identified as part of this: "[Aboriginal people] have a long, multi-generational history of colonization, marginalization and displacement from our Homelands, and rampant abuses that has forced many of our sisters into prostitution" (AWAN n.d.).

Feminist conversations on sex work are, however, splintered. Some feminists have reassessed sex work (Rickard and Store 2001), listened to industry workers and integrated sex workers' discourse into their analysis (cf. van der Meulen, Durisin, and Love 2013; O'Doherty, 2011; Bruckert and Chabot 2010; Brock 2009; van der Meulen and Durisin 2008; Parent 1994, 2001; Parent and Bruckert 2010; Jeffrey and MacDonald 2006; Mensah 2006; Ross 2006; Lewis and Shaver 2006; Shaver 2005; Bruckert, Parent, and Robitaille 2003).[3] In contrast to the sex-work-as-violence perspective, this literature both assumes as a point of departure that sex work is an income-generating activity and recognizes that broader socio-economic stratifications and scripts (including gender, economic resource distribution and racialization) condition the range of options open to sex workers — thus creating situations in which some individuals engage in sex work in the context of constrained choice alternatives (cf. Jeffrey and MacDonald 2006;

Kinnell 2002; Weldon 2006; Namaste 2005; Scambler 2007). In this respect there is a recognition that restricted choice does not negate agency: "choosing" this particular work in the context of limited and often unpleasant choices does not mean that sex work is more of a survival tactic than choosing to take on other available jobs. Moreover, a diversity of factors enters into play; some women are compelled (or perceive themselves to be compelled) to engage in the sex trade by their abusive partners, their substance or drug use, their fear of deportation or their abject poverty. For these women, prostitution is "work," although it is not necessarily as much of a job as one of a number of other income-generating activities in which they participate. In this regard the issue of substance use/abuse is key (see Parent and Bruckert 2006). While many women workers in the sex industry are not drug consumers and others maintain a professional labour relationship to the industry despite being consumers of illicit substances, for a small minority of women sex work is intertwined with drug consumption patterns. They will, unlike the women whose relationship to the industry is one of work, exchange sex for drugs.

While the literature reflects on the role of racialization and the impact of colonization on Aboriginal women, we need also to recognize that colonization plays a role in the exclusion of sex workers as women with agency. As Sarah Hunt (2013: 87) notes, "In discussions about colonial violence Indigenous sex workers are often invoked as nameless, voiceless, placeless victims, in memory of past in-justices." As Hunt explains, "The lives and voices of Indigenous sex workers are obscured by discourses of victimization that, on the surface, aim to draw attention to marginalization and colonial violence but fail to provide a space for Indigenous sex workers to speak for themselves and define their own struggles" (2013: 89). We need, in other words, to acknowledge racialized and Indigenous sex workers as women with agency and provide a space from which they can speak for themselves and define their own struggles.

Our work here, which straddles labour theory and criminology, is situated within this emerging body of literature. Labour theory not only reflects the subject position of workers in the industry, but also allows us to step outside of the traditional criminological analysis of deviance to examine these jobs as jobs. A recognition of sex work as gendered labour that occurs in a broader context of racialization immediately places the industry and its workers within a dynamic socio-economic context. In this sense we need to consider what the economic restructuring of the last three decades (intensified by the global economic downturn of 2009) means for Canadian women in general while attending in particular to how some women's choices are conditioned by intersections of gender with racialization and/or class location. In Canada not only do working-class women continue to be ghettoized in sales, service and clerical occupations (Statistics Canada 2010), but the post-industrial labour market is also increasingly characterized by "McJobs" (Ritzer

2004: 148): low-paid, deskilled, monotonous and highly monitored service-sector work that offers workers neither satisfaction nor stability — nor, for that matter, a living wage (Ritzer 2004: 108–15). Moreover, at the same time another parallel trend is obvious. Women increasingly inhabit a precarious labour-market location characterized by temporary and part-time work (Williams 2010). The practice exacerbates marginality: women workers in these labour situations not only experience greater gender income disparity than do their counterparts in the traditional labour market, but are also denied the security and benefits traditionally associated with employment. That said, even full-time women workers between the ages of twenty-five and fifty-four earn just 76 cents to the male dollar (Stienstra 2010: 4). Importantly, the gender income gap is considerably greater for racialized women. For example, in Ontario racialized women have higher rates of unemployment, and those who are employed earn just 53.4 percent of what non-racialized men and 84.7 percent of non-racialized women earn (Block 2010: 3). It is within the context of these constraints and alternatives that women are "choosing" to work at McDonald's, in the retail sector — or in the sex industry.

The labour lens also allows us to shift our focus from structure to practices — or what workers do (Phillips 1997) — and positions us to consider the nature of the labour. It allows us to render skills and competencies visible, examine social and work relations, and reflect on how workers experience the physical, emotional and sexual dimensions of their labour. This attention to grounded experience also speaks to specificity within the broadly defined sex industry, thereby providing an antidote to the tendency to unquestionably conflate the divergent labour practices of cam-girls,[4] peep-show attendants, phone-sex operators, street-sex workers, escorts, erotic dancers and massage parlour/brothel employees under the rubric of "moral transgression."

While invaluable, labour theory, in and of itself, is incomplete — sex work may be work, but it is work that is marginalized, stigmatized and criminalized. It is imperative that we integrate into the analysis the unique configuration of challenges, problems, and difficulties confronted by women working in sectors of the labour market characterized by social, moral and criminal justice regulation. By bringing criminology into labour theory, we can attend to the ways in which social and legal discourses and practices influence the organization of labour and the labour process, increase the danger and stress negotiated by workers, and shape the relations of workers to their social and personal worlds.

It is also imperative that we integrate race and class into the analysis. Sex work, its organization and how it is subjectively experienced are conditioned by the intersection of class, gender and race. Race/ethnic (much like class) stratifications have "always been one of the bedrock institutions of Canadian society embedded in the very fabric of our thinking, our personality" (Shadd 1991: 1). As numerous authors have demonstrated, Canadian society is characterized by discriminatory immigration policies, systemic racism, stereotypical media portrayals and racist discourses that have resulted in a distribution of economic, social and discursive resources that put racialized Canadians generally and women in particular at a disadvantage (Henry et al. 2000; Dhruvarajan 2002). Put another way, race intersects with class and gender to condition women's choices and opportunities both in the broader labour market *and* in the sex industry.

A recognition of racialization raises a number of important questions. How do racializing discourses and racialized spaces structure the incall sex industry? How do racializing practices and discourses condition the experience of racialized women labouring in the sex industry? At a more theoretical level we can ask, how can we analytically separate race and class and produce an analysis that attends to intersectionality while avoiding the pitfalls of cumulative or essentialist approaches (Joseph 2006)?[5]

INCALL SEX WORK AS (CRIMINALIZED) WOMEN'S WORK

Incall work can be broadly defined as women providing sexual services in establishments. But the variety of these services — ranging from marginal to illegal — makes classification problematic. Some of the establishments are massage parlours that offer non-contact erotic entertainment and visual titillation only (such as vibrator and hot-tub shows); others offer erotic massage and manual (and in some cases oral) stimulation; others are brothels in which massage is rare but complete sexual services are available. Still other businesses are dungeons, devoted to domination and submission and allowing clients to self-stimulate only. In short, considerable variety exists in work that falls under the rubric of incall sex work.

That diversity is echoed in the women's perspectives. Some of the women we interviewed had jobs that did not require them to have sex, and that aspect was a precipitating factor in their decisions to work in that sector of the industry. Jacqueline, a Toronto-area dungeon worker specializing in domination, explained: *"Escort work I never really considered. I don't know, I'm just not entirely comfortable with the idea of actually having sex."* Other workers did actively engage with sexuality, and many took pleasure in the exploration of this element of the labour. As Crystal, a massage-parlour worker, told us: *"I love sex. I can really let myself go at work. I like to experience new things and try out new things."*

The Regulatory Context

In Canada, although prostitution per se is not (and has never been) illegal, the industry and the workers are criminalized and sex workers are vulnerable to charges of communicating for the purposes of prostitution (s. 213.1(c)), procuring/living off the avails of prostitution (s. 212.1(j)), or under the common bawdy house provisions (s. 210). Women working in massage parlours, brothels or dungeons are most frequently criminalized under the bawdy house provision 210.1(b), which stipulates that being an inmate (a resident or regular occupant) of a common bawdy house is an offence punishable by summary conviction. Sex workers can also be charged as "keepers" of a bawdy house (a much more serious offence under section 210.1(a)) if they exercise some measure of control (that is, they answer the phone or lock up at the end of the night) (Bruckert and Law 2013).[6] Notably, on December 20, 2013, the Supreme Court of Canada ruled these provisions to be unconstitutional because they infringed on sex workers' liberty interests contrary to section 7 of the *Canadian Charter of Rights and Freedoms*. Sex workers' hopes of a decriminalized industry are, however, unlikely to be realized because the federal government indicated that it would introduce new legislation prior to the ruling taking effect on December 20, 2014.

In addition to the criminalization of their labour (or more specifically, of their labour site), some workers in the incall sex industry (unlike their colleagues who solicit clients on the street, for example, but like erotic dancers) are also regulated in a number of municipalities through by-laws pertaining to the body-rub (and sometimes the holistic health) industry. A body-rub is defined as the "kneading, manipulating, rubbing, massaging, touching, or stimulating by any means, of a person's body or part thereof, but does not include medical or therapeutic treatment" (City of Toronto 2010) — activities that could well be defined as prostitution under Canadian jurisprudence. In effect, this means that there is a layering of regulation over criminalization — a situation that does not work in the interests of sex workers. On this point Emily van der Meulen and Mariana Valverde (2013: 321) explain, "It's rare for people working in licensed sex industry establishments to speak out against abuses as any attempt to rectify exploitative working conditions could lead to federal criminal charges, by-law fines, license cancellation, or even the closure of the business itself." Similarly, Jacqueline Lewis and Eleanor Maticka-Tyndale (2000: 445) concluded that "municipal licensing appears to increase police presence in the lives of escorts and to disempower escorts and their employers from taking action to enhance health and safety." While in principle these by-laws could create a safe and controlled space for workers, in practice they extend the regulation, impose additional levels of control and offer few benefits (van der Meulen and Valverde 2013).

Labour Structure

Despite the diversity of the incall sex industry, broad organizational similarities are apparent in third-party-managed establishments. In general, workers are scheduled for relatively long shifts of ten to twelve hours, although some places have eight-hour shifts and others allow women to select either long or short shifts.

In many establishments, workers are expected to do receptionist duties — which can include answering the phone, booking appointments, explaining the services offered (using more or less explicit code), describing the workers, identifying and declining undesirable clients, and engaging in laundry duties. In addition to these tasks, the women are required to remain on the premises for the duration of their shifts, although they are free to fill their time according to their personal inclinations — sleeping, cooking, reading, studying, socializing.[7] They are also expected to meet the standards of grooming (such as nail policy, makeup) and appearance (such as type of attire) established by the agency. As Moxie, a brothel worker, explained:

> You were expected to have lingerie. You were expected to keep your nails done at all times. You're expected that your hair should be done. And one place I worked all of the girls wore eyelashes and white eyeliner. I don't know where that came from.

The establishment sets rates, with workers receiving between 40 to 60 percent of these rates, an amount that supplements the income they generate through tips and/or the provision of "extras" (although some agencies have "no-extra" rules). The workers appreciated the potential revenues — they spoke of their ability to adequately support themselves (and in some cases their children) through sex work. Workers also found that working for an agency made fiscal sense and said they benefited from the agency fees:

> They were in charge of paying the bills, cleaning, all of the day-to-day operations that I may not want to deal with. And also the legal liability for them was higher because they owned the place on paper … It was having, like, a personal assistant — that was the concept that I was going after was having someone to deal with all the bullshit, and I just had to show up … Being independent, you're working all of the time. Like, you're constantly answering emails, cleaning your location, shopping for new things. There's so much that goes into it that it's easier just to pay a third party sometimes. (Trina, massage parlour worker)

The women who shared this information, whose highly variable incomes ranged from $40 to $800 per day, can be understood as own-account, self-employed workers operating within a fee-for-service structure without benefit of a guaranteed income. While independent vis-à-vis income, they are nonetheless dependent contractors to the extent that they are reliant on, and required to meet the expectations of, a single operator for the physical space, equipment, supplies, advertisement and sometimes the services of support staff. These labour sites appear, then, to be consistent with the trend toward non-standard labour arrangements. While not all non-standard workers[8] are vulnerable (Saunders 2003), for working-class women this labour-market position is, generally speaking, precarious. In many cases the jobs operate as "no more than disguised forms of casualized wage-labour, often marked by dependency on capitalist employers through some sort of sub-contracting system" (Bradley 1996: 49).

The disadvantages of the labour structure notwithstanding, workers see some positive elements in addition to the income potential. Most of the women interviewed appreciated the flexibility that allowed them to integrate and manage the many components of their lives (school, children, art, for example). Of course, the desirability of non-standard labour arrangements must be understood within the context of the steady erosion of the welfare state since the 1980s, which has expanded poor women's burdens. Women are increasingly required not only to assume extra labour but also to organize their employment in a manner that allows them to meet their myriad obligations. Women workers who need to satisfy increasing family and financial obligations as the state decreases its levels of support may therefore embrace non-standard labour arrangements, including contract and self-account work.

As dependent contractors, the women are in a paradoxical position. On the one hand, incall sex workers in commercial establishments, like erotic dancers, aestheticians, massage therapists and hair stylists, are managed as employees — even though they are not wage labourers in the traditional sense but are exchanging a percentage of their earnings for legal protection and access to the necessary legitimizing context, physical space, equipment and technical support. In short, these workers, like other similarly positioned workers such as hair stylists who rent a chair/booth (Gonzales 2010), are exploited in a Marxian sense of having "free" labour extracted and receiving less remuneration than the value that their labour adds to the product/service (Marx 1974 [1859]). On the other hand, as "disguised" employees, incall sex workers are denied the security and access to statutory protection and legal recourse traditionally associated with employment. The precarious labour-market situation of incall sex workers, like that of many other workers employed in non-standard labour arrangements, is at least in part a function of their exclusion from social-security protection (such as Employment Insurance, Canadian Pension Plan), non-statutory benefits (health and dental plans, disability benefits, paid sick leave) and statutory rights (minimum wage, holiday and overtime pay, job protection, notice of termination).

The issue is even more complicated when their labour-market position intersects and interacts with stigma, marginality and criminal law. Not only are workers vulnerable to criminalization, but the illicit status of their labour site (bawdy house) also de facto excludes them from gaining access to their rights not only as workers (for instance, health and safety, labour regulations/agreements) and professionals (to form provincially authorized associations, as do realtors or massage therapists), but also as citizens (to have police protection, for instance). Their position is simultaneously hyper-regulated and unregulated, with many implications for their well-being (Gillies 2013).

Labour Practices

Paying closer attention to labour practices and skills in commercial incall sex work does a couple of things: first, it makes the invisible visible; and second, by exploring the intersections of class, gender and race we can highlight the role of criminalization and stigmatization in conditioning the work of women in this sector of the sex industry.

Like much service-sector employment, incall sex work is physically demanding labour that requires stamina, physical strength and endurance. In stark contrast to the discourse suggesting that sex work is somehow "natural" and therefore not really work (and certainly not skilled work), our research found that success in this area is contingent on a particular and not uncomplicated set of skills and necessitated mastering the rules and expectations of an employer. Christina told us when she was hired she was *"emailed a list of about four pages of procedures and what's expected of you. Whether or not you should work when you're on your period — the answer was no. What to do if you got a yeast infection. Things like that."* Another worker, Crystal, explained that in her job at a massage parlour, *"You learn every day and learn new things every day."* Like waitresses, hair stylists and other women employed in the service sector, successful incall sex workers have to be sociable, patient, courteous and polite, and they have to be capable of dealing with a variety of people. They must present a pleasant and professional demeanour to clients.

Success also calls for a number of more specialized prerequisites, including creativity, an open attitude toward sexuality and a positive assessment of men. In addition, workers must have basic anatomic/sexual knowledge, be able to master massage and sexual techniques, create and maintain an erotic and pleasing presentation of self, discern and respond to clients' (often non-verbalized) needs or wishes, and promote or sell their service. Crystal and Maud, another massage parlour worker, explained that their work necessitated performance skills not only to *"become the whore at work"* but also to put *"on a mask and play a certain character."* They need to be able to improvise a role play based on their reading of the expectations of clients or on the (sometimes detailed) "scripts" of clients.

Women who work in domination require additional knowledge. They must be trained to use the equipment in a safe and effective manner as well as know how to clean and care for it. They must also learn where to strike without leaving marks or doing damage. They need to know anal training techniques, recognize code words (such as yellow for caution, red for stop), and know how to instruct clients. As one of them, Anaïs, noted, providing domination services in a dungeon is a job that requires both openness and insight: *"It's more than just being aggressive and angry. It's about understanding where the bottom's [the client receiving domination services] coming from."* According to Charlotte, another dungeon worker, this specialization also requires finely tuned sensitivity so that the worker is *"able to gauge, you know, how light or heavy they [the clients] are, 'cause for a lot of them it's just visual ... They think they're very heavy into it, but they're not really."* Charlotte also spoke about the need to *"contact your anger"* when necessary. Her strategy was to recall her experience, many years earlier, of being raped by three men: *"That's how I get into the roles sometimes if I'm having trouble with it."* Some workers, like Anaïs, can, despite being bound and *"submissive,"* retain control and *"top the scene from the bottom."*

Incall sex work is not only physically demanding skilled labour, but can also be dangerous. This is, of course, characteristic of many working-class jobs that — computerization and automation notwithstanding — extract a physical toll from workers (Shostak 1980; Houtman and Kompier 1995: 221). Here, however, we see a particular cluster of risks. Workers in the incall sex industry risk exposure to infectious diseases (including, but not restricted to, sexually transmitted infections). Additionally, a number of respondents spoke of the ever-present potential for clients to be sexually and/or physically aggressive. Workers implement strategies to minimize these risks. In the case of the health risks, their tactics include the use of condoms, gloves and lubricants, the visual inspections of clients' sexual organs, washing hands with antiseptic soap, and disinfecting equipment. Third parties can mediate the potential for physical/sexual aggression through measures such as maintaining zero-tolerance policies and bad date lists, the collection and verification of personal information (for example, name, phone number, employer of clients), requiring references, matching clients to workers, hiring on-site or oncall security persons, training workers in exit and conflict avoidance strategies, establishing emergency protocols in addition to such things as the presence of others in the location, a monitored entrance, security camera, no-locked door policies, and a two-call system and client screening. This last strategy sometimes includes profiling on the basis of race and class (Bruckert and Law 2013). Workers also endeavour to mitigate risk through their own labour practices (including the refusal to participate in submission, abstaining from alcohol or drugs at work, carrying pepper spray, and creating a "virtual" bouncer).[9]

A number of respondents evoked the language of gendered sensibility when they spoke of refusing men whom they "intuitively" perceived to be threatening — an ability based on the knowledge of experience, which allows the workers to perceive and interpret numerous minute signs of potential danger. Karen, reflecting on her own experience as a massage parlour employee, noted that workers are *"thinking all the time; you gotta be quick in case any of [the clients] try to pull something on you."*

Women who offer submission services are in a particularly vulnerable position. The implications of a client's incompetence, ignorance or maliciousness range from bruises to welts to permanent organ damage.

Sex work can also be emotionally demanding on a number of different levels. The women must cope with the valorization of youth and "lookism." Women who are older or whose appearance does not conform to narrow conventions of attractiveness may find work hard to come by. As Maxine, a massage parlour worker, commented: *"I'd have weeks without work because the parlour didn't advertise my body type or whatever. They'd just be like, 'Oh, yeah, and this is Maxine.' ... 'Well, she's a larger girl.'"* As a result, Maxine told us, *"I would question myself, and I'm like, 'Should I sell out?' 'Should I get fake tits?' 'Should I go on a diet?'"* In addition to sizeism and ageism, racism also plays out in the clandestine space of the sex industry — which occurs in particular in the framing of racialized workers as the erotic/exotic Other. Trina, a massage parlour worker, explained: *"The wording that they used was always the same ... Like, you know, Black girls were always referred to as chocolate. Or ebony. And Asian was always exotic."* Incall sex workers also spoke of agency quotas on racialized workers. Lee, a Black sex worker in Toronto, spoke of *"being told by agencies because I'm Black that I may not get calls, or I'm not popular, or I'm difficult to market."*

In addition, like other direct-service employees — including waitresses (Paules 1991) and domestics (Salzinger 1991) — sex workers must retain a positive self-concept in the face of clients who, according to Jacqueline, a dungeon employee, *"don't seem to realize that you're another person."* Moreover, Angelica explained that sometimes her clients at the massage parlour *"assume I'm really stupid ... Like, I'm pretty much an object or a service."* Moreover, like women workers in other service sectors of the labour market (including bartenders and hair stylists), incall sex workers also sometimes have to deal with manipulative clients who, to procure extra services, pout, nag, flatter or threaten to take their business elsewhere. In the sex industry the stakes are high and the process is complicated by the ever-present spectre of criminalization. Not only are some clients seeking sexual services that the woman is not prepared to offer and that may endanger her (sex without a condom, for instance), but she is also operating in a non-institutionally structured space in which the rules and expectations are difficult to enforce.

At other times workers are required to engage in emotional labour (Hochschild 1983). Some clients seek more than sexual services; they seek personal intimacy. Crystal explained that as a worker in a massage parlour: *"You got to be sweet and all that. You gotta really play the role."* Occasionally clients are seeking companionship. Jade, who works in a brothel, recalled her experience: *"There was a guy, seventy-six years old, who took two hours at a time. I took off my top but kept my bra on and we played cards ... we drank wine. The guy was all alone and his kids didn't see him ...*

Some I've seen for five years and we did nothing.[10] This aspect of the work requires workers to engage in "deep acting," recreating personal experiences to "induce or suppress feeling in order to sustain the outward countenance that produces the proper state of mind in others" (Hochschild 1983: 7) in a commercial setting. This demanding expectation is hardly unique to sex workers; arguably, it is increasingly a job requirement of women working in numerous other areas of the service sector, including beauticians (Sharma and Black 2001), flight attendants (Hochschild 1983) and nurses (Lopez 2006; Molinier 2003).

Unlike some of those other sectors, incall sex workers are positioned to negotiate the nature and extent of their emotional labour. In a brothel, a dungeon, or, for that matter, a beauty salon, clients receive a technical service (intercourse, domination, a pedicure) and may anticipate additional intimacy and interpersonal interaction. This condition is not, however, an inherent one within the institutional confines of the service encounter. The workers are left with the choice of whether or not they will engage in emotional labour to improve the service encounter — and they might choose to do so either out of a personal inclination or to secure a regular clientele.[11]

Incall sex work thus requires workers to vigilantly guard against physical and/or sexual danger, to maintain their personal boundaries at the same time as they create an environment of intimacy, and to strive to realize the sexual (and sometimes interpersonal) fantasy of their clients. Not surprisingly, as Wendy Chapkis (1997: 79) points out, an ability to distinguish between the work domain and the personal realm is imperative for maintaining emotional equilibrium. Catherine explained that as a worker in an erotic establishment, *"You really have to be mentally strong ... You have to dissociate from your private life. You have to see it as a job."* Many sex workers are able to draw on their professionalism to mediate the emotional expectations of clients. Angelica described her work in a massage parlour: *"You can actually, like, give someone what they need emotionally but still be disconnected. It's a pretty amazing thing ... But it's not taking a lot out of me. Like, it's my work."*

The stresses of the demands of the job are further exacerbated by the illegal nature and stigmatic assumptions of outsiders. The illegality means that workers are susceptible to charges under section 210 of the Canadian Criminal Code, which necessitates continual vigilance, assessment of clients and self-monitoring because, as Angelica pointed out, *"One day you could say the wrong thing to the wrong person."* In establishments in which owners endeavoured to circumvent the law through wilful blindness (often municipally licensed agencies that operate under the pretence that no sexual services are being offered), workers are not able to discuss challenges with colleagues or their employer. They must be vigilant in their communications with clients and discreet about their use of safer sex equipment. As Robyn, a massage parlour worker, remarked, *"You weren't allowed to have condoms in the room. Like, if they found condoms in the garbage that was a big issue because we would get inspected by the police."* Ultimately, one of the more disconcerting findings of our research was the lack of accurate legal knowledge on the part of many sex workers. As a result of misconceptions, women took ineffectual precautionary measures (such as not touching the money prior to engaging in the sex act and refraining from intercourse).

Importantly, the women's vulnerability to arrest denies workers potential resources in their negotiations with clients. Among other things, the fear of denunciation by disgruntled customers complicates workers' maintenance of their personal boundaries. Moreover, women are hesitant to turn to the police for protection or to report violent clients. Karen, a massage parlour worker, noted:

> *It would feel a lot safer [with decriminalization] because you'd know that if anything happened, people would listen to you and there'd be a place to go. You wouldn't have to worry about going to jail or telling a cop. Maybe people wouldn't try stuff as much as they do.*

Criminalization also denies workers the ability to negotiate labour conditions with their employers through professional organizations or organized labour action, or by evoking their statutory labour rights.

Moreover, although numerous workers — including morticians, custodians and some sectors of the sales force — labour in stigmatized occupations, when they leave the labour site women in the incall sex industry must cope with the condemnation that accompanies the stigma of "whore" (Pheterson 1989). Annabelle, a massage parlour worker, recognized: *"It is not easy to fight against a whole population and against ideas so deeply entrenched in people's heads."* According to Karen, who also works in a massage parlour, this stigma necessitates that a woman *"not let it get you down and take your work home with you … Don't view yourself the way society views you."* Consequently, some workers seek to isolate themselves from public censure by closeting their occupational location, creating fictitious jobs, and separating their work and private lives (including not associating with other sex workers).

Unfortunately, these tactics also mean a lack of insider support. Angelica, who had been working in a massage parlour for five months, found that her counterculture friends were carefully non-judgmental. Nonetheless, she bemoaned her lack of a network:

> *It's hard to get a certain type of support. People who don't do it are always, like, "well, just stop doing it," "why are you doing it if it's hard?" It's like, "well, everything is hard!" You know? Like, if you're working, you're making six dollars an hour at a coffee shop, you're gonna have to deal with people you hate, but that's part of your job.*

In practice, it appears that workers must negotiate and maintain a balance between what emerges as competing objectives of anonymity and support. While workers are, for the most part, able to find a personally suitable space on the spectrum — with anonymity/no support at one end and strong social support/ vulnerability to public and private condemnation at the other — the conditions nonetheless increase the day-to-day stress, and, regardless of any compromise position adopted, the women are left in a precarious situation. Moreover, the experience of stress is intensified when the worker lacks social support in the home (Levi, Frankenhauser, and Gardell 1986: 55). As Meg Luxton and June Corman (2001) point out, a lack of support has particular relevance for women whose role and labour-force challenges may not be fully acknowledged within social and familial areas — which is certainly the case for sex workers, whose job is frequently not even acknowledged to be work.

Still, despite the myriad challenges and stressors confronted by these women workers, all of our respondents identified positive aspects of their jobs. While the financial benefits that allowed them to participate in the social sphere were foremost, they also identified a number of other benefits, including flexibility, free time and a pleasant, relaxed work environment.[12] Moreover, they also noted a wide range of intrinsic rewards. Anaïs saw her job in a dungeon as being *"entertaining, it's fun sometimes and it's very mundane, but you know usually you don't know what to expect so it's kind of fun. It's exciting."* Some women appreciated the skills they develop. For Maud, a massage parlour worker, this included learning *"how to take control and assert limits."* Others highlighted pleasurable social and/or sexual interactions with clients. For Anaïs the work was also *"a legit way of expressing resistance against society."* Similarly, for Angelica, who had experienced sexual harassment throughout her life, the work allowed her to *"manipulate this [sexism] for my own benefit ... I feel like I'm beating the man, you know? I literally get to beat the man!"* Perhaps these features are all the more striking in contrast to the monotonous, repetitive and unsatisfying alternatives readily available to young working-class women — the "McJobs" (Ritzer 2004).

THE COMPLEXITIES OF SEXUALIZED COMMERCE

We are left, then, with the question of the suitability of the term "sex work" — and the critiques from radical feminists as well as from the conservative right that the sex industry does not constitute work, either because it is sexual exploitation or because the prerequisite competencies are natural and therefore do not constitute skills. Is the concept, as Sheila Jeffreys (2005) maintains, simply an attempt to make the industry more palatable through "euphemistic neutral terms"?

Stepping outside of normative assumptions, we can listen to workers such as Lea, who has a job in a massage parlour and asserted: *"It's a service that I offer."* We can make links to "reputable" jobs by applying a labour analysis. In doing this a number of commonalities emerge. On a structural level these jobs are consistent with the broader trend toward women's increased participation in service-sector employment and non-standard labour arrangements that position women workers outside of the stability and protection traditionally associated with employment. We also see how the sex industry echoes the broader social stratifications in the marginalization of and discrimination against racialized workers. When we shift to labour process, we see that like other working-class women's work in the consumer-service sector, the job of sex-trade workers requires the application of (rarely acknowledged) skills.[13] It is physically demanding and potentially dangerous and stressful, and requires workers to undertake emotional labour. It is certainly not an easy job. In the course of their workday, workers must confront and negotiate a myriad of challenges and stressors. Moreover, many workers in the commercial incall sex industry who labour for third parties are, in a Marxian sense, exploited workers.

In light of these commonalities, the pivotal question becomes: does the sexual component mark the industry as being outside the framework of labour? Despite the challenges introduced by the sex radical discourse twenty years ago (Califia 1994; Johnson 2002), the private/public and sex/labour dichotomies continue to be so firmly embedded in our consciousness that the term "sex work" is virtually an oxymoron. This approach is reproduced in labour studies in which work-site sexuality is either invisible or an inherently harmful expression of patriarchal power that renders the atmosphere oppressive (Hearn and Parkin 1995; Lobel 1993).

Arguably, this positioning is highly problematic. On the one hand, "[s]exuality is a structuring process of gender" (Adkins 1992: 208), and gender and sexuality are central "to all workplace power relations" (Pringle 1988: 84). The traditional skills that women are required to bring to the labour market include the ability to assume an attractive "made-up" appearance so that "part of the job for women consists of looking good" (Adkins 1992: 216). However, more than just a good appearance is required. Increasingly, the prerequisite presentation of self is sexualized so that much of the labour that working-class women undertake has a visible sexual subtext and necessitates the negotiation of a sexualized labour terrain. On the other hand, our sexuality — in our private and professional lives — is subjectively experienced, and we must take care to acknowledge not only that class may condition the approach and meaning ascribed to sexuality (Aronowitz 1992: 62),[14] but also that there are a variety of positions vis-à-vis labour-site sexuality that speak to a spectrum of engagement.

For some working-class women, the distinction between sex work and other consumer service work may be one of degree and explicitness. This is a connection that Angelica made when she reflected on her previous labour experiences:

I've been a cocktail waitress and that was sex work too, but it's just over the table sex work that the government supports ... Basically, you're hired 'cuz you're pretty. Start there. Then ... the money you make is based on the shifts that you work, the shifts you get. So in order to get the good shifts you have to sell the most drinks. In order to sell the most drinks you have to be flirtatious. So, it's totally sex work.

In short, the many points of convergence support the conceptualization of women employed in sexualized commerce as working-class women workers in the new economy, and they lend support to the linguistic shift toward the term "sex work." The illegal/illicit status of the labour not only raises the spectre of criminalization, but also facilitates an additional level of exploitation in that it inhibits workers from gaining access to both their statutory labour rights and their rights as citizens. Moreover, many of the challenges and stressors of the job do not emerge from the labour itself, but are a by-product of discourses of immorality, the lack of recognition as workers, limited social and interpersonal support, a lack of police or legal protection, criminalization and stigma.

The sex industry's long tradition of adapting both to changing market, social and moral conditions and to technological innovations[1515] has resulted in increasingly varied industry practices and structures, which in turn have opened up the industry to new workers (Bernstein 2007). Today a sex worker may be a stay-at-home mother who responds to erotic telephone calls (Flowers 1998) or a high-school student who types erotic messages on the Internet and exchanges pictures for gifts (Robinson 2004). She may be an administrator subsidizing her wages by working as an erotic dancer two nights a week (Law 2011). She could be a woman on social assistance who makes ends meet through street sex work (Parent and Bruckert 2006) or a full-time worker, either independent or working for or with a third party, offering sexual services in a brothel or hotel room. All of this diversity destabilizes stereotypical assumptions about sex workers; it also highlights the problems of an occupational classification that encompasses such a range of labour structures and processes.

The problem, then, lies not with the term "sex work," but with the imposed limits embedded in its application. On the one hand, the term continues to situate the industry in question outside of women's work, obscuring how the jobs inhabit a particular location on the axis of sexual labour and emotional labour characteristic of much women's work. On the other hand, it fails to capture the complexity of "sex industry" labour practices, in which sexuality is but one component. The solution may not be to abandon the particular vocabulary but to destabilize the dichotomies by inserting the private, the sexual and the intimate into the language of labour. In this manner, we can develop a more nuanced and inclusive analytic framework of sexualized commerce to make sense of the labour of women workers — both in and outside of the industry.

Notes

1   In this discussion we draw on empirical data from two qualitative research projects. The first, on the incall sex industry, was undertaken in 2002 (Parent and Bruckert 2005). The research was guided by the feminist commitment to methodological approaches that centre the voices and experiences of women. Accordingly, the questions we posed were designed to illicit information regarding labour structure and process and to reveal how that work is subjectively experienced. Using snowball sampling, we conducted a series of fourteen in-depth semi-structured interviews (in French and English) lasting between one and three hours during the summer and fall of 2002. The women were all employed, or at least very recently employed, in the incall sex industry in Montreal (eight) and Toronto (six). Respondents ranged in age from twenty-one to forty, and with between four months to seven years of experience; the majority of women where white (twelve), one woman was Asian, and another Black. The second research project, which we use to "fill out" the picture, was a SSHRC-funded study on sex-industry management. We draw on a subsample of the data — twenty-four focus group interviews that took place in Toronto, Halifax, Ottawa and Montreal during spring 2012 with sex workers who work(ed) for or with third parties in the incall sex industry. The participants, who ranged in age from twenty-one to fifty-seven (average age thirty-three), had between one-and-one-half and forty-four years of experience in the industry. As in the previous study the majority of the workers we interviewed were white (thirteen), two were Black, two Aboriginal, two identified as Aboriginal/White, and one was Aboriginal/Black (three participants did not indicate their race/ethnicity). Collectively these thirty-eight respondents from the two research projects represent a diverse cross-section of industry workers and offered rich insights.

2   The initial analyses that situated the sex trade within questions of class, gender and economic vulnerability were quickly displaced by concerns about the white slave trade (Walkowitz 1980; Rosen 1982; DuBois and Gordon 1983). Within this framework, these feminists started to demonize individual men as being threatening to "innocent womanhood" and campaigned for greater regulation and laws. The attempts by these earlier feminists to help prostitutes — all the while condemning prostitution — had disastrous consequences for women in the trade (Rosen 1982: 102). For an overview of later feminist positions on prostitution, see Tong 1984, Järvinen 1993, and Parent 1994.

3   Some workers have also reasserted sexuality into the debate, challenging the appropriation of sexuality of women by men and asserting their right to control their bodies and to define their sexuality outside both traditional moral discourse and the feminist discourse that associates feminine sexuality with love and warmth. In short, these sex workers are part of a broader rethinking of sexuality as a contested terrain, the site and source of subversion (Aline 1987; CORP 1987; McClintock 1993; Chapkis 1997).

4   "Cam-girls" exchange revealing photos for "gifts" with individuals they have contacted

through the Internet (Robinson 2004).

5   See Bannerji (2005) for a discussion of the pitfalls of feminist anti-race theorizing.

6   The Criminal Code defines a common bawdy house as "a place that is a) kept or occupied or b) resorted to by one or more persons, for the purposes of prostitution or the practice of acts of indecency" (s. 197). Canadian jurisprudence specifies that the definition of "prostitution" does not require actual sexual intercourse, nor need there be physical contact. This very broad definition has led to convictions under section 210 of the Criminal Code of women who worked in strip clubs where dancers gyrated on the laps of fully clothed patrons (R. v. Caringi, O.J. 2002), massage parlours that offered full body massages (including manual masturbation) but no oral, vaginal, or anal sexual intercourse (R. v. Brandes, O.J. 1997); and sado-masochism dungeons in which neither intercourse nor masturbation was offered.

7   The women working in one establishment (a dungeon) were (unless they booked off for a set period) expected to be available to be paged seven days a week, twelve hours a day, in addition to working one receptionist shift per week without pay. With the exception of this receptionist shift, they were not required to be on-site.

8   Non-standard or precarious labour arrangements are relationally understood to standard employment — which is defined as the "employment of individuals for wages and salaries by a single firm, where individuals work full time on the employer's premises, and expect (and are expected) to be employed for an indefinite period of time" (Canada 1999: 2) — and includes part-time, seasonal, short-term contracts, temporary employment and own-account work.

9   A number of establishments did employ security personnel, but even when no such individual was on-site the women workers sometimes led clients to believe that this was the case.

10   The interview quotations from Jade, Catherine, and Annabelle have been translated by the authors.

11   By contrast, for dancers in "straight" strip clubs, where physical contact is prohibited, the technical service oftentimes is the interaction so that emotional labour becomes a job requirement (Bruckert 2002; Wood 2002).

12   Whether or not a job meets middle-class standards of "interesting" or "rewarding," it may have non-economic benefits. It may offer women social contacts and friendships (MacDonald and Connelly 1989: 66), and recognition of their labour that is not afforded full-time homemakers (Reiter 1991: 106). Greater economic contribution can also be correlated to power within the family (Feree 1984: 75), independence, status, and a sense of self-worth and self-esteem (Penney 1983: 21).

13   That skills are largely dismissed or rendered invisible is not unique to incall sex workers, but characterizes many working-class women's jobs. It does, however, affirm once again the relative and subjective nature of what are defined as skills. Class and gender continue to be associated with skills in complex ways (Gaskell 1986).

14   For example, sexual interaction may not necessarily be understood as sexual harassment (Westwood 1984). Ethnographic accounts offer a very different image of such practices as sexually explicit shop-floor banter (Barber 1992: 81). Furthermore, positioned to recognize the costs of capitalism and patriarchy, working-class women may deconstruct the advantages afforded by an asexual presentation of self (Feree 1990).

15 For example, the trajectory of strip clubs and the transformation of dancers from performers to service workers speak to the intersection of broader market forces and marginal labour. Between 1973 and 1995 the work of erotic dancers was "de-professionalized"; workers went from being salaried performance artists to service-sector employees labouring for tips (Bruckert 2002). In a similar vein, the sex industry's use of print media, telephones and the computer speaks to its adaptability. Certainly, Internet technology has had a major impact, transforming both existing practices (many escorts now advertise and interact with clients via the Internet) and facilitating the emergence of new practices (such as cam-girls).

References

Adkins, L. 1992. "Sexual Work and the Employment of Women in the Service Industries." In M. Savage and A. Witz (eds.), *Gender and Bureaucracy*. Oxford: Blackwell.

Aline. 1987. "Good Girls Go to Heaven, Bad Girls Go Everywhere." In F. Delacosta and A. Priscilla (eds.), *Sex Work: Writings by Women in the Sex Industry*. Pittsburgh: Cleis Press.

Aronowitz, S. 1992. *Politics of Identity*. New York: Routledge.

AWAN (Aboriginal Women's Action Network). 2007. *Aboriginal Women's Statement on Legal Prostitution*. Vancouver: AWAN. <prostitutionresearch.com/aboriginal%20 statement%20on%20legal%20prostitution.pdf>

Bannerji, H. 2005. "Introducing Racism: Notes towards an Anti-Racism Feminism." In B. Crow and L. Gotell (eds.), *Open Boundaries: A Canadian Women's Studies Reader* (second edition). Toronto: Pearson.

Barber, P. 1992. "Conflicting Loyalties: Gender, Class and Equality Politics in Working Class Culture." *Canadian Woman Studies* 12, 3.

Barry, K. 1979. *Female Sexual Slavery*. New York: New York University Press.

Bernstein, E. 2007. "The Sexual Politics of the 'New Abolitionism.'" *Differences* 18, 5.

____. 2012 "Carceral Politics as Gender Justice? The 'Traffic in Women' and Neoliberal Circuits of Crime." *Theoretical Sociology* 41.

Block, S. 2010. *Ontario's Growing Gap: The Role of Race and Gender*. Ottawa: Canadian Center for Policy Alternatives.

Bradley, H. 1996. *Fractured Identities: Changing Patterns of Inequality*. Cambridge: Polity.

Brock, D. 2009. *Making Work, Making Trouble: The Social Regulation of Sexual Labour* (second edition). Toronto: University of Toronto Press.

Bruckert, C. 2002. *Putting it On, Taking it Off: Women Workers in the Strip Trade*. Toronto: Women's Press.

Bruckert, C., and F. Chabot. 2010. *Challenges: Ottawa Area Sex Workers Speak Out*. Ottawa: POWER.

Bruckert, C., and T. Law. 2013. *Beyond Pimps, Procurers and Parasites: Management in the Incall/Outcall Sex Industry*. Ottawa: Management Project.

Bruckert, C., C. Parent, and P. Robitaille. 2003. *Erotic Service/Erotic Dance Establishments: Two Types of Marginalized Labour*. Ottawa: The Law Commission of Canada.

Bryan, J. 1965. "Apprenticeship in Prostitution." *Social Problems* 12.

Califia, P. 1994. *Public Sex: The Culture of Radical Sex*. Pittsburgh: Cleis.

Canada, Public Service Commission, Research Directorate. 1999. "The Future of Work:

Non-Standard Employment in the Public Service of Canada." Ottawa: Policy, Research, and Communications Branch.

Carter, V. 2004. "Prostitution and the New Slavery." In C. Stark and R. Whisnant (eds.), *Not for Sale: Feminists Resisting Prostitution and Pornography*. Sydney: Spinifex.

Chapkis, W. 1997. *Live Sex Acts: Women Performing Erotic Labour*. New York: Routledge.

City of Toronto. 2010. *Toronto Municipal Code, Chapter 545 Licensing, Article XXXII*. Toronto, ON: City of Toronto.

CORP. 1987. "Realistic Feminists." In L. Bell (ed.), *Good Girls, Bad Girls: Sex Trade Workers and Feminists Face to Face*. Toronto: Woman's Press.

Day, S. 2008. *Prostitution: Violating the Human Rights of Poor Women*. Ottawa: Action Ontarienne contre la violence faite aux femmes.

Dhruvarajan, V. 2002. "Women of Colour in Canada." In V. Dhruvarajan and J. Vickers (eds.), *Gender, Race and Nation: A Global Perspective*. Toronto: University of Toronto Press.

Dubois, E., and L. Gordon. 1983. "Seeking Ecstasy on the Battlefield: Danger and Pleasure in Nineteenth-Century Sexual Thought." *Feminist Studies* 9.

Farley, M. 2003. "Prostitution and the Invisibility of Harm." *Women & Therapy* 26, 3/4.

____. 2004. "'Bad for the Body, Bad for the Heart': Prostitution Harms Women Even if Legalized or Decriminalized." *Violence Against Women* 10, 10.

Feree, M. 1984. "Sacrifice, Satisfaction and Social Change: Employment and the Family." In K. Sacks, and D. Remy (eds.), *My Troubles Are Going to Have Trouble with Me*. New Brunswick: Rutgers University Press.

____. 1990. "Between Two Worlds: German Feminist Approaches to Working-Class Women." In J. Nielsen (ed.), *Feminist Research Methods*. Boulder: Westview Press.

Flexner, A. 1920. *Prostitution in Europe*. New York: Century Co.

Flowers, A. 1998. *The Fantasy Factory: An Insider's of the Phone Sex Industry*. Philadelphia: University of Pennsylvania Press.

Gaskell, J. 1986. "Conceptions of Skill and Work of Women: Some Historical and Political Issues." In R. Hamilton, and M. Barrett (eds.), *The Politics of Diversity: Feminism, Marxism and Nationalism*. London: Verso.

Gillies, K. 2013. "A Wolf in Sheep's Clothing: Canadian Anti-Pimping Law and How It Harms Sex Workers." In E. van der Meulen, E. Durisin, and V. Love (eds.), *Selling Sex: Experience, Advocacy, and Research on Sex Work in Canada*. Vancouver: UBC Press.

Glover, E. 1969 [1943]. *The Psychopathology of the Prostitute*. London: Institute for the Study and Treatment of Delinquency.

Gonzales, J. 2010. "Booth Rental: Is It Right for You?" Hairdresser Career Development Systems. <hcds4you.com/blog/booth-rental-is-it-right-for-you/>.

Greenwald, H. 1958. *The Call Girl: A Social and Psychoanalytic Study*. New York: Ballantine.

Hearn, J., and W. Parkin. 1995. *Sex at Work: The Power and Paradox of Organization Sexuality*. New York: St. Martin's Press

Henry, F., C. Tator, W. Mattis, and T. Rees. 2000. *The Colour of Democracy* (second edition). Toronto: Harcourt Brace.

Heyl, B. 1977. "The Training of House Prostitutes." *Social Problems* 24.

____. 1979. *The Madam as Entrepreneur: Career Management in House Prostitution*. New Brunswick, NJ: Transaction Books.

Hochschild, A. 1983. *The Managed Heart: Commercialization of Human Feeling*. Berkeley:

University of California Press.

Holsopple, K. 1999. "Pimps, Tricks, and Feminists." *Women's Studies Quarterly* 27, 1/2.

Houtman, I., and M. Kompier. 1995. "Risk Factors and Occupational Risk Groups for Work Stress in the Netherlands." In S. Sauter and L. Murphy (eds.), *Organizational Risk Factors for Job Stress*. Washington: American Psychological Association.

Hunt, S. 2013. "Decolonizing Sex Work: Developing an Intersectional Indigenous Approach." In E. van der Meulen, E. Durisin, and V. Love (eds.), *Selling Sex: Experience, Advocacy and Research on Sex Work in Canada*. Vancouver: UBC Press.

James, J. 1977. "The Prostitute as Victim." In J. Chapman and M. Gates (eds.), *The Victimization of Women*. Beverly Hills: Sage Publications.

Järvinen, M. 1993. *Of Vice and Women: Shades of Prostitution* (translated by K. Leeander). Oslo: Scandinavian University Press.

Jeffrey, L., and G. MacDonald. 2006. *Sex Workers in the Maritimes Talk Back*. Vancouver: UBC Press.

Jeffreys, S. 1985. "Prostitution." In D. Rhodes and S. McNeil (eds.), *Women Against Violence Against Women*. London: Onlywomen Press.

____. 2005. "Different Word, Same Dangers from Trade in Women." *Sydney Morning Herald*, April 20.

Johnson, M. 2002. "Jane Hocus, Jane Focus." In M. Johnson (ed.), *Jane Sexes It Up*. New York: Thunders Mouth Press.

Joseph, J. 2006. "Intersectionality of Race/Ethnicity, Class and Justice: Women of Color." In A. Merlo and J. Pollock (eds.), *Women, Law and Social Control*. Boston: Pearson.

Kinnell, H. 2002. *Why Feminists Should Rethink on Sex Workers' Rights*. UK Network of Sex Work Projects, Beyond Contract Seminar Series. <nswp.org/sites/nswp.org/files/KINNELL-FEMINISTS.pdf>.

Koyama E. 2002. *Instigations from the Whore Revolution*. Portland: Confluere Publications.

Lakeman, L., A. Lee, and S. Jay. 2004. "Resisting the Promotion of Prostitution in Canada: A View from the Vancouver Rape Relief and Women's Shelter." In C. Stark and R. Whisnant (eds.), *Not for Sale: Feminists Resisting Prostitution and Pornography*. Melbourne Australia: Spinifex Press.

Laner, M. 1974. "Prostitution as an Illegal Vocation." In C. Bryant (ed.), *Deviant Behaviour*. Chicago: Rand McNally.

Law, T. 2011. "Not a Sob Story: Transitioning Out of Sex Work." M.A. thesis, University of Ottawa.

Levi, L., M. Frankenhauser, and B. Gardell. 1986. "The Characteristics of the Workplace and the Nature of Its Social Demands." In S. Wolf and A. Finestone (eds.), *Occupational Stress: Health and Performance at Work*. Littleton: PSG.

Lewis, J., and E. Maticka-Tyndale. 2000. "Licensing Sex Work: Public Policy and Women's Lives." *Canadian Public Policy* XXVI, 4.

Lewis, J., and F. Shaver. 2006. *Safety, Security and the Well-Being of Sex Workers: A Report Submitted to the House of Commons Subcommittee on Solicitation Laws*. Windsor: Sex Trade Advocacy and Research.

Lobel, S. 1993. "Sexuality at Work." *Journal of Vocational Behavior* 42.

Lombroso, C., and E. Ferrero. 1885 [1985]. *The Female Offender*. New York: Appleton.

Lopez, S.H. 2006. "Emotional Labor and Organized Emotional Care: Conceptualizing

Nursing Home Care Work." *Work and Occupations* 33, 2.

Luxton, M., and J. Corman. 2001. *Getting By in Hard Times: Gendered Labour at Home and on the Job.* Toronto: University of Toronto Press.

MacDonald, M., and M.P. Connelly. 1989. "Class and Gender in Fishing Communities in Nova Scotia." *Studies in Political Economy* 30.

Marx, K. 1974 [1859]. *Capital* (Volume 1). New York: International.

Mensah, M.N. 2006. "Débat feminist sur la prostitution au Québec: Points de vue des travailleuses du sexe." *The Canadian Review of Sociology and Anthropology, Special Issue: Casting a Critical Lens on the Sex Industry in Canada* 43, 3.

McClintock, A. 1993. "Maid to Order: Commercial Fetishism and Gender Power." *Social Text* 37.

Mignard, A. 1976. "Propos élémentairessur la prostitution." *Les Temps Modernes* 356.

Millett, K. 1971. *The Prostitution Papers: A Candid Dialogue.* New York: Avon.

Molinier, P. 2003. *L'énigmede la femme active. Égoïsme, sexeet compassion.* Paris: Payot.

Namaste, V. 2005. *Sex Change, Social Change: Reflections on Identity, Institutions and Imperialism.* Toronto: Women's Press.

O'Doherty, T. 2011." Criminalization and Off-street Sex Work in Canada." *Canadian Journal of Criminology and Criminal Justice* 53, 2.

O'Hara, M. 1985. "Prostitution Towards a Feminist Analysis and Strategy." In D. Rhodes and S. McNeil (eds.), *Women Against Violence Against Women.* London: Onlywomen Press.

Parent, C. 1994. "La Prostitution ou le Commerce des Services Sexuels." In L. Langlois, Y. Martin, and F. Dumont (eds.), *Traité de Problèmes Sociaux.* Québec: Institut québécois de recherche sur la culture.

____. 2001. "Les Identités Sexuelles et les Travailleuses de l'Industrie du Sexe à l'Aube du Nouveau Millénaire." *Sociologie et Sociétés* 33, 1.

____. 2005. "Le Travail du Sexe dans les Établissement de Service Érotiques: Une Forme de Travail Marginalisé." *Déviance et Société* 29, 1.

Parent, C., and C. Bruckert. 2006. "Répondre aux besoins des Travailleuses du Sexe de Rue: Un objectif qui passé par la décriminalisation de leurs activités de travail." *Reflets* 11.

____. 2010. "Le Travail du Sexe Comme Métier." In C. Parent, C. Bruckert, P. Corriveau, M.N. Mensah, and L.Toupin (eds.), *Mais Oui C'est un Travail! Penser le Travail du Sexe au-delà de la Victimisation.* Québec: Presses de l'Université du Québec.

Paules, G. 1991. *Dishing It Out.* Philadelphia: Temple University Press.

Penney, J. 1983. *Hard Earned Wages: Women Fighting for Better Work.* Toronto: Women's Press.

Pheterson, G. 1989. *A Vindication of the Rights of Whores.* Seattle: Seal Press.

Phillips, P. 1997. "Labour in the New Canadian Political Economy." In W. Clement (ed.), *Understanding Canada: Building the New Canadian Political Economy.* Montreal: McGill-Queen's University Press.

Poulin, R. 2004. *La Mondialisation des Industries du Sexe: Prostitution, Pornographie et Traite des Enfants.* Ottawa: L'Interligne.

Pringle, R. 1988. *Secretaries Talk.* London: Verso.

Raphael, J., and B. Myers-Powell. 2010. *From Victims to Victimizers: Interviews with 25 Ex-Pimps in Chicago.* Chicago: Schiller DuCanto & Fleck Family Law Center of DePaul University College of Law. <newsroom.depaul.edu/pdf/family_law_center_report-final.pdf>.

Raphael, J., J.A. Reichert, and M. Powers. 2010. "Pimp Control and Violence: Domestic Sex Trafficking of Chicago Women and Girls." *Women & Criminal Justice* 20, 1.

Reiter, E. 1991. *Making Fast Food.* Kingston: McGill-Queen's University Press.

Rickard, W., and M. Storm. 2001. "Sex Work Reassessed." *Feminist Review* 67.

Ritzer, G. 2004. *The McDonaldization of Society.* Thousand Oaks: Pine Forge.

Robinson, M. 2004. "Cam Girls are the New 'It' Girls of the Sex Industry." *Fulcrum* 65, 13.

Rolph, C. 1955. *Women of the Streets: A Sociological Study of the Common Prostitute.* London: Secker and Warburg.

Rosen, R. 1982. *The Lost Sisterhood.* Baltimore: Johns Hopkins University Press.

Ross, B.L. 2006. "'Troublemakers' in Tassels and C-Strings: Striptease Dancers and the Union Question in Vancouver, 1965–1980." *Canadian Review of Sociology and Anthropology* 43, 3.

Salzinger, L. 1991. "A Maid by Any Other Name." In M. Burnaway (ed.), *Ethnography Unbound.* Berkeley: University of California Press.

Saunders, R. 2003. "Defining Vulnerability in the Labour Market." Paper presented at CPRN/LCC Roundtable on Vulnerable Workers. June 17. Ottawa.

Scambler, G. 2007. "Sex Work Stigma: Opportunist Migrants in London." *Sociology* 21, 6.

Shadd, A. 1991. "Institutionalized Racism and Canadian History: Notes of a Black Canadian." In O. McKague (ed.), *Racism in Canada.* Saskatoon: Fifth House.

Sharma, U., and P. Black. 2001. "Look Good, Feel Better: Beauty Therapy as Emotional Labour." *Sociology* 35, 4.

Shaver, F. 1996. "Traditional Data Distort Our View of Prostitution." <walnet.org/csis/papers/shaver-distort.html>.

Shostak, A. 1980. *Blue Collar Stress.* Menlo Park: Addison-Welsley.

Stienstra, D. 2010. *Fact Sheet: Women and Restructuring in Canada.* Ottawa: CRIAW/ICREF.

Statistics Canada. 2010. "Experienced Labour Force 15 Years and Over by Occupation and Sex, by Province and Territory." <statcan.gc.ca/tables-tableaux/sum-som/l01/cst01/labor45a-eng.htm>

Tong, R. 1984. *Women, Sex and Law.* Savage: Rowman and Littlefield.

van der Meulen, E., and E. Durisin. 2008. "Why Decriminalize? How Canada's Municipal and Federal Regulations Increase Sex Workers' Vulnerability." *Canadian Journal of Women and the Law* 20, 2.

van der Meulen, E., E. Durisin, and V. Love. 2013. *Selling Sex: Experience, Advocacy, and Research on Sex Work in Canada.* Vancouver: UBC Press.

van der Meulen, E., and M. Valverde. 2013. "Beyond the Criminal Code: Municipal Licensing and Zoning By-laws." In E. van der Meulen, E. Durisin, and V. Love (eds.), *Selling Sex: Experience, Advocacy, and Research on Sex Work in Canada.* Vancouver: UBC Press.

Velarde, A. 1975. "Becoming Prostituted." *British Journal of Criminology* 15, 3.

Walkowitz, J. 1980. "The Politics of Prostitution." *Signs* 6, 1.

Weldon, J. 2006. "Show Me the Money: A Sex Worker Reflects on Research into the Sex Industry." *Research for Sex Work* 9.

Westwood, S. 1984. *All Day Every Day.* London: Pluto Press.

Williams, C. 2010. "Economic Well-Being." *Women in Canada: A Gender-Based Statistical Report.* Ottawa: Statistics Canada.

Wilson, E. 1983. *What Is To Be Done About Violence Against Women?* Harmondsworth: Penguin.

Wood, E. 2002. "Working in the Fantasy Factory." *Journal of Contemporary Ethnograpy* 29, 1.

Wynter, S. 1987. "Whisper." In F. Delacoste and P. Alexander (eds.), *Sex Work: Writings by Women in the Sex Industry*. Pittsburgh: Cleis Press.

Cases Cited

Bedford v. Canada (Attorney General) [2013] SCC 72.

R v Caringi, [2002] OJ No 2367

Legal Facta

Bedford v. Attorney General of Canada and Attorney General of Ontario, [2011]. (Factum of the Intervener Women's Coalition) OCA C52799 and C52814.

Bedford v. Attorney General of Canada and Attorney General of Ontario, [2009]. (Factum of The Christian legal Fellowship, REAL Women of Canada and The Catholic Civil Rights League) OSCJ 07-CV-329807 PDI.

Chapter 15

BAD GIRLS LIKE GOOD CONTRACTS
Ontario Erotic Dancers' Collective Resistance

Suzanne Bouclin

From: *Victim No More: Women's Resistance to Law, Culture and Power,* pp. 46–60 (reprinted with permission).

In most Canadian jurisdictions there has been a shift in the labour performed by female erotic dancers from visual entertainment (stage dancing) to more individualized services (lapdancing) (Frank 2002). This requires additional physical and emotional investment from dancers and renders them more vulnerable to sexual and economic exploitation (DERA 2002). Given their ambiguous employment status, dancers also lack access to employment protections and common law remedies. This is compounded by the stigma associated with their work and the fine line dancers walk between legal and illegal sex acts. In light of the aforesaid conditions of constraint, some dancers have organized to craft more meaningful choices for themselves.

This chapter first provides an overview of the feminist methods and theories that guide my research on dancers' collective resistance. I then outline the efforts of Ontario-based dancers to respond to unfair labour practices, arguing that affiliations have emerged as a venue through which women can exercise agency and subvert the oppressive structures of their workplace. I go on to discuss the barriers marginalized and stigmatized workers face when attempting to organize. I conclude that, in conditions that foster individualism and competition, support systems for dancers can lead to sophisticated political and legal campaigns to change the erotic industries.

METHODOLOGY, METHODS AND THEORETICAL FRAMES

This research project was conceived in 2002, when I attended a Stigmatized Labour Support Network (SLSN) meeting and met members of the Dancers' Equal Rights Association (DERA). In light of the marginalized and stigmatized nature of the Canadian erotic dance industry, a history of the women working within it is not readily accessible. As a result, my core findings draw upon semi-structured interviews with five primary and five secondary research participants. The former are DERA members: current and former dancers in their mid-twenties to their mid-thirties, who identify as English-speaking and white and who live in Ottawa. Two are in long-term relationships; two are single-parent heads of households; four were experiencing financial difficulties at the time of the interviews. Secondary informants include an SLSN member (a nurse providing outreach in clubs), two former dancers, a legal studies professor and a labour organizer. Finally, I also engaged in considerable correspondence via e-mail with women in other jurisdictions who are championing the rights of sex trade workers through STELLA (Montreal), the International Union of Sex Workers (England) and the Exotic Dancers' Alliance (U.S.). I collected information on four Ontario-based groups: Canadian Association of Burlesque Entertainers, Exotic Dancers' Alliance, Association for Burlesque Entertainers and DERA. Members of these small, fairly homogenous affiliations share a commitment to changing labour practices. However, the approaches taken by these groups have not always resonated with the broader dancer community, as they tend to focus on the needs of a privileged minority of dancers (white, young, English-speaking and who have some formal education). While these limitations do not render their activism fatally flawed, they do speak to the generalizability of my findings.

In terms of theories, this research is influenced by feminist re-readings of the concept of resistance. Briefly, during the early eighties, a debate emerged among North American feminists around the rhetorics of choice/constraint as they related to the sex trades (Bell 1987; Chandler 1999). More recently, these binaries have been challenged for being caricatured:

> The simplistic binary constructs that my culture gives me to interpret these events, passive victim versus active agent, do not encompass my experience. I was both and neither, something different, something to be located in the underlying play of differences between the dichotomy of victim and agent. (Ronai: 1999: 126)

A recurring project in more recent feminist theorizing has been to move away from binary categories to emphasize how women resist oppressive systems that regulate their lives. Feminist postmodern/poststructuralist theorists deconstruct the unitary notion of the female subject and accentuate the shifting nature of identity (Alcoff 1991; Butler 1990; Cixous 1983). This is reflected and reproduced in more recent readings of erotic dancing, which, for example, can be personally and financially rewarding, but may also be experienced as exploitive and oppressive. More likely, the work of an erotic dancer is located between these two extremes (Bouclin 2004; Bruckert 2002; Egan 2003; Sanchez 1997), and dancers individually and collectively negotiate choices for themselves within their workplace. In this context, resistance refers to tactics or strategies that individuals employ in order to contest the conditions of constraint in which they exist. Indeed, dancers do engage in everyday individual acts of resistance within the Foucauldian (1976) understanding of power and agency. For instance, not unlike waitresses and flight attendants, there is an expectation reinforced by employers and customers that dancers will engage in emotional labour (Hochschild 1983; Montemurro 2001). For instance, Julie recounts how dealing with customers is draining at times: *"They try to touch you when you say not to touch you basically. And at the same time you're on friendly vibe so it's very taxing you know? And there are ones who get all depressed and tell you sob stories, you know, and you can't leave."* However, with time and experience, she adopted a more *"abrupt and professional"* approach: upon receiving gratuities, she would *"just stand up in the middle of a sentence, smile and say 'okay then have a great night'"* and walk away. Erotic dancers also engage in performative defiance (Wood 2000) when negotiating customers who cross the line. Sam explains that she would adopt a highly erotic disciplinarian persona to communicate what she would and would not tolerate: *"Just talk to them like puppies — good boy, sit, stay."* However, the strategies available to some dancers are not available to others. Heather outlines the characteristics that might leave dancers with less space in which to manoeuvre:

> *I know that some girls are afraid because ... they don't have any education or another job or they don't have anything to fall back on, they're worried about supporting their families, they would be afraid of losing their jobs.*

Everyday acts of resistance are to a large extent contingent upon one's cultural markers. It seems however that some dancers are cognizant of the disconnect between everyday acts and effecting changes in strip clubs. They have looked to collective strategies to bring about conditions in which they can exercise more meaningful choices in relation to their labour practices. The remainder of my discussion focuses on this collective form of resistance, which finds its roots in a more traditional Marxian blueprint for social change.

GETTING ORGANIZED:
DANCERS RESIST LICENSING

In 1975, the Supreme Court of Canada determined that performing nude in a cabaret theatre was not an immoral act (*R. v. Johnson*). While local ordinances on nudity varied, generally dancers could only remove their clothing down to a G-string in a manner that did not offend public decency under sections 163 and 170 of the Criminal Code. They would perform five stage shows per six-hour shift and their average weekly remuneration was $300 (Bruckert and Parent 2004). Between shows entertainers were strictly forbidden from fraternizing with customers in order to avoid being charged with soliciting for the purposes of prostitution (*Re Sharlmark Hotels Ltd v. Municipality of Toronto* 1981). Flying in the face of sanctions against nudity, clubs threatened dancers with dismissal if they did not disrobe entirely (Tracey 1997). With this and the move toward more seedy entertainment such as mud wrestling and wet T-shirt contests (Bruckert 2002), striptease emerges as a "social problem" to be controlled, mainly through municipal licensing. Dancers began to organize to challenge industry changes and intrusive regulation.

In 1978, Toronto proposed a bylaw that would require all club owners, operators and dancers to obtain licences. The city claimed this measure would protect workers, provide them with professional credibility and ensure better regulation of the industry. However, in order to obtain licences, women were required to produce medical certification that they were free of sexually transmitted infections, submit photo identification, establish that they did not have a criminal record and pay an annual fee (Cooke 1987; Johnson 1987). A group of Toronto-area dancers led by Diane Michaels organized to challenge the licensing scheme. In 1979, the Canadian Association of Burlesque Entertainers (CABE) was recognized by the Canadian Labour Council and became Canada's first and hitherto only union-backed association of dancers in Ontario. CABE went before city council arguing, according to former president Merri Johnson (1987), that licensing would push the most marginalized dancers — older dancers and those with criminal records — out of the clubs into the much more precarious street-level sex work. With the exception of having dancers' stage names on licences rather than their real names, CABE's submissions were ignored and the licensing scheme passed (Cooke 1987).

Despite this defeat, CABE remained vocal, and in 1981 it sued clubs for having barred its members from entry into clubs. In rendering its decision, the Labour Board grappled with whether dancers were employees (CABE v. Algonquin Tavern). CABE argued in the affirmative because of the managerial control over dancers' working conditions (attire, music, clients with which dancers interact, hours of work). The taverns argued that dancers were independent contractors and the Board agreed: dancers were not an "integral" part of taverns' business. Rather they were one of many forms of entertainment (like musical, comedic and sporting events) that clubs promoted. In short, dancers were ancillary to clubs' primary income-generating activity: food and alcohol sales. Moreover, dancers worked for a number of establishments at once and were not economically dependent on one specific employer. As a result, they were denied the safeguards and benefits afforded to employees through protective legislation (maximum work hours, minimum pay, wage protections, overtime benefits, notice for termination and vacation time). CABE was nevertheless successful on one front: the Board drew a distinction between freelancers and housegirls. Freelancers worked according to their own schedule and received no base salary, so even though they were required to meet a basic four-hour requirement, they could be considered independent contractors. Housegirls (scheduled dancers), on the other hand, received a weekly wage in addition to being required to work six to eight hours a shift; they were deemed employees. However, CABE was unable to mobilize enough housegirls to enforce their employee status (Weagle 1999). CABE therefore shifted its resistance strategy and moved from the courtroom back to the political realm. It began lobbying the municipal government to implement a bylaw requiring dancers to wear a G-string. The city responded favourably and attempted to legislate. The bylaw was unsuccessfully challenged by a coalition of club owners; its pith and substance dealt with the regulation of a business and was well within municipal authority. However, in 1985, the Ontario Court of Appeal struck down the law because its dominant purpose was regulating public morals — a matter squarely within federal jurisdiction (*Re Koumoudouros*).

CABE disbanded only three years after its inception. Amber Cooke, who worked in the industry in Toronto during the 1980s, argues that the group's favouring of the G-string law may have led to loss of confidence in its leadership, and it could "not act from a position of strength" (1987: 96). Despite its inability to present a collective voice for dancers, CABE nonetheless contributed to challenging societal assumptions about dancers as victims. It presented women as labourers working to effect changes. As well, it remains the only Ontario-based dancers' affiliation to forge formal bonds with a union.

THE SHIFT TO MORE PERSONALIZED SERVICES

After CABE folded, a hiatus in organizing followed. During the eighties, there were nonetheless a number of broad societal shifts that shaped and are reflected within the micro-level of the strip club. With the global move toward neo-liberalism, the Mulroney government emphasized deregulation of the private sector and downsized the public sector (Timpson 2001). Canada's economy suffered a severe decline, which forced working-class women from scarce manufacturing jobs to the service sector, with correspondingly low wages, little employment security and long hours (Vosko 2000). In light of these conditions, a number of (primarily white, working-class) women who met the standard of sexiness promoted within the stripping industry opted for erotic dancing or other forms of commodified sexual labour as an alternative to working for minimum wage (Bruckert 2002). With an increase of available workers, erotic dancers' labour shifted: table dances were standardized and wages atrophied. With table dancing, women would sell a one-on-one, no-contact dance for five dollars. Stage shows, while still a core element, gave way to the more personalized interactions and became a form of advertisement. With the exception of feature dancers (who tour cities and are paid at a higher weekly rate) remuneration for housegirls went from a per-show basis to per-shift basis (on average $40 a shift). According to Cooke, women were strongly encouraged to provide "hands-on entertainment rather than dance in order to make their money" (1987: 98). Dancers who refused to table dance were fined by the clubs (an egregious practice still current today) or scheduled for less lucrative shifts. Valerie found that with de facto mandatory table dances, women had slim options: *"table dance and maybe lose the ability to choose to 'cross the line' with some customers,"* refuse to table dance and take the decrease in income or leave the industry altogether.

In the early nineties, the erotic dance industry underwent additional changes. First, clubs began requiring dancers to pay a ten- to thirty-dollar "stage fee" for every shift they worked. Clubs promoted the idea that dancers engaged in contracts for service (independent contractors) rather than in contracts of service (employees) (Weagle 1999). Management argued that they rented out the venue in which women sold titillation and company; dancers simply paid the fees for access to the club's customers. Second, owners substantially decreased the number of scheduled dancers. As Christina explains: *"They just stopped putting me on schedule. I was a regular girl with four shifts a week. Then one day I go into work and there's no more schedules."* Third, the creation of champagne rooms (cubicles) for personalized interactions at a higher cost (usually ten to twenty dollars) and the emergence of contact dances (lapdancing) vitally altered the labour performed by dancers. In principle, a lapdance involves a naked dancer gyrating on a patron's lap (facing him or with her back to him). In practice, the extent of contact between a patron and a dancer varies according to dancers' personal boundaries and social location, customer preference, the presence or absence of seclusion, the amount of money exchanged and club rules. Of these shifts, lapdancing has without doubt been the most contentious, and there have been considerable legislative efforts to regulate it. Specifically, in *R. v. Mara and East,* police officers charged two men (the club owner and manager) with allowing an indecent performance under section 167 of the Criminal Code at a Toronto tavern. Officers witnessed mutual masturbation between patrons and dancers and what appeared to be cunnilingus. At trial, Judge Hachborn found that while this behaviour may have offended community standards in other contexts, it was innocuous by comparison to the conduct dealt with in an earlier case (R. v. Tremblay), though, but for that earlier decision, the conduct would have likely been subject to regulation. With that, he dismissed the charges. Almost two years later, the Ontario Court of Appeal unanimously reversed that decision. First, it held that the judge had not properly applied the community standard of tolerance (R. v. Butler). Instead, the higher court held that lapdancing is harmful to society because it degrades and dehumanizes women, is incompatible with the dignity of each human being, predisposes persons to act in an antisocial manner and presents a risk of real physical harm to women. Second, the court found that the facts could be distinguished from those in Tremblay. In that case, the physical contact between patron and dancer was strictly prohibited and the explicit nudity took place in a booth rather than in the middle of the club. The Supreme Court upheld the appellate judgment.

Between the trial and the Supreme Court ruling, clubs began promoting lapdancing as legal; this in spite of the fact that many were being charged and found guilty of keeping a common bawdy house (R. v. Caringi). As one owner remarks: "Following the decision lapdancing became a popular form of entertainment at most clubs in Ontario as dancers and club owners had a judicial decision that touching between patrons and dancers would not constitute criminal behaviour" (affidavit of Mr. Koumoudouros in OAEBA v. Toronto 1997). Simultaneously, two anti-lapdancing discourses emerged. Some opponents of lapdancing argued that it was inherently harmful to the moral order and disrupted the nuclear family. Others argued that it was harmful to the health and well-being of women (Lewis 2000). Certainly, while some dancers felt that lapdancing provided them with an additional income, others felt that it decreased their ability to negotiate unwanted physical contact with patrons. Two Toronto-area groups organized in response to the Hachborn decision. It is noteworthy that although both challenged ideas about dancers' victimization, they also reproduced the "harm to dancers" discourse.

TORONTO DANCERS ORGANIZE

The Association for Burlesque Entertainers (ABE) formed to lobby Toronto's municipal authorities around lapdancing. The bylaw campaign was spearheaded by ABE's president, Katherine Goldberg, and was backed by the provincial New Democratic Party (Ferguson 1995). On behalf of its 200 members ABE went before city council with country-wide complaints that dancers experienced lapdancing as disempowering and were being coerced into "upping the ante." As one dancer explains:

> I remember the very first night we lapdanced … we were driving home from the club and we were crying our eyes out. We both felt like this is not what we were brought up to do. These strangers' fingers all over you … it was really nasty. (cited in Lewis 2000: 10)

In 1995, Toronto became the first municipality to ban lapdances and its bylaw was immediately challenged by a coalition of club owners. The Ontario Adult Entertainment Bar Association (OAEBA) sought an order quashing it on the basis that it was beyond the city's jurisdiction and encroached upon the federal government's power to enact criminal law (*OAEBA v. Toronto*). Two dancers intervened and argued that the ban infringed their freedom of expression under section 2(b) of the Charter of Rights and that they derived personal rewards and economic gains from the new labour practice: "I chose to participate in close contact or lapdancing for a number of reasons … I could make more money doing close contact dancing. I also enjoyed the personal contact that I developed with my customers doing close contact dancing" (affidavit of Ms. Johne in *OAEBA v. Toronto*: 651). Relying on the testimonies of ABE members, the city submitted that the law was enacted for health and safety reasons and that lapdancing increased the likelihood of violence within clubs and the transmission of infections:

> I'm not saying all exotic dancing is bad, but lapdancing and prostitution in bars is bad … I don't think lapdancing can be controlled. I urge you to get rid of it … lapdancing hurts everyone. For instance, a man fingers a girl and has a cut finger … and he gives her AIDS or venereal diseases … she goes home and gives it to her husband. (ABE 1995, cited in Lewis 2000: 11)

The judge held that the purpose of the bylaw was in fact the protection of health and safety in adult entertainment parlours and that no Charter rights were violated (contact dancing was not a constitutionally protected form of speech). On appeal, the trial judge's decision was upheld and appeal to the Supreme Court denied.

In the aftermath of this success, ABE's membership declined significantly. First, several dancers, including Goldberg herself, were banned from working at the club for their involvement in anti-lapdancing initiatives (Highcrest 1995). Additionally, its focus on lapdancing may have alienated some dancers and overshadowed other issues. As one former member comments: "No one is talking about other workplace issues such as filthy change rooms, long hours, and the whole wage structure. When we could lapdance we had some choice in how we worked" (Dawn in Highcrest 1995). However, a number of Toronto-area dancers held positions similar to ABE's. In one dancer's words: "I had enough of men saying to me I'll give you fifty bucks for a blow job … I hated the way it made me feel. So I'm actually enjoying dancing more since the ban [on lapdancing]" (cited in Lewis 2000: 211).

ABE folded after the Supreme Court found lapdancing to be within community standards of tolerance (*R. v. Pelletier*). But as late as 1998, members were still
appearing before city councils across the country and successfully lobbying for
municipal bans on lapdancing. ABE's evidence was also relied upon by lower level
courts in other provinces in finding that lapdancing constituted a health risk for
dancers and for patrons (*563080 Alberta Ltd*). To this end, ABE's primary strength
lies in its use of an adjudicative approach, which encouraged dancers to participate and engage the courts in a meaningful way (especially interesting given the
marginalizing impact the adversarial system often has on women). Finally, to date,
ABE is the only Ontario-based dancers' organization to actively pursue activism on
a national level rather than limiting its scope to regional issues; thus its members
also destabilized traditional stereotypes about dancers by presenting themselves
as pan-Canadian labour rights advocates.

Around the same time as ABE's inception, another Toronto group began to organize. In 1994, a woman working in the region initiated a series of regular meetings
between dancers, health workers and government officials to strategize around
health and safety issues relevant to the industry. The result was twofold. First, a pilot
program was implemented in three strip clubs; once a month a public health nurse
would go into clubs to do intake with dancers. Primarily, the nurse would provide
methods for minimizing the risk of transmission of disease (e.g., best methods for
removing dried semen, blood and other bodily fluids from furniture and props)
(EDA 2001). The program emphasized that it was not dancing in and of itself that
rendered women vulnerable to infections, but the nature of their labour practices
and work environments (Lewis 2000). Second, a group of dancers received funding
in 1995 to form an association, the Exotic Dancers Alliance, to champion erotic
dancers' rights (EDA 2001). Mary Taylor, EDA's first executive director, had been
active in trying to change dancers' working conditions for several years. In fact,
in 1992, Taylor and thirteen other dancers "marched in G-strings, bras and little
coats" to a Scarborough area bar to denounce a club's decision to raise deejay fees
from $10 to $20; they negotiated management down to $15 (Hendly 1999). Ms.
Taylor left the industry when lapdancing became an occupational requirement:
"Everybody has their line they've gotta draw … I didn't like it in the end and I
would only go to work out of desperation when I needed to pay bills" (cited in
Snug 2000: 1). Shortly thereafter she became involved with EDA and helped draft
its mission statement with the objectives of building solidarity among dancers,
developing programs and services and ensuring fair treatment of dancers within
the judicial system (EDA 2001).

EDA was successful at generating public attention around issues of concern to
dancers primarily through workshops and burlesque shows that demystified the
industry (Reid 2001). They also attempted to raise awareness around violence

against women and systemic sexism within policing. For instance, they approached reporters to cover a story about a Toronto-area dancer who had her head smashed against the wall by a gang of young men. When the police arrived they did not offer the woman assistance, but counter-charged her with assault for biting her assailant in self-defence (Reid 2001). The association's primary networking and information-sharing tools were, until recently, its website and monthly newsletter, "The Naked Truth," through which dancers could access basic legal information and links to social services. In the first volume (2001), EDA printed a list of demands for better work places (lockers, ventilation, doors on bathroom stalls and cleanup of the unhygienic conditions). However, lack of funding led EDA to shut down both of these services and even disconnect its phone line. However, since June 2002, it has made use of an Internet group as a means of increasing communication among dancers. Members discuss issues from legal questions and coping with coercive managers or patrons, to beauty tips and advice for interpersonal relationships. The interactive and informal format allows dancers to engage at their convenience and to post their opinions with anonymity. However, its easy access means that custom-ers and club owners can also log on and dancers may self-censor for fear of being banned. That said, contentious questions do arise, especially around lapdancing and other sex acts that occur in clubs. For instance, one member, known as Dancer on Tour, posted the following on October 14, 2004, in an attempt to spur on col-lective action by "real dancers":

> I am proud to be a "clean" dancer who does everything to prove to the world that not all dancers are whores ... It's a shame that there are so many dancers [who] are more interested in "cut-throating" each other than pulling together to get better conditions and a fair wage or at the least an abolishment of "fines" and "stage fees."

Clearly, in objecting to lapdancing, dancers sometimes overlook other relation-ships of privilege and exploitation that further complicate women's decision to engage in certain labour practices. In other words, the anti-lapdancing discourse produces and reproduces hierarchies among women occupying different social locations. Moreover, while interactive communication technology holds the potential to bring about new affiliations between dancers as well as attract a more diverse constituency to the discussion, it is limited to women who have access to the Internet and may exclude more marginalized women who are most vulnerable to exploitation: poor women, older women and women for whom English is not their first language.

At its peak EDA's paper membership was at less than twenty (Hendly 1999). Because the EDA was labelled an anti-lapdancing organization by owners and managers, most members have been banned from a number of clubs (Prittie 1999). Further, in 2000, Ms. Taylor left EDA due to infighting. In her opinion, power had become centralized, communication among members had broken down, and some dancers were more concerned about getting media attention than continuing to struggle for better working conditions for dancers (Personal communication). Rhonda Collins, a health care practitioner, has taken the helm. Under her direction EDA has forged greater alliances with social workers, community groups and the police in efforts to improve dancers' working conditions and general health (Thesenvitz 2002). Most recently EDA supported a joint licensing effort between itself, the Peel Region's Health Department and the local police. Unlike CABE, EDA feels that the long-term aim of licensing could ultimately be a self-regulating system whereby dancers themselves would administer the licenses and city council and police would be able to access the database of files when necessary, in cases of missing women, for example (Weagle 1999). However, dancers have consistently been against licensing and fear that it will result in greater regulation of women rather than increased protection.

Lewis and Maticka-Tyndale (2003) found that the most successful work done by EDA at its peak (in the late 1990s) was outreach in clubs in conjunction with local health units. To this end, they argue that the approach favoured by EDA was more service oriented than a grassroots model of organizing. Unfortunately, most of its service provision has been abandoned and it seems to have moved toward a pro-regulation approach. The emergence of EDA should nonetheless be read as a success. First, until recently, EDA's leadership and membership was always limited to current and former dancers, which enabled it to maintain its credibility as a legitimate voice within the dancer community. Second, whereas ABE engaged in more politicized action and challenged legal regulation and oppressive labour struggles within a courtroom setting, EDA centered its action around service-provision, information-sharing, coalition-building and the creation of support networks, which may have effected a more direct impact on dancers' everyday lives.

OTTAWA DANCERS RESIST LAPDANCING

While normalized in clubs since the nineties, it is only with the Supreme Court's ruling in Pelletier that lapdancing was deemed legal (R. v. Pelletier). Pelletier owned a club that enforced strict touching rules: patrons could touch the dancers' buttocks and breasts only and only in the context of a private dance in a champagne room. In 1997, two undercover police officers visited the bar and purchased lapdances. The dancers did not offer additional sexual services, nor did they permit the officers to touch them in a manner that would breach club rules. Nonetheless, Pelletier was charged with bawdyhouse offences under sections 197 and 210 of the Criminal Code.

The judge held that these acts were not indecent and that the club, under Ms. Pelletier's constant supervision, enforced strict rules to which both dancers and patrons complied. The Court of Appeal reversed the acquittal and entered a conviction with a fine. That decision was overturned by the Supreme Court in 1999. It determined that the trial judge had thoroughly considered all relevant factors in analyzing the community's standard of tolerance and made no error of law in his application of that test. With this ruling, lapdancing was effectively legal, subject to municipal ordinances banning it. Since the early 1990s, the city of Ottawa had a bylaw in place that prohibited lapdances. As in other jurisdictions with similar proscriptions though, the bylaw had never been systematically enforced and by the late 1990s all Ottawa area clubs offered lapdancing (DERA 2002). According to my participants, some dancers were in favour of the new industry practice and felt it was a sustainable way to increase their income, though most emphasized the economic motives that position women who want to work as erotic dancers with little alternatives: *"It's a harsh reality. They really don't think they have a choice — if they want to make money. In a strip club right now you have to get touched if you want to make money"* (Raye Ann). Others experienced increased vulnerability to economic exploitation and sexual or physical violence. It is the latter concern that spurred Samantha Smyth, a former Ottawa-area dancer, to found the Dancers' Equal Rights Association (DERA).

According to Ms. Smyth, lapdancing has become the defining feature of the erotic dance industry and has resulted in "the abuse, mistreatment and exploitation of women working in [Ottawa]" (DERA 2002: 1). DERA's objective is to further dancers' labour and human rights; it was incorporated in 2000 and received its first grant from the United Way in 2001. Drawing upon the work of previous such groups, DERA's specific goals include the promotion of health and safety standards in clubs, the harmonization of municipal regulation of clubs and the eradication of de facto mandatory lapdancing (DERA 2003). Its approach is unique in that shortly after mobilizing it forged a coalition with service providers, health care workers, lawyers, academics and students in order to increase DERA's visibility and to help counter the stigma of being an organization of "deviant" workers. The SLSN was formed in March 2002 to assist DERA in achieving its objectives and to provide resources for DERA members and other women working as erotic dancers. While SLSN's members come from divergent backgrounds, most advocate the decriminalization of sex work and are all working toward the destigmatization of erotic dancing. As with DERA, the SLSN's key spokesperson is Ms. Smyth. In many ways then, DERA and SLSN can be viewed as two halves of one organization: the former is exclusive to dancers and provides a safe space for information-sharing; the latter is comprised of community groups who are working with dancers in order to effect changes within the industry. Some DERA/SLSN initiatives include public education (speaking at conferences, organizing roundtable discussions between government officials and community members), coalition-building, political lobbying, establishing a dancer support group, fundraising and promoting in-club health programs (based on the EDA model).

At the fore of DERA's more recent activism is its work to establish clear labour practice guidelines and to harmonize Ottawa's adult entertainment bylaws. In 2004, the city of Ottawa met with various stakeholders including DERA and after considerable discussion proposed a bylaw that would have required clubs and dancers to obtain licences (upon the provision of photo identification). DERA opposed municipal licensing because of the risks inherent in providing governmental bodies and club owners with personal information (and specifically whether or not a dancer has a criminal record). As Sam explains:

> *If you've been convicted of prostitution and you don't want to be a prostitute anymore where else are you going to get a job? I think she should have the right to choose not to be a prostitute.*

A public health nurse working with DERA adds that licensing will be used as a "tracking device" that will further marginalize dancers:

> *People don't get licensed for nothing. There has to be something in it for them. So what do women gain by being licensed. Healthcare? Decent wages? No. It's just a way to keep track of the women ... I see the ultimate goal as protecting men. It's so that the guys that go to the clubs know that they are clean so they know that they are not taking anything home to their wives.*

Despite being against licensing, DERA agreed to endorse the bylaw so long as other key concessions were made, namely, a strict no touching/no lapdancing policy implemented and elimination of champagne rooms. City council accepted their arguments and removed licensing from the agenda. Yet, in August of that same year, it passed a bylaw eliminating champagne rooms in order to prevent lapdancing and other forms of sex acts from occurring between patrons and performers.

In June 2005, club owners, managers and dancers associated with the nine Ottawa clubs applied to have the bylaw quashed (*AEAC v. Ottawa*). They claimed that DERA did not represent their interests and the city was wrong in relying on the evidence its members put forth. They added that the city had not undertaken empirical studies to determine whether lapdancing posed a serious risk to the health and safety of club attendants. A number of dancers deposed that they had never engaged in sex acts with customers and that they were unfairly portrayed as vulnerable and in need of protection.

Judge Hackland of the Court of Justice dismissed the application and held that the city was reasonable in relying upon DERA's submissions as representative of the interests of performers. The objections to the law mirrored those expressed by DERA, namely increased regulation of women. Basing his judgment on the *OAEBA v. Toronto* decision, Justice Hackland found that the no-touch provisions were within municipal jurisdiction and did not violate the Charter. The decision is currently under appeal and may well find itself before the Supreme Court within a year.

This is a substantial success for DERA, which managed to gain momentum and mobilize community members in spite of considerable backlash from clubs owners, who not only banned members from their clubs but who threatened to fire any dancer who voiced opposition to lapdancing. This may help to explain the reality that despite its success, as with the other erotic dancer affiliations I have researched, DERA has experienced difficulties in recruiting members. To date, estimates of membership vary from five to ten current and former dancers, in spite of an estimated 750 currently working in Ottawa clubs.

BARRIERS TO ORGANIZED RESISTANCE

The groups I examined draw their legitimacy primarily by virtue of their "insider claims-maker" status (Best 1987). That legitimacy is subject to challenge though when we consider that their membership rates have been and continue to be relatively low. What follows then is a discussion of the barriers to mobilizing dancers.

First, dancers are highly independent and autonomous and for the most part view themselves as self-employed. As such, attempts to collectively lobby around labour issues may not seem relevant. My findings support the research of others (Bruckert 2002; Cooke 1987) who have found that for many dancers, the energy required to organize does not seem worthwhile:

> *It's difficult for them to make a commitment … A lot of dancers are like that. It's difficult to approach dancers at work because a lot of them [are] just there to make money and they don't want to talk about, or get into this stuff at work. They just want to make their money and do their thing. (Heather)*

For a number of dancers, particularly those who see their labour as pleasant, short-term and lucrative, maintaining the status quo is more important than getting involved with dancers' affiliations, advocating broader changes within the industry or assuming the working-class militant persona (Sangster 1997). As Raye Ann explains: *"The girls don't care. They don't care. This is the way it is. I'm not going to be here very long. Don't care. Don't want to know."* This may be due to the perception from dancers that they stand to earn a better income through gratuities from lapdancing than through minimum wage and table dances (Heather). To this end, dancers need incentives to get organized. For instance, Christina argues that were clubs to eradicate lapdancing, dancers would need to receive something in return, namely, increased income:

> *If they got rid of lapdancing, I think that the price of regular non-touch dancing should be upped. A lot of the $20 dancers are not going to want to go down to $10 a song — that's a fifty percent [decrease] each song and that's always going to be going through their mind.*

Second, many of the key spokespersons no longer work in the industry. Heather, an active DERA member, is keenly aware that because of this, the group risks becoming "out of touch" with dancers' day-to-day work experiences:

> *We need to know more what they want. Sam and I aren't in the clubs anymore. We need girls who are actually working in the clubs right now so that we know exactly what's going on, what they need, and what they want.*

Third, dancers do not want to be associated with the group for fear of reprisal by owners and, specifically, of losing their jobs. As noted earlier, this concern is not unfounded given that the women at the helm of all four Ontario-based organizations have been banned. In short, those dancers who are highly independent or who view their work, in its current form, as an enjoyable and viable means of making a living, are difficult to integrate into a collective resistance strategy. That said, these findings should not be read as suggesting that dancers' affiliations are not legitimate voices. Instead, they contextualize the activism in which they engage and highlight the reality that even within subversive forms of organizing some voices overshadow others.

CONCLUSION

The object of this inquiry has been to document and to tease the potential of dancers' affiliations as a venue for collective resistance. My findings are framed within the understanding that erotic dancers are labourers who operate within constraints: poor working conditions, limited access to labour protections and collective bargaining mechanisms, social marginalization and stigmatization. They are also often subject to hostile state regulatory practices. However, dancers exercise agency through their collective efforts to reshape labour practices that they have determined, limit their individual choices. Documenting these attempts in Ontario, and discussing the extent to which formal resistance enables dancers to craft better working conditions, contributes to the growing literature on the striptease industry. Despite their near absence from historical records, Canadian women, and working-class women specifically, have a long history of collectively resisting oppressive systems of class, race and gender in order to promote their fundamental human rights under Canadian law. Through a feminist lens that centres labour and resistance, mine is an attempt to engage with the paradigm shift in theorizing around women working as erotic labourers from seeing them as either "sex radicals" or "victims." Instead, I grapple with more nuanced readings of women's labour and their occupational choices and ability to resist exploitation as something that is fundamentally influenced by their individual social location. What I have learned is that despite limited resources for formal organizing, Ontario-based erotic dancers have consistently mobilized in response to particular labour concerns and sometimes even in an attempt to fundamentally change their work environments. They have found that in order to respond to changes in the way their work is organized and in industry standards, they must work together so that they can make choices about how to earn a wage. For instance, Sam argues that getting organized can assist women in gaining the support needed to resist the stresses of their working life, overcome feelings of powerlessness and fight for better treatment by club owners and managers:

> There are strengths in numbers. It gives a big sense of empowerment ... A lot of women don't even know they have rights. [DERA aims to] educate each and every single dancer on what their rights are, what they can say no to, and eventually set up standards and guidelines that reflect the dancers.

Without doubt, by rejecting notions of individualism and competition, groups like EDA and DERA are collectively resisting conditions of constraint. They have assisted dancers in subverting stereotypes encrypted upon their occupational choice and provide a space in which they can emerge as workers rather than victims.

References

Alcoff, L. 1991. "The Problem of Speaking for Others." *Cultural Critique* 20.

Bell, Laurie (ed.). 1987. *Good Girls/Bad Girls: Sex Trade Workers and Feminists Face to Face.* Toronto: Women's Press.

Best, J. 1987. "Rhetoric in Claims-Making." *Social Problems* 34.

Bouclin, S. 2004. "Exploited Employees or Exploited Entrepreneurs? A Look at Erotic Dancers." *Canadian Woman Studies/les cahiers de la femme* 24: 3.

Bruckert, Chris. 2002. *Taking it Off, Putting it On: Women in the Strip Trade.* Toronto: Women's Press.

Bruckert, Chris, and Colette Parent. 2004. *Erotic Service/Erotic Dance Establishments: Two Types of Marginalized Labour.* Ottawa: Law Commission of Canada.

Butler, Judith. 1990. "Performative Acts and Gender Constitution: An Essay in Phenomenology and Feminist Theory." In S. Case (ed.), *Performing Feminisms: Feminist Critical Theory and Theatre.* Baltimore: Johns Hopkins University Press.

Chandler, C. 1999. "Feminist as Collaborators and Prostitutes as Autobiographers." *Hastings*

Women's Law Journal 1, 10.

Cixous, H. 1983. "The Laugh of the Medusa." In R. Warhol and D. Herndel (eds.), *Feminisms: An Anthology of Literary Theory and Criticism.* New Brunswick, NJ: Rutgers.

Cooke, A. 1987. "Stripping: Who Calls the Tune?" In L. Bell (ed.), *Good Girls/Bad Girls: Sex Trade Workers and Feminists Face to Face.* Toronto: Women's Press.

DERA (Dancers' Equal Rights Association). 2002. "Current Issues Concerning Exotic Dancers." Unpublished Document. Ottawa.

____. 2003. Mission Statement.

EDA (Exotic Dancers Alliance). 2001. *The Naked Truth.* Winter (1). Toronto

Egan, D. 2003. "I'll be your Fantasy Girl, if you'll be my Moneyman: Mapping Desire, Fantasy and Power in Two Exotic Dance Clubs." *Journal for the Psychoanalysis of Cultural and Society* 8, 1.

Ferguson, Rob. 1995. "Harris Stalling on Election Promise to Ban Lap Dancing, Critics Say." *The Montreal Gazette* August 2: A5.

Foucault, Michel. 1976. *Histoire de la sexualité.* Paris: Gallimard.

Frank, Katharine. 2002. *G-Strings and Sympathy: Strip Club Regulars and Male Desire.* London: Duke University Press.

Hendly, Nate. 1999. "Live Girl Productions." *The Eye* July 1.

Highcrest, Alexandra. 1995. "Exotic Dancers Lose Regardless of Who Lays Down the Law." *The Eye* October 19.

Hochschild, Arlie. 1983. *The Managed Heart: The Commercialization of Human Feeling.* UCP, Berkeley: CA.

Johnson, Merri. 1987. "CABE and Strippers: A Delicate Union." In Laurie Bell (ed.), *Good Girls/Bad Girls: Sex Trade Workers and Feminists Face to Face.* Toronto: Women's Press.

Lewis, J. 2000. "Controlling Lap Dancing: Law, Morality, and Sex Work." In R. Weitzer (ed.), *Sex for Sale, Prostitution, Pornography, and the Sex Industry.* New York: Routledge.

Lewis, J., and E. Maticka-Tyndale. 2003. "Peer Research in the Sex Trade." *Research Bulletin: Centers of Excellence for Women's Health* 4, 1.

Montemurro, B. 2001. "Strippers and Screamers: The Emergence of Social Control in a Non-Institutional Setting." *Journal of Contemporary Ethnography* 30, 3.

Prittie, Jennifer. 1999. "Exotic Dancers Fight for Rights: Conditions 'Filthy.'" *National Post* September 11. <groups.msn.com/ExoticDancersAlliance/Exposureshow.msnw> accessed February 15, 2006.

Ronai, Rambo C. 1999. "The Next Night: Sous Rature: Wrestling with Derrida's Mimesis." *Qualitative Inquiry* 5, 1.

Sanchez, L. 1997. "Boundaries of Legitimacy: Sex, Violence, Citizenship in a Local Sexual Economy." *Law & Social Inquiry* 22.

Sangster, J. 1997. "Telling Our Stories: Feminist Debates and the Use of Oral History." In V. Strong-Boag and A. Fellman (eds.), *Rethinking Canada: The Promise of Women's History.* Toronto: Oxford University Press.

Snug, Hannah. 2000. "Peel & Play Professor of Strip Mary Taylor Empowers Women by Showing Them how it's Done." *Varsity* October 10.

Thesenvitz, J. 2002. "Exotic Dancers: Not so Hard-to-Reach After All." *The Update* Health Communication Unit at The Centre For Health Promotion University of Toronto (THCU). Available at <http://www.thcu.ca/infoandresources/newsletters/

sprng2002%20final.pdf> accessed November 14, 2008.

Timpson, Anis. 2001. *Driven Apart: Employment Equality and Child Care in Canadian Public Policy*. Vancouver: UBC Press.

Tracey, Lindalee. 1997. *Growing up Naked: My Years in the Bump and Grind*. Vancouver: Douglas and McIntyre.

Vosko, Leah. 2000. *Temporary Work: The Gendered Rise of a Precarious Employment Relationship*. Toronto: University of Toronto Press.

Weagle, Robert. 1999. "Human Resource Issues in the Exotic Dance Industry." Unpublished M.A, Queen's University. Kingston.

Wood, E. 2000. "Working in the Fantasy Factory: The Attention Hypothesis and the Enacting of Masculine Power." *Journal of Contemporary Ethnography* 29, 1.

Cases Cited

563080 Alberta Ltd. (c.o.b. Body Shoppe) v. Calgary (City) [1997] A.J. No. 269.

AEAC *(Adult Entertainment Association of Canada) v. Ottawa* (City) [2005] O.J. No. 3626.

CABE *(Canadian Association of Burlesque Entertainers) v. Algonquin Tavern* [1981] O.L.R.B. Rep. 1057.

OAEBA *(Ontario Adult Entertainment Bar Association) v. Metropolitan Toronto (Municipality)* (1997), 118 C.C.C. (3d) 481, aff'd. (1996), 27 O.R. (3d) 643.

R. v. Butler [1992] 1 S.C.R. 452 (S.C.C.).

R. v. Caringi [2002] O.J. No. 2367 (Ct. J.).

R. v. Johnson [1975] 2 S.C.R. 160 (S.C.C.).

R. v. Mara and East [1997] 2 S.C.R. 630 (S.C.C.); aff' D (1996), 88 O.A.C. 358 (C.A.).

R. v. Pelletier [1999] 3 S.C.R. 863 (S.C.C), over'd [1998] J.Q. no 4316 (C.A).

R. v. Tremblay [1993] 2 S.C.R. 932 (S.C.C.).

Re Koumoudouros and Toronto (1985), 52 O.R. (2d) 443 (C.A.), ov'ed (1984) 45 O.R. (2d) 426 (Div. Ct.).

Sharlmark Hotels v. Municipality of Toronto [1981], 32 O.R. (2d) 12.

DRUGS

Chapter 16

REPRESENTATIONS OF WOMEN IN THE DRUG TRADE

Susan C. Boyd

From: *Criminalizing Women: Gender and (In)Justice in Neo-liberal Times*, 2nd edition, pp. 131–151 (reprinted with permission).

In a popular representation of today's drug trafficker, a man of colour flashes his wealth, gangsta style. He is portrayed in a violent, hypermasculine form, as a menace to society. Sometimes he is joined by other popular stereotypes: cartel drug traffickers and traffickers with links to organized crime and "terrorist groups."

Strangely, these common depictions of drug traffickers do not reflect Canadian criminal justice drug-arrest statistics. In Canada the majority of drug traffickers arrested are poor, street-level dealers. Since the enactment of our first narcotic legislation, the prime police target for drug offences has been poor people and people of colour. A significant number of women have also been charged, and are serving time, for drug offences. Moreover, today most drug offences in Canada involve cannabis, and the bulk of charges laid are for simple possession rather than trafficking. In Canada it is the cannabis user who is most at risk for arrest (Desjardins and Hotton 2004: 3).

While men involved in the drug trade have been represented in a hypermasculine form, women have not escaped similarly gendered representations. This chapter explores the historical and contemporary representations of women as traffickers, importers and users of illegal drugs that shape public imagination and policy — moving through the background of contemporary drug regulation in

Canada (including the colonization of First Nations peoples and the representation of Aboriginal women as well as the targeting of other racialized groups and the "protection" of moral white women) and contemporary representations of the drug trafficker — and then provides a feminist analysis of representations of women as drug users, traffickers and couriers in the context of the economic, social and political structures that shape women's lives. I also look at the criminal justice response to women in the drug trade, highlighting two recent groundbreaking Canadian drug courier cases that are significant in illustrating the typical situations of women involved in importing drugs.

THE ROOTS OF DRUG REGULATION IN CANADA

Colonization and Representations of Aboriginal Women

The regulation of drugs is not new. During the colonization of what is now Canada, Christian missionaries condemned a wide array of spiritual, healing and shamanic practices, which the state later criminalized. Although the colonizers brought their drug of choice — alcohol — and introduced it to Indigenous people in Canada, they took several measures to ensure that alcohol's legal use was reserved for non-Aboriginal peoples.

One of the provisions of Canada's Indian Act in 1886 prohibited Aboriginal people from consuming alcohol. Those categorized by the state as "Status Indians" were prohibited from buying or possessing alcohol — an aspect of the legislation that was not completely repealed until 1985. While a hundred years of prohibition did not stop Aboriginal people from drinking, it did change the way they drank. Thousands of Aboriginal people were arrested and jailed for alcohol-related offences (Maracle 1993).

Aboriginal women arrested for public drunkenness were constructed as being more immoral and deviant than both their male counterparts and white women. They were accused of contributing to "race suicide" by setting up house with non-Aboriginal men and producing "mixed-race children." Their adult children were also accused of being the "kingpins" of the illegal alcohol trade (Mawani 2002a; Nelson 2002). For instance, between 1930 and 1960, many Aboriginal women were charged and convicted under the Ontario Female Refuges Act (FRA) for alcohol-related charges and sexual immorality. Originally enacted in 1897, the FRA was broadened in 1919 to enable women to be incarcerated by police, parents, welfare agents and the Children's Aid Society for being "out of sexual control" (see Minaker 2014). Most of the women charged under the FRA were white; however, as Joan Sangster (2002: 47) points out, "The legal and social understandings of 'promiscuity' — so central to the FRA — were racialized." Sangster states that by the end of the nineteenth century, "political and media controversies" served to promote and maintain negative stereotypes of Aboriginal women in the public imagination. Aboriginal women were represented as easily corrupted, lacking morality, sexually promiscuous and a "threat to public 'morality and health.'" They were also depicted as wild, able to lead others astray, and in need of containment (Sangster 1999: 43, 44). Moral reformers ignored the negative impact of colonization, law, and religion. Legal, psychiatric, and social work discourses fuelled the practice of incarcerating Aboriginal women.

Opium Laws and Racial Profiling

Canada's second drug law — and the country's first legislated control of narcotics — was enacted in 1908 to regulate opium production, even though no pharmacological evidence existed at the time to support the need for this new legislation. There is little debate that this law, enacted to limit the use of opium smoking by Chinese labourers in Western Canada, was fuelled by moralism, racism, gender and class conflict (King 1908; Solomon and Madison 1976–77; Small 1978; Comack 1986).

Capitalists had brought Chinese labourers to Canada as a cheap labour source to supply the large projects of industrialization (such as the building of the national railway system). Following the Anti-Asiatic Riot in Vancouver in 1907 — an event sparked by the economic fears of white labourers toward their Chinese counterparts — William Lyon Mackenzie King, then Canada's deputy minister of labour, was sent to settle damages for what the federal government had defined as a labour conflict. After discovering that the opium trade was unregulated, and hearing the complaints of several affluent Chinese Canadians about the opium industry, King proclaimed, "We will get some good out of this riot yet" (Boyd 1984; Comack 1986).

King subsequently submitted a report on the smoking of opium to the federal government. In response, Parliament passed Canada's first Opium Act (King 1908: 7, 8). King's report drew heavily from newspaper reports depicting opium as corrupting the morality of white women. In particular, King (1908: 13) represented the smoking of opium as an "evil" that threatened the "principles of morality" that should "govern the conduct of a Christian nation." He provided no evidence to support his claims about the dangerousness of this form of opium use and the subsequent breakdown of morality.

The public at large, believing the claims that only a small minority group would be affected, raised little opposition to this early piece of legislation, subsequent amendments or the related broadening of police powers (Boyd 1984; Green 1979; Solomon and Green 1988). Indeed, racialized groups were easily targeted, and drugs associated with these groups increasingly came under attack (Boyd 1984, 1991; Comack 1986). Early arrest patterns in Canada suggest that between 1908 and 1930, Chinese and Black men were the ones singled out by the police for arrest. Clayton Mosher's (1998) study of systemic racism in Ontario's legal and criminal justice systems examines how Black and Chinese drug users were subjects of a "white paternalism" that was expressed in more lenient sentencing. In contrast, those convicted of selling to white people were sentenced harshly (Mosher 1998: 157, 159). Drug traffickers, especially people of colour, were depicted as preying on innocent white victims.

Before criminalization took effect, the prevailing profile of the opiate user was as a law-abiding, upper-class, Anglo-Saxon woman taking the drug for a variety of ailments ranging from reproductive problems to nervousness (Berridge and Edwards 1981; Gray 1999; Kandall 1996). Patent medicines containing opiates, cocaine and cannabis (which were not included in early narcotic legislation) were advertised in Eaton's and Sears, Roebuck and Co.'s mail-order catalogues. Given that most Canadian women lived in rural areas and could not afford the services of doctors, many of them relied on home remedies and patent medicines to treat themselves and the family members in their care (Kandall 1996; Mitchinson 2002: 31).

During the late nineteenth and early twentieth centuries, significant historical, political, economic and social shifts were occurring in Western nations. In Canada and the United States, industrialization, social unrest and non-Protestant immigration threatened Protestant hegemony, and it was against this backdrop that the temperance and anti-opiate movements emerged in the nineteenth century, overlapping and intersecting with moral reform and social purity movements. Moral reform movements were both national and religious. Anti-opiate and temperance groups claimed that controlled use of opium and alcohol was impossible (Berridge and Edwards 1981), and by the early nineteenth century, self-control, morality and sobriety had become the template of white, Anglo-Saxon, middle-class respectability as well as the model for the imperial subject. Western Protestants adopted religious dedication and temperance as symbols of social status and self-control, and labour and material wealth were viewed as signs of "God's favour." As Max Weber (1976: 72) commented, the capitalist system "so needs this devotion to the calling of making money." The Women's Christian Temperance Union in Canada, for instance, regarded sobriety and morality as innate in the female gender; yet women could be easily corrupted because of their fragile characters. As a result, temperance and anti-opiate reformers constructed alcohol and the smoking of opium as two of the main culprits of many of society's ills — such as poverty, criminality and violence. Moral reformers were concerned with what they perceived as the "breakdown" of the family and the abandonment of white, middle-class, Christian morality (Hannah-Moffat 2001; Valverde 1991). They thus set out to transform immoral individuals. Such practices were therefore intrinsically linked with the nation-building and state reform of the late nineteenth- and early twentieth-century period (Hunt 1999b; Valverde 1991).

A Drug Policy for the Protection of White Women

Canadian views on certain drugs, and individuals and groups who used and sold drugs, would shift dramatically by the early 1920s, partially due to the efforts of moral reformers such as Emily Murphy. Hailing from Edmonton, Murphy was the first woman in Canada to be appointed a juvenile court judge. Along with other moral reformers, she produced and disseminated significant new materials about drug users and traffickers. In 1922, her book *The Black Candle* was published. Serialized in Canada's national *Maclean's Magazine*, the book was intended to educate Canadians about drug issues (Murphy 1973; Anthony and Solomon 1973).

Murphy's representation of the male drug trafficker is that of a non-white, deranged villain bent on destroying the Anglo-Saxon way of life, corrupting the morality of white women, and taking over the world. She targeted Chinese and Black men for enslaving white women and contributing to "race suicide." While Murphy (1973: 162) constructed male drug traffickers as devious people who were "active agents of the devil," the mixing of the races and the moral downfall of white women were central to her argument. Women's moral downfall was measured by their proximity to, and enslavement by, men of colour. Beneath a photo of a white woman and a Black man lying in what looks like an opium den, Murphy wrote, "When she acquires the habit, she does not know what lies before her; later, she does not care" (1973: 30). Murphy went on to assert that all women who are seduced by men of colour become addicted and degraded, and all of them also become liars. She claimed, "Under the influence of the drug, the woman loses control of herself; her moral senses are blunted, and she becomes 'a victim' in more senses than one" (1973: 17). For Murphy and others of her ilk the woman drug user was an immoral, promiscuous being who was contributing to the breakdown of the family and Anglo-Saxon society.

Canada's drug legislation, then, was grounded not only in the class interests of industrial capitalism, but also in the Eurocentric view of morality, gender, race, family and nation-state. The image of white women as fragile and vulnerable to moral corruption sharply contrasts with the images of Aboriginal women as promiscuous, unruly, prone to public displays of drunkenness and in need of confinement. What are the contemporary images of women in the drug trade and how do current socio-political agendas underpin the regulation of these women?

CONTEMPORARY REPRESENTATIONS OF THE DRUG TRAFFICKER: THE WAR ON DRUGS

Representations and Regulation

Contemporary representations of the drug trafficker have not strayed far from the writings of Emily Murphy. Indeed, drug laws in Canada have become increasingly severe, justified by police efforts to secure broader powers to capture and punish the drug trafficker and importer. Both the Opium and Drug Act of 1908 and the Narcotic Control Act of 1961 underwent many amendments (Giffen, Endicott, and Lambert 1991). Today certain drugs (excluding tobacco and alcohol) are regulated under the federal Controlled Drugs and Substances Act (1997). Few Canadians are aware of the content of this act and of the maximum penalties for possession, trafficking and importation/exportation of drugs, which include: seven years for possession of drugs such as cocaine and heroin; life imprisonment for importing or trafficking these drugs; five years less a day for possessing less than thirty grams of marijuana; and life imprisonment for importing or trafficking more than three kilograms of cannabis. It is rare for a Canadian judge to impose a maximum penalty for a drug offence, especially because our legal system has first-time offence guidelines. Nevertheless, sentencing is not always lenient, especially in relation to importation charges. In addition, a series of minor offences or probation violations and failure to pay fines can snowball into a lengthy prison sentence.

Until the late 1950s and the emergence of the Beat and sixties countercultures, representations of illegal drug use and drug trafficking were constructed solely by police, judges, politicians, the medical profession, social workers, academics and the media. The Beat writers of the 1950s and the political movement of the 1960s challenged official representations of the illegal drug user and, to a lesser degree, the drug trafficker. For millions of youth, use of drugs, especially marijuana and psychedelics, was considered to be a positive thing and a challenge to "rational consciousness" (Wagner 1997: 14). Illegal drug use was associated with altered states of consciousness and political dissent.

Despite these forms of resistance to dominant representations of drug use and users, several "drug scares" have been generated to rationalize increased drug regulation, including: heroin in the mid-1950s; marijuana and psychedelics in the 1960s; cocaine in the 1970s; crack cocaine in the mid-1980s; ecstasy in the 1990s; and, most recently, methamphetamine and marijuana grow-operations. Each drug scare has had a similar narrative, with similar actors: an epidemic of use that is spreading and in need of containment; criminal groups with links to organized crime (and now terrorist groups); criminalized spaces, such as inner-city neighbourhoods; vulnerable victims (especially youth) — and ruthless traffickers, importers and producers.

Each drug scare embodies narrow representations of traffickers, importers and producers as racialized, foreign Others operating outside the law. For instance, in a drug strategy recently adopted by the City of Vancouver, *A Framework for Action: A Four-Pillar Approach to Drug Problems in Vancouver*,[1] drug traffickers are racialized and seen as a threat. They are constructed as males who have ties to organized crime and cartels outside of the nation-state. In the report, drug traffickers are described as "masters of manipulation and impersonation, [who] can blend into mainstream society quite easily" (MacPherson 2001: 54). The report also singles out Asian, Colombian and Italian-based groups that are thought to be active in the Canadian drug trade (although no evidence is provided). Since these groups are represented as being able to operate anywhere at any time, arguments are presented for the imposition of special police powers.

Like the earlier period, then, myths and narratives about the drug trafficker and importer continue. "Foreign" traffickers and importers are still seen as a threat to "Christian" nation-states. Since the terrorist attacks on the World Trade Center and the Pentagon on September 11, 2001, we have been told by the RCMP and politicians — particularly President George W. Bush and his supporters — that the war on drugs is linked to the war on terrorism. Both wars converge, instrumentally intensifying racial profiling and eroding civil rights. In Canada, 90 percent of all state funding for drugs goes to criminal justice (Nolan 2003: 187), and drug arrests continue to increase (Desjardins and Hotton 2004).

Drug Statistics

Historically, repressive drug laws have been supported by myths, narratives, and representations of the drug trafficker that intensify the regulation of women. We are told continually that the government, police and drug agencies need more special powers, budgets and repressive laws so that we can be "protected" and the drug trafficker can be caught. However, the statistics tell a different story about who is really using drugs and who is being profiled by the police.

Contrary to media, government and enforcement claims, the drug user in Canada is most often using legal drugs such as alcohol, tobacco, prescribed drugs and over-the-counter products (CCSA/CCLAT 2004; Gagnon 2002; Single et al. 1999). In 2002, Canadians spent $12.3 billion on prescription drugs (Gagnon 2002). In 2004, about 17 percent of women and 23 percent of men reported being current tobacco smokers (Health Canada 2004). In Canada's 2004 national drug survey, 79 percent of Canadians surveyed reported having used alcohol in the previous year. Women reported drinking slightly less than men (77 percent versus 82 percent for men).

Illegal drug use in Canada is primarily centred on cannabis use. In the 2004 survey, 14 percent of the Canadians surveyed reported using cannabis in the previous year. Women were less likely to use cannabis over the previous year (10 percent versus 18 percent for men). Contrary to depictions of illegal drug use by the poor, high income is correlated with a higher lifetime prevalence of cannabis use, and up to 70 percent of Canadian youth from eighteen to twenty-four years of age have tried cannabis at least once (CCSA/CCLAT 2004). Curiously, the national drug survey does not include usage rates for tobacco, our most toxic drug. However, it does include a conflated annual rate of 1.3 percent for speed, ecstasy and hallucinogens. The survey gives a past year usage rate of 1.9 percent for cocaine/crack (CCSA/CCLAT 2004).

These statistics demonstrate that Canadians are drug users. Their drug use is most often confined to legal drugs — such as alcohol, tobacco, and prescribed drugs — and, to a lesser degree, illegal drugs such as cannabis. Yet the Canadian media, some politicians and enforcement agencies would have us believe otherwise. We are inundated with representations of drug users as people who consume cocaine/crack, heroin or methamphetamines, even though the statistics reveal that these users represent a small percentage of drug users.

Charges for drug offences increased steadily in Canada between 1981 and 2002, except from 1987 to 1989 (Dell, Sinclair, and Boe 2001: 60; Desjardins and Hotton 2004: 3). Cannabis offences increased by 81 percent between 1992 and 2002, most of them involving charges for possession (Desjardins and Hotton 2004: 1). In 2002, 76 percent of all drug offences in Canada were for cannabis and 66 percent were for possession (Desjardins and Hotton 2004: 3). About 14 percent of all drug charges involved women. Yet, according to 2004 statistics from the Correctional Service of Canada, about 30 percent of female federal prisoners were serving time in federal prison for drug-related offences, compared to 18 percent of men.[2] The incarceration rate for women is higher than for men, even though men serving prison terms for drug offences such as trafficking and importation have "more extensive criminal history backgrounds" than do their female counterparts (Motiuk and Vuong 2001: 27). Importation offences make up about 1 percent of all drug charges, and more men than women are serving federal prison time for this offence. However, the total percentage of women serving time in federal prison in 2004 for importing charges is three times higher than it is for men. Similarly, the percentage of female federal prisoners serving time for drug trafficking is 11 percent, compared to 9 percent of male prisoners.[3]

Numerous Canadian studies point out that the female prison population has tripled since 1970 and that First Nations and Black women are overrepresented in federal prisons (Hannah-Moffat and Shaw 2000b; Statistics Canada 2001a). According to the findings of the 1995 Commission on Systemic Racism in the Ontario Justice System, drug trafficking and importing dominate the increased number of admissions at the Vanier Centre for Women (VCW). White women made up the majority of women admitted for drug trafficking and importing charges in 1986–87, but by 1992–93 most of the women admitted were Black. White women and Black women admitted to VCW for drug trafficking and importing charges between 1986–87 and 1992–93 increased by 667 percent and 5,200 percent, respectively (Commission on Systemic Racism in the Ontario Criminal Justice System 1995: 25, 26). Similarly, research indicates a 20 percent increase in the number of female federal offenders serving drug-related sentences since 1997 (Correctional Service of Canada 2002–03).

Although state and police officials maintain that they are committed to arresting top-level drug traffickers, the makeup of the female prison population — the majority of whom are racialized, poor, undereducated, single parents — belies their claims. We need to ask, therefore, what is the current (neo-liberal) construction of women involved in the drug trade? How can we understand women's participation in the illegal economy in relation to a socio-economic context characterized by the disappearance of the social safety net, decreased opportunities for women, the increased stratification of social classes? And how are both women's engagement with the drug trade and the state response to that engagement shaped by race and class?

A FEMINIST ANALYSIS

One explanation for the increasing criminalization of women for drug offences lies in the economic, social, and political structures that shape women's lives (Wagner 1997). In these terms, the central factors in understanding rising incarceration rates and "coercive state violence against women" are the racialized feminization of poverty related to neo-liberal globalization, the tough-on-crime agendas of political parties, the transnational war on drugs, and the global prison-industrial complex (Sudbury 2005b: 168). Feminist researchers have brought to our attention the situations of women around the world who are involved in the drug trade, imprisoned for drug-related crimes and hurt in other ways by the war on drugs (Boyd 2004; Boyd and Faith 1999; Da Cunha 2005; Diaz-Cotto 2005; Faith 1993, 2000; Green 1996, 1998; Heaven 1996; Huling 1992, 1996; Joshua 1996; Martin 1993; Roberts 2005; Sudbury 2005a). They seek to situate women's involvement in the drug trade against the backdrop of international and national political, economic and social factors that have an impact on the lives of women — an impact that has been experienced most acutely in the regulation of reproduction.

Bad Mothers

Historically, women who use, sell, and import illegal drugs have been constructed as being doubly deviant for transgressing both their proper gender role and the criminal law. They have been seen as a risk to themselves, their children, society and the nation-state. In more recent times, mothers suspected of using illegal drugs continue to be depicted as immoral, dangerous and driven by their addiction (Boyd 1999, 2004; Campbell 2000; Humphries 1999; Martin 1993; Murphy and Rosenbaum 1999; Roth 2000). Indeed, women's bodies have become the newest terrain of the "war on drugs," as law and order pundits seek to criminalize maternal drug use. This situation has been further exacerbated since the 1980s by the intersection of the war on drugs and the war on abortion and women's reproductive rights. Drug policy has been shaped by discourses about good and bad mothers — about sexuality, reproduction and morality.

Women's gains in reproductive autonomy, including legal access to birth control and abortion in Canada and other Western nations, were accompanied by a counter-discourse about the fetus as a legal person who is separate from the pregnant woman and in need of protection. Feminist activists and researchers state that advances in fetal rights have culminated in a situation in which women's bodies are under attack (Boyd 1999, 2004; Paltrow 2001; Roth 2000). Unsubstantiated fears about maternal drug use have culminated in increased social-service, legal and medical surveillance of women since the 1960s. The United States "crack scare" of the mid-1980s, for instance, centred on lurid, unsubstantiated tales about "crack babies" and unfit mothers (Humphries 1999).

In Canada social workers have expanded their domain of regulation through the regulation of drug use, including maternal drug use. A number of legal cases in the 1980s and 1990s highlighted their shifting practices to "apprehend" the fetus in order to protect it from suspected drug use by pregnant women (Maier 1992; Turnbull 2001). In challenging the legal definition of the term "child," these cases highlighted social workers' interest in expanding their domain and extending legal rights to the fetus. Anti-abortion and fetal-rights advocates have also been pressing for the fetus to be granted legal rights. They view the establishment of legal personhood as an important strategy toward criminalizing abortion and regulating women's activities during pregnancy and birth. Since the 1970s, neo-liberal discourses represent poor single mothers on public assistance as morally deficient and producing social problems, including damaged children (Bashevkin 2002: Boyd 2004). Individualized responsibility and self-sufficiency emerged as the neo-liberal solution to systemic poverty, social inequality, and racialized and sexualized welfare policy. Poor women were increasingly represented as draining the national coffers, and as immoral, promiscuous, dishonest and unwilling to work. Further, they were depicted as a danger to their children and to the health of the nation. Negative representations of women on assistance were accompanied by cutbacks and shifts in social work practice. Rather than support, surveillance of families and accountability to management became central to social work practice (Bashevkin 2002). State apprehension of children is one of the most punitive practices that social workers employ against women who live in poverty, especially those mothers who are racialized (Swift 1995). The discourse centres on individualizing single mothers' personal behaviour, rather than on the impact of racialized and gendered welfare policy and the neo-liberal economic and social restructuring that shapes the lives of women and their children.

One 1996 case received considerable media attention, in turn illuminating the effect of negative representations of racialized single mothers on welfare who are suspected of using drugs. The case involved a young, pregnant First Nations woman who was being forced into treatment for solvent abuse by Winnipeg Child and Family Services. The media and the social workers involved argued that this woman had already had two damaged children due to her solvent use. They assumed, without evidence, that solvent use is linked to fetal damage during pregnancy (Medrano 1996). In hearing this case, the Supreme Court of Canada ruled that the courts cannot detain and order drug treatment for pregnant women to protect the fetus. The Court also ruled that the unborn child does not possess legal rights (*Winnipeg Child and Family Services [Northwest Area]* v. *G[D.F.]* 1997). This ruling has not stopped legal challenges from occurring, even though it did send an important message to legal, moral and social service reformers who seek to limit women's reproductive autonomy.

The battle continues over women's bodies, drugs and reproductive autonomy in the political arena as well. In 2002, Canadian Alliance MP Keith Martin (now a Liberal) introduced a private Member's bill, Bill C-233, to amend the Criminal Code. The bill — which was not ratified — was intended to amend the code to extend legal personhood to the fetus. It would have made it an offence for a woman who is pregnant to consume a substance harmful to a fetus that she does not have a fixed intention to abort. The bill sought to provide legal protection for the health of the fetus before it is born. It also "authorized" the courts to make orders to confine a woman in a treatment facility during her pregnancy, and to have her report to a physician weekly upon her release in order to protect the fetus. In the United States, over 200 women have been arrested and held criminally liable for the outcomes of their pregnancies (Paltrow 2001).

Such efforts to criminalize maternal drug use are shaped by discourses about unfit mothers, the dangerousness of certain drugs, and welfare moms who drain limited economic and social supports. Illegal drug use by mothers is viewed as plac-ing the child at risk, thus as justifying state intervention. It is mistakenly assumed that drugs are the only variable that brings about negative pregnancy and maternal outcomes. The main problem with this is that moral panic about maternal drug use deflects our attention from poverty, one known social factor that has a negative impact on pregnancy. In Canada the numbers of poor women have been growing as social and economic supports decrease. Today more children live in poverty than was the case twenty years ago (Bashevkin 2002). The 1996 case in Winnipeg is a prime illustration of this point. Focusing attention solely on the culpability of a young, poor, Aboriginal woman to provide proper care for her fetus ignores the broader social and economic conditions that women in her situation confront in their struggle to make a life for themselves and their children.

Negative portrayals of mothers also ignore the wealth of research that clearly demonstrates that drugs are only one variable that influences pregnancy outcomes and that women who use illegal drugs can be adequate parents. In fact, when non-judgmental prenatal care and social and economic supports are provided, maternal outcomes improve (Boyd 1999; Colten 1980; Murphy and Rosenbaum 1999; Hepburn 1993). When these supports are in place, women using illegal drugs have had the same maternal outcomes as non-drug using women from the same socio-economic background (Hepburn 1993, 2002). Medical professionals maintain that while maternal drug use is a risk, it is a manageable risk.

Women, Drug Trafficking and Importing

When we think about women who sell drugs, many of us think of women living in inner-city communities and working in the sex trade or selling drugs on the street to finance their addiction. While this may be true for a small percentage of women, the full picture is much more complex. Most women who use and sell illegal drugs are not driven by addiction. Economic factors such as cutbacks in housing and welfare assistance compel women to find alternative ways of making money. I am not suggesting that poor women are more involved in the drug trade than are middle- or upper-class women. Rather, I would argue that poor women are more likely to come into contact with the law due to their visibility, police-profiling and increased intervention by social services and other state and non-state agencies that seek to regulate them.

Feminist sociological studies from Canada, Australia, the United States and Britain tell a different story about women who traffic and import drugs. Marsha Rosenbaum's (1981) research in San Francisco provided the first feminist ethnographic sociological study of women heroin users, paving the way for other feminist studies about women who use and sell drugs. A growing body of research findings differs from conventional research that sees the female drug user and dealer as more deviant, immoral, pathological and criminal than are male users and dealers. In contrast, critical and feminist research shows that many women "drift" into drug dealing, often pooling their money to get a better deal or to buy larger quantities (Waldorf, Reinarman, and Murphy 1991). Most women deal drugs in order to support themselves and their families, not to finance their addiction.

Patricia Morgan and Karen Ann Joe (1997), in their study of women who sell methamphetamine in three United States cities, found that women engage in drug selling and transporting in order to avoid dependency and to provide for their children in a world that provides few avenues of support for them. They challenge stereotypes of women who are involved in the drug trade, and argue: "Most women who use and sell illegal drugs are not from minority disenfranchised populations living in inner city communities, and most women who use and sell drugs have not, and will not engage in prostitution and other crimes outside of illegal drug sales" (Morgan and Joe 1997: 107).

An Australian study by Barbara Denton (2001) found that women's drug dealing was not driven by their drug use, but instead was seen by them as a viable way of making money. In my study on mothers (from diverse class and ethnic/race backgrounds) who use illegal drugs in Canada, the women revealed that they saw drug dealing as the most viable option for earning money to supplement inadequate incomes (Boyd 1999). However, Lisa Maher (1995) notes in her ethnographic study of women crack smokers in Brooklyn in the 1990s that for poor Black and Hispanic women, selling crack did not provide "equal opportunity employment." Women were more stigmatized and more subject to violence than were men (Maher 1995).

Women living within and outside of Canada have also been recruited or have chosen to import drugs into Canada. These women — labelled drug couriers or mules — are subject to long prison terms if they are caught — which sometimes happens in places where they do not speak the language and do not know the criminal justice system. They are more often than not imprisoned far away from their families. It is hard to conceive of anyone volunteering to carry or ingest drugs, because the profits are small and the risks are very high. Many women who "choose" this job are desperate. The research suggests that most women who are convicted of either importing drugs into or transporting within a nation rarely own the drugs they ingest or carry. They are paid a flat fee and most often do not share in the potential profits (Green 1998; Huling 1992; Wedderburn 2000).

Tracy Huling's 1992 study of female drug couriers who were arrested at the JFK airport in New York helped pave the way for a fuller understanding of women drug couriers by providing qualitative detail about the lives of the women involved. Huling noted that these women were sometimes used as decoys. They were usually first-time offenders, rarely released on bail upon arrest, and unable to develop an effective defence. The women in Huling's study were too poor to hire a lawyer, so they had to rely on court-appointed or legal aid lawyers with huge caseloads and limited budgets. Regardless of their innocence or guilt, the women were often advised to plea bargain to reduce their sentences — which meant an admission of guilt. Like other researchers, Huling (1992) found women drug couriers to be motivated by poverty and familial concerns rather than greed (see also Green 1996).

Between 1999 and 2001, Julia Sudbury (2005) interviewed twenty-four women in three prisons in Britain. Her findings confirm earlier studies about Black British women, Caribbean women and working-class women serving sentences for drug-importing charges. While women are often naive about the drugs they carried, it would be a mistake to see all drug traffickers and couriers as lacking agency and being dupes of the drug trade. Rather, it is illuminating to look more closely at the ways in which women support themselves and their families when faced with social and structural inequalities, and state and male violence.

Despite this body of feminist research, misrepresentation of the female drug courier still persists. A British study of 1,715 drug couriers caught at Heathrow Airport between July 1991 and September 1997 asserted that female drug couriers carried more drugs "in terms of weight and value" than did their male counterparts (Harper, Harper, and Stockdale 2002). The women were also more likely to be carrying Class A (heroin and cocaine) than Class B (cannabis) drugs. Women made up 28 percent of the sample in the study. The authors expressed surprise that the female drug couriers appeared to be engaging in risk-taking and dangerous roles most often associated with criminalized men — thus subjecting themselves to greater penalties. They speculated that seeing women as risk-takers in these roles is counterintuitive to conventional gender stereotypes that construct women as subordinate dupes (Harper, Harper, and Stockdale 2002: 101, 106).

This study had several limitations, however. It provided no information about race/ethnicity or class, and no data indicating whether the women and men arrested at the airport were aware of the quality of the drugs that they carried. A number of other studies suggest that female couriers are usually unaware of the exact weight and quality of the drugs they carry, which become significant factors as trial evidence (see Green 1996). Further, the study offered no significant analysis as to why women are increasingly carrying Class A drugs. One might speculate that both cocaine and heroin, being less bulky than cannabis, are more easily transported and that flat rates for carrying cocaine and heroin are usually higher. It might also be the case that some women are more likely to be coerced to take more risks due to threats or intimidation.

When looking at women's involvement in the drug trade, we also need to examine the drug economy against the backdrop of the global economy. Poor women are exploited in both the drug economy and the global economy. They are the most "poorly remunerated" and the most "disposable of workers" (Sudbury 2005: 175). Neo-liberal economic structuring of the global economy ensures that some people will remain poor and exploited. Choices to participate in the drug trade are framed by global and national political and economic concerns, as well as by Western demand for and consumption of specific drugs. Poor women with little access to social and economic supports or to legitimate work with adequate wages may turn to the drug trade to provide for themselves and their families.

Although most drug traffickers and drug couriers are men, gender and racial profiling comes into play at a key entry point for illegal drugs: airports. Huling (1992) described how Black and Hispanic women were profiled by New York airport customs officers. The Drug Enforcement Agency (DEA) in the United States claims that Black women are ideal drug mules (Weich and Angula 2000: 3), and their profiling and enforcement practices are shaped by this belief. In 1999, Black women coming into a New York airport were nine times more likely to be X-rayed than were white women and two times more likely to be strip-searched than were other women (Ekstrand and Blume 2000: 2, 12). However, Black women were less likely than other women to be carrying contraband. In fact, Black women were half as likely as white women to have contraband on them. Only 4 percent of the total searches were successful, which means they had a 96 percent failure rate (Ekstrand and Blume 2000: 10). Since 2002, the war on terrorism has increased racial profiling by customs agents in the United States, Canada and Britain.

The focus on drug couriers serves to deflect attention from the tons of drugs imported into Canada, the United States and Britain via airplanes, ships and trucks. These vessels hold significantly larger quantities of illegal drugs than those found on and in bodies. It also serves to deflect attention from the impacts of Western drug consumption and economic, military, and political initiatives on both Western and Third World nations and the people who live in them, especially poor women and women of colour.

In sum, narratives and representations of the drug trafficker and courier by criminal justice and moral reformers fail to capture the lives of most women in the drug trade. Feminist and critical drug research demonstrates that drug trafficking is not limited to the poor or people of colour. It is a normalized activity in many strata of society and can be found outside inner-city spaces. This research demonstrates that by expanding our analysis and challenging popular misconceptions, we can better understand how women in the drug trade — of all classes — derive rewards, especially monetary ones, from their work.

The makeup of our prison population demonstrates that race, class and gender inequality do come into play for women who sell and import drugs by limiting their choices and closing avenues to legitimate work. These factors of inequality also come into play in relation to police-profiling, arrests, convictions, and sentencing. When poor women and women of colour — people who are the most vulnerable to arrest and conviction — come into contact with the drug economy, it is often at the lowest level, a position that mirrors their status in society.

THE CRIMINAL JUSTICE RESPONSE: *R. V. HAMILTON*

In Canada drug couriers are typically sentenced harshly, but two recent Canadian cases had a different outcome (see *Hamilton* 2004). In both cases, women were arrested at Toronto's Pearson International Airport after returning from visits to Jamaica. Marsha Hamilton was arrested in 2000, and Donna Mason in 2001. The trial judge sought to place the participation of both of these women as drug couriers against a backdrop of race, gender, poverty and inequality. His analysis of the cases speaks to the social conditions that shape women's conflict with the law.

Marsha Hamilton is a Black woman with a Grade 9 education. At the time of her arrest she was unemployed and living in Canada, with family in Jamaica. She was twenty-eight years old and a single parent with three children under the age of eight. She had made a trip home to Jamaica and, in preparation for returning to Canada, had swallowed ninety-three pellets of cocaine with an estimated $69,000 street value. She almost died on the trip because the pellets leaked cocaine into her body. Marsha had no prior arrests or police record, and she stated that she had committed the crime for financial reasons.

Donna Mason is a Black woman with a Grade 12 education. At the time of her arrest she was thirty-three years old and living in Canada. She had three children whom she solely supported on a limited income. Prior to the birth of her third child, she had worked full-time at a Wendy's restaurant for $8 an hour, supplemented by welfare assistance. She was also the choir leader at her church. Before returning to Canada from Jamaica, she had swallowed under one kilogram of cocaine pellets. She had no prior arrests or police record, and she also said that financial hardship was the main reason she committed the crime.

Both women pleaded guilty to importing cocaine, in an amount of under one kilogram, from Jamaica. Both were Black women of limited economic means. Both had dependent children. Both were first-time offenders. Their "profile" is similar to that of other women in prison for drug importation in Canada, Britain and the United States. In 2003, Mr. Justice S. Casey Hill of Ontario's Superior Court of Justice sentenced both women. Their cases are groundbreaking because both women were given conditional sentences and not sent to prison. Hamilton was sentenced to twenty months; Mason to twenty-four months less a day.

The defence in each of these cases highlighted the role of the judiciary, and specifically the sentencing judge, in addressing injustices against Aboriginal peoples in Canada — injustices recognized in *R. v. Gladue* (1999). The defence argued that Black women should be granted similar consideration when the evidence presented at the trial suggests a history similar to that of Aboriginal women — of poverty, discrimination and overrepresentation of Black women in the criminal justice system (*R. v. Hamilton* 2003). In contrast, the arguments in the Crown's case drew from conventional law and order discourses related to concern for the protection of youth and narcoterrorism and organized crime. The Crown argued that cocaine is a dangerous drug and that schoolchildren in Canada would have been at risk if the cocaine that the women carried had reached the streets. They also noted the prevalence of narcoterrorism in Jamaica, stating that huge profits were to be made by gangs participating in the illegal drug trade.

In analyzing the two cases, Justice Hill did not confine himself to the arguments advanced by the Crown and the defence. Rather, the judge drew from his own observations in the courtroom, as well as the findings of the Report of the Commission on Systemic Racism in the Ontario Criminal Justice System (Ontario 1995) to explain how systemic social and economic circumstances shaped the lives of Hamilton and Mason and other Black women moving through the criminal justice system.

The judge's ruling and the defence lawyer's arguments suggest that some criminal justice professionals in Canada understand that women's lived experience and their conflicts with the law are shaped and defined by race, gender and class. The *Hamilton* and *Mason* cases exemplify the "typical" situations of women involved in importing. Poverty, discrimination, and race and gender inequality shape women's lives.

Nevertheless, the Crown appealed the decisions. In August 2004, the Court of Appeal for Ontario ruled that the trial judge had erred in his sentencing decision and in his "holding that systemic racial and gender bias justified conditional sentences" (R. v. Hamilton 2004: 34). However, the Court of Appeal declared that "the administration of justice would not be served by incarcerating the respondents for a few months at this time. They have served significant, albeit, inadequate sentences" (R. v. Hamilton 2004: 39). Marsha Hamilton and Donna Mason were therefore allowed to complete their conditional sentences.

Neither Marsha Hamilton nor Donna Mason fit mainstream media and law and order representations of the drug trafficker or importer. Representations of well-organized, male, high-level drug traffickers who are a threat to the nation-state deflect our attention away from larger political actions and from gendered, racialized and class-biased drug policy. Conventional representations of the drug trafficker also ignore the plight of women and the structural inequalities that shape their participation in the drug trade. The *Hamilton* case, therefore, holds a potential for change. Justice Hill's decision was significant for its recognition of systemic factors in the imposition of conditional sentences and for challenging the representations of women in illegal drug trade discourse. However, the Crown's successful appeal and the 2004 ruling of the Court of Appeal for Ontario demonstrate that much more needs to be done to challenge the law and order discourse of judges and prosecutors, as well as gendered, racialized, and class-biased drug policies.

Furthermore, none of the legal decisions, including Justice Hill's argument for leniency, challenged Canada's draconian drug laws and the representation of cocaine as a "dangerous" drug.[4] Nor did the legal decisions recognize the criminal justice system as a site of conflict and oppression. However, Sophia Lawrence and Toni Williams (forthcoming) argue that the "criminal justice system is an agent" in these women's subordination. They also note that in Justice Hill's argument, culpability is reduced if Black women suffer from poverty and systemic racism and gender bias. Such an argument, they claim, contributes to mythologized negative representations of impoverished Black single mothers as "drug criminals." They point out that Hill's argument builds on a discourse about poor Black single mothers who are trapped by their social and economic situation and thus pushed into crime. Black women are depicted as "prone to swallowing and smuggling" illegal drugs.

PUBLIC IMAGINATION AND
THE DECRIMINALIZATION OF DRUGS

To address issues relating to women and drugs, we have to look more closely at the discourses that surround the drugs themselves, the user, the trafficker and the importer, and how such discourses support the criminalization of particular drugs and the expansion of police budgets and power. Since the emergence of the anti-opiate movement and the enactment of our first drug laws, drugs associated with racialized peoples have been depicted as being "outside the border" and more "dangerous" and "evil" than are the drugs associated with white, Anglo-Saxon, Christian, Western nations. Critical and feminist researchers point out that legal categories are cultural and social fabrications. Most illegal drugs are grown and produced locally (marijuana, for example) and share the same pharmacology as legal drugs (morphine and codeine are both opiates). Nevertheless, negative representations about criminalized drugs and the people who sell and import them continue to inform the public imagination. Those who engage in drug trafficking are depicted as the most dangerous, because they are seen as foreign, greedy, corrupt and threatening the health and security of the nation. Women who use illegal drugs and those who participate in the drug trade are represented as being even more immoral and criminal than are their male counterparts for transgressing their gender role and the law. Racialized women, especially Aboriginal women, have historically been represented as being more easily led astray, and more desperate, immoral and dangerous than their white counterparts. These negative representations inform and shape policy. Even as we explore the possibility of decriminalizing or legalizing marijuana in Canada, our discussions about drug reform are accompanied by arguments about the dangerousness of those involved in the drug trade and their perceived threat to the nation. Thus, harsher sentencing for trafficking and production (such as marijuana grow-operations) and increased law enforcement funding are recommended at the same time as decriminalization of personal use is considered.

Many feminist activists around the world oppose the so-called war on drugs. They consider criminal justice and military initiatives to be in direct opposition to peace and social justice. Drug wars are linked to domestic and international economic instability (Boyd 2004). One practical response would be to legalize drugs. Legalization can be regulated (as in the case of alcohol). We would thus see an end, or at least a decrease, in the illegal market and in drug-trade violence. Furthermore, women's bodies would no longer be used as the newest terrain for advancing the war on drugs. Legalization of drugs would also limit the number of overdoses and lower the transmission of infectious diseases such as Hepatitis C and HIV/AIDS. It would strip drug use of its pathologized, racialized, sexualized and criminalized status. It would remove drug use from punishment industries and contribute to the emptying of prisons.

As we see more and more belt-tightening cutbacks to economic and social services, the criminal justice, the military, and the prison industries are all expanding. Legalizing drugs could save billions of dollars — dollars that could be diverted to socially beneficial services. Women like Donna Mason and Marsha Hamilton would be supported by a caring society, rather than left to fend for themselves in a free-market economy.

Notes

I would like to thank Arlene Wells, Elizabeth Comack, Gillian Balfour and an anonymous reviewer for their thoughtful editorial comments.

1   *A Four-Pillar Approach* is a compilation of data from a series of public forums in Vancouver and does not represent the author's opinion. It is interesting to note that the number of crime control "initiatives" increased between the first public draft and the final report.

2   C. McGregor, Media Relations Officer, Correctional Service of Canada (Personal communication March 18 and May 20, 2004).

3   Ibid.

4   See Coomber and South 2004, especially the editors' chapter, "Drugs, Cultures and Controls in Comparative Perspective" (pp. 13–26) and Alison Spedding's chapter, "Coca Use in Bolivia: A Tradition of Thousands of Years" (pp. 46–64). See also Morgan and Zimmer 1997.

References

Anthony, B., and R. Solomon. 1973. "Introduction." In E. Murphy, *The Black Candle*. Toronto: Coles Publishing.

Bashevkin, S. 2002. *Welfare Hot Buttons: Women, Work, and Social Policy Reform*. Toronto: University of Toronto Press.

Berridge, V., and G. Edwards. 1981. *Opium and the People: Opiate Use in Nineteenth-Century England*. London: Allan Lane.

Boyd, N. 1984. "The Origins of Canadian Narcotics Legislation: The Process of Criminalizaton in Historical Context." *Dalhousie Law Journal* 8.

Boyd, S. 2004. *From Witches to Crack Moms: Women, Drug Law, and Policy*. Durham, NC: Carolina Academic Press.

____. 1999. *Mothers and Illicit Drugs: Transcending the Myths*. Toronto: University of Toronto Press.

Boyd, S., and K. Faith. 1999. "Women, Illegal Drugs and Prison: Views from Canada." *The International Journal of Drug Policy* 10.

Campbell, N. 2000. *Using Women: Gender, Drug Policy, and Social Justice*. New York: Routledge.

CCSA/CCLAT. 2004. *Canadian Addiction Survey (CAS). Highlights*. Ottawa: Canadian Centre on Substance Abuse.

Colten, M. 1980. "A Comparison of Heroin-Addicted and Nonaddicted Mothers: Their Attitudes, Beliefs, and Parenting Experiences." In *Heroin-Addicted Parents and Their Children: Two Reports*. (National Institute on Drug Abuse Services Research Report). Washington, DC: U.S. Department of Health and Human Services; Public Health Service; Alcohol, Drug Abuse, and Mental Health Administration.

Comack, E. 1986. "'We Will Get Some Good out of this Riot Yet': The Canadian State, Drug Legislation and Class Conflict." In S. Brickey and E. Comack (eds.), *The Social Basis of Law: Critical Readings in the Sociology of Law*. Toronto: Garamond.

Commission on Systemic Racism in the Ontario Criminal Justice System. 1995. *Report of the Commission on Systemic Racism in the Ontario Criminal Justice System: A Community Summary*. Toronto: Queen's Printer for Ontario.

Coomber, R. and N. South. 2004. "Drugs, Cultures and Controls in Comparative Perspective." In R. Coomber and N. South (eds.). *Drug Use and Cultural Contexts: 'Beyond the West.'* London: Free Association Books.

Correctional Service of Canada (CSC). 2002–03. *Department Performance Report, 2002–03*. <http://www.csc-scc.gc.ca/text/pblct/dpr/2003/section_3_overview_of_changes_e.shtml>. Accessed June 10, 2005.

Da Cunha, M. 2005. "From Neighborhood to Prison: Women in the War on Drugs in Portugal." In J. Sudbury (ed.), *Global Lockdown: Race, Gender and the Prison-Industrial Complex*. London: Routledge.

Dell, C., R. Sinclair, and R. Boe. 2001. *Canadian Federally Incarcerated Adult Women Profiles Trends from 1981 to 1998*. Ottawa: Research Branch. Correctional Service of Canada.

Denton, B. 2001. "Property Crime and Women Drug Dealers in Australia." *Journal of Drug Issues* 31, 2.

Desjardins, N., and T. Hotton. 2004. "Trends in Drug Offences and the Role of Alcohol and Drugs in Crime." *Juristat* 24.1.

Diaz-Cotto. 2005. "Latinas and the War on Drugs in the United States, Latin America, and Europe." In J. Sudbury (ed.), *Global Lockdown: Race, Gender and the Prison-Industrial Complex*. London: Routledge.

Ekstrand, L., and J. Blume. 2000. *U.S. Customs Service, Better Targeting of Airline Passengers for Personal Searches Could Produce Better Results*. Washington, DC: General Accounting

Office.

Faith, K. 1993. *Unruly Women: The Politics of Confinement and Resistance.* Vancouver: Press Gang Publishers.

____. 2000. "Seeking Transformative Justice for Women: Views from Canada." *Journal of International Women's Studies* 2, 1.

Gagnon, L. 2002. "Rising Drug Costs in Canada." *Federations* 2, 4.

Giffen, P., S. Endicott, and S. Lambert. 1991. *Panic and Indifference: The Politics of Canada's Drug Laws.* Ottawa: Canadian Centre on Substance Abuse.

Gray, M. 1999. "Long Day's Journey into Night." *The Drug Policy Letter* 39.

Green, M. 1979. "The History of Canadian Narcotics Control." *University of Toronto Faculty Law Review* 37.

Green, P. 1996. "Drug Couriers: The Construction of a Public Enemy." In P. Green (ed.), *Drug Couriers: A New Perspective.* London: Quartet Books.

____. 1998. *Drugs, Trafficking and Criminal Policy: The Scapegoat Strategy.* Winchester, UK: Waterside Press.

Hannah-Moffatt, K. 2001. *Punishment in Disguise: Penal Governance and Federal Imprisonment of Women in Canada.* Toronto: University of Toronto Press.

Hannah-Moffat, K., and M. Shaw. 2000b. "Introduction." In K. Hannah-Moffat and M. Shaw (eds.), *An Ideal Prison? Critical Essays on Women's Imprisonment in Canada.* Halifax: Fernwood Publishing.

Harper, R., G. Harper, and J. Stockdale. 2002. "The Role and Sentencing of Women in Drug Trafficking." *Legal and Criminal Psychology* 7, 1.

Health Canada. 2004. *Canadian Tobacco Use Monitoring Survey* (CTUMS). Summary of Results for the first half of 2004 (February to June). <http:www.hc-sc.gc.ca/hecs-sesc/tobacco/research/ctums/2004/summary_first.2004.html>. Accessed April 13, 2005.

Heaven, O. 1996. "Hibiscus: Working with Nigerian Women Prisoners." In P. Green (ed.), *Drug Couriers: A New Perspective.* London: Quartet Books.

Hepburn, M. 1993. "Drug Use in Pregnancy." *British Journal of Hospital Medicine* 49, 1.

____. 2002. "Providing Care for Pregnant Women Who Use Drugs: The Glasgow Women's Reproductive Health Service." In H. Klee, M. Jackson, and S. Lewis (eds.), *Drug Misuse and Motherhood.* London: Routledge.

Huling, T. 1992. *Injustice Will Be Done: Women Drug Couriers and the Rockefeller Drug Laws.* New York: Correctional Association of New York.

____. 1996. "Prisoners of War: Women Drug Couriers in the United States." In P. Green (ed.), *Drug Couriers: A New Perspective.* London: Quartet Books.

Humphries, D. 1999. *Crack Mothers: Pregnancy, Drugs, and the Media.* Columbus: Ohio State University Press.

Hunt, A. 1999a. "The Purity Wars: Making Sense of Moral Militancy." *Theoretical Criminology* 13, 4.

____. 1999b. *Governing Morals: A Social History of Moral Regulation.* Cambridge: Cambridge University Press.

Joshua, L. 1996. "Nigeria, Drug Trafficking and Structural Adjustment." In P. Green (ed.), *Drug Couriers: A New Perspective.* London: Quartet Books.

Kandall, S. 1996. *Substance and Shadow: Women and Addiction in the United States.* Cambridge, MA: Harvard University Press.

King, W.L.M. 1908. "The Need for the Suppression of the Opium Traffic in Canada." Ottawa: S.E. Dawson.

MacPherson, D. 2001. *A Framework for Action: A Four-Pillar Approach to Drug Problems in Vancouver*. Vancouver: City of Vancouver.

Maher, L. 1995. "Dope Girls: Gender, Race and Class in the Drug Economy." Unpublished doctoral dissertation. Rutgers, The State University of New Jersey.

Maier, I. 1992. "Forced Cesarean Section as Reproductive Control and Violence: A Feminist Social Work Perspective on the 'Baby R' Case." Unpublished Master's thesis, Simon Fraser University, Burnaby, BC.

Maracle, B. 1993. *Crazywater: Native Voices on Addiction and Recovery*. Toronto: Penguin.

Martin, D.1993. "Casualties of the Criminal Justice System: Women and Justice Under the War on Drugs." *Canadian Journal of Women and the Law* 6, 2.

Mawani, R. 2002a. "In Between and Out of Place: Mixed-Race Identity, Liquor, and the Law in British Columbia, 1850–1913." In S. Razack (ed.), *Race, Space, and the Law: Unmapping a White Settler Society*. Toronto: Between the Lines.

Medrano, M. 1996. "Does a Discrete Fetal Solvent Syndrome Exist?" *Alcoholism Treatment Quarterly* 14, 3.

Minaker. J. 2014. "Sluts and Slags: The Censuring of the Erring Female." In G. Balfour and E. Comack (eds.), *Criminalizing Women: Gender and (In)Justice in Neo-liberal Times,* 2nd edition. Halifax and Winnipeg: Fernwood Publishing.

Mitchinson, W. 2002. *Giving Birth in Canada 1990–1950*. Toronto: University of Toronto Press.

Morgan, J., and L. Zimmer. 1997. "The Social Pharmacology of Smokeable Cocaine: Not All It's Cracked Up to Be." In C. Reinarman and H. Levine (eds.), *Crack in America: Demon Drugs and Social Justice*. Berkeley: University of California Press

Morgan, P., and K. Joe. 1997. "Uncharted Terrain: Contexts of Experience Among Women in the Illicit Drug Economy. *Women and Criminal Justice* 8, 3.

Mosher, C. 1998. *Discrimination and Denial: Systemic Racism in Ontario's Legal and Criminal Justice Systems, 1892–1961*. Toronto: University of Toronto Press.

Motiuk, L., and B. Vuong. 2001. "Profiling the Drug Offender Population in Canadian Federal Corrections. *Forum on Corrections Research* 13, 3.

Murphy, E. 1973 [1922]. *The Black Candle*. Toronto: Coles.

Murphy, S., and M. Rosenbaum. 1999. *Pregnant Women on Drugs: Combating Stereotypes and Stigma*. New Brunswick, NJ: Rutgers University Press.

Nelson, J. 2002. "'A Strange Revolution in the Manners of the Country': Aboriginal-Settler Intermarriage in Nineteenth-Century British Columbia." In J. McLaren, R. Menzies, and D. Chunn (eds.), *Regulating Lives: Historical Essays on the State, Society, the Individual and the Law*. Vancouver: University of British Columbia Press.

Nolan, P. 2003. *Cannabis: Report of the Senate Special Committee on Illegal Drugs*. Toronto: University of Toronto Press.

Ontario. 1995. *Report of the Commission on Systemic Racism in the Ontario Criminal Justice System*. (M. Gitten and D. Cole, Co-Chairs). Toronto: Queen's Printer.

Paltrow, L. 2001. "The War on Drugs and Abortion: Some Initial Thought on the Connections, Intersections and the Effects." *Southern University Law Review* 28, 3.

Roberts, M. 2005. *Using Women*. London: DrugScope.

Rosenbaum, M. 1981. *Women on Heroin*. New Brunswick, NJ: Rutgers University Press.

Roth, R. 2000. *Making Women Pay: The Hidden Costs of Fetal Rights*. Ithaca, NY: Cornell University Press.

____. 2004. "Searching for the State: Who Governs Prisoners' Reproductive Rights?" *Social Politics* 11, 3.

Sangster, J. 1999. "Criminalizing the Colonized: Ontario Native Women Confront the Criminal Justice System, 1920–1960." *The Canadian Historical Review* 80, 1 (March).

____. 2002. "Defining Sexual Promiscuity: 'Race,' Gender and Class in the Operation of Ontario's Female Refuges Act, 1930–1960." In W. Chan and K. Mirchandani (eds.).

Single, E., M. Van Truong, E. Adlaf, and A. Ialomiteanu. 1999. *Canadian Profile: Alcohol, Tobacco and Other Drugs*. Toronto: Canadian Centre on Substance Abuse and Centre for Addiction and Mental Health.

Small, S.J. 1978. "Canadian Narcotics Legislation, 1908–1923: A Conflict Model Interpretation." In Wm. Greenway and S. Brickey (eds.), *Law and Social Control in Canada*. Scarborough: Prentice-Hall.

Solomon, R., and M. Green. 1988. "The First Century: The History of Nonmedical Opiate Use and Control Policies in Canada, 1870–1970." In J. Blackwell and P. Erickson (eds.), *Illicit Drugs in Canada*. Toronto: Methuen.

Solomon, R., and T. Madison. 1976–77. "The Evolution of Non-Medical Opiate Use in Canada, Part I, 1870–1929." *Drug Forum* 5.

Spedding, A. 2004. "Coca Use in Bolivia: A Tradition of Thousands of Years." In R. Coomber and N. South (eds.). *Drug Use and Cultural Contexts: 'Beyond the West.'* London: Free Association Books.

Statistics Canada. 2001a. *Women in Canada*. Ottawa: Canadian Centre for Justice Statistics Profile Series. Catalogue no. 85F00033MIE.

Sudbury, J. (ed.) 2005a. *Global Lockdown: Race, Gender, and the Prison-Industrial Complex*. London: Routledge.

____. 2005b. "Introduction: Feminist Critiques, Transnational Landscapes, Abolitionist Visions." In J. Sudbury (ed.), *Global Lockdown: Race, Gender, and the Prison-Industrial Complex*. New York: Routledge.

Swift, K. 1995. *Manufacturing "Bad Mothers": A Critical Perspective on Child Neglect*. Toronto: University of Toronto Press.

Turnbull, L. 2001. *Double Jeopardy: Motherwork and the Law*. Toronto: Sumach Press.

Valverde, M. 1991. *The Age of Light, Soap, and Water: Moral Reform in English Canada 1885–1925*. Toronto: McClelland and Stewart/Oxford.

Wagner, D. 1997. *The New Temperance: The American Obsession with Sin and Vice*. Boulder, CO: Westview Press.

Waldorf, D., C. Reinarman, and S. Murphy. 1991. *Cocaine Changes*. Philadelphia: Temple University Press.

Weber, M. 1976. *The Protestant Ethic and the Spirit of Capitalism*. London: George Allen and Unwin.

Wedderburn, D. 2000. *Justice for Women: The Need for Reform*. London: Prison Reform Trust.

Weich, R. and C. Angula. 2000. *Justice on Trial: Racial Disparities in the American Criminal Justice System*. Washington, DC: Leadership Conference on Civil Rights and Leadership Conference on Education Fund.

Cases Cited

R. v. Gladue. 1999. 1 S.C.R. No. 699.

R. v. Hamilton. 2003. 172, C.C.C. (3d) 114, 8 C.R. (6th) 215 (S.C.J.).

R. v. Hamilton. 2004. 186 C.C.C. (3d) 129, 241 D.L.R. (4th) 490, 22 C.R. (6th) 1, 72 O.R. (3d) 1 (C.A.).

Winnipeg Child and Family Services (Northwest Area) v. G., (D.F.). 1997. 3 S.C.R. 925. Available at <http://www.lexum.umontreal.ca/csc-scc/en/pub/1997/vol3/html/1997scr3_0925.html>. (Accessed July 2, 2003.)

PRISON

Chapter 17

REGULATING WOMEN

Gillian Balfour

From: *Criminalizing Women: Gender and (In)Justice in Neo-liberal Times*, 2nd edition, pp. 158–176 (slightly revised and reprinted with permission).

Conditions of poverty, racism and misogyny very much characterize the lives of criminalized women. The historical and contemporary narratives that construct women as errant females, prostitutes, street gang associates and symbols of moral corruption mask their restricted choices and how the conditions of their lives have always been embedded in the socio-political context. Women — as prisoners, patients, mothers and victims — have been disciplined, watched, drugged, restrained, managed, corrected and punished.

The current regulation of women is founded on the legacy of moralizing discourses from the late nineteenth and early twentieth centuries — discourses that continue to shape contemporary regimes of control, such as the punishment and "correction" of women in prison. The more conventional view of criminalized women casts them, historically, as "correctional afterthoughts" (Ross and Fabiano 1985) or as "high need and high risk" (Laishes 2002), therefore requiring intensive management and control. The analysis presented below provides a different view. As Kelly Hannah-Moffat (2001) suggests, criminalized women have been at the centre of the state's preoccupation with punishment and public order. Indeed, a close look at the history of the regulation of women in both institutional and public spaces exposes deeply gendered, racialized, sexualized and class-based forms of social control.

THE IMPRISONMENT OF WOMEN

The history of women's imprisonment in Canada is "a mixture of neglect, outright barbarism, and well-meaning paternalism" (Cooper 1993: 33). Throughout the nineteenth century, criminalized women were oftentimes housed in the attics of men's prisons and treated as inconveniences or difficult to manage. These unruly women were subjected to "cruel treatment such as starvation and excessive corporal punishment" (Beattie 1977: 152–54). Recognizing the special needs of women prisoners, early prison reformers began advocating for separate prisons for women. Inspired by the work of Elizabeth Fry in England, maternal feminists sought to "domesticate" the female prisoner by relying on "maternal images (domesticity, motherhood, parental discipline, caring and nurturing) and pastoral strategies of spiritual redemption and guidance" (Hannah-Moffat 2001: 31). The infamous Prison for Women (P4W) was finally opened in 1934 adjacent to the Kingston Penitentiary for Men, and until 1995 was the only federal prison for women in Canada.

Nevertheless, numerous government commissions — one of which, the Archambault Commission, reported only four years after the prison opened — denounced P4W as "unfit for bears, much less women" (Canada 1977). The facility was repeatedly condemned for closure as government officials saw the ethos of punishment as unduly harsh and unlikely to reform the "fallen women" who were being confined within its walls. Many of those imprisoned in P4W during its first decades were young working-class white women — often unwed mothers — deemed in need of moral correction by the matrons who enforced strict regimes of domesticity framed as a maternal ethic of care. For example, one of the matrons who worked at the P4W for over two decades "recalled stories of teaching prisoners domestic skills such as knitting, sewing, cooking, and housekeeping" and relied on "benevolent maternal techniques" such as placing an angry or upset prisoner in the bathtub until she cooled off instead of administering punishment (Hannah-Moffat 2001: 88). Essentialized as wayward rather than exploited and impoverished, young women were imprisoned indefinitely for acts such as vagrancy and prostitution (Sangster 1999).

Outside the prison walls, the regulation of young women in public spaces took on a decidedly classed and racialized edge. Between 1920 and 1950, the criminalization of Aboriginal and white women for prostitution-related offences, vagrancy and public drunkenness increased as part of a "broader web of gendered moral regulation articulated through law" (Sangster 1999: 34). By the 1950s, 72 percent of all charges against Aboriginal women were alcohol-related. Between 1940 and 1950, the Female Refuges Act was more vigorously used to incarcerate Aboriginal women than it was for white women. The FRA enabled the imprisonment of women aged sixteen to thirty-five, sentenced or even "liable to be sentenced" under any Criminal Code or by-law infractions for "idle and dissolute behaviour" (see Sangster 1996: 239–75, 2002; Minaker 2014). Joan Sangster (1999: 40) links this increase in the use of criminalization and incarceration of Aboriginal women to the migration of women in the 1950s into urban centres from reserves, leading to "spiralling economic deprivation and social dislocation." Reserve communities had been devastated by the impact of residential schools, which included physical and sexual abuse and the denigration of Aboriginal cultures and languages, compounded by the lack of economic development and education on reserves. Young women fled the isolated reserves hoping to escape extreme poverty, only to find themselves facing racism, destitution and homelessness in the city.

Sangster suggests that policing and sentencing practices were informed by racialized and gendered images of the "drunken Indian," but were also deeply sexualized and class-based. Aboriginal women's public drinking and presumed sexual promiscuity offended middle-class sensibilities, but their sanctioning as the "degenerate Other" also retrenched the boundaries of a white middle-class femininity and hegemonic masculinity (Razack 1998: 38). Homeless and destitute Aboriginal women were viewed as "licentious wild women that symbolized sexual excess and need for conquest and control" (Sangster 1999: 44). Social workers and prison matrons described incarcerated Aboriginal women as "degenerate," "dirty" and "backward." In contrast, they responded much differently to young white women often convicted of similar types of offences of prostitution and public drunkenness (Boritch 1997: 177; Oliver 1994). White women received the "partial justice of degradation and humiliation and the positive elements of reform and discipline" (Dobash, Dobash, and Gutteridge 1986). Poor white women were seen as unfortunate, childlike victims in need of protection. Nicole Rafter (1985b: 176) suggested, "Reformatories were designed to induce childlike submissiveness, and inmates were regarded as recalcitrant children."

Early twentieth-century prison reforms were shaped by the broader socio-political context of Victorian moral regulation. Alan Hunt's (2002) study of social surveys from 1902 to 1919 shows how dance halls, movie theatres, ice cream parlours, skating rinks, department stores and city parks were all sites of systematic disciplinary supervision. State and non-state agencies attempted to regulate the heterosexual lives of young working-class women and men — focusing, in particular, on the respectability of women — through the enforcement of bylaws and curfews. As Hunt (2002: 17–18) notes:

> The controls instituted by authorities did not directly regulate sex, but rather regulated the time, places and contexts in which young people could engage in heterosocial encounters. In particular these controls operated

through selecting women as the primary targets of regulation in a system which functioned to responsibilize women for their sexual conduct.

Interestingly, middle-class white feminists were instrumental in generating sexual purity campaigns to suppress prostitution and the spread of disease. These campaigns directly targeted young poor women and single women working as clerks in department stores (Hunt 1999; see also Valverde 1991). The early strategies embraced by prison reformers and maternal feminist organizations such as Elizabeth Fry Societies and the Women's Christian Temperance Union were rooted in this wider context of moral regulation and of chasteness and propriety.

By the 1970s, however, explanations for the causes of women's lawbreaking, as well as strategies for prison reform, were being shaped by the liberal feminist notion of formal equality; that is, that women should have the same rights and entitlements as men. The federal government's correctional plan for the women prisoners had cycled through various configurations. Throughout the 1970s and 1980s, some women prisoners were held in provincial jails under exchange of service agreements so that they could remain close to their families and work toward their community reintegration; or they were confined in Kingston's Prison for Women and expected to participate in treatment programs inside men's prisons (Berzins and Hayes 1987). Both approaches failed to meet the needs of women prisoners for gender-appropriate addiction treatment, educational and vocational training, and support in overcoming the trauma of abuse (Clark Report 1977; MacGuigan Report 1977; Needham Report 1978; Chinnery Report 1978; Canadian Advisory Council on the Status of Women 1981; Jackson 1988). Prison reformers quickly abandoned their attempts to address women's correctional programming needs by arguing for an "equality of sameness," and instead focused on the growing crisis within P4W of prisoner suicides and incidents of self-harm.

In 1988, the tragic suicide of Marlene Moore inside P4W proved to be a profound moment in the history of the prison. Marlene had been raised in extreme poverty and was a victim of incest and rape (see Kershaw and Lasovich 1991). Institutionalized from the age of thirteen inside training schools and juvenile detention centres for status offences, such as incorrigibility and running away, she eventually became the first woman to be declared a dangerous offender in Canada — even though she had never killed anyone. Rather, she was a repeat offender who was deemed not amenable to treatment. Marlene had attempted suicide many times and was a "cutter" — someone who uses self-injury as a way of managing profound emotional crises of fear or anxiety brought on by an overwhelming sense of powerlessness (Heney 1990; Fillmore and Dell 2000). A coroner's inquest was called to determine if prison protocols for the treatment of women in crisis contributed to Marlene's death. The Canadian Association of Elizabeth Fry Societies

(CAEFS) was granted unprecedented legal standing at the inquest. Their strategy was to implicate the prison regime and staff in Marlene's suicide. CAEFS believed that the security protocols at P4W had contributed to Marlene Moore's death by failing to provide her with the necessary therapeutic supports to prevent her from harming herself. Instead, prison security tended to treat women who self-injure as threats to institutional security and attempted to control women by placing them in segregation.

Following the inquest, the Correctional Service of Canada (CSC) announced the first-ever national Task Force on Federally Sentenced Women (TFFSW) to examine the conditions of women's imprisonment, their experiences in P4W and their programming needs. The Task Force proved to be the most significant study of women's imprisonment in Canada, and served as a blueprint for what was to be unprecedented change in the treatment of criminalized women.

THE TASK FORCE ON FEDERALLY SENTENCED WOMEN

The striking of the TFFSW in 1989 was shaped by increased activism within the prison system by organizations such as CAEFS and its regional membership, Aboriginal women's organizations and social justice groups. The socio-political context of the 1980s beyond the prison walls also reflected a broader awareness of issues affecting women's lives, an awareness underscored by the growing prevalence of feminist research in the areas of domestic violence, sexual assault, the feminization of poverty, single-parenting and sexual harassment in the workplace. Feminist research methodologies began to reshape the analytical frameworks of activists and academics. Women's standpoint of their lived experiences of domestic violence, sexual assault, poverty, and racism began to define the agendas for change. In this way, the TFFSW was driven by a fundamentally new approach that called for the inclusion of women's experiences of criminalization and imprisonment, and emphasized the importance of community alliances in the development of a new, women-centred correctional model. A growing Aboriginal self-government political agenda also influenced the structure and aims of the TFFSW, illustrated by the inclusion of Aboriginal women (both prisoners and their advocates) on the Task Force and the commissioning of a survey of federally sentenced Aboriginal women in the community (see Sugar and Fox 1989; Hayman 2006).

The survey of federally sentenced women conducted for the Task Force (Shaw et al. 1991) was unlike most research on offenders in that it was a qualitative study that positioned federally sentenced women as experts. The women's narratives of their prison experiences provided a testament to the inadequate and damaging effects of a male model of corrections that "classified risk, prioritized needs, and fitted offenders into pre-structured programs" (Shaw et al. 1991: 55). From these narratives came the groundbreaking report *Creating Choices* (TFFSW 1990), which revealed the prevalence of physical and sexual abuse in the lives of criminalized women and how abuse intersected with other difficulties such as drinking and drugging, violence and mental illness (Shaw 1994a, 1994b). While many of its recommendations focused on the immediate aims of addressing the therapeutic needs of women as victims, the report acknowledged the women's experiences as being compounded by the social context of poverty and racism. The relationship between women's victimization and their own use of violence — or what Karlene Faith (1993: 106) calls the "victimization-criminalization continuum" — was instrumental in defining a new gender-responsive correctional model.

Released in April 1990, *Creating Choices* called for the closure of P4W and the construction of four new regional facilities and a healing lodge for Aboriginal women. Programming within each facility would focus on a holistic, women-centred correctional model emphasizing five fundamental principles: empowerment to raise women's self-esteem; meaningful choices involving a variety of diverse programs in the prison and the community; respect and dignity to cultivate self-respect and respect for others; a supportive and nurturing environment; and shared responsibility among the woman prisoners, staff, and community. A series of key recommendations in the report also called for the development of a community release strategy that would offer increased resources for both the accommodation and treatment of women in the community.

THE IMPLEMENTATION OF *CREATING CHOICES*

While the federal government accepted in principle the report's main recommendations, the implementation of those proposals quickly deteriorated as CSC became more interested in a hierarchal top-down model as opposed to a tripartite consensus-building model involving the community stakeholders, Aboriginal groups and the government. Fears about public safety and a growing public backlash against prisoner rehabilitation also undermined the implementation process. CSC was required to enter into exchange of service agreements with the provinces in which the regional facilities were to be built, and municipal and provincial governments were under increasing public pressure from local people not to allow the construction of a women's prison close to their communities, especially without a perimeter wall, uniformed staff or a traditional static security design. On one hand, the backlash from local communities was driven by a wider neo-conservative political agenda of law and order and an increasingly vocal victims' rights lobby. On the other hand, neo-liberal economics had taken hold in most provinces, calling for fiscal restraint in the spending of public dollars.

CSC further undermined the implementation of *Creating Choices* by excluding the Elizabeth Fry Societies from the National Implementation Committee, instead offering CAEFS a limited role in programming subcommittees. With this diminished status, CAEFS was quickly marginalized by the federal government, and less able to advocate for implementation of the recommendations of the Task Force report (Faith and Pate 2000). In 1992, CAEFS made the difficult decision to withdraw from the implementation process altogether to signify the organization's serious concerns over the CSC's shift in strategy in abandoning many of the principles of *Creating Choices* (see Hayman 2006).

While the implementation process was underway, conditions inside the P4W began to deteriorate. After the decision to close the P4W had been announced, the CSC's budget for P4W had been cut back to put money into the new facilities, and senior staff had begun transferring out of the prison. These changes resulted in programming reductions and increased overtime hours for junior officers who had little knowledge of or experience in dealing with women prisoners. Meanwhile, the women prisoners were becoming increasingly frustrated with inconsistencies in the prison's management and the absence of programming. They were also anxious about the lack of information related to their eventual transfer to another province. This anxiety was heightened by the amount of time it was taking to implement reforms. While the government had announced in 1990 that the P4W would be closed by September 1994, the prison actually remained in operation until July 2000.

These conditions created a tense environment that sparked a confrontation between six prisoners and front-line staff in April 1994, resulting in the all-male Institutional Emergency Response Team (IERT) being sent into the segregation unit of P4W in riot gear to conduct "cell extractions" and strip-search the women (see Faith 1995; Pate 1999; Shaw 2000). Shortly afterward, an internal Board of Investigation quickly produced a report, which included fifteen pages focusing on the profiles of the women prisoners involved in the incident, emphasizing their violent histories and institutional records. The report described the events inside P4W as "a planned attack on staff, perpetrated by a group of violent women who were attempting to escape" (Shaw 2000: 62), thereby justifying the use of force by male officers against women prisoners. The report made no mention of the strip-searching of the women prisoners by male guards or the IERT videotape made (as per "official policy") of the cell extractions. References to the women being strip-searched by male guards and the existence of the video had been edited out of the report. In addition, the report stated that the women had been given blankets and mattresses upon their return to their cells, which was untrue. The women were left for twenty-four hours dressed only in paper gowns. Only after the CBC's *The Fifth Estate* obtained and aired a copy of the videotape were calls for a full inquiry into CSC's handling of the matter acted upon.

The report of the Commission of Inquiry into Certain Events at the Prison for Women in Kingston, headed by Madam Justice Louise Arbour (1996), described women in prison as "high needs/low risk." It also contained a critique of the CSC for what Justice Arbour termed its violations of the rule of law. Arbour described the correctional system as being "out of control" and the behaviour of the male IERT as "cruel, inhumane and degrading." The CSC's response to the incident, according to Arbour, was to "deny error, defend against criticism and to react without a proper investigation of the truth." The report made some hundred recommendations, including the creation of the position of a deputy commissioner for women, stopping the practice of using male riot squads in women's prisons, and putting an end to the long-term segregation of women prisoners.

Between 1995 and 1997, the new regional prisons in Edmonton, AB, Kitchener, ON, Joliette, QC, and Truro, NS, as well as the Okimaw Ohci Healing Lodge in Maple Creek, SK, became operational. But it soon became clear that simply building new facilities was not enough to transform women's experiences of imprisonment. The CSC's response to several incidents involving suicides, slashings, walkaways and disturbances at the regional prisons[1] was to implement a heavily securitized approach to the management of women prisoners — one that involved the reassertion of control and punishment (Shaw 2000). In 1996, the CSC announced that all women classified as maximum-security would be moved to separate maximum-security units in three of the men's prisons, the P4W or the Regional Psychiatric Centre in Saskatoon. While this was to be a temporary measure (lasting eighteen months to two years), it was not until some six years later — in February 2003 — that women classified as maximum-security were moved to "enhanced security units" inside four of the women's facilities.

In 1997, CSC set up a new Mental Health Strategy for Women Offenders. The strategy adopted a broad definition of "mental illness" and "mental disorder." For instance, women could be identified as having mental health needs if they had a history of relationships characterized by abuse, dependent children, low educational attainment and limited job opportunities, or significant long-term substance abuse. In short, social marginalization was being transformed into a "mental health need" (Hannah-Moffat and Shaw 2001: 47). After commissioning a series of reports on the treatment and security needs of maximum-security women and those with acute mental health needs, CSC announced in 1999 the implementation of an Intensive Intervention Strategy for managing these two groups of women (see Laishes 2002).

Creating Choices took the position that women should not be held in the kind of secure environment that the P4W provided. It advocated cottage housing units, with an "enhanced" security unit to be used only on a temporary basis when required. Because women were seen as high need/low risk, they required support instead of security. Rather than classification, *Creating Choices* advocated an assessment of treatment needs and the use of a holistic as opposed to hierarchical model. Following the opening of the new facilities, however, CSC adopted an Offender Intake Assessment process. Initiated by cognitive psychologists for male prison populations, this scheme is based on an assessment of both risk and need, especially as these relate to rehabilitation prospects and the effectiveness of particular types of treatment. In addition to risk-based security placement and release decisions, the system assigns different levels and types of treatment based on a prisoner's "criminogenic needs." As Kelly Hannah-Moffat (2000) notes, what this approach does is redefine "need" as a "risk factor." Dependency, low self-esteem, poor educational and vocational achievement, parental death at an early age, foster care placement, constant changes in the location of foster care, residential placement, living on the streets, prostitution, suicide attempts, self-injury, substance abuse and parental responsibilities: the system considers all of these as characteristics that give rise to criminogenic needs (Hannah-Moffat 2000: 37).

Several of CSC's decisions also undermined the implementation of the healing lodge for Aboriginal women prisoners — and these decisions again violated the principles of *Creating Choices.* The initial plan for Aboriginal women at the healing lodge was to address the disconnection and dislocation experienced as a result of residential schools, child welfare apprehensions and the Indian Act (Monture-Angus 2002). Instead, the healing lodge appeared to be governed by CSC's agenda of risk management through imprisonment, rather than the approved principles of healing and meaningful choices aimed at reconnecting Aboriginal women to their land, cultures and communities (Monture-Angus 2002: 52). For example, because the healing lodge was deemed a minimum- to medium-security-level prison, Aboriginal women classified as maximum-security — who made up 46 percent of this group of women prisoners (CAEFS 2003) — were denied access to the facility.

By 1998 it was clear that the programming for women prisoners was not going to be linked to a feminist analysis of the systemic nature of women's needs as envisioned in *Creating Choices.* Instead, CSC was implementing a system of cognitive behavioural programming, a therapeutic approach premised on the notion that "criminal offending is a result of the offender's inability to think logically, reason appropriately and to make rational decisions" (Pollack 2004: 694). Such an approach considered structural inequalities as irrelevant — it viewed any discussion of poverty, racism or gendered experiences (such as rape) as the context of women's criminal behaviour as a denial of personal responsibility. Kathleen Kendall (2002: 183) argues that the cognitive behavioural paradigm of self-regulation "is consistent with neo-liberal strategies of individualizing social problems." Shoshana Pollack (2000, 2004) found in her research that many Aboriginal and Black women prisoners were often confined to maximum-security units because they did not comply with the cognitive behavioural program. Women resisted program requirements of submitting to orders by security staff that were demeaning or humiliating. For women in maximum-security, non-compliance to security protocols resulted in long-term confinement in segregation, strip-searches, involuntary transfers, limited human contact — and death.

EMPOWERMENT AND RESPONSIBILIZATION

In 2004 CSC introduced a new correctional plan for female offenders that re-entrenched the view of criminalized women as being in need of cognitive therapy to address their criminal thinking. The plan considered women to be a greater risk because of their need for intensive treatment given the impact of severe childhood trauma of abuse and neglect upon their decision-making skills — causing them to "choose" drugs and alcohol, prostitution and violence (see Fortin 2004). In short, women needed to learn how to take responsibility for their choices rather than challenge the conditions under which they must make such choices. Prisoners considered "difficult to manage" or unamenable to treatment because of their criminal personalities were to be managed under Dialectical Behavioural Therapy (DBT), which pathologizes women's experiences of victimization; women prisoners are not able to regulate their own emotions because of the impact of childhood sexual abuse.

DBT, the centrepiece of the Correctional Service of Canada's correctional planning for women prisoners, is grounded in the essentialized view of women as defined by their familial and intimate relationships. Women are psychologically damaged when these relationships are characterized by trauma (for example, sexual victimization or neglect). These experiences of trauma become "pathways" to addiction and criminal conduct (Bloom, Owen, and Covington 2003). DBT is an example of a gender-responsive correctional plan wherein women must take responsibility for their relationships through learning proper emotional regulation, anger management, and effective communication skills (Bloom, Owen, and Covington 2003). Hannah-Moffat (2010: 201) points out how gender responsive programming "inadvertently creates insidious and invasive forms of governing. Relationships, children, past victimizations, mental health, self-injury and self-esteem have all become correctional targets in the pursuit of normative femininity and gender conformity." Gender-responsive programming does not consider how women's lives are also structured by pathways of poverty and racism. Indeed, women's low self-esteem and emotional vulnerability, which can lead to abusive relationships, may stem from unstable housing or precarious employment, yet are framed as risk factors (Hannah-Moffat 2010; McKim 2008).

How can we make sense of the more regressive and punitive response of CSC toward federally sentenced women — despite the progressive recommendations of *Creating Choices* and the dramatic findings of the Arbour inquiry? In part, it would seem that CSC has become emboldened by an angry and fearful public, which was increasingly influenced by media that never seem to tire of images and stories of violent women and girls, leading to ceaseless demands for protection through a punitive criminal justice response to crime. But in addition to such neo-conservative law-and-order sentiments, the dismantling of the welfare state under the sway of neo-liberalism had ushered in a new model of crime control whereby offenders were to be "empowered" to take responsibility for the consequences of their choices (O'Malley 1992, 2010; Hannah-Moffat 2000). Within this new model, ideas such as empowerment — so central to the philosophy of *Creating Choices* — take on new meaning.

As Hannah-Moffat (2000, 2002, 2010) points out, feminist reformers invoked the language of empowerment as a way of recognizing women's power to make choices. The neo-liberal discourse, however, translates empowerment to mean that incarcerated women are responsible for their own self-governance and requires them to manage their own risk to themselves (Pollack 2009). In short, under neo-liberal risk-management schemes, women are now being "responsibilized." Yet this correctional discourse has also enabled the state to coercively — and in some instances to illegally — punish women (Kerr 2013). Starting in 2003, the Office of the Correctional Investigator (OCI) has reported on the overclassification of feder-ally sentenced women, especially Aboriginal women and women with untreated mental illnesses, as maximum-security inmates. The OCI also reported that male guards held front-line positions at all regional facilities, despite continuing griev-ances by women prisoners of sexual harassment, abuse and assault.

Disregarding these concerns, in 2003 CSC implemented a Management Protocol that enabled prison authorities to place women deemed "high risk to institutional security" in indefinite solitary confinement — a practice that is actually illegal under the Corrections and Conditional Release Act, the legislation that governs federal prisons in Canada. OCI has noted that almost all women inmates held on this protocol are Aboriginal. The protocol was subsequently the subject of two court cases. In *R. v. S.L.N.* (2010), the court commented, "The Management Protocol is a mechanism whose principal element is just that: extensive, prolonged isolation. While it is intended as an effective means of managing the most danger-ous and disruptive of inmates, there seems little doubt that it is entirely capable of inflicting great damage on those to whom it is applied" (para. 63). In *Worm v. Attorney General of Canada* (2011; see also Balfour and Comack 2014), the B.C. Civil Liberties Association successfully argued that the Management Protocol was unconstitutional and constituted illegal conditions of confinement. In light of this legal action, CSC rescinded the Management Protocol in 2011. Troublesome practices, however, have continued. In 2014, a coroner's jury returned a finding of homicide in the death of prisoner Ashley Smith. Evidence presented throughout the inquiry revealed the systematic use of chemical restraints, such as Seroquel, in addition to relentless deprivation of human contact that served to antagonize Ashley, causing her to lash out against her captors.

In addition to the inhumane treatment of women prisoners documented in these cases, OCI has also reported a striking lack of compliance by CSC to internal procedures for reporting use of force incidents:

> It is troubling to note that CSC auditors found that national and regional direction and oversight is lacking with respect to the frequency and appropriate use of physical restraint equipment in the Treatment Centres. On a number of occasions, the Office has provided its views on these matters only to be informed that revised policy directives are "under review" or "being consulted." It bears reminding that the same compliance issues, governance and accountability problems noted in the January 2011 audit have prevailed since the death of Ashley Smith in October 2007. This situation is simply untenable. (Sapers 2011: 16)

The conditions in provincial lock-ups also continue to deteriorate as provincial governments look for more ways to manage the increasing numbers of criminalized men and women struggling with drug addiction and mental illness, a situation compounded by a lack of community treatment services and affordable housing. As neo-conservative governments denounce the cost of government delivery of human services as an unfair demand on middle-class taxpayers, all the while building prisons to increase jobs in economically depressed voter-rich regions, provincial jail populations have swelled, leading to problems of overcrowding. In September 2013, for instance, all of the jails in Manitoba were overcrowded. While the total capacity of the province's institutions is 1,982 beds, 2,433 adults were being held in custody (123 percent of capacity). The Women's Correctional Centre (WCC), which opened in February 2012 as a replacement to the aged Portage Correctional Institution (built in 1893 for male prisoners), has an official capacity of 168 inmates. As of September 2013, the WCC's inmate count was already at 211 — or 126 percent of its official capacity (Owen 2013).

Concerned social justice organizations and advocates have exposed the disregard for women prisoners, such as the case of Julia Bilotta, who gave birth to her first child while held in segregation in the Ottawa-Carleton Detention Centre. Bilotta was held in remand custody on fraud charges for forging cheques after being denied bail. She was eight months pregnant and requested medical attention because she was experiencing labour contractions. Bilotta was told by the prison nurse that she had indigestion and was experiencing false labour, and then was told to "shut up" because she was moaning too much. Her son's birth was breech, and as a result he experienced significant respiratory problems; Bilotta also required a blood transfusion. A formal complaint was filed with the Ontario College of Nurses, and Ontario's Corrections Ministry initiated formal disciplinary proceedings against the involved staff (Pedwell 2013).

In 2013, the Ontario provincial Ombudsman released a report on his special investigation into prisoner complaints of excessive force used by staff in various provincial jails. The Ombudsman's review of inmate complaints revealed systemic disregard for the rights of prisoners and a culture of silence among correctional staff with regard to prisoner abuse. One of the cases detailed in the report involved the story of "Helen," a woman admitted to the Sarnia Jail on August 31, 2011. Suffering the effects of drug withdrawal, Helen was housed in an area containing a single cell. On being escorted to her cell the next day, she stopped to ask a manager if she could be placed in a different location. The next thing she knew a correctional officer attacked her. Helen only disclosed what had happened when she was being readied for transfer to another facility.

The Correctional Investigation and Security Unit's investigation into Helen's complaint confirmed that a correctional officer had pushed her against a wall, pinned her by the neck, and later repeatedly hit her with a closed fist while she was restrained on her bunk. The correctional staff who witnessed the incident omitted these damning details in their initial reports of the incident. It was not until much later that four officers told the truth about what they had seen. In this case, the code of silence among the prison staff was particularly powerful. The culprit was extremely influential in the jail and the local corrections community. Two officers closely connected to him had also engaged in a campaign of harassment to ensure that the witnesses kept silent and didn't "rat out" their colleague. The officer who injured Helen and his two code of silence enforcers were dismissed. But even after the Ministry removed the chief instigators from the jail, officers who had told the truth continued to face reprisals from their peers, leading one of them to resign her job (Ombudsman of Ontario 2013).

WOMEN IN CAGES

While crime rates are down in Canada, women are the fastest-growing group of prisoners, as they are throughout the world. Julia Sudbury (2005a: xvii) argues that the "global lockdown" of women inside immigration detention centres, psychiatric hospitals and prisons is the manifestation of global capitalism's prison industrial complex, intended to "warehouse those surplus to the global economy and creating profits for private prison operators and corporations servicing prisons." Sudbury's analysis of this global lockdown reminds us of the many facets of the coercive power in Western capitalist democracies — such as the colonization (and criminalization) of Indigenous peoples, the creation of legislation to combat the "war on drugs," which has incarcerated more women than men for trafficking of drugs, and the privatization of prisons, which has created much private profit — and how these tactics aggressively affect women all over the world.

It has been over two decades since *Creating Choices* was written, rooted in the findings of the survey of federally sentenced women. Since that time, more women are federally incarcerated than ever before. In 2002–03, there were 359 federally incarcerated women (accounting for only 3 percent of all penitentiary inmates). By 2012–13, the population of women in federal prisons was at 579, an increase of just over 60 percent. One in three federally incarcerated women is Aboriginal. The number of Aboriginal women increased by over 80 percent in ten years — from 104 in 2002–03 to 191 in 2012–13 (Sapers 2013: 35–36). Does this mean that women are becoming more dangerous and engaging in serious crimes? Or do the numbers tell us something about the criminal justice response to women and the lack of accessible services for women in our communities?

When we look at the personal histories of federally sentenced women, we come to understand that most of these women have long-standing mental health and addiction issues — which call for effective treatment, not lengthy criminal records. In their report on federally sentenced women, Meredith Barrett, Kim Allenby, and Kelly Taylor (2010) document that approximately two-thirds of women prisoners are serving sentences of between two and five years, and "one out of every five women in the federal correctional system presents with mental health problems, a proportion that has increased by 61% since 1997" (Barrett, Allenby, and Taylor 2010: 21). The authors also report that 48 percent of women were identified at intake as having a previous or current drug addiction; over 80 percent of women self-reported histories of physical abuse and 68 percent reported sexual abuse (an increase of 10 percent since the original survey on federally sentenced women). Just under half of women report having engaged in self-harming behaviour as a means of coping with emotional pain. Moreover, almost 77 percent of women inmates have children; 64 percent of women reported supporting themselves and their children financially through paid employment, yet more than half of the women reported having less than a high-school education (Barrett, Allenby, and Taylor 2010). Clearly, criminalized women face economic disadvantage, for the most part supporting their children through poorly paid work, and are vulnerable to exploitation and abuse.

Prisoner advocate and feminist Kim Pate (2003) explains the connection between women's increased economic marginalization under neo-liberal provincial governments and increased reliance by provincial and territorial governments on prisons:

We know the increasing numbers of women in prison are clearly linked to the evisceration of health, education, and social services. We also know that the cycle intensifies in times of economic downturn. It is very clear where we are sending the people who are experiencing the worst in the downturn in the economy and social trends. Jails are our most comprehensive homelessness initiative. In terms of the rate at which women are charged, however, there has been a 7 percent decrease overall in the number of women charged with criminal offences. In particular, we are seeing a decrease in the number of violent crimes committed by women yet there are increases in the number of women in prison. These increases have occurred within the context of increased cuts to expenditures for social services, health, and education throughout the country. (Personal communication, Oct. 3, 2005)

A consequence of the closure of the P4W and the construction of the healing lodge and regional prisons is that more women are being sentenced to longer periods of incarceration so that they can supposedly benefit from the treatment programs available. Prior to the closure of P4W, fewer women were receiving federal sentences because judges were loath to send women to a prison so widely condemned. Ultimately, as more women are sentenced to prison "for their own good," the public will come to view criminalized women as being more and more dangerous (Shaw 1993).

BEYOND THE PRISON WALLS

Given the deteriorating conditions of confinement, what do women's lives look like after they are released from prison? Most women are released from federal custody on parole or conditional release, and many of them convicted of criminal offences end up "doing time on the outside" (Maidment 2006) in the form of sentences to be served in the community (typically with numerous conditions attached).[2]

In the early 1980s, criminologists recognized that social-control mechanisms aimed at inducing conformity operated both inside and outside of the criminal justice system (Cohen 1985). These mechanisms are networks of professionals, such as social workers and counsellors, along with non-profit social-service agencies, such as halfway houses, detox centres and food banks. Each agency or expert engages in the supervision and reinsertion of the non-conformist (prisoner, addict, street person) back into the social-control matrix of family and work. Over time many of these agencies — such as church-based and charitable organizations — became an extension of the criminal justice and mental health systems, competing for operational funding to house, feed, treat and supervise ex-prisoners and patients. Although neo-liberalism seeks to make individuals responsible for solving or handling their own problems, whatever those problems might be or wherever they spring from, it also seeks to put communities into the hands of "the market" for the delivery of social services. This approach to service delivery, which is touted as being more financially prudent, is rationalized as a matter of community capacity-building and of empowering communities to take responsibility for their own problems and populations (Andersen 1999).

Critical criminologists such as Edwin Schur (1984) and Pat Carlen (2003) refer to the relocation of punishment into the community as "transcarceration," and feminist criminologists recognize that the transcarceration regimes are profoundly gendered. Through transcarceration the reach of regulatory (rather than criminalizing) agencies governs women's relationships and bodies "at a distance." Social-control networks of surveillance and observation within the community have expanded the gaze of the state through the use of halfway houses, shelters for battered women, food banks, probation officers, and community policing (Maidment 2006); and women's relationships in the community are "assessed for their criminogenic potential" (Hannah-Moffat 2010: 203). The strategies and tactics of parole supervision mirror those of the gender-responsive correctional model. Women's risk of recidivism (reoffending) is assessed according to a gendered logic. Women's risk to reoffend is determined by their relational lives with their children and partners. Relationships are "risky conditions" unless women have received proper interventions, such as anger management or cognitive behavioural therapy to take responsibility for their relationship choices. Parole board members utilize records of women's past experiences of domestic violence — especially for those who have resisted abuse — as a possible predictor for future violence (Hannah-Moffat and Yule 2011; Turnbull and Hannah-Moffat 2009; Pollack 2007).

More recently, criminologists have begun to take seriously the non-legal forms of "governmentality" — the process of social control in which the state works through civil society, not upon it (Garland 2001; O'Malley 1996). For example, low-income women on welfare are the target of moral scrutiny under the social assistance laws of Ontario. For example, if they are deemed to be living in an unreported supportive relationship with anyone (the so-called "spouse in the house" rule), they are cut off state benefits (Mosher 2014; Little and Morrison 1999; Little 1998). According to governmentality theorists, the work of regulation is more diffuse across private and public domains; it involves technologies of surveillance and risk assessment that are often not administered by the criminal justice system (Ericson and Haggerty 1997).

INVESTIGATING THE REGULATION OF WOMEN

Others have explored the historical and contemporary regulation of women. Robert Menzies and Dorothy Chunn (2014) tell the story of Charlotte — a woman who defied many of the normative sexual and gendered expectations of the early twentieth century. Charlotte, who was imprisoned for most of her life as a patient/prisoner, was forced to endure brutalizing treatments for her undisciplined independence and resistance. Menzies and Chunn map out the gendered, class-based and sexualized regulation of women that overshadows contemporary regimes of control inside and outside of the criminal justice system.

Illustrating the historical continuity of control over women by the state, Dorothy Chunn and Shelley Gavigan (see Chapter 12) outline the transformation of welfare laws in Ontario since the rise of neo-conservative social politics and neo-liberal economic policies under Premier Mike Harris's government of 1995–2002. During that period, law and order rhetoric coupled with the individualism of neo-liberal economics resulted in the creation of new crime categories and a broadening of the regulatory powers of the state to properly discipline welfare recipients. Poor women with children were most vulnerable to these new policies, which ushered in a sharp reduction in welfare benefits, the ratcheting up of eligibility criteria, work-for-welfare policies, the creation of a welfare snitch line, investigations into the personal, intimate lives of welfare recipients, and the creation of welfare fraud as a criminal offence. In the end, neo-liberal governments — seemingly committed to smaller government — have increasingly relied upon the expansion of the criminal justice system to implement their policies.

The expanding reach of the state to govern women's lives through psychiatrization as criminalization, or welfare dependency as welfare fraud, is taken up by Amanda Glasbeek and Emily van der Meulen (2014) in their examination of CCTV — closed circuit television installed in large urban centres under the pretence of public safety. CCTV functions as a form of security that works in complex ways across women's lives; both as crime prevention and criminalization. Racialized and poor women experience technological surveillance of urban spaces for reasons of public order and safety as a "paradox of visibility." Cameras serve to govern spaces in which women are at risk of victimization, yet they also become a means of both state surveillance of women's street work and of private eroticized surveillance of women's washrooms.

Jennifer Kilty (2014) takes us into the segregation cells of Grand Valley Institution, spaces of coercive surveillance and disciplining of women. In her analysis of the conditions leading to Ashley Smith's death in custody, Kilty argues that therapeutic regimes such as cognitive-behavioural programming operate as modes of punishment, legitimating the excessive use chemical and physical restraints to achieve compliance.

The spaces and strategies used for the regulation of women are hauntingly familiar. Historical sociologists, socio-legal scholars and criminologists demonstrate how the state, through the criminalization or treatment of women "for their own good," responds to their resistance to social isolation due to a potent mixture of poverty, racism, maternalism, and/or heterosexism. What emerges across all the narratives of criminalized and imprisoned women's lives is the profound impact of poverty and violence — and what happens to women when they choose to resist.

Notes

1   For instance, between January and March 1996 two suicides and a series of slashings occurred at the Edmonton Institution. In April 1996, seven women walked away from the prison; and in a media release following the "escapes," CAEFS asserted that the women who had left did so to see their families and were apprehended only a few blocks away. A disturbance occurred at the Truro prison in September 1996.

2   Conditional sentences, for example, which were implemented by Parliament in 1996 with the passage of Bill C-41, gave judges the option of imposing a community-based sentence for an offence that does not carry a mandatory minimum prison term, and if the judge would otherwise have sentenced the offender to imprisonment for less than two years (the Conservative government added further restrictions on applicable offences in 2007 and 2012; see Yalkin and Kirk 2012). A conditional sentence will have mandatory conditions attached to it (keeping the peace and being of good behaviour, appearing before the court when ordered to do so, reporting regularly to a supervisor, remaining within the jurisdiction). It can also have optional conditions attached (abstaining from drugs and/or alcohol, firearms prohibition, performing up to 240 hours of community service, attending counselling or treatment programs, abiding by a curfew). Offenders who breach their conditions serve the remainder of their sentence in custody.

References

Andersen, C. 1999. "Governing Aboriginal Justice in Canada: Constructing Responsible Individuals and Communities through 'Tradition.'" *Crime, Law and Social Change* 31.

Arbour, The Honourable Justice Louise (Commissioner). 1996. *Commission of Inquiry into Certain Events at the Prison for Women in Kingston.* Ottawa: Solicitor General.

Balfour, G. and E. Comack. 2014. "Introduction." In G. Balfour and E. comack (eds.), *Criminalizing Women: Gender and (In)Justice in Neo-liberal Times,* 2nd edition. Halifax and Winnipeg: Fernwood Publishing.

Barrett, M.R., K. Allenby, and K. Taylor. 2010. *Twenty Years Later: Revisiting the Task Force on Federally Sentenced Women.* Ottawa: Correctional Service Canada.

Beattie, J.M. 1977. *Attitudes towards Crime and Punishment in Upper Canada, 1830–1850: A Documentary Study.* Toronto: University of Toronto, Centre of Criminology.

Berzins, L., and B. Hayes. 1987. "The Diaries of Two Change Agents." In E. Adelberg and C. Currie (eds.), *Too Few to Count: Canadian Women in Conflict with the Law.* Vancouver: Press Gang Publishers.

Bloom, B., B. Owen, and S. Covington. 2003. *Gender Responsive Strategies: Research,*

Practice, and Guiding Principles for Women Offenders. Washington: National Institute of Corrections.

____. 2005. *Gender Responsive Strategies for Women Offenders: A Summary of Research, Practice and Guiding Principles for Women Offenders.* Washington: National Institute for Corrections.

Boritch, H. 1997. *Fallen Women: Female Crime and Criminal Justice in Canada.* Toronto: Nelson.

CAEFS (Canadian Association of Elizabeth Fry Societies). 2003. "Submission of the Canadian Association of Elizabeth Fry Societies (CAEFS) to the Canadian Human Rights Commission for the Special Report on the Discrimination on the Basis of Sex, Race and Disability Faced by Federally Sentenced Women." Ottawa: CAEFS. <caefs.ca/wp-content/uploads/2013/04/CAEFS-Submission-to-the-Canadian-Human-Rights-Commission-for-the-Special-Report-on-the-Discrimination-on-the-Basis-of-Sex-Race-and-Disability-Faced-by-Federally-Sentenced-Women.pdf>.

Canada. 1977. *Report to Parliament by the Sub-Committee on the Penitentiary System in Canada.* Ottawa: Supply and Services.

Canadian Advisory Council on the Status of Women. 1981. *Women in Prison: Expanding Their Options.* Ottawa.

Carlen, P. 2003. "Virginia, Criminology, and the Antisocial Control of Women." In T. Bloomberg and S. Cohen (eds.), *Punishment and Social Control.* New York: Aldine De Gruyter.

Chinnery Report. 1978. *Joint Committee to Study Alternatives for Housing Federal Female Offenders.* Ottawa: Ministry of Solicitor General.

Clark Report. 1977. *Report of the National Advisory Committee on the Female Offender.* Ottawa: Ministry of Solicitor General.

Cohen, S. 1985. *Visions of Social Control.* Cambridge: Polity.

Cooper, S. 1993. "The Evolution of the Federal Women's Prison." In E. Adelberg and C. Currie (eds.), *In Conflict with the Law: Women and the Canadian Justice System.* Vancouver: Press Gang.

Dobash, R.E., R. Dobash, and S. Guttridge. 1986: *The Imprisonment of Women.* Oxford: Basil Blackwell.

Ericson, R.V., and K.D. Haggerty. 1997. *Policing the Risk Society.* Toronto: University of Toronto Press.

Faith, K. 1993. *Unruly Women: The Politics of Confinement and Resistance.* Vancouver: Press Gang Publishers.

____. 1995. "Aboriginal Women's Healing Lodge: Challenge to Penal Correctionalism?" *Journal of Human Justice* 6, 2.

Faith, K., and K. Pate. 2000. "Personal and Political Musings on Activism." In K. Hannah-Moffat and M. Shaw (eds.), *An Ideal Prison? Critical Essays on Women's Imprisonment in Canada.* Halifax: Fernwood Publishing.

Fillmore, C., and C.A. Dell. 2000. "A Study of Prairie Women: Violence and Self Harm." *The Canadian Women's Health Network* 4 (Spring). <pwhce.ca/pdf/self-harm.pdf>.

Fortin, D. 2004. *Program Strategy for Women Offenders.* Ottawa: Correctional Service of Canada.

Garland, D. 2001. *The Culture of Control: Crime and Social Order in Contemporary Society.*

Chicago: University of Chicago Press.

Glasbeek, Amanda, and Emily van der Meulen. 2014. "The Paradox of Visibility: Women, CCTV, and Crime." In Gillian Balfour and Elizabeth Comack (eds.), *Criminalizing Women: Gender and (In)Justice in Neo-liberal Times,* 2nd edition. Halifax/Winnipeg: Fernwood Publishing.

Hannah-Moffat, K. 2000. "Prisons that Empower: Neo-Liberal Governance in Canadian Women's Prisons." *British Journal of Criminology* 40, 3 (Summer).

____. 2001. *Punishment in Disguise: Penal Governance and Federal Imprisonment of Women in Canada.* Toronto: University of Toronto Press.

____. 2002. "Creating Choices: Reflecting on Choices." In P. Carlen (ed.), *Women and Punishment: The Struggle for Justice.* Cullompton: Willan Publishing.

____. 2010. "Sacrosanct or Flawed: Risk, Accountability, and Gender-Responsive Penal Politics." *Current Issues in Criminal Justice* 22, 2.

Hannah-Moffat, K., and M. Shaw. 2001. *Taking Risks: Incorporating Gender and Culture into the Assessment and Classification of Federally Sentenced Women in Canada.* Ottawa: Status of Women Canada.

Hannah-Moffat, K., and C. Yule. 2011. "Gaining Insight, Changing Attitudes and Managing 'Risk': Parole Release Decisions for Women Convicted of Violent Crimes." *Punishment & Society* 13, 2.

Hayman, S. 2006. *Imprisoning Our Sisters: The New Federal Women's Prisons in Canada.* Montreal and Kingston: McGill-Queen's University Press.

Heney, J. 1990. *Report on Self-Injurious Behaviour in the Kingston Prison for Women.* Ottawa: Solicitor General.

Hunt, A. 1999. "The Purity Wars: Making Sense of Moral Militancy." *Theoretical Criminology* 13, 4.

____. 2002. "Regulating Heterosocial Space: Sexual Politics in the Early Twentieth Century." *Journal of Historical Sociology* 15, 1.

Jackson, Michael. 1988. *Justice Behind the Walls.* Ottawa: Canadian Bar Association.

Kendall, K. 2002. "Time to Think Again About Cognitive Behavioural Programmes." In P. Carlen (ed.), *Women and Punishment: The Struggle for Justice.* Cullompton: Willan Publishing.

Kerr, L. 2013. "Solitary Confinement and the Question of Judicial Control of Punishment." J.S.D. dissertation, New York University School of Law.

Kershaw, A., and M. Lasovich. 1991. *Rock-A-Bye Baby: A Death Behind Bars.* Toronto: Oxford University Press.

Kilty, Jennifer. 2014. "Examining the "Psy-Carceral Complex" in the Death of Ashley Smith." In Gillian Balfour and Elizabeth Comack (eds.), *Criminalizing Women: Gender and (In)Justice in Neo-liberal Times,* 2nd edition. Halifax/Winnipeg: Fernwood Publishing.

Laishes, J. 2002. *The 2002 Mental Health Strategy for Women Offenders.* Ottawa: Correctional Services of Canada: Mental Health Services. <csc-scc.gc.ca/publications/fsw/mhealth/toc-eng.shtml>.

Little, M. 1998. *No Car, No Radio, No Liquor Permit: The Moral Regulation of Single Mothers in Ontario, 1920–1997.* Toronto: Oxford University Press.

Little, M. and I. Morrison. 1999. "Pecker Detectors" Are Back: Regulation of the Family Form in Ontario Welfare Policy." *Journal of Canadian Studies/Revue d'Études*

*Canadiennes*34, 2

MacGuigan Report. 1977. *Report to Parliament: Subcommittee on the Penitentiary System in Canada.* Ottawa: Ministry of Supply and Services.

Maidment, M. 2006. *Doing Time on the Outside: Deconstructing the Benevolent Community.* Toronto: University of Toronto Press.

McKim, A. 2008. "Getting Gut-Level: Punishment, Gender and Therapeutic Governance." *Gender and Society* 22.

Menzies R. and D. Chunn. 2014 "The Making of the Black Widow: The Criminal and Psychiatric Control of Women." In Gillian Balfour and Elizabeth Comack (eds.), *Criminalizing Women: Gender and (In)Justice in Neo-liberal Times,* 2nd edition. Halifax/Winnipeg: Fernwood Publishing.

Minaker, J. 2014. "Sluts and Slags: The Censuring of the Erring Female." In G. Balfour and E. comack (eds.), *Criminalizing Women: Gender and (In)Justice in Neo-liberal Times,* 2nd edition. Halifax and Winnipeg: Fernwood Publishing.

Monture-Angus, P. 2002. *The Lived Experience of Aboriginal Women Who Are Federally Sentenced.* Submission of the Canadian Association of Elizabeth Fry Societies to the Canadian Human Rights Commission. Ottawa: Canadian Association of Elizabeth Fry Societies.

Mosher, J. 2014. "The Construction of 'Welfare Fraud' and the Wielding of the State's Iron Fist." In E. Comack (ed.), *Locating Law: Race/Class/Gender/Sexuality Connections* (third edition). Halifax and Winnipeg: Fernwood Publishing.

Needham Report. 1978. *Report of the National Planning Committee on the Female Offender.* Ottawa: Ministry of Solicitor General.

Oliver, P. 1994. "'To Govern by Kindness': The First Two Decades of the Mercer Reformatory for Women." In J. Phillips, T. Loo, and S. Lewthwaite (eds.), *Essays in the History of Canadian Law* (Volume V). Toronto: Osgoode Society.

O'Malley, P. 1992. "Risk, Power and Crime Prevention." *Economy and Society* 21, 3.

____. 1996. "Risk and Responsibility." In A. Barry, T. Osborne and N. Rose (eds.), *Foucault and Political Reason: Liberalism, Neo-Liberalism and Rationalities of Government.* Chicago: University of Chicago Press.

____. 2010. *Crime and Risk.* Los Angeles: Sage.

Ombudsman of Ontario. 2011. *Ombudsman's Report: The Code.* Ontario: Ombudsman's Office. <ombudsman.on.ca/Resources/Reports/The-Code.aspx>.

Pate, K. 1999. "csc and the 2 Per Cent Solution." *Canadian Women's Studies* 19, 1 and 2.

____. 2003. "Prisons: The Latest Solution to Homelessness, Poverty and Mental Illness." Women Speak Series, Calgary, September 18.

Pedwell, T. 2013. "Baby Born on Prison Floor: Ontario Corrections Ministry Opens Disciplinary Procedure." *Toronto Star,* February 6. At <thestar.com/news/canada/2013/02/06/baby_born_on_prison_floor_ontario_corrections_ministry_opens_disciplinary_procedure.html>.

Pollack, S. 2000. "Reconceptualizing Women's Agency and Empowerment: Challenges to Self-Esteem Discourse and Women's Lawbreaking." *Women and Criminal Justice* 12, 1.

____. 2004. "Anti-Oppressive Practice with Women in Prison: Discursive Reconstructions and Alternative Practices." *British Journal of Social Work* 34, 5.

____. 2007. "I'm Just Not Good in Relationships: Victimization Discourses and the

Gendered Regulation of Criminalized Women." *Feminist Criminology* 2, 2.

____. 2009. "You Can't Have It Both Ways: Punishment and Treatment of Imprisoned Women." *Journal of Progressive Human Services* 20, 2.

Rafter, N.H. 1985a. *Partial Justice: Women in State Prisons, 1900–1935*. Boston: Northeastern University Press.

____. 1985b. "Gender, Prisons, and Prison History." *Social Science History* 9, 3.

Razack, S. 1998. "Race, Space and Prostitution: The Making of the Bourgeois Subject." *Canadian Journal of Women and the Law* 10.

Ross, R., and E. Fabiano. 1985. *Correctional Alternatives: Programmes for Female Offenders*: Ottawa: Ministry of Solicitor General Programmes Branch.

Sangster, J. 1996. "Incarcerating 'Bad Girls': The Regulation of Sexuality through the Female Refuges Act in Ontario, 1920–1945." *History of Sexuality* 7.

____. 1999. "Criminalizing the Colonized: Ontario Native Women Confront the Criminal Justice System, 1920–1960." *The Canadian Historical Review* 80, 1.

Sapers, H. 2011. *Annual Report of the Office of the Correctional Investigator, 2010–2011*. Ottawa: Office of the Correctional Investigator. <oci-bec.gc.ca/cnt/rpt/pdf/annrpt/annrpt20102011-eng.pdf>.

____. 2013. *Annual Report of the Office of the Correctional Investigator, 2012–2013*. Ottawa: The Correctional Investigator Canada.

Schur, E. 1984. *Labeling Women Deviant: Gender, Stigma, and Social Control*. New York: Random House.

Shaw, M. 1993. "Reforming Federal Women's Imprisonment." In E. Adelberg and C. Currie (eds.), *In Conflict With the Law: Women and the Canadian Justice System*. Vancouver: Press Gang.

____. 1994a. *Ontario Women in Conflict with the Law: Community Prevention Programmes and Regional Issues*. Toronto: Ministry of the Solicitor General and Correctional Services.

____. 1994b. "Women in Prison: Literature Review." *Forum* 6, 1 (Special Issue on Women in Prison). <csc-scc.gc.ca/publications/forum/e061/061d_e.pdf>.

____. 2000. "Women, Violence, and Disorder in Prisons." In K. Hannah-Moffat and M. Shaw (eds.), *An Ideal Prison? Critical Essays on Women's Imprisonment in Canada*. Halifax: Fernwood Publishing.

Shaw, M., K. Rodgers, J. Blanchette, T. Hattem, L.S. Thomas, and L.Tamarack. 1991. *Survey of Federally Sentenced Women: Report of the Task Force on Federally Sentenced Women*. User Report 1991–4. Ottawa: Corrections Branch, Ministry of Solicitor General of Canada.

Sudbury, J. (ed.). 2005a. *Global Lockdown: Race, Gender, and the Prison-Industrial Complex*. London: Routledge.

____. 2005b. "Introduction: Feminist Critiques, Transnational Landscapes, Abolitionist Visions." In J. Sudbury (ed.), *Global Lockdown: Race, Gender, and the Prison-Industrial Complex*. New York: Routledge.

Sugar, F., and L. Fox. 1989. "Nistem Peyako Seht'wawin Iskwewak: Breaking the Chains." *Canadian Journal of Women and the Law* 3, 2.

TFFSW (Task Force on Federally Sentenced Women). 1990. *Creating Choices: The Task Force Report of the Task Force on Federally Sentenced Women*. Ottawa: Correctional Service of Canada.

Turnbull, S., and K. Hannah-Moffat. 2009, "Under These Conditions: Gender, Parole and the Governance of Reintegration." *British Journal of Criminology* 49.

Valverde, M. 1991. *The Age of Light, Soap, and Water: Moral Reform in English Canada 1885–1925.* Toronto: McClelland and Stewart.

Yalkin, T., and M. Kirk. 2012. *The Fiscal Impacts of Changes to Eligibility for Conditional Sentences of Imprisonment in Canada.* Ottawa: Office of the Parliamentary Budget Officer.

Cases Cited

R. v. S.L.N. [2010] BCSC 405

Bobby Lee Worm v. Attorney General of Canada, [2011] BCSC. Notice of Civil Claim. <bccla.org/wp-content/uploads/2012/03/20110303-BCCLA-Legal-Case-BobbyLee-Worm.pdf>.

Chapter 18

REFORMING PRISONS
FOR WOMEN?

Carolyn Brooks

From: *Marginality and Condemnation: A Critical Introduction to Criminology,*
3rd edition, pp. 323–349 (reprinted with permission).

Another day I'm confined...
Inside of being confined,
Another day I am undefined...
With feelings of love and hate combined.
Another day I analyze...
I try to bend and compromise,
While fighting back tears from my eyes...
My faith dangles and my spirit dies...
　　　　　　　— *Summers 2011, Another day [in prison] series*

Canada's treatment of women prisoners is said to "reveal a sad legacy of harsh, cruel, and discriminatory treatment" (Boritch 2002: 309). The media representations of women and crime contrasts sharply with the reality of women who have come into conflict with the law and how they have been treated in the criminal justice system. The treatment of federally sentenced women and the history of the Prison for Women in Kingston is one filled with harshness and cruelty. Both are also in sharp contrast to *Creating Choices: The Report of the Task Force on Federally Sentenced*

Women, which is largely only symbolic of feminist engagement with the state. While we acknowledge the importance of documents such as *Creating Choices* as catalysts for broad-ranging transformations in federal corrections for women, and applaud the commitment and energy of those involved, we question the success of their implementation. Twenty-five years later, the realization of a new feminist-based prison system remains limited, both theoretically and practically.

MEDIA IMAGES VS. CRIME STATISTICS AND WOMEN'S STORIES

Media images often viscerally influence how we think and feel about women in trouble (Faith 2011, 1993; Schissel 2006). The resulting public perceptions influence public policy and criminal justice measures (Schissel 2006; Garland 2001). However, these perceptions rarely reflect reality.

Images in Film

The mid-twentieth century saw the rise of a genre of very crude prison films portraying incarcerated women as sexualized, demonized characters. Beginning with the infamous film *Caged* in 1950, the next four decades saw women presented as monsters and depicted as masculinized — often lesbian — predatory maniacs who are born criminals. Faith (1993, 2011) described this as an invention of women that bears no resemblance to real women actually locked inside prisons:

> The monster-criminal woman of fifties movies was the anonymous woman, the shadow woman, a killer so primitive as to lack an individual identity … They and the psychotic lesbian matron are evil and terrifying, especially to the predictably white, pretty goody-goody who got there by mistake, the only character with whom the intended audience can identify. (1993: 258)

These demonized characters are starkly contrasted with women who are wrongly convicted; we are thus set up with images of good (innocent) and evil (guilty). Explicit, pornographic scenes add a component of Madonna (innocent) versus whore (guilty) as well as compliant versus dangerous.

I have shown part of the 1985 movie *Reform School Girls* in my classrooms and asked students what they see. Students talk about innocent young women corrupted by "wicked" "monster" "predators," routine physical damage amongst the women, disproportionate numbers of the women seen as lesbians, false images of lesbian women, brutal prison guards and staff and sexualized scenes. Many of the students in my classes throughout the years have pointed out that women in real prisons "likely don't wear lingerie or look like the women in the films."

These misrepresentations of incarcerated women create a misinformed ideological framework for understanding real women in trouble. The women in these films are shown punching each other in the face and raping and violating each other. These films exploit classism, racism and homophobia. Women with darker complexions or who are lesbians are depicted as being more dangerous, inviting hostility towards lesbian and racialized women (Faith 1993; Lawston 2011). Faith (2011, 1993) points out that few women prisoners are lesbians and few lesbian women are "sex-crazed." Such stereotypes reify dangerous and false images of women behind bars.

In the later 1980s and the 1990s, images in film shifted and introduced what Faith (2011, 1993) calls the "super-bitch killer beauties." These films had villains whose beauty was undermined by an evil nature. Faith describes the character of Alex Forest, played by Glenn Close in *Fatal Attraction* (1987), who rages against her loving and supposedly (except for the adultery) idyllic happy family:

> [Forest] is the image of the beautiful, solitary, ominous, male-identified, childless, pathologically obsessive woman, "liberated" in anti-feminist terms, who would take what she wants at any cost. (Faith 1993: 265)

Other examples include:

- *The Hand That Rocks the Cradle* (1991) — A deceptive, beautiful villain captures the heart of the family she is also seeking to destroy;
- *Single White Female* (1992), *Single White Female 2: The Psycho* (2005), *The Roommate* (2011) — These movies all portray beautiful young women trying to violently steal their roommate's life and soul; and
- *Basic Instinct* (1992), *Basic Instinct 2* (2006) — These homophobic dramas feature a deceptive and manipulative bisexual woman with stunning female lovers; the female characters violently destroy men's bodies and minds.

As Cecil (2007: 305–306) points out, "Because the correctional system is rarely depicted in the media … images in 'babes-behind-bars' films are detrimental in that they negate the issues surrounding women in prison." Although these characters are so far-fetched to be barely believable, they may influence how the public understands female crime (Cecil 2007; Clowers 2001). Faith (2011, 1993) argues that fear of the unruly women shown in many female prison films has helped justify maximum-security prison construction.

Images in the News

The news tends to focus on the most hardcore, violent women criminals. For example, Karla Homolka, Aileen Wuornos and Susan Smith all received extensive mass media coverage and all were labelled as "monsters" by the media. Karla Homolka is a Canadian serial killer who was convicted of manslaughter in the rape-murder cases of her own sister and two other teenage Ontario girls. Along with her husband, Paul Bernardo, Homolka was convicted of abduction and rape, but she was found guilty of manslaughter while Bernardo was found guilty of murder. This case dominated the news and one of the main stories was the prosecution's deal with Homolka to serve only a twelve-year sentence if she testified against her husband. The news stories used two narratives of Karla Homolka as a morally depraved dangerous woman versus a passively innocent woman in danger of an abusive spouse (Banwell 2011). Aileen Wuornos was convicted of six counts of murder in the first degree and put to death by lethal injection in 2002. Susan Smith is an American woman sentenced to life for murdering her four children.

Faith and Jiwani (2015) point out that women who commit fatal violence, especially against strangers, receive attention-grabbing and intense media coverage. As they note, in a study of newspaper stories about criminalized women in Saturday editions of five regional Canadian newspapers, 50 percent concerned serious violence; however, less than 0.5 percent of all criminal charges actually laid against women are for serious violence. No articles concerned shoplifting, despite it being most commonly committed crime by both genders.

Chesney-Lind and Eliason (2006: 29) argue that the attention on violence of women and girls in all forms of media lend legitimacy to female punishment and even execution through a "'masculinization' of certain girls and women." They write, "A review of the media fascination with 'bad girls' and crime provides clear evidence of the assumption that if women begin to question traditional femininity, they run the risk of becoming like men, that is more violent and sexually 'loose' (often conflated with interest and involvement in lesbian activities), particularly in prison settings" (2006: 31).

WOMEN AND CRIMINALITY

In contrast to the images of female criminals in film and news stories, women in actual conflict with the law in Canada are overwhelmingly young, poor, uneducated mothers with little or no work experience or vocational training, and they are generally victims of physical, sexual and/or emotional abuse and racial discrimination (Hannah-Moffat and Shaw 2000; Boritch 2002, 2008; Hotton-Mahony 2011; Barrett, Allenby, and Taylor 2010).

Research consistently reveals that the lives of most women prisoners are characterized by disadvantages of every kind and reflect the prevailing subordinate status of women in society (Boritch 2002, 2008; Comack 1996, 2006; Barrett, Allenby, and Taylor 2010). As a group, female inmates are socially and economically marginalized and have often been victimized by family members and intimates. The experiences of abuse, poverty and substance abuse are their most common pathways to crime (Boritch 2008). The Canadian Human Rights Commission (2003: 5) offered this visual snapshot of federally sentenced women:

- Disproportionately Aboriginal
- First-time offenders
- Under thirty-five years of age
- Survivors of physical and sexual abuse
- Single mothers with one or more children
- Significant substance abuse problems

Education and Work Experience

The majority of federal and provincial female offenders have only a high school education, and many have considerably less, particularly Aboriginal women (Delveaux, Blanchette, and Wickett 2005: 27). Eighty-eight percent of Aboriginal women and 67 percent of non-Aboriginal women were unemployed at the time of their arrest. Twenty-eight percent of Aboriginal women and 13 percent of non-Aboriginal women had less than a Grade 8 education, and 87 percent of Aboriginal women had no high school diploma at the time of intake into the correctional system, compared to 35 percent of non-Aboriginal women. Aboriginal women scored lower than non-Aboriginal women with respect to all categories of employment needs. The work experience of sentenced women is generally characterized by low skill, low wage employment with little room for advancement (Boritch 2002, 2008).

Women Offenders Are Actually Non-violent

An additional indication of women lawbreakers' impoverishment is the nature of their crimes. "Over 80 percent of all incarcerated women in Canada are in prison for poverty related offences" (Jackson 1999, cited in Comack 2006: 67). Although female crime generally and female crimes against the person are increasing, the majority of charges against women continue to be petty property offences. Crimes against the person are those that involve threatening of violence or the use of violence against another person. These include homicide, attempted murder, assault, sexual assault and robbery (Hotton-Mahony 2011). Property crimes, or offences/crimes against property, are acts considered unlawful that do not involve threat or violence but are done to gain property, including theft, fraud and break-and-enters. Petty property offences are those charged with theft under $5,000. Women have over time been shown to have a high percentage of theft-related charges. Historical data from Statistics Canada in 1993 and 1994 show that 66.8 percent of female crimes were property crimes and theft related (cited in Boritch 2002). More recent data reflect the same trend:

> In 2009, approximately 233,000 females and 776,000 males (adult and youth) were accused by police of having committed a *Criminal Code* offence in Canada. Females accounted for more than one quarter (28 percent) of youth (under 18 years of age) accused by police and more than one fifth (22 percent) of adult accused. The most common offences for which females were accused were theft under $5,000, assault level 1, and administration of justice violations (e.g., failure to appear in court, breach of probation, etc.). (Hotton-Mahony 2011: 19)

Put simply, women have consistently comprised a very small proportion of adults charged with violent offences. Women account for only 16 percent of persons charged with violent crimes, with 62 percent of these charges being level one common assaults, the least serious form of violence.

Abuse

Crimes committed by women against the person — assaults, manslaughter, murder and sex offences — become more understandable in the context of the history of violence in these women's lives. Evidence of physical, sexual and/or emotional abuse prior to incarceration is overwhelming. The *Report Back to All Federal Women in the 1989 Survey of Your Views* indicates that 68 percent of women prisoners were physically abused and 53 percent were sexually abused; 89 percent of the entire female prison population indicated some experience of abuse. Comparing these numbers to the profile of federally sentenced women twenty years later, these figures have either remained the same or have worsened. In *A Profile Comparison of Federally Sentenced Women 1991–2010,* Barrett et al. state:

> In terms of victimization, the majority of women (86 percent) reported being physically abused at some point in their lives. As compared to the original survey this represents a significant increase as in 1991 68 percent of the women reported experiencing physical abuse. In general, a greater proportion of women were abused as adults. (2010: 2)

The numbers are even higher for Aboriginal female inmates, with 90 percent being victims of physical abuse and 61 percent disclosing sexual abuse. Helen Boritch summarizes the harsh realities of female offenders:

> These statistics paint a dismal portrait of the life experiences of most

women prisoners, the stories of individual women prisoners tell us of
women who have endured fractured childhoods of neglect, abandonment
and abuse and gone on to struggle with often unimaginably painful and
violent circumstances. (2002: 317)

There is no clear evidence of whether victimization of women is a direct predictor of criminality, but the prevalence of victims of violence, substance abuse and
addiction and mental health issues among criminalized women cannot be ignored
(Barrett et al. 2010). In addition, some women retaliate to violence against them
by fighting back in kind, dealing with anger and aggression by using drugs and
alcohol or through violence as a learned behavior. Evidence suggests a connection
between the condition of women in society, and their exposure to violence and
poverty, and criminal behavior. For example, in *Women in Trouble* (1996), Elizabeth
Comack interviewed twenty-four incarcerated women and revealed experiential
evidence of the interconnection between their imprisonment and their histories
of violence and abuse. She suggests that these connections may be as direct as
women imprisoned for manslaughter for resisting abuse against them. She tells
the story of Janice, for example:

> *I was at a party, and this guy, older guy, came, came on to me. He tried telling*
> *me, "Why don't you go to bed with me. I'm getting some money, you know."*
> *And I said, "no." And then he started hitting me. And then he raped me. And*
> *then [pause] I lost it. Like, I just, I went, I got very angry and I snapped. And I*
> *started hitting him. I threw a coffee table on top of his head and then I stabbed*
> *him. (cited in Comack 2006: 37)*

Racism and Colonization

There is a notable intersection of race, class and gender in the lives of criminalized women as well as a connection between Aboriginal over-incarceration and
the historical forces of colonization (Comack 2006). Boritch (2002: 316) states,
"Among female prisoners, Aboriginal women are even more disadvantaged than
non-Aboriginal women along virtually every conceivable dimension, because they
have also endured the formidable burden of racism and oppression throughout
their lives." Aboriginal women are subject to a lack of opportunities as well as more
overt racism. As Monture-Angus writes, "Often, what [Aboriginal women] can
experience in the city (from shoplifting to prostitution, drug abuse to violence)
arising from their experiences of poverty and racism, leads to contact with the
criminal justice system" (2000: 57). Aboriginal women are the fastest growing
population in Canada's federal prisons, increasing over 80 percent in the previous decade; they represent 33.6 percent of all incarcerated women (Office of

the Correctional Investigator 2013). High rates of incarceration are linked to the history of colonialism, systemic discrimination including racial prejudice, social and economic disadvantages, violence, trauma and intergenerational factors, all of which is documented in R. v. Gladue (1999) and R. v. Ipeelee (2012):

> Courts must take judicial notice of such matters as the history of colonialism, displacement, and residential schools and how that history continues to translate into lower educational attainment, lower incomes, higher unemployment, higher rates of substance abuse and suicide, and of course higher levels of incarceration for Aboriginal peoples. (Justice LeBel for the majority in R. v. Ipeelee 2012, cited in Office of the Correctional Investigator 2013).

The overt racism within the justice system has become prominent with the call for an inquiry into Canada's missing and murdered Aboriginal women. The Commissioner of the RCMP led a study of incidents on murdered and missing Aboriginal women in Canada and found that between 1980 and 2012 there have been 1017 police reported Aboriginal female homicides and an additional 164 missing Aboriginal women. Tragically, the disappearance and violence against Aboriginal women has not demonstrated significant formal interest. In comparing the dreadful occurrence of missing women from Vancouver's Downtown Eastside, where so many women disappeared and where there was comparably little formal attention, politicians and researchers are asking important questions, such as, "Do you think if 65 women went missing from Kerrisdale [and affluent Vancouver neighborhood] we'd have ignored it so long?" (cited in Hugill 2010: 10).

THEORETICAL CONSIDERATIONS

Traditional criminological theories and some feminist inquiries have attempted to explain "female criminality," but in doing so they have often contributed to stereotypical definitions of criminals by scientifically justifying harmful myths. Early theories of female criminality perpetuate delinquent behavior amongst women by justifying treatment that reinforces traditional gender stereotypes. Any theory of crime must begin with an understanding of the position of women — including racialized women — in the larger society.

Biology

The so-called classical work of Lombroso and Ferrero, The Female Offender (1895), represents the first "scientific" inquiry regarding women and crime. Using a biological determinist perspective, they define criminality as a pathology originating from the biological make-up of individuals. Central to their thesis is the notion of "atavism," which they use to suggest that criminals are genetically deficient and evolutionarily regressive. Atavists are identifiable through certain physical features that symbolize genetic deficiency.

Lombroso began his work by defending the use of anthropometry, measuring bodies and studying abnormalities. His analysis detected that "criminal women" had smaller cranial capacity than non-criminal women. The criminal woman was also said to have a heavier and masculine jaw. This work also identified physical abnormalities depending on the type of crime. Baez explains:

> Criminal women, particularly in murder, theft and prostitution, are close to or above the average female weight but are rarely of average height. For prostitutes, the proportion of arm span to height is smaller than other women … prostitutes had disproportionately larger hands and shorter and narrower feet. (2010: 3–4)

The descriptions become quite bizarre and even included the color of hair, suggesting that criminal women are usually dark haired and go grey faster. Women who are involved in crime are also said to have vivid wrinkling and resemble images of witches.

According to Lombroso and Ferrero, some of these features are harder to distinguish among women criminals because women are in general "less evolved" than men. They argue that women's biologically determined nature is antithetical to crime but, because of the woman's lower form, she makes up for her lower crime rate in the cruelty and vileness of her crimes. Lombroso and Ferrero write:

> We also saw that women have many traits in common with children; that their mental sense is deficient; that they are revengeful, jealous, inclined to vengeance of a refined cruelty. In ordinary cases these defects are neutralized by piety, maternity, want of passion, sexual coldness, by weakness and an undeveloped intelligence. (Lombroso and Ferrero 1895: 151)

Although Lombroso and Ferrero's biological explanations have been largely discredited, parallels still exist in more recent works. *Delinquency in Girls* (Cowie, Cowie, and Slater 1968) argues that female crime requires a biological explanation whereas delinquency in boys requires a socio-economic explanation. The authors include social and environmental causal factors as predisposing boys to delinquency. In contrast, biological factors are maintained as more important than environmental factors for young women:

> Pathological psychiatric deviations are much more common in delinquent girls than boys … Delinquent girls more often than boys have other forms

of impaired physical health; they are noticed to be oversized, lumpish, uncouth, and graceless, with a raised incidence of minor physical defects. (cited in Burns 2006: 123)

They also note that "pathological psychiatric deviations are much more common in delinquent girls than boys" (cited in Burns 2006: 166).

Dalton (1978) and Pollack (1979) also provide biological explanations for female delinquency. In her study of imprisoned women, Dalton claims that a relationship exists between the criminality of women and women's menstrual cycles. Pollack similarly argues that women are more likely to commit crime during hormonal changes, especially during pregnancy and menopause (Pollack 1979). Dalton states:

> [Three] women successfully pleaded diminished responsibility or mitiga-tion due to premenstrual syndrome in crimes of manslaughter, arson, and assault. All had long histories of repeated misdemeanours, which contin-ued while in prison. Police and prison records confirmed the diagnosis of premenstrual syndrome. The women were successfully treated with progesterone, and their behaviour returned to normal. (1978: abstract)

According to these theories, women pose a risk for committing crimes for approxi-mately 75 percent of their lives.

Role Theory

Role theory moves away from solely biological explanations, offering the notion that individual pathologies are induced by society and can, therefore, be modi-fied by society. Role theorists consider sociological factors such as inequality and utilize concepts such as "diverse socialization." Inadequate socialization becomes an individual pathology, which can be cured through re-socialization.

Hoffman-Bustamente (1975) argues that boys are encouraged to be aggressive while girls are encouraged to be passive and non-violent. Freda Adler, in *Sisters in Crime* (1975), suggests that the women's liberation movement allowed women to challenge traditional sex role stereotypes and to enter into fields that were once restricted to men. A problem in Adler's argument is that she attributes female crime to an increase in masculine qualities but fails to explain why males commit crime. Role theory in general does not discuss structural origins of differential roles in society (Smart 1976; Currie 1986). These theories reify and obscure the social and political processes underlying criminality (Currie 1986). It was feminists who insisted on digging deeper into the social and political inequality that is related to crime, criminality and criminal justice.

Feminist Theory

Early feminist criminological theories mainly critiqued prior attempts to include women in mainstream criminology, labelling such work as sexist and making efforts to revise it (Smart 1976). The mission to revise differential association theory, labelling theory, social control and conflict theory (see Brooks and Schissel 2015) were criticized as an "add women and stir" approach (Schram and Tibbetts 2014). Critical feminist theories refute these explanations and argue that understanding women and crime must be located in a socio-economic, gendered and racialized context. Critical feminists (including standpoint feminist work, such as Comack 1996) introduced more qualitative research, attempting to provide women a voice, instead of male academics telling us about women's lives, in order to better understand their conflict with the law. The intention of this critical, empowering research was to place women at the center of the inquiry in order to learn from the voices of experience. Much of the research that foregrounded criminalized women's voices identified strong links between women's crimes and victimization, poverty, racialization and violence against them (Comack 2006).

Feminist criminology often cautions against quantitative approaches towards understanding female crime, favouring women-centred narrative approaches to research (see Comack and Balfour 2006; Wattanaporn and Holtfreter 2014). Critical feminist theories identify the importance of including women's voices while recognizing that women's agency (their capacity for independent action) is shaped by — and also shapes — larger relations of power and social control. Feminist-based theories engage the question of the interaction between human agency and social structure — essential to understanding the different meaning of empowering women in conflict with the law and the impact their stories will have on the social forces that affect their lives.

Some critical feminist theories give primacy to certain social structures, such as patriarchy. Others give primacy to agency while acknowledging that women's lives are shaped by social structures such as colonialism, patriarchy and capitalism. Comack argues that feminist research studies the dynamics of class, race and gender and how these play out in the everyday lives of women, while still acknowledging that all of these categories are socially constructed. Comack (1996: 34), for example, emphasizes that what we know of the world is conditional upon one's social location:

> In taking the women's lives as my starting point, my aim has been to develop a way of knowing ... that is capable of shedding light on the factors and conditions which brought them into conflict with the law. Central to the formulation of this standpoint is the attempt to situate their lives within the nexus of the class, race and gender relations of our society.

Critical feminist criminology also offers a critique of prisons, noting that they provide women few opportunities to either challenge or overcome racial, sexual or class barriers. As Carlen writes:

> In so far as prisons debilitate, women's prisons feed off their own product ... it is an indictment of society at the end of the twentieth century, and not of the penal system itself when women tell me that they will go out to a world that has even less to offer them than prison. (1988: 163)

From the critical feminist perspective, prison and its reform may be seen as a furthered mechanism of social regulation over women.

WOMEN IN PRISON

Women have often been deemed as "too few to count" (see Adelberg and Currie 1987) as they constitute such a small percentage of adult offenders in correctional systems in Canada. Women accounted for only 16 percent of criminal offences by adults in 1998 and 9 percent of admissions to provincial/territorial and federal prisons (Thomas 2000, cited in Boritch 2008). This number has only slightly increased over time from 10 percent in provincial and federal custody in 1999–2000 to 12 percent in 2008–09 (Hotton-Mahoney 2011).

Historically, only one prison held federally sentenced women in Canada compared to over forty federal facilities for men. Prior to the building of the Prison for Women, women were housed in the Kingston penitentiary for men, where they were confined to a very small area in the attic above the mess table of the male inmates and moved frequently to serve the needs of the male offenders. Since its inception in 1934, the Prison for Women at Kingston (P4W) was criticized for being dark, foreboding and dysfunctional. More than a dozen government reports[1] denounced the P4W for a number of factors; all but one called for the closure of the prison. These examinations of women's prison(s) indicted its centralized location, the over-classification of inmates with respect to security risk, the lack of programming, the inadequate provisions for francophone and Aboriginal inmates and its insufficient recognition of the special needs of incarcerated women. The single location of the P4W, in Kingston, Ontario, meant that pretty well all Canadian imprisoned women were removed from their communities and support systems. At the time *Creating Choices* was published, only 60 of the 130 women inside the P4W were from communities in Ontario (CSC 1990: 74). In addition, access to Kingston was very difficult for visitors, and the trip could be costly, leaving many families unable to visit. Moreover, many of the imprisoned women remained geographically stranded upon their release (Boritch 2002, 2008).

The neglect of the needs of women was, in part, the result of the maximum security design of the P4W. Many historical documents note that tight security conditions are unsuitable for most women offenders. For example, the *Report of the Standing Committee on Justice and Solicitor General* reviewed sentencing, conditional release and related aspects of corrections, noting that "concern[s] that large numbers of women prisoners across the country are being detained in facilities which provide much higher security than most of them require and that most of them would be subjected to if they were men" (Canada 1977: 135). The correctional programs offered at the P4W were highly lacking with respect to both quantity and quality. For example, the *Report to Parliament* (Canada 1977) disclosed the lack of recreation, adequate programs and space for an activity centre. Counselling services were minimal, and, in the case of drug and alcohol rehabilitation, programs were developed based on a correctional philosophy for men. The *Report on Self-Injurious Behavior in the Kingston Prison for Women* (Heney 1990) revealed that 98 percent of the prison population and 93 percent of the correctional staff thought the counselling services at the P4W were inadequate. Many prisoners had suffered physical, sexual and emotional abuse in their lives, yet programs failed to address their immediate psychosocial or medical needs (Kendall 2000). Mental health services at the P4W were only available during regular hours, leaving segregation units as the alternative for after-hours crises. Moreover, the counselling available in the prison generally only addressed coping with confinement and the resulting emotional distress (Kendall 2000). Prison programming reflected the needs of prison management, and limited help was available for imprisoned women to deal with the root of their problems (Kendall 2000; Boritch 2002, 2008).

Specific services pertaining to Aboriginal and francophone women at the P4W were almost non-existent. Aboriginal women had access to mainstream psychological services but these were limited in cultural awareness and not readily available (Heney 1990). Similarly, the cultural needs of francophone women were ignored, especially in terms of the absence of French programs.

PAIN OF IMPRISONMENT FOR WOMEN

Compared to their male counterparts, women in prison are more strictly supervised and are charged for behavior that is less serious (Shaw 2000). In one woman's words, "You come in here as an adult and you leave as a child" (CSC 1990). Women prisoners reported feeling a lack of respect, favouritism regarding staff relations, discrimination and arbitrary rules, all contributing to a feeling of worthlessness and pain (McDonagh 1999). Yvonne Johnson, a prison activist who spent time in the P4W, wrote that "by law they must keep our bodies alive in here, but what will we be when we're released? The human need for kindness, grace — it's impossible in prison" (Wiebe and Johnson 1998: 326). Prison rules and regulations that limit inmate movements and interactions, especially the rules of solitary confinement, created a feeling that women have described as "powerlessness" (Heney 1990; Kendall 2000). The correctionalist alternative to counselling in the P4W was a policy of isolation for punishment and behaviour modification (Kendall 2000).

Incarcerated women's experiences differ from men's, especially when they are housed in a prison that is very far away from their families. Female inmates experience no greater pain of imprisonment than separation from their children, and they worry about losing their children to child welfare and about the placement of their children in foster care. In contrast, male inmates often have partners or family members to care for their children. P4W rules and policies created a situation in which it was often very difficult for the women inmates to see their children (Martin 1997).

Imprisoned women have greater emotional and mental health problems than male prisoners, which is manifested in suicide attempts and other self-injurious behavior (Daigle et al. 1999). For women prisoners, cutting is a long-standing problem linked to both life situations of abuse and enduring the pain of imprisonment; it offers distraction from the tension and anger caused by conditions of imprisonment (Hoffman and Law 1995). In the words of one prisoner at the P4W, "Prison is frustration and anger so intense that cutting into the arteries of my own arm only alleviates some of the pain" (CSC 1990: 6, cited in Boritch 2002: 320).

The suicides of four Aboriginal women — Marlene Moore, Lorna Claira Jones, Careen Daigneault and Sandy Sayer — are evidence of the personal pain experienced by female prisoners and the horrific conditions at the Prison for Women. These suicides were labelled by the news media as a "form of liberation" (*Star Phoenix* March 23, 1991) and an "escape from the pain of imprisonment" (*Ottawa Citizen* 1991). These tragedies received national attention, and feminist reformers began using the law to demand better treatment for female prisoners. *R. v. Daniels* was a landmark decision in which the Supreme Court agreed that a federal prisoner's right to life and security would be violated under the *Canadian Charter of Rights and Freedoms* if she were sentenced to the P4W because of the high risk of suicide (Arbour 1996: 246).

CHANGING WOMEN'S PRISONS: CREATING CHOICES

The impetus for the Canadian government to assess the needs of federally sentenced women came from a number of suicides of women at the P4W, a shifting mentality towards female prisoners as "high needs/low risk," the enactment of the *Canadian Charter of Rights and Freedoms* and an increased feminist voice relating to inequality, poverty, racism and violence against women (Shaw 1993; Kershaw and Lasovich 1991, cited in Boritch 2002). The result was the completion and implementation of *Creating Choices: The Report of the Task Force on Federally Sentenced Women* (1990).

The Task Force

With continued pressure by groups outside the government, the Correctional Service of Canada (CSC), in partnership with the Canadian Association of Elizabeth Fry Societies (CAEFS), appointed the Task Force on Federally Sentenced Women in March 1989. The mandate of the Task Force was "to examine the correctional management of federally sentenced women ... and to develop a plan which will guide and direct the process in a manner that is responsive to the unique and special needs of this group" (CSC 1990).

This Task Force was exceptional due to its composition: it included seventeen members from women's groups and voluntary organizations outside of the government as well as two federally sentenced women. In total thirty-eight of the forty-two members were women. The steering committee and the working group had more community representatives than government representatives. As Shaw observes:

> No previous government inquiry into women's imprisonment had included so many voluntary sector representatives, or Aboriginal or minority groups, and certainly no women who had personal experience of prisons. And many of those in the voluntary sector reflected the feminist perspectives. (1993: 53)

Notably, the Native Women's Association of Canada (NWAC) was initially not interested in becoming involved with the Task Force. The NWAC was reluctant in part because of its volunteer involvement in other grassroots issues and also because it disagreed with the differentiation being made between men and women. First Nations Elders convinced the NWAC that their voices were essential to the Task Force. Ultimately, five Aboriginal women were appointed to the steering committee and two to a working group. Two of these seven Aboriginal women were federally sentenced women who had served time in P4W. Patricia Monture, however, cautioned that the participation of Aboriginal women in the Task Force "must never be viewed as a recognition that the jurisdiction of the federal government of Canada ... in the affairs of our Nations is valid" (CSC 1990: 17, cited in Hayman 2000: 46).

The participation of women with experience as prisoners at P4W was particularly unique, and the report gave these women (and those still at P4W) a voice:

> I and women like myself, who contribute to this chapter [of *Creating Choices*] are the flesh that has fed the need for this Task Force. Our pleas are drawn from our hearts and souls. We are witnesses to the human pain, the tears and the blood spilled within traditional prisons in the name of justice. (Prisoner at the Kingston Prison for Women) (CSC 1990: 13)

Shaw describes the committee as passionately dedicated to major changes for federally sentenced women and frustrated because of the "enormity of the task" (1993: 53). The Task Force members were particularly affected by suicides of two Aboriginal P4W inmates in 1989 and the suicides of four Aboriginal P4W inmates in 1990.

TASK FORCE RESEARCH AND CONCLUSIONS

Creating Choices was largely based on extensive interviews with federally sentenced women. This consultation and research was "groundbreaking" (Shaw 1993: 54), framing female offenders within their social context of inequality, dependency and discrimination. The report emphasized that the vast majority of women in prison were "low risk/high needs" — referring to the low risk of reoffending posed by federally sentenced women as well as the enormity of the physical, emotional and sexual abuse in these women's lives. Statistics demonstrated a clear link between socio-economic status and criminality of women, with federally sentenced women tending to be undereducated, poor, young, addicted to alcohol and/or drugs, victims of abuse and emotionally and financially dependent on abusive partners (CSC 1990). These conclusions have held steady through years of additional research. See, for example, Helen Boritch (2002); Elizabeth Comack (1996) Hannah-Moffat and Shaw (2000), Colleen Dell, Catherine Fillmore and Jennifer Kilty (2009) and Ferrari (2011), to name but a few.

Considering the experiences of the federally incarcerated women, the Task Force members agreed that imprisonment had failed to provide the support female offenders needed to avoid recidivism. The Task Force concluded that fundamental changes within the women's correctional system were required, with the long-term goal of restorative justice options and an Aboriginal system of justice (CSC 1990: 95).

Reiterating the many problems cited in previous investigations — over-classification regarding security, ignoring women's special needs, geographic dislocation, inadequate services, ignoring needs of Aboriginal and francophone women — *Creating Choices* recommended that P4W be closed and replaced by a Healing Lodge for Aboriginal women (in Saskatchewan) and four regional correctional facilities (in Alberta, Ontario, Québec and Nova Scotia).

Guiding Principles and Recommendations

The overall statement of principle guiding *Creating Choices* was the following:

> The Correctional Service of Canada with the support of communities, has the responsibility to create an environment that empowers federally sentenced women to make meaningful and responsible choices in order that they may live with dignity and respect.

The women-centred philosophy of *Creating Choices* has been viewed as transformative for women's corrections in Canada. The Task Force critiqued the traditional male model, with its focus on assessing inmates as either high, medium or low security risk, pre-structured programming and the prioritizing of needs, and replaced it with a new model emphasizing the assessment of imprisoned women's needs and the holistic treatment of these needs. Five new guiding principles were stressed:

1. creating meaningful choice;
2. empowerment;
3. respect and dignity;
4. supportive environments; and
5. sharing responsibility (with community and corrections) for the incarcerated women's welfare.

The Task Force defined empowerment as a means to help the women raise their self-esteem and overcome inequalities brought about through poverty, racism and abuse. The recommended training and vocational facilities, for example, illustrated a move away from limited traditional gender roles. Education at all levels was to be offered, including adult education, university and other post-secondary education. The Task Force emphasized the importance of incarcerated women gaining respect for others and to be given respect in return. The Task Force insisted that women could not fit into existing programs designed by correctional staff but should identify their own needs and subsequently have them fulfilled through physical space and programming. This became a "resources approach," in which programming responds to the "multifaceted, inner-related nature of women's experience" (csc 1990: 103). The regional women's facilities and Healing Lodge were meant to emphasize individual healing and wellness and offer programming according to the needs of women, addressing such issues as addiction, childhood sexual, physical and emotional abuse, domestic abuse, spirituality, independent living, self-reliance and positive interaction. In support of self-determination and self-esteem, the Task Force maintained the emphasis of staffing shifts from traditional security to dynamic security and support. In the "Report of the Task Force on Security" (csc 2008), it is recommended that "the term 'dynamic security' be defined and understood as 'those actions that contribute to the development of professional, positive relationships between staff members and offenders.'"

Discrimination against Aboriginal women led the Task Force to conclude that Aboriginal people should not be dealt with as add-ons inside corrections, but instead they must be handled through an Aboriginal-directed approach. A Healing Lodge in Maple Creek, Saskatchewan, was proposed — and implemented — with

program offerings to include Aboriginal teachings and spiritual ceremonies, culturally sensitive counselling services and frequent contact with Elders and Aboriginal
staff. The Task Force clearly stated that this had to be adopted by and developed
by Aboriginal people for it to be most effective.

Sharing Responsibility

The Community Release Strategy was an extremely important component within
the Task Force plan. Increased facilities were intended to accommodate women
upon their release from prison and provide treatment within communities. This
included halfway houses, community-based residences, Aboriginal centres and
home placements. Each woman was to have a personalized release strategy, developed in conjunction with correctional staff, the woman herself and community
workers.

Regional Facilities

The new regional facilities aimed to approximate norms of community, emphasize
the development of self-sufficiency in daily living, provide holistic and sensitive
programming including counselling and treatment for abuse and substance abuse
problems, provide educational and vocational development, provide family visits,
recognize spirituality and use the local communities for support and services. The
new facilities were designed to promote wellness through natural light, space,
privacy and colour. The facilities included cottage-style houses that could accommodate six to ten women as well as a family visiting facility for women and children
to live together in, all situated on several acres of land.

IMPLEMENTATION OF CREATING CHOICES REPORT

> *Creating Choices* is probably one of the most powerful things that has ever
> been written by so many women, but it's still only a piece of paper. And
> sometimes I look at it and think it's not worth the paper it's written on.
> (Prisoner, Edmonton Institution for Women, cited in Gironella 1999: 35)

Creating Choices was published in April 1990. A few months later, the Solicitor
General formally and publicly announced that P4W would close by 1994 and that
$50 million would be available to implement the Task Force recommendations,
including the construction of the four new regional facilities and the Healing Lodge
as well as improvements to and expansions of community services and halfway
houses (Shaw 1993). By 1997, new prisons were opened in Joliette, Québec,
Kitchener, Ontario, Edmonton, Alberta, and Burnaby, British Columbia, and a
Healing Lodge for Aboriginal women was established on the Nekaneet Reserve
in Saskatchewan. The Prison for Women was closed officially on July 6, 2000.

Safeguards were built in by the Task Force to ensure that the plan was enacted as intended. These included an implementation committee that would be externally based as well as an Aboriginal advisory committee, both of which were to oversee the implementation process (Shaw 1993). However, various events during and since the implementation of the Task Force Report suggest that it was modified beyond recognition (Hannah-Moffat and Shaw 2000; Boritch 2008; Dell et al. 2009). The implementation of *Creating Choices* is attributed largely to the efforts of a constellation of people acting when feminism had impacted the highest levels of government (Hayman 2000). When *Creating Choices* was submitted, the situation at P4W had become so severe that not acting would have been inimical to everyone, including the officials from corrections. Ole Ingstrup, the Commissioner of Corrections at the time, was prepared to give those outside of correctional institutions a voice. Specifically, he listened to the Canadian Association of the Elizabeth Fry Societies (CAEFS). Although CAEFS' relationship with the Correctional Service of Canada (CSC) was difficult, and their preference was not to be involved in creating new prisons for women,[2] Bonnie Diamond, the executive director of CAEFS at the time, recognized that Ingstrup was willing to hear alternative ideas and did not want to miss this window of opportunity for change.[3] CAEFS especially did not want to see any more federally sentenced women lose their lives through suicide.

Many criticisms of this Task Force implementation suggest that the feminist ideals were undermined by the Correctional Service of Canada in response to concerns of the public, false stereotypical perceptions of women in conflict with the law (Hayman 2000; Shaw 1993) and shifting strategies of managing risk and need (Hanna-Moffat 2000; Shaw 2000). Indeed, many problems identified with the federal Prison for Women remained unresolved (Boritch 2002, 2008; Monture-Angus 2000; Shaw 2000; Dell et al. 2009; Sapers 2008; Ferrari 2011). The commitment of the Healing Lodge Circle (Ke-kun-wem-kon-a-wuk) to manage the Healing Lodge, and to base the Healing Lodge on Aboriginal cultural principles, was also not upheld (Ferrari 2011).

While many of the main Task Force recommendations were accepted in principle, the recommendations concerning implementation were not. A number of problems with implementation are discussed more detail below.

The Choice of Sites

The Task Force stressed the importance of the establishment of a prison in a community with women's support services and good transport facilities. However, the choices of Truro, Nova Scotia, (a small rural community approximately ninety kilometers away from Halifax), Joliette, Québec, and Kitchener, Ontario, were heavily criticized for lacking community resources for inmates and adequate travel facilities to prevent costly journeys for family and visitors. In response to the sites chosen, one federally sentenced woman said, "My spirit was engulfed in deep shame for having contributed to the work that was intended to assist in positive change for Federally Sentenced Women but was now politically sabotaged" (Joanne Mayhew, CAEFS Newsletter, Spring 1992).

Community Release Strategies

Another major concern of the Task Force and public sectors was that the government was building the new facilities with less attention towards the community release strategy and less money for development of community resources. The government announced that the money for community development was not intended to come from the $50-million budget but must be found at the local level.

Failure to Address Needs of Violent and High-security-risk Women

Creating Choices portrayed women as victims of violence, but it is criticized for failing to address violent and high-security-risk women (Hannah-Moffat and Shaw 2000; Ferrari 2011; Dell et al. 2009). Correctional Services of Canada responded to difficulties in the new prisons with the prevailing view of women as dangerous and violent. For example, the Edmonton Institution, which opened on November 20, 1995, had difficulties from the outset. In February 1996, investigations began regarding several incidents of self-injurious behavior. On February 29, Denise Fayant, a 21-year-old Saskatchewan woman, was found hanging in her cell, and another inmate was charged with her murder. More self-injuries and suicide attempts were documented in the following days, as well as assaults on staff and three escapes.

Problems with violence in the new regional facilities led correctional authorities to quickly fall back on punitive measures (Shaw 2000; Boritch 2002; Dell et al. 2009; Ferrari 2011). In Edmonton, Correctional Services of Canada responded to these concerns by redefining the women as dangerous, transferring the maximum and medium security women out of the facility and increasing their own security, including installing security cameras and an eight-foot perimeter fence with barbed wire. Unfortunately, the women heard the news of the transfers from the media rather than from prison officials. This resulted in two women slashing their own necks and the police riot squad using pepper spray to extract the women from their rooms (CAEFS 1999).

The failure of *Creating Choices* to deal with women labelled as maximum security was most acute with respect to the Healing Lodge. Aboriginal women were (and continue to be) disproportionately labelled high risk/maximum security, but because the Healing Lodge has been deemed a medium-security facility, many Aboriginal women were not offered the chance to benefit from the Healing Lodge (Monture-Angus 2000). Therefore, those most in need of reformed conditions are confined in men's institutions; they were also those left the longest in P4W prior to its closing in July 2000. As Monture-Angus (2000: 55) notes, "Unfortunately, many of the women that the Lodge was visioned around will never serve their sentences at the Lodge as the institution is now too full, and clearly, selection is based on the borrowed notion of security classification."

Principles of Law and Order

The issue is even more complicated when we consider the time frame of the opening of the first three regional prisons for women: the Healing Lodge, the Edmonton Institution for Women (EIFW) and the Nova Institution for Women in Truro. In the mid-1990s, an overall increased emphasis on law and order was emerging in politics and the media (Hayman 2000; White 2002). Media scrutiny and public concerns found their way to the EIFW, which witnessed severely hostile local community reactions to prison escapes, murder and self-mutilation. As a result, the EIFW was temporarily closed on May 1, 1996. This was followed by intense political pressure — especially from the Reform Party and the public — to address the fear that women who were potentially dangerous were escaping into the community. Not one woman who escaped from the prison committed an illegal offence while absent from the facility. The public believed the facility closed because the women were too violent to be held there (Hayman 2000). Moreover, the escapes from the EIFW affected more than just the inmates in Edmonton. All of the regional prisons — except the Healing Lodge — increased security measures, "signalling that all the imprisoned women were potentially dangerous ... every federally sentenced woman paid the price for the misbehaviour of the few" (Hayman, 2000: 44).

When the EIFW reopened on August 29, 1996, medium-security inmates were re-admitted. The CSC spent $289,000 at the Saskatchewan Penitentiary and $222,000 at the Regional Psychiatric Centre in Saskatoon, Saskatchewan, to accommodate the remaining maximum-security inmates who were not eligible for the regional facilities. As Hayman notes, "This happened despite the fact that *Creating Choices* envisaged that all federally sentenced women, regardless of their security level, would be housed in the new regional facilities" (2000: 44).

The Canadian Association of the Elizabeth Fry Societies (1999, 2000) affirmed that women in the regional prisons continued to be subjected to strip searches, excessive force and interventions of emergency response teams. Minimum-security women prisoners have been shackled when being escorted into the community. One regional prison used pepper spray and stripped a woman naked when she cut herself; she was subsequently left in handcuffs and shackles on a steel bed frame with no blanket for several hours (Boritch 2002). The consequences of incidents in Edmonton (among others) as well as the re-introduction of security classification schemes contributed to the expansion of physical security measures in many of the regional facilities as well as the holding of some female inmates in isolated units in prisons for men (Boritch 2002; Dell et al. 2009). In 2005, the deputy wardens of Canada's federal prisons for women recommended ceasing strip searches for women for two reasons: the searches traumatize women, conjuring up histories of sexual assault against them, and they yield little or no contraband from the women (Pate 2011).

Recent events have drawn additional attention to the increased use of security priorities and control in women's prisons and that the suicides, deaths and disturbances are still frequent. Segregation continues to be used in women's prisons to separate those who are disruptive or misbehaving and the practice is unable to address the psychological, behavioural and emotional needs of the women (Sapers 2008; Dell et al. 2009). The use of segregation in the Ashley Smith case was strongly challenged (Sapers 2008). It has been reported that Ashley Smith spent more than two thirds of her time in prison in segregation, which also means being excluded from participating in programming (Sapers 2008). It was clear that Ashley Smith required specialized care and that she had been in segregation for unthinkable time frames, which meant her treatment for her self-harming and mental health concerns were left unaddressed (Sapers 2008; Ferarri 2011).

Power Imbalances between Staff and Inmates

Programming in the regional prisons was designed to empower female inmates and offer choices that are meaningful in a supportive atmosphere. Yet Shaw (2000) argues that power imbalances between staff and prisoners in these new facilities made the aim to empower the women and increase their self-esteem unattainable. The women prisoners have said the correctional workers were unable to apply the new women-centred approach, did not apply the rules inconsistently and often had very little knowledge of policy (Ferrari 2011). As one prisoner noted, "Person-to-person, staff to staff, shift change to shift change, everybody interprets the rules and regulations of this institution the way they want to, for whatever their purposes" (Gironella 1999: 58). Six women interviewed at the Edmonton regional facility all complained about the negative relationships with staff and said that, because of the unpredictability of outcomes, they would rather be at the Prison for Women in Kingston (Gironella 1999).

The women also complained that they did not have choices concerning the selection of the programming yet were penalized if they failed to meet rehabilitation expectations (Boritch 2002; Monture-Angus 2000). If a woman refused to participate in programs such as parenting, vocational, educational and substance abuse programming, she was labelled as a risk and assigned a higher security classification (Hannah-Moffat 1999). This again led to women being classified as unreformable and moved into conditions that were more secure (including men's facilities). Thus, many federally incarcerated women have not benefitted from the women-centred model proposed in *Creating Choices*.

Correctional Strategies of Empowerment

Creating Choices was intended to promote a woman's power to make her own choices and to negate the traditional paternalistic and maternal correctional-ist regimes (Hannah-Moffat 1999; Faith 2011, 1993). This included allowing women to regain control of their lives through the development of self-confidence, autonomy and an influence over social conditions in life. Yet, upon implementation of *Creating Choices*, the notion of empowerment was compromised by the penal culture (Dell et al. 2009; Ferarri 2011). *Creating Choices* in practice was criticized by feminists such as Hannah-Moffat as being reflective of a wider shift in governing "wherein governments and corporations with little or no interest in granting real power to dispossessed groups have merely adopted discourses of empowerment" (2000: 31).[4] This is a strong criticism linking the empowerment politics of *Creating Choices* to neo-liberal strategies, questioning whether empowerment is possible (Rose 1996, 2000).

More specifically, the Correctional Service of Canada defined empowerment as "the process through which women gain insight into their situation, identify their strengths, and are supported and challenged to take positive action to gain control of their lives" (CSC 1994: 9, cited in Hannah-Moffat 2000). However, after the closure of P4W, women's choices within this model of empowerment continued to be limited to those deemed by prison administration as being responsible and meaningful. In other words, to escape and run to see their children was not a choice, yet the choice to participate in Alcoholics Anonymous was responsible. Critics argue that this interpretation of empowerment simply shifts the old management strategies onto the women inmates, in effect, to have them police themselves. As Simon writes, "The new techniques [like empowerment] do not so much replace these traditional measures as embed them in a far more comprehensive web of monitoring and intervention" (Simon 1994 cited in Hannah-Moffat 2000: 33).

STRATEGIES OF RISK MANAGEMENT

There is a recent trend towards standardized correctional practice through the clas-sification of prisoners (developed through the new Offender Intake Assessment process) that is contradictory to *Creating Choices* and the differential treatment of women. Characteristics such as low self-esteem, poor education, foster care place-ment, residential placement, prostitution, suicide attempts, substance abuse and others now represent both risk *and* need. Correctional researchers have linked these characteristics to violent recidivism and argue that this constitutes risk; this is in direct contrast to feminist researchers who argue these are mental health concerns that constitute the need for treatment (Heney 1990).

Task Force members and others[5] claim that risk categories are not highly relevant for female prisoners. Hanna-Moffat suggests that the discussion to date about the needs of female inmates relies not on feminist interpretations of needs for women but rather "depends on correctional interpretations of women's needs as potential or modified risk factors that are central to efficient management of incarcerated women" (2000: 38). This points once again to a wide discrepancy between the intentions of *Creating Choices* and the current practice within correctional settings.

Gendered Risk

In theory, crime can be reduced through scientific determination of a prisoner's risk score and classification for security. However, this calculation has been criticized as gendered and racialized (Hannah-Moffat 2000). Boritch (2002) demonstrates how this calculation is gendered — the labelling of the risk level of offenders lowers the bar for women in the calculation of dangerousness. Evidence for this is found by examining the label of dangerous offender and the actions of the women who acquire this label versus the actions of men. For example, Lisa Neve was labelled a dangerous offender yet her most serious crime was aggravated assault; this fails to compare to the types of offences committed by men who are labelled as dangerous offenders, which are typically murder, serial sexual assault and pedophilia. The same discrepancy is noted with security risks and those deemed high security. In 1999, 31 percent of incarcerated women were deemed to be maximum security; only 22 percent of men shared this label despite men being sentenced for more violent crimes overall (Correctional Service of Canada 1999).

Racialized Risk

Ideas regarding risk are racialized, highlighted by the disproportionate labelling of Aboriginal women as maximum security. Risk-prediction scales, responsibility and need dimensions are problematic for Aboriginal offenders. Individualization of risk does not address colonial impacts and the oppression of Aboriginal women, and offender-based notions of responsibility are lopsided from an Aboriginal view.

Racism is also a key factor of discrimination in security classification and risk assessment. For example, the Case Needs Identification and Analysis protocol identifies need dimensions based on seven categories: "employment, marital/family, associates, substance abuse, community functioning, personal/emotional and attitude" (Motiuk 1997, cited in Monture-Angus 2000: 57). These dimensions are problematic because colonialism has led to Aboriginal communities that are not defined as healthy or functional, which leads to a failure to score well in this category as well.

The idea of responsibility embraced by correctional structures is lopsided from the Aboriginal point of view because it is solely based on the offender (Monture-Angus 2000: 55). Relationships are central in First Nations legal practices, whereby healing of individuals and healing of communities are co-constitutive. All of this has been eroded by concerns for security and standard correctional agendas (Monture-Angus 2000).

This concept of risk management adds to earlier explanations of why twenty women remained at P4W until it closed in July 2000. It also helps to explain why these so-called high-risk and high-need women are now housed in men's maximum-security institutions around Canada. Women who are resisting the new women-centered vision are demonized and pathologized; moreover, many of these women are Aboriginal and therefore not able to benefit from the regional cites.

SUMMARY

Rich and diverse feminist approaches attempt to assess the reform efforts of *Creating Choices* and the meaning of justice for women in trouble. Much of this discourse remains optimistic about the potential of *Creating Choices* even while acknowledging problems with its implementation (Hannah-Moffat 2000; Hayman 2000; Shaw 1993). Other feminist authors question whether feminist prisons are possible or even desirable (Faith, 2011, 1993; Comack 1996; Boritch 2002; Shaw 2000). While *Creating Choices* is viewed as making fundamental changes in women's federal corrections, criticisms force a rethinking of the original vision.

The key criticisms of *Creating Choices* are that the voices of the federally sentenced women have not been heard and the report has not been not implemented as intended. This is evident in the definition of empowerment; the classification of risk versus need; forced participation in programming; the negative relationships with staff; the continued use of segregation, handcuffs, pepper spray and strip searches; and the ranking of commitments to correctional and cultural programming.

The critical position is that implementation strategies must therefore be revisited with attention to need versus risk, proper hiring and instruction of staff, women's voices and agency and the renouncement of harmful operations such as segregation, pepper spray and strip searches. Planning for the long-term sentences of the federally sentenced women at the Healing Lodge must be linked to the increased involvement of the Nekaneet Band, Elders and their teachings. The initial vision, which stated that the Healing Lodge "must [be] developed by and connected to Aboriginal communities" (CSC 1990: 122), should therefore be revisited. "Connected" here means more than just placing the facility on Aboriginal land, which simply becomes the "prisonization" of the Healing Lodge (Monture-Angus 2000: 54). Much more research is also necessary to uncover the needs of more violent women, especially given the abundance of stereotypical and false information in the news media (cf. Faith 2011, 1993; Faith and Jiwani 2015). New strategies are also needed to measure risk and responsibility. As DeKeseredy (2011) points out, women who are violent are most often reacting to violence against them.

There has also been a shift in how women offenders are perceived, which has affected their treatment since the closure of P4W. The idea that women are high need yet low risk has been replaced with the perception of women as high need and high risk. Characteristics of the women, such as their history of abuse and self-injurious behaviour, are now used to justify higher security classifications rather than as reasons supporting the need for therapeutic intervention.

This chapter has examined the social control of criminalized women through the criminal justice system, media, education, violence and the law. The relationship between women's criminalization and social justice issues was explored in relation to race, gender and class. We have drawn attention to the contrast between the image of the "monster woman" in film and the news and the statistical reality of criminalized women whose crimes are generally not violent and who have often experienced economic marginalization, racism and violence. By focusing our attention on Canada's most violent and notorious women offenders — such as Karla Homolka — and creating false and hateful pornographic images of female prisoners, we forget how class, race and gender inequalities affect women's criminalization.

Themes of criminal responsibility and dangerous social groups are criticized in feminist literature as ideological tools that attempt to manage the most vulnerable people (Morris 2000; Shaw 2000). The criminal justice system and the media function as powerful hegemonic tools that convince the majority that the poor and marginalized must be feared as the most dangerous and criminal class (Collins 2014).

Critical feminist literature also provides an in-depth critique of the complex nature of law and order politics. These critical views also show ways that P4W and the new regional prisons have failed to reduce the incidence of female criminality because they fail to address problems such as violence against women and children, poverty, continued racism and inequality of opportunity. Prisons cannot address these broader structural, economic, social and political problems. This chapter suggests that we cannot limit our discussions to criminal justice or penal reform; rather, we have to also query the relationships between law, legislative reform and social regulation.

Critical feminist authors such as Karlene Faith (2011, 1993), Helen Boritch (2002, 2008) and Margaret Shaw (2000) argue that reform within the prison system risks expanding and justifying the use of incarceration for women. *Creating Choices* offers feminist reforms that may negate the offering of socially informed alternatives to imprisonment for women. The goal for feminist reformers must be to reduce reliance on imprisonment for women in trouble and to push for the implementation of non-carceral correctional approaches.

We cannot (in good conscience) conclude by arguing that *Creating Choices* has simply failed to achieve its vision upon implementation and is doomed. *Creating Choices* has improved some women's lives and may, with much continued effort, help (not hinder) reform-minded feminists in their efforts towards eventually de-institutionalizing women, using restorative and community initiatives and addressing structural inequalities and issues of human rights. Critical feminists attest that we must not abandon prison reform for women; however, more research and consciousness-raising must be done to demonstrate that female offenders are relatively low risk, that their lives are characterized by abuse, poverty and inequality and that ill-designed systems can be reformed. Considerations of the power of both the media and out-dated criminological theory in shaping public opinion must also be considered with respect to the social regulation of criminalized women.

Women in prison, academics and activists continue to call our attention to the voices of women in prison and the importance of protecting their real human rights:Tears have long since been subdued

My waters have run dry
I just might come unglued
As I start to cry.

Time is suffocating
My flow
I'm tired of waitin
I'm ready to go!
                    —*Summers 2011: Another Day [in prison] Series*

Notes

1   Canadian Corrections Association, Brief on the Woman Offender (Canada 1968); Report of the Canadian Committee on Corrections (Canada 1969); Report of the Royal Commission on the Status of Women (Canada 1970); Ministry of the Solicitor General, Report of the National Advisory Committee on the Female offender (Canada 1976); Report to Parliament by the Sub-Committee on the Penitentiary System in Canada (Canada 1977b); Canadian Association of Elizabeth Fry Societies, "Brief on the Female Offender" (1978); Brief to the Solicitor General (Canada 1978); Ministry of the Solicitor General, Report on the National Planning Committee on the Female Offender (Canada 1978); Ten Years Later (Canada 1979); Women for Justice, "Brief to the Canadian Human Rights Commission" (Canada 1980).

2   CAEFS' philosophy supports the eventual abolition of prisons for women.

3   Ole Ingstrup had been commissioner for six months, with the average term being three years.
4   Governing has moved from the regulation of an individual's behaviour in the more coercive institution, towards strategies of empowerment which rely on self-governing and creates prudent subjects who are responsiblized (who take responsibility for their own behaviour) (Rose 1996, 2000).
5   See also, for example, the Arbour Commission, Public Hearings 1995.

References

Adelberg, E., and C. Currie. 1987. *Too Few to Count: Canadian Women in Conflict with the Law.* Vancouver: Press Gang.

Adler, Freda. 1975. *Sisters in Crime: The Rise of the New Female Criminal.* New York: McGraw-Hill.

Arbour, Honourable Louise. 1996. "Commission of Inquiry into Certain Events at the Prison for Women in Kingston." *Ottawa: Public Works and Government Services Canada.*

Baez, H. 2010. "Lombroso, Cesare: The Female Offender." In F. Cullen and P. Wilcox (eds.), *Encyclopedia of Criminological Theory.* Thousand Oaks, CA: Sage Publications.

Banwell, Stacey. 2011. "Women, Violence and the Gray Zones: Resolving the Paradox of the Female Victim-Perpetrator." *Internet Journal of Criminology* ISSN 2045-6793. <internetjournalofcriminology.com/banwell_women_violence_and_gray_zones_ijc_september_2011>.

Barrett, Meridith Robeson, Kim Allenby and Kelly Taylor. 2010. "Twenty Years Later: Revisiting the Task Force on Federally Sentenced Women." *Correctional Service Canada* July. <csc-scc.gc.ca/005/008/092/005008-0222-01-eng.pdf>.

Boritch, Helen. 2002. "Women in Prison in Canada." In B. Schissel and C. Brooks (eds.), *Marginality and Condemnation: An Introduction to Critical Criminology.* Halifax and Winnipeg: Fernwood Publishing.

____. 2008. "Women in Prison in Canada." In C. Brooks and B. Schissel (eds.), *Marginality and Condemnation: An Introduction to Criminology* (second edition). Halifax and Winnipeg: Fernwood Publishing.

Brooks, Carolyn, and Bernard Schissel. 2015. "Theorizing Crime: Introduction." In Carolyn Brooks and Bernard Schissel (eds.), Marginality and Condemnation: An Introduction to Criminology, 3rd edition.

Burns, Jan. 2006. "Mad or Just Plain Bad? Gender and the Work of Forensic Clinical Psychologists." In Jane M. Ussher and Paula Nicolson (eds.), *Gender Issues in Clinical Psychology.* New York: Routledge.

CAEFS (Canadian Association of Elizabeth Fry Society archives). 2014. "Fact Sheets and Newsletters." <caefs.ca/resources/fact-sheets-in-pdf/>.

Canada. 1977a. *Report on the Standing Committee on Justice and Solicitor General on its Review of Sentencing, Conditional Release and Related Aspects of Corrections.*

____. 1977b. *Report to Parliament by the Sub-Committee on the Penitentiary System in Canada.* Ottawa: Supply and Services. 1977.

Canadian Human Rights Commission. 2003. "Protecting Their Rights: A Systemic Review of Human Rights in Correctional Services for Federally Sentenced Women." *Canadian*

Human Rights Commission, December. <caefs.ca/wp-content/uploads/2013/05/fswen.pdf>.

Carlen, P. 1988. *Women, Crime, and Poverty.* Milton Keynes, Philadelphia: Open University Press.

Cecil, Dawn K. 2007. "Looking Beyond Caged Heat: Media Images of Women in Prison." *Feminist Criminology* 2: 304–26.

Chesney-Lind, Meda, and Michele Eliason. 2006. "From Invisible to Incorrigible: The Demonization of Marginalized Women and Girls." *Crime, Media and Culture* 2: 29–47.

Clowers, M. 2001. "Dykes, Gangs, and Danger: Debunking Popular Myths about Maximum-Security Life." *Journal of Criminal Justice and Popular Culture* 9, 1: 22–30.

Collins. Rachael. 2014. "'Meet the Devil… He'll Chill You to the Bone' Fear, Marginalization, and the Colour of Crime: A Thirty-Year Analysis of Four Canadian Newspapers." <ecommons.usask.ca/handle/10388/ETD-2014-03-1491>.

Comack, Elizabeth. 1996. *Women in Trouble.* Halifax: Fernwood Publishing.

____. 2006. "The Feminist Engagement with Criminology." In Gillian Balfour and Elizabeth Comack (eds.), *Criminalizing Women: Gender and (In)Justice in Neo-Liberal Times.* Halifax: Fernwood Publishing.

Correctional Service of Canada. 1990. *Creating Choices: The Report of the Task Force on Federally Sentenced Women.* Ottawa: Correctional Services Canada, April.

____. 1999. "Profile of Incarcerated Women Offenders: September, 1999." <www.csc-scc.gc.caa/text/releases00-07-06e.shtm>.

____. 2008. "Report of the Task Force on Security." <www.csc-scc.gc.ca/text/pblct/security/toc-eng.shtml>.

____. 2013. *Coroner's inquest touching the death of Ashley Smith.* <csc-scc.gc.ca/publications/005007-9009-eng.shtml>.

Cowie, John, Valerie A. Cowie and Eliot Slater. 1968. *Delinquency in Girls.* New York: Humanities Press.

Currie, Dawn. 1986. "Female Criminality: A Crisis in Feminist Theory." In B. MacLean (ed.), *The Political Economy of Crime.* Scarborough: Prentice-Hall.

Daigle, Marc, Mylene Alaire and Patrick Lefebvre. 1999. "The Problem of Suicide Among Female Prisoners." *Forum on Corrections Research* 11, 3.

Dalton, Katharina. 1978. *Cyclical Criminal Acts in Premenstrual Syndrome.* Elsevier.

Dekeseredy, Walter. 2011. *Violence Against Women: Myths, Facts and Controversies.* Toronto: University of Toronto Press.

Dell, Colleen Anne, Catherine J. Fillmore and Jennifer M. Kilty. 2009. "Looking Back 10 Years After the Arbour Inquiry: Ideology, Policy, Practice, and the Federal Female Prisoner." *The Prison Journal* 89, 3: 286–308.

Delveaux, K., K. Blanchette and J. Wickett. 2005. *Employment Needs, Interests, and Programming for Women Offenders.* Ottawa: Correctional Service of Canada.

Faith, Karlene. 1993. *Unruly Women: The Politics of Confinement & Resistance.* Vancouver, BC: Press Gang Publishers.

____. 2011. *Unruly Women: The Politics of Confinement & Resistance.* New York: Seven Stories Press.

Faith, K., and Y. Jiwani. 2015. "The Social Construction of 'Dangerous' Girls and Women." In Carolyn Brooks and Bernard Schissel (eds.), Marginality and Condemnation: An

Introduction to Criminology, 3ʳᵈ edition. Halifax: Fernwood Publishing.

Ferrari, J. 2011. "Federal Female Incarceration in Canada: What Happened to Empowerment?" <qspace.library.queensu.ca/bitstream/1974/6352/3/Ferrari_Jacqueline_201104_MA.pdf>.

Findlay, Isabel, James Popham, Patrick Ince and Sarah Takahashi. 2013. *Through the Eyes of Women: What a Co-operative Can Mean in Supporting Women During Confinement and Integration.* Saskatoon: Centre for the Study of Co-operatives, University of Saskatchewan.

Garland, E. 2001. *The Culture of Control: Crime and Social Order in Contemporary Society.* Chicago: Oxford University Press.

Gironella, Fiona D. 1999. "Creating Choices or Redefining Control? Prisoners from the Edmonton Institution for Women Share Their Standpoint." Edmonton: University of Alberta.

Hannah-Moffat, K. 1999. "Moral Agent or Actuarial Subject: Risk and Canadian Women's Imprisonment." *Theoretical Criminology* 3, 1: 71–94. Reprinted 2006 by the International Library of Essays in Law and Society, in P. O'Malley (ed.), *Governing Risks.* Ashgate Publishing Ltd. <tcr.sagepub.com/content/3/1/71.abstract>.

Hannah-Moffat, K., and M. Shaw. 2000. "Gender, Diversity and Risk Assessment in Canadian Corrections." *Probation Journal* 47, 3: 172. <prb.sagepub.com/content/47/3/163.abstract>.

Hayman, Stephanie. 2000. "Prison Reform and Incorporation: Lessons From Britain and Canada." In Kelly Hannah-Moffat and Margaret Shaw (eds.), *An Ideal Prison? Critical Essays on Women's Imprisonment in Canada.* Halifax: Fernwood Publishing.

Heney, J.H. 1990. *Report on Self-Injurious Behaviour in the Kingston Prison for Women.* June (revised). Submitted to the Correctional Service of Canada.

Hoffman, L.E., and M.A. Law. 1995. "Federally Sentenced Women on Conditional Release: Survey of Community Supervisors." Ottawa: Federally Sentenced Women Program, Correctional Service of Canada.

Hoffman-Bustamente, D. 1973. "The Nature of Female Criminality." *Issues in Criminology* 2.

Hotton-Mahony, Tina. 2011. "Women and the Criminal Justice System." Statistics Canada Catalogue no 89-503-X. *Women in Canada: A Gender-Based Statistical Report.* April. <statcan.gc.ca/pub/89-503-x/2010001/article/11416-eng.pdf>.

Hugill, David. 2010. *Missing Women, Missing News: Covering Crisis in Vancouver's Downtown Eastside.* Halifax and Winnipeg: Fernwood Publishing.

Kendall, K. 2000. "Psy-Ence Fiction: Inventing the Mentally-Disordered Female Prisoner." In Kelly Hannah-Moffat and Margaret Shaw (eds.), *An Ideal Prison? Critical Essays on Women's Imprisonment in Canada.* Halifax: Fernwood Publishing.

Kershaw, Anne, and Mary Lasovich. 1991. *Rock-a-Bye Baby: A Death Behind Bars.* Toronto: McClelland and Stewart.

Labrecque. R. 1995. *Study of the Mother-Child Program.* Ottawa: Federally Sentenced Women Program, Correctional Services of Canada.

Lawston, Jodie. 2011. "From Representations to Resistance: How the Razor Wire Binds Us." In Jodie Lawton and Ashley Lucas (eds.). *Razor Wire Women: Prisoners, Activists, Scholars and Artists.* Albany: State University of New York Press.

Lombroso, Cesare, and Guglielmo Ferrero. 1895. *The Female Offender.* New York: D.

Appleton and Company.

Martin, M. 1997. "Connected Mothers: A Follow-Up Study of Incarcerated Women and Their Children." *Women and Criminal Justice* 8, 1.

McDonagh, Donna. 1999. "Maximum Security Women: 'Not Letting the Time Do You.'" *Forum on Corrections Research* 11, 3.

Monture-Angus, Patricia. 2000. "Aboriginal Overrepresentation in Canadian Criminal Justice." In David Long and Olive Patricia Dickason (eds.), *Visions of the Heart: Canadian Aboriginal Issues*, second edition. Toronto: Harcourt Canada.

Morris, Ruth. 2000. *Stories of Transformative Justice.* Toronto: Canadian Scholars' Press.

Office of the Correctional Investigator. 2013. "Aboriginal Offenders – A Critical Situation." <oci-bec.gc.ca/cnt/rpt/oth-aut/oth-aut20121022info-eng.aspx>.

Pate, Kim. 2011. "When Strip Searches Are Sexual Assaults." <http://www.caefs.ca/wp-content/uploads/2013/05/October_2011_Kim_Pate_When_strip_searches_are_sexual_assaults.pdf> accessed June 2014.

Pollack, O. 1979. "The Masked Character of Female Crime." In Adler and Simon (eds.), *The Criminality of Deviant Women.* Boston: Houghton Millin.

Rose, N. 1996. "Governing Advanced Liberal Democracies." In A. Barry, T. Osborne and N. Rose (eds.), *Foucault and Political Reason: Liberalism, Neo-Liberalism, and Rationalities of Government.* Chicago: University of Chicago Press.

____. 2000. *Government and Control.* Oxford and New York: Oxford University Press.

Sapers, Howard. 2008. "A Preventable Death: Correctional Investigation into the Death of Ashley Smith." Canada: Office of the Correctional Investigator.

Schissel, Bernard. 2006. *Still Blaming Children: Youth Conduct and the Politics of Child Hating.* Black Point, NS: Fernwood Publishing.

Schram, Pamela, and Stephen Tibbetts. 2014. *Introduction to Criminology: Why Do They Do It?* Thousand Oaks, CA: Sage Publication.

Shaw, Margaret. 1993. "Reforming Federal Women's Imprisonment." In Ellen Adelberg and Claudia Currie (eds.), *In Conflict with the Law: Women and the Canadian Justice System.* Vancouver: Press Gang.

____. 2000. "Women, Violence and Disorder in Prisons." In Kelly Hannah-Moffat and Margaret Shaw (eds.), *An Ideal Prison? Critical Essays on Women's Imprisonment in Canada.* Halifax: Fernwood Publishing.

Smart, Carol. 1976. *Women, Crime and Criminology: A Feminist Critique.* London: Routledge and Kegan Paul.

Star Phoenix. 1991. "Dying to Get Out of P4W: In Kingston's Prison for Women Some Natives Find Death a Form for Liberation." March 23.

Strange, C. 1985. "The Criminal and Fallen of Their Sex: The Establishment of Canada's First Women's Prison, 1874–1901," *Canadian Journal of Women and the Law* 79.

Summers, Tammica L. 2011. "Stories So Strong They Crumble Concrete." *Another Day Series.* <womenandprison.org/poetry/view/another_day_series/>.

Thomas, Jennifer. 2000. "Adult Correctional Services in Canada, 1998–99." *Juristat* 20, 3. Canadian Center for Justice Studies.

Wattanaporn, Katelyn A., and Kristy Holtfreter. 2014. "The Impact of Feminist Pathways Research on Gender-Responsive Policy and Practice." *Feminist Criminology* 9: 191–207.

White, R. 2002. "Restorative Justice and Social Inequality." In B. Schissel and C. Brooks (eds.), *Marginality and Condemnation: An Introduction to Critical Criminology*. Halifax: Fernwood Publishing.

Wiebe, Rudy, and Yvonne Johnson. 1998. *Stolen Life: The Journey of a Cree Woman*. Toronto: Alfred A. Knopf Canada.

Legal Cases

R. v. Gladue. 1999. 1 SCR 688

R. v. Ipeelee. 2012. SCC 13, [2012] 1 S.C.R. 433.

Chapter 19

EXPERIENCING THE INSIDE-OUT PROGRAM IN A MAXIMUM-SECURITY PRISON

Monica Freitas, Bonnie McAuley and Nyki Kish

From: *Criminalizing Women: Gender and (In)Justice in Neo-liberal Times*, 2nd edition, pp. 303–313 (reprinted with permission).

INSIDE-OUT AND ITS EFFECT ON MY IMPRISONMENT: MONICA FREITAS

Sitting in my cell, I reflect on the past two years of my life and the intense emotions I have experienced within the Canadian judicial system. Many women experience very low self-confidence and quite frankly do not see any way out of the crime cycle that most are accustomed to in order to survive life's hardships. Having harmful thoughts, negative self-talk, and experiencing marginalization, oppression and constant judgment at the hands of the people that are supposed to assist us with rehabilitation and reintegration into our communities prove to be very challenging. Due to the numerous challenges that I have been facing — having a criminal record, being away from my supports and loved ones, and experiencing extreme emotions of guilt, shame and loneliness — my efforts and focus during my incarceration have been on obtaining higher education, advocating for and empowering female inmates, and educating our communities about the criminalization of women and its long-term effects on society as a whole. I attribute my passion and fervour for these important causes to the Inside-Out program.

Inside-Out completely changed my perspective on learning and encouraged me both through the class dialogue/activities and essays to challenge myself and others. The course facilitator and her assistant were there to encourage healthy dialogue and a positive environment, where each participant could explore their personal boundaries and perhaps challenge society's perceptions of prisons, punishment and incarcerated women. There was no evidence of anyone exercising power or privilege over one another, as the class had mutually and democratically agreed upon guidelines of conduct at the beginning of the program. By doing this, the facilitator empowered each person to become not only students, but teachers in their own right.

I have concluded during my time behind "the walls" that we all have a plan, whether we chose it or it was chosen for us. We cannot help who, what and where we are, but it is what we do with our lives that differentiates us from becoming oppressed, oppressors and the liberated. I believe that education is necessary from the grassroots level in order to ensure that society creates an environment where all individuals feel respected and equal and have fair access to the basic necessities of life.

"INSIDE THE WALLS":
BONNIE MCAULEY

My name is Bonnie and I am doing a life/twenty-five sentence for the murder of my husband. I completed year eighteen on August 22, 2013. I began my sentence at the Prison for Women in Kingston, Ontario, in 1995 and at that time I also began taking courses from Queen's University by correspondence. I have three adult children and two grandchildren. I was a registered nurse outside and when I obtain this second degree I may be eligible to teach nursing in a college setting. Unfortunately, as the years have passed my chances at bursaries and outside funds for education have decreased considerably. I am now in a financial position where I'm not able to continue my education without financial help from others.

Three years ago the opportunity arose where I was able to apply for a degree course through Wilfrid Laurier University in a program referred to as Inside-Out. My hopes were increased immediately. The course would be compensated entirely by the Lyle S. Hallman Foundation, which awarded Wilfrid Laurier with a substantial amount of money. The course would be funded through Wilfrid Laurier and paid for me in its entirety. Unfortunately, I did not get into the first course. I was devastated. In December 2011, I applied to a social work course called "What Is Family?" and I was accepted into the program. Since then I have applied to and completed three courses — with outstanding marks.

When I started the class in the first Inside-Out course I glanced around at the students and I have to admit that what I saw was mostly upper-class, privileged, educated females who I thought I would never fit in with. But the circle and the icebreakers helped me to get to know and like each person on an equal level. They also made me realize that for the most part these women were just the same as me. The circle also enhanced our learning in the Inside-Out program. It brought university outside to the inside. These wonderful circles became "circles of trust" and it definitely removed that upper-class feeling that I had developed at the beginning. The circle also encouraged dialogue among two very different classes of students.

I am privileged enough to be starting a fourth Inside-Out course on social litera-ture. These courses have helped increase both my self-esteem and self-confidence. I am truly blessed to be part of this wonderful program.

JAIL THE BODY, FREE THE MIND:
NYKI KISH

I spent two years and nearly four months imprisoned within a maximum-security unit at the Grand Valley Institution for Women (GVIW), a multi-security-level women's federal penitentiary in Ontario. In what follows I share the hurdles, rewards, and general experiences I encountered in studying at a post-secondary level from inside a maximum-security prison. I explore issues around participat-ing in a prison educational program during Canada's shift into a "tough on crime" penal policy, and I also attempt to express, through my own experience, how Inside-Out pedagogy and the prison environment interact, and how the two are entirely contradictory in effect.

Being Held in a Maximum-Security Prison
At the time I was introduced to the Inside-Out program, I was being held in a maximum-security wing of the Grand Valley Institution for Women for a mandatory twenty-seven-month period, a sentence stipulation anyone with a life sentence, like myself, must endure. The maximum-security unit, which the Correctional Service of Canada calls the secure unit and which everyone else refers to as "max," is a fifteen-cell, twenty-seven-bed "supermax"-inspired wing, containing three isolated five-cell corridors where women are kept. The small, narrow, fluorescent-lit, self-contained corridors are known as "pods." We spent the majority of our time on the pods; we were allowed out of the unit only to ask for a maximum of one hour outside in the evenings and for visits and programs. On pod, we were locked in the cells for 14.5 hours daily. We were often double-bunked. When I first arrived, I remember clearly my first impression being: How could anyone exist for two years in such a small, uncomforting space? My second impression quickly followed: What meaningful experience could one even craft from such an existence?

All pursuits that interest me, from volunteering, to making art, to connecting to the natural world, were cauterized from my life upon my being put into Grand Valley's max, and I quickly hoped that education could be that time's saving grace. But from a resource and opportunity standpoint, the max offers less than little. An option to privately purchase correspondence courses exists, should an imprisoned woman have access to the $500 to $800 course fees; however, a switch to online learning increasingly limits choices for the select few who can afford this option, as imprisoned people in Canada have no access to the Internet. Further, what available government assistance for post-secondary courses to inmates used to exist in Ontario was also cut from the federal budget in 2012. Indeed, post-secondary pursuits in the Grand Valley Institution's maximum-security unit have always been rare and are increasingly becoming rarer. Further, they are pursuits that, by my experience, are warned against by most of the max staff because of the limitations of the unit.

There are four dated computers installed between two program rooms near the pods that are prioritized for women working through secondary school, not all of which ever steadily work. Accessing them is *always* a challenge. Movement in max is authorized by guard discretion in conjunction with room scheduling, and the two rooms are also used as the library, chapel, gym, court, intervention, psychology and institutional program room, and even the women enrolled in secondary school are denied access regularly. Being able to type, research or even work safely in a calm or quiet environment presented daily hurdles, most of which we never satisfied. As mentioned, the majority of our time was spent on pod and in cell where there are no computers, no working space, and only what study supplies we purchase through the canteen, which are limited to lined paper, pens and erasers.

Access barriers, though significant, were not enough to stop us from wanting to pursue schooling. Beyond structural limitations, however, regular violent disruptions and emotional upheaval occurring between women and staff and among the women make the max one of the most hostile, unstable places a person could study in. In Grand Valley, the secure unit is used to hold not just people with life sentences, but also women with violent histories and women who experience varying mental illnesses and who do not function in the general population. The max offers little for us to do and is not a treatment unit to which those with mental illnesses should be surrendered. The conditions culminate to make max the perfect environment for violence. Moreover, aside from chemically restraining women, discipline and isolation are the utilized responses to any emotion or incident in max, which only perpetuate incidents and chaos on the unit, as emotional responses were, generally, our natural reactions to the intensely regulated, regimented institutional environment. Finally, because of the small size of the pods, when incidents occur, they generally shut down at least the involved pod, if not the entire unit, affecting us all.

Such was the daily reality of being kept in the max. Still, as Inside-Out was being introduced into Canada and into GVIW, organizers were quite careful in pushing for the inclusion of max women, and included we were.

I completed the first four Inside-Out courses that were offered at GVIW while imprisoned in the max; it was Canada's very first Inside-Out class that I shared as my first experience with the program. "Diversity, Marginalization, and Oppression" was the course title, and with this course began the most meaningful experience I had during my imprisonment in max.

The Inside-Out Program's Pedagogy and Format

Inside-Out pedagogy promotes a collective, dialogue-based experiential learning. Every class takes place with university students who are both imprisoned and not imprisoned. A supportive rather than competitive tone is encouraged and equality in voice is promoted. Assigned readings are discussed, usually in one large class circle, followed by dialogue-based activities that are carried out within smaller class groups to deepen our analyses. The large circle is generally re-formed to end each class with personal reflection on the session. The opening, dispersing, regrouping ritual of the large and small circles in Inside-Out created something of a sacredness to the classes for me. Inside-Out as a whole does not follow conventional education mechanics, but presents instead as a transformative life and academic experience.

Toward the end of each course, a final project is developed by the entire class. Final projects are usually action-oriented and are often produced with themes of social justice and advocacy. By the end of the courses strong bonds tend to form between the imprisoned and outside students, both because of the starkly unconventional nature of the program that we students mutually experience, and because syllabi tend to be tailored to be relevant to issues of imprisonment (for example, the courses I participated in studied prisons, punishment, human rights and oppression, which always gave us amply solid grounds upon which we became united and galvanized).

My Experiences with the Inside-Out Program

The courses are held in the medium-security compound of the prison, meaning that in order to attend I had to be taken off pod by guards, frisk-searched, and escorted to and from the classroom, while during class being under constant supervision of prison staff. During class I sat among all the students, both the women in this prison and as well, the outside students. In that setting and *only* in that setting there was no way to identify me as a maximum-security prisoner. At the time of our very first class, I had been in a max pod for eight months, and I remember feeling instantly more human than I had since being convicted. It was not long after that first Inside-Out class when I realized how compromised my social skills had become as a result of my living conditions. I was no longer, by that time, accustomed to being spoken to with respect, or having any atmosphere where my thoughts were valued or where I could express my opinions unpenalized. The allowance of my being able to have the limited periods of free expression that came through Inside-Out ultimately became invaluable to my surviving the max, and I stress that this aspect of the program will continue to be invaluable to any imprisoned women being held in the max who engages in Inside-Out.

The supermax style of imprisonment that Canada has embraced within several aspects of the country's prison industry is, in my opinion, inherently dehumanizing. Supermax-style units are not built with anything but containment, control and minimized maintenance in mind, and this led to atrocious effects on the hearts and minds of those of us who were subjected to exist within their walls. Very rarely did I ever get the opportunity to connect with others in any way that was not superficial or quite guarded in nature. And while no prison guards are stationed on pod with us, women in the max are watched all day through multiple cameras; as well, all of our conversations can be listened to by staff through a speaker system. What we said and did on the pods was constantly monitored, scrutinized and used to determine our "institutional progress." Such control over ideas and casual conversation left me wary to engage at all, and I spent the majority of my first twenty months in the prison in the cells to which I was assigned. Even when I did interact with the other women on pod, because the pods only typically imprison three to five other women, the environment was always extremely isolating and socially strenuous.

Contrary to the max environment, it has consistently been my experience that there is a healing quality to the circle setting that Inside-Out embraces. In class circles there was no hierarchy and there were not the power struggles that dominated my experience with both guards and other imprisoned women in max. In class circles I felt safe to think and share and interact, and especially as our class read texts and poetry relevant to oppression, criminalization and issues of imprisonment, I began to find something I had lost in the trauma of experiencing the penal system: my voice. Even the simplest activities that occur within the Inside-Out setting, such as reading aloud, listening and being listened to within a group of people, and being encouraged to disagree and challenge ideas, counteracted the negative impacts of imprisonment in max. Being allowed to be this way during classes reminded me of the self I developed before my imprisonment, and class after class, slowly but surely, I regained confidence, vitality and drive that I was not aware I had lost. I finished my first Inside-Out class feeling like I had found liberation from within prison walls. It has been echoed to me by other participants that such is the case for many Inside-Out students, both imprisoned and not.

Public Perception, Deservingness and Stigma

The trend of labelling criminalized people as "undeserving" of education and other opportunities is neither new nor undocumented, and with our having access to the limited, however meaningful, post-secondary education that the Inside-Out program offers comes a great degree of carefulness and public relations management on the part of the prison administration and involved universities. While forces within both institutions vocally proclaim the program internally, frequent were our class conversations which navigated toning down, tailoring to "public perception," and properly presenting the products our classes produced through the final project of the Inside-Out course. Within CSC, almost every change that is implemented is announced to the prison population with a clause about how said change interacts with Canada's public perception of this prison system. Indeed, public perception is most often the guise under which we as an imprisoned population are denied even the most basic human rights and dignities. It is the excuse given to keep computers from being purchased and from allowing the ranges to be air-conditioned (though we endure soaring temperatures regularly), and it is the most common reason we are given when we are told what a gift it is that a few of us are able to learn. I do not dispute that under our current system, programs like Inside-Out are indeed a privilege; I dispute that they ought to be.

The acceptance on the part of imprisoned participants that we were receiving a privilege in our ability to study university courses comes about in relation to the arguments that we are imprisoned and learning while many non-imprisoned Canadians are never able to engage in university, and that the costs of these courses for imprisoned students are largely carried by the program. It is said to us that much of the public does not believe imprisoned people should have meaningful opportunity. This argument against meaningful opportunity for imprisoned people generally stands upon the logic that imprisoned people should be experiencing punishment in a setting undesirable enough and reduced enough from the average quality of existence in Canada to deter the next citizen from partaking in crime, rather than being able to develop oneself in any positive, significant manner. This logic of course rests upon the notion of individualized responsibility within a reactionary approach to the social issue of crime; it does not consider that imprisoned people might experience imprisonment as a result of lack of opportunity and marginalization. Nor does this logic consider the ripple social effects of an institution that would return educated people into communities rather than people who have only experienced trauma, isolation and deprivation for extended periods of time.

In this prison we often listen to mainstream media expressing supportive narratives about Canada's turn away from an alternative, non-punitive penal system toward the neo-liberal, reactionary, "tough on crime" prison industrial phenomenon that has spread globally. I have been imprisoned through the implementation of the Stephen Harper government's 2012 Omnibus Crime Bill C-10; I have experienced, since my conviction, the increasing social aggression being imposed upon the marginal and most often impoverished identities that comprise the majority of Canada's women's prison population. I have felt the devastation, and I do not use the word lightly, of existing within a cage within a society that is accepting a drastic policy overhaul of one of its dominant institutions, its prison system, without understanding the changes or their immediate or long-term effects. It has felt inexpressibly awful. We were told in the max that the public essentially wants us to suffer, that suffering is what we deserve, and that this is why max is so structurally suppressive. Even though the Inside-Out program began in Canada in the fall of 2011, just as the Conservative "tough on crime" agenda was producing its effects, the program can only ever reach a small portion of the women in this prison, even fewer of the max population. For those few of us who are eligible and allowed to participate from max, maintaining the security clearance to attend in the medium-security compound presented itself as a constant hurdle, one which I always found to be nearly too stressful to maintain.

No Security: The Constant Threat of the Max Unit's Level System
Because there is a constant surveillance of us in max, even our most menial actions and interactions are documented, assessed and used by staff to guide decisions about how our time is spent. Decisions impact all of us — from long-term realities, such as parole, to our immediate quality of life. Most significantly, the max unit operates with every prisoner being represented by a level, in a four-level system, with level one offering the most restrictions and level four offering the most privilege. Level one prisoners may not leave the unit without being shackled and handcuffed and without being escorted by several guards. Level four prisoners can leave the unit without any handcuffs or shackles and with only one CSC staff, who does not necessarily have to be a guard (for example, a teacher or prison psychologist may escort a level four maximum-security prisoner throughout the medium-security compound). Levels are assessed weekly at staff meetings and provide the max staff an enormous, immediate and generally arbitrary form of control over our realities. Only at level four may one participate in most programs institutionally, including Inside-Out, and throughout my participation in four separate Inside-Out courses I was not able to maintain a level four status.

I did maintain the required level four for three courses; it was during the fourth course my level four was reduced. There had been several prior occasions when staff had threatened to reduce my level. Levels could be reduced on grounds as generic as "deteriorating behaviour," and the standard of our behaviour was determined largely by the opinions of our jailers. The jeopardy of Inside-Out always being taken from me created a permanent tension in my prison life; Inside-Out was the only meaningful activity I had access to during the two-year-plus period I was imprisoned in the max. There were countless weeks that I worried whether or not I would even be able to participate, let alone worrying about accessing the computers or having a safe space to study.

The actual course material never caused me stress, though I often found myself wishing that I was not involved in the program so that the prison would have nothing to constantly threaten me with. Still, readings and essays became my escape from prison reality; through Inside-Out I found a way to engage about issues that matter to me. I sat in many cells and read Freire and Foucault and felt in those moments connected to the world, not isolated, both physically and in ideas and beliefs. I continually regained confidence through Inside-Out courses. In hindsight, the contradiction of the confidence and social skills I was able to rebuild during class against the low self-worth, guardedness and social anxieties I developed through time in max highlight how the living conditions of the max unit are entirely detrimental to human emotional and mental health. Being isolated, monitored, deprived of community, and constantly scrutinized and put down for so long was traumatic in a sense that I do not yet fully comprehend (it has presently been three months since I left max). I was extremely fortunate in my ability to use Inside-Out, aside from an opportunity to develop academically, as the tool with which I rebuilt and maintained some social skills and normalcy.

When I was finally pulled from completing my fourth course, although I was able to finish with a pass, I was devastated. This was the human rights course and it was unfortunately ironic that the only access to education that I had was being taken; that the staff would rather keep me on the unit and for all purposes — mentally and socially broken — than to be participating in a meaningful, productive social and academic experience. But such is the reality of the max unit. Such is the reality of the general attitude behind the Canadian penal system. The Inside-Out program was and continues to be one of the only substantial opportunities available to women imprisoned at GVIW, let alone the max, and it is only available because of the prolonged determination of outside forces. Nothing similar has been developed within the institution; the majority of the women in max sit from periods of months to periods of years with absolutely nothing to do. The majority of us are not even eligible to participate. If there is any emotion expressed by an imprisoned person in max, let alone violence (which most women in max experience), the Inside-Out program would be not more than something one or two of the women's pod-mates left to do once weekly.

Inside-Out as a Stepping Stone

The Inside-Out Prison Exchange program does and will continue to get nothing but support from me, but in praising it I will not let the system within which it exists be overshadowed. Long-term isolation is a difficult experience to express; I strongly urge anyone studying or interacting in the Canadian penal system to look at programs like Inside-Out as stepping stones away from the effects of isolation, and more generally as movement away from the development (or permanence) of a mass, industrialized imprisonment culture. Few know what women are sentenced to when shipped to any of Canada's maximum-security prisons, and I certainly did not foresee that such trauma could be inflicted upon me by the state, nor that a private organization could provide such a profound experience that my deterioration in max could be managed. I held onto the Inside-Out program for the majority of my imprisonment in the max as the reason and meaning by which I endured. Several peers of mine in max collapsed and became entirely institutionalized through the lack of dignity and opportunity we experienced, and many are still in max today as result. I do not doubt whatsoever that without my having had the ability to hang onto Inside-Out as I did, as a routine, as a source of hope for a potential future for myself, and as a healthy social setting, I too would have broken down long ago in that unit.

There is an abundance of literature on the benefits of imprisoned people studying, and surely as the Inside-Out program ages, bodies of literature will arise to support the effects of imprisoned people studying through the experiential form that the program provides. But the unfortunate reality is that in the majority of places where Inside-Out exists, the imprisoned people who could benefit the most deeply will not be institutionally supported to engage.

In Canada and in penal culture globally, there is increasing support for punitive systems. However a punitive system nearly broke me, and in sharing my experience I hope readers are imbued with the importance of programs like Inside-Out within these systems, if these systems must exist. The inclusion of maximum-security prisoners in the Inside-Out program was thankfully not overlooked at GVIW. Let it not be overlooked anywhere as the program expands and finds roots in the Canadian prison system.

Custom Textbooks from Fernwood Publishing

Custom textbooks are for instructors and professors who want to hand-select material for their students from every Fernwood Publishing title. Teaching a course on Indigenous social work? Labour unions in Canada? Racism and the law? We have content on a huge range of topics in the social sciences and humanities that can be combined to fit your course.

HOW IT WORKS

We will compile individual chapters from any title we've previously published and deliver a professionally printed and bound book to be used in your course. No photocopies, and no coiled binding. You need only provide us with the titles of the chapters from our books that you want to use. Because the material is already published by us, we can create these custom texts quickly and cost effectively.

You can browse our full title list on our website (www.fernwoodpublishing.ca) for more detailed information as well as the tables of contents, and we're happy to provide examination copies if you need a closer look.

If you have a course but you need some help with choosing material, please contact us at marketing@fernpub.ca.

THE FINE PRINT

We need at least six months notice prior to the course start date to create your custom textbook. The minimum number of students enrolled is 40. Retail price is based on the number of students enrolled in the course and length of the book.

For more information, please contact marketing@fernpub.ca.